DIRECTED BY

Vincente Minnelli

. . . .

DIRECTED BY

Vincente

• • • • • • • • • • • • • • • • • • • •

Minnelli

STEPHEN HARVEY

Foreword by

LIZA MINNELLI

THE MUSEUM OF MODERN ART, NEW YORK
HARPER & ROW, PUBLISHERS, NEW YORK

• • • • • • • • • • • • • • • • • •

Published on the occasion of the exhibition
"Directed by Vincente Minnelli."
The Museum of Modern Art, New York
December 15 1989 – January 28 1990

The exhibition is part of *American MovieMakers*,
a major film retrospective and restoration program
sponsored by AT&T.
This publication has been supported in part by
funding from AT&T.

Library of Congress Catalogue Card Number: 89-63633
ISBN 0-87070-474-5 (MoMA clothbound)
ISBN 0-06-016263-5 (Harper & Row trade edition, clothbound)

Edited by Patricia Warner
Designed by Emsworth Design
Production by Bill Luckey
Typeset by Dix Type, Inc.
Printed by Murray Printing Company

Cover: Fred Astaire and a blonde-wigged Cyd Charisse in
"The Girl Hunt" ballet from *The Band Wagon* (1953)
Title Page: Vincente Minnelli directing Kay Kendall and
Rex Harrison in *The Reluctant Debutante* (1958)

The Museum of Modern Art
11 West 53 Street
New York, New York, 10019

Harper & Row, Publishers, Inc.
10 East 53 Street
New York, New York 10022

• •

Grateful thanks are due Turner Entertainment Co. for permission to print illustrations of the following films: *Meet Me in St. Louis*, © 1944 Loews' Inc., Ren. 1971 Metro-Goldwyn-Mayer Inc.; *Ziegfeld Follies*, © 1946 Loews' Inc., Ren. 1973 Metro-Goldwyn-Mayer Inc.; *Yolanda and the Thief*, © 1945 Loews' Inc., Ren. 1972 Metro-Goldwyn-Mayer Inc.; *Till the Clouds Roll By*, © 1946 Loews' Inc.; *The Pirate*, © 1948 Loews' Inc., Ren. 1975 Metro-Goldwyn-Mayer Inc.; *Madame Bovary*, © 1949 Loews' Inc., Ren. 1973 Metro-Goldwyn-Mayer Inc.; *Tea and Sympathy*, © 1956 Loews' Inc., Ren. 1984 MGM/UA Entertainment Co.; *Some Came Running*, © 1958 Loews' Inc. and Sol C. Siegel Productions, Inc., Ren. 1986 MGM/UA Entertainment Co. and Sol C. Siegel Productions, Inc.; *Undercurrent*, © 1946 Loews' Inc., Ren. 1973 Metro-Goldwyn-Mayer Inc.; *Two Weeks in Another Town*, © 1962 Metro-Goldwyn-Mayer Inc. and John Houseman Productions, Inc.; *The Sandpiper*, © 1965 Metro-Goldwyn-Mayer Inc. and Venice Productions Inc.; *An American in Paris*, © 1951 Loews' Inc., Ren. 1979 Metro-Goldwyn-Mayer Inc.; *Lovely to Look At*, © 1952 Loews' Inc., Ren. 1980 Metro-Goldwyn-Mayer Inc.; *The Band Wagon*, © 1953 Loews' Inc., Ren. 1984 Metro-Goldwyn-Mayer Inc.; *Kismet*, © 1944 Loews' Inc., Ren. 1971 Metro-Goldwyn-Mayer Inc.; *Gigi*, © 1958 Loews' Inc. and Arthur Freed Productions, Inc., Ren. 1986 MGM/UA Entertainment Co. and Arthur Freed Productions, Inc.; *Designing Woman*, © 1957 Loews' Inc., Ren. 1985 MGM/UA Entertainment Co.; *Brigadoon*, © 1954 Loews' Inc., Ren. 1982 Metro-Goldwyn-Mayer Inc.; *Cabin in the Sky*, © 1943 Loews' Inc., Ren. 1970 Metro-Goldwyn-Mayer Inc.; *I Dood It*, © 1943 Loews' Inc., Ren. 1970 Metro-Goldwyn-Mayer Inc.; *Father of the Bride*, © 1950 Loews' Inc., Ren. 1977 Metro-Goldwyn-Mayer Inc.; *The Courtship of Eddie's Father*, © 1962 Metro-Goldwyn-Mayer Inc., Euterpe Inc. and Venice Productions Inc.; *The Bad and the Beautiful*, © 1952 Loews' Inc., Ren. 1980 Metro-Goldwyn-Mayer Inc.; *The Cobweb*, © 1955 Loews' Inc., Ren. 1983 MGM/UA Entertainment Co.; *Lust for Life*, © 1956 Loews' Inc., Ren. 1984 MGM/UA Entertainment Co.; *Home from the Hill*, © 1959 Loews' Inc. and Sol C. Siegel Productions, Inc., Ren. 1987 Turner Entertainment Co. and Sol C. Siegel Productions, Inc. We also thank 20th Century-Fox and Paramount Pictures, Inc., for the use of stills from *Goodbye, Charlie* and *On a Clear Day You Can See Forever*.

. . . .

Foreword

S everal years ago, when Stephen Harvey told me he was writing a book on my dad, I thought, "Oh terrific!" But I had no idea it would turn out to be the definitive study of Vincente Minnelli the man, the artist, the perfectionist. Nothing I had imagined had prepared me for this in-depth, fascinating, unsettlingly honest portrait of my father's life's work.

You see, my father was obsessed with his own special way of storytelling. He believed in magic and he fought for truth and, above all, he believed with all his heart that the combination of those two elements on the screen was art. Mr. Harvey has caught all of this; and even if I disagree with some of his opinions, his extensive research and obvious love of Minnelli movies are formidable. My heartfelt thanks to Stephen Harvey and The Museum of Modern Art Department of Film for helping to share my father's dreams and love of the art form with audiences for years to come.

I loved my father more than I can ever express. He taught me that anything was possible just as long as you went about it the right way, as long as you used your mind and always tried to be as good as you could be. That was one of the things he left me. But I think his greatest legacy was that he made me very proud to be a woman. I never wanted to be anything else. He also gave my mother a great gift. He guided her through a change most child stars never achieve—from awkward adolescent to lovely young woman. You can see his love for her in every frame of Meet Me in St. Louis. That's the film where they met and would ultimately fall in love. It's my favorite, for when all is said and done I wouldn't be here if it hadn't been for that movie.

My father gave me my dreams. In fact, through his movies he gave a lot of people their dreams, and it's comforting to know that even though Daddy is gone his pictures will always be there. Wherever I am, whenever I see one of his movies, I inevitably nudge the person next to me and say, "Hey . . . my father *thought of that.*"

LIZA MINNELLI

Contents

Acknowledgments

Throughout the course of this project, the entire Minnelli family has given unstintingly of their time and encouragement. From the time I began work in 1982 until Mr. Minnelli's death four years later, he valiantly defied frail health to offer me the benefit of his insight and the warmth of his friendship. Through the years since our first meeting, his widow Lee Anderson Minnelli has shown extraordinary generosity and support, which I deeply appreciate. Despite the demands of a punishing work schedule, Liza Minnelli has always found an opportunity to share her recollections of her father with me, and her kindness has been a sustaining force in seeing this book to its completion.

Much valuable information on Minnelli's theatrical career in the 1930s was made available to me at The Shubert Archives, the Radio City Music Hall archives, The Museum of the City of New York, and the Lincoln Center Library for the Performing Arts. Deborah Russell of the administrative staff of the Delaware, Ohio, school system, in consultation with the Delaware Historical Society, provided me with vital data on Mr. Minnelli's early years. Most of the factual information on the making of the Minnelli films came from the vast array of contracts, production files, memos, letters, and statistical information preserved at the MGM Legal Department, covering his entire twenty-six-year tenure at the studio. I am extremely grateful to Deanna Wilcox, Richard Kahn, and particularly Herbert S. Nusbaum for allowing me access to this invaluable material. This was supplemented by additional research at the Margaret Herrick Library of the Academy of Motion Picture Arts and Sciences and the Film Study Center of The Museum of Modern Art. Accurate financial records on the box-office returns of movies from the 1940s through the '60s are often frustratingly unreliable or incomplete. The data cited in the text came mostly from the MGM files, supplemented by the annual gross tabulations in *Variety* and the statistics on films produced by the Freed Unit as cited in Hugh Fordin's book *The World of Entertainment;* when discrepancies between these arose, generally figures from the studio records were used. In addition to her work on the bibliography, Catherine A. Surowiec assisted mightily in organizing the historical material for this book.

Photographs accompanying the text came from the following sources: The Museum of Modern Art Film Stills Archive, Mrs. Vincente Minnelli, Ms. Liza Minnelli, MGM/UA, the Academy of Motion Picture Arts and Sciences, the British Film Institute, the Turner Entertainment Co. and Photofest. Many of the color frame enlargements in the book were photographed by Francene Keery.

Both during the writing of this book and the preparation of the accompanying film retrospective at The Museum of Modern Art, the cooperation of the Turner Entertainment Co. has been exemplary. Roger L. Mayer and Richard P. May have never hesitated in providing us with access to first-rate prints of the Minnelli films from the Turner collection; without their support, the project would truly not have been conceivable. Additionally, for making possible the preservation of *Meet Me in St. Louis,* I thank the Turner Entertainment Co. and the Film Department of George Eastman House, Rochester, for providing film materials, and Pete Comandini and Richard Dayton of YCM Laboratories for preparing new negatives and prints. As sponsor for the Minnelli retrospective, AT&T demonstrated its leadership as a corporate supporter of the arts with a generous financial grant; I would especially like to thank Zack Manna for his enthusiastic support.

It is impossible for me to cite all those friends and professional colleagues, and the associates of Mr. Minnelli, whose advice and encouragement carried me through the writing of this book. However, I must thank James H. Dunn, Carrie Rickey, Alden Cohen, Vito Russo, Martin Scorsese, Meredith Brody, Meade Roberts, donfeld, Katsumi Sasahara, John Michael Strange, and Jay Padroff for their special help. My co-workers at The Museum of Modern Art have shown great forbearance during this entire period, and I would like to thank Charles Silver, Ron Magliozzi, Terry Geesken, Peter Williamson, Rachel Gallagher, Laurie Rigelhaupt, Jeanne Collins, and Sarah Eaton. Mary Corliss, Assistant Curator in the Department of Film, organized the superb wall show to accompany the film retrospective at the MoMA. I owe a special debt to my colleagues in film programming—Larry Kardish, Adrienne Mancia, Robert Beers, and Jytte Jensen—for their patience and comradeship beyond the call of duty.

Harriet Bee and Nancy Kranz of the Museum's Publications Department have been stalwart supporters of this project from the beginning; I am also grateful to Rick Kot of Harper & Row for his enthusiasm, and to Tony Drobinski, whose design for the book is as elegant as its subject. I feel extraordinarily lucky to have been matched up with an editor like Patricia Warner, who proved to be a superb collaborator. Working under enormous time pressures, she brought clarity and freshness to a harried author and his unwieldy text— her contribution to this book is incalculable. A note of appreciation to our proof readers, who did such great work in record time.

Finally, I offer my most heartfelt thanks to Mary Lea Bandy, Director of the Department of Film at The Museum of Modern Art. Through all the years of work, her guidance, understanding, and determination to see it through has been an unwavering source of strength. I would like to dedicate this book to her, to my family, and to Karl Phillip Carlock, the staunchest of friends.

S. H.

1 ·
Introduction

The history of Hollywood during the height of the studio system is littered with tales of individualistic directors in a fight to the death with intransigent moguls—the former dedicated to making movies with a personal imprint, the latter determined to manufacture an assembly-line product with the broadest possible appeal. Whether biased toward the notion of cinema as art or movies as pop culture, numerous film historians and critics have relied on this equation to chart their terrain. The work of directors such as John Ford, Alfred Hitchcock, and Ernst Lubitsch is lionized for its triumph over the conformist dream-factory mentality, whereas that of Orson Welles and Erich von Stroheim is lamented because they were vanquished by it. These directors' mark of genius is measured by the extent to which they avoided the neutralizing stamp of their employers. A Hitchcock movie is still indisputably his own creation, whether it was produced by David O. Selznick or at 20th Century-Fox; John Ford's westerns look the same whether the interiors were shot on the sound stages of Republic or RKO. In contrast, biographies of the legendary producers tend to portray directors as little more than efficient hired hands.

All of the above fails to account for much that is ambiguous about American film history. If the impulse to express a private vision was antithetical to the needs of mass entertainment, the enduring achievements in such popular genres as the musical, the screwball comedy, film noir, science fiction, and the western would have never been realized. It would be sentimental and misleading to view the creative lives of that era's most gifted directors as something out of a Frank Capra plot about lone idealists tilting against the crass and powerful. As hard-working professionals, they knew that, onerous and compromise-ridden as the studio system was, it provided a base which allowed them to function and even flourish.

In this context, the career of director Vincente Minnelli is an anomaly in the annals of American filmmaking. In thirty-four films made between 1943 and 1976,

Minnelli's work is as visually audacious and emotionally resonant as that of any of his contemporaries; although their thematic range is astonishingly varied, Minnelli's films express a sensibility unmistakably his. Yet more than for any other director of comparable status and achievement, his professional life was inextricably connected with the fortunes of one studio, Metro-Goldwyn-Mayer, whose trademarks, stylized opulence and an unruffled confidence in the supremacy of the crafted-in-Hollywood product, found their most glittering expression in Minnelli's movies.

Minnelli was contractually linked to this studio for twenty-six years, and all but three of his films were produced at MGM. That he even became a film director was due in large measure to the perception and patience of his employers. Before arriving in Hollywood in 1940, at the age of 37, Minnelli had been a successful theater director and set designer on Broadway, specializing in musical comedies and revues. His previous experience with the film industry had been an abortive six-month tenure at Paramount three years earlier. Recognizing his relative inexperience, MGM launched Minnelli on a three-year apprenticeship, during which time he was encouraged to learn production methods and to advise on the staging of song-and-dance numbers for the studio's constant stream of movie musicals. Once his on-the-lot training was completed to everyone's satisfaction, Minnelli was entrusted with the direction of two films that represented considerable financial and creative risks to MGM: *Cabin in the Sky,* a fantasy with an all-black cast which had been a commercial failure on the stage, and *Meet Me in St. Louis,* an expensive period piece that recorded four seasons in the lives of a provincial American family. For the next twenty years, Minnelli's pictures were among the studio's most prestigious and popular films. As one regime succeeded another in the executive offices of MGM's Irving Thalberg Building, he would enjoy a degree of confidence and respect remarkable for its endurance and continuity. The stacks of contracts, memos, budget reports, and production schedules preserved at the studio which relate to Minnelli and the thirty-one films he made there testify with rare unanimity to the long, harmonious working relationship between this painstaking filmmaker and his employers.

Louis B. Mayer gives his blessing at the wedding of Judy Garland and Vincente Minnelli, 1945

OPPOSITE:
Arthur Freed and Fred Astaire celebrate Minnelli's birthday on the set of Yolanda and the Thief *(1945)*

The timing of Minnelli's debut at MGM was fortuitous for all concerned. The early forties was a period of transition and prosperity for the studio. Spurred on by Arthur Freed, a lyricist turned executive who had been granted his own production unit after yeoman work as associate producer of *The Wizard of Oz,* MGM toiled to establish itself as Hollywood's nonpareil creator of movie musicals. At this time, reliable staples like the Jeanette MacDonald–Nelson Eddy operettas and Eleanor Powell tap marathons were waning in appeal, and 1939's *The Wizard of Oz,* which indicated a future direction for the studio to explore, was still years away from showing a profit. The only director then on the studio roster with any real affinity for the musical was Busby Berkeley, whose talent for kaleidoscopic production numbers adorned otherwise perfunctory movies, and whose most imaginative achievements lay in the past with the Warner Bros. *Gold Diggers* series. (One of Minnelli's first tasks on the MGM lot was to stage an intimate song sequence which Berkeley would shoot, in the Garland–Rooney *Strike Up the Band.*)

Simultaneously, MGM was embarking on the production of an increasing number of films in Technicolor, after a tentative start with the MacDonald–Eddy *Sweethearts* in 1938. During the late thirties, the studio was more cautious than its competitors in utilizing the new three-strip Technicolor process. After Technicolor's feature film debut with *Becky Sharp* in 1935, the most prominent early color films were Paramount's *The Trail of the Lonesome Pine;* 20th Century-Fox's

Ramona, and David O. Selznick's *The Garden of Allah, Nothing Sacred,* and *A Star Is Born.* In the early forties, MGM continued to film its popular Mickey Rooney–Judy Garland vehicles in black and white, while Fox, its principal movie-musical rival, routinely glorified Betty Grable, Alice Faye, and Carmen Miranda in full color. Apart from the expense and technical hurdles involved, there were few in Hollywood who could use the process creatively. Thus, the results tended toward paintbox garishness or at best a lush but literal-minded pictorialism; even *The Wizard of Oz* was widely criticized for what many then felt was a visual approach too earthbound for fantasy. Yet from *Meet Me in St. Louis* onward, black and white musicals became the exception. All pertinent to Minnelli's imminent role in the movies; for, during his rapid rise on Broadway in the 1930s, Minnelli's productions were acclaimed for their artistic cohesion—his mastery of a theatrical palette that blended every element of mise-en-scène into boldly hued stage images with a striking unity of design. Properly translated to the screen, this was a gift of great value to the studio which had lured him west.

Within a short time, Minnelli managed to fulfill that promise, and then to surpass it. Over the next decade, MGM groomed many accomplished directors of musicals, such as Charles Walters, George Sidney, Stanley Donen, and the versatile Gene Kelly. The first of his generation, Minnelli was the one against whom their achievements were, and still are, measured. As the most influential and warmly praised screen musical of its decade, *Meet Me in St. Louis* had something of *Oklahoma!*'s éclat in the theater. Like the Rodgers and Hammerstein work, it was sophisticated populism par excellence, celebrating ordinary lives out of the American past without losing sight of everyday human conflicts and unobtrusively incorporating music into a simple story so that the fusion illuminated rather than confined its characters.

Meet Me in St. Louis, Ziegfeld Follies, Yolanda and the Thief, and *The Pirate* established that, as a colorist, Minnelli was without peer in the Hollywood of the forties. His hallmark, in film as in the theater, was the selectivity of his eye. Sensitive to the overpowering brightness of the Technicolor process, he carefully mutes *Meet Me in St. Louis'* color scheme to convey the cozy parochialism of a middle-class family and its time. The house interiors are blue and mustard plush, with ochre-colored wood trim and genteel lace accessories—welcoming but traditional. The Smith family, dressed for a spring outing, are shimmering white-robed figures against an emerald green lawn; reminding us that 1904 was not only the year of the St. Louis Exposition, but also the age of Auguste Renoir. No other Technicolor movie shot on Hollywood backlots so successfully conveyed the look of these places and those times.

Shifting from the relative naturalism of *Meet Me in St. Louis* to fantasy, Minnelli continued to saturate the screen with a few key colors, consciously limiting his range to magnify their impact. At first, the effect of this was merely picturesque: in *Ziegfeld Follies,* black-garbed jewel thief Fred Astaire pursues white-gowned debutante Lucille Bremer in a crimson-and-twilight blue tableau; in *Yolanda and the Thief,* the Astaire–Bremer "Coffee Time" production number is aswirl in shades of café au lait to espresso. By *The Pirate,* Minnelli is aiming beyond gorgeousness—in the "Mack the Black" ballet, the colors of smoke and midnight blue with orange flames, are exhilarating, sexy, and scary—the colors of its virginal heroine's erotic hallucination.

Minnelli's first film, *Cabin in the Sky,* demonstrated his understanding of a concept somewhat foreign to his theatrical training—the three-dimensional use of film space. As a novice moviemaker, Minnelli was expected to use the sound stage as an unusually spacious proscenium arch, the camera eye poised from the best seat in the house. But from the outset, Minnelli realized that the camera was more than just a recording device; in movement it could shape and even transform what passed in front of its lens. He was hardly the first Hollywood filmmaker to be aware of this, yet it's odd how little this concept had been explored in the movie musical in the decade after the early talkie-era experiments of Ernst Lubitsch (*The Love Parade, Monte Carlo*) and Rouben Mamoulian (*Applause, Love Me Tonight*). In most notable musicals, the camera keeps a discreet distance from the dancers, who provide all the motion that matters, as in the Astaire–Rogers movies, or else

miniaturizes them into figures in a geometric pattern, as in Busby Berkeley extravaganzas (*Gold Diggers of 1933, Dames*). Minnelli devised a collaboration between the performers and his camera eye that uniquely combined these two seemingly opposite approaches. The sequence from *Ziegfeld Follies* cited contains an astonishing early example of this. Throughout a stately, graceful routine, the two stars have performed a mutual seduction in dance, alternately propelled by gliders set in the stage floor and their own footwork; suddenly, the camera soars around them and up into a diagonal arc, completing their choreographed movement and accelerating it. The collaboration between subject and camera becomes the essence of dizzying romanticism.

This was the kind of showmanship a director's employers could appreciate—particularly when a movie turned out to be as profitable as *Ziegfeld Follies.* Minnelli's talents flourished in an era when the studios boasted that the entire world could be reproduced within their confines; thus, his camera eagerly probed the possibilities of this self-contained universe. In the fifties, when actual location shoots became more prevalent, Minnelli searched for the metaphoric truth behind surface verisimilitude. In *Lust for Life,* it's less pertinent that Van Gogh actually lived and worked in these precise settings, than that they could be shaped to look like his paintings set in motion. The main difference between the non-ballet sections of *An American in Paris* (filmed wholly on the Culver City lot) and *Gigi* (shot primarily on location in France) is that the former emulates Utrillo's paintings, while the latter is inspired by the *belle époque* caricatures of French illustrator, SEM.

If MGM's executives were dazzled by Minnelli's refined yet marketable sensibilities, they appreciated even more his boundless capacity for hard work and cooperative attitude which befitted a member of MGM's efficient corporate "family." Ever since the squabbles between Erich von Stroheim and producer

Minnelli (at top) on the set of The Clock *(1945). Robert Walker and Judy Garland, center rear*

OPPOSITE:
Minnelli at MGM, smoking as usual

Irving Thalberg over *Greed* and *The Merry Widow* in the twenties, MGM had been inhospitable to those renegades convinced that they knew more about moviemaking than the moguls, and who didn't hesitate to say so. Artistic temperament notwithstanding, a certain hierarchy had to be respected—if directors called the shots on the set, it was executives and producers who could and did dictate the final form. This was the system that prevailed throughout Hollywood at this period, and as the film industry's most powerful studio, MGM epitomized it. Filmmakers accustomed to a degree of autonomy tended to find it an uncongenial place to work; directors like William Wyler, John Ford, and John Huston hit and ran at MGM, completing the occasional prestigious free-lance assignment at Culver City before moving on to less restrictive regimes.

Vincente Minnelli rarely challenged the ground rules. As a contract employee at MGM, he was expected to execute the assignments chosen for him, without recourse to the luxury of spurning projects he might feel were unworthy of his time and trouble. The internal correspondence devoted to Minnelli still extant at the studio shows not a single example of legal coercion. Naturally, it was in the best interests of the studio to try to match Minnelli with material suited to his talents. When a producer such as Arthur Freed decided that Minnelli alone was capable of realizing a property important to the studio but which the director found uncongenial, as happened with the film versions of Broadway's *Kismet* and *Brigadoon,* persuasion was used. Minnelli's compliance in return bought MGM's acquiescence on issues that truly concerned him. Minnelli accepted *Kismet* on the understanding that it would not interfere with the forthcoming *Lust for Life,* a project the studio had tried to make for a decade and one to which the director was deeply committed. And when it became imperative to start production on the Van Gogh biography or lose its European locations for another year, Minnelli left *Kismet* without a qualm for Stanley Donen to complete.

Although Minnelli was the studio's premier director of musicals, the genre constituted only a small proportion of MGM's annual production schedule and slightly more than a third of Minnelli's total output. As far as the studio was concerned, his ability to handle everything from domestic comedy to literary and theatrical adaptations to stylized melodrama was an asset underscored by Minnelli's phobia for idleness. Throughout the 1950s, scarcely a week elapsed between the completion of one Minnelli project and the start of preproduction for the next. On rare occasions, Minnelli worked on two films simultaneously; during a six-week shutdown on *An American in Paris* to construct the massive and complicated sets for the ballet, he shot *Father's Little Dividend,* the sequel to his highly popular *Father of the Bride.* This second Spencer Tracy–Elizabeth Taylor vehicle may not figure as one of his more enduring movies, but it is far from ignominious. As for the *American in Paris* ballet, it indisputably shows Minnelli at the height of his creative vigor—not a frame betrays a man suffering from battle fatigue.

His working regimen was such that if retakes were necessary on a completed film, someone else frequently had to be found to direct them, for Minnelli would be elsewhere (often on a different continent) shooting his next project. Thus, George Cukor essayed a few days' work on *Lust for Life* while Minnelli filmed *Tea and Sympathy,* and Charles Walters retouched *Gigi* on the lot when Minnelli was back in Paris engrossed in *The Reluctant Debutante.* He clearly accepted this as part of the established order in Hollywood, so long as the resulting footage didn't clash with his own, or be substituted for it. (When some of the Walters' *Gigi* material supplanted his, the usually docile Minnelli asserted himself with such vehemence that his original work was restored.) In a few instances, Minnelli himself returned the favor, most notably on a 1952 remake of the thirties musical *Roberta,* retitled *Lovely to Look At,* which called for a lavish fashion-show finale. Although he declined a screen credit, the sequence is saturated with Minnelli trademarks—a lush and daring use of color, the seamless fusion of music and camera movement, and a decorative scheme that mates the cast with inanimate objects in voluptuous counterpoint, all combined into a spectacle which is half high-Hollywood, half Venetian masque. *Lovely to Look At* is a prime example of Hollywood's collaborative system of moviemaking at its most efficient. However, the contrast between Minnelli's footage and the tameness which

precedes it is also a one-picture primer on the justness of the auteur theory.

If MGM had good reason to be satisfied with a contract director as professional and amenable as Minnelli, the benefits he reaped from his relationship with the studio were just as considerable. MGM provided him with continuity and structure; as one picture was completed, there was always another project waiting for him. The stability of the studio personnel also favored his working routine. His rapport with studio producers like Arthur Freed, Pandro S. Berman, John Houseman, and, later, Sol C. Siegel helped buffer Minnelli from the front office. By his account, Minnelli rarely met and scarcely knew Louis B. Mayer, who presided over MGM from 1924 until he was deposed in 1951. When Mayer was supplanted by Dore Schary, and Schary himself was ousted five years later, it was the lesser executives who had reason to tremble—Minnelli was as usual too busy on the set to pay much attention. As vital to Minnelli as Freed or Berman was the pool of craftspeople who worked at MGM for as long as the integrated studio system lasted. In addition to their extraordinary skill and diligence, these artisans needed psychic powers to work with a director like Minnelli. In translating his ideas from the abstract to the concrete, he was renowned for being as inarticulate as he was demanding. After years of experience, art directors like Preston Ames and Jack Martin Smith and cameramen of the caliber of George Folsey and John Alton understood Minnelli's ways, and knew how to bring his schemes into the realm of the practical.

With these and other key members of MGM's creative army, Minnelli managed to exploit the studio's production facilities to the fullest, while slyly subverting the aesthetic formulas that were MGM's pride. From the late twenties, studio style accentuated the gloss of its contract stars and the profligacy of its production values. These last were supervised by Cedric Gibbons, for decades head of the art department, and the man who pioneered the use of Art Deco in Hollywood design. He was intolerant of those directors who questioned his acumen. Gibbons' visual principles were prescribed according to the general subject matter at hand—cluttered coziness for small-town Americana in the Andy Hardy vein and cosmopolitan swank for upscale comedies and romances.

With his own extensive background in scenic design, Minnelli was bound to clash with an authoritarian figure like Gibbons, and the skirmishes began during his first film. They escalated in *Meet Me in St. Louis* with Minnelli's insistence that the Smith family's carpenter-Gothic house should be designed from scratch, rather than a refurbishment of something on the lot. Subsequently, Gibbons objected to the red and green motif Minnelli devised for one sequence, on the grounds that these hues were discordant in Technicolor, and too redolent of Yuletide in any case. Minnelli stood firm with the retort that somebody should have told God these colors clashed when He invented roses; besides, in the scene in question it was Christmas Eve. Thereafter, Gibbons largely relinquished to his subordinates the chore of dealing with Minnelli. In the future, when a particularly ambitious design challenge was in store, Minnelli implored his producers to hire free-lancers with whom he felt in tune—Irene Sharaff for *Ziegfeld Follies* and the *American in Paris* ballet, Oliver Smith for *The Band Wagon,* and Cecil Beaton for *Gigi.*

Generally his supervisors acquiesced, in the forlorn hope Minnelli might reduce the time inevitably spent redressing his sets before exposing a foot of film. It was a vain wish, according to the legions of actors who turned slowly to stone while an oblivious Minnelli was absorbed in touching up the requisite atmosphere: Lucille Bremer shriveled in a gilded tub while Minnelli thought about the bubbles; Leslie Caron persevered in lipsynching the chorus to "The Parisians," until the swans behind her glided in the proper alignment; Frank Sinatra and company languished outdoors all night in an Indiana hamlet before Minnelli decided that yes, the Ferris wheel at the rear would have to be moved six feet, after all. There is a revealing and funny candid photograph of the director on location in France for *The Four Horsemen of the Apocalypse.* In the midst of the most expensive and complicated production of his career, a wild-eyed Minnelli is clutching a mound of hay while he berates a crestfallen hireling who has failed his standards for photogenic hay-strewing.

The incident testifies to an ethos central to Minnelli's entire oeuvre, that no visual detail is ever too trivial to matter. The director believed his characters' true natures are revealed—often more tellingly than they can ever know—by the surroundings in which they live. If the settings are anonymous and interchangeable, then their fictional inhabitants can never rise above the level of mere movie archetypes. The specificity of Minnelli's decors could define, and occasionally indict, his protagonists before a word of dialogue is uttered. It's no denigration of Jennifer Jones' remarkable performance in Minnelli's version of *Madame Bovary* to note that his mise-en-scène is the key to Emma Bovary's mortal plight. His Emma desires above all that her world be filled with beauty—a longing never to be fulfilled because, in essence, the lady has no taste. As a new bride, she decorates her home in the suffocating luxe of the petit bourgeois. A glimpse at the fashions set by the local gentry brings a fleeting awareness of her own myopic standards, but before long she reverts to form, exulting in the chiffon hangings, potted palms, and bric-a-brac that adorn the hideaway her law-clerk lover has provided for their trysts. When later the disgruntled Léon retorts, "I hate the vulgarity of this room," he deals a fatal blow to her pride. In the end, the only consoling memory of Emma's whole frustrated life is the vision of herself at her one formal ball, encircled by men of pedigree and gazing at her reflection in an oval baroque mirror too lovely for her ever to own.

Minnelli's eye is no less acute when rendering the delusions and aspirations of his own country. In the cheerful marital comedy *The Long, Long Trailer* that he made with Lucille Ball and Desi Arnaz in 1953, the third protagonist is the trailer of the title. Technologically sleek and comfortable, it represents the newlyweds' hopes for a contented middle-class future. Yet before long their treasured mobile home threatens the harmony of their marriage. The couple is literally weighed down by the burden of their possessions. A few years later, Minnelli directed *Home from the Hill,* which remains one of the most penetrating of all American movies about troubled family life. The clue to the permanent rift between husband (Robert Mitchum) and wife (Eleanor Parker) is that although they live together, the rooms they inhabit are separate domains. Hannah Hunnicutt's province is dainty, polished, and fairly sterile, while her husband's lair boasts walls hung with guns and hunting trophies, and hounds lounging at his booted feet before an open flagstone hearth. Their embattled son Theron has his own retreat: a bedroom cluttered with chemistry sets and rock collections—boyish things he should have outgrown years before.

The Cobweb is a melodrama about a few days in the lives of a mental institution's inmates and keepers and

OPPOSITE:
Minnelli directing Louis Jourdan and Jennifer Jones in Madame Bovary *(1949)*

their families, in which the choice of a set of new drapes for the sanitarium library is the pivot of the story's conflicts. The chief psychiatrist's wife, a midwestern Emma Bovary, favors a fussy flowered chintz that is beyond the hospital's means; the spinster administrator's selection of cheap plain cotton betrays her puritanical nature. Meanwhile, a compassionate occupational therapist promotes the designs of her gifted and troubled patient, whose Ben Shahnesque silkscreen pictures attest both to his creativity and his despair. Without a hint of irony, Minnelli makes it plain that questions of taste are no trifling matter. Minnelli's is a world in which sabotage, adultery, attempted suicide, and general insurrection can be ignited by a dispute over a swatch of fabric.

Minnelli's sense of style was his last resort to transcend the most resistible MGM assignment. Throughout *Kismet,* he reveals his contempt for the subject with visual effects that defiantly upstage the songs and script. The tenor's soliloquy, "Night of My Nights," is the excuse for a procession of dromedaries and jeweled caravans to pass between Moorish minarets and a still, reflecting pool. From opposite ends of the Cinema-Scope screen, juvenile and ingenue sing their callow hearts out in rapture at finding a "Stranger in Paradise," while the audience's eye is riveted to a mute white peacock busily preening its plumage smack in the center of the frame.

Under more auspicious circumstances, Minnelli's mise-en-scène and the material it interprets are so integrated that one becomes indistinguishable from the other. *The Bad and the Beautiful,* a movie à clef about a dynamic, despotic film producer, pays tribute to the tunnel vision of those Hollywood denizens who subordinate every aspect of their lives to the love of their craft: neurosis redeemed by professionalism. Throughout the film, Minnelli blurs the distinction between his characters' career struggles and personal travails by shooting both in precisely the same way. Whether the setting is producer Jonathan Shields' Hollywood studio or his Beverly Hills mansion, the same strident chiaroscuro prevails, orchestrated to the meter of a camera in perpetual and sinuous motion. Heroine Georgia Lorrison's moment of supreme emotional catharsis—a berserk drive from the scene of her lover's betrayal—is the occasion for some headlong celluloid hocus-pocus. The interior of her car lurches about on what must be a sound-stage turntable, as the camera swerves around the driver's seat in reeling counterpoint; flashes of light punctuate her distress, while sham rain pelts the windows of the sedan on a night that minutes before had been bathed in clear moonlight. Compared to this, the sequences we've watched of a movie-within-a-movie that made Georgia a star—some lofty nonsense about White Russians buffeted by the Revolution—is neorealism undiluted. The fun of *The Bad and the Beautiful* is in attempting to match its dramatis personae with their Hollywood antecedents: Turner's Georgia as Diana Barrymore melded with Jennifer Jones plus a hint of Monroe; Kirk Douglas' Shields combining the legend of David O. Selznick with a chapter from the life of B-picture wizard Val Lewton. Although the movie includes fictionalized cameos of such directors as Hitchcock and von Sternberg, little of Minnelli's own personality intrudes visibly into the script. Yet in the truest sense, this movie is more tellingly autobio-

Minnelli with Jack Buchanan (as Oedipus), Louis Calhern, and Arthur Freed in 1952 on the set of The Band Wagon *(1953)*

*Lucille Ball, Desi Arnaz,
Vincente and Liza Minnelli
on location for* The Long,
Long Trailer *(1954)*

graphical than his memoirs, published two decades later. No less than his Jonathan Shields or Georgia Lorrison, Vincente Minnelli is besotted with the enclosed world of the film industry and transported by the challenge of fabricating artifice—or even art—within its gates. (*Two Weeks in Another Town,* the follow-up to this film, made nine years later, reflects the decline of the system that nurtured him more poignantly than Minnelli could have realized.)

The idea that the satisfactions of hard work can compensate for personal unhappiness recurs in a number of Minnelli films. It is central to *Lust for Life,* his biography of Van Gogh, and is the main undercurrent to the script of *The Band Wagon,* one of his finest musicals. *Lust for Life,* the midwestern melodrama *Some Came Running,* the romantic *An American in Paris,* and the ebullient *Bells Are Ringing* all focus on artists or writers alienated from others by their creative urges, yet are stalled and thwarted by the work they do. It can't be entire coincidence that these films were made during the decade of Minnelli's most intense professional activity as well as in a period of considerable personal turmoil—the dissolution of his first marriage, to Judy Garland, and a second union which swiftly ended in divorce. In his autobiography, Minnelli described these events tersely and with a decorum altogether missing from the films he made at the time. His memoirs also pass quickly over his rather rootless midwestern youth, as the only child in a family of struggling tent-show performers. In *The Pirate,* Minnelli evoked the life of

the itinerant player with stylized gusto; from *Meet Me in St. Louis* through *Home from the Hill,* his treatment of family relations and small-town American life is considerably less fanciful. Following the warmth and cohesiveness of the Smith ménage in *Meet Me in St. Louis* and the middle-class solidity of the Banks clan in *Father of the Bride,* Minnelli's vision of the family was to grow progressively bleaker. *Lust for Life, Some Came Running,* and *Home from the Hill* all pivot on a tormented relationship between two brothers, one a conformist and one an outcast, whose rift can never be healed. In *Meet Me in St. Louis,* family unity manages in the end to resolve all crises, however grave. By *Home from the Hill,* Minnelli's perspective has darkened considerably. In this film, the love of two parents (who hate each other) saps the will of their son and finally destroys him.

For a self-made sophisticate like Minnelli, there's poignance in this compulsion to reimmerse himself in the realities of parochial America, following such cosmopolitan diversions as *The Reluctant Debutante* and *Gigi.* Minnelli's compassion for ordinary people is palpable, but so is his relief at having escaped the constraints that bind them. *Some Came Running* and *Home from the Hill,* lengthy sagas of familial and class strife in the heartland, both fade out to credits against the same eloquent image—a tombstone. These two movies, made back to back at the MGM lot and on location in Indiana and Mississippi, sum up a key moral conflict: the clash between suffocating respectability and creative anarchy. As a conscious aesthete working within an avowedly materialistic industry, Minnelli was highly sensitive to the attractions and pitfalls of these opposites, and his films reflect the difficulty of trying to reconcile them. In *The Cobweb* and *Tea and Sympathy,* the artistic temperament runs the risk of being equated with neurosis and effeminacy; but when thwarted, as in *Some Came Running,* it leads to aimless dissipation. Whatever salvation there may be for these movies' troubled heroes comes from the devotion of a woman: genteel, omniscient, and at once both mother and lover. Because these poised creatures—Deborah Kerr in *Tea and Sympathy* and Martha Hyer in *Some Came Running*—are the most stilted characters in the Minnelli canon, one questions how much faith the director himself had in their restorative powers.

If the idiosyncratic beauty of Minnelli's style transcended MGM's trademarked gloss, the fundamental pessimism of his viewpoint just as surely sabotaged their upbeat ethic. Whether shepherded by Louis B. Mayer or Dore Schary, MGM movies stood for the celebration of an idealized status quo based on fixed moral values and a positive outlook. The seductive sur-

faces of Minnelli's movies, and the fact that so many were musicals or comedies and therefore innocuous by definition, deflected attention from their disturbing content, and this continues to be so whenever they're revived. The extraordinary charm of *Meet Me in St. Louis* camouflages the fact that 5135 Kensington Avenue is located far from utopia. The head of the household is a boor, shielded from all emotional upheavals by his wife and children. The movie's most distinctive character is five-year-old Tootie, whose fascination with thoughts of violence and death lead her to "kill" her dolls and bury them, accuse her sister Esther's heartthrob, the archetypal boy next door, of molesting her, and to batter her family of snow people into oblivion on Christmas Eve. The central set piece of *The Pirate,* another escapist musical, is a fantasy rape ballet sufficiently metaphorical to have blinded industry censors to its implications. Another nightmare disturbs the caustic good cheer of *Father of the Bride:* Spencer Tracy imagines himself flailing impotently on the undulating floor of a church nave as his gargoyle-faced friends and family recoil in disgust, in a sequence more redolent of Ingmar Bergman's *Hour of the Wolf* than *Ziegfeld Follies.* Minnelli's last domestic comedy, *The Courtship of Eddie's Father,* is in fact about bereavement and acceptance, the period of adjustment endured by a widower and his son after the death of the child's mother. As for *Gigi,* Maurice Chevalier's twinkle and Cecil Beaton's Art Nouveau furbelows are the icing on what is in truth a rather unsavory tale. Minnelli's biggest box office hit and the film which won him his Oscar is, after all, about a girl schooled from childhood to be a kept woman, but who opts instead for the more palatable alternative of marriage to the aimless if attractive plutocrat for whom she had been groomed. That Minnelli was able to shape this material into what many consider the ultimate MGM musical is as much a measure of his deviousness as of his directorial genius.

Contradictions like these are what link Minnelli's movies and help give them their substance. The melancholy underlying many of Minnelli's ostensibly lighter films imbues them with an unexpected depth of feeling and observation, just as a kinetic grace elevates his best melodramas from the turgid hokum they might have become. Minnelli's enduring achievement was to give vigor, eloquence, and refinement to the popular

values of his time, until these themselves changed beyond his recognition.

In the mid-to-late fifties, when Minnelli was at the peak of his directorial activity, his unbroken association with one studio was an anachronism in Hollywood. By then, the major production companies had largely divested themselves of the burden of long-term contracts with high-paid craftspeople, and many directors welcomed the autonomy their new free-lance status gave them. Minnelli resisted this shift for as long as possible, and with good reason. As a salaried MGM employee, this was the period in which he directed several of his most idiosyncratic and compelling movies, including *Lust for Life, Gigi, Some Came Running,* and *Home from the Hill.* Afterward, his fortunes were linked to the fate of a studio in decline, just as they had been during its triumphant years. At Culver City,

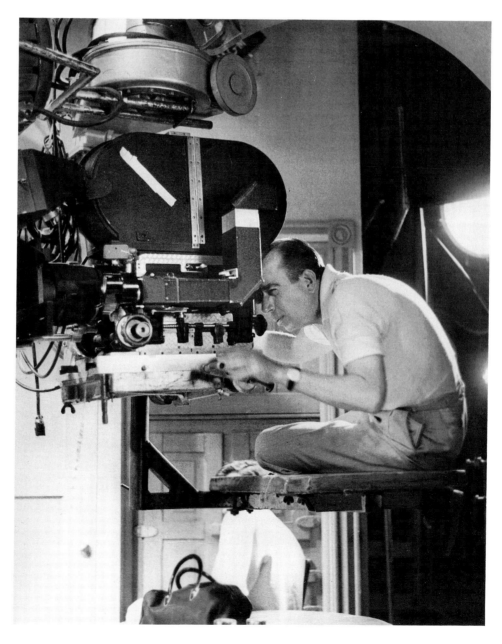

Minnelli at work, circa 1958

2 Overtures

"The biographer of his early years is hard put to sift fact from legend. He was born in Delaware, Ohio, in 1906, but was implicated almost immediately in a shady episode revolving around a piece of zwieback, and had to leave town at the age of one."

—S. J. Perelman, "That Felli Minnelli," *Stage* Magazine, April, 1937

S. J. Perelman's parody portrait of Minnelli, written at the height of the young director's Broadway fame, is more blithely fictitious than the satirist ever intended. The episode is one of many apocryphal events in this account, for Minnelli was born neither in Delaware, Ohio, nor in 1906. Even his first name was an artful invention. Eager to cultivate his image as a precocious prodigy/aesthete, Minnelli began shaving years off his age while still in his twenties. A generation later, some accounts of his life misidentified his birthday by as much as a decade.

The photocopy of a birth certificate preserved in the MGM files records the arrival of one Lester Anthony Minnelli in Chicago on February 28 1903, the last of five children born to Vincent Charles Minnelli and his wife, Mina Le Beau, and the only offspring to survive infancy. This sad circumstance apart, baby Lester's origins were the stuff that launched a dozen Arthur Freed backstage musicals. His father was a musical conductor, sometime composer, and co-impresario of the Minnelli Brothers' Tent Theater, which plied the midwestern circuit for the better part of twenty years early in the century. In that era, tent shows constituted the lowest order of legitimate show business—ramshackle troupes barnstorming provincial towns in melodramas like *Uncle Tom's Cabin* and disguised tab versions of recent Broadway hits. In cold weather, the Minnellis packed away their canvases and looked for pick-up work in stock and vaudeville. During one such engagement, Vincent Minnelli met and married a singer-actress with the stage name of Mina Gennell, familiarly known as May, who became the leading lady of the Minnelli Brothers' troupe. Their son arrived in the middle of a winter hiatus, and just like in the movies, he joined them on the boards as soon as he could toddle, making his debut as Little Willie in *East Lynne*. However, a star wasn't born on that fateful occasion,

for the child had neither the inclination nor the talent for an acting career.

Nevertheless, Minnelli spent his childhood summers on the road with his parents, and the rest of the year deposited at one boarding school or another or shuttled between his grandmothers in Chicago and the town of Delaware, where his late grandfather Minnelli had taught music at Ohio Wesleyan University. This itinerant life was just as precarious but certainly less romantic than the mountebank hijinks he would depict so lovingly in *The Pirate* four decades later. As Minnelli recalled in his autobiography, his mother regarded her theatrical career as a distasteful economic necessity, while his father's lack of success also embittered him toward the profession. The last thing they wanted for

OPPOSITE:
Minnelli with the model for a set from Ziegfeld Follies of 1936

Lester Anthony Minnelli, circa 1910

ABOVE:

Minnelli's mother May, in costume as Lady Babbie in The Little Minister

RIGHT:

Little Lester and a cousin pose in front of the Minnelli Brothers' Tent Theater, circa 1907

their surviving son was for him to follow in their footsteps. In the mid-1910s, the Minnelli Brothers' Tent Theater folded permanently, doomed like other itinerant theaters by the silent-movie emporia now being erected in even the smallest of hamlets. The Minnellis settled for good in Delaware, while Vincent Senior eked out a living as a free-lance musician. Delaware, circa 1915, was a pretty town of Victorian gingerbread —the kind of American heartland *Meet Me in St. Louis* later evoked. But the Minnellis were hardly middle-class pillars of the community like MGM's Smith family, and Lester by no means a typical midwestern kid. His family couldn't afford the plush trappings of the local burghers. With his lifelong obsession for decor, sixty years later Minnelli could recall the contrast between the "bilious green overstuffed sofas, tiny rosebuds in . . . ceilings and wallpaper" in the homes of their social betters, and the "golden oak furniture and chintz fabrics" of his mother's modest home.

After rootless years with the tent show, May Minnelli settled gladly into this stable if penurious existence, but her son dreamt of other things. Minnelli later described his younger self as a solitary, introverted boy with a voracious taste for literature and a flair for drawing. While still in his early teens he began to supplement the family income as an apprentice sign painter, his most ambitious assignment being the show curtain at the local movie house. After three terms at St. Mary's Parochial School, Minnelli spent his senior year at Delaware High School, where he distinguished himself as Dick Deadeye in the class production of *H.M.S. Pinafore.* "Les" Minnelli, also known by the sobriquet of "Taxi," graduated from Delaware in 1921; beneath his smiling portrait in the class yearbook ran the cryptic legend, "From the crown of his head to the sole of his foot he is all mirth." Small-town life was too confining for an adolescent of his restless, imaginative temperament, so he quickly set off for Chicago, where he boarded with his grandmother Le Beau and spinster Aunt Amy.

Minnelli wanted to pursue an artistic career, but in the meantime he needed some tangible means of earning his keep. Soon after his arrival in the big city, Minnelli's portfolio of sketches won him a job as fourth-assistant display artist at the Marshall Field Department Store. This modest professional start had a far more telling effect on his development than the handful of classes he attended at Chicago's Art Institute. In its limited way this was his first experience with mise-en-scène—arranging merchandise, lights, and backdrops into arresting tableaux. It trained his eye to solve practical three-dimensional problems, while, on a personal level, he was relieved to meet "normal" male colleagues who shared his creative bent. "Talking to the other display men . . . I saw by their example that one could happily function as the male animal and still give vent to his so-called feminine traits," Minnelli recounted in his memoirs. "As a result, I wasn't cowed at this impressionable age into more conventionally male avenues of expression." Certainly, the stylized epiphanies of his later movie musicals were a kind of display art at its most glorified. Something of this teen-aged window dresser endured in Minnelli throughout his directorial career—during his twenty-odd years at Metro he was notorious for frantically rearranging the props on his sets until they coalesced perfectly into the images he had in his head.

After New York, Chicago was the nation's hub of live entertainment. With his show-business roots, Minnelli naturally found himself drawn after working hours to the first-class touring companies that played the Loop. To supplement his income he began to do caricatures and costume sketches of the famed stage artists who appeared in town. These caught the attention of photographer Paul Stone, who specialized in society and theatrical portraits. Admiring the young Minnelli's lively pictorial eye, Stone offered him a job as his assistant at better wages than Marshall Field's. The work helped develop Minnelli's gift for visual texture and composition. On shooting assignments, Minnelli learned to both stroke the egos and embellish the charms of the performers who passed through Stone's studio—talents which would prove extremely useful later in life.

Minnelli now felt that his real future lay as a theatrical costumer. Armed with a sheaf of sketches and photographs, he talked his way into the post of chief costume designer for the Balaban and Katz organization, Chicago's premier movie theater chain. Its downtown showplace, the Chicago Theater, featured unit revues as opulent as anything the New York movie palaces could offer. Getting this job was a coup for an inexperienced young man scarcely in his twenties, and he plunged enthusiastically into the grind of designing a weekly extravaganza for the Chicago Theater and its neighborhood satellites. Before long he was responsible for the sets as well, his baptism being a riot of tinsel and feathers called "A Birdland Fantasy." Every show required some dazzling central gimmick, but Minnelli seemed to thrive under the pressure of dreaming something up in time for every Monday's change-of-bill. The work demanded boundless energy and theatrical imagination, and was the perfect training for the challenges to come.

Once Minnelli had made a name for himself on

Minnelli at Radio City Music Hall, circa 1934

Broadway, his publicity tried to convey that this midwestern apprenticeship passed with astonishing swiftness. In fact, he spent about a decade in Chicago preparing for the chance to test his craft in the big time. The opportunity came in 1931, after the Balaban and Katz theaters merged with the Paramount-Publix chain, and Minnelli was asked to join the organization in New York, at the then princely salary of $150 a week. During these early Depression years, the larger movie houses still supplemented their feature attractions with live entertainment; Paramount-Publix was bigger and more compartmentalized than Minnelli's former employer, and assigned him to create costumes exclusively. Local guild regulations prevented him from designing sets, so he crammed to gain his union card in the Society of Painters and Paper Hangers. (One of the test requirements was to sketch and diagram a "modern interior" with mantelpiece, as well as the balcony scene from *Romeo and Juliet;* applicants were also asked to name "two modernistic painters.")

With this challenge met, the indefatigable young designer began casting about for free-lance work to sup-

plement his twelve-hour days in the Paramount Building. His first Broadway assignment came from impresario Earl Carroll, whose annual *Vanities* rivaled the *Follies* in masses of peekaboo pulchritude if not marquee talent. Minnelli was drafted to design a show curtain for the 1931 edition, which would also inaugurate Carroll's sleek Art Deco theater. He came up with a green and silver scheme punctuated by dangling chorines in shades of coral. His inspiration was the lush-hued combinations Leon Bakst had devised for the Ballets Russes, and won Minnelli his first notices from the New York press, not all of them to his liking; writing in the *New Yorker,* Robert Benchley dismissed what he termed a "decidedly Negroid sense of color." Carroll nonetheless was sufficiently impressed to rehire Minnelli to do all the sets and costumes for the 1932 *Vanities.* Its principal attractions were Harold Arlen's sultry ballad "I Got a Right to Sing the Blues," and a Minnelli production number of Carroll cuties holding glass tubes which turned kaleidoscopic colors with every fluorescent light cue. While the *Vanities* was running, Minnelli discarded Art Deco for Louis Quinze on

*Minnelli set for Radio City
Music Hall stage show, 1934*

OPPOSITE:
*Minnelli at work in his New
York studio, circa 1935*

his first book show, *The Dubarry,* an Anglo-Viennese operetta imported as a crossover vehicle for the young Metropolitan diva Grace Moore. He also found the time to make his debut as a book illustrator, embellishing a new edition of Casanova's memoirs in the naughty High-Victorian style of Aubrey Beardsley. By the end of 1932, he was performing double duty for Paramount's stage spectacles as well, designing these tab-show sets in addition to all the costumes. With his base of operations transferred to Paramount's East Coast production facility at Astoria, Minnelli got his first vicarious glimpse of moviemaking, which didn't particularly tempt him to change metiers.

Up to then, Minnelli's ample salary from Paramount-Publix and his free-lance jobs had insulated him from the rigors of the post-market crash economy, but in early 1933 the Depression finally caught up with him. Paramount was on the verge of receivership, and the first luxury to go was its lavish stage shows, replaced by the cheaper expedient of touring big bands. Suddenly Minnelli was out of a job and without prospects, until the fledgling management of Radio City Music Hall summoned him for an interview.

It was lucky timing both for Minnelli and the Music Hall, as this gleaming new showplace was in serious trouble after its gala unveiling on December 27 1932. The centerpiece of the still-incomplete Rockefeller Center complex, Radio City Music Hall wasn't built to show movies at all. Under the direction of legendary Theater Guild designer Robert Edmond Jones, the intention was to create a temple for vaudeville's triumphant last hurrah. Featuring such diverse attractions as Ray Bolger, Martha Graham, a tabloid *Carmen,* and the flying Wallendas, this first top-heavy bill attracted scant attendance and a bewildered press. Something else was fast needed to fill those 6,200 seats; the management quickly decided on the more standard mix of a Hollywood attraction with a mini-revue, a policy that

endured uniquely at this house for the next forty-five years. But in the wake of this first fiasco and Jones' precipitous departure, a new production staff had to be assembled from scratch.

Minnelli replaced Jones' costumer, James Reynolds, at the end of February 1933—just days before F.D.R.'s Bank Holiday. Even more elaborate than the Paramount-Publix shows, the Music Hall spectacles required weekly costume changes for its corps de ballet, glee club, and assorted soloists, in addition to that phalanx of precision *danseuses* then known as the Roxyettes—in tribute to the Music Hall's presiding showman, "Roxy" Rothafel. Although buffeted by blasts of the notorious Roxy temper, Minnelli clearly pleased the Music Hall's bosses. A short four months after his arrival, Roxy's art director Clark Robinson had quit abruptly, and Minnelli was tapped to take over. For his first assignment, the week of July 6 1933, he devised a "Water Lily" ballet setting in green atop a chromium turntable; a Cuban potpourri illustrated with a backdrop of gargantuan fighting cocks; a Big Top interior for a circus number, and a Rue de la Paix dress shop to display the high-kicking Roxyettes. From the start of his tenure, Minnelli's designs had an up-to-the-minute dash which amused the Music Hall's more sophisticated patrons, as well as the impressionable hordes of regular movie fans. If Rockefeller Center and the Music Hall had been conceived as the ne plus ultra of urban contemporaneity, his bold stage pictures exalted the moderne-to-the-hilt aesthetic with every weekly change-of-bill. Eager to find any press angle to promote this expensive showplace, Music Hall publicists flacked its youthful design wizard as a fresh new force in the lively arts. In one 1934 dispatch, reprinted in the New York *Herald Tribune,* the Radio City press office breathlessly reported, "As art director at the Music Hall for the past ten months, Minnelli's modes in settings and costumes were always in the mood moderne. Instead of a face on a backdrop, Minnelli would paint one eye, suggesting a face. Instead of a saloon scene with a bar . . . an empty bottle and an upturned glass. Young and, confessedly, a modernist, Minnelli revels in the mediums of modernistic dance, torch songs, music from the heart of Harlem and picturesque angular furniture.''

While the Music Hall trumpeted his professional achievements, Minnelli worked to establish himself as a colorful personality-about-town. He had long since discarded his hick first name for his father's more euphonious one, Latinized with a final ''e.'' His first bachelor flat was on Perry Street in Manhattan's downtown Bohemian quarter, and he affected a wardrobe to match. As a 1937 *Esquire* profile described Minnelli in these early years, ''he was the incarnation of our preconceived notion of a 'Village type'—flat black hat with a wide brim, loose collar and looser tie around his thin neck . . . the cut of his long coat a triumphant marriage of Harlem and the Left Bank.'' In his naive fashion, he aspired to become a sort of latter-day James McNeill Whistler—an artist as equally celebrated for his personal style as his worldly attainments. Minnelli's cosmopolite longings overcame his native shyness, and before long he became a social fixture in the theatrical smart set of the day, initiated by his closest new chums, Ira Gershwin and his wife, Lee.

Once ensconced at the Music Hall, Minnelli exchanged his Village studio for an apartment on East 52nd Street, assuming a more debonair image to suit the move uptown. Visiting reporters marveled at his ''modernistic'' apartment with its blue-and-white color scheme set off by a bright-red bathroom; its most picturesque accessory was Hara, Minnelli's ''little Japanese valet,'' in the patronizing tones of the *New York American*, ''his severest critic . . . who sees all the shows and minces no words.'' All pretty heady stuff for this son of show-business never-weres forced to settle for a life of pinchpenny respectability. Minnelli remained an idiosyncratic elegant for the rest of his life; in Beverly Hills his perennial uniform of choice became

a black turtle-neck with a sports jacket in his favorite shade of canary-yellow—a cigarette permanently attached to his tapering fingers.

Meanwhile, in late 1934, the Music Hall gave him the chance to expand his art-direction duties by conceiving and directing his own stage shows on a monthly basis. The first of these, called ''Coast to Coast,'' took Music Hall patrons on a fanciful tour of the Mediterranean (the Côte d'Azur), the races at Ascot (the Gold Coast), Africa (the Ivory Coast), and honky tonk San Francisco (the Barbary Coast), to words and music by such notables as Duke Ellington and lyricist ''Yip'' Harburg. Having visited none of these places except via books, paintings, and travelogues, Minnelli imagined them with a sort of wide-eyed chic ideally suited to the huge Music Hall stage. His Ascot revelers were orange-feathered Rockettes in white attended by chorus boys in gray morning suits; the Ivory Coast number featured the looming totems of moderne Africana he favored in one set after another during the thirties. But it was the Riviera section that really left them breathless. Punctuated by white cut-out palm trees, the Dufyesque set anticipated the look of his *American in Paris* ballet by fifteen years. Against the backdrop's neutral tones he gave his profligate palette a real workout. ''And here is a grouping of colors too luscious,'' gushed *Variety's* reviewer. ''Girls come on in gray satin with cerise scarves, and henna gowns with chartreuse scarves.'' The show-business weekly proclaimed that ''Vincente Minnelli is to be congratulated upon his first stage show for Radio City. Never has this huge theater had such a beautiful offering.''

While still devising weekly decors for the Music Hall shows, Minnelli maintained his standard with six more of these monthly cornucopias. It was a regimen bound to take its toll on his creative energies sooner or later —there were just so many corners of the globe he could recycle, however modernistically, week after week. Minnelli began to cast his eye from Sixth Avenue to Broadway, where he could gain greater public recognition while working at a more reasonable pace.

His chance came in the spring of 1935, when an offer arrived from an unexpected quarter—Lee Shubert, one

Minnelli backdrop for
Ziegfeld Follies of 1936

OPPOSITE TOP:
*Minnelli design for "Death in
the Afternoon" ballet,* At
Home Abroad *(1935)*

OPPOSITE BELOW:
Minnelli backdrop for At
Home Abroad *(1935)*

half of the legitimate stage's indomitable Shubert brothers. To maintain their stranglehold on Broadway's real estate, the Shuberts were indefatigable producers, known equally for their shrewd business acumen as for their negligible taste. During the prosperous twenties, they'd specialized in schmaltz and cheesecake: the *mittel-europäisch* refrains of *Blossom Time* and *The Student Prince* on the one hand, and girlie shows like the *Artists and Models* series, notorious as the nudest entertainments this side of burlesque, on the other. So long as these formulas worked, the Shuberts disdained those theatrical artists whose tastes ran to the opulent or highbrow, and this contempt was mutual.

However, between the advent of the talkies and the Depression, Broadway's diminished audiences had become far more exacting. In the early thirties, the taste for operetta was fading fast and the 50-chorines-50 extravaganzas had become both economically perilous to mount and a Hollywood commonplace. In their wake came a new vogue for streamlined revues, largely sparked by 1929's surprise hit, *The Little Show*. Tailored around glittering personalities like Libby Holman, Beatrice Lillie, Clifton Webb, and the Astaires, these entertainments accentuated urbanity over flash and flesh. A few bristled with barbed allusions to current events, but most were content to sport the freshest-minted of bon mots and melodies in settings of restrained luxe. Unlike the glorified vaudevilles of the twenties, the best of these revues (generally conceded to be 1931's *The Band Wagon* and the 1933 Irving Berlin–Moss Hart collaboration *As Thousands Cheer*) were as unified in style as any book musical. After a shaky start with the 1932 show, *New Americana* (which introduced the song

"Brother, Can You Spare a Dime?" and the Broadway debut of Charles Weidman and Doris Humphrey's modern dance troupe), the Shuberts adapted successfully to the new order two years later with *Life Begins at 8:40*, whose attractions included Bert Lahr and Ray Bolger, with swanky revolving settings by Albert Johnson, and jaunty Harold Arlen tunes such as "You're a Builder-Upper" and "Let's Take a Walk Around the Block."

Having sharpened his skills over two years at Radio City, Minnelli was the perfect choice to preside over a series of smart new Shubert revues. Promised complete artistic autonomy with billing to match, Minnelli signed a contract with the Shuberts to create three musical shows over eighteen months. Accordingly, he left Radio City in April 1935, although his fortunes would be linked with the Music Hall in one way or another for the rest of his career. His designs continued to adorn its stage for decades to come, and after he transferred his activities to the screen, he remained Radio City's director of choice. From *Yolanda and the Thief* through his last, *A Matter of Time*, seventeen Minnelli movies would play a record total of eighty-five weeks at the self-billed Showplace of the Nation.

Minnelli's Broadway directorial debut was planned for the fall 1935 theatrical season. In the meantime, he set up working quarters in a townhouse next to The Museum of Modern Art, which waggish friends christened "The Minnellium." As his ideas for the revue took shape, it became a full-length variation on that first all-Minnelli stage show at the Music Hall. Like *Coast to Coast, At Home Abroad* was an around-the-world musical cruise, and he and the Messrs. Shubert assembled a very classy crew for the occasion.

The stars of At Home Abroad *(from top, clockwise) Eleanor Powell, Ethel Waters, Beatrice Lillie, Herb Williams*

Revue specialists Howard Dietz and Arthur Schwartz were hired to compose the score, with Dietz also contributing some of the comic sketches. Heading the troupe were the peerless comedienne Beatrice Lillie and Ethel Waters, whose long apprenticeship as a blues singer and Broadway personality had finally brought her stardom in *As Thousands Cheer,* in which she outshone no less a luminary than Marilyn Miller. *At Home Abroad* also boasted the tap-dancing of Eleanor Powell, fresh from her movie debut, and the highflown terpsichorean Paul Haakon, from the Radio City Ballet troupe; Briton Reginald Gardiner was the show's principal funnyman, abetted by vaudevillian Eddie Foy Jr., and Hoosier radio personality Herb Williams.

The most peripatetic passenger was the top-billed Miss Lillie, whose ports of call included London, where she impersonated an imperious matron trying to purchase One Dozen Double Damask Dimity Napkins; Paris, the adopted city of a languid *diseuse* "born in Prrrrovidahnse, Rhode Island"; the Swiss Alps, where she out-yelled a stageful of yodelers, and Japan, where she's transformed into an impish geisha who confided in song, "It's better with your shoes off." Ethel Waters' appearances were generally confined to such equatorial climes as the British West Indies and the Congo; in the latter, she played a "Hottentot Potentate" called the Empress Jones, who has converted the locals to the modes of Paris and Manhattan. (In the words of Dietz' deliciously convoluted rhyme scheme, she "gave them some hot-cha/je-ne-sais-quoit-cha.")

Minnelli's job was to bring a measure of stylistic coherence to this polyglot gaiety. As a magazine profile explained, he deployed the stage throughout as "a flat design like a map, filling in the spaces with clear colors." There were the usual alarums during *At Home Abroad*'s rehearsal and Boston tryout. It took all Minnelli's powers of diplomacy to mediate between his two stars, who loathed each other; what was worse, for its out-of-town opening the show spanned thirty numbers running nearly three and a half hours. Dietz wanted to cut two dance numbers of which Minnelli was especially proud—a spy-movie pastiche for Powell in which the white-garbed dancer tapped out messages in whirlwind code, and a matador ballet featuring his most dramatic lighting effects in forced-perspective and blood-red tones. Minnelli insisted on pruning elsewhere, thus "The Lady with the Tap" and "Death in the Afternoon" both remained, to become showstoppers once *At Home Abroad* dropped anchor at Broadway's Winter Garden Theater on September 19 1935.

Despite a few demurrals that Ethel Waters' material didn't match her Irving Berlin songs in *As Thousands Cheer*, first-nighters acclaimed *At Home Abroad* as superior entertainment. The *Times'* Brooks Atkinson wrote, "Without resorting to opulence, [Minnelli] has filled the stage with rich, glowing colors that give the whole work an extraordinary loveliness. Nothing quite so exhilarating as this has borne the Shubert seal before. Under his direction, the revue has such unity of appearance that it is more difficult than usual to pluck out the best numbers." He singled out the Jamaican setting for the Waters song "Loadin' Time"—"that looks like a modern painting." Other reviewers favored Minnelli's all-white Matterhorn first-act closer, with a papier-mâché mountain smothered in confetti snowflakes. It was Minnelli's particular triumph that nobody before had simultaneously staged and designed a Broadway musical. Or, in the words of the *New Yorker*,

"at least nobody has tried it and got away with it." At 198 performances, *At Home Abroad* ran for nearly six months on Broadway, a considerable achievement in those economically troubled times. (In a season encompassing such notable shows as Cole Porter's *Jubilee*, the Billy Rose spectacle *Jumbo*, and the Gershwins' *Porgy and Bess*, the only musical that ran long enough to make a profit on its investment was Rodgers and Hart's *On Your Toes*.)

When *At Home Abroad* premiered, Minnelli was already at work on his second Shubert assignment, in which he took a slightly less conspicuous role. After the death of Florenz Ziegfeld in 1932, the Shuberts contracted with his widow, Billie Burke, to revive the *Follies*, uniting their funds with her name as producer. For the 1936 edition, they'd chosen as director, John Murray Anderson, a man renowned for tasteful revues since his *Greenwich Village Follies* series in the twenties. More recently, Anderson had salvaged the first post-Ziegfeld *Follies* during its disastrous out-of-town tryout, and gone on to stage the Shubert hit *Life Begins at 8:40*. Minnelli was much influenced by Anderson's approach to the theater, and felt honored to take a backseat to his mentor on this occasion; just as graciously, Anderson sought out Minnelli's help in staging several *Follies* numbers.

In the best Ziegfeld spirit, the Shuberts belied their reputation for stinginess by assembling a scintillating roster of talent. As in 1934, the score was written by Vernon Duke to lyrics by Minnelli's friend Ira Gershwin. Responsibility for the dance numbers was split between Robert Alton—later a mainstay of the Freed Unit in Hollywood—and the young George Balanchine, making his Broadway choreographic debut with a brace of "surrealistic" ballets. Fanny Brice, the clowning star of seven previous *Follies* dating back to

Minnelli set for Josephine Baker sketch, Ziegfeld Follies of 1936

the 1910s, provided the main link to the receding Ziegfeld era; her supporting cast was headed by torch singer Gertrude Niesen, the fast-rising Bob Hope, and a sardonic beauty named Eve Arden, to whom Hope addressed the show's biggest hit tune, "I Can't Get Started." Lesser spots were reserved for Ozark comedienne Judy Canova and that matchless tap-dancing team, the then teenaged Nicholas Brothers. But the most eagerly awaited performer was Josephine Baker, making a much-heralded return home after a decade as the ascendant queen of French music hall.

In the New Year, *At Home Abroad* moved down Broadway to the Majestic to accommodate the *Follies'* January 30 premiere. Minnelli's new show lacked the tenuous thematic thread of his previous hit, but the glorified-girl motif of all Ziegfeld revues gave him what he needed—these *Follies* would shimmer with the droll elegance of a high-fashion layout in the manner of Cecil Beaton. Minnelli found Baker a particularly inspiring mannequin for his fanciful sense of chic. In a bow to her music-hall image as the pagan icon of exotica, he bared Baker in a bikini-dentata of white tusks for the Duke–Gershwin song "Island in the West Indies"; elsewhere, he draped her in saris as a maharani at the race-track and a gold-metallic gown in a sketch representing her weary-of-it-all existence in Paris. The press, however, proved far less enamored of Baker than Minnelli was, attributing to her lots of star attitude but not the goods to go with it. Apparently there was room for only one black musical personality in the Broadway of the 1930s, and New Yorkers preferred the earthier talents of Ethel Waters.

Otherwise, the *Ziegfeld Follies of 1936* had everything theatergoers could ask for in mid-Depression escapism, even at the then-exorbitant seat price of $5.50 top. Brice convulsed her fans as her trademark Baby Snooks, a Yiddish-inflected Martha Graham disciple, and in the "Sweepstakes Ticket" routine which she preserved for posterity in the MGM *Ziegfeld Follies* a decade later. Among Minnelli's most striking stage effects was a Balanchine number in abstract forms of green and black featuring Harriet Hoctor, the contortionist toe-dancer who had an inexplicable vogue in the mid-thirties. His pièce de résistance was the first-act finale, an extended parody of the Busby Berkeley–Warner Bros. backstage musical, starring "Ruby Blondell" (Brice), "Bing Powell" (Hope), and "Dolores Del Morgan" (Niesen). The epic unfolded in sets and costumes of stark black-and-white until the big finish in glorious "Techniquecolor" promoting a new dance craze, "The Gazooka." To approximate the brazen tints of early Technicolor, Minnelli covered his sets and performers alike in bright-hued cellophane. It was such a witty ersatz-movie effect that during the *Follies'* out-of-town tryout, Boston critic Elliott Norton wrote, "If you are one of those who love the legitimate stage, you are urged to utter a fervent plea to the deities of the theater that the bogeymen of Technicolor don't get him for a while at least." Norton added heretically that as far as he was concerned, the Minnelli *Follies* was more visually sophisticated than anything Ziegfeld himself had ever concocted. If his New York confreres didn't go quite so far, the 1936 *Follies* nevertheless confirmed Minnelli's reputation as the musical stage's reigning colorist. The show ran out the season at the Winter Garden, returning in the fall for another three months with a new supporting cast for Brice's antics.

Having staged his share of Caribbean tableaux by now, Minnelli decided it was time to see the place firsthand; after the *Follies* opened, he sailed to the West Indies in the company of Ira and Lee Gershwin for the first real vacation of his life. On return, Minnelli began work on his most ambitious revue. *The Show Is On* united Beatrice Lillie with her greatest male counterpart, Bert Lahr, in a satirical survey of the entertainment world, from the Bard and burlesque to swing bands and lieder. Many of the people who had contributed to *At Home Abroad* were reassembled for the occasion, including Reginald Gardiner and Paul Haakon on stage and Minnelli's favorite sketchwriter, David Freedman, behind the scenes, here collaborating with no less a Broadway luminary than Moss Hart.

To his brother J. J.'s dismay, Lee Shubert encouraged Minnelli to shoot the works with *The Show Is On*. Accordingly, Minnelli solicited musical contributions from virtually every top Broadway composer of the day: Rodgers and Hart supplied "Rhythm" for Lillie as a bebopping band singer; Dietz and Schwartz wrote a Shakespeare parody in Tin Pan Alley slang, and Harold Arlen and "Yip" Harburg provided Bert Lahr with the nonsensical "The Song of the Woodman," which prefigured their joint merriment three years later for *The Wizard of Oz*. But "Little Old Lady," by Hoagy Carmichael and Stanley Adams, proved the revue's breakaway hit, performed by the Eleanor Powellish Mitzi Mayfair, and a young hoofer named Charles Walters, who would subsequently follow Minnelli to MGM's Freed Unit as a movie-musical director of distinction. But it was the Gershwins who gave *The Show Is On* its most enduring song with "By Strauss," a back-handed tribute to Viennese schlag in three-quarter time. ("Let the Danube flow along, and *Die Fledermaus*/Keep the wine and give me song, By Strauss!") This was an unexpected bonbon from the most determinedly modern of popular composers (and sadly, the last melody he ever wrote for the Broadway stage; George Gershwin died suddenly in Hollywood six months after *The Show Is On*'s premiere.) Fifteen years later, Minnelli would sentimentally include the song in his Gershwin cavalcade, *An American in Paris*.

Minnelli filled *The Show Is On* with tongue-in-cheek nostalgia for the show-business staples of his own childhood. In memory of the ballad-singing lady-in-the-moon, who glided over the audience in the first

Minnelli set for Ziegfeld
Follies of 1936

vaudeville show he ever saw, he placed Lillie on a swing, with a saucy invitation to the audience to "Buy Yourself a Balloon" as she flung garters at the gentlemen's heads. The first-act finale, "Parade Night," was a lavish evocation of the cakewalking Tom Shows which stormed the hinterlands in the era of the Minnelli Brothers' Tent Theater. With *The Show Is On,* Minnelli exceeded the expectations raised by *At Home Abroad* and the *Follies.* Boston's Elliott Norton was his staunchest fan, dubbing Minnelli "the Broadway theater's major magician of the moment." On the morning after the revue's Christmas 1936 premiere at the Winter Garden, the New York critics vied with each other for superlatives to bestow on the "Minnelli touch," with the *New York American* praising his "patrician taste and fine wit, transmitted to paintbrush and pencil," while the *Journal*'s Douglas Gilbert proclaimed, "He has changed the old vulgar form of the musical into a charming composite of pageantry, humor, and artistic good sense, and I salute him as a pioneer."

The Show Is On ran a triumphant seven months prior to a national tour with a less notable cast; among musicals, only the Rodgers and Hart *Babes in Arms* was more popular that season. In the few years since his arrival in New York, Minnelli had made a special niche

for himself in the tonier reaches of popular entertainment. At a time when such contemporary designers as Jo Mielziner, Donald Oenslager and Boris Aronson were generally raising the standards of Broadway decor, Minnelli's painterly playfulness summed up the theatrical taste of the moment. Of all his much-bruited "modernistic" impulses, the most striking was his penchant for blurring the distinctions between high and low art. Thanks to his voracious self-education, Minnelli had absorbed the influences of artists as diverse as Fragonard, Hokusai, and De Chirico, and as a director he retranslated them into vivid, organic stage pictures.

With his third revue for the Shuberts, Minnelli felt he'd taken the form as far as it could logically go. To pursue it further would risk repeating himself; the moment was propitious to test his gifts in another medium. As soon as *The Show Is On* was on its feet, Minnelli did precisely what sages like Elliott Norton had predicted—he left the stage behind to make a new beginning as a producer-director of Hollywood musicals. But a false start out west led to a six-year wait before he again grabbed the spotlight in the movies.

3 ········· *Musicals*

As Minnelli himself explained in his autobiography, Arthur Freed's offer to join the MGM talent roster seemed, at the time, to be a decidedly mixed blessing. In 1940, Minnelli was 37 years old, and had spent a decade pursuing a theatrical career in New York. Through unstinting work and a shrewd sense of publicity, Minnelli had forged an identity as one of the liveliest minds on the musical stage—an aesthete with a strong pragmatic bent who managed to translate his esoteric notions of beauty into punchy Broadway vernacular. But as the decade waned, Minnelli's professional momentum in the theater perceptibly stalled. At the end of 1936, with his hard-won stage reputation at its peak, Minnelli left New York to accept a lucrative contract as a producer-director for Paramount Pictures. This initial Hollywood sojourn proved the first debacle of Minnelli's professional life. After six months on the Paramount lot, Minnelli had nothing to show but an inflated bank account; studio executives bypassed his pet project, a script entitled *Times Square*—which would link scenes from current Broadway hits with a mystery plot—but gave him nothing else to do. Minnelli's one contribution to Paramount's 1937 lineup was the concept for a production number entitled "Public Melody Number One," eventually performed by Louis Armstrong and Martha Raye in Raoul Walsh's *Artists and Models.* Not permitted to direct it himself, Minnelli felt the result was a chaotic travesty of his original notion. His relationship with the studio was a classic example of the uneasy symbiosis between Broadway and Hollywood that marked the thirties. Paramount admired Minnelli's theatrical pedigree but found his tastes too cultivated for mass movie audiences; Minnelli in turn was impressed by Hollywood's technical wizardry and its richness of indentured talent, but balked at expending his energies on classing up Paramount's *Big Broadcast*s or even worse. So when the Shuberts offered him another stage project, Minnelli bought out his screen contract and returned to New York.

Yet Broadway too had changed during Minnelli's brief exile, and he was hard-pressed to catch up. With the beginning of the Roosevelt administration's second term, even bourgeois West 45th Street began to mirror the values of the entrenched New Deal, as exemplified by Rodgers and Hart's affectionate F.D.R. spoof, *I'd Rather Be Right,* and the ILGWU-sponsored *Pins and Needles,* the sleeper musical hit of the late thirties. Chic escapist revues of the Minnelli sort were fast waning in fashion, and he tried to adapt to the changing order with an anti-rearmament satire set to music and entitled *Hooray for What?* This was the first book musical he had directed, and Minnelli's relative inexperience and his fundamental disinterest in political issues were apparent in the show's final form, a loose pretext for the patented antics of its star, Ed Wynn.

Minnelli next proposed a *soi-disant* surrealist revue entitled *The Light Fantastic.* Intended as a vehicle for Beatrice Lillie, it was essentially in the same mold as *At Home Abroad* and *The Show Is On,* and never got past the discussion stage. He turned next to a suggested musical-comedy version of the S. N. Behrman–Enid Bagnold comedy *Serena Blandish* with an all-black cast, in which Minnelli planned, prophetically, to team Ethel Waters and an unknown café singer named Lena Horne. This too was never realized. After a year of professional frustration, Minnelli was signed to direct the Jerome Kern–Oscar Hammerstein II musical, *Very Warm for May.* Generally dismissed as a ponderous retread of the Rodgers and Hart hit *Babes in Arms, Very Warm for May* achieved the shortest run of any Kern show in well over a decade.

In retrospect, its Broadway failure proved Hollywood's boon. Kern retreated permanently to the West Coast, to devote his energies to the screen; he was never again to write for the theater. Minnelli, with his Broadway career clearly stagnating, was tempted to make a second assault on Hollywood; at the same time, he realized that a repeat of his experience with Paramount might do permanent damage to his professional reputation.

When he expressed these fears to Arthur Freed, the producer and Minnelli devised a novel arrangement intended to minimize this risk: at a nominal salary by Hollywood standards, Minnelli would join MGM on a short-term basis which could be canceled or renewed at regular intervals by mutual consent. During this time, Minnelli would offer his expertise while studying the studio's production methods. He would be given responsibility for a film of his own when both he and the studio felt he was ready, at which time a standard director's contract would be put into effect.

The first agreement between Minnelli and MGM, drawn up on March 27 1940, stipulated a guaranteed ten weeks' employment at $300 per week salary, plus round-trip transportation from New York. MGM's legal department was initially confused as to what it was that Minnelli actually did, listing him as a "dance director" before learning that, versatile though he was, Minnelli never claimed to be a choreographer. A revised contract, signed by Minnelli on April 20, specified that he would serve "in a general advisory capacity in connection with the preparation of and production of photoplays which contain musical numbers and/or dance sequences. . . ." His duties were to include, at the studio's discretion, "the staging or mounting of musical numbers, your services as co-director, the collaboration, preparation and writing of musical numbers, treatments, adaptations and continuities with dialog of the literary material which is to serve as the basis of said photoplays." On the standard accounting forms for MGM employees, one Vincenti Minelli [sic] was listed under the category of "Musicians," which applied to all those hired to work on the studio's musicals who were not producers, directors, screenwriters, or performers. In June 1940, this rather ambiguous status was extended an additional ten weeks, an arrangement which lasted another two years.

The studio wasted no time putting their new musical ideas man to work. In March, the MGM legal department noted that Minnelli was drafted to contribute to the current Marx Brothers' picture (presumably *The Big Store,* released in 1941) and to *Strike Up the Band,* Arthur Freed's second Mickey-and-Judy-put-on-a-show extravaganza; both entered production as Minnelli arrived at the studio. Any contribution Minnelli made to *The Big Store* has gone unrecorded, but his work on the Freed picture was widely noticed, around the studio at least, and boosted his stock with the front office. When he learned that *Strike Up the Band*'s director, Busby Berkeley, was stumped for a novel way to stage a number called "Our Love Affair," Minnelli suggested a Lilliputian orchestra made out of fruit and vegetables—a double-bass player with an orange for a head sawing on a half pineapple; a leek organist thumping an asparagus console, and so on. Everyone agreed that this idea was exceedingly cute, and it was adopted. As Minnelli recalls, studio head Louis B. Mayer was particularly impressed—anyone who could confect a major production number from the contents of a shopping cart was his kind of genius.

Nevertheless, his apprenticeship at the studio proceeded slowly. During the last half of 1940, MGM continued to renew Minnelli's option, but had no particular assignments for him; most of his time was spent as part of the expanding creative entourage of the Freed Unit, although other producers of musicals, such as Jack Cummings and Pandro Berman, availed themselves of his services when the occasion arose. At the

Ann Sothern and chorus,
Panama Hattie *(1942)*

Ethel Waters and Butterfly McQueen (far left) in Cabin in the Sky *(1943)*

beginning of 1941, he was sent back to New York at MGM's expense to survey the current crop of Broadway musicals, including *Pal Joey, Lady in the Dark, Panama Hattie,* and *Cabin in the Sky.* Back at the studio, along with a brace of other writers, he provided an uncredited polish to the screenplay of Freed's *Lady Be Good;* later that year, he rewrote the opening pages for the Berman remake of the Ziegfeld musical *Rio Rita.*

A revision in his agreement with the studio, drawn up in March 1941, reflected MGM's faith in Minnelli's prospects; the clause confining his labors to the studio's musical output was eliminated, and it was further noted that he was "to render services as a director, producer, associate producer and writer as the producer may direct." Yet his status was in effect to continue for another eighteen months. As the new Rooney–Garland vehicle, *Babes on Broadway* (directed, as usual, by Berkeley), went into production in the summer of 1941, Minnelli was once again requested to devise a fresh, intimate musical sequence for the stellar pair, with the 1000-Girls-1000 routines being left to Berkeley's fevered imagination. Minnelli came up with the "Ghost Theater" number—Mickey and Judy, inspired by their discovery of some musty theatrical trunks in an abandoned Broadway theater, perform a medley of legendary showstoppers by the likes of George M. Cohan, Harry Lauder, Blanche Ring, and Fay Templeton.

As executed by Berkeley, the sequence was somewhat precious and labored. Although coached by Elsie Janis, herself one of the great vaudeville stars of the 1910s, Rooney and Garland understandably had trouble conjuring up the spirit of performers whose style they could scarcely have known firsthand, and Minnelli himself was dissatisfied with the outcome. Increasingly, his tenure at MGM was turning into a reprise of his thwarted stint at Paramount, the congenial esprit de corps of the Freed Unit notwithstanding.

His next assignment signaled an improvement in his prospects at the studio. Two years after his arrival on the West Coast, Minnelli was finally allowed to direct, and was given screen credit for the first time. Cole Porter's *Panama Hattie,* produced on Broadway in 1940, was a saucy confection snugly tailored to the contours of Porter's favorite interpreter, Ethel Merman. Its book was nothing more than a personality showcase: the tale of a lovably vulgar chanteuse working in a Central American dive, who strives to clean up her act when she falls for a handsome young plutocrat. Porter's score contained such lower-case standards as "Let's Be Buddies" and "Make It Another Old Fashioned, Please," but the show was scarcely his most distinguished. Thanks to Merman, it ran a year on Broadway and, perversely, MGM bought the film rights to the property while deeming its star a mite overpowering for the screen.

The Freed Unit went to work on the film version of *Hattie* in the fall of 1941. With Ann Sothern in the lead and directed by Norman McLeod, it was essentially a high-budget variation on her *Maisie* series of B-pictures for the studio. The first sneak preview was so calamitous that Freed took the unusual step of ordering a complete overhaul of the picture. A new script was commissioned; Roy Del Ruth was called in to replace McLeod and Minnelli was brought on to stage the musical sequences. Added to the cast was Lena Horne, a Minnelli acquaintance from New York, who had just been signed by the studio.

When *Panama Hattie* was released in 1942, the press was underwhelmed; Bosley Crowther of the *New York Times* quipped, "*Panama Hattie* was finished last fall. At several sneak previews, it cast a great pall. Metro revised it, with scissors and pen, but couldn't put *'Hattie'* together again" (10.2.42). Nevertheless, MGM viewed it as a highly creditable salvage job; understandably, because the film proved to be one of the studio's most popular attractions of the year. In retrospect, this only seems to prove how hungry audiences were for diversion at the outset of the war. Noisy but sluggish, *Panama Hattie* stumbles through long sieges of would-be mirth from Red Skelton, Rags Ragland, and Ben Blue, occasionally interrupted by a perfunctory romantic plot involving Sothern and a non-dancing Dan Dailey.

Minnelli's contribution amply demonstrated his professionalism under pressure, but the film rarely rises above the polished mediocrity which marked most of the Freed Unit musicals during the early forties. Its opening number, Porter's "I've Still Got My Health" (spliced together with Roger Edens' "Hattie from Panama" from footage shot by McLeod), suffers from Sothern's low-wattage belting. The finale, a would-be rouser called "The Son of a Gun Who Picks on Uncle Sam," combines post-Pearl Harbor jingoism with staging reminiscent of a 100% All-Talkie production number from the late twenties: brightly smiling, the entire cast (minus the black specialty artists) faces front in a static long shot, to render such urbane lyrics as "We've got a wood kimono for the Mikado/We've got a mausoleum for Mussoleen."

The movie's scant distinction is found in the two numbers which showcase Lena Horne. At least with this movie Minnelli can be credited with shaping the screen image of the most anomalous star performer of the era. The first black woman packaged for glamour by Hollywood, Horne was presented as a smouldering sophisticate—exotic but unthreatening. Since the racial politics of the time wouldn't permit her to share the screen with white colleagues, Horne spent most of her 1940s film career relegated to guest appearances. While she became an official star at a time when such niceties of billing were taken very seriously, Horne's on-screen time rarely exceeded five minutes per movie.

Her sequences in *Panama Hattie* display the two facets of Horne which MGM would promote for the rest of the decade. For the novelty item she shares with the high-flying gymnastics of the Berry Brothers, timid ethnicity is the key: adorned in black net with ball fringe, Horne applies a variety of Caribbean accents to her tongue-twisting lyrics extolling "a tricky, icky dance they call the Sping." However, "Just One of Those Things," borrowed from Cole Porter's Broadway score for *Jubilee,* is vintage early Horne. Lovingly framed by Minnelli's camera, Horne adds her own banked fires to the creamy vocalism required of forties movie chanteuses. It's the one memorable moment from *Panama Hattie*—a cornerstone of Horne's occasionally glorious, generally frustrating MGM career, if only a footnote to Minnelli's.

. . . .

1943 CABIN IN THE SKY

Minnelli's refurbishment of *Panama Hattie* did not go unrewarded. His confidence behind the camera persuaded Freed that after two years at the studio, Minnelli was ready for his first comprehensive directorial assignment. The project marked the producer's first attempt at something novel for the Hollywood musical and was a prime opportunity for Minnelli to explore his own particular sensibilities on film. With a score by Vernon Duke and John Latouche, *Cabin in the Sky* had been a modest success of Broadway's 1940-41 season. A prettified fable set in the rural black South, where the minions of Satan and the angels of De Lawd battle for possession of the saintly Petunia's scapegrace husband, Little Joe, the show's principal attractions were songs such as "Taking a Chance on Love" and "Honey in the Honeycomb." Choreography was by Katherine Dunham and George Balanchine, and a notable cast featuring Dunham, Dooley Wilson, Todd Duncan, and Rex Ingram supported the incandescent Ethel Waters. In June 1942, two months after *Panama Hattie* was completed, MGM acquired the film rights to the show for Freed for the sum of $40,000.

Although modestly budgeted for an MGM musical (at a total cost of $679,260, it was Freed's cheapest production of the decade), *Cabin in the Sky* was viewed as a risky screen venture. Hollywood films with all-black casts had rarely found favor with white mass audiences; in fact, *Cabin* was only the fourth such venture by a major studio since the coming of sound. (In 1929, MGM produced King Vidor's heartfelt and skillful *Hallelujah,* while Fox came up with its All-Shuffling/All-Coonshouting musical, *Hearts in Dixie,* and seven years later, Warner Bros. released a film adaptation of the stage sensation *The Green Pastures*.) Moreover, by the war years, civil rights organizations and the black press were increasingly attentive to the movies' depiction of minorities, and might subject *Cabin* to a scrutiny potentially embarrassing to the studio.

Freed persevered nonetheless, with Minnelli as his logical choice to direct. At a time when black themes and artists were marginal to mainstream show business, Minnelli had long since established his credentials with this kind of "exoticism." As one of the commercial theater's most progressive directors in the 1930s, he had displayed a bold affinity for African and West Indian motifs in many of his stage designs. Additionally, Minnelli had directed the notoriously temperamental Ethel Waters without mishap on Broadway in *At Home Abroad*. With a score by Vernon Duke, an old colleague from the *Ziegfeld Follies of 1936*, and the addition of Lena Horne to the cast, this was the very combination of talents Minnelli had tried to forge when *Serena Blandish* foundered three years before.

Production began on *Cabin in the Sky* at the end of August 1942 with only Waters and Rex Ingram, as the devil's chief emissary, retained from the Broadway cast. (Dooley Wilson was considered to repeat his stage role, but it was felt that Eddie "Rochester" Anderson's name meant more to screen audiences.) With contract player Horne supplanting Dunham as the satanic temptress Georgia Brown, the part was expanded and the focus shifted from dance to song. Harold Arlen and E. Y. Harburg were commissioned to write a sheaf of songs to add to the Duke–Latouche score—there were three by each team in the final version of the film. Marc Connelly, creator of *The Green Pastures*, polished Joseph Schrank's screenplay, but requested that he remain uncredited. The relatively constricted scale of this production was reflected in the salaries paid to the "colored artists," as the cast was referred to in the studio's interoffice correspondence. Ethel Waters' recompense was approximately $25,000. Because she feared that MGM sought to enhance Horne at her expense,

*Lena Horne and Eddie
'Rochester'' Anderson in*
Cabin in the Sky *(1943)*

Waters stipulated in her contract that ''no member of the Negro race [is] to appear in size of type larger than that used to portray her name.''

On the film's release in April 1943, the reception accorded *Cabin in the Sky* was everything Freed could have hoped for. If anything, the film was more uniformly praised than the stage version; the press universally cited its novelty and skill, qualities less than apparent in Freed's recent *Lady Be Good* and *Panama Hattie.* While less than for any Freed project at the time, *Cabin in the Sky*'s box-office receipts of $1,606,624 were eminently respectable in light of its low production costs. The principal beneficiary of *Cabin*'s success was Minnelli; this project's unusual nature gained him immediate notice as a distinctive addition to the industry. And if the freshness of his eye was appreciated on the lot as well as in the press, Minnelli's employers were likewise pleased to note that his classy visual sense hadn't clouded his professionalism. The fact that he had succeeded first time out in making a widely admired A-product of what was for MGM a B-budget film, proved to the studio that Minnelli was as efficient as he was artistically resourceful.

With the rise of racial self-assertion in the media as well as in other aspects of American life, subsequent decades were not kind to properties such as *Cabin in the Sky.* In retrospect, there's no denying the essentially patronizing nature of the material Minnelli was working with. Like *The Green Pastures,* Dubose Heyward's *Porgy,* and other well-meant white visions of black culture of the day, *Cabin in the Sky* founders on the notion that colored folks are simply more primal than the over-civilized Caucasian and, thanks to their essential simplicity, they embody moral absolutes of good and evil devoid of the complex shadings of white society. The competing lures of Heaven and Hell are far more urgent an issue in *Cabin in the Sky* than the stresses of every day. Those concrete depredations imposed on blacks by a white majority are never alluded to; by a soothing stroke of fantasy, whites are invisible and therefore irrelevant. Poverty is seen as the eternal lot of God's children, who will reap their reward in the hereafter.

Hence, in *Cabin in the Sky,* the heroine Petunia is glorified for qualities which would have seemed saccharine and impractical in an equivalent white character—exceeding piety, serene resignation to her place in the world. (As the title song expresses, even Petunia's vision of Heaven is a replica of her life on earth—only now her cabin will be on a cloud ''as the angels go sailing by.'') Similarly, the sensuality and acquisitiveness of her nemesis Georgia Brown is viewed as an unholy threat—as such an assertive black woman would seem to much of white society. The absence of anger and disaffection are precisely what made a movie like *Cabin* palatable to white audiences; it was comforting to pretend, for 99 minutes anyway, that Negroes would be content with so much less in life than they had.

Considering this premise, it's remarkable how little of *Cabin in the Sky* is really discomfiting to watch more than four decades later; principally, a John Bubbles solo dance entitled "That's Why They Call Me Shine" and Waters' last chorus of the title song, filmed on a sound-stage hillside and pond, with the star framed by a chorus of bandanna'd mammies and urchins in the style of *The Green Pastures*. Otherwise Minnelli's tactful treatment of these ersatz folklore creatures avoids the worst stereotypical excesses. Waters may strain a little too hard for beatitude in her solo songs, but surely few other actresses could spend so much time on their knees with eyes uplifted without cloying. The hushed urgency of her entreaties to the Lord and her blunt drollery in vanquishing the Devil's earthly emissaries make Waters' Petunia a model of judicious understatement. "Rochester's" gravel-voiced dismay and pop-eyed befuddlement is given a human dimension generally absent in his other movie turns as Jack Benny's valet and miscellaneous domestics. Described by Rex Ingram's Lucifer Jr. as "one of Pappy's favorite daughters," the mantrap Georgia Brown was, astonishingly, to be Lena Horne's only acting role in her seven years at MGM. Its demands are admittedly modest, requiring Horne to slither, coo, and undulate her bare midriff while those dark eyes blazed, but Minnelli embellishes it with a number of witty, alluring touches. For example, Georgia snatches a plate-sized magnolia from a nearby tree, fashioning it into a hat meant for seduction. Hell's minions, including the robust, bellow-voiced Ingram (pretty low-down after his stint as De Lawd in the Warner Bros. *Green Pastures*), a non-musical Louis Armstrong as the Devil's chief ideas man dressed in a harlequin bathrobe, and that unflappable

scamp, Mantan Moreland, make far more entertaining companions than Kenneth Spencer in the role of God's goody-goody. With competition like this, no wonder Petunia has to sweat and suffer so to keep Little Joe inscribed in Heaven's ledgers.

Rex Ingram and Lena Horne in Cabin in the Sky *(1943)*

ABOVE:
Minnelli directing Eddie "Rochester" Anderson and Lena Horne in Cabin in the Sky *(1943)*

Given this roster of talent, many of Metro's contract directors might have made an entertaining screen transcription of this well-crafted stage property. What made *Cabin in the Sky* something more was Minnelli's gift for integrating these figures into a coherent (and kinetic) vision of his own devising. Budgetary constrictions clearly put a damper on his concept of a sepia afterlife, with Hell consisting of one cramped white-deco office suite in Hotel Hades, while Heaven is a painted staircase to infinity surrounded by dry ice and dotted with incidental black cherubs resting on broken Greek (or plantation?) columns. Petunia's earthly paradise, however, is less claustrophobic than microcosmic. At least half the action takes place on the set representing her cabin, yet the movie never feels constricted, thanks to Minnelli's gift for filling this realistically small space with a lived-in aura of fantasy. From the oil lamps that flare with the arrival of messengers from beyond, to the lacy iron bedstead on which a delirious Little Joe awaits his fate, every object in Minnelli's frame is imbued with qualities at once homely and fantastic. His meticulousness on this score prompted the first of his many disputes with MGM art director Cedric Gibbons, whose own notions of shanty life were far more prosaic. It was this ability of Minnelli's which gave *Cabin in the Sky* its requisite note of stylization, without which the enterprise would have been impossibly arch.

Minnelli sought this strength of detail in his years as a designer and director for the theater, and there are moments in *Cabin in the Sky* which smack of theatrical tableaux, like the title number; Little Joe and Petunia's ascent into Heaven. Yet, throughout this maiden effort, Minnelli keeps exploring the camera's active potential for shaping the mood of the material, rather than merely recording it. The musical sequences are filmed with an unobtrusive succinctness, and a judicious use of closeups: Waters bathed in a saintly key light from above for songs like "Happiness Is Just a Thing Called Joe" and a radiant Horne emerging from a froth of white plumes for "Honey in the Honeycomb." Yet in *Cabin in the Sky*'s first number, the Sunday-meeting "Little Black Sheep," Minnelli's camera describes a zigzag track backward through the church, pausing to focus on the hymn's soloists and gossiping parishioners, until it rests on the subject of both the song and the attendant chatter—Petunia, with her errant husband ready for salvation. Here Minnelli strives to meld song meter with camera movement, all in the service of dramatic purpose. His mastery of this technique was soon to mark him as the most cinematic of all directors of movie musicals.

Throughout *Cabin in the Sky*, there are tantalizing hints of themes and images that would preoccupy Minnelli for the rest of his career. In his later work, mirrors become the most emotion-fraught objects in Minnelli's universe, whose gaze exposes his protagonists' worst fears about themselves. Here, all three principal characters have their moment before the looking glass to reveal their true natures, more for our benefit than theirs. We see Little Joe's moral ambivalence, Georgia's preening self-satisfaction, and Petunia's unstinting faith. On a broader level, *Cabin in the Sky* was the first Minnelli movie to use fantasy as palatable sublimation for very real human conflicts—which, as his later films will underscore, is a very different matter from undiluted escapism. There is considerable pain underlying *Cabin in the Sky*'s sprightly surface; after all, the plot is propelled by greed, adultery, and a double homicide before all is resolved. The bulk of the action takes place within the framework of a dream, its structure reminiscent of MGM's 1939 *The Wizard of Oz*, even to a cyclone as the *deus ex machina*. But for Minnelli, that only enhanced this story's power to disturb. For as he was to prove so often later on, dreams can turn truth into beauty—and also into terror.

• •

1943   I DOOD IT

MGM rewarded Minnelli for his successful labors on *Cabin in the Sky* in two ways. Immediately after it was completed, they assigned him the unappetizing task of directing *I Dood It,* a Red Skelton–Eleanor Powell vehicle (her last for the studio), previously announced for Roy Del Ruth, and sweetened the deal by doubling his wages of five hundred dollars a week. Neither decision was reached capriciously. Amid a flurry of internal memos on the subject of Minnelli's compensation, I. H. Prinzmetal of the legal department noted, "Vincente Minnelli was originally a stage and art director in New York in relationship to the spoken stage. His function was primarily in connection with the presentation of musical numbers. . . . He showed remarkable ability to go beyond this function and was assigned to direct feature pictures. He completed the direction of *Cabin in the Sky* and he showed such remarkable talent we are now assigning him regularly to the function of directing important A-productions. . . . The proposed salary is less than that paid to other per-

Red Skelton and Eleanor Powell in I Dood It *(1943)*

sons who do a similar type of work and compensation paid directors of comparable ability generally runs from $1,500 to $4,000 a week . . . we have been able to hire people on an experimental basis who have always been assured that when they reached success, their success would be rewarded, and they would not be tied down to a contract not commensurate with their proven ability.''

It's unlikely that the studio considered this tacky enterprise either a waste of Minnelli's time or a back-handed insult to his ''remarkable talent.'' After all, he was being entrusted with a moderately important release on their 1943 schedule, at nearly twice the budget of *Cabin in the Sky;* MGM was in the entertainment business, and its contract artists were expected to apply their skills to the task with as little grumbling as possible. The fact that Minnelli had been assigned to the helm of a million-dollar-plus picture was the studio's main rationale for adjusting his salary.

Minnelli started work on *I Dood It* in November 1942, three weeks after completing *Cabin in the Sky.* In December he was inducted into the army, and MGM frantically set about arranging an emergency furlough so he could complete the film. (Months earlier, the studio had tried to get Minnelli exempted from the draft, on the grounds that ''the production of motion pictures has been declared an essential industry by the War Manpower Commission, and that the activity of Mr. Minnelli will be of a nature essential to the war effort.'' Eventually, he was reclassified for physical disabilities.)

I Dood It is a loose remake of Buster Keaton's last silent film, the 1929 *Spite Marriage.* As before, Red Skelton is a tailor's assistant enamored of a Broadway star (Eleanor Powell), who impulsively marries him to pique her sullen sweetheart, played by John Hodiak. To update the plot, the 1943 version has the comedian winning the lady's devotion once he exposes Hodiak as a spy for the Axis forces. Skelton was an inveterate Keaton admirer, if perhaps not his comic equal, and pallid traces of the film's source turn up intermittently throughout *I Dood It;* notably in a long slapstick routine in which the hero maneuvers the dead weight of his comatose bride onto their nuptial bed. In Keaton's version, his human prop is merely drunk; here, Powell mistakenly downs the mickey she'd coolly concocted to knock out Skelton on their wedding night. When the heroine's self-centered callousness collides with the game Skelton's masochism, *I Dood It* sours into genuine unpleasantness, particularly Skelton's suicide attempt, foiled because the gas lines have been turned off—a sequence with no equivalent in Keaton's film.

Producer Jack Cummings must have hoped that Minnelli could infuse this nonsense with a little style, but even visually *I Dood It* is indistinguishable from a dozen other Metro mediocrities of the day. Although he'd previously collaborated with Eleanor Powell on the stage for *At Home Abroad,* her vaudevillian gymnastics were not Minnelli's forte. Attentive fans will have noticed that several of her solos were snipped wholesale out of previous Powell extravaganzas (a hula dance from *Honolulu,* the cannons-and-poop-deck rou-

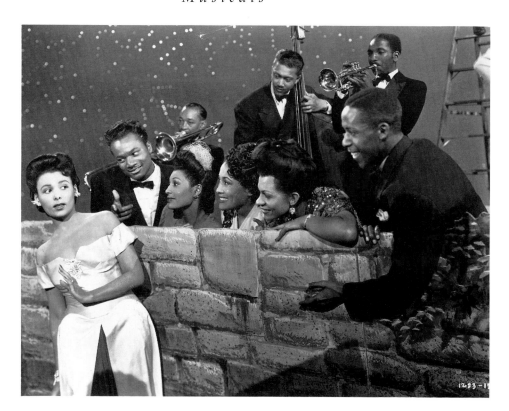

tine from *Ship Ahoy,* or was it *Born to Dance*?). Although "So Long, Sarah Jane," her cowgirl-with-a-lariat specialty, was concocted specifically for this movie, Minnelli later disclaimed responsibility for that as well.

The one spark of Minnellian flair is a kind of Penthouse-in-the-Sky routine which he shot and inserted three months (and three tepid sneak previews) after the rest of the film was in the can. Framed as a producer's audition for Powell's new show—and easily excisable to placate those Southern exhibitors discomfited by the sight of all those uppity colored performers dressed to kill—it takes shape as a battle between black pop divas Hazel Scott and Lena Horne. First Scott launches into "Taking a Chance on Love" as a mock

concerto turned boogie-woogie, while Minnelli's camera describes 180-degree arcs around her baby grand. Then, against a starry cyclorama, a white-gowned Horne sweeps in, exclaiming "I'm terribly sorry, I just *couldn't* find a taxi"—a line to prompt bitter mirth from the balcony of the Loews' Victoria. What follows is a Café Society version of the fall of Jericho, as a genteel Horne and her lowdown chorus belt out the swinging harmonics of a characteristic Kay Thompson arrangement.

Still, this one vibrant note is small recompense for enduring the rest of *I Dood It.* Minnelli's one consolation was that, after the triumph of his next picture, never again would he have to give such abject proof of his fealty to Ars Gratia Artis.

• •

1944   MEET ME IN ST. LOUIS

During the spring and summer of 1943, several projects engaged Minnelli's attention. The studio asked him to direct Lena Horne's cameo in *Thousands Cheer,* MGM's wartime all-star super-vaudeville to compete with Paramount's *Star Spangled Rhythm* and Warner Bros.' *Thank Your Lucky Stars.* His shimmering staging of "Honeysuckle Rose" was his last professional collaboration with Horne, and his first opportunity to work in Technicolor. Shortly thereafter, he

served as script doctor and production advisor during the Los Angeles tryout of a stage revue, *Laugh Time,* which featured Ethel Waters and was produced by Fred Finklehoffe, an MGM screenwriter then at work on the project which would establish Minnelli's reputation for good.

The film was *Meet Me in St. Louis.* Initially conceived by the studio as a modest programmer for the family trade, by the time Minnelli was brought in, it was shaping up as one of MGM's most important pictures for the coming year. Under the title "5135 Kensington," Sally Benson's stories of her midwestern childhood ran serially in the *New Yorker* from June 1941 to May 1942 before being consolidated in book form with an additional four chapters. MGM acquired the rights in January 1942; justifying the purchase, studio executive I. H. Prinzmetal noted, "I think the stories are somewhat similar to the 'Life with Father' stories . . . in making the pictures as I contemplate, we will want to make them something like the Hardy series." With this in mind, in addition to the $25,000 purchase price,

MGM offered Benson a $10,000 option on the use of her characters for future sequels.

The author was brought out to the studio to write a screen treatment, and for the next year, several staff screenwriters, including Victor Heerman, Sarah Y. Mason, and William Ludwig, tried their hands at turning these nostalgic, virtually plotless stories into a workable scenario. One early treatment opted to punch up the story by making heroine Esther Smith the victim of a blackmail/kidnapping scheme. Arthur Freed fortunately decided that this was emphatically the wrong approach. He voted to preserve the simplicity of the

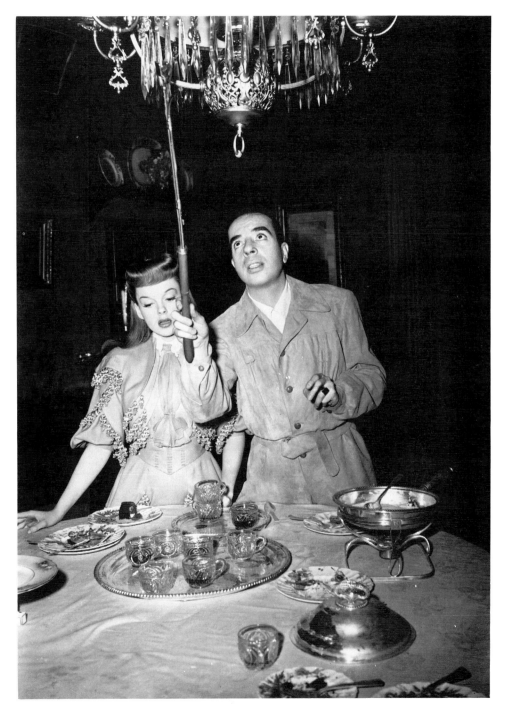

Minnelli directing Judy Garland in Meet Me in St. Louis *(1944)*

Kensington stories while expanding the package into a Technicolor vehicle for Judy Garland, with songs carefully integrated into the fabric of the family's domestic pleasures and disappointments. His enthusiasm was shared by none of the other executives in the Thalberg Building; the idea strayed too far from the norm to justify the proposed expenditure. Nevertheless, L. B. Mayer was prepared to back up Freed. His faith in the producer's discernment was encouraged perhaps by a happy accident of timing—in March 1943, an unheralded musical opened on Broadway that also exalted life in the American heartland at the turn of the century. Rodgers and Hammerstein's *Oklahoma!* in which MGM had a substantial investment, became the theatrical sensation of the decade. If Broadway's patrons could thrill to heroine Laurey's indecision over her date for the church social, MGM had reason to hope that the moviegoing masses might sigh along with Esther Smith, pining her heart out for the boy next door.

Freed now drafted the team of Finklehoffe and Irving Brecher to write a script according to his specifications and offered the property to Minnelli to direct. Minnelli's enthusiasm was instantaneous; not only was this an opportunity to expand the possibilities of the movie musical, but the period and locale had a special resonance for the director—the film was set in the year of his birth in a suburban setting reminiscent of his own midwestern origins. Once the studio gave the go-ahead to *Meet Me in St. Louis,* Minnelli was given ample time to prepare a film to match Freed's aspirations. The project was assigned to him eight months before shooting began in December 1943. Minnelli used the time working in close collaboration with Brecher and Finklehoffe on script revisions and drafting the studio's research department to amass all the visual documentation they could muster on turn-of-the-century America. This accomplished, he set about recreating this world in concert with Lemuel Ayers, *Oklahoma!*'s set designer, whom Arthur Freed had lured to Culver City when MGM's art department persisted in viewing the film as another *Love Finds Andy Hardy*, with Victorian trim.

Minnelli's most urgent task at this stage was persuading Judy Garland that *Meet Me in St. Louis* was worth doing at all. After a protracted screen adolescence, by 1943 Garland had begun to play grown-up heroines in such musicals as *For Me and My Gal* and *Presenting Lily Mars*. The prospect of playing another tremulous seventeen-year-old given to wistful lines such as "I've waited all my *life* to be a senior!" struck her as a step backward, however illustrious the context. This, coupled with her perennial suspicions of the studio's motives in her behalf, prompted Garland to enlist Minnelli in her campaign to get the movie cancelled. As he later recalled, his excitement over *Meet Me in St. Louis* surprised Garland, but at this early point in their professional and personal relationship, it failed to sway her. It was only at Mayer's insistence that Gar-

land relented and reported for work, and for the first weeks of shooting Minnelli tactfully fought her instinct to satirize a character she felt she'd long since outgrown. Casting the rest of the Smith family was a relatively easy matter; apart from Joan Carroll, the child veteran of Broadway's *Panama Hattie* who was cast as Agnes, all the principals were MGM contract players. While Van Johnson was the announced choice to play Esther's love interest, he was eventually supplanted by Tom Drake. Making her screen debut as Rose, the eldest Smith daughter, was Lucille Bremer, a former New York night club dancer and Freed protégée. Never again in her brief tenure at the studio would she be as aptly cast.

Metro's craftsmen endured an object lesson in Minnelli's stubborn exactitude during the four months it took to shoot *Meet Me in St. Louis*. He had definite, time-consuming notions about such niceties as camera movement, lighting, and decor. In this he had a treasured ally in MGM's veteran cinematographer, George Folsey, who achieved some of the most fluid and evocative work of his career with this film. Others were less patient when an apparently simple sequence like Esther's shy courtship of the boy next door while extinguishing the lights in the parlor and landing took four days to light and stage to Minnelli's satisfaction. Furthermore, the muted palette Minnelli sought was persistently challenged by color consultant Natalie Kalmus, whose unwanted presence was a contractual inevitability on any picture utilizing Technicolor camera equipment.

Yet the longueurs of shooting *Meet Me in St. Louis* were due less to Minnelli's perspicacity than to other factors beyond his control. As meticulously documented in Hugh Fordin's book on the Freed Unit, *The World of Entertainment,* the shooting schedule was constantly interrupted by illness among the cast, from Garland and screen mom Mary Astor to Joan Carroll and Margaret O'Brien, whose mother was simultaneously wrangling with the studio over her daughter's punishing work schedule for a mere $250 per week. (When the film was finished, MGM granted O'Brien and Minnelli substantial bonuses for hard work well done.)

The *Meet Me in St. Louis* company finally completed production on April 7 1944; the total cost of the film was $1,883,289.14, making it one of the studio's most expensive that year. Minnelli's major squabble was still to come and, surprisingly enough, it was a clash with his most loyal supporter at the studio, Arthur Freed. Upon viewing the final cut, Freed insisted on excising Minnelli's favorite and most exactingly executed sequence—Tootie's Halloween adventure—on the grounds that it was inessential to the plot and slowed up the picture. Fortunately, somehow it stayed in for the film's first sneak preview in June and was retained thereafter. In the end, the only major trim was the excision of a Rodgers and Hammerstein song, "Boys

Lucille Bremer and Judy Garland harmonize on the title song, Meet Me in St. Louis *(1944)*

and Girls Like You and Me," interpolated into Ralph Blane and Hugh Martin's score. Previously dropped from *Oklahoma!* here it was sung by Garland immediately following the "Trolley Song" number, on a set representing the uncompleted St. Louis fairgrounds.

On its release in November, the film's reception surpassed everyone's high expectations. In box-office returns and the unanimity of critical praise, *Meet Me in St. Louis* was the most successful Freed production to date, exerting an influence on the development of the movie musical which was to last well into the next decade. The attempt to shape an intimate, period chronicle of a "typical" American family in musical terms very soon became a Hollywood commonplace, as often as not entrusted to the unlikeliest of directors. 20th Century-Fox's 1946 *Centennial Summer,* with Otto Preminger at the helm and a Jerome Kern score, followed *Meet Me in St. Louis'* example nearly to the point of plagiarism. MGM itself tried to recreate the magic with its 1948 release, *Summer Holiday,* a musical reworking of Eugene O'Neill's *Ah, Wilderness!* In the early 1950s, Warner Bros. drafted its own in-house singing ingenue, Doris Day, for a pair of Booth Tarkington adaptations, *On Moonlight Bay* and *By the Light of the Silvery Moon,* while budget-conscious Universal produced a modest equivalent with Douglas Sirk's *Has Anybody Seen My Gal?* Yet none of these variations on Minnelli's theme has enjoyed anything like the enduring resonance of *Meet Me in St. Louis.*

In basic outline the film reflects MGM's original impulse to confect its own version of the *Life with Father* formula. Like Howard Lindsay and Russel Crouse's

stage hit (which had also been adapted from a series of personal reminiscences published in the *New Yorker*), *Meet Me in St. Louis* depicts a comfortably situated turn-of-the-century household, whose perennially irascible patriarch is constantly outwitted by his apparently submissive wife and their numerous offspring. At a period when American family life was challenged by the social upheavals and enforced separations of wartime, the cozy solidarity of the fictional Smiths—and even the marked uneventfulness of life at 5135 Kensington Avenue—had a special poignance for audiences during the mid-forties. In keeping with the hallowed precepts of *New Yorker* fiction, Benson's original stories are deliberately undramatic. Each of her monthly sketches climaxes with a small family epiphany, of which many found their way intact into the finished film, with some chronological rearrangement—Rose's long-distance call from a far-off beau, the Smith girls' parlor musicale, a suburban Halloween, and the exhilarating family visit to the fairgrounds—along with a surprising amount of the original dialogue. The Kensington stories have a deliberately placid tone; nothing that happens to the Smith family in the course of this year ever seriously threatens their domestic harmony. What distinction these stories have comes from Benson's fastidious gift for description—her near-photographic recall of traditional midwestern decors and decorum, which give a persuasive specificity to these childhood recollections.

It was the screenwriters' task to preserve the evanescent charm of these stories while infusing them with a certain narrative focus and momentum. Structurally,

Brecher and Finkelhoffe compressed Benson's twelve monthly vignettes into four acts representing the seasons from summer, 1903 to spring, 1904. A more delicate problem was the need to reshape the family ensemble to meet the exigencies of the Metro star system, without distorting its balance. In the stories, Esther's character is less delineated, but as a property for Judy Garland in *Meet Me in St. Louis* she emerges first among equals, achieved primarily by focusing on her blossoming romance with the Boy Next Door (who doesn't exist in Benson's stories). Also, the role of Tootie was expanded at Agnes' expense to showcase the precocious virtuosity of Margaret O'Brien. Originally, Agnes was the Halloween heroine of the hour, and it was she who triumphantly disrupted the big kids' party with her enthusiastic cakewalk. Absurd though the brainstorm to abduct and ransom Esther might have been, some kind of dramatic conflict was clearly required. In the end the screenwriters sagely took their cue from a minor incident buried in the original stories. In Benson's text, the threat of the family's move from St. Louis to New York is raised and dismissed in a brief three pages; here it becomes a serious prospect and provides the film's emotional fulcrum, wreaking despair as the Smiths suddenly realize how fragile their domestic happiness really is.

Punctuated throughout with sprightly and idiomatic dialogue, Brecher and Finklehoffe's adaptation proved one of the handful of truly satisfactory screenplays ever to grace the American movie musical. It afforded Minnelli the ideal occasion to explore more fully the impulses first expressed in *Cabin in the Sky:* the quest for a new kind of lyric cinema through imagery of painstaking sophistication applied to an everyday context. The opening sequence of *Meet Me in St. Louis,* conjuring up one hot summer afternoon at 5135 Kensington Avenue, shimmers with a deceptive simplicity that only the most cultivated eye could produce. After a black-and-white family album snapshot of the Smith house springs to color and animation, George Folsey's camera tracks down the bustling, unpaved suburban street, then reverses direction to follow a young man (son Lon) riding his bicycle onto the Smith lawn. Inside the house, Mrs. Smith and Katie the maid are engrossed in their ketchup-making; Lon casually hums a few bars of the title song as he sets down the groceries, while the second-youngest, Agnes, enters the kitchen—her bloomers still wet from a swim—and picks up the tune while sauntering through the hallway and up to the second floor as the camera trails behind her. From inside the bathroom, Grandpa continues the refrain; their paths cross as he waltzes past the upstairs landing into his room and tries on some samples from his lodge-cap collection. Outside, Esther and her crowd are heard completing the chorus, and from Grandpa's window we see her alighting from a horse cart and entering the house.

Back in the kitchen, there's more bickering over the ketchup recipe and Esther exhorts Katie to make sure dinner is served an hour earlier than usual as eldest sister Rose, unmarried at twenty, is expecting a long-distance call from an admirer in New York. "Personally, I wouldn't marry a man who proposed to me over an invention," retorts Katie. "There's the poor old maid now," she announces as we see a coquettish Rose sauntering up the front steps. The object of her languorous gaze is a young man of impeccable, frat-man allure, standing on the neighboring lawn with his pipe firmly clenched in his teeth. Cued by "The Boy Next Door" melody on the soundtrack, she persuades Esther to join her on the porch for a peek. Nonchalantly, the two girls take in the view; oblivious, the young man withdraws and so do they. Rose drifts disdainfully upstairs for her shampoo, as Esther reminds her of the fateful phone call to come. "My dear, when you get to be my age, you'll realize there are more important things in life than boys," she retorts. Unconvinced, Esther gazes dreamily toward the camera and in the direction of her unwitting beloved. "The moment I saw him smile/I knew he was just my style," Esther muses in the lushest Garland tones, as she ambles toward the window seat that faces neighboring 5133 Kensington Avenue. She pauses after the first chorus of "The Boy Next Door" to primp and prance in the hallway mirror and then, resuming her vantage point, completes this soliloquy of longing. A rapturous closeup of Esther greets the last bars; the white muslin curtain she'd held back from the window slowly descends before her face to cap the moment.

Minnelli dissolves from this visual valentine to a closeup of the tureen of ketchup in the kitchen as Grandpa pronounces it "Too thick!" Agnes bursts into the kitchen searching for her cat, which Katie boasts of having kicked down the cellar stairs: "I could hear its spine hit on every step," she murmurs. "Oh, if you killed her I'll kill you!" cries the infuriated Agnes, but it's a joke—there's Lady Babbie in the corner. Slicing cabbage at the sink, Mrs. Smith advises Rose to keep her impending phone call a secret from Mr. Smith, due home shortly from work. Esther enters and asks where the youngest daughter, Tootie, is. "Oh, she's probably working on the ice wagon," replies Mrs. Smith nonchalantly, and the scene dissolves to a shot of Tootie, bleating a few bars of the hymn "Brighten the Corner" while perched on Mr. Neely's horse cart as it plods down Kensington Avenue. A pint-sized Lucretia Borgia, Tootie is aglow with pleasure over the moribund state of her favorite doll, Margaretha. "She has four fatal diseases," she proudly informs the iceman. "And it only takes one," he muses. After enumerating the delights of the funeral to come, Tootie shifts to her second favorite preoccupation—her precocious hometown pride. Gently, she rebukes Mr. Neely, who has called St. Louis "quite a town" and mispronounced it in the bargain. "It isn't a town, Mr. Neely, it's a city. It's the only city that has a world's fair. My favorite city. Wasn't I lucky to be born in my favorite city!"

Back home, Esther waltzes around the parlor in her post-shampoo bloomers to a reprise of the fair's anthem, accompanied by Rose at the family piano. As she rejoins her sister at the keyboard for a second chorus of close harmony, Minnelli shifts to a tilted, low-angle shot, exquisitely counterpointing the two girls with a ceramic miniature of twin Victorian damsels on top of the piano. The enchantment of the moment is lost on Mr. Smith, seen trudging wearily up the walk to the house. "For heaven's sake, stop that screeching," he barks as he enters the parlor. Collapsing into a chair, Mr. Smith mutters, "That song. The fair won't open for seven months . . . I wish everyone would meet at the fair and leave me alone." He's troubled by the court case he's lost that day, and the fact that the womenfolk hovering around him in his distress can't seem to get into the properly dolorous spirit. "If losing a case depresses you so, papa, why don't you quit practicing law and go into another business?" Esther queries blandly. This practical solution is lost on Mr. Smith, who flares up again when he learns that dinner will be served early. Asserting his last shred of authority over his brood, he informs them they will eat when he is ready and not a moment before, and storms upstairs for a cool, restorative bath.

These first few minutes of *Meet Me in St. Louis* are a model of deft economy. From the very first shot, Min-nelli makes it clear that the real protagonist of this movie is an inanimate one—the Smiths' house, whose sturdy idiosyncrasies reflect and sustain the unity of the family sheltered inside. In a leisurely tempo, Minnelli manages to sketch in the characteristics of all ten members of the Smith clan and their relationship to each other, prefiguring the strains to come. Tootie's homicidal bent over her toys will become more primal when she has a real motive for anguish. As the patriarch whose life is centered outside the confines of 5135 Kensington Avenue, Mr. Smith is less head of the household than its disruptive outsider.

Minnelli's subtlest accomplishment here is his plausible fusion of these elements with the genre requirements of the movie musical. Romance is as intrinsic to the Smiths' daily world as ketchup-making. Anything that happens in the house prompts (or interrupts) a burst of song, since singing is as natural an expression of family sentiment as kitchen gossip or bickering in the parlor. Minnelli's successful pursuit of the values of the so-called "integrated" musical, only recently patented on the stage by Rodgers and Hammerstein, is what immediately sets *Meet Me in St. Louis* apart from the five years of Garland star vehicles which preceded it. Apart from the *sui generis The Wizard of Oz,* her films had been sketchily conceived affairs, with thin back-stage plots interrupted by overproduced vaudeville. At the center of these movies Garland was also a divided creature—a gauche, unprepossessing kid in the prosy episodes, blossoming suddenly into a vocal dynamo

The youngest Smiths prepare for Halloween. Joan Carroll and Margaret O'Brien in Meet Me in St. Louis *(1944)*

whose poise springs from nowhere once Mickey gives her the downbeat from the onscreen orchestra pit. The part of Esther represents a definitive break from all those "ordinary" girls revealed as musical freaks of nature. Photographed as never before, and directed to bring forth all her reserves of wit, charm, and confidence, Garland also modulates her singing to a more human key. When Esther makes music, she's not trying to slay the crowd but to divert her St. Louis neighbors or comfort a kid sister, or simply to let out her feelings in a way which is second nature to the most gifted in a family of parlor virtuosi.

If *Meet Me in St. Louis* was the least overtly showbizzy of Garland movies to date, it also remains Minnelli's least stylized musical. Clearly, the film acknowledged certain Broadway traditions—carefully woven into the fabric of the text, "The Boy Next Door" is a superior example of the singing ingenue's Act I declaration of longing and purpose dear to every self-respecting stage musical since Jerome Kern. There is virtually nothing in *Meet Me in St. Louis* that resembles a standard production number. The closest thing is Blane and Martin's arrangement of "Skip to My Lou" during Lon's going-away party, the occasion for Es-

Marjorie Main, Judy Garland, Mary Astor, and Lucille Bremer comfort an injured Margaret O'Brien, Meet Me in St. Louis *(1944)*

ther's first meeting with stalwart John Truitt. However, this hoedown is the antithesis of the stock Busby Berkeley spectacular. It's staged entirely within the confined space of the Smith parlor, with a cast of perhaps a dozen of Esther's pals, and underscores the character traits of its soloists while nudging the plot along. Fickle Rose flits from one dance partner to another; Esther and John are gently pushed together where they belong at the end of the dance. The *Oklahoma!* influence is particularly apparent in this sequence, from its rustic rhythms (tempered by Kay Thompson's urbane vocal arrangements) to the Girl-Who-Falls-Down quotation from Agnes de Mille's *Oklahoma!* ballets at the number's conclusion. But it's Minnelli's dancing camera that gives "Skip to My Lou" its unifying verve, sashaying in turn from one reveler to the next in a web of movement that enriches the intricate patterns of Charles Walters' choreography.

This scene and the Christmas ball toward the end of the picture are anomalous moments in *Meet Me in St. Louis;* elsewhere, Minnelli mounts his camera boom to stress the tension of the dramatic episodes and underscores the intimacy of the songs by framing them as unobtrusively as possible. Esther and Tootie's cakewalk to "Under the Bamboo Tree" doesn't stop the show—it perks up the party. Minnelli's staging throughout strikes a note of homely spontaneity: the girls' dispute over how to start the number, their slightly ragged harmony on the chorus, even the sudden exasperation which clouds O'Brien's face when Garland makes a move she didn't anticipate. The child's deadpan minstrel shuffle is irresistible because she lacks the mechanical aplomb of a Shirley Temple; O'Brien captures instead the clumsy exhilaration of a kid allowed to stay up late and show off for her elders; Garland subdues her usual clarion pitch so as not to drown out her screen sister.

"The Trolley Song," however, finds her at full throttle, belting out her tale of a flirtation with a handsome stranger to vent her nervousness until her real love sprints onboard to join the crowd bound for the fairgrounds. Meanwhile, Minnelli visually lowers the pitch by making Esther the neutral center in a swirl of colors. Garland, hatless in a black outfit trimmed with white, is surrounded by a bevy of her chums sporting pastel shirtwaisters and flowery headgear.

Meet Me in St. Louis feels most like a musical during its summery first act, before all manner of darkness descends upon the Smith family. The autumn and winter sections of the film take place almost exclusively at night, the better to reveal the discordant undertones threatening the household's harmony. It is here that Minnelli soundly shifts the focus of the film from Esther to five-year-old Tootie. Too young to understand her elders' precepts of "civilized" behavior, the child constantly blurts out her observations on the unsavory aspects of adult life—drunkenness, violence, sudden death—which her genteel family seeks to suppress and ignore. Thanks to her near-morbid sensitivity and lurid imagination, Tootie of all the Smiths realizes just how easily shattered their domestic idyll can be, which is why she's so traumatized when it's really threatened.

Characteristically, Tootie's favorite holiday is Halloween, celebrated in her St. Louis neighborhood by taking revenge on all those repressed grown-ups who force their offspring to act like little ladies and gentlemen the rest of the year. Dressed (or, more usually, cross-dressed) like gruesome parodies of their parents, the children's goal is to "kill" the adults by throwing flour in their faces while telling them how hateful they are. Appropriately attired in the drag of a "horrible ghost"—her father's castoff coat and bowler hat, plus a gnarled rat's snout over her nose—Tootie gleefully anticipates the fun, until her plans are dashed by the older kids, Agnes included, who declare that she's too young to take part. Defiantly, she volunteers to lay siege to the most fearsome household on the block, inhabited by a man who allegedly poisons cats when he tires of his other pastime, beating his wife with a hot poker.

From his first framing shot of the house—now ominously Gothic in the late October darkness, the windows eerily lit with a yellow-orange light—Minnelli fuses a child's sense of creepiness with an adult's retrospective detachment. Tootie's approach toward the feared Brokoff house is filmed in one long, sustained traveling shot, her quivering frame passing zombie-like through the blackness of the night. We know she's not in any real danger, but the crescendo of terror in her stunned eyes is chilling nonetheless. After she's "killed" her quarry (greeted by a paternal chuckle which Tootie never hears), Minnelli speeds up the tempo with a reverse traveling shot of Tootie scampering back to safety, her tattered disguise flapping in the wind. "I'm the most horrible, I'm the most horrible!" she exclaims with pride, piling more debris on the kids' bonfire—a symbol of savage conformity the director will use with more ominous intent in *Tea and Sympathy* a dozen years later—as Minnelli pulls away with a triumphant crane shot of Tootie as princess of the suburban primitives.

However, as the autumn sequence progresses, Tootie's fears assume proportions even the grown-ups can't quite ignore. Moments later, as Esther is marveling over Rose's latest conquest, Tootie is heard screaming offscreen. Carried sobbing into the house, a bloodied Tootie whimpers, "He tried to kill me." Mrs. Smith decides to summon the doctor rather than her husband ("What could he do?" she declares airily), and accompanied by a closeup of a horrified Esther, the child announces that John Truitt was the culprit. The doctor finds a tuft of man's hair clenched in Tootie's fist. "It must have been quite a struggle fighting him off," he announces, with an implication too disturbing to be acknowledged out loud under the Hollywood Production Code, for Tootie has barely escaped being molested.

Thus having hinted at serpents in Metro's imperturbable American Eden, Minnelli immediately retreats to a jocular note. With a pizzicato violin arrangement of "The Boy Next Door" over the soundtrack as caustic counterpoint, Esther storms across the lawn to confront the upstanding ogre who'd "pick on a girl." After she's socked, shaken, and bitten him, she returns home to find a pampered and petted Tootie giggling with Agnes over their exploits. It seems the pair had stuffed an old dress and laid it on the trolley tracks. "It looked just like a body. A *live* body, too," Tootie exclaims with pride. John had only tried to hide Tootie from the police, an unnecessary precaution, for, as she points out, cops never pay attention to little girls anyway. "You're nothing less than a murderer, you might have killed dozens of people,'' Rose declares, but the giggle in her throat betrays her. All ends well as Esther rushes next door to apologize and receives her first kiss as reward.

Now is the moment for father the intruder to return home and present his family with a threat more tangible than anything Tootie's imagination could dream up. He announces that he's being sent to New York on business. Misinterpreting the implication, they cheerily anticipate his departure: ''They'll all be safe with me,'' Grandpa promises, ''I've got twelve guns in my room.'' When Mr. Smith makes it clear that they'll all be leaving for good right after Christmas, the mood darkens as the Smiths contemplate the unthinkable. ''It'll take me at least a week to dig up my dolls from the cemetery,'' protests Tootie, and her elders point out soberly that in New York she's unlikely to have room for a new cemetery at all. As an appalled Rose remarks, in New York only rich people live in houses: ''People like us live in flats, hundreds of flats in the same building.''

Just as they had during the summertime squabble with Papa over Rose's long-distance call, the Smiths assert their rebellion from his benign tyranny by refraining from food; only he can find the appetite to wolf down a slice of Katie's special Halloween cake. Music is the means through which family unity is reinforced. With determination, Mrs. Smith moves to the parlor piano and sounds the first bars of ''their song,'' which prompts her husband's firm baritone (loaned to Leon Ames for the occasion by none other than Arthur Freed himself). In a beautifully composed deep-focus shot, the alienated Smith offspring are seen drifting back downstairs and into the dining room, pensively taking their places to listen to the music. Minnelli infuses the scene with a wealth of telling behavioral details—Mr. Smith struggling with the tune until his wife transposes it to his key; an absorbed Esther unconsciously waving Tootie's hand out of her cake plate and feeding the child with a fork. For the last chorus, Anna Smith accompanies her husband in two-part harmony: ''Through the years, we'll still be together, you and I,'' they sing, and with the family peacefully assembled in the home they love, a fragile, wistful truce is forged as the film's autumn segment fades to winter.

Meet Me in St. Louis' climactic section begins cheerily enough, with a Currier-and-Ives vision of horse-drawn sleighs and youngsters sledding down the lawns of Kensington Avenue in the bright sunshine. This dissolves to a view of the Smith girls laughing at Tootie's snow people—lumpy caricatures of her own family with a polar bear pet. The two eldest daughters are preparing for the big Christmas dance; in their bedroom, Rose tightens Esther's corset-strings to the point of asphyxiation. Their aim is to achieve maximum allure and utterly efface one Lucille Ballard, an alleged Eastern snob who has snared Rose's beau Warren for the evening, condemning Rose to the ignominy of being escorted to the dance by her brother. Before their

vanity mirror, the girls steel themselves for conquest. ''We can certainly handle twenty men,'' Esther declares with a quaver, ''I should hope.''

However, the descending night brings trouble, as it usually does at 5135 Kensington Avenue. John arrives with the news that his dress suit is locked at the cleaners, leaving Esther dateless until Grandpa gallantly offers to stand in. For her the dance is a mixture of slapstick humiliation and an encroaching sense of loss. It is Esther who is stranded with the stag line of losers, and the dance band's selections, from ''Goodbye My Lady Love'' to ''Home, Sweet Home,'' are painful reminders of her dreaded departure from the town that nurtured her. ''It's our last dance in St. Louis,'' she sighs, her head nestled in her grandfather's shoulder: ''I feel like I'm going to cry.'' As he waltzes her behind the massive Christmas tree for a surprise reunion with a belatedly gussied-up John, the camera pulls back to reveal the whole glittering Yuletide assembly, but Minnelli's mood is more elegiac than exultant. John's long-anticipated proposal, delivered under a leafless tree in the ice-blue moonlight, is an unexpectedly melancholy occasion. Their youth, his college plans, and her imminent move cast a pall on their ardor. ''Even if I did go to New York, we could still work something out,'' Esther says tentatively, and leaves him alone in the dark as the Christmas church bells sound.

Throughout the film, Esther has been straining to maintain a pose of precocious adulthood—composed, ladylike, and a mistress of her emotions. Too small for such pretense, it is Tootie who saves the family by venting the misery everyone else is too well-mannered to betray out loud. Esther finds her waiting for Santa Claus at the windowsill and wondering how he'll know where to find the Smiths next year. ''I'm taking all my dolls, the dead ones too,'' Tootie declares, while Esther points out that her snow people will have to stay where they are. To console her, Esther sings a holiday song of quixotic wishful thinking, accompanied by Tootie's dancing-bear music box. ''Have yourself a merry little Christmas, let your heart be light. Next year all your troubles will be out of sight,'' she promises, but the teary gleam in her eyes and the solemn throb in her voice reveal that she's not fooling anyone. Least of all Tootie, tearstained and sobbing in Minnelli's inserted closeup as Esther concludes her anthem of hope.

When the song is done, Tootie breaks away from her sister's embrace to lay siege to her snow family outside—decapitating them all with a stick, then pummeling their torsos in a frenzy. ''I'd rather kill them if we can't take them with us,'' she cries, but the act is really murder-by-proxy of all those grown-ups who have heedlessly conspired to make her miserable. The convulsive savagery of her impulse is far scarier than any of Tootie's Halloween antics, since this is no mere rite of childhood bravado. Once again, Minnelli has allowed the placid surface of the Metro musical to be shattered by naked emotion, as startling to the witnesses on-screen as it is to the audience. From his bedroom window, a dismayed Mr. Smith stares down at the wreckage, and from his perspective we see a long shot of Esther vainly comforting her sister, encircled by snow corpses. Minnelli moves in closer for the real thrust to the heart—Tootie blinded by tears as a kneeling Esther clasps her in an embrace, vainly murmuring that "the main thing is that we're going to be together." Tootie knows better, and for the rest of the scene the unthinkable happens—the voice of Judy Garland is drowned out by her keening co-star, who simply cannot stop crying.

Inside the house, Minnelli shifts his attention to Mr. Smith, stunned by the chaos he has unwittingly caused. As Esther leads a spent and whimpering Tootie upstairs to bed, he surveys their once comfortable home now in forlorn disarray, with the grandfather clock swathed in newspapers and bald patches on the wallpaper where the family pictures used to be. Wrapped in sadness, he sits in his armchair, igniting his hand instead of the cigar in his mouth as the sound-track surges with the repeated first bars of the title song. With a start, he summons the family downstairs. Over a group shot of their expectant faces, his voice announces, "We're going to stay here until we rot!" As their jubilation peaks, Rose's beau Warren bursts in and blurts out his determination to marry her whether she likes it or not. "That's final. I love you," he declares, and vanishes. (Mr. Smith, characteristically, hasn't the slightest idea who this young man is.) Comforted by her husband, Mrs. Smith weeps with relief in the foreground while their children exclaim over their gifts behind them, and the winter segment fades to a bittersweet calm.

Meet Me in St. Louis' springtime chapter finds the Smith family back in the sunlight, their high spirits restored. By far the briefest of the film's four acts, it's essentially a swift epilogue to the family's saga, now resolved. Its dazzling moment is the fade-in showing

Margaret O'Brien, Judy Garland, and the snow family on Christmas Eve, Meet Me in St. Louis *(1944)*

the Smith girls arrayed in their whitest finery outside 5135 Kensington Avenue while awaiting the carriage that will take them to the fair. This was Minnelli's first movie opportunity to pay homage to the painters he admired—a frequent theme in his stage designs—and this brief tableau is an exquisite distillation of Renoir in motion.

The remainder of the sequence is, visually at least, more anticlimax than postscript. During the war, the federal government had imposed severe restrictions on the amount of money and materials the studios could devote to the construction of new sets, and in *Meet Me in St. Louis* the allotment was wisely lavished on the Smith household itself. Accordingly, the fair's would-be dazzler is more Monogram than Metro—the illumination of the Palace of Electricity represented by a miniature, one-dimensional cyclorama before a pool the size of a mixing bowl. As an offscreen chorus reprises the title song for the last time, the Smith family and an assortment of fiancés gather to bask in the spectacle. For the final fadeout, Minnelli's camera dollies in close to frame Esther's rapt face, with John at her side. Like Dorothy in *The Wizard of Oz*, she glows with relief that her midwestern utopia has been regained, with a still-brighter future in store "right here in St. Louis."

With this conclusion, Minnelli leads the audience back to a comforting affirmation of the MGM ethos—the belief that change is frightening, and happiness is found by staying put in the embrace of one's family. *Cabin in the Sky* extolled a similar notion, and what makes both films more persuasive than MGM's usual no-place-like-home propaganda is Minnelli's specific vision. Home isn't an abstract ideal, but a tangible place whose idiosyncrasies reflect the character of the people who inhabit it.

Still, this is an odd theme for an artist who, without a backward glance, fled his own small-town hearth before he was out of his teens. In this instance, time and distance lent enchantment, because never again would Minnelli view this terrain with the same placid equanimity. Over the next twenty years, he would direct many such scenes of provincial family life, from *la France profonde* in the mid-19th century *(Madame Bovary)*, to contemporary American suburbia *(Father of the Bride)*, to rural Texas *(Home from the Hill)* and to insular midwestern towns rather like the one where he was born *(The Cobweb, Some Came Running)*. The subterranean strains which rumble intriguingly throughout *Meet Me in St. Louis* will soon erupt in full view, and Minnelli's sympathies will shift instinctively to those misfits and bohemians who find well-mannered middle-class life a suffocating purgatory. Those who willingly submit to its strictures—from Dr. Bovary to the hero's appalling relatives in *Some Came Running*—are only half-alive anyway. Mr. Smith's triumphant pledge that the family is "going to stay here till we rot" becomes no idle threat in Minnelli's later movies. From then on, people who remain behind muddle through from crisis to crisis in such happy-ending entertainments as *Father of the Bride*, while in the melodramas, they earn a tombstone to commemorate their misdirected lives.

Imitated though it was by other directors, *Meet Me in St. Louis* was the last Minnelli musical with a domestic setting. Too perfect to duplicate, in the end it was also, of course, too good to be true. Before *Meet Me in St. Louis* was made, the studio feared its subject was too humdrum for fantasy; after he'd completed the film, apparently Minnelli decided that it was really too disturbing to gild. Thereafter, his musicals would take flight either in cloud-cuckoo-land renderings of Baghdad, the West Indies, and the Scottish Highlands, or in the New York and Paris of his imagination. For Minnelli knew that out there in the sticks was where everyday nightmares took place.

· · · · · · · · · · · · · · · · · · · ·

1944   ZIEGFELD FOLLIES

Minnelli's next assignment was as distinct from *Meet Me in St. Louis* as a movie musical could be—an opulent vaudeville conceived as the studio apotheosis of Technicolor escapism. MGM owned the celluloid patent for the celebrated Ziegfeld name, already exploited in two MGM screen spectacles—the 1936 biography of the showman, *The Great Ziegfeld,* and the 1941 *Ziegfeld Girl,* a melodrama with songs tracing the disparate fortunes of three Broadway chorines, played by Hedy Lamarr, Lana Turner, and Judy Garland. This time, Arthur Freed decided to revive the plotless revue for the first time since the early talkies—the ultimate Ziegfeld extravaganza in movie terms, featuring virtually the entire Metro roster of singers, dancers, and comedians.

With a then-breathtaking budget of three million dollars, from a production point of view this was the most complex undertaking the Freed Unit had tackled to date. Between endless bouts of reshooting, recutting, and reshuffling the cornucopia of material Freed prepared for this movie, more than two years passed between the start of production on *Ziegfeld Follies* and its general release in the spring of 1946.

Freed's problems with *Ziegfeld Follies* had begun months before Minnelli became involved. When filming commenced on January 24 1944, the film had been assigned to George Sidney, like Minnelli a relatively unseasoned director whom MGM was nurturing. After three months of shooting, nobody concerned was particularly pleased with the footage completed thus far, Sidney included, and he asked Freed to release him from the picture. (Undaunted, Sidney immediately went to work on what became one of his best-liked musicals, the Gene Kelly vehicle *Anchors Aweigh.*) Freed summoned Minnelli to take over, which he did one day after finishing *Meet Me in St. Louis.*

One can only wonder why Freed hadn't simply waited for Minnelli in the first place. Certainly, of all the directors at his disposal, Minnelli had impeccable credentials for the job; he had made his Broadway reputation as the mastermind of the chic Broadway revue, and his art direction for the *Ziegfeld Follies of 1936* had been a particular triumph.

Hugh Fordin's study of the Freed Unit, *The World of Entertainment,* gives a detailed account of *Ziegfeld Follies'* bewildering shooting history. For efficiency's sake, various production numbers and comic routines were filmed simultaneously. Obviously Minnelli couldn't be present on two sound stages at once, so certain sequences were given to other directors, most of whom were duly credited in the title cards introducing their respective sketches. Only about fifty percent of the movie in its final release form was actually directed by Minnelli. Some of Sidney's work remained more or less intact as well—Red Skelton's bibulous "When Television Comes" monologue and, most indelibly, the "Bring on the Beautiful Girls" opener, a sado-masochistic sideshow in which ringmistress Lucille Ball, wearing cherry-vanilla spangles, brandishes her whip at a cageful of panther ladies dressed in black. Additionally, production records indicate that Sidney also stood in for Minnelli for an odd day or two of shooting when Minnelli was otherwise engaged.

In an era when production costs were sufficiently manageable to afford such luxury, far more material was shot than could ever be incorporated. For instance, when production began, MGM announced that Jimmy Durante would be featured in three *Ziegfeld Follies* sequences; two were shot, but none turned up in the release print. Among episodes filmed but not used (mostly executed by other directors) were an Astaire dance to a song he wrote himself called "If Swing Goes, I'll Go Too"; a setting of the Gershwin song "Liza" sung by Avon Long to Lena Horne; and what would have been the one filmed record of Fanny Brice's celebrated stage and radio creation, Baby Snooks.

For Judy Garland, Minnelli exhumed the "Reading of the Play" sketch, a Beatrice Lillie highlight in his 1936 hit revue, *The Show Is On*, but apparently it was never even shot. One of the first numbers Minnelli staged was a duet for Garland and Mickey Rooney entitled, "Will You Love Me in Technicolor? (As You Do in Black and White)." Considering the insider jokiness of the lyrics ("Since you have seen my pan in a House of Westmore tan, I'm so afraid you'll put me on the shelf," parries Rooney, to which Garland ripostes, "You never were such an eyeful till you had a Natalie Kalmus dip") only stockholders in the Technicolor Corporation can have mourned its excision. Even the finale, an amphibian tableau featuring several tons of iridescent bubbles filling Metro's biggest sound stage, was drastically revised before the patrons ever saw it. The bubbles remained, but the stars, including Fred Astaire, Lucille Bremer, Lena Horne, and James Melton, were beached on Albert Akst's cutting-room floor.

Principal photography for *Ziegfeld Follies* was completed in mid-August of 1944, four months after Minnelli started work on it, but MGM's efforts to shape this superproduction were far from over. The reaction to the first sneak preview in November of that year was at best tepid, and more cutting and reshooting was ordered by Freed after a second preview in the spring of 1945. After the film's roadshow premiere in Boston that August, the studio contemplated further changes before its national release, but in the end decided to leave well enough alone. After this protracted out-of-town tryout *Ziegfeld Follies* finally achieved its Broadway roadshow run in April 1946. Total expenditure on the film was calculated at $3,403,388.93—an astronomical figure in those years (even *Gone with the Wind* had cost scarcely a few hundred thousand dollars more), but the public responded enthusiastically to this cornucopia of stars and music; the final domestic return was over five million dollars.

In retrospect, the principal appeal of this film lay in its novelty. For that vast majority of moviegoers who had seen none of the fabled Ziegfeld revues, Metro's *Follies* recreated them on a scale more opulent than even that profligate showman could have achieved. Yet there was good reason why *Ziegfeld Follies* remained an experiment the studio never ventured to repeat. The notion of mounting a celluloid *Follies* was an anachronism by the mid-forties, and not merely because the great man had been dead for some fifteen years. His mainstream formula of stars and showmanship had long since been supplanted on Broadway by a more streamlined approach to the form. It is in the nature of the revue to be a series of showstoppers interrupted by stage fillers. In its heyday between the two world wars, the best examples—such as Minnelli's own *At Home Abroad* and *The Show Is On*—disguised the grab-bag nature of the form by applying one stylistic concept throughout. No such approach marks the MGM *Follies*, whose unequal components are linked only by Minnelli's striking color schemes and theatrical imagination, and the richness of the Metro contract roster.

This lack of integration accentuates the mustiness of most of the comic interludes. In the liveliest Broadway revues, topical satire and sexual naughtiness sparked the laughs between production numbers, but both were anathema in L. B. Mayer's prudish domain. Hence the *Follies'* creators resorted to innocuous vaudeville routines, some of which, like the Victor Moore–Edward Arnold "Pay the Five Dollars," had been chestnuts for decades. However, while Roy Del Ruth's rendering of the venerable "Sweepstakes Ticket" sketch at least provided a gleeful showcase for Fanny Brice's madcap virtuosity; the rest virtually invited the patrons to flee to the lobby for popcorn and a smoke while waiting for Garland or Astaire to sweep on screen.

Even here, the canned perfection of Metro's justly fabled craftsmanship subverts much of what made the form so appealing in the theater. After all, the primary allure of the great revues lay less in the showgirl tableaux than in the personal interplay between great entertainers and a live public—something the intimacy of early television, amplified by a vociferous in-studio audience, managed in part to recapture with its variety shows a few years later. What made the top musical stars of the screen special was the fusion of their singing and dancing gifts with those distinctive quirks of personality revealed during the long stretches between songs. While *Follies* strives to reveal new facets of their gifts—Garland's sophisticated spoofery, Astaire's touching mime—the sheer intricacy and magnitude of the production surrounding them overwhelms any sense of spontaneity and dilutes the fun.

If there is one preeminent star in *Ziegfeld Follies*, it is Minnelli's mise-en-scène. This was the first of three successive movie musicals in which he labored to elevate the form to new heights of stylization. Seeking to expand upon the lessons learned on Broadway in the thirties, he added a new kind of filmic energy to his special flair with color and composition. On stage, all sense of movement is provided by the performers, as was largely true in the best Astaire movies of the 1930s. Minnelli's looping crane shots and the performers' choreographed routines fuse into a new synthesis of motion. His stars may remain at the center of Minnelli's frame, but they don't monopolize it—they're simply its most vivid elements.

The first Minnelli segment in *Follies* is fourth in the film's running order, preceded by a ponderously fey prologue of Ziegfeld in heaven, directed by Norman Taurog and featuring William Powell in a quick reprise of his turn in *The Great Ziegfeld;* Fred Astaire introducing Lucille Ball and her bullwhip; and a fragment with Esther Williams frolicking around the faux coral before she darts up among the lilypads for air, breathing through her nose as her grinning mouth fills with water. Finally comes Minnelli's rendering of the Verdi "Libiamo" from *La Traviata*. That it doesn't meet Minnelli's standard of intoxicating glamour can be attributed to the low wattage of his assigned performers and the blandness of Merrill Pye's set. The duet is coolly sung by Marion Bell (subsequently the leading lady of Broadway's *Brigadoon*) and opera/radio tenor James Melton. The sound stage is (barely) dressed with massed curtains and chandeliers in the same stark-white hue. Minnelli tried to distract the eye with a waltzing chorus arrayed in Irene Sharaff's hoop skirts appliquéd with butterflies and pine cones, but the bland abstraction of the setting is a far cry from the fevered romance of Violetta's demimonde.

The next sequence is pure Minnelli territory: "This Heart of Mine" (song by Harry Warren and Arthur Freed) is a plotted ballroom-dance ballet, reminiscent of the indelible Astaire–Rogers' "Let's Face the Music and Dance" from *Follow the Fleet*. In movement and mime, it tells of a gentleman-thief (Astaire at his most

courtly) who crashes a society ball and woos a bejeweled princess (Lucille Bremer, all icy languor). After their dance, his greed clashes with his awakening love, but as they exit, he wins both the diamonds and Lucille. Among Astaire's great romantic duets, "This Heart of Mine" doesn't rank very high, and although she's a supremely accomplished dancer, Bremer is a little too self-contained to evoke the rapturous chemistry Astaire created with Ginger Rogers, Rita Hayworth or Cyd Charisse. However, this number gleams with that inimitable visual élan which was Minnelli's most obvious contribution to the movie musical. The first shot is unmistakable Minnellian swank: a close-up of a black-masked, glistening-white pixie figure (sculpted by the director's favorite plaster fantasist, Tony Duquette) gazing with frozen amusement at the mortal revelers below. The camera pans to reveal an enclosed dance pavilion in a shade of cerise that came to be known around the Metro lot as "Minnelli red" (later it would adorn both Gigi's garret and *Lust for Life*'s Red Café). The human mannequins bustling within are arrayed in black, white, and Minnelli's second color of choice, a buttercup yellow. The director underscores the glamorous but claustrophobic artifice of the scene by excluding all human sound—the majordomo announces new arrivals with bleats from the MGM Orchestra, and guests vent their party mood in bursts of frantic pantomime.

As Astaire and Bremer make their escape, the pavilion portals divide and the camera retreats to reveal an abstract winter landscape of cobalt sky and Duquette's gargantuan papier-mâché courtiers guarding (or im-

Judy Garland, "A Great Lady Has an Interview," Ziegfeld Follies *(1944)*

Fred Astaire and Gene Kelly, "The Babbitt and the Bromide," Ziegfeld Follies *(1944)*

ated for the screen, and the closest thing to pure cinema in all of *Ziegfeld Follies*; devoid of dialogue, encapsulated in a world of three-dimensional artifice, the sequence combines the heightened pathos of Griffith-era silent films with a dazzling sound-and-light show out of the Freed Unit at its most audacious.

The number is structured as a romantic tragedy interrupted by a delirious reverie. In London's dockside Limehouse district, a strolling half-caste girl (Lucille Bremer), appraised by a slimy plutocrat (Robert Lewis, who also helped stage this sequence), captures also the eye and heart of a solitary Chinese coolie (Fred Astaire). She pauses momentarily at a shop window to admire a fan displayed within. Once she has moved on, her humble admirer gazes longingly at the object of her desire, only to be gunned down in the shuffle when a pair of robbers raids the store. Lying wounded, he conjures up a fantasy of riotous chinoiserie, featuring himself and his beloved as its stellar fan dancers—the type of dream only a habitué of the Odeon Whitechapel could imagine. The illusion fades as he regains consciousness for the last time. Oblivious to her languishing admirer, the girl returns to the shop with her would-be protector in tow; she retrieves the fan from the floor, only to recoil from the stains of blood which now mar it. And while the worldly couple sets forth for their evening's pleasures, death spasms overtake this martyr of unfulfilled longing.

Although Bremer's amused exotic evokes Anna May Wong rather than Lillian Gish, "Limehouse Blues" pays explicit homage to *Broken Blossoms,* with Astaire assuming the mask of mute longing formerly worn by Richard Barthelmess. The mid-forties was the last moment when it was still possible for Hollywood Caucasians to don minstrel face with impunity, or assume a Westmore Brothers' version of the physiognomy of the East. (Across the lot, Katharine Hepburn was then impersonating a patrician Chinese in *Dragon Seed.*) But such masquerades ill-suited Astaire, whose most sublime illusion was the effortlessness of his art.

Astaire aficionados understandably prefer the numbers where his genius effaces the world around him. Yet here, he is simply the most eloquent human figure in a Minnellian panorama of London mezzotints and pastel orientalia. Conjured up from leftover sets built for Metro's *The Picture of Dorian Gray,* Minnelli's pipe-dream London is poetically sordid—painted in dank shades of fog brown and coal-fume gray, illuminated only by the sudden apparition of Bremer herself in shimmering yellow. Music dictates the rhythms of the sequence and the movements of the camera. As it relentlessly dogs his traces, Astaire is propelled toward his fateful encounter with Bremer by the music-hall medley that animates Limehouse—a gaslit Edwardian singer in a basement pub behind him, a Victrola wheeled in a baby-carriage down a fetid alleyway and cheery buskers singing for coppers in the little square

prisoning) the merrymakers from without. Alone with his quarry, Astaire finds his voice and seduces Bremer in song; the first chorus of the dance duet which follows is a skillful if slightly dispassionate retreat to Astaire-and-Rogersland, with Minnelli's camera deferring tactfully to the polished exuberance of his dancers. As their courtship grows, Minnelli adds more movement than two mere human figures can provide. First the floor beneath them comes to life and a treadmill sweeps them back and forth, as their high-society mating dance picks up steam; then Astaire and Bremer scamper downstage to a revolving turntable, gradually surrounded by a soigné chorus of ladies in shades of magenta-to-flame and their escorts in black, posed against white branches. Here the camera performs its own pirouettes, and in one ecstatic shot it sails diagonally away from the rapturous pair to catch up with the chorus, taking its turn to glide majestically past the dance pavilion.

Minnelli's velvety, kinetic exploration of depth and space in this number is its own reward. With "Limehouse Blues," Minnelli stirs the froth more deliriously yet, into a whirlpool of nightmarish luster. This mini-melodrama in dance and mime is the most ambitious (or pretentious) musical sequence Minnelli had yet crein which he first sees her. The compelling image here is not Bremer in her Eurasian splendor, but the mute desire of Astaire's reaction to her—the way his back arches with longing as he gazes in her direction.

The palette changes radically for Astaire's reverie of choreographed glory. Surrounded in the dark by a swarm of human pagodas in metallic gray-blue, he grasps in vain for the fan picked out by a narrow spotlight, until he touches the unseen Bremer's hand and the whole scene is suddenly bathed in a blaze of golden light. Designed by Irene Sharaff in anticipation of her "Small House of Uncle Thomas" ballet from *The King and I*, the scene is a collage of Far Eastern exotica seen through Occidental eyes, populated by silk-draped lute players, pole-bearing revelers and masked chorines. Bathed in another Minnelli trademark, a fringed-sunburst spotlight, Astaire and Bremer stalk each other and flick their fans, punctuated by a series of breathtaking cartwheels by the infinitely adaptable master of dance. Throughout, the number celebrates the duo's astonishing precision. As a persuasive display of real exuberance and spontaneity, the fan dance was a warm-up for the exhilarating "Coffee Time" sequence from Astaire and Bremer's next and last collaboration, *Yolanda and the Thief*.

What's interesting about this number is the way certain rather disturbing emotions lend a discordant undertone to its splashy, haute-show biz style. The Astaire we see in "Limehouse Blues" is an abrupt departure from his previous screen image as the movies' treasured emblem of brash elegance and high-spirited optimism. These traits will never entirely disappear from the Astaire persona, but with the star now in his mid-forties and embarking on a new contract at MGM, something additional was required to launch this transitional phase in his career. It was Minnelli who explored a more contemplative aspect of Astaire, which seems to have fused elements of the dancer's offscreen temperament with the director's own affinities. The new Astaire is a rueful, solitary figure, thwarted in the quest for human contact by his own shyness, dubious of future happiness after the memory of an emotionally bleak past. It's a portrait which will deepen with *Yolanda* and especially in their masterpiece, *The Band Wagon*. All are shaped by Minnelli's particular insight that beauty is achieved only at an emotional cost, and always informed by an inexplicable sense of loss.

With "A Great Lady Has an Interview," immediately following "Limehouse Blues," Minnelli refurbishes the screen personality of his favorite star, Judy Garland. The sketch was written by Freed's resident cosmopolites, Roger Edens and Kay Thompson, and conceived as a gentle parody of MGM's Greatest Lady, Greer Garson. When she declined it as *lèse-majesté*, Freed's troupe reworked the idea to mark Garland's definitive transformation from everyone's favorite gamine next door to grown-up sophisticate.

She impersonates a generic screen legend meeting the press to announce her latest project, "a monumental biographical tribute to a monumental biographical woman," i.e., one Madame Crematon, who starved and slaved in a Dutch garret to give birth to her brainstorm, the safety pin. This dig at Garson's taste for bio-pics notwithstanding, if Garland conjures up any specific star, it's Tallulah Bankhead. As an imperious coquette, she charms her courtiers with endearments in throaty Culver City Oxbridgisms, striking attitudes of picturesque hauteur as one immaculately coiffed curl straggles purposefully across her forehead. Until the rhymed prose gives way to rhythmic song this routine is pretty arch going. It's premature camp where Garland is concerned; at the age of twenty-three or thereabouts, she strains to conjure up the requisite note of mock-dragonlady chichi. Moreover, her own unmistakable youth and freshness nullify the point of the joke. Flouncing around contemplating the allure of cheesecake over Oscars, the Star muses, "What does Betty Grable have that I have not? And what is Ginger Rogers that I am not?"—which merely tempts the viewer to ponder, "What, indeed?"

Yet once the number begins in earnest, Garland loosens up considerably, buoyed by Thompson–Edens' eccentric brand of Persian Room gospel. In fervent recitative, she sums up Madame's travails and triumphs, a cappella save for the staccato applause of her hipster hallelujah chorus, bounding over each others' shoulders the better to attend the Star. Garland's tribute to "the lady with the great invent" is peppered with delicious stage business—her genteel bump and grind with eyes cast heavenward, as she declares "No baby can do without it"; her look of peeve as, in the midst of a climactic high note, *les boys* encircle her to insist on another final chorus. The acrobatics of Charles Walters' choreography is delightfully suave, but it's Minnelli's camera work that gives the song its exhilarating momentum. Throughout the number, there is no internal cutting—the last half of the sequence is filmed in one long shot lasting three minutes, the camera swooping around Garland and the cast up to the last instant, when it tracks through a thicket of ecstatically thrust arms to a closeup of this droll Legend, simpering beguilingly above a swarm of white feathers.

This and "Limehouse Blues" were the two *Ziegfeld Follies* episodes that had show biz reverberations beyond the natural life of this movie. "Limehouse"—itself influenced by *Oklahoma!*'s innovations in the theater—set the example for a decade of screen dream ballets. Meanwhile, the sound and style of Garland's virtuoso turn was recapitulated by Kay Thompson herself in her celebrated cabaret act of the fifties and echoed in the Broadway of the sixties with Stephen Sondheim's opening number in the 1964 musical *Anyone Can Whistle* as a direct, affectionate homage. At the time, it simply signaled a triumphant step forward in

Garland's evolution as the silver screen's most prodigal musical star.

The subsequent "Babbitt and the Bromide" is memorable less as an artistic milestone than as a footnote in the annals of show business—save for a brief reunion three decades later on *That's Entertainment II,* it marked the one on-screen teaming of the movies' nonpareil male dancers, Fred Astaire and Gene Kelly. The occasion was a reprise of a sprightly Gershwin duet Astaire had danced with his sister Adele in the 1927 Broadway hit *Funny Face.* The recording the Astaires made at the time confirms the possibilities in Ira Gershwin's caustic account of two mediocrities' infinite gift for cliché, both on earth and during their final posthumous encounter.

On film the song is preceded by an exceedingly coy foreword, in which Astaire professes not to recognize his co-star. When Kelly lists his most conspicuous screen credits, Astaire queries, "You're not Rita Hayworth?" to which Kelly wittily parries, "No, I'm not, Ginger." Thereafter, Minnelli subordinates the satirical point of the Gershwin lyrics to the dance—which, breathtakingly executed though it is, remains vaguely unsatisfying. This was an unique opportunity for the two dancers to face off in their opposing choreographic styles—Kelly's sinewy athleticism versus Astaire's weightless grace. Instead, they meet diplomatically in a cautious middle ground. After some brief, competitive hoofing, as the song progresses to its climax, Astaire and Kelly pair off in a stately same-sex waltz, a mock jitterbug, and a synchronized, hip-swiveling tap. The ironic result is that while the song mocks the paralyzing effect of unstinting good manners, the Astaire–Kelly dance is itself an anemic model of proper etiquette in motion.

Minnelli makes the most of what wit remains by subliminally upstaging the dancers with his wry decor. He had already begun to show his penchant for using works of sculpture to mirror the hapless struggles of the mortals they loom over. Here the set is dominated by a vast equestrian statue that changes form to reflect the three stages of existence through which pass these two dancing fools. In their straw-hatted prime, the bronze steed rears up lustily, doves soaring around his head; as they face middle-age, in bowlers and moustaches, the rider and mount form a Remington tableau of weariness on the prairie—the encircling doves transformed into limp-winged crows. And as Astaire and Kelly prepare for their maker in morning coats and gray goatees, horse and rider spring into the afterlife—glistening white, each sporting his own harp.

Ziegfeld Follies' conclusion is frankly a mess—a phantasmagoria of mixed metaphors. First the simpering Kathryn Grayson trills a bland Warren–Freed song called "Beauty," amid a distinctly ominous landscape of gnarled tree trunks and back-projected clouds in atomic hues. A blob of orange foam covers the lens as the camera segues into remnants of the aborted bubble number, in which Cyd Charisse and her tutued corps de ballet pirouette gamely through iridescent columns of suds.

This vision dissolves, literally, into Minnelli's tour de force, a weird hallucination of loveliness if there ever was one. It's a Daliesque landscape of slate-colored skies and a tilted, forced-perspective desert floor—but instead of melting clocks, the mirage is populated with anesthetized voluptuaries in gold-lamé gowns. This kind of glossy, Condé Nast surrealism had been an upscale rage for well over a decade; and engrossed as always by current trends in art and psychology, Minnelli had already mined this vein repeatedly in the theater, most prominently in his design for "Words without Music," a Balanchine ballet for the 1936 *Follies.* At least, Minnelli gives movement to an essentially static canvas by snaking his restless camera around these lunar-landscape odalisques to the shrill, off-screen voice of some Queen of the Night. The movie fades out on a more conventional note—Grayson atop a pedestal, hitting someone else's dubbed high C. But Minnelli's sudden descent to earth is deceptive; for as his next musical proved, he wasn't ready to awaken from his fevered dream quite yet.

• •

1945   **YOLANDA AND THE THIEF**

Even before Minnelli started work on *Ziegfeld Follies,* Freed was immersed in planning *Yolanda and the Thief,* a Latin-baroque reverie which, compared to the *Follies,* was an easy package to assemble. The original tale by Ludwig Bemelmans and Jacques Thery—a screen treatment fobbed off as a short story—was published in *Town and Country* magazine in July 1943. At Freed's urging, it was immediately procured by MGM for $23,000; Freed himself was paid $25,000 to compose the score, with lyrics by his usual collaborator during the forties, Harry Warren. Bemelmans was spirited to Hollywood to work on the script, and in the usual Metro manner, it went through several other hands over the succeeding months until Freed was satisfied. He had conceived it as an ideal property for Astaire and Minnelli, and the studio first announced this

*Lucille Bremer and Mary
Nash in* Yolanda and the
Thief *(1945)*

lineup in March 1944. Two months later, MGM announced that Lucille Bremer was to play Yolanda, a logical choice considering Freed's particular interest in her progress at the studio, and the fact that she was proving a most congenial dance partner for Astaire in the *Follies,* then in production.

Minnelli assumed this would be his next picture after *Ziegfeld Follies,* but an unforeseen—though to Minnelli not unwelcome—studio crisis intervened. *The Clock,* the first dramatic picture for both Freed and Garland, had stalled under the direction of Fred Zinnemann. The star vehemently suggested that Minnelli replace Zinnemann, and he commenced work on it three days after principal shooting ended on *Ziegfeld Follies. Yolanda and the Thief* subsequently started production on January 15 1945, more or less on schedule; filming was completed about four months later, at a cost of $2,443,704.

With *Yolanda,* Minnelli had carte blanche to unleash his visions of subtropical luxe, paganized Catholicism, and nocturnal hallucinations of guilty desire. Certainly no previous movie musical had ever looked anything like it, and Minnelli's riotous palette was admired in many quarters. Where the press was concerned, its

vaulting ambitions made *Yolanda* a film they wanted to embrace more enthusiastically than they actually did. The public's response was less ambivalent—*Yolanda* was the first major commercial flop for the Freed Unit. Certain of Minnelli's most unswerving admirers have claimed that *Yolanda*'s failure was to its retrospective credit, the film was too rarefied, too exquisite to please the wartime mass public. Indeed, the daring of Minnelli's 108-minute headlong plunge into idiosyncrasy is the film's one enduring distinction. Even at its most unsatisfying, *Yolanda* is preferable to the anonymous mediocrity of, say, *I Dood It,* which was more closely attuned to the average taste. Nonetheless, *Yolanda* remains a laborious collage of ill-assorted parts, disguised if rarely transcended by Minnelli's visual audacity.

The project's weaknesses began with Bemelmans and Thery's published outline, which was fleshed out with unusual fidelity in the final screenplay. Bemelmans had a whimsical bent which was most palatable when accompanied by his own sprightly illustrations, as in such juvenile books as *Madeline;* when writing for adults, his tone curdled into faux-naiveté.

Subtitled "A Scenario for a Latin-American Movie," "Yolanda and the Thief" is told in sound-stage jargon which must have seemed a tiresome gimmick to *Town and Country's* civilian readers. Minnelli could ignore the presumption of such bald directions as "the CAMERA moves from Yolanda and the duenna to the other end of the car where several passengers are seated . . . the CAMERA dwells upon two gentlemen who play a considerable part in our story." What couldn't be so easily dismissed was the platitudinous cuteness of the plot, or the fleshless archetypes who populated it.

Yolanda takes place in some Hispano-American utopia (called "Latino" in the story, "Patria" on screen). This happy land's assets are in the hands of the Aquaviva clan, whose last descendant, the orphaned heroine, has reached legal majority and hence must leave the protection of the convent to take charge of the family legacy and fulfill her personal destiny. The Mother Superior exhorts the girl to pray for guidance to her own guardian angel; Yolanda's fervent chant is overheard by a cynical American conman, who persuades the credulous creature that he is the angel of her prayers and convinces her to put all her affairs in his celestial hands. Her virginal heart is as stirred by this apparition as if he were a mortal man; he in turn starts to find his avarice clashing with his latent finer instincts. Unknown to them both, their alliance has been shadowed by one of God's own minions, who engineers the hero's conversion to honesty and his joyous wedding at the fadeout to the tremulous Yolanda.

The skeletal plot and schematic characters betray its authors' patronizing view of what a successful movie scenario should be. It self-consciously strives for the charm of an up-to-date fairy tale, but Bemelmans' abundant miscalculations leave an acrid aftertaste. They begin with the specifics of its setting. With Paris, Vienna, and the rest of Europe long off-limits as backdrops for musical fantasy, by 1945 the notion of Latin America as a song-and-dance playland had been mined to exhaustion. Nobody wanted any gloomy political truths to erupt in an escapist diversion like *Yolanda;* even so, the sight of all those mimosa-waving peons cheering Yolanda as Pan-American Monopoly Queen has a reactionary tinge which sours this Technicolor fantasy.

Arguably, this comes with the territory; for all its South of the Border tints and rhythms, *Yolanda's* heart is in that Middle-European principality where operetta languishes. What should have been apparent to *Yolanda's* creators is the unpleasant chemistry of the protagonists' romance, which has something to offend practically everyone. While the heroine's blind belief in an angel's intercession seems more imbecilic than endearing, his exploitation of her credulity is patently

cruel. Throughout, Yolanda prostrates herself before this unworthy idol, beseeching forgiveness for her lack of faith and guilty rumblings of desire. His patronizing manner in the face of her abasement betrays a darker side of sexual politics unacknowledged in this movie. As the plot winds down to its inevitable happy conclusion, nothing can quite dispel the inherent nastiness of it all—not the hero's increasingly tormented conscience, nor even his ultimate pledge to treasure his new bride faithfully for the rest of their lives.

Before it reached the screen, the *Yolanda* script was amended by several of the Freed Unit stalwarts: George Wells, Joseph Schrank *(Cabin in the Sky),* and Robert Nathan (responsible with Schrank for *The Clock),* with final screen credit accorded to Irving Brecher, who had co-written *Meet Me in St. Louis.* Their combined efforts gave flesh to the Bemelmans–Thery sketch without bringing depth to it. At times the screenplay borrows from a far more pungent example of the shyster-fleeces-dupe plot, *The Lady Eve*—particularly early on when the hero sizes up the competition aboard a train bearing him and his quarry toward their destiny. The role of the thief's cohort in crime was tailor-made for Metro's erstwhile Wizard of Oz, Frank Morgan; he's a fumblesome fraud, described in the script as "the only bank embezzler in history who successfully juggled the books and then forgot to take the money." Yolanda's dithery Aunt Amarilla, played by Mildred Natwick as a brunette Billie Burke, was imbued with the sort of high-toned wackiness that appealed to Minnelli's taste for the fanciful. Her command to "Do my fingernails immediately and bring them to my room at once" is reminiscent of that musical comedy treatment for *Serena Blandish* Minnelli had longed in vain to mount a few years before. What's missing is the emotional center to give ballast to all this attendant giddiness.

In any case, the scenarists needed more help than they received from Warren and Freed's interpolated score, the weakest for any Minnelli musical save *I Dood It.* The picture opens with a boy soprano chorus singing the "Patria" anthem's notably insipid lyrics ("This is a day for love, this is a day for song. And all together we will merrily walk along"). Yolanda's "Angel" number is a burbling beguine, pallidly reminiscent of Kurt Weill's "Speak Low" from the then-recent *One Touch of Venus;* later, hero Johnny counters with a harp-accompanied "Yolanda" in the same vein, while his nightmare in dance is underlined by "Will You Marry Me?" a ditty sung by Bremer, featuring a ridiculously convoluted rhyme scheme. "Come and share with me/ Connubiality" goes one deathless couplet. The one rouser comes toward the end of the picture—a refurbishment of an old Freed tune, "Java Junction," now called "Coffee Time." Although patently out of sync with the movie's Latin setting, this infectious big-band jitterbug inspires *Yolanda's* only really spirited sequence, heightened by Minnelli's vivacious staging.

Judy Garland and Lucille Bremer in the Yuletide colors that drove Cedric Gibbons crazy, Meet Me in St. Louis *(1944)*

BELOW:
Tom Drake and Judy Garland, "The Trolley Song," Meet Me in St. Louis *(1944)*

Manuela gets into the act.
Judy Garland and Gene
Kelly in The Pirate *(1948)*

BELOW:
Judy Garland in the opening
scene from The Pirate *(1948)*

"I'll Build a Stairway to Paradise." Georges Guetary in An American in Paris *(1951)*

Georges Guetary (foreground left) and Gene Kelly (rear center) team up on "S'Wonderful" while Minnelli rides his boom. An American in Paris *(1951)*

69

The Furies stalk the lovelorn artist. Gene Kelly in the ballet from An American in Paris *(1951)*

BELOW:
A Cohan strut in the Rousseau square. Gene Kelly and Leslie Caron in the ballet from An American in Paris *(1951)*

Leslie Caron, Gene Kelly in the ballet from An American in Paris *(1951)*

RIGHT:
Action in Van Gogh yellow. The ballet from An American in Paris *(1951)*

*"Triplets." Fred Astaire,
Nanette Fabray, and Jack
Buchanan in* The Band
Wagon *(1953)*

LEFT:
*LeRoy Daniels and Fred
Astaire. "Shine on Your
Shoes" from* The Band
Wagon *(1953)*

*Fred Astaire and Cyd
Charisse "Dancing in the
Dark,"* The Band Wagon
(1953)

The fashion show finale from
Lovely to Look At *(1952)*

BELOW:
The fashion show finale from
Lovely to Look At *(1952)*

Leslie Caron and Louis Jourdan in Gigi *(1958)*

Hermione Gingold, Louis Jourdan, Leslie Caron in Gigi *(1958)*

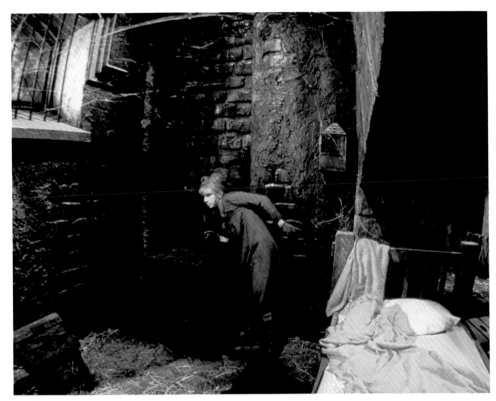

Melinda escapes the orphanage. Barbra Streisand in On a Clear Day You Can See Forever *(1970)*

BELOW:
"Things with good lines—like things from Klein's." Judy Holliday outswanks the swells in "Drop That Name" from Bells Are Ringing *(1960)*

Minnelli (left) in 1969 at the Central Park Zoo directing Barbra Streisand (center) in a sequence cut from On a Clear Day You Can See Forever *(1970)*

BELOW:
John Richardson takes a nibble on Barbra Streisand in a Brighton flashback from On a Clear Day You Can See Forever *(1970)*

The material ill-served its two leads, who labored hard to infuse it with life. The film was to launch Bremer as a star, and its failure was attributed in part to her lack of warmth as a screen presence. (Following *Yolanda, Till the Clouds Roll By* marked her last appearance in a Freed musical, and shortly thereafter she left the studio. Bremer retired from the screen in the late forties after a few B-melodramas, one of which, Edgar G. Ulmer's *Ruthless,* cast her strikingly as a hardbitten adulteress.) Yet *Yolanda* was an insuperably treacly part; that it might have been more appropriate for, say, Kathryn Grayson is no insult to Lucille Bremer. As the script has it, Yolanda has a postulant's soul in a siren's body. In fact, her awestruck queries on the hierarchy of heaven would have stuck in the throat of Margaret O'Brien and—coming from Bremer—all this seems downright perverse. A compliant if less than spontaneous actress, Bremer dutifully modulates her voice to the requisite ardent quaver, but it's obvious that her strawberry-soda mane and Bette Davis eyebrows were made for other worldlier things.

Yolanda suited Astaire scarcely better than it did his co-star, although the film did prepare the ground for his glorious resurgence as an MGM star over the decade to come. Astaire's gifts as a straight actor are here plumbed more fully than his dancing genius; besides the ballet and the jitterbug, Astaire performs only one brief tap solo during the second chorus of "Yolanda." Ironically, he's too persuasive for the script's own good, conveying the doleful avarice of his character so thoroughly that he accentuates how unsavory the plot really is. Released in November 1945, this film introduced audiences to an unabashedly middle-aged Astaire. Every nuance of his performance betrays this awareness on the part of Astaire and Minnelli alike—his pouched eyes are the emblem of a man wearily on the lam again after a lifetime of fraud. It's the subliminal content of *Yolanda* which, more fully explored, would fuel his best future portraits in dance—the solitary man wary of emotional entanglements, transformed into half-surrogate father, half-Pygmalion to a woman young enough to reawaken his lost illusions.

Although *Yolanda*'s conceits stifled its star players, its vacuity inspired Minnelli to conjure up his own brand of magic. Since the script takes place nowhere on earth, geographically or psychologically, his playful task was to create his own imaginary world—a free-association daydream of Hispanic exotica overlaid with an exaggerated colonial splendor translated into the Esperanto of high-Hollywood.

In the prologue, a rumpled schoolmaster with an Austro-Hungarian accent leans against a reclining llama, while lecturing his class of well-scrubbed peasant lads on the geography of Patria. The setting is an emerald valley illuminated by a sound-stage cyclorama sunset in volcanic-sundae hues. The artifice is so hermetic that Minnelli's sudden cut to an outdoor set lit

Fred Astaire and Frank Morgan, Yolanda and the Thief *(1945)*

by actual sunshine is a real jolt, and one that's rarely repeated in the rest of the film.

Patria's inhabitants look the sort that would vanish into the smog if they ever left their sound-stage Brigadoon. The natives affect pastel bowlers in a Peruvian mode or sub-Mexican serapes and sombreros according to their sex and inclination, while the students at Yolanda's convent retreat are distinguished by their class uniforms in vibrant Minnelli red. The Aquaviva hacienda is a testament to Old World nostalgia far madder than anything Werner Herzog later conjured up for his *Fitzcarraldo*. Its reception hall is a transplanted Mediterranean *settecento* fantasy in peach-ochre stucco, replicated in the snoods and ribbons of Yolanda's retinue of maids. The other public rooms, in a variety of tints, are crammed with enough gilt-dripping furniture to fill Charles Foster Kane's Xanadu.

All of this is austere compared to Yolanda's private bathroom-boudoir. Lined with frescoes of baroque arches framing pink clouds in a turquoise sky, its pièce de résistance is the enormous sunken bathtub fed by a stepped artificial brook into which runs a trompe-l'oeil rendering of Venetian canals and bridges. This is where Minnellian fancies wed standard dream-factory notions of glamour. Poured into MGM couturier Irene's black-lace negligee gown or a "peasant" frock in Minnelli yellow, Bremer is a generic classy pinup in motion, her diction homogenized to match; she even refers to herself as Yolahnda. Her first languid levee as mistress of the house commences with a dunk in a tubful of bubbles left over from *Ziegfeld Follies.* Refreshed, she poses picturesquely while trilling of her anticipated meeting with her own Angel; meanwhile, a silent gaggle of chambermaids unfurls a cascade of tulle trimmed in ermine for her dressing gown, then a piece of black lace passes between the camera and Bremer's radiant countenance, before being affixed to her lacquered coiffure. Neither Gloria Swanson in her de Mille days nor Jeanette MacDonald as Ernst Lubitsch's Queen of Sylvania ever had it so good.

Yolanda's plot is a convenient pretext for Minnelli to use sculptures as icons of human aspirations—serenely chaste figures of angels are everywhere: in the puppet show marking Yolanda's farewell to childhood, in the garden of her family manse, leading the climactic carnival procession. Minnelli also indulges an urge to clutter the screen with exotic fauna—shampooed llamas nuzzle their way through the throngs of dress extras, upstaging their biped betters, as would the peacocks in *Kismet* and the Bois de Boulogne swans in *Gigi* later.

Minnelli's imagination truly runs riot for the film's two profligate set pieces, during which the story thankfully lurches to a halt. First, and most thematically am-bitious, is the hero's nightmare which plays out his conflict between the lure of ill-gotten wealth, his growing attraction to Yolanda, and his fear of the strictures of wedlock. The sequence begins with insidious trickery, deliberately blurring the audience's perception of the divide between wakefulness and the dream state. In his hotel room at night, a grim, sleepless Astaire stubs out a bedside cigarette, and the camera tracks 180 degrees across the room to a red flower in a glass—an image which anticipates the start of the *American in Paris* ballet a half-dozen years later. His hand grabs the flower, and as a marimba version of "Angel" plays softly on the soundtrack, he changes from pajamas to street clothes. His entrance onto the town market square tips us off that something even stranger than *Yolanda*'s concept of reality is going on. Astaire's progress through the square replicates his activities of a few hours earlier, with some disturbing variations. The bum who cadges a cigarette from him gradually sprouts six arms bearing smouldering butts; after Astaire scatters coins to a group of street urchins, a cloudburst of gold rains down on him from the heavens.

Lucille Bremer and Fred Astaire dance "Coffee Time," Yolanda and the Thief *(1945)*

From then on, he's definitively entered the realm of the abstract. On a curved golden path in an unearthly twilight, he stumbles onto a group of seductive washerwomen scrubbing their laundry to the sound of ominous percussion. In an intriguingly choreographed section, the women languorously stalk him along the stepping stones of the brook, enclosing him in a taut triangle of sheets; then they regroup in parallel lines, turning their sheets into dangerously billowing waves, through which Astaire must painfully pass.

Having made his escape, Astaire finds himself in a turbulent tan landscape, where a strange apparition confronts him—a female figure swathed in windswept veils emerges like a Daliesque Venus from an obsidian-dark pool. The scene shifts to art director Jack Martin Smith's most breathtaking creation—a sound-stage desert in bleached-bone hues, dominated by huge crenellated rock formations in papier-mâché. Deep in the background, the amphibious lady stands motionless, waiting to be unveiled by Astaire. It's Bremer herself, transformed into one of Minnelli's statues, and coming to life at Astaire's touch. As they pirouette behind a massive rocky arch, she hands Astaire the girdle of golden coins from her hips; attended by three would-be bridesmaids, she pleads in song for a wedding, which prompts a joyous dance duet over and around the steep mounds of the desert floor.

Their idyll is interrupted by a burst of insidious harem music: a quartet of soignée sirens in neon-satin dresses grab Astaire's arm to lure him to join the horsey set betting on a race mimed by two dancing jockeys. The race ended, Astaire pulls out his empty pockets and is snubbed by the swells. Bremer rematerializes, one foot posed on her hope chest; he revives her with dance for the second time, the sunburst spotlight illuminating them in the sudden dark. As Minnelli's camera describes delirious arcs around the pair, her attendants prepare Bremer for her nuptials. Astaire tries to escape toward the camera with her booty in tow, but his bride's chiffon scarf wrapped around his neck halts him in his tracks. As walls of rock close in on both sides, he retreats backward, trapped in her silken web. In a dissolve, Astaire is revealed breathless in bed, strangling in the tangle of his own sheets.

For all its exciting imagery, the number is mainly interesting as a somewhat overwrought blueprint for the dance dramas Minnelli created so seamlessly in later musicals. However novel its use here, the symbolic content of the sequence is too obvious for eloquence, emphasized by the disjointed manner with which it's expressed. The transitions are abrupt and arbitrary; the intended mood is further dashed by the intrusion of Bremer's banal song in the midst of the otherwise voiceless ballet. This general unevenness of tone extends to Loring's choreography. Once Astaire escapes his coven of laundresses, the dancing is a mingling of watered down ballet with a standard sample of

an Astaire ballroom duet, and the mini-Ascot Gavotte that distracts him from his nightmare bride is more earthbound yet. Under the circumstances, Minnelli's soaring diagonal shots upstage the dancing, to compensate in movement and momentum for what the choreography lacks.

Minnelli's aspirations for "Coffee Time" are more modest. What he's aiming for here is to create a knockout blend of color and motion, and the result is one of the most breathtaking set pieces in any Minnelli film, or other MGM musical. The carnival scenes which precede it are pretty spectacular in themselves, reflecting his wide-eyed enchantment with the rites of sophisticated pagans. Abetted by Charles Rosher's deeply saturated Technicolor camera work, the density of detail is extraordinary. Each merrymaker has a distinct identity: reincarnated Versailles courtiers jostle mestizos; plumed llamas mingle among creatures with human faces topped by red antlers; a majordomo with a green visage hurls confetti at the mouths of people who rile him. All of which is deliberately stranger than anything from Astaire's subconscious in the dream ballet.

Following this brief fantasia, Minnelli subdues his palette for the production number, which takes place not in Astaire's head but in musical-comedy heaven. Flanked by a quartet of gargantuan, 18th-century figures (first cousins to the ones in the *Follies'* "This Heart of Mine"), the set's an op-art floor of undulating black-and-white waves à la the sidewalks of Copacabana. Gradually this space is invaded by a mixed chorus of hand-clapping Latin hepcats, arrayed by Sharaff in graduated earth tones. The seas part as Astaire gives Bremer a twirl, and the camera rushes up joyously to greet them. Minnelli's wedding of shifting tempos and light schemes is the height of show biz sensuality: the couple's hip-swinging, side-by-side adagio framed by simulated moonbeams on a set drenched in sapphire; the sudden blaze of noon that greets a second invasion of the chorus; orange and white dappling the floor as Astaire and Bremer sail into a double-time series of jive pirouettes. This time, Minnelli's unfettered camera is integral to the choreographic design, echoing and amplifying the aplomb of Astaire at home in his own idiom at last, graced with a partner who is up to every thrilling step.

Unfortunately, after this climax a lot more footage must unreel before *Yolanda* heads toward its final fadeout. *Yolanda*'s premise may owe something to *Cabin in the Sky*—they both celebrate heroines whose religious convictions inspire the reformation of their errant, nightmare-prone men—but the resemblance ends there. For where Petunia's devotion seems genuine, *Yolanda*'s is an unconvincing tale of faith. While the movie proves that Minnelli can create intermittent magic in a vacuum, other, better films find his fantasy soaring higher as the subject inspires real passion on his part.

TILL THE CLOUDS ROLL BY

1946

With *Yolanda* in the can, Minnelli had a happy personal event in store. On June 15 1945, three weeks after production on the film was completed, he and Judy Garland were married. The wedding—his first, at the age of forty-two—took place in the Beverly Hills home of Garland's mother. Ira Gershwin served as Minnelli's best man; also conspicuously in attendance was L. B. Mayer, relishing his role as surrogate father of the bride. The couple embarked on a two-month honeymoon in New York, absorbing the atmosphere they had so successfully counterfeited on the Metro backlot the previous year for *The Clock*. On their return, the Minnellis set to work on the first of the two sole professional collaborations during their marriage.

Arthur Freed was preparing a mammoth musical biography of Jerome Kern, entitled *Till the Clouds Roll By*. To the all-star cast culled from MGM's roster, Freed had assigned the studio's top singing attraction, Judy Garland, to play Broadway's supreme musical comedy luminary of the twenties, Marilyn Miller. Casting the picture turned out to be the least of Freed's difficulties. One month after production began, in early October 1945, Kern died suddenly, necessitating a frantic rewrite of the screenplay. In the six months it took to shoot the picture, Freed lined up one director after another with a nonchalance more usually endured by the studio's screenwriters.

At the film's inception, choreographer Robert Alton was drafted to stage the musical numbers, and he managed to stay on board throughout; however, the film's shamelessly kitsch song-medley finale, concluding with Sinatra in white tails atop a tiny pedestal crooning, "Ol' Man River," was apparently directed without credit by George Sidney. First on hand to direct was Busby Berkeley—an odd choice, since his forte was the spectacular production number. He lasted but a few weeks, supplanted by Henry Koster, who also contributed little to the finished film. Halfway through the shooting schedule, with most of the film's dramatic spine still to be filmed, Richard Whorf was brought in to complete the picture, and it was he who snagged the dubious credit as its director. None of this affected Minnelli, who took on Garland's sequences alone, with appropriate acknowledgment in the opening credits. This material was among the first to be wrapped up, for a most pragmatic reason—in October 1945, the star was four months pregnant with their daughter, Liza.

The fact that *Till the Clouds Roll By* betrays little of its behind-the-scenes confusion is a tribute to the efficiency of the Freed Unit. Minnelli's sequences aside, this musical is a homogenized product of moviemaking-by-committee. *Till the Clouds Roll By* was the first and probably the dullest of several bio-pics MGM was to make on the lives of Broadway's top composers; still to come were tributes to Rodgers and Hart (*Words and Music*, 1948), Kalmar and Ruby (*Three Little Words*, 1950), and Sigmund Romberg (*Deep in My Heart*, 1954).

The plot focuses on Kern's transatlantic courtship of his future wife and his lifelong friendship with a song arranger named James Hessler. A semblance of conflict is provided in the person of Hessler's rebellious child, a would-be actress. (Inexplicably, *Till the Clouds Roll By* never acknowledges the existence of Jerome Kern's own real-life daughter; the celluloid Kerns are apparently childless.) The script, worked over by at least seven scriptwriters, slumbers under the anesthetic of Freed's reverence for Kern. A man known for his high-spirited charm, Kern is played by Robert Walker with a solemn dignity bordering on the comatose, and as his pal Van Heflin merely looks very bored throughout. The role of Eva Kern was assigned to an anonymous blonde named Dorothy Patrick, a wooden actress who was about as English as Jeanne Crain in *State Fair*. Lucille Bremer, cast as Hessler's petulant offspring, is the only one of the central quartet to display any energy, although her persuasive portrait of singleminded egotism boded ill for her future as a sympathetic star of Metro musicals.

Audiences expected the story to be a protracted stage wait between musical specialties, but the numbers are scarcely livelier. The tab version of *Show Boat* which opens the film (featuring Lena Horne in her one crack at Julie Laverne, the role of her dreams) is so perfunctory as to make the studio's lackluster full-length 1951 remake seem definitive. Throughout, the film's brace of popular balladeers—Horne, Dinah Shore, Kathryn Grayson, Tony Martin—dutifully hit their marks and make pretty sounds while projecting as little personality as possible. A few numbers muster some surface vivacity—Angela Lansbury's Edwardian music-hall turn, a brace of songs from Kern's Princess Theater musicals of the 1910s, featuring June Allyson and Ray McDonald—but Alton's staging never exceeds the boundaries of decorous good cheer.

The three sequences Minnelli contributed come about halfway through the picture; their freshness emphasizes the brain-fatigue of everything else. When we first meet Garland as Marilyn Miller at the opening-night intermission of her 1920 triumph, *Sally*, the setting is essence of Minnelli; the anteroom to the star's dressing room is a cherry-red chamber littered with white Grecian busts, all crowned askew by the top hats of Miller's admirers. Inside, she's the calm center of a civilized maelstrom—acknowledging the praises of her well-wishers, planning the next quick change with her dresser, humming a new arrangement with the con-

*Judy Garland as Marilyn
Miller singing "Look for the
Silver Lining," Till the
Clouds Roll By (1946)*

ductor, all the while orchestrating her transformation into the smudge-browed Sally, kitchen drudge with dreams of glory. In one extraordinary lateral take, Minnelli follows Garland as she strides through the wings past the flies and multicolored spotlights onstage toward the unlit set—a restaurant sink topped with an Everest of dirty dishes. After checking the placement of her props with the stage manager, the lights hit her and Garland is on. After all the backstage tumult, in a quiet, plaintive voice, she sings "Look for the Silver Lining." The staging of this song has been cited elsewhere as a clever ruse to hide Garland's pregnancy; in fact, this is a near-exact reproduction of Miller's original rendition a quarter-century earlier. But it's Garland's own directness and simplicity that give the number its special pathos. The wistfulness of the lyric is underscored by her fierce concentration on the mundane tasks at hand —keeping her hair out of her face and her sleeves out of the suds as she tackles the next mound of plates.

This is the film's one number with any emotional content, and thanks to the way Minnelli shaped it, there's a dual message at work. Up to now, every song had been staged as an immaculate tableau seen from the audience's perspective, concluding with stock shots of dress extras clapping with rapture. But here the public's presence is indicated only by the play of lights on Garland's face as the curtains close and swirl back as she basks in applause. Shot from the performer's point of view, the sequence is about the process of making musical-comedy magic—the combination of professionalism-under-pressure and generosity of talent which made Marilyn Miller the star she was, and Judy

Garland, in that happy phase of her career, a legend in the making. Everyone else in this movie may be wax mannequins, but Minnelli ensures that Garland is both flesh and blood, and triumphantly larger than life.

From the hushed intimacy of *Sally*, Minnelli plunges into the spectacular for a pair of numbers from the next Kern–Miller collaboration, the 1925 *Sunny*. The show's circus setting prompts him to out-dazzle Busby Berkeley with the title song. The sequence opens with a vertiginous flourish—from atop the offstage rafters, Minnelli focuses on a stagehand riding a spotlight flashing red, then the camera plummets to earth as the set comes ablaze with light. And what a set it is, a center ring of baroque fantasy done in scarlet and white, summing up all his tent-show childhood dreams of the big time. There's a marching band in Minnelli red; gold-sprayed elephants surrounded by attendants in pastel Indian silks; tightrope walkers picked out in silhouette against the big-top's canvas, and at the center of it all is the main attraction—Garland, posing daintily in white tutu before her screen double leaps in one bound onto her pony's back for a speedy canter around the gold-sawdust ring. Minnelli's matchless gift for blending an infinite number of seemingly random details is a marvel of visual harmony, keyed with hair's-breadth precision to the meter of the music. In the guise of paying tribute to the magic of the circus, Minnelli revels in the screen's possibilities for spectacle, climaxing with a dizzying final image—with the camera at bird's-eye level, and on the final note of the song, a spinning female aerialist suddenly catapults herself aloft in great arcs over the earthbound antics below.

From the gaudiness of the title song, Minnelli dissolves to a subdued palette for "Who?" showcasing Garland as Miller, the dancing sophisticate. On the set, Oscar Hammerstein's lyrics proved an occasion for mirth, as the expectant Garland crooned, "Whoooo stole my heart away?" to a bevy of ardent chorus boys, doffing their top hats one by one. Nevertheless, she maintained her sangfroid while the cameras were turning. Although far more elaborately staged, "Who?" prefigures Minnelli's "I'll Build a Stairway to Paradise" from *An American in Paris.* Garland glides airily down a white wrought-iron staircase, flanked by the men, and descends to the stage floor to execute a carefree solo romp around the sound stage during the orchestral chorus. Robert Alton's choreography attains a buoyant elegance here, accentuated by the monochromatic chic of Minnelli's concept—abetted by a mixed chorus in black and white, Garland in yellow chiffon is the only spot of color on the set. "Who?" derives its momentum from the ever-shifting mobility of Minnelli's camera work. While Alton's own numbers elsewhere founder in their inflated staginess, this one makes no pretense of being proscenium-bound, as Minnelli recaptures the luster of a bygone theatrical era by translating it into the most fluent screen terms.

· ·

1948 THE PIRATE

It was a foregone conclusion that Minnelli's next musical for the Freed Unit would be another showcase for Garland, but the impending birth of their daughter took precedence over these plans. Meanwhile, Pandro S. Berman requested Minnelli for a project outside the bounds of his accustomed forte—a psychological melodrama entitled *Undercurrent.* Once it was finished, Minnelli again immersed himself in preparations for the project that would return Garland to the screen after her confinement—a musical version of S. N. Behrman's flamboyant costume romp *The Pirate,* in which Alfred Lunt and Lynn Fontanne had scored their usual personal triumph under the aegis of the Theater Guild.

In his memoirs, Minnelli recalled that it was he who urged the studio to acquire this property specifically for Garland, in tribute to her ripening gifts as a comedienne. Behrman's brand of highflown whimsy had a special appeal for Minnelli; it was this playwright's *Serena Blandish* which he had sought to adapt for the musical stage just before joining MGM. Minnelli's enthusiasm may have prompted the studio to reshape this straight play into a song-and-dance divertissement. However, production records indicate that Metro had owned *The Pirate* long before he had anything to do with it, and initially at least, the studio's intentions for the screen version were quite different.

Back in November 1942 (when Minnelli had just finished directing his first picture, and had but a slight professional acquaintanceship with Judy Garland), the studio was busily negotiating the film rights for *The Pirate* on the eve of its Broadway premiere. As indicated in a letter from Loews Inc. executive J. Robert Rubin to the top brass on the West Coast, there was a surprising wrinkle; the Lunts wanted to be included in the package, despite the fact that they were notoriously movie-shy since making their joint talkie debut in *The Guardsman* at MGM a decade before. The prospect of these wonderful but now distinctly middle-aged thespians gamboling across the screens of the Loews' circuit didn't thrill MGM's executives. Studio story editor Kenneth MacKenna wired back that while interest in the property was running high, it was absolutely no to the Lunts. In a subsequent cable he reported that, "*The Pirate* was told to a full executive story meeting and was unanimously liked for a broad comedy. Mr. Mayer was particularly enthusiastic. It was talked of in terms of [William] Powell, [Hedy] Lamarr and [Charles] Laughton. Pan Berman is the leading contender for it among several producers who have expressed a wish to make it." And when Mr. Mayer was particularly enthusiastic, MGM's largesse was considerable: *The Pirate* was soon theirs for the then-staggering sum of $225,000.

Preparations for this songless farce began immediately. While *The Pirate* was still running on Broadway (it closed in March 1943 after 176 performances), the studio proposed taping a live sound recording of the stage version to gauge its laugh quotient, as MGM had done for *The Philadelphia Story.* However, the miffed Lunts requested an extortionate sum for their services, and the idea was dropped. Next, according to MGM's timeworn custom, the property was sent along the screenwriters' assembly line. The first adaptation was crafted by house sophisticate, Joseph L. Mankiewicz, in one of his last assignments before moving to 20th Century-Fox and greater glory as a screenwriter-director. This version was supplanted by another confected by Myles Connolly and director Henry Koster, with Myrna Loy replacing Hedy Lamarr as *The Pirate*'s prospective heroine, still opposite William Powell. A third script treatment was produced by MGM veteran

Frances Marion and one H. E. Rogers. Two years had now passed since Behrman's play was purchased, and while the studio dithered, Samuel Goldwyn produced a comic swashbuckler with Bob Hope and Virginia Mayo entitled *The Princess and the Pirate,* whose premise was dismayingly similar to Behrman's—though not sufficiently so to warrant a plagiarism suit.

Freed then proposed that the project be reactivated as a musical under his supervision, directed by Minnelli with a Cole Porter score. Mayer agreed, but the problem of a workable script remained. Anita Loos and Joseph Than spent the first six months of 1946 toiling over the story, and in a burst of desperate creativity, they upended Behrman's basic premise in a manner that exasperated everyone concerned. At some point, Sally Benson, Freed's favorite script doctor, Robert Nathan, and Freed himself had a crack at this resistant yarn. The final, filmed version was credited to Frances Goodrich and Albert Hackett, the married screenwriting team responsible for *The Thin Man* series among many other movies. Minnelli supervised the writers' progress closely, urging them to blend their own shrewd eye for movie construction with Behrman's ear for flamboyant high camp. At last, both he and Freed pronounced their satisfaction with the script, and over the years, Goodrich and Hackett became among the director's most esteemed collaborators.

With the script in trustworthy hands, Minnelli immersed himself in that phase of preproduction he relished most—imagining the particular look the film would have. MGM veterans chuckle at the memory of ''Vincente's paper dolls.'' Minnelli would spend weeks at a time holed up in his office surrounded by cutouts and torn pages from his personal cache of art books, period fashion engravings, and architectural photographs, augmented by the vast resources of the studio research library. From these he'd assemble a collage of images to inspire the appropriate vision in his art director and costumer—in this instance, Jack Martin Smith, whose contribution to *Yolanda* captivated Minnelli, and Mme. Karinska, already legendary for her work in ballet and musical theater. With their collaboration, plus the virtuosity of cameraman Harry Stradling, Minnelli's *Pirate* would become an extended visual metaphor for its heroine's private dilemma—a seductive carnival of Afro-Latin exotica invading the pastel decorum of the languishing colonials.

Unfortunately for Minnelli, the fun stopped there. A trouble-ridden project from the start, *The Pirate* proved the most emotionally taxing film of his whole career. Principal shooting alone took six months, from February to August of 1947; adding preproduction, plus the extensive retakes and revisions deemed necessary before its release, Minnelli spent the entire year on this one assignment. In present-day Hollywood this would be in the normal nature of things. However, in the movie-factory heyday, the studios expected tireless productivity from its contract directors. Hence this was viewed as rather indulgent behavior expended on what was after all just another musical, albeit one more ambitious than most.

The situation was doubly painful for Minnelli as his sound stage became the setting for his own domestic tragedy. Subsequent Minnelli films may unconsciously reflect his personal conflicts; in times to come, the studio often served as a kind of refuge, where his decisive creativity on the set compensated for his bafflement over an often turbulent personal life. (Among its more explicit themes, *The Bad and the Beautiful* is a celebration of that very process.) On *The Pirate,* his emotional and professional dilemmas collided in the person of Judy Garland, then assailed by the most painful crisis to date of her young life.

Garland's various hagiographers have recorded this period in voluminous detail; the best-documented account can be found in Christopher Finch's even-handed and intelligent biography, *Rainbow.* Suffice it to say that, once more in the throes of an increasingly uncontrollable dependence on barbiturates, for the first time in her life she succumbed utterly to the strain. Garland's frailty was generally ascribed to the studio's punishing regime of overwork, a plausible rationale that explains her final exile from MGM four years later, following her inability to complete three out of four successive movies in which she was to appear. Yet ironically, her breakdown during *The Pirate* followed over a year of professional idleness, and was presumably prompted by Garland's anxiety at once again confronting the daily rigors of her career. Almost from the first, the star's difficulties made the projected shooting schedule for *The Pirate* a hypothetical prospect at best. Literally months were spent vainly trying to shoot around her absences and illnesses—or worse, making do when she did appear on the set, obviously ill-equipped to meet the demands facing her.

With Minnelli cast in the role of her anguished husband as well as her exasperated director, the mutual distress of the situation can only be imagined. (For Minnelli, the pain was deepened by the sudden loss of his father, two years after the death of his mother.) As an increasingly irrational Garland needed to assign someone the blame for her troubles, Minnelli was the logical target. Resenting the easy professional rapport he had established with *Pirate* co-star Gene Kelly, she accused Minnelli of sabotaging her and throwing the picture to Kelly at her expense.

Although this couldn't have been farther from Minnelli's intent, in retrospect one can understand what prompted her claim. Even in the Behrman play, Serafin is by far the more active and colorful part. While Lynn Fontanne's wit and glamour may well have obscured this, the role of Manuela is just the foil/catalyst to the hero's acrobatics and ham grandiloquence. From its inception it was clear that *The Pirate* was never destined to be another regulation Garland vehicle.

In the films they made together, Minnelli's attempt to extend her range as an actress was a challenge with an undertone of danger for a performer as notoriously insecure as Garland. Other directors with whom she had worked—Norman Taurog, Busby Berkeley, George Sidney—weren't so particular about working with Garland as to make the characters she played fit some larger, unifying concept; their task was to create a snappy musical setting in which the star could shine. Although it was clear that her work with Minnelli was the most distinguished of her adult career thus far, increasingly the Garland he sought to nurture subverted the screen Judy whom she and her fans alike had come to treasure. If she had thus far epitomized the heartland virtues, her evolving persona gently mocked such romantic assumptions. In *Ziegfeld Follies* Minnelli playfully contrasted his "real" star as an arch fabulist in a shimmering gown, posing before an oil portrait lampooning the audience's own Judy—the gamine in a ragged gray frock. In *The Pirate,* the veiled and sequestered virgin who dreams of abduction by a lusty buccaneer is a satiric comment on the naive ardor of Esther

Judy Garland (standing left)
and friends, The Pirate *(1948)*

Smith, longing to hold hands on the front porch with that respectable boy next door. For an actress who had trouble differentiating her screen self from her own sense of identity, Minnelli's well-intended efforts could have dire consequences. No wonder Garland had so many problems in bringing Manuela to life; with her illnesses and absences, she was too busy acting out her resentment toward her husband's role as Svengali.

Never the most self-effacing screen presence, Kelly, at this new peak in his form, couldn't help but dominate every scene he's in. All three of Kelly's virtuoso dance numbers reached the screen triumphant and intact, whereas two of Garland's solos—"Voodoo" and the main chorus of "Love of My Life"—were deemed wanting and excised from the release print. (In the case of "Voodoo," Garland's emotional state may have rendered it too intense for comfort; as preserved on Hugh Fordin's LP of numbers cut from movie musicals, her eerie glissando makes the release of Manuela's id sound more like an exorcism.) By this time, Garland's own phantoms were too menacing to be banished by a Freed happy ending. At the final fadeout of *The Pirate*, Manuela gleefully flees her old life by joining Serafin as the new adornment of his madcap troupe; however, the only escape open to Garland in real life was a temporary sojourn in a California sanatorium.

The movie's ill fate extended to its popular reception. In a time of industry-wide retrenchment prompted by the postwar decline in moviegoing, *The Pirate* cost MGM a total of $3,768,014—a million dollars more than the studio would spend on *An American in Paris* three years later. *The Pirate* needed to provoke a sensation at the box office to make any money, and no such miracle happened. After its release, MGM assessed the deficit at upwards of two million dollars; of all Garland's MGM pictures, it was the only one which lost money for the studio.

The movie's critical reception focused on Minnelli's heady aestheticism, which to some reviewers loomed large over the film's perceived weaknesses of script and score. Others tweaked him for making *The Pirate*'s pictorial virtuosity an end in itself—a charge frequently repeated throughout his career by those who deemed naturalism the highest aim to which the screen could aspire. No cavils greeted Gene Kelly's irrepressibly stylized performance. Although the dancer's screen specialty was the brash American Joe with a touch of Pierrot in his heart, Serafin's passionate self-love in satin breeches proved another profitable vein, from Kelly's D'Artagnan in the MGM version of *The Three Musketeers* to *Singin' in the Rain*'s film-within-the-film "The Dueling Cavalier."

Considering *The Pirate*'s obvious affinities to Minnelli's previous and similarly unprofitable *Yolanda*, the fact that it was made at all says much for MGM's faith in Freed and his director. Both films take place in some uncharted torrid zone Shangri-La, whose stucco and cobblestones are as triumphantly fake as the sun streaming down from the sound-stage rafters. In each, the chatelaine of this domain is an orphaned, auburn-haired, somnambulant beauty stirred by reveries of the ideal male who will give her life meaning; instead, she is seduced by a scapegrace liar. The psychological dynamic of the tale is expressed almost identically in both films. Midway through both *Yolanda* and *The Pirate*, the action is interrupted by a Minnelli specialty, the hallucinatory ballet, in which the dreamer's mingled feelings of fear and desire toward the person threatening his waking equilibrium are played out with choreographed clarity. This undercurrent of erotic danger notwithstanding, we are still securely within the boundaries of an MGM musical fantasy. Which means that for both Yolanda and *The Pirate*'s Manuela, disillusionment will be brief, followed by the joyful awareness that the romance of a tangible mortal, however fallible, is more fulfilling than any dream.

Although *The Pirate*'s commercial failure dis-

heartened everyone concerned, in retrospect this movie justified their initial faith. It's easy to point out its deficiencies as conventional entertainment, which, like *Yolanda*, commence with Minnelli's need to overcompensate visually for an indifferent quotient of songs. By the late forties, the destiny of the movie musical was already threatened by the increasing paucity of first-rate original scores. Most great masters of the American popular song were dead, in decline, or devoted exclusively to the theater. Unfortunately for Freed and Minnelli, Cole Porter's final, decade-long burst of creativity started just after *The Pirate*, with his 1948 score for *Kiss Me Kate*. When Porter composed this film, he was yet to emerge from a fallow period which comprised such forgettable stage work as *The Seven Lively Arts*, *Mexican Hayride*, and *Around the World in Eighty Days*. The songs for *The Pirate* are indisputably more sophisticated than Harry Warren and Arthur Freed's contributions to *Yolanda and the Thief*. Still, this is Porter as determined pro rather than inspired songsmith; the score bears a hollow echo of the insinuating sensuality that was his trademark.

Moreover, the chemistry between Garland and Kelly never quite fuses, which makes the movie's central theme of mutual longing and fulfillment seem theoretical at best. *Yolanda*, too, was blunted due to an ill-considered match between the stars and their respective roles, but at least Astaire and Bremer were sublimely in tune as soon as they joined forces on the dance floor. On *The Pirate*, the situation was more complicated; Garland was incapable of connecting with anyone on the set—she was concentrating on her own survival, not on the fate of her character. In the finished film, it's obvious that Garland's protracted absences disrupted Minnelli's visual schemes for the film —group scenes are frequently stitched together from shots of the rest of the troupe intercut with Garland reciting her lines in isolation, picked up in those instances when she was capable of performing. Thanks to her reserves of professionalism and the protective measures of *The Pirate*'s film editor, we watch as Garland goes through the requisite motions, her Manuela lurches between hauteur and antic apprehension. Yet the spirit is missing; her puppetlike animation is betrayed by the hollow cast of her eyes in many scenes, Garland's wiry frame shrinking inside the whimsical flounces of all those Karinska-executed gowns.

Furthermore, Garland and Kelly's only number together is the slapstick reprise of "Be a Clown" at the finale. Until this point, she sings alone and he dances with everybody but his co-star, from anonymous Caribbean temptresses and brigands to the talented Nicholas Brothers. This ignores a fundamental principle of the genre that song and movement are metaphors for sex. If the stars do their stuff solo, alienation is bound to upstage romance.

Nevertheless, *The Pirate* is a far more ingratiating example of that brand of Technicolor fantasy Minnelli first explored with *Yolanda and the Thief*. If the songs are slight, as a dance musical *The Pirate* was the studio's liveliest achievement to date; the athletic sexuality of Kelly and Robert Alton's choreography brought a new language to this screen idiom. Despite its false starts, the Goodrich–Hackett script is superior to that of *Yolanda* and to the Behrman play itself. The threat of censorship forced certain alterations in the text; originally, Manuela was the restive wife of portly Don Pedro, but as the Production Code would never have sanctioned Judy Garland as an adulteress, here she is his anxious fiancée. Other minor changes included changing Manuela's avaricious parents to a dithery aunt and uncle (played by Gladys Cooper and Lester Allen), and omitting a comic romantic subplot between Manuela's black maid and one of Serafin's fellow thespians (one of the Nicholas Brothers in the movie).

At the same time, the film script features a vastly improved structural change. In the play, Serafin recognizes Don Pedro as the true pirate in Act I and tells Manuela of her husband's dark past less than halfway through the play, which turns the Act III finale of Pedro's public exposure and humiliation into a distinct anticlimax. The film makes these revelations more gradually, which both infuses the plot with some suspense and changes Manuela from an object of seduction to a woman torn between infatuation and propriety. Goodrich and Hackett even allow the now-bourgeois brigand a measure of tragic dignity he never possessed in the play. Whereas Behrman's villain unwittingly exposes his former crimes during the Act III trial for Serafin's life, in the film Don Pedro (Walter Slezak) deliberately confesses, hoping to awaken Manuela's love for the scoundrel inside him, even if he must hang for it. Though much of the playwright's epigrammatic wit remains, the tone of the film script is more expressly romantic than Behrman's. Minnelli's eye for color both amplifies the wit and clarifies the conflict between the luxurious dullness of Manuela's daily life and the wild, terrifying freedom Serafin represents.

Throughout *The Pirate*, Minnelli creates a new synthesis of visual elements from his previous pictures—this daydream to music is a peach-stucco world of parasoled ladies of leisure and black-veiled duennas mingling with villagers in jungle-plumage bandannas and soldiers arrayed in primary-color finery. His ersatz-Caribbean frescoes are further enlivened by his racial sensitivity, unusually acute for that time and place; by the

Judy Garland mesmerized by Gene Kelly, The Pirate *(1948)*

OPPOSITE:
Gene Kelly extolling "Niña," The Pirate *(1948)*

nonchalant racial mix of its dress extras, *The Pirate* rebukes the all-white tropicana featured in most movie-musical versions of the torrid zone during the forties and fifties. Characteristic of him, if unique in the Hollywood of the time, is the way he teams up Kelly and the Nicholas Brothers in the film's first rendering of "Be a Clown." Dressed in the same blue-and-yellow motley, they form an equilateral acrobatic triangle in constant motion—a distinct change from the segregated specialties the screen's greatest male dance team usually performed in their decade of glory.

For all *The Pirate*'s escapist spirit, Minnelli's visual schemes have a psychological purpose foreign to the usual Arthur Freed entertainments. The way his camera frames Garland and Kelly is as revealing as the performances of the actors themselves. It closes in ever tighter on the perennially sequestered Manuela, then speeds to keep up with the vagabond Serafin. As long as she stays in her own milieu, the heroine remains at dead center of a series of overdecorated still-lifes. Manuela is first seen pacing the narrow enclosure of her guardians' wrought-iron veranda, framed by a retinue of contented virgins. (When the girl's aunt interrupts her reverie with the news that she has procured her a husband, Manuela can only murmur plaintively, "Is it anybody I know?") As a bride, she will take her place as the most exquisite possession in Don Pedro's mansion. Manuela's future as a thing of inert beauty is summed up as she poses for an artist in profile behind a lace-bordered sheet of muslin, her silhouette captured forever for her fiancé's delight.

Minnelli's ambivalence over the allure of the material is especially pronounced in *The Pirate*. As a sensualist, he's intoxicated by the tints and textures of beautiful objects; yet as in such contrasting films as *The Long, Long Trailer* and *Home from the Hill*, Minnelli the moralist is compelled to acknowledge that the accumulated weight of all these things can crush the soul. It's no accident that we first see Serafin the trouper climbing triumphantly aloft the shipping crate bearing Manuela's trousseau from the Old World; in this one shot, Minnelli establishes the free-spirited hero's supremacy over the seductive trappings which are the sum total of Don Pedro's appeal to Manuela.

From then on, the unfettered Serafin bounds energetically through the artificial world of this movie, the camera sailing along beside him in animated synchrony. "Niña," the movie's first, rhumba-laced production number, celebrates the hero's chronic restlessness, both erotic and athletic. Sauntering down the port city's main street, Serafin is an equal-opportunity seducer, pausing to play with fruit vendors, highstrung demoiselles, and flirtatious trollops alike. Unfazed by gravity and untroubled by vertigo, he turns the town into his own set of monkey bars—snaking up and down balconies; suspended from a window while wrapped in a brief, passionate embrace; reclining ca-

sually atop a stone archway to serenade yet another damsel, conveniently equipped with a flamenco guitar. After shimmying down to earth, he bestows a kiss on a smouldering Carmencita after purloining her cigarette with his lips. As the brass of the MGM Orchestra switches to percussion and snake-charmer woodwinds, Serafin's mood shifts to flamenco. In a barber-pole-rigged gazebo he subdues a new group of dancing Niñas, who swirl their skirts and snatch his hat to fan themselves into further delirium.

Throughout this sequence, Minnelli exploits his fondness for invisible cutting, using the longest possible takes composed of lateral pans and tracking shots to emphasize the fluidity and momentum of the dance. In the number's climax, he creates circles within circles; as Minnelli's camera vaults around the curvilinear set, he's constantly redefining the space between the dancers and their immobile props, in a manner that anticipates the matchless Place de la Concorde fountain pas de deux from the ballet of his next musical, *An American in Paris*.

The "Mack the Black" ballet, a puff of smoke from Manuela's (and Minnelli's) overheated imagination, distills the contrast between her ennui and Serafin's irrepressible energy. She is seen in a tight closeup at her window, trying in vain to close the shutters against her visions of the brigand's reckless exploits. Meanwhile, with a Douglas Fairbanks rope trick, Serafin-as-Macoco plummets down to earth from the mast of his ship; as the blood-and-charcoal backdrop lights up with rhythmic blasts of flame, he careens about his ravaged domain, wielding a large pole to daunt burly rivals and feminine conquests alike. The link between sex and mortal peril (which Minnelli later parodied in *The Band Wagon*'s "The Girl Hunt" ballet) is blatantly explicit here, starting with the inelegant image of Macoco "castrating" the prostrate Manuela by slicing off the topknot of her white headdress.

Manuela—and the camera's treatment of her—comes alive once she begins to reject decorum and plumb her instincts. This, too, is dangerous; to surrender to passion is to court madness, a notion underscored in Porter's score with lyrics rhyming Serafin's quest for Niña with neurasthenia and schizophrenia, or Manuela's tribute to her phantom pirate, sung under hypnosis amid Serafin's troupe. Relieved for once from the pins and trusses befitting a lady, she prowls the stage arrayed in a simple blouse and skirt, her hair flying free as she proclaims, "And I'm loco/For Mack the Black, the Black Macoco!"

The risk is moot, since neither his hypothetical Niña nor her longed-for buccaneer with Gene Kelly's physique really exists. Which is fortunate for them, for between his quest for a wench of elusive, indifferent beguilement and her desire for a man who'll "swoop down on me like a chicken hawk and carry me away" leaving "a flaming path of masculinity," their ideals of the erotic other are equally masochistic. Serafin and Manuela are not opposites at all, but mirror images reflecting the same fundamental urges. He needs a partner to complement his life onstage and off; always pragmatic in his fashion, he woos Manuela with the demurral, "It isn't essential for you to love me to be in the troupe. It helps, but it isn't essential." Similarly, Manuela will find true fulfillment only in playacting, despite her claim that "there is a practical world and a dream world . . . I won't mix them." For her, the artifice of the stage is more honest and spontaneous than that "practical world" of bourgeois propriety. At first she turns her latent gifts against Serafin to punish him for his own subterfuges. In a sly seduction scene, Manuela vamps the sham pirate with a rapier thrust to his thespian ego, professing his theatrical guise "unspeakably drab." (Aptly enough, Manuela's dramatic debut is also Garland's first sustained scene of assured comic playing in the picture.) In a set piece more noteworthy for dogged energy than hilarity, Manuela next turns furious farceuse, hurling a barrage of Don Pedro's gilded loot at Serafin's offending head. Now it's his turn to criticize her performance, wailing, "You're overdoing this!" as the remnants of an oil painting dangle from his shoulders.

In fact, Manuela's flair for slapstick, that most "unfeminine" of the theatrical arts, will prove the key to her happy future as star and partner in Serafin's itinerant troupe. Once the plot has been resolved (the lovers' flair for histrionics having saved Serafin from the noose), it's on to the serious business of putting on a show. In their unisex costumes, their faces disguised with the same black-and-white masks of merriment, the hero and heroine reappear to perform a reprise of "Be a Clown"—a riot of pratfalls, ear-wigglings, and gleefully klutzy dodges from an avalanche of juggler's pins cascading from all sides. In the end, it's teamwork, not passion, which is celebrated in *The Pirate*'s upbeat fadeout.

All of this goes far to explain why *The Pirate* is a more stimulating flight of fancy than *Yolanda*, for it's borne aloft by an idea that stirred Minnelli profoundly. In a curious way, this movie is a form of autobiography in code, with the director's memories and longings filtered through both leading roles: in his childhood, Minnelli was drawn in turn to the raffish allure of his parents' traveling tent show and the security of his grandparents' respectable small-town home. Although he'd revisit the latter in memory with, for example, *Meet Me in St. Louis,* he chose the life of pink gels and canvas scrims, far from the stifling calm of Ohio. Moreover, it's easy to read the romance between Serafin and Manuela as a wistful vision of the bond between Minnelli and his own particular star and partner—one based on a mutual nurturing of their talents, and a shared understanding of the volatile nature of the artistic spirit.

Like his fictional counterparts in *The Pirate,* Minnelli had found himself by defying the humdrum life to conjure up his own brand of magic. In his musicals of the forties after *Meet Me in St. Louis,* this urge for Technicolored enchantment took form in an inimitable blend of the urbane and the naive. There's an innocence to

The Pirate's artifice that Minnelli never quite summoned up again, and even its rococo Macocoisms were severely tempered henceforth. Evidently, the rupture of his partnership with Garland and the resounding failure of this movie taught him that Manuela wasn't the only one who needed to learn how to tell the practical world from the world of dreams. From now on, there were no more tropical mirages left for Minnelli. In their place, his musicals unreeled a Minnellian version of the tangible world—the Paris of *An American in Paris* and *Gigi,* the New York of *The Band Wagon* and *Bells Are Ringing.* When his employers did force him to conjure up Never-Never-Land again with movies like *Brigadoon* and *Kismet,* the strain was evident. *The Pirate* represented Minnelli's last moment as a freewheeling fabulist, and for all the backstage angst and turmoil, it was a lovely time while it lasted.

· ·

1951   **AN AMERICAN IN PARIS**

The rigors of making *The Pirate* marked the start of a frustrating period at the studio for Minnelli; for a while it seemed that his rise to eminence at MGM had been checked for good. Oblivious as usual to all but the work at hand, Minnelli was slow at first to pick up the cues of impending trouble. With principal shooting completed on *The Pirate* in late summer of 1947, he turned to a new and tantalizing musical project—an Irving Berlin cavalcade called *Easter Parade.* For this property, Freed had again summoned much of *The Pirate*'s roster of talent; in addition to Minnelli, the lineup included Garland and Kelly as stars, the scriptwriting team of Goodrich and Hackett, Robert Alton as choreographer, and Harry Stradling behind the camera. But *Easter Parade* sought to avoid *The Pirate*'s wanton fancies for a more emotionally nuanced approach—in outline it was a kind of Tin Pan Alley Pygmalion, set in the New York of the early 1910s. The finished film proved one of the most popular musicals Freed ever produced, but a series of behind-the-scenes crises combined to make it a very different package from the one he had initially envisioned.

Rehearsals for *Easter Parade* began in September 1947, with Minnelli, Alton, and Kelly conferring on the latter's prospective dance routines; at this point, Garland was still recuperating from her breakdown. On her return everything was serene as far as Minnelli could tell, until the day he was summoned to Freed's office and told that, on the advice of Garland's psychiatrist, it would be best for all concerned if somebody else directed the picture. Minnelli's shock at the news was increased by what he viewed as Garland's subter-

fuge—her unwillingness to level with him personally. Yet, after all their miseries at home and at the studio during *The Pirate,* the logic of this decision should have been obvious to everyone; the surprise is that, by his own account, it had never occurred to Minnelli.

His replacement was Charles Walters, the young former choreographer, who had made a successful directorial debut with Freed's remake of the 1920s college musical, *Good News.* There were more defections to come—Gene Kelly broke an ankle, and Fred Astaire was persuaded to emerge from a short-lived retirement to partner Garland. In the role of Garland's rival, Cyd Charisse was supplanted by Ann Miller, making her MGM debut as the studio's second-lead tap dancing soubrette; along the way, the Goodrich–Hackett script was substantially refurbished by Sidney Sheldon.

With production on *Easter Parade* under way in earnest, Minnelli and Garland were briefly reunited on the lot for *The Pirate*'s last batch of retakes. What followed was a particularly bleak stretch for Minnelli. If Garland had suffered most from the too-intense link between their private and professional lives, now he was the principal victim. Showing remarkable resilience, she was happily at work on a satisfying project he had coveted; meanwhile, for the first time since *Cabin in the Sky* Minnelli was idle, with no assignments in view. While still receiving $2,500 a week from his 1946 contract, for a full year he marked time by directing screen tests of potential MGM talent. Minnelli feared that he was being punished for Garland's mishaps and *The Pirate*'s subsequent failure, and he may have been right. Certainly he was a convenient target for blame, since in the studio-system cosmos, directors were expendable commodities; whatever their caprices, Metro's stars had a value more tangibly measured at the box office.

Toward the end of 1948, Minnelli's anxieties were at last dispelled when Pandro Berman offered him *Madame Bovary*—an assignment which was to cinch his claim as a first-rate director of serious films as well as musicals. Three years were to pass between *The Pirate* and Minnelli's next movie in the genre that had made his reputation.

A quick summation of Freed's musicals from this period explains why Minnelli's talents were temporarily superfluous. Freed's choicest work-in-progress was the screen adaptation of *On the Town,* whose slangy exuberance didn't suit Minnelli's temperament, and which was planned in any case to serve as Gene Kelly and Stanley Donen's joint directorial debut. This aside, the Freed Unit's most intriguing prospects—*The Barkleys of Broadway* and *Annie Get Your Gun*—had been assembled specifically for Garland, although in the end each was played by someone else. All that remained were *Take Me Out to the Ball Game,* an uninspiring Kelly–Sinatra baseball musical, plus Esther Williams' *Pagan Love Song.* Minnelli must have been relieved when Freed didn't draft him for these.

Fortunately, the producer had something special in mind for bringing Minnelli back into the fold. In 1949, Freed had a vague notion for a spectacular new musical—an all-Gershwin songfest about an expatriate Yank living in France. So far, this resembled a matched bookend to Freed's recent Irving Berlin medley, *Easter*

Parade. However, Freed upped the ante with his brainstorm for a smash finale—a full-length ballet set to the Gershwin orchestral suite "An American in Paris," which would also provide the film's title. Even this was not the novelty it might seem; after all, Freed musicals, from *Yolanda* and *Ziegfeld Follies* on, had featured extended dance sequences of a certain pretension. In the interim, the unexpected box office success in the States of the Powell–Pressburger *The Red Shoes* indicated that audiences might sit still for something even longer and unabashedly *en pointe,* with highbrow music to match.

The surviving Gershwin brother, Ira, was easily persuaded, and the music catalogue—including rights to the *American in Paris* title—was acquired for $158,750, plus a handsome fee to Ira to provide new or revised lyrics as needed. Initially, Freed was undecided between Fred Astaire and Gene Kelly as *An American in Paris'* dancing star, but Kelly's immediate enthusiasm for the concept made the film his from an early stage in its development. The producer knew whom he wanted to shape his blurred outline into a semblance of a movie-musical plot: Alan Jay Lerner, then Broadway's brightest young lyricist/librettist—save possibly the team of Betty Comden and Adolph Green, already under contract to Metro thanks to Freed. If the Comden–Green forte was puckish satire, Lerner specialized in worldly sentiment. After a less-than-taxing movie baptism on *Royal Wedding,* Freed figured Lerner was now ready to tackle this.

Minnelli was clearly the right choice to direct this project. A Francophile artist himself, he had no trouble

Georges Guetary and Gene Kelly, "S'Wonderful," An American in Paris (1951)

Nina Foch and Gene Kelly,
An American in Paris
(1951)

identifying with the aspirations of *An American in Paris'* hero. No Hollywood filmmaker was as conscious of the painterly aesthetic as he was—Minnelli's work had always sought to use light and color in a cinematic homage to the canvases he loved. He had enjoyed a close personal association with the Gershwin family dating back to his early Broadway days, and he'd proved how mutually inspiring his teamwork with Kelly could be. Most of all, Freed's *idée fixe* for the finale made the drafting of Minnelli a foregone conclusion. In its final form, the ballet would be a kaleidoscopic dance collage inspired by a half-century of French painting; it would run 17 minutes and cost half a million dollars to shoot, sufficient in 1950 to produce a modest full-length feature. On the Metro lot or else-

where, nobody but Minnelli could boast the requisite taste and experience to bring it off.

In February 1950, the studio issued a publicity release officially announcing Minnelli's selection as director of *An American in Paris*. Lerner had already turned in a longish first draft of the script; while trimmed substantially to accommodate the Gershwin songs and a running time of under two hours, it reached the screen essentially unchanged. Lerner's plot consists of two intersecting romantic triangles. Jerry Mulligan is an artist studying in Paris under the GI Bill; he finds a patroness in fellow expatriate Milo Roberts, a restless heiress whose interest in Jerry is amorous as well as professional. Meanwhile, he becomes smitten with youthful Parisienne Lise Bourvier, unaware at first that she is the fiancée of a local friend, music-hall star Henri Baurel, who had sheltered Lise when she was orphaned during the war. Linked by guilt and obligation to the wrong partners, Jerry and Lise bid a painful farewell, only to be reunited in a rapturous clinch at the fadeout. The story doesn't exactly shine with originality, and came in for a goodly share of critical carping once the film was released in November 1951. Nevertheless, Freed, Minnelli, et al., deemed it a better than serviceable hook for the movie's principal attractions—Kelly's dances, the Gershwin songbook, and the picturesque Gallic setting.

Matching these roles with the right performers tested the resources of Freed and Minnelli, since MGM's roster of contract players, still fairly ample in 1950, comprised no one suited for *An American in Paris* save star Kelly. The part of Mulligan's caustic pal, an indigent pianist/composer named Adam Cook, was tailored specifically to suit longtime Gershwin crony Oscar Levant; Nina Foch, once Queen of the B's across town at Columbia, was an early choice to play the mercurial Milo. Henri Baurel had been conceived as Maurice Chevalier's return to the American screen after an absence of fifteen years; even his age would have been an asset, emphasizing by contrast the youthful ardor of Lise and Jerry. Contradictory reports survive to explain why Chevalier's comeback had to wait several years longer. Minnelli has cited a conflict with Chevalier's concert schedule—an unlikely reason, considering the star's eagerness to reestablish himself with the vast movie public. A more plausible motive was MGM's fear of controversy over the rumors of Chevalier's collaboration with the occupying forces during the war. Lerner's autobiography further cites whispers of Chevalier's alleged postwar leftist affiliations. In this, however, he probably confused Chevalier with Yves Montand, another prospect for Henri, whom Warner Bros. the previous year had considered then rejected for a contract on similar grounds; a decade would pass before Montand at last made his Hollywood debut. Studio executives suggested Carl Brisson. This was logical enough; because, while best known in 1950 as Rosalind Russell's father-in-law, in the thirties he had served for a time as Paramount's second-string Chevalier upon the latter's departure from the studio. Yet Freed passed, settling instead on Georges Guetary, the youngish *vedette* of a series of minor stage and screen musicals in Paris, who at the time was enjoying a moderate success on Broadway in *Arms and the Girl.*

The casting of Guetary was greeted by everyone on the picture as a case of *faute de mieux;* his name meant nothing to the American public and not much more abroad, nor did he pose a threat to Kelly in the charisma department. As things turned out, Guetary seemed inspired by those continental capons perfected by Georges Metaxa in the Fred-and-Ginger movies of the thirties; nevertheless, his spirited rendition of "I'll

Build a Stairway to Paradise" proved one of the movie's undeniable highlights.

Finding the right young actress for the poignant Lise was the main puzzle, and it was Kelly who solved it. The studio suggested such conveniently local talent as Cyd Charisse or Vera-Ellen, but Freed and company insisted on finding *une vraie française.* The front runner was a rising ingenue named Odile Versois; then Kelly remembered a teenaged ballerina he'd seen perform in the Paris Ballet des Champs-Elysées two years before —a certain Leslie Caron. While Caron had no prior acting experience, like Versois she was simultaneously being considered for the female lead in Marcel Carné's newest film, *Juliette ou la Clé des Songes;* moreover, she was rumored to speak passable English. In 1950, Kelly was dispatched to Paris to direct tests of both. When the *American in Paris* team viewed the results back in Culver City, the decision was unanimous, and MGM offered Caron a long-term contract. Soon thereafter a not-yet-eighteen-year-old Leslie Caron landed in America, to make her screen debut speaking English as Gene Kelly's partner in the year's most anticipated song-and-dance spectacular. It was a daunting prospect, but the result was something that happens often in celluloid folklore and rarely in Hollywood reality— Caron became a genuine overnight sensation.

Assembling the right production team was an easier task. While the studio system was increasingly threatened by a host of new economic circumstances— shrinking postwar audiences and the rise of television, the divestiture of studio-owned theater chains and the increasing power of the film industry's craft unions— the impact had yet to reach the army of specialized technicians that MGM had been accumulating since the twenties. Supervising art director, Cedric Gibbons, assigned Preston Ames of his team to design the sets. As recounted in Donald Knox's *The Magic Factory,* an invaluable oral history on the making of this film, Ames felt that the years he'd spent as an architecture student in Paris helped in his selection for this project. In any event, it was a fortuitous choice. Metro's production designers often found working with Minnelli a frustrating experience, for he was known to be at once exigent and inarticulate. This was Ames' first experience on a Minnelli musical, and the two proved instantly congenial. In subsequent years, he contributed his talents to every musical Minnelli was to make at MGM.

The studio chose Adrienne Fazan as *An American in Paris'* film editor, and she too was someone whose sensibility was in tune with Minnelli's; eight years later, she would salvage *Gigi* after supervising editor Margaret Booth slashed at it before its premiere. Minnelli was less satisfied with Alfred Gilks, the cinematographer who was set to photograph the film. According to Minnelli, his quest for visual nuance clashed with Gilks' instinct for expediency—whatever the emotional texture of the scene, Gilks' solution was to flood the set with light. This marked Minnelli's first serious rift with the cinematographer of one of his pictures. He insisted that Gilks be taken off once the book was completed and the ballet was ready to shoot, replacing him with John Alton, with whom he'd just made *Father of the Bride*. This was a daring move, for with Technicolor experts such as Harry Stradling, Charles Rosher, and George Folsey at his disposal, Minnelli opted instead for a cameraman known as a specialist in film noir. While Alton's lack of experience with color struck many as a liability, Minnelli realized that his evocative style wouldn't be tempered by preconceptions as to what the Technicolor cameras could or couldn't achieve.

Responsibility for assembling the score was assumed by John Green, then head of MGM's music department and an alumnus of Gershwin's stage musicals of the thirties. His executive duties forced Green to entrust much of the work to staff orchestrator Saul Chaplin; together, they spent weeks in concert with Freed, Minnelli, Kelly, and Ira Gershwin poring through the Gershwin canon for the songs that would best mesh with Kelly's choreographic ideas and Lerner's script. Among the final selections were songs that carried a special resonance for the *American in Paris* team. "Our Love Is Here to Stay," the occasion for Kelly and Caron's romantic pas de deux in the film, was George Gershwin's last song, left partially incomplete at his death in 1937, and the mock-Viennese "By Strauss" had been written for Minnelli's last Broadway revue.

As usually happened at this stage, more songs were envisioned than the release version of *An American in Paris* could accommodate. Some projected musical sequences were apparently never shot—an Oscar Levant piano rendition of "Liza" and a second dance duet for Kelly and Caron to "Somebody Loves Me." Others were recorded and photographed but cut from the movie after the first sneak preview, specifically Kelly's version of "I've Got a Crush on You," reportedly one of his favorite moments in the film, and a pair of songs for Guetary—"Love Walked In" and "But Not for Me." Leslie Caron was spared this by default. Superlative dancer though she was, Caron had no gift for song whatsoever; rather than introduce her to the screen with a borrowed voice, it was decided she should remain mute during the film's musical interludes. These scenes were handled so deftly that when *An American in Paris* was released, no one seemed to notice what an anomaly it was, for it is the only important musical of the era with an all-male vocal score.

As preproduction work accelerated in the spring and early summer of 1950, one crucial issue was still unresolved—whether *An American in Paris* would be shot entirely at Culver City, or become the first MGM picture filmed in *la Ville Lumière*. For authenticity's sake, the director and star campaigned hard for the latter;

Kelly cited the success of the previous year's *On the Town*, due in no small part to the freshness of its New York locations. The notion of shooting such a complex and expensive film off the lot would have been inconceivable even shortly before this, but runaway production was becoming an increasingly attractive prospect, for reasons of showmanship and economics alike. Two of the studio's most imposing releases for 1950-51, *King Solomon's Mines* and *Quo Vadis*, were both filmed abroad; the latter was MGM's costliest film to date and the first to be shot in Rome since the silent *Ben Hur* was begun there a quarter century earlier. Producing a musical so far from home posed a variety of logistical problems—as Preston Ames pointedly asked Kelly, "Have you ever danced on cobblestones?" Still, the idea persisted until the last possible minute. On July 20, less than two weeks before shooting was to begin, Culver City informed MGM's New York headquarters that the *American in Paris* company would depart at the end of August for several weeks of Paris location work. Finally, with Freed's assent, the studio opted to reduce its foreseeable risks—Paris would be recreated in California in the usual Metro manner. Under Ames' supervision, MGM's craftsmen constructed facsimiles of the Left Bank *quartier* where Kelly lives; a Montmartre street below Sacré-Coeur; the Café Bel Ami near the Seine (a set which turned up again in Minnelli's *Four Horsemen of the Apocalypse*), and the quai behind Notre Dame—*without* cobblestones. Peter Ballbusch, a second-unit director specializing in location work, was dispatched to Paris to shoot exterior footage for insertion in the film where needed; this was used mostly for the opening montage, and the establishing shot of Milo's Paris pied-à-terre, the Hotel Ritz.

Paradoxically, the decision to confine *An American in Paris* to the studio only liberated its creative team, at least as far as the climactic ballet was concerned. At this stage, Minnelli and Kelly's conception for the sequence was still exceedingly vague. Had they been bound to the notion of dancing through a succession of Parisian parks and boulevards, the result might well have been déjà vu with a twist—a kind of *On the Town* in berets. Instead, the need to conjure up a dream Paris with lights and canvas prompted a far bolder leap of the imagination. Like the paintings it evokes, Minnelli's sound-stage Place de la Concorde has a distilled magic which no attempt at pictorial realism could rival. Many later Hollywood movies gave audiences the treat of savoring the real Paris—particularly Minnelli's own, resplendent *Gigi*. Yet nothing would ever surpass the *American in Paris* ballet for bright-hued, delirious abstraction. Both music and choreography are a joyful projection of the city's essence as only an outsider's senses could perceive it. By combining exuberant American brushstrokes with a Gallic palette, the ballet's style and substance fuse into a remarkable cross-cultural whole.

Gene Kelly, An American in Paris *(1951)*

Once shooting finally began, on August 1 1950, *An American in Paris* sped along with amazing efficiency; Minnelli finished shooting the book and most of the musical numbers in exactly six weeks. Production then closed down as Minnelli and Kelly sweated out their ideas for the ballet. While the sets were being constructed and Kelly worked on the choreography, Minnelli absented himself to fulfill an obligation to the studio to direct *Father's Little Dividend,* a sequel to his previous hit, *Father of the Bride.* Constantly interrupted to consult with his *American in Paris* team, he nevertheless completed the film with breathtaking speed to return to the bigger challenge ahead. Minnelli started *Father's Little Dividend* on October 6 and finished it on the first of November. In fact, filming the two-reel ballet took longer than this feature-length comedy. Shooting resumed on *An American in Paris* December 6, and with a short Christmas break it closed production on January 8 1951.

As *The Magic Factory* documents, the making of this film summoned forth that cooperative energy which was the studio system's greatest virtue. To fulfill Minnelli's visions, Preston Ames' designs were executed and embellished by George Gibson and his team of painters; on the set, Metro's master set decorator, Keogh Gleason, fleshed them out with the attention to vivid detail Minnelli always demanded. If Ames' inspiration occasionally flagged, another member of the art-direction team was quickly drafted; it was Minnelli regular Jack Martin Smith who came up with the black-and-white scheme the director wanted for the

Beaux Arts Ball that precedes the ballet. Meanwhile, *An American in Paris'* distinctive sound was determined by a harmonious triumvirate. Conrad Salinger was responsible for orchestrating the score assembled by Green and Chaplin, a task to which they also contributed when the occasion warranted. As each of them attested, it was almost impossible to detect where their work ended and Salinger's began.

On *An American in Paris,* Gene Kelly served as sole choreographer as well as the film's principal player; he was, moreover, a burgeoning director in his own right. As such, Kelly took an active role in shaping the film from its inception, and his ideas were eagerly sought and usually incorporated by Minnelli. Both the dance medley to "Embraceable You," which introduces Leslie Caron, and the staging of Guetary's "I'll Build a Stairway to Paradise" exemplify their close collaboration. To showcase the contradictory facets of Lise's character in a series of contrasting dance vignettes was Kelly's idea, reprising Vera-Ellen's "Miss Turnstiles" montage from *On the Town.* What made it distinctive was Minnelli's visual concept—keying each sequence to a different monochromatic color scheme and architectural style. Yet the sequence was actually shot by Kelly, while the director was busy elsewhere. Guetary's big moment also underscored their complementary sense of musical-comedy staging. Kelly had the notion of illuminating the music-hall staircase with each tread of Guetary's springy step. Minnelli's colliding vertical designs gave the number its propulsive energy, combined with deliberate haute-vaudeville kitsch—his camera tilted vertiginously as descending showgirls engulf an ascending Guetary, the whole framed by a brace of human candelabra composed of chorines arrayed in faux-Grecian drapery.

The ballet itself proved the mettle of their partnership. Minnelli and Kelly wrote the seven-page continuity for the ballet and submitted it to the studio for approval on September 6 1951. If Kelly's choreographic concepts provided the essence, it was Minnelli who had to turn this *coup de théâtre* into a cinematic whirlwind through his mastery of color, framing, and movement. To spark his imagination, Minnelli once more sought out the superlative Irene Sharaff, who had created the costumes for *Meet Me in St. Louis, Yolanda and the Thief,* and *Ziegfeld Follies,* as well as the overall design for the ''Limehouse Blues'' sequence in the latter. Officially, Sharaff's task here was to design the five hundred-odd costumes for the ballet, but her real contribution was far more significant. Working with Minnelli, it was she who determined the overall visual scheme for the ballet—her own Impressionist-saturated sketches were the blueprint for Ames' fleshed-out designs.

At this point, Gibson's scenic art department was left with the trickiest problem—how to render the values of these Dufy/Renoir/Utrillo/Rousseau/Van Gogh/Toulouse-Lautrec sketches in backdrops at a hundred times the scale. Nothing quite like this had ever been tackled by MGM's artisans; they simply had to learn by doing, and in the matter of a few short weeks. Meanwhile, Henry Greutert, a sculptor in the plaster department, was given the job of concocting a Dufyesque Place de la Concorde fountain for Caron and Kelly to dance through. The translucent plastic object he dreamed up dismayed Cedric Gibbons, who missed the artist's tints and brushstrokes; but an enchanted Minnelli overruled these objections—with the lighting scheme he and Alton devised, the sculpture would out-Dufy the master.

Minnelli was just a powerless bystander during the most crucial behind-the-scenes wrangle. According to the corporate executives of Loews Inc., the budget allocated to the ballet was an extortionate sum to film what was essentially a glorified production number. As always, Freed had the staunch support of L. B. Mayer, but by 1950, that was a devalued commodity. After a quarter century heading studio operations, Mayer's credibility with the money men had waned, and the following year he was forced out of the studio for good. In the meantime, he was being overtaken by Dore Schary, then the studio's new vice president in charge of production, and the first person to hold that title since Irving Thalberg in the thirties; soon Mayer's post too would be his. Although Schary's taste ran more to black-and-white civics lessons, Freed prudently campaigned for his help as well. A flattered Schary backed him up, but the ballet was threatened once more when

the New York office screened the completed film for the first time; Nicholas Schenck suggested hacking away at the sequence to hurtle the movie faster toward Kelly and Caron's final embrace. Schary's demurral and the vast sum already lavished on the ballet convinced them, grudgingly, to leave it alone.

A technical glitch sabotaged *An American in Paris'* first sneak preview—the theater's amplification system expired, and Kelly and company sounded as if performing from the bottom of a deep well. The second preview proved triumphant, but with the film's final cut completed in May 1951, several changes had been made. Much of Kelly's ''I Got Rhythm'' was reshot with a new cinematographer (Hal Rosson), and Minnelli's black-and-white bacchanale was pared down drastically so as not to crowd the ballet. When *An American in Paris* was released in the fall, the critical consensus proved benign but muted. Kelly, Caron, and the ballet garnered lavish praise, while its dramatic continuity prompted mild scorn at best. Although the film enjoyed an overwhelming popular response (total returns of over $8 million against production costs of $2,723,903), it was generally viewed as just another big MGM musical, with a classier score than most plus a socko conclusion.

Nevertheless, when the Academy Award nominations were announced, *An American in Paris* was cited eight times. In addition to the expected sheaf of technical nods, Lerner's original screenplay was honored, as was Minnelli's work, the first time the Academy had nominated the director of a musical since *Yankee Doodle Dandy's* Michael Curtiz in 1942. More startling was *An American in Paris'* Best Picture nomination, something no Freed production had ever received. Few in the trade seriously expected the film to win. While favored perhaps over the studio's own gargantuan *Quo Vadis* and the intelligent but unimposing war melodrama *Decision Before Dawn,* its chances were overshadowed by the race between 1951's two most prestigious dramatic hits, *A Place in the Sun* and *A Streetcar Named Desire.* Between them, this pair had divided most of the critics' year-end prizes, and it was felt each represented a bold new Hollywood, bent on tackling new themes beyond the grasp of the timid if seductive home screen. Hence, it was anticipated that Oscar night would turn into an orgy of back-patting in tribute to the industry's own newfound foresight and daring.

However, there was a sudden switch in the scenario on the night of March 20 1952. As already announced, special recognition was accorded Arthur Freed and Gene Kelly; Freed received the Irving Thalberg Award for the body of his work as a producer, and Kelly a special statuette for his contribution to dance on film. While a rebuff to the critics, Lerner's Oscar for best original screenplay wasn't so startling, as the most admired films of the year were all adaptations of plays and novels. Yet when *An American in Paris* was announced as the year's Best Picture, radio audiences heard a collective gasp run through Hollywood's Pantages Theater. Only twice before had a musical snared this prize—1929's *The Broadway Melody* (with lyrics by Arthur Freed) for its novelty, and 1936's *The Great Ziegfeld* for its luxe and weight.

Clearly, *An American in Paris* was rewarded for striving so hard to expand the boundaries of the movie musical. Its triumph with Academy voters testified also to their nostalgia for the conservatism it represented, as the summation of a form of entertainment slowly perfected since the advent of talkies. At a time of increasing pessimism and retrenchment in the movie business, the irrepressible confidence and frivolity of this movie—its sheer Hollywoodness—seemed an increasingly endangered and treasurable legacy. If *An American in Paris* exemplified moviemaking at its most traditional, it stood to reason the director in question was just an industrious worker ant on the job, duly fulfilling a collective vision. It's not surprising, therefore, that after six other Oscars were bestowed on *An American in Paris,* Minnelli was passed over. (George Stevens' award served as *A Place in the Sun*'s consolation prize, while *Streetcar* swept three of the four acting Oscars.) Significantly, the other directors nominated for the 1951 prize—John Huston, William Wyler, Elia Kazan, and Stevens—were either producer/directors or represented that year by independently packaged films.

Minnelli was proud nonetheless of his long-term association with MGM at a time when many prestigious filmmakers were fleeing these ties, and demonstrated it by signing a new five-year contract starting at $3,000 a week during the making of *An American in Paris.* He knew that his status at the studio afforded him all the artistic latitude and variety of projects he could ask for in Hollywood's uncertain climate. Still, the notion that he was a well-compensated Metro-Goldwyn minion rankled, especially where *An American in Paris* was concerned. Throughout his life, Minnelli was reticent rather than unduly modest when it came to proclaiming his own gifts. In this instance, however, he was uncharacteristically blunt. "Some erudite types point to *An American in Paris* as the perfect example of the studio-as-auteur theory. I disagree," he declared in his autobiography. "Though I don't minimize anyone's contributions, one man was responsible for bringing it all together. That man was me."

If *An American in Paris* was conceived to meet Arthur Freed's cultural aspirations and then tailored to suit Gene Kelly's screen persona, it was Minnelli who unified the whole with his special thematic preoccupations and formal grace. Despite Kelly's contribution to it, the ballet is a pure product of Minnelli's vivid imagination. As a director in his own right, Kelly's later experiments in this form, from the "Broadway Melody" sequence in *Singin' in the Rain* to *Invitation to the Dance,* simply can't compare in richness or momentum. The fact that the rest of the film hasn't worn as well as many other Minnelli musicals is due in large part to the director's own lapses, including the tendency to indulge Kelly's more exasperating movie mannerisms.

For most of its length, *An American in Paris* shows Minnelli's skill at disguising its retrogressive thrust as the epitome of the modern movie musical. Despite Alan Jay Lerner's allusions to the GI Bill and the legacy of the Occupation, the script fits uneasily into a contemporary 1950s context. The film's theme of the expatriate rush to France to find personal freedom and artistic inspiration conjures up the previous postwar generation of the 1920s, and the use of Gershwin songs from that decade reinforces the connection. Lerner's characters are kin to the slumberous ghosts who populated his own *Brigadoon*—on the picture-postcard street where they live, nobody seems to have told them that the post-Atomic era has arrived with a bang. Hero Jerry Mulligan's portfolio of ersatz Utrillos and Renoirs (executed for the film by painter Gene Grant) wouldn't have been the last word in modernity in 1920, let alone during the age of Existentialism, and Henri Baurel's dismissal of a song like "Fascinating Rhythm" (composed in 1924) as earsplitting noise marks him as more fossil than romantic.

These anachronistic tastes are matched by *American in Paris'* backlot-Left Bank settings; spruced up though they are with the last word in Perrier and Marie-Claire ads, they're in direct line of descent from that Paramount version of Paris that adorned movie screens throughout the Depression. (The hoped-for casting of Chevalier would have made this *hommage* complete.) This made sense, for while Minnelli loved the idea of Paris, in 1950 he scarcely knew the city first-hand, having alighted there but once briefly on the eve of World War II. Hollywood's Paree, however, was a more vivid memory—Rouben Mamoulian's 1932 *Love Me Tonight* was the film which first persuaded Minnelli that the movie musical could rival the stage in style and innovation. Hence Minnelli may be pardoned for filling the screen with types who are more Frenchified than French—tubby, grinning concierges and goateed *professeurs* sporting floppy foulards. At best, Gene Kelly's newfound *copains* resemble refugees from an ersatz Pagnol movie.

Not that Kelly's all-American archetype seems any less synthetic. *An American in Paris* is probably the most complete expression of the star image Kelly strained so hard to project—the lovable, regular guy who just happens to be a genius. Oddly enough, the latter proposition is the easiest to stomach here; if Jerry Mulligan's painterly prowess underwhelms, the variety and virtuosity of Kelly's dancing fulfills the metaphor of star-as-artist. However, too much of *An American in Paris* is bent on proving that the movie's hero is the most disarming American export since the Marshall Plan.

Everybody in the world of this movie, save hapless

heiress Foch, is the lucky recipient of Kelly's Yankee goodwill. He flirts with old ladies to whom gallantry is but a distant memory—waltzing with a white-haired florist transported by the fragrance of a dreadnought tourist. When this palls, Kelly assumes the role of scout leader to the worshipful kids of the quarter, a strutting chewing gum dispenser who gives lessons in American slang and the body language of Hopalong Cassidy. As in most Kelly pictures, he's happiest when carousing with his chums, even if his joy is prompted by the new love in his life. Kelly and pals do a powerful lot of musical male bonding in this picture. Fully three numbers are devoted to Kelly's strenuous notions of *fraternité*—a Teutonic trio harmonizing on "By Strauss"; Kelly bounding through his garret while Levant pounds out "Tra-La-La"; Guetary and Kelly's stentorian "S'Wonderful," as they stroll arm in arm out of the Café Huguette into the Parisian sun, with big grins to match.

To paraphrase Celeste Holm in *All About Eve,* it's a little, as the French say, *de trop.* Kelly's confreres are hard-pressed to emulate his insistent boyishness—particularly Levant, appropriately self-billed here as "the world's oldest prodigy." Kelly's elfin mode doesn't become Minnelli either. "By Strauss" in particular exults in a brand of cuteness rarely found elsewhere in the director's musicals; only the most unregenerate of fans could delight at Kelly mincing about in a checked-tablecloth shawl and then bumping tummies with an obese character danseuse. Minnelli is Kelly's passive accomplice here. The best he can do under the circumstances is stay out of Kelly's way as much as possible, and indeed for most of the number, the camera is placed at a discreet, neutral distance from all this false bonhomie.

Minnelli asserts himself more successfully when exploring the rueful undertones in Alan Jay Lerner's script. Thwarted love is the plot device which propels virtually every movie musical, but here this theme carries real pain and guilt in a manner that is particularly characteristic of Minnelli. Notwithstanding the strictures of the industry's Production Code, it's implied that Jerry and Lise are both kept creatures, whose future in practical terms depends on the continued good humor of their respective patrons. Each is too ashamed to confess why their meetings must be so brief and furtive, although the reason is obvious—his afternoons belong to Milo and her evenings to Henri. At the same time, the latter pair are not just the impervious, disposable second leads of musical comedy lore. In their way, they feel as deeply as the young lovers and, unlike other musicals, this one has no consolation prizes waiting for them in the wings at the final fadeout.

Cheerily obtuse though he may be, Henri is the kindest person in Lerner's script, infinitely forebearing where Lise is concerned. Milo's motives may be baser, but the keynote to her character is suffering, much of it self-

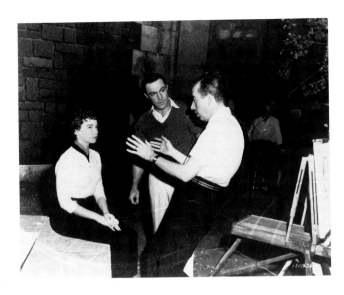

inflicted. Her desperation for intimacy inevitably scares off the object of her desire; when she's thwarted, Milo's last weapons are aggression and ill-temper, which alienate her quarry all the more. Jerry and Lise know their romance inflicts hurt on others, but they can't help themselves; beneath its sprightly surface, *An American in Paris* is largely about the ruthlessness of love. While Lise is merely thoughtless, skipping Henri's triumphant music-hall turn to dance on the quai with her American suitor, Jerry is outright callous to Milo. He flirts with Lise on his first night out with his patroness, and later makes love to the susceptible Milo when he thinks Lise has left his life for good.

Minnelli gives this conflict all the dignity it deserves, so much so that Milo and Henri's plight threatened to dominate the film in its rough cut. Originally, the Beaux Arts Ball contained Henri's melancholy rendition of "But Not for Me," and a monologue for Milo recounting her history of failure with the opposite sex. Both had to go, lest Jerry's romance seem the culmination of his selfishness rather than the happy ending he and Lise deserve. As it is, Minnelli and Nina Foch make Milo the most complex, if not necessarily the most ingratiating, character in the film. Befitting her worldly demeanor, she is the only person endowed with a semblance of wit; on meeting Jerry, she breezily serves up the provenance of her name "as in Venus de" and the source of her wealth ("My family is in oil . . . sun-tan oil"). Milo's creamy smile and silken diction work overtime to camouflage the terrified glint of her gaze, but she fools no one. Returning home in her limo from the *cave* where Jerry has first spied Lise at an adjoining table, she pours out her wounded pride in a torrent of invective which jolts the viewer as much as the hero. The naked, dangerous anger of this brief scene shatters the decorum of the Arthur Freed ethos, edging the film closer to the neurotic world of Minnelli's melodramas.

Lise's moodiness may be less forbidding than Milo's

*Gene Kelly and Leslie
Caron in the Renoir flower
market, the ballet from* An
American in Paris *(1951)*

OPPOSITE:
*1950, Minnelli directing
Leslie Caron and Gene Kelly
in* An American in Paris
(1951)

guile and volatility, but she's not exactly a figure of comic relief either. Between Caron's lack of experience before the cameras and her toothy, roundcheeked good looks, her casting was a stroke nearly as unconventional as the *An American in Paris* ballet itself. Years later, Caron would complain that Minnelli scarcely directed her at all, constantly repeating the platitude, "Just be yourself, darling." In fact, Minnelli knew exactly what he was doing. For the offscreen Caron was a rather solemn girl, and the insecurities of this novice actress perfectly conveyed the youthful confusion that defines this character. Minnelli's empathy for the character Lise gives the movie its moments of real tenderness. We're told that both parents were killed during the war while she hid under Henri's protection, yet her present situation hasn't brought Lise much joy either. She spends the first part of the picture trying to quell Jerry's advances, and the rest of it in a state of remorse for having succumbed. The carefree, radiant creature who pirouettes and cancans at will is a fantasy projection by the men who love her—both Henri's schizoid portrait in dance at the beginning of *An American in Paris* and Jerry's concluding ballet of the girl who (almost) got away. The reedy quaver of Caron's voice betrays the "real" Lise's introverted self-doubt. Her tentative smiles are always clouded by intimations of loss, and an inability to level with either of the men in her life. As with Milo, despair catches up with Lise in the backseat of a car shuttling between the Right and Left Banks. Frightened to tell Jerry why their rendezvous are so difficult, she pleads, "Can't we have our own special world and not talk about anything that

happens when we're apart?" The lines may be arch, but the artless way the words tumble out is heartbreaking. MGM's campaign to launch Caron packaged her as irrepressibly pert, but in fact this debut performance owes more to Lillian Gish than to Fifi D'Orsay.

While these travails dominate the movie, Minnelli never loses sight of the romance that really intrigues him—Jerry Mulligan's relationship to his canvas. *An American in Paris* is a rare movie musical about a man with a vocation other than headlining at the Palace, and it's the first time Minnelli touches upon a premise central to such subsequent films as *The Bad and the Beautiful, Some Came Running,* and *Lust for Life*—the urge to find order and meaning in work as compensation for the unpredictable messes of one's personal life. It's not surprising that Minnelli found the hero of this film such an appealing figure. He'd harbored hopes of becoming a painter in his youth, and throughout his lifetime he turned out Impressionist-inspired canvases of considerable skill. Jerry's feckless flight to Europe for inspiration was clearly an unrealized dream for a resolute Francophile like Minnelli, but he's also too much the realist to portray this quest as unalloyed rapture. Like the later artist-heroes in Minnelli movies, Mulligan is a perfectionist thwarted by his awareness of the limits to his talent. When Milo offers Jerry the prospect of a one-man gallery show, his first reaction is panic, until she hushes him with the reminder, "You've got to face the critics sometime."

What follows is one of the most buoyant passages in the movie—not a song-and-dance anthem to the pleasures of love, but an effervescent montage of Jerry at

The ballet. Leslie Caron can-cans with Gene Kelly as Chocolat in the Toulouse-Lautrec café, An American in Paris *(1951)*

the easel, abandoning himself to his work. You can always tell when a passage particularly stirs Minnelli, as the camera itself describes arcs of excitement, bearing down close to peer at a detail, then retreating backward for a better look at the whole. As Jerry labors to interpret a host of subjects—the cityscape of the Place de l'Opéra; a little girl grasping at a toy; Lise, coquettish, holding a red flower like the one which will spark the beginning of the ballet—Minnelli focuses less on the artist than on the process of making art. His eye shifts restlessly between the swirl of colors on the palette, the object being painted, and the unfinished work on the easel, marveling at the way materials and subject are fused into a new separate creation. The sequence ends in an artist's dream of triumph—an overhead shot of Jerry in his atelier, standing in the middle of a concentric circle of his finished paintings.

The unexpected seriousness of the movie—like the disturbing undercurrents in *Meet Me in St. Louis*—helps explain why *An American in Paris* was such a break from the movie-musical routine in 1951. Even the one Kelly–Caron dance duet that isn't set in a dreamscape is more elegiac than exhilarating. ''Our Love Is Here to Stay'' is the most Fred-and-Gingerish moment in the film, although in Kelly's dance vocabulary ballet upstages the ballroom. As with the Astaire movies of the thirties, the immediate chemistry they feel during this first dance together cinches the stars' romance, but the mood here resembles one of those penultimate-reel Astaire–Rogers adagios of parting. Lise and Jerry meet at night on the quai, bodies stirring to a string orchestration so muted at first it can scarcely be heard. The two

circle each other in a crescendo of movement and music leading to the longed-for embrace, but the finale is subdued—a wistful stroll hand-in-hand away from the camera as the music drops to a hush. This conclusion adds a post-coital sadness to the chaste eroticism of Kelly's choreography. The lovers are speechless and spent, under the same sound-stage moonlight where Esther Smith and John Truitt pledged their betrothal, with the same oddly melancholy result. In Minnelli musicals, the dark is both liberating and spooky, inviting confidences that wouldn't be risked in the glare of daylight, and giving premonitions of trouble to come.

An American in Paris also shares with *Meet Me in St. Louis* its intimate scale. Minnelli's collaboration with Lerner prompted a return to the premise of the so-called integrated musical patented by Rodgers and Hammerstein in the forties. Unlike *Yolanda* or *The Pirate*, this movie is set in a recognizable facsimile of a real place on the map, in which the songs spring instinctively from relatively ordinary folks who live there. Even the unrestrained fancies of the dream ballet adhere to the rules of the genre—according to this mock-realistic school of progressive musical comedy, the spectacular happens only in the realm of the subconscious. Thus Leslie Caron bounds from *tours jetées* to the Charleston in Henri Baurel's pipe dream projected on a café mirror, and Oscar Levant as idle pianist Adam Cook muses on a triumphant performance of the ''Concerto in F'' played, conducted, and bravoed by a hundred of himselves in a theater filled with a shadowy mist of Minnelli yellow.

No miracles are allowed to occur in the backlot reality of *An American in Paris'* here and now. Minnelli draws the audience in by building the film like one long iris shot—focusing on a small detail, and once that's taken in, gradually expanding his vision until the screen is saturated with the color and movement of this ersatz Paris. Kelly's Jerry Mulligan is first seen through the window of his claustrophobic garret, and within this confined space, Minnelli paints him with ambiguous strokes. On the one hand, Jerry seems a cheerful, resourceful guy who turns this tiny room into a Rube Goldberg wonderland of objects that disappear and materialize at will. However, there's a note of self-doubt; Jerry's first order of business on this new day is to wipe out the self-portrait adorning his easel. On the street below, we meet Henri Baurel, whose burbling confidence is also shakier than it seems—he pauses before a mirror to reassure himself that he's still the dapper music-hall idol despite the encroaching years.

In a musical, the hardest challenge comes first—convincing the audience that the most prosaic of circumstances will compel these people to sing and dance. Minnelli cannily seduces the audience by small, tentative strokes. First comes a brief musical false start—Adam tinkling at his piano upstairs prompts a few bars of "Nice Work If You Can Get It" from Henri, as his calling card from the street. Henri's reunion with his old pal Adam and the news of his engagement leads to the Five Guises of Lise, danced and scored to "Embraceable You." Besides heralding the virtuosity of Leslie Caron and the MGM music department's team of orchestrators, the number serves a multitude of structural purposes. Since it's only happening inside Henri's head, "Embraceable You" doesn't challenge the viewer's sense of what's believable.

But, by the time it's over, we're prepared to leap the breach between speech and music with these characters. Only then does Minnelli let loose Kelly, Levant, and Guetary to camp it up with the café's denizens on "By Strauss." Having earned our complicity, Minnelli bolsters it by holding fast to the rules he himself has set. Henri Baurel is a performer by vocation, so he can sing anywhere—with his pals at the Café Huguette or from the music-hall stage that is his natural domain. Jerry is an amateur who dances because he feels like it; his stage is the street or his attic room, his public whoever happens to be around when the urge to move can't be repressed any longer. Minnelli underscores the difference in the way he frames these two performers. As the onstage orchestra strikes up "I'll Build a Stairway to Paradise," he takes in the spectacle from afar, with Baurel a lone figure within two receding proscenium arches—the real one of the stage and the illusion of one made by the borders of the camera lens. Even this, the film's one conventional production number, conforms to Minnelli's yardstick of movie-musical naturalism. Although the sequence is built through cutting and camera movement, this is a rare Hollywood version of a vaudeville turn that could plausibly fit on an actual stage.

Since Jerry dances only for his own enjoyment, Minnelli is always right on his heels lest we miss any of the private fun. Until the imaginary ballet, Jerry's stages are more constricted than Henri's—a sidewalk, his room in the pension—which only spurs the resourcefulness of dancer and director alike. During Kelly's tap-dancing English lesson to "I Got Rhythm," Minnelli's camera scampers along beside him, like one of the enraptured kids following Kelly down the block. While prompted by love-at-first-sight to warble "Tra-La-La," Kelly doesn't have the space to do any serious strutting—between his room and Adam's adjoining flat you can barely swing an easel. So he dances toward us within the director's deep-focus frame, from one cramped room into another. Throughout the movie's blend of song and plot, Minnelli sustains this minimalist note so rigorously that his rare deviations earn a special punch by dint of the surprise. A modest number like "S'Wonderful," with Kelly tripping merrily along the sidewalk to Guetary's whistled accompaniment, is just the buildup to Minnelli's staggering fadeout—a huge retreating boom shot of the entire Left Bank street set, with the two men belting out the final notes from opposite ends of the screen.

Minnelli controls his instinct for the spectacular until the Beaux Arts Ball, when the film's romantic entanglements have reached a final impasse. Party scenes are a climactic staple in a dozen Minnelli films of all genres, and the mood is usually more ominous than festive—the riotous merrymaking of the anonymous revelers underscores the loneliness of the misfit protagonist, who'd rather be anywhere else. That was obviously Minnelli's intent here, as his four disillusioned romantics contemplate their private miseries while offscreen minions hurl black and white confetti in their faces. Visually, this passage is a decolorized throwback to *Yolanda's* fiesta scene, with the bleached tree branches left over from *Ziegfeld Follies'* "This Heart of Mine" thrown in for good measure. As before, dress extras merge into a decadent sea of masks and motley; the Parisian novelty being that shrieking girls hurtle themselves off balconies into the arms of their feckless escorts on the dance floor below. (There's so much going on here that the Production Code obviously missed a few savory details—such as the sailor who scampers eagerly out of camera range with his ballerina-clad boyfriend in tow.)

In fact this is one Minnelli party that got out of hand. He'd already confected a vivid black-and-white ball once before as the dramatic centerpiece of 1949's *Madame Bovary,* and ironically that was the one endowed with all the rhythmic momentum you'd associate with Minnelli's best musicals. This passage is spatially inert, with everyone jumping up and down in place while the stunned camera tries to take it all in. With so much of the scene's continuity hacked out to speed things up, the best he and Adrienne Fazan could hope for was to give some sort of sequential order to the shots. The result is fatiguing—you're glad to join Kelly away from the pandemonium on his perch under the Paris cyclorama, nursing his broken Harlequin heart while the ballet sets are hammered together on an adjoining sound stage.

At Minnelli's request, Lerner contributed a last-minute revision to conclude the ball sequence with a new monologue for Kelly. To a tearful departing Lise, Mulligan declares, "Now, what have I got left? Maybe that's enough for some, but it isn't for me anymore, because the more beautiful everything is, the more it'll hurt without you." These are the last words spoken in the film, with nearly twenty minutes left to run. The speech is the cue for Minnelli's magical transition from the real to the imaginary, expanding gradually outward from the miniscule to the gargantuan, black and white dissolving slowly into a blaze of Technicolor. Since thwarted love has soured Mulligan's art and his affair with Paris, the dream ballet begins with his ripped-up charcoal sketch of the Place de l'Etoile. In a brooding tracking shot, the pieces are swept along the gutter in a whirlwind of confetti until they suddenly re-fuse and dissolve into a Kelly-sized backdrop of the same design. As the set is bathed in the red, white, and blue of the French flag, a black-garbed Kelly materializes in the foreground, grasping Caron's discarded red rose with piteous intensity (Kelly has claimed credit for this particular self-conscious image, and he is welcome to it). Gradually, the screen is invaded by clusters of voluptuous Furies who stalk him with feline swipes of their talons. The hues might be different, but Kelly's prelude to delirium conjures up Astaire's skirmish with the laundresses in the *Yolanda and the Thief* nightmare. Those peasant mesmerizers in beige lured Astaire to the edge of a vast and ominous landscape for a fateful meeting with a mystery female; this time, Parisian Circes in swirls of red and white tulle lead Kelly to the congested expanse of the Place de la Concorde. While Astaire was helpless prey to a phantom sweetheart, Kelly is the enthralled pursuer whose prize dissolves into smoke even in the throes of a danced embrace.

Minnelli had done a lot of thinking about the movie-ballet idiom since the days of *Yolanda*. The latter wandered uncertainly from one discreet movement to the next, a hybrid of song and dance within a monochromatic setting. Six years later he created an authentic screen symphony, whose tonal variety always serves the fluid momentum of its larger design. To defy the restive attention span of a ballet-shy mass public, the dance is shrewdly structured in eight fleet sections, of which only the flower-market pas de deux uses an exclusively traditional classical ballet vocabulary. There's no plot as such—a Yank chases after his French dream girl through the Paris of his favorite artists, her identity constantly shifting as dictated by the alternating moods of Gershwin's orchestral suite. (In this sense, the ballet is a mammoth variation on the "Embraceable You" medley which introduced Caron at the film's beginning.) Throughout, Minnelli's inexhaustible spectrum of colors exalts the infinite diversity of Kelly's dance styles, and the transitions from one texture to the next are perhaps the ballet's most breathtaking accomplishment. What unifies the whole is a sense of continuous, velvety movement, in which the invisible editing of Minnelli's roving camera work propels all these contrasting episodes toward a seamless fusion.

The opening segment in the Dufy-style Place de la Concorde is a vision of exhilarating chaos, with outsider Kelly in black the focal point amid a human sea of red and blue. Minnelli's genius for design attains the miraculous here. Each figure in his frame of vision—all these *pompiers* and *zouaves* cascading against a tide of disdainful Parisiennes—has its own idiosyncratic identity, while all merge into an abstract and constantly shifting canvas. Gorgeous as this is, Minnelli isn't satisfied with the merely picturesque. As the excitement builds, he raises the stakes with a sudden infusion of dangerous undertones. In an instant, Minnelli plunges the screen from the glare of noon into a searchlit midnight; the camera teeters with queasy speed toward the fountain and to escape artist Caron, beaming as she disappears.

A night fog dissolves into the mist of dawn, and the camera retreats to reveal Kelly alone at the flower market, a dappled, gauzy place of pastel blues and greens replicating Renoir's painting of the Pont Neuf. Minnelli keeps the background static; as Caron drifts into view *en pointe* to be partnered by a gallant Kelly, the vendors and their customers are frozen eerily in place, their faces painted an oily, opaque patina. The quietest, most intimate section of the ballet, it's also subliminally the creepiest. At the end, she dissolves in his arms into a whirling bouquet of flowers; the scene shifts to an Utrillo-like street in Montmartre—the set a masterwork of forced perspective in the wan sun of late afternoon. This sequence, the only one in which Caron doesn't appear, shows Kelly at his most characteristic. Joined by four GIs on French leave, he's back on the town, doing a carefree prance with the guys. Straw hats and blazers magically leap off a store window's dummies onto their bodies, a cue for what Kelly called "the Cohan strut"—with torsos bent forward in a jerky vaudevillian march, they doff their chapeaus and grin with brash American pride.

Suddenly we're in a Rousseau-inspired square *en fête*, replete with menagerie, Punch-and-Judy show, acrobats and gendarmes on holiday. In this faux-naif setting, the red-white-and-blue motif connotes Franco-American amity, an occasion for the boisterous tourists to teach the locals an innocent trick or two. Caron leads a blithe squadron of tiptoeing schoolgirls when the Cohan quintet enters the scene, preceded by their wrist-flicked boaters. Kelly shuffles to her side and, prompted by her flirtatious example, all Paris starts imitating *le tip-tap à l'Americain,* and Caron proves it's even more charming in toe shoes. She's not the only one captivated by these Yank high spirits—the sprinting diagonals Minnelli executes turn a production-number tableau into a three-dimensional celebration.

Minnelli then shifts from playful flirtation to erotic steam in the most breathtaking segue from any of his musicals, or anybody else's. With the screen plunged again into darkness, Kelly looms over Caron in silhouette, yellow mist pouring through their legs; in a seamless cut, we are back at the Place de la Concorde fountain at night, with a languid Caron in tattered blue chiffon cradled in Kelly's arms, swaying to the throb of a Gershwin trumpet solo. This sinuous mating dance around the pagan gods of the fountain is really a trio—Kelly, Caron, and Minnelli's camera as dogged voyeur. In his autobiography, Minnelli describes his way of shooting dance numbers thus: "Many short takes using several cameras from different angles tended to interrupt the flow of movement. . . . Sometimes I might use as many as twenty different stops on the camera to accommodate different details. But it was always done with one camera moving all over the place." Here he's like a sculptor: as the two dancers strike a succession of Rodinesque poses, he encircles their bodies to capture every curve of their embrace, retreating to survey the tableau he's created and then darting inward again to concentrate on his models' blissful faces. Since his medium is celluloid, not stone, the interplay of light

also shapes his creation, bathing the figures in alternating waves of red, blue, and shaded charcoal.

The sequence proves that Fred Astaire's preferred rule for dance—the camera as tactful observer from the middle distance—isn't an absolute after all. For the fanciest footwork comes from Minnelli, to the greater glory of his dancers. His camera becomes the ultimate choreographer, to draw a dizzying succession of concentric circles, enclosing and transforming Kelly's movements and the arc of the fountain with the sweep of his lens.

In a fade to black, the camera dollies backward to the merriment of a Van Goghesque Place de L'Opéra in autumnal ochres and oranges. This section serves as a parenthesis to a café out of Toulouse-Lautrec; a mass of prancing sophisticates surging across the foreground against the forced-perspective of the set. A sandwichman's poster of Toulouse-Lautrec's *Chocolat* dissolves into Kelly striking the same pose; his jazzy cakewalk is the centerpiece of Minnelli's playful riff on the vivacious flat surfaces of Toulouse-Lautrec's poster art. Minnelli doesn't just recreate this style—he uses the camera's powers of depth and movement to exploit the artist's virtuosity in two dimensions. The café habitués are a surreal mix of painted figures on a backdrop, wax effigies, plus real dress extras as picturesquely frozen as their inanimate neighbors at the next table. Minnelli slithers through this assortment of archetypes in their gaslight-yellow tableau, reveling in his own layers of artifice. As in the original posters, the café-concert patrons are fixed objects in a smoky interior, but Minnelli is able to go Toulouse-Lautrec one step further, for his

The ballet finale, An American in Paris *(1951)*

star performers really can burst into movement. The interplay between Kelly's sinewy Chocolat and a brace of blonde cancan girls led by Caron at her sauciest makes for the ballet's liveliest episode, paced by the tempo of Minnelli's own restless eye.

But Kelly has a rendezvous with disenchantment at the finale. Minnelli lures him and Caron backward into the Opéra set toward a line of twirling mirrors—always ominous props in a Minnelli movie. A closeup of pirouetting skirts in shades of Van Gogh ochre cuts to the same image in Minnelli/Dufy red—the return of the Furies. The subsequent long shot of the Place de la Concorde is the ballet's one Busby Berkeleyish image—apparently hundreds of dancers in red, white, and blue, leaping in place and swinging their arms heavenward. Minnelli turns the ballet's last few seconds into a mirror image of its beginning, retreating from the panoramic to the microcosmic. In a startling unseen cut, the colorful crowd dematerializes, with Kelly a melancholy black dot in a white landscape. This too disappears, leaving the disoriented dreamer once more haunted by his blown-up sketch of a deserted Paris. The camera zooms in for an enormous closeup of the dew-specked red rose in his hand, and as the last chords of the suite build to a crescendo, the rose dissolves into Kelly's lovelorn face.

After all this, the movie's fadeout is cannily too brief for anticlimax. As Jerry gazes down to the street in misery, he sees Lise giving Henri a grateful farewell kiss; absolved at last, the lovers race into an ecstatic clinch on their own stairway to paradise. (This last scene is a marvel of Metro fakery. All Minnelli had to work with was one meager backlot flight of thirty steps or so, but thanks to a glorious matte shot this Montmartre stairway seems endless—the intercut takes of Kelly clambering down, Caron scampering upward, their embrace at mid-landing and final descent are simply the same cramped outdoor set photographed four times with the actors duly running in place.) In the final shot, Minnelli creates his last bit of Culver City trompe l'oeil—a pan upward to the twinkling scrim of a sapphire Paris skyline.

As Minnelli had hoped, the concluding two reels ignite all the currents of exuberance, apprehension, and rapture which the film's first ninety minutes convey only fitfully. The greatness of the ballet lies not in its fealty to High Art, but in the headlong excitement Minnelli felt for his own hybrid medium. Paradoxically, with this state-of-the-art production number, Minnelli conjured up the primal eloquence silent films once had—moving images as pure sensuality and emotion, freed from the limitations imposed by words. On the set, Minnelli found speech an infuriating barrier between the pictures forming inside his head and the artisans ready to realize them, if only their lip-twitching boss could blurt out exactly what they were supposed to look like. After years of collaboration, he and the Freed Unit achieved a new level of telepathy this time, and for a magical seventeen minutes not one stammered syllable intrudes to break the spell.

. . . .

1953   # THE BAND WAGON

Eighteen months passed between the completion of *An American in Paris* and the commencement of Minnelli's next musical of note, the superlative *The Band Wagon*. Minnelli was anything but idle during this period, but spent most of 1951 rueing the lowly caste of directors in the MGM hierarchy. The occasion for this discontent was Arthur Freed's proposed song-and-dance *Huckleberry Finn*, destined to founder on the rocks of studio miscalculations and star intransigence, with Minnelli stranded on the sidelines.

Back in the late thirties, MGM had filmed a forgettable version of the Twain classic with Mickey Rooney. Freed had coveted the idea of a remake with music and color for nearly a decade, but the notion seemed ill-omened from the start. In July 1944, the producer assigned his *Meet Me in St. Louis* team of Sally Benson, Hugh Blane, and Ralph Martin to concoct a new script and original score; their efforts failed to excite Freed, and by 1946 the project was postponed indefinitely. The producer resuscitated the idea in 1950, drafting a new trio of writers even more prestigious than the first—studio veteran Donald Ogden Stewart for the scenario and (after Harold Arlen's demurral) the composer/lyricist team of *Finian's Rainbow*, Burton Lane and E. Y. Harburg, who were trusted Freed alumni. Despite their impeccable qualifications, in light of the times, Freed's choice was quixotic to say the least. Both Stewart and Harburg were well known for their left-liberal political sympathies, and Hollywood was then bracing itself for the House Un-American Activities Committee's second and more relentless round of hearings on alleged Red infiltration of the film industry. Stewart and Harburg completed their assignments by May 1950, but as the year wore on it was obvious that,

*"Dancing in the Dark." Cyd
Charisse and Fred Astaire in*
The Band Wagon *(1953)*

whatever its merits, their work would never be used. On January 18 1951, Rudi Monta of the MGM legal department distributed a memo confirming that Harburg had been relieved of his duties, ostensibly due to a "Broadway commitment." With this episode, the Hollywood careers of both writers came to an end.

That same day, two weeks after *An American in Paris* finished shooting, Minnelli was announced as the film's director. With Burton Lane the sole surviving member of Freed's writing team, the producer decided to reunite him with Alan Jay Lerner, who had contributed screenplay and lyrics to Lane's score on *Royal Wedding*. A more troublesome problem for Freed at this stage was the casting of the picture. An MGM musical on this scale needed star names, an axiom thwarted by Twain's inconvenient focus on Huck and Jim. Since the Hollywood of the fifties wasn't promoting the box office clout of child actors, much less blacks, Freed sidestepped the issue by expanding the roles of the pair's roguish traveling companions, the Duke and the Dauphin. He thus succeeded in luring Gene Kelly and Danny Kaye to loan their talents and name value to the project. In the case of Kaye, who was not under contract to the studio, the price for his prestige was a then-remarkable $200,000.

As things turned out, this seeming coup became *Huckleberry Finn*'s final undoing, but for several months the Freed team was too engrossed in preproduction work to notice. Freed and Minnelli rounded out the cast with MGM contract moppet Dean Stockwell as Huck and William Warfield, fresh from Freed's *Show Boat*, to play the runaway slave. Margaret O'Brien, now in her early teens, was to return to MGM after a few years' absence in the role of Polly Grangerford. In July 1951, Minnelli went to New York to confer with Lerner on script revisions; on his return, he and Irene Sharaff labored over the visual design of the film. Rehearsals officially started at the end of August, with Kelly conspicuously absent. To accommodate Kaye, who was scheduled to make *Hans Christian Andersen* elsewhere at the end of the year, the studio perversely insisted on starting *Huckleberry Finn* while Kelly was still busy as star, choreographer, and co-director on *Singin' in the Rain*. With assistant dance director Ernie Flatt on hand to supervise Kelly's routines, Minnelli put the company through its paces for three weeks while the sets were being constructed.

Suddenly on September 21, to Minnelli's bafflement, production shut down indefinitely. According to a wire from West Coast publicity chief Howard Strickling to the New York office, the snag was Kaye's looming commitment to Samuel Goldwyn: rather an obvious pretext, since everyone concerned had been aware of this timetable for months. The truth was that both stars wanted out. Accustomed to top-banana treatment, Kaye increasingly realized that no act of will would turn *Huckleberry Finn* into *The Dauphin Steps Out*. Kelly may have had similar qualms, but his main objection was a practical one—after his triple labors on *Singin' in the Rain*, he was simply too exhausted to throw himself into dancin' on the levee. The studio then proposed to pick up production in six months' time, but that too ran up against Kelly's plans. A soon-to-lapse legal loophole permitted Americans to work abroad tax-free for eighteen months, and Kelly set a year-end departure to take advantage of it. (The creative result of this European interlude was *The Devil Makes Three*, an obscure melodrama shot in Munich, and Kelly's dream project, the virtually unheeded *Invitation to the Dance*.)

For a long time, Freed and MGM refused to give up on the project. Two years later, in 1953, MGM announced that under the new and snappier title of *The Boys from Missouri*, the erstwhile *Huckleberry Finn* would be Kelly's next vehicle after *Brigadoon*. In January 1954, Alan Jay Lerner submitted his third and final draft of the script. But the momentum had dissipated beyond recall, and Freed at last admitted defeat; in 1955, MGM closed its books on the Freed *Huck*, at a loss of $966,855.62. Five years later, the studio assembled a lower-case adaptation of the Twain novel featuring Eddie Hodges and former boxer Archie Moore. A few yellowing portions of the Lerner/Lane score were exhumed from the files and staged for this version, despite its distinctly unmusical cast; by the time the movie was released, the songs had been excised and consigned to molder forever in the back shelves of the MGM music department.

This debacle riled *Huckleberry Finn*'s thwarted creators for years thereafter. Lerner and Lane later claimed this was among the best work they had ever penned for the movies. For Minnelli, it was a lost opportunity to re-explore that vein of vivid yet rueful Americana he'd last conjured up with *Meet Me in St. Louis*, abetted by much of the troupe who had collaborated so well on *An American in Paris*. Twain's antiheroic outcasts bucking the smugness of the midwestern heartland struck a profound chord in Minnelli, later to resound through several of the melodramas he made during the decade to come. He was convinced that this could have been a very special film, although in fact it's hard to imagine a happy alliance between the rambunctious fervor of Mark Twain and the Kaye/Kelly minstrelsy dictated by Arthur Freed. This Huck-that-never-was gave further disquieting proof of a director's lowly estate in a system built on stars. Had Minnelli proved intransigent he would doubtless have been replaced, but his actors were rewarded for their lapses—Kaye won his release and a nice chunk of money, and Kelly snared a European busman's holiday. A director got to call the shots only after the names above the title consented to grace the set. Until then, Minnelli was left with his dusty sheafs of drawings and cutouts, and daydreams of a movie that never would be, left to unreel inside his head.

Kathryn Grayson, Howard Keel, and Tony Duquette's human chandeliers in the finale from Lovely to Look At *(1952)*

While Minnelli had been busy rehearsing *Huckleberry Finn*, Mervyn LeRoy was filming *Lovely to Look At*, the second screen version of the Jerome Kern musical *Roberta*, under the aegis of Freed rival Jack Cummings. With the bulk of the picture completed, LeRoy was suddenly needed elsewhere, so the studio asked Minnelli to concoct the musical climax—a long and opulent Kern medley dress parade for the finale. Loathing idleness, and amused by the chance to upstage one of the studio's most laureled directors, he agreed. With nonchalant largesse, Minnelli agreed to forego screen credit for this job, but once on the set he insisted on his usual perquisites. Shooting a Minnelli production number was serious business, and he wasn't going to let the studio forget it. Cummings had figured on a couple of days to polish off the fashion show to his satisfaction. Minnelli calmly dismissed the art department's preliminary set sketches, gathered up a few trusted accomplices, mounted his camera boom, and stayed there for three weeks.

All of which proved what a shrewd studio diplomat he could be. The *Lovely to Look At* finale is a footnote in Minnelli's movie musical career, but its dazzle and energy showed MGM once more what an indispensable fixture he was. Up to this point in the film, *Lovely to Look At* is not merely inferior to its 1935 predecessor, but ominous evidence of MGM's stubborn refusal to acknowledge that the world was changing outside its Culver City Brigadoon. The score and script (perfunctorily refurbished for the occasion) were nearly twenty years old, and the cast assembled entirely from the studio's diminishing contract roster; again Cedric Gibbons and his crew struggled to dream up a new way to counterfeit the Right Bank on Washington Boulevard.

With *Lovely to Look At*, the standard musical-comedy model bows to the law of ever-diminishing returns. Populated by Hollywood's second generation of musical-comedy stars, the movie shows how decadent the line had become. Marge and Gower Champion have all the endowments of Astaire and Rogers except the essential magic; pouty Kathryn Grayson's shrill tremolo only added luster to the memory of RKO's original Irene Dunne. The chemistry wasn't enhanced by a regrettably desexed Howard Keel, or Ann Miller and Red Skelton trotting out their perfunctory high spirits and low comedy. (Skelton's big moment—an endless lampoon of an Irish concert singer doing an American folk tune—reaches a new low in mirthlessness, even for him.)

Still, the elements behind *An American in Paris* also had a dated air before Minnelli took hold of them. Jack Cummings was a far less demanding producer of musicals than Freed, and the curious choice of Mervyn LeRoy to direct ensured that *Lovely to Look At* would fulfill its torpid promise. Never the most lightfooted director since his arrival at Metro in the late thirties, LeRoy hadn't the slightest affinity for the movie musical, as his later *Rose Marie* and *Gypsy* proved. Without half trying, he made this movie ugly to look at, depressing to know, and heaven to miss.

Working with the same cast and one of LeRoy's leftover sets—the stone courtyard of the *hôtel particulier* that houses Grayson's dressmaking establishment—for ten minutes Minnelli transports this movie to another realm. After the drabness that preceded it, the kitschy flamboyance of Minnelli's coda is a jolt to the senses. Abetted by his sculptor-decorator pal Tony Duquette, who'd dressed up parts of *Ziegfeld Follies* and *Yolanda and the Thief*, Minnelli crams the screen with his most characteristic calligraphy. On this Minnellian Mars, sunburst spotlights and illuminated obelisks are natural light sources. Versailles and Vienna jostle Broadway and the Taj Mahal; Louis Seize courtiers and masked harlequins intersect with human candelabra and stag-antlered Pegasuses. As mannequins for the House of Roberta, stony-faced showgirls in drop-dead frocks stalk this landscape with the aplomb of Technicolor marquesas. Their deadpan allure gives the number a twitch of subversive wit. Fashion Victim Number One is Red Skelton as the hapless MC, given to utterances like "Enter, oh priestesses of beauty" before vestal chorines mummify him in streams of white chiffon.

The score, the stars, even Adrian's creations are all subsumed in Minnelli's obsessions with dizzying tints and celluloid geometry. From *The Women* to *Easter Parade*, fashion shows provided the chic dead spot at the center of a succession of MGM movies. His brainstorm was to replace the couture still-lifes with a whirlwind montage of Minnellian hues. A tableau of lavender shifts to aqua and then turquoise and white, interrupted by an Adrian parade in neutral shades to refresh

Jack Buchanan as Jeffrey Cordova, star, director, and adapter from the Greek of "Oedipus Rex," The Band Wagon *(1953)*

the palate. In the 1935 *Roberta,* the finale's highlight was the wistful Astaire–Rogers duet to "Smoke Gets in Your Eyes"; here, Minnelli showcases the Champions, but trusting less to their chemistry, he surrounds them with eye-popping splashes of color. Skelton orates, "It is the morn, bright youth of day when sunlight fills the world and hope is born," and, to Cedric Gibbons' undoubted horror, Minnelli focuses on a blood-red doorway framed by walls bathed in violent green. As red-antlered chorus boys and white-zombie models draped in ebony prowl the set, a black-garbed Gower Champion does a variation on Astaire's jewel-thief ballet from *Ziegfeld Follies.* To a jazz-tinged arrangement of Kern's "Yesterdays," he and a scarlet-gowned Marge execute an athletic dance of greed and seduction, filching rhinestone trinkets from the models and each other before lust gets the better of them.

To give the Champions room Minnelli allows them the run of the set, plunged in darkness except for a brace of ruby-red antlers. The rest of the time, he keeps the sequence flowing with a succession of tight compositions in an array of triangles and semicircles, described by the chiffon panels and pillars borne by his ever-mobile dress extras. Minnelli confuses the eye by constantly redefining this playing space—in a reversal of the usual production-number technique, the cutting and musical underscoring take a backseat to Minnelli's ever-shifting sets and roving camera in buoying the rhythms of the sequence. Kathryn Grayson enters to warble a few bars of "The Touch of Your Hand," and you know the number is drawing to a conclusion because Minnelli bathes the set in his favorite sunshine

yellow. While the film's stars waltz in the foreground, Minnelli's backdrop effortlessly dwarfs them—pavilions and chandeliers lit like diamonds against a golden light. On assignments like this and the subsequent *Kismet,* Minnelli's task was to conjure up magic in an aesthetic void, but his quest for beauty often courted the absurd; without any textual emotions waiting to be expressed, his inimitable taste is reduced to affectation. Still, *Lovely to Look At* confirmed that in the realm of grandiloquent glitter, no one could match Minnelli.

Minnelli felt secure enough to decline the next musical MGM proposed. As the first solo star vehicle for Leslie Caron, studio contract writer Helen Deutsch had composed a delicate fantasy-with-songs called *Lili,* about a provincial French waif who joins a traveling carnival. Minnelli was the obvious choice to direct it. As far as he was concerned, this notion was just too predictable. After *An American in Paris* and *Lovely to Look At,* Minnelli was weary of that corner of the Metro backlot which was forever France. When he declined, the studio assigned *Lili* to Charles Walters, who was used to picking up Minnelli's leavings. As it happened, everyone benefited from Minnelli's refusal. With a modest but original script and score, *Lili* was an unusual musical for MGM in the early fifties. It suited Walters perfectly and proved an unexpected hit at a time when the studio desperately needed one.

By then Minnelli was too busy to regret his decision. During the first half of 1952, he filmed one story for the omnibus film *The Story of Three Loves* and completed his first dramatic feature in three years, *The Bad and the Beautiful.* As shooting wound to a close, Minnelli was already engrossed in preparations for Arthur Freed's first production since *Singin' in the Rain*—a backstage musical cued by the song portfolio of Howard Dietz and Arthur Schwartz.

Freed had a special taste for confecting musicals around composer anthologies, and the Dietz–Schwartz catalogue held a particular nepotistic appeal. For nearly three decades, Howard Dietz had sustained a prosperous dual career. By day he was Loews Inc.'s vice-president in charge of MGM publicity, forever immortal as the man who thought up the studio's Leo the Lion logo; by night Dietz had gained wider personal fame as the lyricist half of one of Broadway's most respected songwriting teams. While many songs in the Dietz–Schwartz canon were popular standards, few had reached the screen till then, thanks to a curious anomaly in their joint stage career. Dietz and Schwartz had never written a truly successful book musical—alone among their peers, their metier was the plotless revue, a form that rarely traveled to Hollywood. (One of these, the 1935 *At Home Abroad,* served as Minnelli's Broadway directorial debut; although one of its songs was used for *The Band Wagon,* it didn't make the final cut.) Productions such as *The Little Show* (1929), *Three's a Crowd* (1930), *Flying Colors* (1932), and particularly Dietz and Schwartz' 1931 entry, *The Band Wagon,* had set their era's standard for high-toned escapism, while serving as glittering showcases for the brightest revue stars of the day: Clifton Webb, Libby Holman, Fred Allen, and Fred and Adele Astaire, who made their final joint appearance in the first *Band Wagon.*

In 1949, 20th Century-Fox produced a film called *Dancing in the Dark,* using much of the stage *Band Wagon's* score; curiously, its stars were the unmusical William Powell and Betsy Drake, and the movie was quickly forgotten. Fox's failure further convinced Freed that he was the man to give the Dietz–Schwartz collaboration the distinguished setting it deserved. Just as the jazzy exuberance of the Gershwins immediately suggested Gene Kelly, the moody sophistication of the Dietz–Schwartz style was made for Astaire, and Freed conceived the project with him in mind from the first. The problem was finding a plot framework that would support the score and star alike. The producer's first, fruitless attempt centered on an original story by screenwriter Peter Viertel entitled "Strategy of Love," which MGM acquired at Freed's request for the sum of $15,000. After several months of pondering, Freed discarded it, and in a memo to Kenneth MacKenna, head of the MGM story department, he declared, ". . . in my judgment it was wrong to do a straight love story with Astaire." The one thing retained for the time being was Freed's title for his Dietz–Schwartz property—*I Love Louisa,* from one of their 1931 songs. He summoned Betty Comden and Adolph Green and instructed them to start over, with this title as inspiration.

After the triumph of *Singin' in the Rain,* the choice of Comden and Green was an easy one—after all, it too had an entirely new screenplay surrounding a stack of old songs by Nacio Herb Brown and Freed himself. This time, they came up with perhaps the only workable solution. Just as they had linked Brown and Freed's MGM-spawned catalogue to a tale about the movie business, Comden and Green set the Dietz–Schwartz material to a backstage yarn about making a Broadway musical. If the premise was banal, their irrepressible wit and specificity of observation lifted it far above the ordinary, for Comden and Green knew this milieu intimately. Moreover, like Minnelli's just-concluded Hollywood movie à clef *The Bad and the Beautiful, The Band Wagon* was sparked by its provocative allusions to actual show business personalities—most pertinently, Astaire himself.

The script's protagonist, Tony Hunter, is a dramatically heightened portrait of the Astaire whose career temporarily ebbed in the mid-forties—a somewhat aloof, middle-aged movie hoofer whose taps seem out of sync with the times. With no movie offers forthcoming, he ponders a return to the stage at the behest of Lester and Lily Martin, a musical comedy writing team that bears a certain resemblance to Comden and Green themselves, with the marital bickering of the likes of Ruth Gordon and Garson Kanin added for spice. The catalyst for this would-be Broadway extravaganza is magnetic director/impresario/star-thespian Jeffrey Cordova. Some people discerned touches of Orson Welles and George S. Kaufman in this character; however, the main inspiration was Jose Ferrer, who in the previous Broadway season had directed himself in *The Shrike* and staged two other productions between his own performances. The real-life model for Hunter's co-star, ballerina Gabrielle Gerard, is more vague in outline— one plausible source was crossover dancer Zizi Jeanmaire, just then making a mainstream movie debut with *Hans Christian Andersen.* Gaby's scowling choreographer/Svengali, Paul Byrd, might well have been based on Jeanmaire's husband, Roland Petit; but for Broadway mavens with long memories, Byrd also conjured up George Balanchine, who had staged the dances for former wives Tamara Geva and Vera Zorina when they defected to musical comedy in the thirties and early forties.

In consultation with Minnelli, Freed, and his staff, Comden and Green spent the spring and summer of 1952 refining the script. Freed discarded his working title for the less-confining *The Band Wagon;* in summoning up the memory of Astaire's distant stage triumph, it deepened the movie's resonance as an autumnal valentine to the screen's premier dancing legend. Meanwhile, Freed assigned his associate producer, Roger Edens, the task of selecting the movie's score from the wealth of Dietz–Schwartz material at their disposal. Both Freed and Minnelli were determined to break from precedent by making one backstage musical that would really connote Shubert Alley rather than Washington Boulevard. They summoned two Broadway artists with no prior movie experience to lend *The Band Wagon* an authentic theatrical aura: choreographer Michael Kidd, late of *Finian's Rainbow* and *Guys and Dolls,* and designer Oliver Smith, drafted to work with Cedric Gibbons' art department on the film's production numbers. (Among many other credits, Smith had designed and co-produced Comden and Green's *On the Town* and *Billion Dollar Baby*.)

To support Astaire, Freed and Minnelli selected a cast as novel for movie audiences as the team behind the scenes. The one really familiar note was struck by Freed pal Oscar Levant, whose malingering private personality meshed with the role of comic-neurotic Lester Martin. Opposite him, Freed chose vivacious Broadway leading lady Nanette Fabray, who had recently adorned the stage musicals *High Button Shoes, Love Life* and (opposite Georges Guetary) *Arms and the Girl.* As a teenager named Nanette Fabares she had played a few bit parts in movies and in later years would return in character roles; regrettably, *The Band Wagon* would prove Fabray's only screen appearance in the genre in which she excelled.

The Band Wagon now seems inconceivable without Cyd Charisse, arguably the most sensuous and technically expert partner Astaire ever had. Yet casting her was an act of faith on Freed's part. During eight years at MGM, she had largely been used as a sort of Caucasian Lena Horne, whose specialty numbers were inserted as added showmanship into otherwise unrelated musical extravaganzas. Although Charisse had played occasional second leads and scattered non-dancing parts, she was yet to prove she could sustain the star role in a film of this scale. *The Band Wagon* confirmed that while her acting skills were a little uncertain, in motion Charisse was one of the screen's irreplaceable movie-musical artists—the last great song-and-dance personality ever developed at MGM. She was to become a particular Minnelli favorite; in the post-musical era a decade later, he insisted on casting her as the perilous seductress in *Two Weeks in Another Town.*

Jeffrey Cordova was the most colorful part in the script, but Freed had difficulty finding a star to play it. Everybody's first choice was Clifton Webb, who in recent years had gained his widest fame as a prissy character star in 20th Century-Fox comedies. In the twenties and thirties, however, he'd been Astaire's closest rival in the arena of dapper dancing and the stellar attraction in a trio of Dietz–Schwartz revues. It was a rich opportunity for Webb to show off his former gifts to a movie public who knew him mainly as the snotty Mr. Belvedere, but he declined the role as too secondary to suit his newfound screen fame.

Nevertheless, he made a substantial contribution to *The Band Wagon*'s success. While Freed considered such possible substitutes as Vincent Price, Webb sug-

gested Britain's epitome of top-hatted panache—Jack Buchanan. A West End fixture for three decades, Buchanan was virtually unknown to the American movie public, having taken his leave of Hollywood after a pair of early talkie musicals in 1930. However, he too was a Dietz–Schwartz alumnus, having starred in the 1937 *Between the Devil,* a flop book musical with a beautiful score. Buchanan's wit, energy, and somewhat neutered charm made him the ideal foil to Astaire, and MGM eagerly signed him for the role.

The backstage format of the Comden and Green script was elastic enough to accommodate an ever-changing array of Dietz–Schwartz songs. By the start of production in late September 1952, Edens had culled twenty of them. An even dozen materialized in the release print of the film: "I Guess I'll Have to Change My Plan" (originally written for *The Little Show*); a brief chorus by the show-within-the-show's gypsies of "Something to Remember You By" *(Three's a Crowd)*; "Shine on Your Shoes" and "Louisiana Hayride" from *Flying Colors*; "You and the Night and the Music" (1934's *Revenge with Music*); *Between the Devil's* "By Myself" and "Triplets"; and a brace of tunes from the first *Band Wagon*—"New Sun in the Sky," "I Love Louisa," and "The Beggar's Waltz," used as background for Charisse's ballet solo; and a short dance-band rendition of "High and Low" in the Central Park sequence, as prelude to "Dancing in the Dark." Additionally, Freed asked Dietz and Schwartz to contribute one new number—a rousing anthem to the lively arts on the order of Irving Berlin's "There's No Business Like Show Business." That very day, the team returned with "That's Entertainment," Dietz' second-best contribution to MGM's greater glory. Two decades later, with the studio in collapse, it furnished the title for MGM's hit anthology of its past musical triumphs.

It's indicative of the latitude given Freed, and the importance accorded this project, that many other numbers were recorded and staged during *The Band Wagon*'s four months of shooting, with no hope that all could be included in the final cut. Among the first to go were an Astaire solo keyed to *Revenge with Music's* "Never Marry a Dancer" and a rehearsal sequence for Astaire and Charisse to "You Have Everything," another song from *Between the Devil.* Two other numbers proved slightly longer lived. *At Home Abroad's* "Got a Bran' New Suit" prompted an intriguing shorn sequence; as described in a memo from Edens to Rudi Monta of the studio's legal department, it showcased the genesis and death of a Broadway production number. Librettist Fabray auditions her song for Astaire, who in an extended montage struggles to devise an appropriate dance setting for it; at last he is satisfied and performs a beguiling tap routine for Fabray and Levant, only to be told that there's no longer any room for it in the show—which turned out in fact to be all too prophetic.

A showcase for Charisse, "Two-Faced Woman" from *Flying Colors,* suffered the same fate. "Lyric refers to a woman who, to say the least, has a highly variegated nature," according to Edens. "Girls in the chorus representing the 'good' side are dressed in white costumes; those representing the 'bad' side are dressed in strong red costumes." Like "Got a Bran' New Suit," this lasted to the rough assembly of *The Band Wagon,* but was excised a few weeks before the first sneak preview in March 1953. However, "Two-Faced Woman" didn't go entirely to waste. MGM was concurrently planning a small-budget musical called *Torch Song* as Joan Crawford's return to the studio after a decade-long absence. So the studio retrieved the "Two-Faced Woman" soundtrack off the cutting room floor and devised a new number around it for Crawford. The result was pretty silly, with the determined diva adorned in mesh stockings and mulatto makeup as well as India Adams' twice-borrowed voice.

After *The Band Wagon*'s sneak preview, Fabray and Levant's version of "Sweet Music," lifted from the first *Band Wagon,* was also judged superfluous. On screen it was performed at a backers' audition, the occasion for one of those Levant piano specialties that were the early fifties' equivalent of Harpo Marx's MGM stringpluckings of fifteen years before. As Edens put it, "the lyrics cleverly make use of Mr. Levant's talent as a pianist, allowing him to play fragments of piano compositions . . . including . . . the coda of the First Piano Concerto by P. I. Tchaikowsky." This time, Freed and company decided that wasn't entertainment, and the backers' audition was streamlined into a Buchanan monologue.

The making of *The Band Wagon* wasn't nearly as tortuous as the out-of-town miseries depicted in the script, but there were problems enough. With their overlapping responsibilities, Oliver Smith and studio mainstay Preston Ames clashed over turf; the studio felt that meticulous cameraman George Folsey succumbed too easily to Minnelli's time-consuming passion for detail, and replaced him with Harry Jackson halfway through shooting to speed up production. The actors were plagued by their own phantoms, many of them self-created. Buchanan was ill much of the time, and Levant exasperated everyone with his constant phobias and complaints. (In retaliation, Minnelli cast him as an out-and-out psychotic in *The Cobweb* two years later.) In Astaire's youth, sister Adele had dubbed him Moaning Minnie in tribute to his pessimistic outlook toward the work at hand. As usual Astaire worried about everything, from Michael Kidd's unconventional choreographic ideas to Cyd Charisse's height, this last inserted as a wry in-joke into the Comden–Green script. Astaire might well have been troubled also by the obvious parallels between the fictitious Tony Hunter and the real Fred Astaire—his advancing age and dour temperament, the perennial fear that after tapping in the spotlight for so many years, he was bound to grow stale and outwear his welcome. As ever, Minnelli was too absorbed in his own task to heed the anguish of his star. In a rare burst of temper, Astaire stormed off the set while his director was rehearsing "I Love Louisa"—a gesture blunted by the fact that Minnelli scarcely noticed he was missing. On his belated return, the star contritely apologized for this unusual breach of professional etiquette. "Oh, that's perfectly all right, Fred," Minnelli replied. "I drive everybody crazy."

The toughest creative impasse concerned *The Band Wagon*'s would-be musical climax. Some sort of pop-music ballet was inevitable, but after *An American in Paris* and *Singin' in the Rain,* this notion was increasingly susceptible to cliché. What eventually emerged was that Broadway *Liebestod,* "The Girl Hunt," which took a week to shoot as production wound down in January 1953. With its playful fusion of wit and sex, this became the one sequence to forever delight even those who are allergic to the movie-ballet form. The narration in particular was a killer. ("She came at me in sections. She had more curves than a scenic highway," quotes Astaire while Charisse slithers around the stage like a black-spangled asp.) It's a supreme example of tongue-in-cheek pastiche particular to Comden and Green. Yet remembered accounts clash as to whose handiwork it really was.

Before they left Hollywood for New York to work on their next stage musical, *Wonderful Town,* Comden and Green wrote the outline of a generic film-noir parody in dance entitled "The Private Eye." Everyone agreed that while the idea was sound, the sketch itself lacked punch and specificity. The next step, according to Freed biographer Hugh Fordin, was Roger Edens' suggestion to shape the ballet into a slapstick homage to Mickey Spillane, with terse, overripe lingo and muscular choreography to match. As this account had it, while Edens assembled a mini-score from Arthur Schwartz themes, Alan Jay Lerner agreed to fashion a brief script as a favor to Freed.

Lerner requested neither payment nor screen credit, but his name appeared as co-author with Edens of "The Girl Hunt" on the soundtrack LP issued on the occasion of the film's release. Minnelli was furious. As MGM's legal files attest, and he reiterated in his autobiography, the director emphatically claimed authorship for himself and instructed his agent, Bert Allenberg, to demand that MGM withdraw all copies of the record and rectify the mistake. This burst of righteous anger must have been sincere on Minnelli's part —it was too uncharacteristic of him to be dismissed as mere directorial pique. Minnelli confined his explosions to those times when the work itself was thwarted; he never fought with the studio over billing and rarely prodded Allenberg to intercede with MGM about anything. When queried by the studio's lawyers, Freed further confused the matter by stating that while Minnelli may have made some contribution, the narration was ''probably'' written ''primarily'' by Lerner with Edens. The studio compromised by releasing the sound track a second time on 45 RPM records with Minnelli's name inserted in place of Lerner's. When Comden and Green objected on their own behalf, MGM dismissed their claim entirely—whoever had plotted ''The Girl Hunt,'' Comden and Green were not the principal suspects.

During the spring of 1953, when *The Band Wagon* was being edited for release, its prospects as the last word in movie-musical artistry were clouded by the latest achievement in screen technology—Cinema-Scope. This wide-screen process patented by rival studio 20th Century-Fox threatened to sweep the industry as rapidly as sound had done in the twenties; MGM feared, with justification, that any of its products which didn't conform to the new screen proportions might seem instantly archaic to a public primed by Fox's campaign to launch CinemaScope. As *The Band Wagon* had already been shot in normal ratio, the New York office thought it prudent to convert all prints to ersatz wide-screen format. Culver City wired back to advise that if this were done, the performers' faces and feet would be cut off from view in most of the musical numbers; thus the studio resignedly set a summer release for *The Band Wagon* in its original form, with Astaire and Charisse fully visible from head to toe. Even so, *The Band Wagon* was the last of its line—all Freed musicals were henceforth shot in the wide-screen process, as was every film Minnelli subsequently made at MGM save the next, his comedy *The Long, Long Trailer.* For a director as sensitive to composition as he, it would impose a fundamental adjustment in his expressive technique—from exploring the depth of a square frame to filling a shallower, panoramic fresco.

During production, *The Band Wagon*'s lavishness prompted some industry gossips to speculate that its final cost would reach an unheard-of five million dollars. Yet according to MGM's tabulations, *The Band Wagon* was brought in for $2,872,581—scarcely more than the studio had spent on *An American in Paris.* The film opened at Radio City Music Hall in July 1953, to the most uniformly enthusiastic press for any Minnelli musical since *Meet Me in St. Louis.* Like *Singin' in the Rain* the year before, it was somewhat overlooked in the Academy Award competitions, garnering nominations for the Comden and Green script, Adolph Deutsch's musical scoring, and Mary Ann Nyberg's costumes and winning none of them. While not the commercial sensation of *An American in Paris, The Band Wagon* stockpiled total rentals of well over five million dollars—the most lucrative Freed musical between *Singin' in the Rain* in 1952 and *Gigi* in 1958. As gratifying to Freed and Minnelli was Howard Dietz' reaction to this tribute to his life's work. At first viewing, he immediately fired off a telegram to Arthur Schwartz,

raving over the home team's accomplishment. If there was one MGM production Howard Dietz was thrilled to promote, *The Band Wagon* was it.

Like the best Minnelli musicals that preceded it, *The Band Wagon* matches lyricism with high spirits, elegant surfaces, and an undertow of sadness. Nevertheless, this movie represents a distinct departure from anything he'd done in the field thus far. Until now, all save the infamous *I Dood It* had attempted in one way or another to redefine the boundaries of the traditional movie musical. By contrast, *The Band Wagon* is a triumphant summation of the genre rather than a sly subversion of it. As with every second Hollywood musical dating back to *The Jazz Singer,* the plot describes the quest for romantic and professional fulfillment in the act of putting on a show; its song interludes adhere to the rules of dramatic plausibility by taking place on a stage rather than inside the performers' secret hearts. *The Band Wagon* wryly deflates Minnelli's own specialty by stressing that dance is a product of straining muscles rather than an overworked subconscious. The closest thing to a nightmare in *The Band Wagon* is the collapse of a production number (devoted to a dream ballet no less) during the out-of-town tryout.

It's a characteristic Minnelli paradox that his most ''realistic'' musical was conceived and shot entirely on the sound stages of Metro. Apart from a few second-unit shots of the 20th-Century Limited, sunshine never penetrates a frame of this movie—not even the arc-light variety. The Central Park trees Astaire and Charisse marvel at while playing hooky from rehearsals are a two-dimensional trick of back-projection, less tangible than an asbestos stage curtain; the only difference between the skyscraper cyclorama looming over their outdoor duet to ''Dancing in the Dark'' and the alleyway backdrop that sets the scene for ''The Girl Hunt'' ballet is that the latter is more candidly phony.

This movie-in-a-bell-jar style is never claustrophobic, because Minnelli creates a completely self-sufficient world within its strictures. Its hermetic quality gives flesh to the basic premise of all backstage musicals—that these people are most alive when they're shut up somewhere performing. Minnelli celebrated this idea in *The Bad and the Beautiful,* which *The Band Wagon* resembles more profoundly than it does his other musicals. This time he took his theme further, in that these characters seem not to have any lives at all outside the range of the footlights. The respective alliances between Lester and Lily Martin or Gaby and dance director Paul Byrd are forged by complementary talent rather than passion. When not at the theater, Astaire's Tony Hunter is almost always alone; after working hours, Jeffrey Cordova and the rest of the troupe emerge squinting from their backstage lairs at night and then dematerialize. The outside world exists only as a novel impromptu setting for trying out a new routine—Astaire and Charisse are irresistibly drawn to

"That's Entertainment!" featuring (clockwise) Nanette Fabray, Fred Astaire, Oscar Levant, Jack Buchanan, The Band Wagon *(1953)*

the clearing in Central Park because it looks like a stage. "They probably don't care whether we have a Damnation Scene or not," murmurs a bemused Tony at the offscreen sight of some nighttime strollers in the park. Such persons are a source of wonderment, products of some unimaginably distant galaxy. Most of the time, those rare non-performers they do encounter belong to but two subspecies—backers and ticket-buyers, both essential, both anonymous.

Throughout *The Band Wagon,* Minnelli adapts our gaze to the dimensions of his characters' tunnel vision. During that Production Code-harassed era, it was a truism that in the movies nobody ever went to the bathroom like ordinary mortals. In the film, such prosaic human activities as sleeping and eating are discreetly banished from view. For Minnelli, decor is psychology, and the peculiar absence of bedrooms and kitchens in this movie indicates how superfluous they are to the lives of these characters. Food, when they think of it, can always be catered; sleep (or sex, for that matter) is that limbo they disappear to in those short hours when they're not on call for the vital business of making theater. One's home is at most a surrogate showplace. Cordova uses his soigné duplex as the stage for his Sutton Place medicine act—spieling would-be backers to part with their money. Tony's hotel suite is a temporary gallery for his collection of Impressionist art—a tip-off that, in Minnelli's eye, he's no mere hoofer but a superior being. Dietz' opening lyric to "That's Entertainment" proclaims, "Everything that happens in life can happen in a show," but Minnelli makes the opposite point. Everything that happens on stage shapes and gives meaning to the lives of the

troupe. The mutual attraction between Tony and Gabrielle springs from their realization that each is the other's ideal equal as a working partner. Offstage, they're both too tongue-tied to express their feelings, until, at the opening night, Gaby declares her love in the terms of a *Variety* stringer—"The show's a hit. . . . We belong together. The show's going to run a long time. As far as I'm concerned, it's going to run forever."

Still, they're only the spotlit figures in a larger theatrical ensemble. Tony and Gaby's long-awaited first embrace naturally takes place on stage surrounded by the rest of the cast, which proceeds to trump the pair by dragging them into a final reprised chorus of the movie's theme song. It's a magically appropriate finale, for the movie is only secondarily a love story with the usual movie-musical happy ending. Just like *The Bad and the Beautiful, The Band Wagon* really celebrates the forging of an entire community. In the former picture, the hero is a has-been producer finally rehabilitated because his talent energizes all who work with him— he needs these people to fulfill his ambitions and reciprocates by bringing out the best in each of them. Under its sprightlier Technicolored surface, *The Band Wagon* traces the same journey. As the film unreels, Tony Hunter evolves from a professionally thwarted, personally alienated loner to the invigorated leader of a circle of comrades and colleagues—his newfound romance is a fringe benefit. What matters most is that he's given the show-within-the show the energy and focus it needed to be a hit, while the admiration of his colleagues has restored his self-esteem.

As a matchless example of movie-musical craftsmanship, *The Band Wagon* exemplifies its own theme—the glories of collaboration. While Minnelli grants proper weight to the movie's more solemn implications, the irresistible verve of Comden and Green's script keeps *The Band Wagon* rolling. This and *Singin' in the Rain* are unquestionably the best-written musicals created for the screen. As movie-struck, relatively youthful outsiders, they brought an impertinent new perspective to the old Hollywood formulas.

Then in their mid-thirties, Comden and Green belonged to that first generation which really grew up on the movies, and realized that Hollywood had a treasurable history rather than a disposable past. Unlike their studio elders who tended to an unabashed amnesia over anything cranked out more than five years previously, Comden and Green adored the silliness and excess of the movies from their youth. So, rather than striving like other exiles from Broadway to elevate the screen's cultural tone, they hoped to restore some of its previous fun. From their earliest collaboration as part of a satirical night club troupe, The Revuers, movie spoofs had played a large part in their repertoire, and it seemed natural to bring that precocious, camp sensibility with them when they started writing for the movies themselves. If their script for *Singin' in the Rain*

was generalized nostalgia at its most extroverted, the self-referential tone of the two films Comden and Green wrote for Fred Astaire is both more specific and more contemplative—a fan's slightly tongue-in-cheek valentine to a living icon. The shaky premise shoring up most of his postwar films was that time had stood still in Astaire's fantasyland. He was still the same brash but elegant guy of the deco Depression years, plus Technicolor and minus Ginger. Instead, *The Barkleys of Broadway* and *The Band Wagon* emphasize the distance he'd traveled in two decades of movie stardom. *Barkleys* is a pastel rendering of the strains that sundered the Astaire–Rogers partnership, updated by a decade and transplanted from RKO to Shubert Alley. *The Band Wagon* takes a darker, more speculative view, in that the star drifts through a changed world indifferent to his receding triumphs. The film begins with a desultory auction of Tony Hunter's personal effects, of which the prize item is the top hat and cane he sported in [sic] *Swinging Down to Panama.* In a later age hungry for pop-culture collectibles, the sale of relics like these would cause a small-scale riot, but in 1953 the past is an embarrassment and there are no takers.

The first half of the script affords a constant series of

humiliations for Astaire/Hunter, reminding him that he is a fossil with the bad grace to wander about among the living. On his arrival in New York, he's nearly trampled in the media crush surrounding the last word in star quality, Ava Gardner; a stroll down 42nd Street (whose easy, honky-tonk atmosphere is positively soothing to contemporary eyes) is like an excursion to Mars. "I just can't understand it," he exclaims, amid the studio mock-ups of grind houses and pinball emporia. "I mean this used to be the great theater street of the town. The New Amsterdam—I had one of my biggest successes there [the hit in question was in fact *The Band Wagon*].... Why, the first show I ever did was at the Eltinge, and I don't even believe that's here any more." Worse awaits him when he encounters his new would-be collaborators. Gaby considers him "practically a historical figure by now," and on their first nervous encounter blurts, "I used to see all your pictures when I was a little girl. And I'm still a fan. I recently went to see a revival of them at the museum." Cordova is even more blunt. In the movie's most somberly delivered speech, he informs Tony, "I've seen every show and every movie you've ever done. But let's face some brutal facts. Times have changed, Tony, and you haven't changed with them. You've gone stale."

For any Astaire admirer these are fighting words, which is precisely what Comden and Green intended. The allusions to his age ambush and disarm the captious in the audience, while cueing some of Comden and Green's better quips. (When Gaby praises an early Degas in his collection, Tony retorts, "Yeah, I swiped it from his desk in school. Was he sore!") Moreover, Astaire's renewed popularity after *Easter Parade* ensured that moviegoers wouldn't take Cordova's ominous epitaph too literally. The screenwriter's sympathies are entirely on the side of the beleaguered hero; for in their view, if there was no longer room for a Fred Astaire in "the world of entertainment" Dietz' lyric describes, then it was show business's loss.

They illustrate this with their most telling contribution to the movie—the clash of artistic purposes that jeopardizes the hero's Broadway comeback. Their onscreen surrogates have written an unpretentious libretto about a children's book author who writes pulp thrillers on the side for extra cash; it's a "light and intimate show . . . with just enough plot to make him do lots of gay and varied numbers." Cordova, the selfanointed high priest of the lively arts, labors to transform it into a modern version of the Faust legend, full of what he calls "meaning and stature."

OPPOSITE:
*Fred Astaire, Cyd Charisse,
and Jack Buchanan, "You
and the Night and the Music,"*
The Band Wagon (1953)

As far as Comden and Green were concerned, if he wins the fight, disaster is bound to follow. In their theater and film work alike, Comden and Green mistrusted the growing impulse to inflate mainstream entertainment into self-conscious mass art; from *On the Town* onward, their Broadway hits had resisted the Rodgers-and-Hammersteinization of the musical theater, evoking instead the breezier diversions of the 1920s and '30s. Once in Hollywood, they incorporated this impulse into every script they'd written. The heavy in Comden and Green's screen musicals is always some poseur bent on seducing the protagonist into sharing the same unseemly pretentions: the fractured-Frenchspouting debutante in *Good News; The Barkleys of Broadway*'s continental playwright who lures Ginger Rogers to stop hoofing and go legit in a kitschy play about Sarah Bernhardt, and *Singin' in the Rain*'s indelible Lina Lamont, that "shining star in the movie firmament" who queens it over the studio rabble in a manner worthy of the tinsel monarchs she impersonates on the silent screen. This time Cordova is their selfdeluded Mephistopheles, leading his hypnotized band into the purgatory of an out-of-town flop in New Haven. (Ironically, three decades later Comden and Green found real backstage life echoing this behindthe-scenes fiction. Under the spell of the eminently Cordova-esque Harold Prince, they penned *A Doll's Life*, a musical of meaning and stature in the thrall of Henrik Ibsen. It proved the overwhelming fiasco of their careers.)

It's here that the parallel between the scripts of *Singin' in the Rain* and *The Band Wagon* is most vivid. On their first public unveilings, both the talkie, "The Dueling Cavalier," and Cordova's Faustian extravaganza are matchless flops. During a sleepless night contemplating the wreckage with their cohorts, both Gene Kelly's Don Lockwood and Astaire's Hunter stave off despair by concocting an impromptu production number for their own amusement. This spontaneous whistling-in-the-dark prompts a brainstorm—why not turn turkey to triumph by substituting showstoppers for ersatz Art? Minnelli masks Comden and Green's selfplagiarism by exchanging the socko directness of Kelly and Stanley Donen for his own brand of oblique irony. Whereas "The Duelling Cavalier" disintegrates before our eyes as the proles snicker in the balcony, only metaphor can convey the ignominy of "The Band Wagon." As the first chords of the "Damnation Ballet" dissolve into the rhythmic moans of an offscreen chorus, three black-and-white engravings fill the screen—shrouded Death rowing toward the River Styx, a steer's skull bleached by the desert sun, and one huge, perfect egg. The theater-lobby doors inch open, and the bejeweled and tophatted first-nighters shuffle, speechless, into the night, hollow stares reflecting the horror of what they've just seen. This is a perfect opportunity for Minnelli to use his bent for art appreciation at its most perverse. With caustic economy, he turns a gallery slide show into a three-act black comedy plus epilogue.

Later that evening, a chastened Cordova hands over the reins to Tony, declaring, "I've learned one thing in the theater and it's this—one man has to be at the helm and the rest take orders." Comden and Green's script serves the same function as Lester and Lily Martin's work does within the film: it supplies a winning context for all those "gay and varied numbers," while Minnelli's job is to provide a unifying style to give the movie meaning, if not necessarily "stature." As the song says, *The Band Wagon*'s onstage specialties do run the gamut—from Oedipus Rex to the dance that's a dream of romance to the dame who is known as the flame of the king of an underworld ring. His toughest challenge was to imbue the backstage "world of entertainment" with the same theatrical charge as all those songs and dances.

Happily, *The Band Wagon*'s plot intersects with one of Minnelli's signature themes—the heady pleasure of immersing yourself in hard work. For the audience's sake, he ensures that the outcome will live up to the false starts and heated bickering that went before it, but it's the process itself that fascinates him. Minnelli's primal identification with this process makes *The Band Wagon* the most romantic of his musicals, sparked by those memories of his own Broadway past which this movie inevitably summoned. Once the show-within-the-show gets on its feet, Minnelli draws a witty distinction between the hyperthyroid anarchy-with-a-purpose only insiders see, and that illusion of unruffled professionalism distilled for the public's pleasure.

In contrast to his other musicals, until the climactic "The Girl Hunt" ballet most of Minnelli's numbers are a model of technical self-effacement within deliberately enclosed spaces—Astaire, Buchanan, and the rest do their respective specialties in front of one-dimensional stage backdrops, the camera fixed at the footlights to record their antics. There are few fancy light cues or vaulting tracking shots—he limits his gaze to the stage, rather than exploding its boundaries to suit his vision. When the troupe is in rehearsal, however, it's circus time, with Minnelli riding the trapeze. In *The Bad and the Beautiful*, his long, sinuous takes shift to a staccato montage once its hero is on the sound stage orchestrating magic; here, the cutting also quickens as rehearsals gain momentum—dancers stumbling through their routines, the Martins slashing at the score between fights, and Cordova trying out new stage illusions.

By the time "The Band Wagon" has staggered to its final dress rehearsals before the New Haven opening, the company is in chaos and Minnelli's camera has gone haywire, dangling from the stage flies, perched on the edge of the front mezzanine to observe this mess with appalled detachment. This is the occasion for Minnelli to poke fun at his own past excesses in musical comedy baroquery. The so-called "Transformation Scene," with a black-and-white set hurtling up, down and around the overburdened stage, is an inchoate mosaic of Minnellian tics, with a few left-over Furies from the *American in Paris* ballet colliding with *Lovely to Look At*'s male chandeliers, as the whole thing collapses with a sickening rip of stage canvas. Damnation comes next, a charcoal void picked out with travesties of his favorite colors: light gels of blood-red and vermilion reprised from Cordova's "Oedipus Rex" and every second Minnelli musical, upstaged by a swath of sickly yellow. "Your cue is 'Dance Fools, Dance,'" intones Cordova, while Tony and Gaby stoically survey the stage within the bleak orbit of Minnelli's biggest sunburst spotlight. An offstage chorus bellows, "You and the Night and the Music fill me with flaming desire/ Setting my being completely on fire!" and in perfect sync with the campiest lyric Howard Dietz ever wrote, Minnelli prods his own pyromania by smothering the scene in enough smoke and fire to stoke two *Pirate* ballets. This time his creation achieves what he never quite managed with Kelly—it completely upstages his wheezing, blinded stars. Minnelli was notorious for ignoring the distress of his performers in pursuit of some knockout movie tableau. With Jeffrey Cordova as his stand-in, this is *The Band Wagon*'s most blissful in-joke, with Minnelli laughing hardest of all.

As the smoke of Cordova's fatuous dream sequence finally clears, Tony and Gaby recover their wits by breaking into a gigglesome improvised time-step. This is the spirit which informs the movie's other musical interludes—working toward that clear-eyed self-control which makes both good theater and common sense. Fun means having a clear idea of what you're doing, and then doing it supremely well. In *The Band Wagon*, breaking into song is neither an instinctive gesture of joy nor is dancing the act of unveiling the depths of the unconscious, as in other Minnelli movies. For the Astaire of *The Band Wagon*, music is a cue for self-discipline; he channels his talent to banish that pessimism always coiled in wait to defeat him.

Astaire's first song in *The Band Wagon* is his wry rebuke to melancholy. Ignored on his arrival at Grand Central Station, with Hollywood and failure behind him and an uncertain future in store, Tony Hunter keeps his spirits up by giving voice to a plaintive Howard Dietz' lyric. "I'll face the unknown," he declares softly. "I'll build a world of my own. No one knows better than I myself, I'm by myself alone." In her later concert days, Judy Garland made "By Myself" one of her applause-begging specialties, building the song into a crescendo of defiant masochism. Astaire, however, is too much the stoic for that. With an ironic chuckle, he muses his way through it in a hushed tone too self-effacing for bathos. At the end, he adds an airy syncopation to the melody, affecting a jaunty stride as he makes his solitary way down the train platform.

In the character of Tony Hunter, Astaire uses the

Cyd Charisse and Fred Astaire in a vignette deleted from "The Girl Hunt," The Band Wagon *(1953)*

song to deflect emotion rather than succumb to it, an impulse which also fuels the more extroverted "Shine on Your Shoes" shortly afterwards. Once more, Tony is frustrated and disoriented, lost in a Times Square turned plebian and tawdry during his exile in California. His instinct for survival prompts him to adapt to the new order and make the best of it, adjusting his mood to match the meter of the taps on his shoes. This number is a variant on that beloved Astaire specialty, the quest for dance inspiration in a host of odd inanimate objects—in this case, the garish gadgets littering a penny arcade. Like so much in *The Band Wagon,* "Shine on Your Shoes" reprises a past peak in Astaire's movie career, specifically his trip through the funhouse with George Burns and Gracie Allen in the 1937 *A Damsel in Distress.* Keyed to a swingy brass arrangement of Schwartz' tune, Astaire scampers from the snapshot booth to a shooting gallery like a kid let loose on the monkey bars.

It's one of the most enjoyable Astaire set pieces of his MGM period, and despite its tenuous connection to the plot, the number also deftly expresses the character's temperament. Hunter brushes aside his own depression by turning instead to the woes of someone else—a bootblack sulking at his deserted shoeshine stand. Since working cheers Tony up, he concludes the same thing will help this other guy. Apart from the sheer pleasure of sweeping away morbid thoughts by exercising his limbs, Tony is buoyed by the fact that after a long absence, he's performing before an audience—the stunned bystanders of the penny arcade, rewarding him with cheers and applause. His lighthearted give-and-take with shoeshine man LeRoy Daniels is even a form of subconscious homework for the serious tasks to come; the stalking interplay of Michael Kidd's choreography between Astaire and Daniels foreshadows dancing detective Rod Riley's pursuit of the mysterious dame in "The Girl Hunt" ballet.

Hunter's obstinate self-doubt is likewise the cue for *The Band Wagon*'s explicit paean to escapism, "That's Entertainment." Certain that there's no place for him in Cordova's "modern musical morality play," Astaire is ready to exit scowling until his colleagues persuade him to stop brooding and start hoofing. "You could be greater than you ever were," proclaims Cordova. "Not just the old trademark with the top hat, tie and tails, but a great artist at the peak of his powers." But tap shoes are better than words, and Cordova shows what he means by executing a Bill Robinson strut up the same staircase where he'd just moved the ticket buyers to tears as Oedipus. With what follows, Minnelli proves "the stage is a world of entertainment" by using the blood-red "Oedipus" flats as the set for the lowest of vaudeville shtick—a three-way time-step which dissolves into an orgy of crushed-toe upstaging, a human pyramid whose base wanders to the footlights to take a bow, cheap disappearing acts, a demure bump-and-grind from Nanette Fabray, and a mimed patriotic crescendo, "the American way," for the finale.

Deliberately, this is a production number without production values. While Cordova's own home resembles a perfect stage set, the backstage area of his theater is a jumble of cardboard and canvas; it takes the right combination of talent and high spirits to transform it into that place where magic is made. Minnelli and Kidd's playful staging pretends to expose the tricks that make theatrical illusions possible, but "That's Entertainment" relies on the oldest gag of all—the notion that Astaire, Buchanan, Fabray, and Levant are just larking around, making it up as they go along. The miseries they endure in mounting their show puncture that musical-comedy myth. In its place Minnelli substitutes another, which holds the director in its thrall as well—that show people are among those happy few for whom work and pleasure are indivisible pursuits.

This idea finds earnest expression when Astaire and Charisse first join forces for "Dancing in the Dark." This may well be his most sensual duet since the 1936 "Never Gonna Dance" with Ginger, yet its emotional subtext is radically different. In the Astaire–Rogers films, he always succumbed to Ginger at first sight, whether she could be stirred to music or not. As these movies unreeled, dancing became a rarefied metaphor for sex; in *The Band Wagon* the sublime formal perfection of Astaire's interplay with Charisse is the end in itself, for if Tony and Gaby can't dance together any relationship between them is impossible. The sentimental urgency of Arthur Schwartz' melody is relevant only as the perfect cue to test their professional compatibility. With Ginger, Astaire was ardent, drawing her into the thrall of his steps. With Charisse he is pensive and gallant, and their duet begins when she indicates the moment is right by breaking out of a measured stroll into a tentative ballet leap.

Pondering the possible wreck of his stage comeback, seduction is the last thing on Tony Hunter's mind. Swaying side by side in their matched cool-white costumes, both dancers appear lost in thought, intent on willing their bodies into the necessary work of complementing each other. She poses on a bench with her arms outstretched, waiting for Astaire to lift her to her toes; he reverently supports Charisse as she surges into a pair of exquisite backbends. Together they create a breathtaking example of professional harmony, and in the world of *The Band Wagon* this is like sex only better. The spare beauty of this sequence is Minnelli's own rebuke to the dry-ice-drenched couplings he'd done in other musicals and satirized here in "You and the Night and the Music." The color scheme is restrained for minimal distraction—Astaire and Charisse are shining figures against a sapphire-blue cityscape. While scrupulously following the Astaire maxim to keep the full figures of the dancers always in view, Minnelli's ecstatic camera movements deferentially shape the dance. It's he who supplies the final pulsebeat at the climax, arching giddily around Tony and Gaby as they reboard the hansom cab that had borne them to this "outdoor" rehearsal space.

Among themselves, *The Band Wagon*'s quintet of performers use their gifts to work through their private doubts, but once they're actually on stage, they just want to pulverize the public. Gabrielle Gerard is the first to be showcased, surrounded by her corps de ballet before Broadway lures her away. She's a far cry from the dangerous voluptuary she will become in "The Girl Hunt"; partnered by a succession of male anonymities as she leaps from one imperious pose to the next, Gabrielle is an ice goddess without soul or sex. Like the little we see of Cordova's Oedipus, Gerard as prima ballerina begs for the coarsening touch of popular musical comedy. (It's hard to know how intentional this was. Michael Kidd can simulate the idiom of classical dance, but Broadway-style jazz is his real beat, and his ballet here is the palest of quasi-Balanchine. Besides, despite her years of serious training, the essential Charisse is less an MGM Margot Fonteyn than Barbara Stanwyck in mesh tights and Capezios.) Until a certain stubborn hoofer brings Charisse's Gaby down to earth, Minnelli uses her as a decorative object. In her cherry-red tutu, she is the focal point of Oliver Smith's saturated-blue dreamscape after Chagall, with the female corps streaming past the lens in a blur of white.

Gaby is still an icon for "New Sun in the Sky" after "The Band Wagon" hits the road, but the context is more Ziegfeld Follies than Ballets Russes. Minnelli dispels the smoke and gloom of the show-within-a-show's New Haven fiasco with three sunbursts—his trademark spotlight, Smith's backdrop, and Charisse herself in a shimmering gold dress with a chiffon ball of fire attached to her arm. This is a generic great-lady-and-*les-boys* production number, with Charisse as glamorous prop. While India Adams' voice pours out through her gracious-star smile, she substitutes body language for real dance—swaying her arms and swirling her skirts while the male chorus (and Minnelli's camera boom) flex their legs. In itself the sequence is nothing much, but it does serve as a confident preview of coming attractions for the improved show to come.

The Band Wagon's best production numbers take up the film's final third. There's a logic to this seeming imbalance, for these sequences mark the progress of the new, de-Mephisthelized extravaganza during its trek through the provinces en route to Broadway. (One unanswered question—which musical-comedy book, however elastic, could encompass this cornucopia of showstoppers?) Starting with the high-gloss cheeriness of "New Sun in the Sky," these specialties hit a wide range of notes in the musical-revue spectrum, from the urbane ("I Guess I'll Have to Change My Plan"), to tongue-in-cheek cornpone ("Louisiana Hayride") and dizzy farce ("Triplets").

What unites them is the performers' unflappable élan, and Minnelli's sensitivity to the special, self-contained qualities of the theater. Having spent the early part of his career staging numbers in a real proscenium, Minnelli rarely chose to fake things in his movies; it was much more intriguing to set his own boundaries, unfettered by the arbitrary proportions of the stage. Yet in this ultimate testament to Broadway's allure, it's the theater's capacity for distilled excitement which he celebrates, rather than the screen's expansive scope. As with "I'll Build a Stairway to Paradise," these sequences are believable facsimiles of stage numbers that nevertheless have been shaped entirely for the camera's eye. Within Minnelli's mock proscenium, his cast gives the illusion of immediacy you get from live performance, enhanced by the proximity of the camera. It's a fusion of the best of both worlds.

"I Guess I'll Have to Change My Plan" is the extreme example of this distilled theatricality. Astaire and Buchanan appear as twin dandies in white tie and tails, thrust forward to the narrow apron of the stage on an abstract set daubed in horizontal bands of pastel shades, which Oliver Smith called his homage to Paul Klee. Everything about the number is as subdued as Smith's color scheme—their languid stride and matter-of-fact crooning of Dietz' lyric on lost love, the muffled synchrony of Astaire and Buchanan's percussion with walking stick and tap shoes. At the end, they toss their top hats to the ends of their canes and miss, for a final note of epicene irony as they march arm-in-arm into the wings. The grace of this routine provides a droll counterpoint to all the backstage turbulence we've seen so far, and buries for good the notion that the Astaire who had dazzled two generations could ever be passé, even in the thoroughly modern 1950s.

"Louisiana Hayride" substitutes Nanette Fabray's belting energy for wit, but it's still the stylized hokum that could only happen in a Broadway production number. Here the set is specific, conjuring up a Dogpatch Arcadia just down the block from Finian's Rainbow. Downstage, soubrette Fabray does her human-choo-choo strut with all the ear-splitting pep that makes stars along Shubert Alley; behind her, a passel of hicks from Actors' Equity clamber up and down the flats with a rustic gusto perfected in the second bus-and-truck tour of Oklahoma! When Hollywood usually tried this, there'd be some faint stab at naturalism—real fake sunbeams thrown from the sound-stage heavens, a back-projection vista of cornfields and hayracks. The charm of "Louisiana Hayride" lies in its unabashed falseness, just as it would in the theater. Strobe lights and waving arms simulate a haycart moving beneath trees, in the kind of I-didn't-think-they-could-do-that stage illusion which always earns applause at the Majestic Theater; chorus kids sport jeans and gingham because it's time for a new showstopper, and April in Paris has been overdone this season.

Astaire, Fabray, and Buchanan then reunite for "Triplets," an authentic vaudevillian showstopper featuring Dietz' most deliriously tongue-twisting set of lyrics. From Easter Parade on, Astaire musicals tended to climax with a comic specialty featuring the star in some incongruous masquerade—tramping with Garland for "A Couple of Swells," as a kilted Scot opposite Ginger in The Barkleys of Broadway, or as a grubby prospector carousing with Betty Hutton in Let's Dance. Here he's one third of a trio of spit-curled brats in high chairs, bawling with sibling rage. It's another of Minnelli's black-and-white numbers, his stars in dainty caps and christening gowns on an ebony set spattered with kiddie graffiti. This time the color scheme has a practical function—to maintain the right pint-sized illusion, the three dance on their knees, their lower legs camouflaged in the same black as the painted floor of the set. Apparently this was one of The Band Wagon's most painful, unpleasant numbers to shoot, but you'd never know it from this trio's blithe capers through Minnelli's stage nursery. While exchanging blistering stares of playpen bad temper, they segue from mock Shirley Templeisms to a toy-soldier march and mutual foot (or knee) stomping. Like "That's Entertainment," "Triplets" is a seamless ensemble routine which makes merry at the expense of star exhibitionism—all three troupers are in perfect sync while pretending to violently upstage each other. As with The Pirate's "Be a Clown," Minnelli proves that slapstick can be elegant as well as funny; this is also one of those rare movie showstoppers that aims for cute and pulls it off.

The best number (or at least the biggest) is saved for the Broadway opening night. There's nothing in "The Girl Hunt" ballet that hadn't been tried some time before, either in New York or Hollywood. The idea of a gangster ballet was minted at least as early as 1936 with Balanchine's "Slaughter on Tenth Avenue" in the stage On Your Toes, and most recently reincarnated in the Freed Unit's 1948 Words and Music. The leaping low-lifes populating the 1950 stage smash, Guys and Dolls, were the triumph of Kidd's choreographic career to date; the chorus boys in fedoras who make life so tough on Astaire here are first cousins to the Broadway gamblers who stopped the show nightly with "Luck Be a Lady." Nor was this slangy idiom unfamiliar to The Band Wagon's stellar dance team. Two years earlier, Astaire went Tenth Avenue wiseguy in Royal Wedding, letting loose with Jane Powell in a Hell's Kitchen Apache routine entitled "How Could You Believe Me When I Said I Loved You When You Know I've Been a Liar All My Life." As for Charisse, the underworld became her like nobody else. Her dance cameo as the gunmoll/dominatrix who kicked Gene Kelly's heart around in the "Broadway Melody" sequence from Singin' in the Rain transformed Charisse from just another fine dancer—a kind of Ann Miller en pointe—to the movies' ultimate seductive split personality. When required to stand still and recite lines, Charisse is refined to the point of rigor mortis; but pour her into a red-spangled gown designed to expose Hollywood's longest and strongest gams, and she's the most hypnotic embodiment of wicked sex this side of James M. Cain.

Schizophrenia is what makes "The Girl Hunt" special, too. It chortles over the fevered lust and sadism of the Spillane school of pop lit., while gleefully mocking the somber, formal body language of ballet. Irony and sensuality wrestle to a draw in every frame of this number; moreover, for all its satirical good cheer, the mayhem of this eight-minute film noir in Technicolor is as insidiously unsettling as the darkest Bogart vehicle. Minnelli usually hints at the quicksand lurking beneath the shiny surfaces of his musicals; so trust him to confect a lyrical, funny production number about an inner-city dragnet for a pathological killer.

Unlike the *American in Paris* ballet, "The Girl Hunt" has a linear plot, but it's as impenetrable as *The Big Sleep*. While cynical detective Rod Riley prowls the city streets, a wide-eyed blonde (danced by Charisse in a wig) who is "scared as a turkey in November" tumbles into his arms out of nowhere. An explosion pulverizes the man who'd been stalking her, leaving three clues —a rag, a bone, and a hank of hair. Pursuing these clues, Riley goes to a salon de couture, where he's vamped by a brunette siren (Charisse again) and tussles with a band of thugs, escaping to pursue Mr. Big—a mysterious type in homburg and overcoat. On a subway platform, the blonde rematerializes and their reverie resumes, interrupted when a bullet meant for Riley snuffs out a passing gangster. Coming upon a masked woman in her bath he's clobbered unconscious; from there he ends up at Dem Bones Café, where he and the brunette perform an underworld fertility dance. A brawl erupts and Rod finally figures out who the killer is, as the hatted figure stalks him with pistol blazing. "It didn't matter anymore. Killers had to die," he spits while pumping bullets into the villain, who is none other than the platinum ingenue. At last he is back in the alley where he started, with the raven-haired tomato in tow. ''She was bad, she was dangerous. I wouldn't trust her any farther than I could throw her. But she was my kind of woman,'' mutters Riley as they saunter off arm-in-arm.

The advent of Spillane's terse, outrageous prose had pushed paperback detective thrillers a step further into decadence, and the genre was overripe for parody by the time The Band Wagon was released in 1953. ''The Girl Hunt'' tweaks the pulp worldview from every angle—the loneliness of the urban jungle, the stoic fatalism of the private-dick hero and his leering misogyny toward those curvy dames who are inevitably deadlier than the male. However, many of the number's sardonic in-references detonate closer to home. ''The Girl Hunt'' set is plastered with posters for a certain movie epic called ''The Proud Land''—the name of the fiasco that ruins Jonathan Shields' career in The Bad and the Beautiful. A bottle of nitroglycerine is ''The Girl Hunt's'' plot McGuffin, and three scenes climax in an explosion of white smoke—a wry use of those flashpots lying around backstage since that Faustian hallucination bombed in New Haven.

This is The Band Wagon's one number which takes poetic license with the unities of the stage. Although a few segments of ''The Girl Hunt'' could conceivably unfold within the confines of a proscenium, it's really constructed like a mini-melodrama in celluloid, with Astaire's voice-over narration in the Dick Powell–Robert Montgomery gunman movie manner hurtling the story through a succession of Oliver Smith cityscapes. (One especially impressive throwaway, on view for less than ten seconds, is a red fire escape stretching up into an infinity of blue sky.)

However, its central events simmer with a steamy, playful theatricality recalling the director's revue days of the 1930s. Rod Riley's visit to the fashion salon is an idiosyncratic Minnelli mix of grandeur, wit, and creepiness. The set is a wash of pink, gray, and sky-blue, dominated by one of Minnelli's forced-perspective louvered doorways. The patrons pose as stock-still mannequins, like the Toulouse-Lautrec café patrons in the American in Paris ballet; the models lunge at the camera like panthers, or those Parisian Furies who stalked Gene Kelly. This is the moment when Charisse comes at Astaire in sections—a siren whose serpentine arms bewitch him into deeper trouble. Riley follows her into the boutique storeroom for a quick smooch and instead becomes embroiled in the most flagrantly surreal moment of any Minnelli musical since Yolanda and the Thief.

The room is littered with the dismembered corpses of dressmakers' dummies camouflaging the live thugs who would dispatch Riley to private-eye heaven. He reaches for what he thinks is the brunette's hand, and it detaches in his grasp; she lures him farther inside, and what seems to be a decapitated plaster bust signals its henchmen to do their worst. Meat cleavers are the weapons of choice, one of which fortunately brains a dummy's head instead of Riley's own cranium. Minnelli often loved to pose his actors as human sculpture against real statues and defy the viewer to distinguish the difference; here he turns this penchant into black comedy Grand Guignol. With those lethal blades flying about, the usual Spillane equation of lust with death becomes another Minnelli hallucination in dance about the perils of castration, like the prelude to The Pirate's ''Mack the Black'' ballet.

This fusion of love and oblivion is kidded into exaltation with the turnstile pas de deux—the most deliciously contrapuntal vignette in any Minnelli musical. The set is the Times Square subway station; upstage, black-suited gangsters leap from the local to the express with their heaters blazing, a parody in dance of the underground shootout in Samuel Fuller's Pickup on South Street. As Astaire waits bewildered on the platform in the foreground, Charisse makes a perfect three-point landing at his feet, gliding from the wings on her knees like an urban Odile. ''There was something about this kid that made you want to protect her,'' he muses at this vision in the gauziest of white-for-ingenue gowns. Oblivious to the cartwheeling gang war behind them, Astaire and Charisse then embark on a duet of the most studied, solemn eroticism this side of ''L'Après-Midi d'une Faune.'' The soundtrack is a collage of gunshots and violins; chorus boy corpses twitch into rigor mortis and litter the stage, but the detective's too busy to conduct a body count now. He lifts the blonde ecstatically to her toes, then watches bedazzled while she plummets slowly downward in an exquisite, orgasmic split. Their final clinch is interrupted when a bullet propels one last mafioso to his death on the subway tracks in the orchestra pit—such are the perils of underworld romance. This indelible interlude is a pinnacle of sophisticated fun in the Minnelli–Freed canon, because it distills the essential idea of the MGM musical —its perilous balancing act between high culture and low entertainment—and does so with a dig in the ribs at its own chutzpah.

But it's the denouement in the gangland dive that people remember best, thanks to Charisse's cooch in scarlet. (This episode mesmerized the Legion of Decency as well; shocked by her brazen expanses of thigh in mesh stockings, it dubbed the film in toto ''Morally Objectionable in Part for All.'') Once again on the prowl for Astaire, this time her mood is staccato rather than adagio. Surrounded by Kidd's assortment of crouching hepcats she seems eight feet tall. Twirling the fringe of her slit dress, she pounds the floor with her killer stiletto heels; it's no wonder that when Astaire locks her in an embrace, one arm cinches her waist while the other grabs at a lethally outstretched leg. Astaire's own limbs are pretty potent weapons themselves, boffing the bad guys in the midst of an extended rumble. He saves his pistol for the climax, when Mr. Big lurches toward him with deadly intent. It's the blonde in drag, stripping it off in a last rictus of agony; with a glazed stare she revives for one last instant, using her dying breath to plant a kiss on his astonished mouth. Now that "all the rats and killers were in their holes" Riley can settle down with the dame he wouldn't trust any farther than he could throw; so the curtain falls on another Minnellian variation on an MGM happy ending—comic catharsis as a salve for intimations of real mortal pain.

Although the spotlight in "The Girl Hunt" seems to be on Charisse's vivid mime, it's Astaire's essence as a performer that sets the stage for her to shine. Early in the film, Cordova likens Hunter to a submerged iceberg, urging his star to show him "the whole eight-eighths!" When Hunter tries to humor him, the result is, intentionally, ludicrous; for all his extraordinary showmanship, reticence was always a fundamental part of Astaire's art. His instinctive restraint perfectly

mirrors Minnelli's impulse to hide turbulent feelings under a chipper façade. Several years later, Astaire made a much-publicized transition to non-dancing character star, but *The Band Wagon* contains the most expressive acting of his career. His touching moments come when anger and disappointment collide with his good manners: Hunter's quiet fury as Cordova and company thwart his talent ("I am not Nijinsky! I am not Marlon Brando!"); his nervous, run-on politesse on learning that Gaby might still succumb to her former Pygmalion. Astaire was never better cast than as this inarticulate master of his field, shy but stubborn, who wants nothing more than to keep that niche in the "world of entertainment" which is his haven from despair. It's a description that's just as apt for Minnelli. In the end, *The Band Wagon* triumphs by communicating that determination and excitement so vigorously to us civilians in the audience, its songs and dances tossed up on the screen like colors flung at a canvas. With this testament to the milieu which nourished his own life, Minnelli gives us the whole eight-eighths.

• •

1954   # BRIGADOON

The Band Wagon marked Minnelli's tenth anniversary as Arthur Freed's most prized director; less happily, it also signaled the end of an age of sustained creativity for the Freed Unit. Until now, the consistent success of these musicals had withstood all the tremors shaking Hollywood during the post-war years, but signs of retrenchment were everywhere; it was inevitable that some of that embattled atmosphere should infect the Freed Unit as well. Thanks to television, moviegoing was becoming an occasional pastime rather than a national addiction. As audiences evaporated and neighborhood theaters were converted into bowling alleys and supermarkets, by 1953 the studio system that made the MGM musical possible had also begun its slow fade to end credits. The days had passed when Freed could persuade the front office to sign fresh talent to long-term contracts. With an ever-shrinking production schedule, the studio opted to capitalize on the here and now rather than plan for an increasingly clouded future.

What really threatened the future of the movie musical had less to do with economics than with the pervasive air of retreat shrouding the genre itself. Freed and his ilk may have viewed themselves as the last defenders of class entertainment against the tide of rock-and-roll and the TV spectacular, but the style and novelty that made his films special faded in the wake

of Freed's growing urge to play it safe. Baffled by an ever-more-fickle public, Hollywood's musical specialists increasingly sought the security of pre-sold hits from the stage, to the detriment of their own Hollywood originals. Samuel Goldwyn and 20th Century-Fox led the trend, snaring the most prestigious New York properties of the decade before—*Guys and Dolls,* and a quartet of Rodgers-and-Hammerstein smashes. MGM soon found itself following their lead, picking up whatever was left; thus, of the six musicals Freed was yet to produce, four were adaptations of stage hits. (Ironically, in this the studio ignored the evidence of its own financial ledgers. The three most popular Metro musicals of the mid-to-late fifties—*Seven Brides for Seven Brothers, High Society,* and Freed's own *Gigi*— were all conceived for the screen.)

Brigadoon gave the first troubling evidence of this creative inertia, although at the time it seemed a perfectly logical pretext for regathering the clan that had made *An American in Paris* so notable. The third New York collaboration between Alan Jay Lerner and Frederick Loewe, this operetta in kilts was a surprise hit of the 1946-47 Broadway season. (Celtic whimsy was apparently all the rage—*Brigadoon*'s main rival for the public's affection that year was *Finian's Rainbow.*) Freed's esteem for Lerner made MGM's acquisition of the property a foregone conclusion. At his behest, the

Cyd Charisse and Gene Kelly,
"The Heather on the Hill,"
Brigadoon *(1954)*

studio had already bought Lerner and Loewe's previous and far less successful show, *The Day Before Spring,* although it never reached the screen. The purchase price for *Brigadoon* was a fairly steep $180,000, and in March 1951 MGM announced that Gene Kelly and Kathryn Grayson would head the cast of the movie version. Kelly's commitments, including his long European sojourn, meant that the studio's plans for *Brigadoon* stalled for over two years, by which point MGM's contract with its resident coloratura had lapsed. The studio then decided to cast a dancer opposite Kelly, and everyone's first choice was Moira Shearer, *The Red Shoes'* superlative star ballerina and herself a Scot. Freed tried hard to get her, but *Brigadoon's* unsettled production schedule made Shearer's employer, the Sadlers Wells Ballet Company, unwilling to commit for fear of jeopardizing its own forthcoming season. Having lost his ideal Fiona, Freed settled happily for Cyd Charisse.

No similar compromise marked Freed's choice of director—for this kind of romantic reverie, only Minnelli would do. Where to shoot *Brigadoon* was a tougher issue to resolve, and one which turned out to be just as crucial to the movie's fate. Minnelli and Kelly strenuously argued for using authentic Scottish locations as extensively as possible, to give a freshness and character to the highland atmosphere the stage version could only suggest. Early in 1953, the trade papers announced that Freed, Minnelli, and Kelly would start *Brigadoon* in Scotland early that autumn, with interiors to be filmed at MGM's English studio at Borehamwood. In March, preparations were made for Minnelli and Freed to travel from Culver City to the Highlands to scout locations, but the joint trip never materialized. That spring, the director was engrossed in preparations for *The Long, Long Trailer,* a comedy in the *Father of the Bride* vein for the same producer, Pandro Berman. So Freed went to Europe by himself to consult with Kelly, and was soon persuaded that the Scottish climate was too unreliable to guarantee a sensible shooting schedule. By the time he returned, he was determined to film *Brigadoon* entirely in California.

The *Brigadoon* company then hoped to compromise by substituting Big Sur for Scotland, but studio administrators vetoed that as well—to forestall further delays and cost overruns on an already expensive property, the film would have to be made on the MGM lot. After all, reasoned the brass, hadn't the technical wizards assigned to *An American in Paris* concocted a city more luminous than the capital itself? After that, the mists and heather of *Brigadoon* surely wouldn't overtax their powers. Minnelli was inclined to agree; he was used to this brand of hothouse stylization and, besides, improbable challenges like this whetted his imagination.

In the meantime, he flew from Los Angeles to New York to confer with Lerner on the script. Lerner's task was not particularly onerous; while following the usual

movie formula of expanding the dialogue and trimming the score, Lerner's screen *Brigadoon* was faithful to a flaw to his stage original. Although Freed sought to persuade Lerner and Loewe to compose a few added tunes for the film, nothing came of this. A more urgent problem was to tailor the balance of song and dance to suit the MGM cast. As with many of the ambitious stage musicals written in the shadow of Rodgers and Hammerstein, *Brigadoon's* principals were singers who couldn't move, complemented by a dance troupe barely required to speak. As pop arias alternated with Agnes de Mille ballets, they rarely shared the stage, brushing kilts in the wings and then again at the final curtain call. Presented with stars whose limbs were more gifted than their larynxes, Lerner trusted to God and Roger Edens that Kelly and Charisse's voice doubles would get through a fairly taxing score. Instead, he concentrated on finding ways to cue Tommy and Fiona's romance in a choreographic key, which freed Lerner from some of the stage libretto's arbitrary restrictions. Originally, the newly met lovers sang about "The Heather on the Hill," but were prevented from a'roamin' through it by a convenient offstage storm; Kelly and Charisse's ecstatic dash around the foothills is one of the movie's true highlights. Likewise, Kelly leaps into action for the climactic chase ballet, whereas the Broadway Tommy sidled impotently backstage for the duration.

Back at Culver City, Minnelli and Freed were busy filling the roster of *Brigadoon's* supporting cast. As Kelly's skeptical, bibulous chum, they considered Kelly's *Singin' in the Rain* co-star Donald O'Connor, Steve Allen, and Bill Hayes, the male lead in Rodgers and Hammerstein's then-current *Me and Juliet.* Instead, they chose Van Johnson, a Metro journeyman star for a decade, who surprisingly proved the movie's most spirited performer. Elaine Stewart, the briefly ascendant MGM starlet whose bitchery enlivened *The Bad and the Beautiful,* got fourth billing for a cameo at the end as Tommy's brittle fiancée. The much-admired American *premier danseur,* Hugh Laing, took a leave from the New York City Ballet for the pivotal role of Harry Beaton, a spurned suitor whose bitterness threatens to destroy Brigadoon forever. Ironically, by the time the final cut was spliced together, Beaton's was primarily an acting part, relying on Laing's melancholy voice and glowering good looks; as a choreographer, Kelly was not generous to other male dancers unless they were cast as his clownish lower-case pal. Albert Sharpe, late of Broadway's *Finian's Rainbow,* appeared as Fiona's father; Welsh character actor Barry Jones was imported to play Brigadoon's pontifical town sage. The only member of the original *Brigadoon* troupe cast in the film was Virginia Bosler as Fiona's sister Jean, whose wedding causes all the trouble.

Behind the scenes, Minnelli assembled the crew of artists who had made *An American in Paris* so beautiful

Van Johnson, Barry Jones, Gene Kelly, and Cyd Charisse, Brigadoon *(1954)*

—Irene Sharaff for the costumes, Preston Ames as art director, and George Gibson to realize the sets. Ames' game plan delighted his director—all of Brigadoon would be constructed on the same enormous sound stage, so that Minnelli's camera could wander uninterruptedly from the town square to the dells and foothills and back at will. Minnelli further decided that he wanted those heather-filled landscapes to look as realistic as possible. Compared to this, *An American in Paris'* outsized Impressionist variations were a snap. These sets would be on view for long stretches of the film, and Gibson's crew of set-painters were hard-pressed to simulate the texture of the great outdoors on artificially lit, one-dimensional cycloramas running the circumference of the sound stage.

By the time *Brigadoon* was ready for production in late 1953, there was no avoiding the technological fads sweeping the industry. *Brigadoon* was Minnelli's first film recorded and released with stereophonic sound; what concerned him more was that it would also be shot in CinemaScope whether he liked it or not. He complained that the traditional squarish proportions of the frame had been good enough for most painters and all filmmakers up to then, but in 1953, this was akin to a silent-film director of 1928 whining that talk would destroy the universal language of the screen—it was a vain argument, resolved by dollars rather than aesthetics. To complicate matters further, Minnelli was required to make the film simultaneously in two versions, one CinemaScope and another in a format MGM called Wide Screen, aimed for theaters not yet equipped to project the trumpeted new process. The

CinemaScope *Brigadoon* was also made in the recently developed Ansco Color, which was less expensive than Technicolor but also muddier in its tones. Fortunately, Minnelli was teamed on this frustrating enterprise with the skilled and adaptable Joseph Ruttenberg, a veteran cinematographer who was clearly a kindred spirit; he later collaborated with Minnelli on *Kismet* and *Gigi.*

In the face of so many imposed compromises, the fun had slowly gone out of this project by the time shooting began on December 9 1953. While no major mishaps ensued during the four months it took Minnelli to complete the film, the dispirited atmosphere hovering over *Brigadoon* never quite lifted. (And, being shut up on the same sound stage week after week hardly helped dispel the gloom in the gloaming.) It was increasingly clear that for the first time in their partnership, Minnelli and his principal star were simply not communicating. The version of *Brigadoon* unreeling in Kelly's mind was a kind of Highland western in dance. Meanwhile, Minnelli was busy exhorting Ames to fill the stage with acres of sumac dressed as heather, and Ruttenberg to light the interiors like Flemish genre paintings. Each accused the other of having lost faith in the material, and under the circumstances, both were probably right.

For Minnelli, the most memorable event of this period had nothing to do with *Brigadoon;* on February 18 (the same day *The Long, Long Trailer* opened at Radio City Music Hall), he married for the second time. His bride was a young woman from France named Georgette Magnani, in town as chaperone to a sister who'd won a beauty contest and a short-term movie contract.

The marriage lasted four years, producing one daughter named Christina Nina. Right after the wedding, it was back to that ruined cathedral on Stage 15 to shoot *Brigadoon*'s ill-omened nuptials. On March 20 1954, Minnelli closed production with the filming of "There But for You Go I," a Kelly–Charisse duet destined for the cutting-room floor. MGM's insistence on economy had succeeded in keeping *Brigadoon*'s cost to a reasonable $2.3 million; after two sneak previews in June, the film was ready for release. In September, the film premiered at Radio City Music Hall, the customary launching pad for Minnelli's movies, to a respectful but decidedly muted critical response. During its first-run release that fall, *Brigadoon* proved moderately popular, eventually grossing a million more than MGM spent to produce it, but not enough to offset what it cost to market and distribute the film. After a pair of hit Minnelli musicals, *Brigadoon* came as a distinct letdown for virtually everyone concerned. And in an act of pure studio one upsmanship, for once the Freed Unit was topped by a rival production team working a similar fake-outoorsy, dance-oriented vein; 1954's most widely acclaimed musical was *Seven Brides for Seven Brothers,* directed by Stanley Donen for producer Jack Cummings.

For unswerving fans of Minnelli and the MGM musical, *Brigadoon* is a movie that makes the occasionally glorious best out of frustratingly compromised circumstances. But it's nevertheless clear that, for the first time, Minnelli was stumped by the inability of his cast and technical crew to infuse magic into a story which defies both logic and enchantment. The most striking moments in the movie—the pre-dawn awakening of the town out of the mists of slumber, the convergence of the clans in the ruined cathedral—are sensuous, nearly abstract tableaux which sprang entirely from Minnelli's inventive eye, orchestrated while his stars and screenwriter were taking a breather in the commissary. Once the lights come up on Kelly gazing in wonderment at several dozen Central Casting Scots posed against CinemaScope-sized canvas landscapes, the spell breaks and the audience dreams of escape, just like poor, disgruntled Harry Beaton. Minnelli's musical fantasies of the 1940s had been as problematic as they were flamboyant, but at least their intentions were clear, and expressed in a consistent style sustained from credits to final fadeout. However, *Brigadoon*'s visual confusion and the clotted contradictions of its plot made this the most uneven movie in the entire Minnelli canon. Part of the problem lies in its locale, found on no map but which still evoked certain expectations in the audience. Since *The Pirate* and *Yolanda and the Thief* were set in some entirely mythical torrid zone somewhere south of Hollywood, Minnelli's blend of exotica and Metro myth created its own rules of plausibility. If Minnelli wanted the *lingua franca* of Patria and Judy Garland's Caribbean isle to be Califor-

nia English, or to drape their citizens in vaguely Third-Worldish raiment in Technicolor hues, only pedants would quibble—these were lovely places to visit, and nobody really lived there anyway.

But the painted-scrim Scotland erected on Metro's Stage 15 was too literal for wistful fancies, and less vivid than any one-reel travelogue. Once confined indoors, Minnelli ought to have indulged his bent for unrestrained artifice, and transformed his *Brigadoon* from a cramped approximation of the Highland retreat to a refuge as intangible as dew, and seductive because it resembled no place on earth. Instead, George Gibson's diorama looks like the world's biggest *nature morte;* distant lochs glint like silver cardboard, unseen clouds cast static shadows on a flat sea of heather.

It's a jolt to see this set fill with real mortals rather than Mme. Tussaud waxworks, until you realize that these people are as fake as their surroundings. Twittering with studied mirth, the extras are stock-company peasants—with a change of costume, they'd just as easily suit Metro's 1954 version of *The Student Prince* (and probably did). Sharaff makes sure the screen is a riot of plaids, but they turn up in the oddest configurations; one of Brigadoon's best-populated clans favors snug tights in tartans of flame and butterscotch, the last word in chorus-boy camp. Another illusion cracks as soon as the denizens of Brigadoon, allegedly sequestered for two centuries, speak in the multiple patois of a backlot Babel. Barry Jones is the most scrupulous stage Scot since Harry Lauder, while Cyd Charisse's burr waxes and wanes like the fog over Brigadoon. The offscreen choir gives out with the sturdy open vowels of the UCLA Men's Chorus; Jean's fiancé (Jimmy Thompson, late of *Singin' in the Rain*) orates like an Encino Jaycee toasting his pals at a stag dinner. *Brigadoon*'s vaunted stereo soundtrack only amplifies these and other incongruities—the booming massed voices have no discernible relation to the kilted swarms running across the huge screen, and the sound man's hypersensitive multiple tracks further expose the pinched noises made by the stars or their vocal doubles.

The aroma of greasepaint clings to most movie versions of Broadway musicals, but perversely, it's even more pungent here thanks to CinemaScope—the very gimmick meant to persuade the mid-fifties public that the movies were bigger and better than any other medium. In fact the long, narrow shape of the CinemaScope screen resembles the form of a huge stage proscenium, and its vastness threatened to throw the visual balance between performers and their surroundings back to theatrical proportions. For decades, the screen's concentration on the human face brought a front-row illusion to every part of the hall. CinemaScope took this democratic impulse even further—when the people on screen were dwarfed by these new, broadened panoramas, everyone in the audience was relegated to the same perch in the rear mezzanine.

Most early CinemaScope productions filled this frame with static horizontal tableaux, and about half of *Brigadoon* looks as if it should be taking place on the stage of Radio City Music Hall rather than on the screen suspended above it. Minnelli was a master of the expressive use of closeups, but there's not a single one in *Brigadoon,* for fear of surrounding one monster-sized head with acres of dead space. The longer dialogue scenes play like the arid patches in a 1929 talkie. The actors pose in rows, feeding each other lines while the cinematographer puts brakes on his boom and the film editor plays solitaire; 'Scope technicians had decreed that on such a gargantuan canvas too much motion or internal cutting within a scene would frazzle the eye. Minnelli ignored their advice much of the time, but early in the film "I'll Come Home to Bonnie Jean" is a textbook example of the newly strait-jacketed, "correct" way to shoot a big production number. As stars Kelly and Johnson pose at dead center, a phalanx of male dancers line up the length of the screen; when Johnny Green's orchestra surges to a frenzy in the final choruses, they leap right and left to disappear briefly into the wings off camera, rematerializing on cue with kilts still swirling. This is an operetta showstopper exactly as the Shuberts would have done it, if they'd only had Arthur Freed's bankroll.

It's not surprising that Minnelli's dullest direction intersects with the most stilted passages in Lerner's text. When the villagers arise for their once-a-century spree, the camera goes to sleep as American tourists Tommy and Jeff settle down for a cozy chat over their maps. As we make their acquaintance, Lerner ladles out big dollops of psychological exposition, positing Jeff's sodden cynicism against sensitive Tommy's despair over the anomie of modern life. "You don't believe in anything, do you?" queries Tommy, which his pal parries with his faith in the tangible "things I can touch, taste, hear, see, smell and swallow." Tommy is looking for something more, although he doubts that love in a Scarsdale split-level is it: "Sometimes I think I'm really not capable of loving," he sighs. "Sometimes I think nobody is any more." As this passage tells us of Tommy's longings for the peace of a netherworld like Brigadoon, Minnelli has no choice but to settle down quietly so we can attend to every spurious word; however, he has placed Kelly and Johnson so far from each other that they'd need megaphones to throw their cues. CinemaScope gives Minnelli the dubious opportunity to upstage his actors with colorful bits of decor, should he (or we) get bored with what they're saying. In this case, it's a huge emerald-hued fern rooted smack in the right foreground, and the most photogenic object in Minnelli's static frame.

No flora intrudes to distract us from the key moment when Tommy learns the secret—or as Lerner's mouthpiece Mr. Lundie puts it, the "miracle"—of Brigadoon. While succumbing to the spell of village maiden Fiona,

the hero spends several reels puzzling over the archaic ways of all those quaint folk around MacConnachy Square; he's particularly baffled by that page in the Campbell family Bible which notes Fiona's birthdate as 1732. Since the town by-laws prohibit Fiona from clearing up the mystery, she delivers Tommy and Jeff to the garrulous schoolteacher for a history lesson. Reclining before the art department's phoniest Highland backdrop, they sit stunned at Lundie's feet to hear this yarn. Minnelli seems dumbstruck too, for this is arguably the archest tableau found in any of his movies.

It seems that in the 18th century, the area was plagued by witches, "horrible, destructive women," who were luring the locals away from the Lord to partake in their pagan ways. So incensed was Brigadoon's wise old minister, Mr. Forsythe, that he implored God for a brainwave to protect his flock from evil, now and forever. Suddenly inspiration struck—why not consign Brigadoon to an eternal coma, from which it could emerge but one day each century? This way his people would retain their toehold on mortality, without tarrying long enough to be corrupted by the terrible world outside. There was one catch in this "contract with God"; if any citizen of Brigadoon dared escape its precincts, the whole place would be cast into everlasting oblivion. The Lord obviously approved, as the plan took effect at once, and for this great favor the minister agreed to pay with his own life.

Luckily, the audiences were too soothed by the velvet cadences of Barry Jones' oratory to pay heed to its meaning, for these are curious words indeed from the pen of a worldly sinner like Alan Jay Lerner. From this moment on *Brigadoon*'s spell, and the motives of its characters, disintegrate for good. This yarn's frail logic is the least of its weirdness; after all, moviegoers were weaned on maxims like Mr. Lundie's "When you love someone enough anything is possible, even miracles." However, its implications are appalling enough to transform *Brigadoon* into a closet horror film. Quite apart from the implications of Lundie's outrage at wanton harpies undermining Scottish morale, this story is an evangelist zealot's vision of bliss. Disdaining all notions of free will, the sweet old man has turned his parish into the valley of the living dead—better limbo on earth than the hypothetical possibility of sin.

What's really disquieting is that nobody in the world of this movie ever questions the generosity of this gesture. The two outsiders are skeptical, but awed; Cyd Charisse's look of wide-eyed blankness here conveys Fiona's wonder at it all. Only love-starved Harry Beaton dares challenge his fate, and he's dismissed as a deranged malcontent. When Beaton is struck down by a misaimed bullet from Jeff's rifle, his father has no tender words to utter over his corpse; all he can mutter is "How could ye be so ungrateful. I'm so ashamed of ye!" With him gone, they're all a race of contented zombies, happy to pace their little acre until a century's

Jimmy Thompson (center) and George Chakiris (at his right) lead the wedding procession in Brigadoon *(1954)*

darkness descends and they can once again crawl under their coverlets for the sleep of the righteous. The only sensible ending would have found Tommy spiriting his beloved away from this pretty purgatory, rather than parting the clouds to join her in slumber.

While the result might have been more interesting, it was not Minnelli's job to examine this script too closely—that would have sabotaged the whole enterprise. From *The Band Wagon* through *Lust for Life, Some Came Running* and *Two Weeks in Another Town,* many of Minnelli's heroes are displaced wanderers like Tommy, ill at ease within their own skin and suspicious of the alien worlds they pass through. At least melodrama gave him some latitude for candor, allowing him to ponder the possibility that, sometimes, there is no balm for the disillusioned. The upbeat rules of the Metro musical are, however, much more circumscribed. In *The Band Wagon,* Minnelli found a persuasive way to reconcile the introverted hero to himself, but here the best he can do is play out the plot to its would-be plaintive fadeout and hope for the best.

So Minnelli obligingly imagines Brigadoon as a heavenly refuge, instead of a dead end engineered by an authoritarian preacher for its inmates' own good. Nevertheless, the design scheme conspires to reinforce this claustrophobic mood. You always know what the outer limits of this dreamland are—they're marked by painted walls looming over the cheerful natives and the two Yanks who wandered haplessly inside. At times, the set literally blocks the path for Minnelli's hemmed-in performers. When a love-smitten Kelly takes a tumble down a papier-mâché hill, the camera

cuts away just before he brains himself on the back wall of the sound stage. In a valiant attempt to reproduce the atmospheric conditions of a real Scottish valley, Stage 15 basks in the gray, shadowless light of a damp terrarium, which only adds to the gloom.

Under these oppressive circumstances, *Brigadoon*'s romantic leads can't be entirely blamed for fumbling the movie's intended spirit. Even an actress more seasoned than Charisse would have been thrown by an ethereal vacuum like Fiona. (At least Moira Shearer wouldn't have had to struggle so with the dialect.) As usual, when not dancing Charisse relies on her air of corseted gentility to do the work, and even in repose she carries herself like the supreme movie ballerina she is. According to the hero, Fiona possesses a guileless warmth extinct in the neon wilderness, but the imperious thrust of Charisse's chin and shoulders defies that notion—she's the kind of girl you trek to the big city hoping to find. To gloss over this mismatch of her limitations with an impossible role, she's used instead as that beautiful, malleable creature, the languorous Minnellian diva. For Act I he drapes her in a buttercup-yellow shawl, replaced in Act II by a gown in Minnelli's own cherry-red. When she moons over the lifemate she's yet to meet, Minnelli rapturously frames Charisse at her windowpane, just as he did with Judy Garland in *Meet Me in St. Louis;* as soon as the strains of a Loewe melody stir her to dance, his camera glides in to accentuate the poetry of her movements. Charisse may not be the ideal Scottish ingenue, but at least Minnelli makes sure her star quality retains its luster.

As *Brigadoon*'s choreographer and an occasional director himself, Kelly was not so pliable. This project would never have been made without him, but its dour whimsy and the star's apparent creative fatigue at this point made for listless movie chemistry. It was hardly fair to expect him to scrape the moss off lines like "There's something about this forest that gives me the feeling of being in a cathedral"; Kelly's brand of lyricism lies in movement, not words. Unfortunately, he fails to bring much conviction to anything else in the film either, his dances included. Kelly turns *Brigadoon*'s hero into a disjointed collage of freeze-frames snipped from his last few movies—Kelly the happy-go-lucky soft-shoe artist of, say, *Summer Stock;* Kelly the mournful lover of *An American in Paris.* His fits of glumness are meant to express Tommy's identity crisis, but what they really convey is the star's slow burn over the way this whole enterprise has gone sour. To snap out of it, in *Brigadoon*'s moments of emotional *extremis* Kelly overcompensates wildly. Thus, if Tommy can't help declaring his love as night falls on Brigadoon, the tears in Kelly's throat constrict his voice from scratchy tenor to throbbing falsetto.

The antic bliss of his solo to "Almost Like Being in Love" is the film's most egregious musical moment. Out of nowhere, he's the Yank boulevardier of *An American in the Rain* up to all of his old tricks. The scenario is familiar enough—Kelly's in love, and he can't help sharing the feeling. So he scampers boyishly over several hundred feet of scenery, his hat shoved with millimeter precision to just the right rakish angle on his brow, his face split by that patented irresistible grin. As there are no ancient French women to flirt with this time, he settles for a pair of long-haired oxen. The frantic cuteness of this star turn is amplified by the strain on Kelly's vocal chords, painfully overpowered by the arching melodic line of the Lerner–Loewe song. In this instance, Minnelli only encourages invidious comparisons to past Kelly showstoppers by reconstructing his own mise-en-scène from *An American in Paris'* "S'Wonderful" within a CinemaScope frame— the camera pulls back from Kelly belting out his joy from the middle distance to his wonderstruck pal posed in the left foreground. Derivative on its own terms, this number shows that Kelly's heart is about as far from the Highlands as it can get. He's the kind of pushy interloper old Mr. Forsythe was trying to ward off in the first place.

While Kelly was credited as the movie's sole choreographer, certain numbers explicitly evoke the style of Agnes de Mille, who'd staged the dances on Broadway—particularly Cyd Charisse's wry minuet with her girlfriends to "Waiting for My Dearie," the kind of coy courtship mime de Mille first coined for *Oklahoma!*'s "Many a New Day." The most exciting production number is the wedding celebration in the ruined cathedral, the only musical sequence which actually propels the story, it is quite unlike anything Kelly had ever done before. As orchestrator Conrad Salinger's bagpipe-and-woodwind reprise of "I'll Go Home with Bonnie Jean" is gradually invaded by martial drums, a graceful nuptial pledge between the bride, groom, and a surprisingly agile Mr. Lundie erupts into a general revel. A virile mass Highland fling is interrupted by the women, who merge into the swirling circles of an accelerating Scottish reel. As the momentum rises, Minnelli abandons his place at stage center, soaring aloft to admire the blurred patterns of plaid coloring the rough cathedral floor. Kelly's ever-accelerating tempos hint at unseen danger, and Minnelli comes in closer for a better look, his glance darting restlessly as the dancers whirl into a greater frenzy. Beaton then bursts into the throng to grapple with Jean, and the party dissolves with a sickening silence. Framed by the smoky dark of a sound-stage night, this rout briefly fulfills the promise of moody enchantment *Brigadoon* elsewhere lacks.

Brigadoon features two duets for Kelly and Charisse that also find the director and his star/choreographer on compatible wavelengths. "The Heather on the Hill" is *Brigadoon*'s one frequently anthologized moment, less for the sensuality of the dance than for the sinuous way Minnelli incorporates it into his own sense of movie space. With this number, he stops genuflecting to the unwieldy proportions of the CinemaScope screen and exploits its vastness for his own ends. As the majesty of moor and hillside is the catalyst for this romance, Minnelli turns Tommy and Fiona into leaping figures in an ever-shifting landscape, racing alongside them as they climb from grove to clearing, suddenly pulling backward to revel in the panoramic view. Unlike Kelly's "Almost Like Being in Love" routine, every step the dancers take is shaped by the contours of the set. The maze of earth-colored rises and dips is an invigorating playground, just made for a flirtatious game of hide-and-seek. In an echo of *An American in Paris'* mating dance at the fountain, Kelly and partner become sculpted extensions of their surroundings, draping themselves about the gnarled trunk of a birch tree. Still, Minnelli's paean to nature-as-aphrodisiac is diluted by the fiberglass-and-canvas quality of the set, which no wind machines can stir to life; Tommy and Fiona may pretend they're transported by the perfume of hay and heather, but we're not so easily persuaded.

Reels later, after the hunt for Harry Beaton, "The Heather on the Hill" is reprised inside the darkened cathedral. This time the mood is more urgently erotic; Charisse languishes with longing as Kelly ardently supports her, his dark-clad body merging with the shadows around them. Just as *An American in Paris* celebrated the post-Impressionists, when night invades Brigadoon Minnelli conjures up the seductively gloomy palette of early 19th-century Romanticism. Pagan nature engulfs the remnants of a decayed civilization, and as Charisse wanders through these crumbling Gothic arches, she too is less flesh than metaphor —in her voluminous shroud-like gown, she is a phantom flickering red in a charcoal fog.

Like the Romantics, Minnelli is intoxicated with the night, which frees instincts too perilous to contemplate in the glare of day. If lighthearted movies such as *Meet Me in St. Louis* and *Father of the Bride* turn unexpectedly somber once darkness falls on the suburbs, *Brigadoon* is the perfect occasion to explore this premise as deeply as the script permits. Minnelli daubs the screen with pinpoints of light amid bands of shadow, and sometimes the effect is sumptuously pictorial. Just before Brigadoon awakens, birds flutter around a vaulted stone bridge backlit by a golden haze; an ox blinks as a spotlight sunbeam penetrates the murk, and thickets of naked branches rustle in a swirling fog. When dusk descends just before the wedding, a distant band of merrymakers streams past a raked-perspective background of looming clouds and cliffs. But Beaton flees toward death in a landscape pitched in darkness, and abruptly Minnelli's pastoral sketches bristle with a primitive intensity. Suddenly, the wedding party has been transformed into a vengeful band of barechested hunters snaking through the underbrush. This gives a strangely homoerotic undercurrent to the chase; implicitly, Harry's rebellion has stirred some unseemly feelings in the heretofore tranquil souls of Brigadoon. As they all scatter from the village, the camera dashes nervously past torchlit brooks and thickets of bramble like an animal jolted from sleep. When a rifle blasts offscreen, Minnelli makes a startling cut to a stag rearing up in terror, but the victim turns out to be Harry, another cornered forest creature felled from his perch in a tree. In the theater, this episode triggered an extended de Mille ballet, but the formality of dance can't convey the primal tension Minnelli is after here. While his shots are orchestrated to the offscreen chorus urging the hunters toward their prey, he discards the moviemusical idiom for a more visceral kind of filmmaking. In fact, this scene points the way to the melodramas which increasingly occupied Minnelli over the next few years. It is a rough sketch for the virtuoso race through the wilderness of *Home from the Hill,* in which the hero confronts death and tests his manhood.

One of *Brigadoon*'s crucial problems is that Minnelli is something of a pagan too; his spirits only soar whenever he breaks out of Lerner's pious little paradise. Tommy's abortive return to New York is the pretext for

a favorite bit of Minnelli anthropology—cocktail hour among the civilized savages. In movies as disparate as *Undercurrent* and *Madame Bovary, Gigi* and *Two Weeks in Another Town*, the premise is the same. Preening glamour girls and their hypertensive escorts make their predatory way through a room filled with giggling prattle, and stranded somewhere in a corner is the mute Minnelli protagonist whose isolation is further buffeted by the waves of hysterical cacophony lapping at his ears.

This time, advertising executives and ladies-wholunch shriek of alimony and psychoanalysis, and Tommy's head fills with Fiona's (dubbed) voice while his New York betrothed guzzles Old-Fashioneds, dishes her friends, and rhapsodizes about their dream house in the outer suburbs. Tommy can't stand the tumult and hypocrisy of it all, but Minnelli is too amused by the scene to share his disgust. In fact, it's a positive tonic after the leaden peace of Brigadoon. These people may be soulless but at least they're alive. Minnelli is far better equipped to instruct his extras in the bad party manners of the martini class than the rustic ways of some eccentric Calvinist sect. For all the delicacy of the movie's final images, the hero's retreat into the void comes as a pale anticlimax.

After the effort that went into *Brigadoon,* its relative failure cast a shadow on Minnelli as well. Now fifty years old and halfway through his active career at MGM, he began to reexamine the assumptions that had sustained his work thus far. The dance-oriented musical had clearly reached an impasse, and *Brigadoon* was the last he ever made. It was time for Minnelli himself to venture out of the enchanted village of Culver City before the magic faded completely, and he found himself wandering alone through its haunted ruins. The repertoire of tricks locked up in the studio art department no longer piqued Minnelli's sensibility, and henceforth he resorted to them only under duress. If MGM could no longer counterfeit all corners of the globe, then he'd have to cart along the accoutrements of Hollywood to capture the world outside. In subsequent years this epitome of the studio-bound filmmaker became Hollywood's best-traveled director, searching everywhere for the right places to match the indelible vistas he carried about with him in his head. In time, Minnelli resembled one of those restless wanderers out of his own movies, less concerned about the journey's end than the paralysis lying in wait if he tarried too long back home.

OPPOSITE:
Vic Damone (center, on horse), "Night of My Nights," Kismet (1955)

· ·

1955 KISMET

M innelli's next announced project seemed an ominous echo of *Brigadoon:* W. H. Hudson's *Green Mansions,* another romance set in a supernatural forest, screenplay courtesy of Alan Jay Lerner, under the aegis of Arthur Freed. This time Minnelli was adamant—it had to be shot on location, and he would search out the perfect setting for Rima, the evanescent Bird-Girl of Hudson's Edwardian pipe dream. In June 1954, Minnelli set out on his first trip abroad on the MGM expense account. A studio memo written before his departure spelled out an extensive itinerary including stops in Mexico, Cuba, British Guiana, and Peru, but Minnelli spent most of his time exploring the jungles of Venezuela in the company of Preston Ames, who had preceded him to South America. While the discomforts of the journey may have brought back wistful memories of the antiseptic greenery he'd left behind on Stage 15, Minnelli was entranced by the vibrant colors of the rain forest and brought back several reels of raw footage for future reference once production began. Back in Hollywood, Minnelli and Lerner set to work looking for the spine of this elusive story about a white man's love for a sylvan sprite possessed of eternal

youth. Meanwhile Heitor Villa-Lobos, the distinguished Brazilian composer, was approached to compose an orchestral score synthesizing the rhythms of tropical birdsong. From the beginning it was obvious that part of the picture would have to be shot at the studio. In September, Freed suggested that Minnelli try out his ideas in an elaborate filmed run-through which would also serve as an audition for Pier Angeli, who longed to play the lead. Edmund Purdom, a stolid male-ingenue under contract to the studio, was to play opposite her, and Minnelli ordered his set decorators to drape cascades of rubber-cement spiderwebs on all those branches left over from the *Brigadoon* set. This mini-spectacle took two weeks and $130,000 to shoot, with the final production slated to start in 1955.

As it happened, neither the test nor Lerner's script were persuasive enough to convince Freed that this fable would translate into mass entertainment. By the end of the year, both scenarist and director were on to other things. Lerner had the forthcoming *My Fair Lady* to think about, while Minnelli started work on a movie as removed from Rima's domain as possible: a mental-asylum melodrama with a *Grand Hotel* cast, entitled *The*

Cobweb. It was just as well—with avian gibberish looped in for all those Scottish burrs, *Green Mansions* threatened to out-whimsy *Brigadoon.* A few years later, rival MGM producer Pandro Berman dusted it off and commissioned a new script, which was filmed with Audrey Hepburn under the direction of her then-husband Mel Ferrer. On its release in 1960, this proved one of the few unalloyed fiascos of her career.

However, Freed had another property he was determined to make, and dispatched it for Minnelli's perusal as soon as *The Cobweb* was in the can. It was *Kismet,* which had already enjoyed an astonishingly long life for such a creaky Arabian Nights pastiche. The original dramatic version, by English playwright Edward Knobloch, had dazzled credulous theatergoers on both sides of the Atlantic just before World War I. Its barnstorming star, Otis Skinner, became indelibly associated with the part of Hajj, wily poet of the Baghdad souks; he starred twice in *Kismet,* once in a 1920 silent movie version and then in an early talkie ten years later. In 1944 MGM concocted a lavish remake as a vehicle for Ronald Colman, adding for extra oomph a cooch-dancing Marlene Dietrich as the sultan's mistress. Nine years later *Kismet* became a stage musical composed, after a fashion, by the team of Robert Forrest and George Wright. They were Metro alumni who'd made their careers giving an updated pop varnish to the musical chestnuts of the past. In the thirties, they'd refurbished the scores of various faded operettas for the Depression-age fans of MacDonald and Eddy; in the forties, Forrest and Wright scored their first Broadway success with *Song of Norway,* a medley of Edvard Grieg's greatest hits. This time they decided that the Asiatic strains of Aleksandr Borodin were as close a match to Knobloch's Baghdad as they could get. After a Los Angeles tryout, this umpteenth *Kismet* opened on Broadway late in 1953 under a benign star; in the main, critics thought it was elephantine kitsch, but a newspaper strike prevented the word from reaching ticket-buyers. Its principal assets were acres of tinselly sets and a magnetic star turn by Alfred Drake, as well as a score that people could hum on their way into the theater. Such streamlined Borodiniana as "Stranger in Paradise" and "Baubles, Bangles and Beads" soon flooded the airwaves, and the show ran for two Broadway seasons.

MGM paid $150,000 to obtain the show for Freed, who, as with *Brigadoon,* entrusted the screen adaptation to its stage creators, hiring Charles Lederer and Luther Davis to rework their own musical libretto. Freed counted on the Minnelli touch from the beginning. After all, when it came to those "peacocks and monkeys in purple adornings" described in Forrest's lyric, who better to hustle them about than his pet director? To his astonishment, Minnelli emphatically declined; he'd seen the show, and found it corny and witless. Besides, by early 1955 he was already deep in preproduction work on *Lust for Life,* a film he was desperately eager to make. But Freed persevered and for the first time in their collaboration went over his head, to production chief Dore Schary. Schary offered Minnelli a genteel form of blackmail—*Lust for Life* would proceed as scheduled, but only after he'd finished *Kismet* for Freed.

Minnelli had no choice. He was determined to shoot *Lust for Life*'s exteriors in the actual places Van Gogh lived and worked; this meant the wheat fields and vineyards of Provence had to be filmed that summer before they were harvested. With *Kismet* not scheduled to start production until late spring, Minnelli would have to direct this musical spectacle in half the usual time. Thus he embarked on the most punishing work schedule he'd faced since *An American in Paris*—planning two films simultaneously and then shooting them back-to-back on two continents with just enough time in between for a long snooze on the plane.

When Freed could distract him from conferences with *Lust for Life* producer, John Houseman, Minnelli sped through the necessary arrangements for *Kismet.* To cast the leads they relied entirely on Metro contract players, 1955 being virtually the last time this would be possible. The stalwart, adaptable baritone Howard Keel, already the movies' specialist in Alfred Drake parts, was the inevitable choice for Hajj. The one time Dietrich role of the ever-horizontal Lalume went to Dolores Gray, singing voluptuary of Broadway and the West End, who'd won her short-term deal with the studio thanks to a test directed by Minnelli. First love was represented by the young Caliph and Hajj's comely daughter Marsinah, played respectively by pop balladeer Vic Damone and Ann Blyth, then being groomed as MGM's next and last Kathryn Grayson. The *Kismet* team's first choice to play the comic villain was Robert Morley, but when he declined, Sebastian Cabot filled the Wazir's ample harem pants instead.

The production troupe was filled with people who understood Minnelli's methods and caprices—Preston Ames for the sets, Adrienne Fazan as editor, and as cinematographer, Joseph Ruttenberg, who first had to fly to Arles to catch the orchards in spring blossom for *Lust for Life.* Meanwhile, somebody had to be found to design *Kismet*'s hundreds of costumes in correct Hollywood-oasis style. Minnelli was relieved when this chore was farmed off to Tony Duquette, the sculptor-decorator whose taste perfectly complemented his own. Jack Cole, like Minnelli an alumnus of the Radio City Music Hall stage shows of the thirties, had choreographed the Broadway *Kismet,* and was brought on to repeat this task for the screen version. Cole was known for his short fuse and scathing tongue, but apparently there were no major eruptions between him and his director. Two years later he'd stage Dolores Gray's numbers in *Designing Woman* and play a large supporting part into the bargain.

Howard Keel (right) sings of "Fate" in a Baghdad market, Kismet *(1955)*

Kismet started shooting on May 23 1955 and closed production a scant two months later. It was all too reminiscent of those frantic Music Hall days Minnelli thought he'd escaped for good twenty years before. Once more he was the hired hand drafted to concoct glitzy tableaux out of shoddy stuff in next to no time. As always, Minnelli's pride in his professionalism saw him through, but he couldn't entirely hide his disdain for the assignment. Usually so meticulous in working out every camera composition, this time he printed first and second takes whenever possible before racing on to the next setup. He was too busy worrying about his timetable to pay much attention to the actors, but most of them were too worn out by the pace to care. Four days before *Kismet* was finished, an exhausted Minnelli flew to London to join Houseman, who'd already spent several weeks in Europe scouting locations and casting possibilities for Minnelli's approval. Freed snared Stanley Donen to take care of the unfinished parts of *Kismet,* including the retakes scheduled for August. (Judging by notes on the production schedule in the studio's legal files, the Keel–Gray harem number "Rahadlakum" was probably shot by Donen.)

The final budget was estimated at $2,751,000—a lavish amount considering that the payroll for the principal cast members came to only ten percent of this total. The studio held two sneaks of the picture in September and October, to a moderately enthusiastic response. One preview card gushed, "This is as good as Lana Turner's pictures!"—as accurate an assessment as any. It premiered as the CinemaScope accompaniment to Radio City Music Hall's annual Nativity Pag-

eant, giving the patrons a double dose of dromedaries that year. The movie won a surprisingly cordial reception from the New York press, but once *Kismet* went into general release, the public proved less indulgent. In the end, box office receipts barely exceeded production costs, resulting in a considerable distribution loss for the studio. Minnelli was usually sensitive to such matters, realizing that the high esteem he enjoyed from his employers depended as much on his movies' profits as on their prestige. This time, however, he didn't much care—*Kismet*'s losses only vindicated his loathing for the project.

Of all the harem-and-minaret bombs in the desert Hollywood ever made, *Kismet* is the hardest to take. At least the Maria Montez movies had a kind of brain-dead innocence—they peddled their shoddy Saturday-matinee attractions with gusto, and besides, scheming against sultans was about the classiest calling you could aspire to on the Universal backlot in the 1940s. It was a different matter for the Caliph of the Freed Unit in 1955. Minnelli felt sullied amid all these déclassé souks and seraglios, and the best he could do was to fling a bolt of yellow silk across the screen every so often to brighten up his temporary exile.

As *Kismet*'s presumed audiences are those frustrated folks who missed the show, he gives them just what they'd expect—a celluloid stage play. Actors stride in from the sidelines to sound-stage center and recite that mock-Arabian syntax with the stiffness it deserves; musical numbers end with Dolores Gray or Jack Cole's showgirls in poses of triumph, as if waiting for the applause to die down in the balcony. Undemanding fans of the genre's free-form exotica get what they want too. The geography of movies like *Kismet* is anywhere-but-here, so Minnelli turns his set into the U.N. Security Council at a charity masquerade. In the Baghdad bazaar, Asiatic fishmongers and black pearl vendors jostle with Chicano Levantines, and Cole's choreography for the concubines is a couscous of Bali, Siam, Port Said, and the Copacabana. But Duquette's high-intensity mixed metaphors outdid them all. Ann Blyth's saris (in yellow or red, of course) and Dolores Gray's Turkish-delight lamé hostess frocks don't belong on the same subcontinent, but the CinemaScope screen is wide enough to encompass them both. He really goes wild with the men's millinery—the palace retinue sports mushroom-cloud turbans, swirls of brass tubing or inverted oil funnels, according to their rank. Vic Damone shrinks painfully inside the billowing folds of his lime-and-white prince-of-the-realm ensemble, which in a different century on the opposite sex would be perfect for cocktails at the Colony.

If Minnelli is trying to amuse anybody, it's the handful of subversive aesthetes in the audience who thinks all this is as dopey as he does. Thus we notice that Marsinah's perfumed garden is landscaped with fluorescent jungle gargantua obviously radioactive or (preferably) carnivorous. While Blyth and Damone sing to each other from opposite ends of the set, Minnelli blocks their view with a white peacock on a perch, trying to sleep despite the interference. To reach their marks for the second chorus, the young lovers must scurry down the garden path behind the star of this scene, who by now has been goosed by some flunky into filling the screen with his spread tailfeathers.

Much of *Kismet* is too garish to be anything but willed sabotage on Minnelli's part. It's as though he wanted to fling his abilities right back in the faces of the people who got him into this. While Ann Blyth tries on her "Baubles, Bangles and Beads" in the merchants' square, Minnelli amuses himself by tossing together enough fuchsia, tomato, and acid-green tints to sicken stronger stomachs than Cedric Gibbons'. Half the movie takes place in the Wazir's throne room, with panels of gold tortured into barbed-wire formations to accent walls of rubber molten-rock the color of lead or dried blood, depending on the light. No wonder poor Ann Blyth starts weeping whenever anyone drags her into the place.

Distracted by feathered fowl and headgear, Minnelli doesn't bother propping up those cast members who can't withstand the competition. In any case, Blyth's plastic poise seems impervious to direction, while Damone is simply hopeless. The one emotion he manages to register is damp terror, whenever the camera comes too close, and princely commands like, "Arise my subjects," are mumbled with all the authority of a parking attendant. A shooting schedule as abbreviated as *Kismet*'s called for Darwinian measures, but Minnelli

showed his respect for the two stars, who had both the assurance and irony to transcend these surroundings.

With his virility and wit, Howard Keel demonstrates once again why he was the MGM musical's most likable male singer until the genre collapsed under him. In addition to his warm baritone, Keel could execute a backward somersault with dash and reel off polysyllabic repartee with spirit, while managing to look good in a beard and sherbet-colored costumes—all essential attributes for playing this beggar turned plutocrat by a twist of destiny. As for Dolores Gray, she treats *Kismet*'s Mesopotamia as a place slightly west of the Persian Room at the Plaza—which is fine with Minnelli, who'd rather be there himself. Her "Not Since Nineveh" is a discordant blast of Broadway under the blazing sun of this ersatz Near East, but Gray's clarion mezzo and nitery snake-charmer stance make you grateful for the intrusion. As she later confirmed in *Designing Woman*, Gray's comic specialty was playing exasperated dames who never dropped their best party manner. She says devastating things in an insinuating velvet hush, extracting the maximum from Lalume's rather threadbare innuendo. Minnelli clearly warms to this and showcases it with those characteristic flourishes *Kismet* otherwise lacks. The movie's opening number, "Fate," finds Keel atop a pedestal dividing transcendence from mortal desperation—tall dervishes whirl serenely behind him and a ragged horde seethes below, stuck in that human gridlock of a typical Minnelli streetscape. His camera becomes a sort of dervish for Lalume's languid mock-ballad "Bored," creeping on cat feet around Gray as she slithers over a recumbent Keel in a sudden burst of blue-white light. There's not a moment of real vitality in *Kismet*, but at least Keel and Gray's sheer pleasure in performing gives it a few jolts of showmanship.

Just once, in the dusk of the Caliph's nuptial "Night of My Nights," Minnelli offers up the spangled spectacle Freed hoped would saturate every frame of *Kismet*. Mirrored in a sable-dark reflecting pool, white steeds and courtiers in pastel silks parade across the CinemaScope screen bearing a cornucopia of Duquette's swankiest accessories—sparklers and canopies and temple altars. The scene is a direct descendant of the costume parades Minnelli had perfected in his earliest professional years, from Marshall Field's display windows to the "Scheherazade Suite" which marked his first art-direction assignment at Radio City Music Hall. Nobody could beat Minnelli at this arcane specialty, but he was weary of proving it with yet another tableau expressive of nothing except his art-history background and innate visual flair. Paradoxically, *Kismet* is both an unmistakable Minnelli artifact and one of the least personal films he ever made. Strokes from his calligraphic scrapbook spatter the screen like graffiti, but his real signature is nowhere to be seen.

· ·

1958 # GIGI

Gigi, the film for which Minnelli was most widely acclaimed during his lifetime, is a work of extraordinary contradictions. From its morally ambiguous story and demimonde setting to its sumptuously recherché style, it is one musical that conceded nothing to 1950s notions of mass taste. Nevertheless, *Gigi* proved to be the biggest moneymaker of all the Minnelli–Freed collaborations. No MGM movie ever radiated more assurance in the expressive and technical powers of high-gloss Hollywood moviemaking, yet it was made in an atmosphere of pessimism and retrenchment, within a community whose decadence was more concrete than that of the turn-of-the-century haut monde waltzing across the screen. Before *Gigi* was finished it was buffeted by threats of censorship, pinchpenny budgets, and the general negativity of a new studio management team skeptical of the old Metro ways but equally wary of innovation. Although this is the least Culver Cityish of all Minnelli's musicals, *Gigi* could never have been conceived anywhere else. Like the movie itself, its success was bittersweet, for by the time it was released, the creative climate that made *Gigi* possible had already faded into memory.

After the *Kismet* debacle, this was an ideal opportunity for Minnelli and Freed to resume their harmonious partnership. *Gigi* combined a number of elements Minnelli had explored in a host of previous movies—an original musical with nuanced characters and a love story balancing sentiment and irony, set in the country that most intrigued him and in an age which summoned up a special nostalgia for Minnelli. The idea of adapting *Gigi* to the American screen first surfaced at the studio in the early fifties, but it was largely Minnelli's enthusiasm which spurred Freed to pursue it.

By then, Colette's novella had caused a considerable international stir for such a fragile piece. One of her last sustained works of fiction, *Gigi* was written during the Occupation as a wistful distraction from the grimness of the times. Commissioned as a magazine serial, it was published in book form in Switzerland during 1944, and in Paris just as the city was liberated. The English translation first appeared in the pages of *Harper's Bazaar* in 1946. Two years later, *Gigi* became a modest French film co-written by Colette herself, featuring Daniele Delorme in the title role and two of the *monstres sacrées* of the French screen, Gaby Morlay and Yvonne de Bray, conspiring over Gigi's fate as Aunt Alicia and Madame Alvarez. Soon after, Anita Loos persuaded Colette to allow her to adapt *Gigi* for the Broadway stage.

So charmed was France's great lady of letters by America's perennial gamine that she even played talent scout for the production. On holiday in the south of France, she spied a young bilingual beauty toiling on a ramshackle Franco-British movie called *Monte Carlo Baby*. Colette immediately cabled New York, declaring

Hermione Gingold, Louis Jourdan, Leslie Caron, "The Night They Invented Champagne," Gigi *(1958)*

that she had found the perfect Gigi in a certain Audrey Hepburn. The stage *Gigi* opened late in 1951 and owed its six-month run primarily to the radiance of its instant star. In a novel twist, Colette herself took Loos's dramatic structure and translated it back into French for its Paris theatrical debut. This was the final coup in an inimitable career; it premiered in February 1954, just seven months before Colette's death.

Freed's serious interest in the project began to build soon thereafter. He knew that scurrying after the rights would be a waste of effort, since first, he had to determine whether the prevailing climate in Hollywood would block *Gigi* from being made at all. The so-called Production Code, though more elastic in the postwar years, was still a formidable weapon of industry-wide self-censorship in the mid-fifties; it would be a tough job to pitch Colette, whose vision of life obstinately refused to conform to its quaint strictures. While far from scabrous, *Gigi* still told of a schoolgirl raised by a family of courtesans to assume her rightful place as kept woman to a wealthy libertine. Apparently, the Production Code's pin-striped Savonarolas were particularly aghast that "all of these people consider a man/mistress relationship perfectly normal and nobody condemns it"—a state of affairs which was, of course, unheard of in Hollywood. Without a guaranteed seal of approval, MGM would never allow Freed to shoot one frame of *Gigi*. It was the studio's task to come up with a palatable compromise. Hence, starting in 1955, members of the story department met with representatives of the Code Board five times over the next two years, constantly stressing the innate virtue of *Gigi*'s heroine and the unimpeachable moral lesson of its ending.

While these skirmishes simmered, in early 1956 Freed went east to see Alan Jay Lerner, with two motives in mind—to cast an eye at *My Fair Lady*, then in its Philadelphia tryout, and to persuade him to write *Gigi*'s screenplay for Minnelli to direct. Despite any disappointment Lerner may have felt over *Brigadoon* and the unmade *Green Mansions*, he readily agreed to start work once he'd taken a break from the rigors of getting *My Fair Lady* on its feet. Freed naturally hoped that Lerner and Frederick Loewe would also write the score. Loewe had never before written directly for the movies and initially rejected the idea, but Freed counted on Lerner to bring him around.

Next came the task of clearing through the thicket of permissions needed to secure this well-traveled property. With the intercession of superagent Irving Lazar, MGM negotiated with the executors of Colette's estate: her widower Maurice Goudeket; Gilbert Miller, the producer of *Gigi* on Broadway; Archie Thomson, who had already optioned the film rights; the possessor of the American negative of the French movie version, plus various other intermediaries. After dispersing a total of $233,000, *Gigi* was theirs. Following nearly two decades as a staff producer on weekly payroll,

Freed now had an independent production company housed on the lot; MGM agreed to finance any projects they found mutually attractive, from which Freed would derive twenty-five percent of the net profits. *Gigi* was to be the second film under this agreement, following the Astaire–Charisse *Silk Stockings*.

Nevertheless, the studio imposed a few exasperating restrictions. A memo from MGM executive Saul N. Rittenberg to Freed dated August 10 1956, confirmed this agreement with one proviso: *Gigi*'s budget was not to exceed $1,800,000, plus $150,000 extra if the lead was played by Audrey Hepburn, the logical first choice for the part. Even in 1956 this was a laughable sum for any musical, much less a film to be shot largely on location abroad. Freed acted with his accustomed shrewdness. In the end, a practical working budget wouldn't be tabulated until the company was assembled in Paris ready to shoot, by which point MGM was in too deep to back out.

In the twenty-two months between the completion of *Kismet* and the start of *Gigi*, Minnelli made *Lust for Life, Tea and Sympathy,* and *Designing Woman,* as well as contributing without credit to a remake of Somerset Maugham's *The Painted Veil* (called *The Seventh Sin*), after director of record, Ronald Neame, fought with the studio and departed the scene. Minnelli had definite ideas to contribute to *Gigi*'s screenplay, which he shared with Lerner as soon as work began on the first draft. He had every confidence that Lerner would restore the delicacy of tone he found lacking in the Loos version. In the play, he thought the character of Gigi's mother strident and redundant, and suggested eliminating her from the script entirely. Lerner readily agreed, and the result was an amusing gag sustained throughout the movie. Maman, a bit player at the Opéra Comique, is heard but never seen, closeted in her room to squeak through her scales like a Gallic Susan Alexander Kane.

With Maman dispatched, Lerner's master stroke was the creation of that dapper old reprobate, Honoré Lachaille. Honoré gets but a passing mention in Colette's story as Gaston's father and a possible former lover of Mme. Alvarez, but he's more conspicuous in the 1948 movie, trading jaded aphorisms with young Gaston. Since Colette had contributed to that screenplay, Lerner decided there could be no objections to including him again this time. Now Gaston's uncle, in Lerner's script Honoré is the calm center of the story, the audience's confidant, who establishes the movie's tone of roguish sentiment from his first appearance. The part seems inconceivable without Maurice Chevalier, down to the way he breaks through the wall between *Gigi*'s fictional world and the spectator by addressing the camera directly—just as he did in the Paramount-Chevalier musicals of the early thirties.

In fact, Lerner had always idolized this music-hall legend, regretted his absence from *An American in Paris,*

Hermione Gingold, Leslie Caron, Louis Jourdan, Gigi *(1958)*

songs. Additionally, MGM staff composer-conductor André Previn, late of Minnelli's *Kismet* and *Designing Woman,* would conduct and supervise the entire score. At Lerner's insistence, after their happy experience with *My Fair Lady,* Cecil Beaton was offered the job of general production designer on *Gigi.* Minnelli always welcomed the fresh approaches that artists like Lemuel Ayers, Irene Sharaff, and Oliver Smith brought to the usual Metro decor conceits, and he was to work very happily with Beaton. Abetted by William Horning, the trusted Preston Ames would create the interiors to be shot in Culver City, under Beaton's supervision.

In the spring of 1957, Lerner brought Loewe back with him to Paris to draft the score while he labored on a new version of the screenplay. In early May, Freed and Minnelli joined them. This gave *Gigi*'s director the unusual luxury of three months to feel his way through the city for the right locations and confer on the script and casting. In fact, both needed a lot of work before shooting could start on *Gigi.* On May 8, Freed sent a note to studio vice-president in charge of production, Benjamin Thau, that was meant to reassure MGM their investment was safe. "The script is opening up with everything we discussed," Freed reported. "In addition to this we heard the first four songs and they are equal at least to their writing in *My Fair Lady* . . . the freshest writing I have ever heard in a screen musical."

However, Walter Strohm, the supervisor of the MGM production department sent to Paris to report back on *Gigi*'s progress, took a darkly pragmatic view. Two weeks after Freed's letter, Thau got a pessimistic cable from Strohm. "As of today there is not a script written other than a six-page outline of the intended framework of the rewrite," he complained. "Both Messrs. Freed and Minnelli are hopeful in having the script in two-three weeks. Enclosed you will find a six-page synopsis and will note this is rather meagre material to begin laying out the production." On hearing this news, the studio sent Minnelli an alarmed letter beseeching him to speed things up while adhering to a reasonable budget. He responded by explaining that "there has been no accurate budget set . . . because many of the songs that affect whole sections are not yet written. . . . I do not think this will take long as Alan works very fast. . . . More than half the picture will be done here. When we get back to Hollywood our only sets will be the three apartments and a few process shots and will involve only our five principals." In this, Minnelli was to prove unduly optimistic.

The other dilemma was that with *Gigi*'s starting date looming, half of the principal cast had yet to be found. Hermione Gingold, at the time primarily known as a revue comedienne, was an imaginative choice for Mme. Alvarez, but suitable candidates for Gaston and Aunt Alicia proved more elusive. The hero in particular required sensitive casting—Gaston is an aloof egoist who must finally seem worthy of Gigi's admiration and

and was determined to have him for *Gigi.* When he informed Freed of his intention to write the script in Paris, the producer asked him to go to work while he was there on Chevalier and Audrey Hepburn, then in France to shoot *Funny Face.* Chevalier agreed immediately, but Hepburn chose not to play Gigi a second time. At Freed's request, Lerner then flew to London in quest of Leslie Caron, who had just done the role in the West End. Caron didn't share Hepburn's qualms, although she did worry about a reunion with Minnelli, whose tongue-tied direction of actors had so exasperated her during *An American in Paris.* In December 1956, Lerner left France with a sketchy first draft and commitments from the two stars. By current standards their fees seem amazingly low—Chevalier was to be paid $100,000 and Caron $75,000, plus the balm of top billing, with the rest of the cast scaled down accordingly.

Everyone agreed that it was vital to shoot as much of *Gigi* in France as possible, as Minnelli had done with *Lust for Life.* Freed scheduled the location work for midsummer, when the annual holiday exodus from Paris made it easier to work. Meanwhile, as Minnelli cleared away his other commitments, Freed assembled such familiar figures for the production team as Ruttenberg and Fazan, with Conrad Salinger to arrange the ours. Number one on the list of possibilities was Dirk Bogarde, then the patrician heartthrob of the British romantic screen; however, he was under contract to the Rank Organisation, which refused to release him. Minnelli tested a few local faces including Michel Auclair, recently the existentialist rotter who tried to seduce Audrey Hepburn in *Funny Face*. When none of these panned out, Louis Jourdan was signed, largely because nobody else came to mind. Since his Hollywood debut in *The Paradine Case* a decade earlier, Jourdan had pursued a fairly steady but not particularly exciting career on the American screen; Minnelli's *Madame Bovary* was one of the few distinguished films he'd made. Yet that air of disdainful composure which kept Jourdan from major stardom was exactly what Gaston needed—it turned out to be the part and the performance of his life.

The role of the retired courtesan who trains Gigi in seduction elicited some tantalizing ideas. Lerner suggested Yvonne Printemps, France's insouciant queen of operetta since World War I; Minnelli countered with Broadway's venerated high comedienne, Ina Claire. Freed in turn proposed a startling piece of casting against type. "We hit on an idea that could be quite wonderful," Freed wrote Thau. "That is for Irene Dunne to play Aunt Alicia. . . . [She] would give the aunt a great stature and take away any salacious or questionable implications from a censorship standpoint and although she might cost us a little more money, she would add immeasurably to the distinction of the cast." As they were all accomplished singers, it's likely that Lerner and Loewe envisioned at least one song for Alicia, but in the end this was a moot point. All three ladies suggested were as definitively retired from their professions as Alicia was from hers, and not even *Gigi* could tempt them. Less than two weeks before production started, the part finally went to London's elegant Isabel Jeans—not quite as glittery in marquee terms, but a perfect fit for the part.

Another matter yet to be resolved was the title for the picture. Fearing that after *Lili* and *Gaby* the public might have had enough of Leslie Caron vehicles tagged with cute Gallic nicknames, MGM's working title for *Gigi* was *The Parisians*, after one of the Lerner–Loewe songs. But this too seemed *déjà entendu*; publicity chief Howard Dietz let it be known that "There have been too many titles about Paris for us to be enthusiastic about *The Parisians*." So in the end *Gigi* was what it remained. However, Minnelli and crew had more pressing concerns. Shooting a musical was an intricate, exacting business, and working on location made this infinitely more difficult, especially with the studio harassing them to wrap it up as speedily as possible. For *Gigi*, many essentials usually taken for granted now had to be improvised as expeditiously as possible. Without the studio's vast wardrobe staff to rely on for the bulk of the shoot, costumes had to be executed and accessorized by a host of Parisian firms. Musical numbers were almost always shot to a complete pre-recorded score. *Gigi*'s cast mouthed their songs to vocal tracks dashed off at a local radio studio with Previn at the piano—back in California, the MGM Orchestra would be dubbed in months later.

But these problems paled beside the rigors of cramming a dozen locations covering at least half the picture into less than a month. Considering Minnelli's penchant for setting up elaborate tracks and booms, plus the usual vagaries of Parisian weather, it was a quixotic task. Shooting started on August 5, and for the next four weeks the *Gigi* company zig-zagged through the city, and a few points beyond. Minnelli chose the cozy Place Furstemberg on the Left Bank as Gigi's *quartier,* while Aunt Alicia lived behind an Art Nouveau façade on the Avenue Rapp. Gaston's family digs were shot in the impeccable period rooms of the Musée Jacquemart-André, and the hero dissected his changing feelings for Gigi before the Tuileries fountains and the Pont Alexandre. Filming the "Thank Heaven for Little Girls" opening and finale and the so-called "Battle of the Flowers" in the Bois de Boulogne posed few problems save the heat and an occasional cloudburst, but the real fin-de-siècle interiors Minnelli chose were another matter. The old Palais de Glace at the Rond-Point of the Champs-Elysées was a musty ruin, which Minnelli and Cecil Beaton were obliged to restore to its former splendor in record time. Two key scenes involving dozens of dress extras and Minnelli's usual serpentine camera movements were set in Chez Maxim, and he had only four days to cover it all. He was delighted with the restaurant's rich decor (in his favorite shade of red, no less), as well as the aplomb with which the local bit players entered the spirit of Belle Epoque revelers. However, Joseph Ruttenberg didn't share his rapture. These rooms were hell to maneuver in; moreover, Maxim's most conspicuous feature was its array of Art-Nouveau mirrors lining the walls, reflecting his lights and the camera itself wherever he moved. Ruttenberg did remarkable work under these conditions; he set up an array of tiny bulbs beneath the faces of Maxim's patrons, giving them the footlit quality of a Jules Chéret music-hall *affiche*.

In the midst of this Minnelli had a personal crisis to face. His wife, Georgette, who had accompanied him to Paris, decided this life was not for her and packed her bags for California and a legal separation. All Minnelli could do was express his regrets and keep on shooting. Then, as August waned and the budget mounted, the studio pulled the plug—Thau ordered Freed to shut down in Paris with the greatest dispatch, and finish up whatever was left on the lot. Minnelli never got to Trouville to shoot Gigi and Gaston's day by the sea; a beach was a beach, MGM decreed, and they could just as well frolic in the waves of the Pacific. Since the swans in California were also deemed as photogenic as their French cousins, Gaston's soliloquy would lurch back and forth between Paris and Culver City whether Minnelli liked it or not.

He didn't, but he had no choice but to make the best of it. Sometimes the seams showed, nonetheless—no backlot swan pond could approximate the Jardin de la Bagatelle, and to save time Minnelli had to use a crude back-projected sunset for the Chevalier–Gingold duet, "I Remember It Well," that ill-matched the authentic fading light of the intercut beach scene. The remaining interiors caused less trouble, and Minnelli closed down the set on October 30 1957.

In November, Previn recorded the full score, with Betty Wand's voice smoothly substituting for Leslie Caron's, to the star's great irritation. On January 20 1958, MGM held *Gigi*'s first sneak preview, with ominous results. The audience warmed to Chevalier and the sets but not much else; one preview card called the cast "just dumb dressed-up dummies," while one woman angrily scrawled, "I am the mother of a very nice girl . . . the movie industry contributes in a major way to the decline in the morals of the young and not so young." The MGM contingent was hardly more sanguine—to them *Gigi* seemed endless and emotionally remote, and Lerner found many of the orchestrations too bombastic. After a few quick trims, a second sneak was scheduled the following week, to a scarcely better response. This time the audience played at market analysis. The consensus among the patrons of the Pomona Fox was that while they were sophisticated enough to appreciate a movie like *Gigi,* the unenlightened masses would never buy it.

Lerner felt some scenes needed pruning and rewriting, and Freed agreed that retakes might fulfill *Gigi*'s obvious promise. The studio balked, until Lerner desperately offered to pay for the changes himself if necessary, pledging to buy the negative from MGM if their faith in its prospects were so shaky. His fervor convinced Thau and MGM president Joseph Vogel that perhaps they had missed something in *Gigi,* and they approved the extra $300,000 Freed needed.

Thus, a nine-day schedule of retakes was set up for the following month—only Minnelli wouldn't be directing them. With fewer directors than ever before on the studio payroll, MGM expected them to earn their keep by shuttling from one picture to another—and Minnelli was the star example. According to the terms of his newest contract he was now worth $4,250 a week, and accordingly was dispatched to Europe to start *The Reluctant Debutante,* two weeks before *Gigi*'s first preview. Under this waning system, directors weren't allowed any proprietary airs about the product they made; they moved right on to the next assignment, like the pros they were paid to be. For Minnelli, it was the most frustrating aspect of a regime that otherwise suited him very well.

In Minnelli's absence Freed predictably turned to Charles Walters, with cinematographer Ray June brought in to substitute for Ruttenberg, who was also busy with *The Reluctant Debutante.* Thirty years later, it's hard to determine exactly what Walters reshot, or how much of his footage appears in the final print. Lerner's autobiography credits "I Remember It Well" and "The Night They Invented Champagne" to Walters, but the evidence refutes this. In the former case, production records prove that none of Chevalier's scenes were redone after Minnelli left. As to the latter, Walters choreographed the scene, but Minnelli filmed it himself. Walters did reshoot sections of the title number, but Adrienne Fazan insisted on restoring Minnelli's version to the film instead. The sporadic closeups of Jourdan that punctuate "She Is Not Thinking of Me" are undoubtedly his, for Minnelli hadn't wanted to disrupt his sweeping panoramas of Maxim's with obvious cutting; much of Gaston's climactic proposal of marriage seems to have been Walters' as well. The one number that can confidently be attributed to him is "The Parisians," apart from the verse and the bridge between the two choruses in which Gigi strides through Paris; Lerner felt that Minnelli's version was too brisk for the lyrics to be intelligible. After more repolishing by Fazan and umpteen re-recordings of Jourdan's soliloquy, *Gigi* was previewed twice more, to mounting enthusiasm.

Freed decided that the best way to showcase *Gigi* was by stressing its kinship to *My Fair Lady,* which wouldn't reach the screen for several years. Thus it opened on May 15 1958, as a reserved-seat attraction at the Royale Theater, a legitimate house in the middle of the Broadway theater district. The strategy worked, for in addition to rapturous reviews the film earned an added cachet needed to sell it at a time when standard-issue musicals had become a box office liability. After a change of theaters in November, its first-run engagement lasted over a year. For added prestige, MGM also campaigned hard to get *Gigi* into the 1958 Cannes Film Festival, where it was given the closing night slot out of competition. The French press was divided, with some predictable bile spilled over Hollywood's nerve at coarsening such a quintessentially French bonbon, but mass-circulation organs like *France Soir* and *Le Figaro* praised it enthusiastically.

Although the New York Film Critics' Award reserved its laurels for the black-and-white uplift of *The Defiant Ones,* *Gigi* became the most honored movie of the year. In addition to a Directors' Guild Prize for Minnelli, *Gigi* earned nine Academy Award nominations, from Best Picture through virtually all the technical categories—an astonishing number considering that none of the actors were cited. (From the standpoint of industry recognition, this was the peak' year of Minnelli's professional life as well as one of his busiest; his *Some Came Running,* which opened in Los Angeles at the end of 1958, garnered four nominations of its own.) In addi-

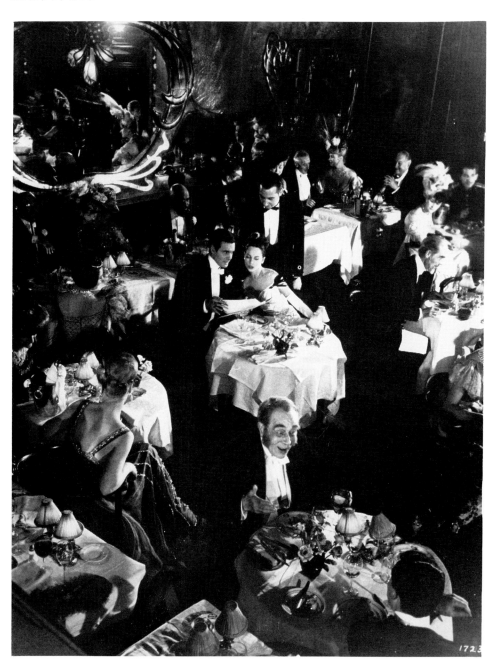

tion to a special citation for Maurice Chevalier, *Gigi* won in every category, according Minnelli the first Best Direction Oscar ever given for a musical.

What gratified the studio even more was its international box office success. By 1962, *Gigi*'s worldwide rentals amounted to $9,965,000 against expenditures of $3,447,000; this left a profit of $4,150,000 which MGM's distribution-fee accounting system reduced to $1,638,000. At the time of these tabulations, *Gigi* was the only one of Freed's five films as an independent producer not to show a loss for the studio. A successful theatrical reissue followed in 1966, and a lucrative sale to television four years later. On a less mercenary note, it was Colette's widower who gave *Gigi* its most unusual accolade. When he finally saw the picture in 1959, M. Goudeket wrote to the studio, conveying

"my heartiest congratulations on *Gigi*'s great success. I was personally enchanted . . . and feel that Colette would have been equally thrilled by the delicate and faithful way her unforgettable story has been handled."

Indeed, Goudeket's kind words weren't just an expression of Old World good manners. For Colette aficionados, *Gigi* is as close to the spirit of its source as a musical in CinemaScope, Metrocolor, and English could be. Minnelli infuses it with a pastel vivacity as specific to Gigi's world as the café-and-garret *vie de bohème* was to *An American in Paris,* or the St. Louis domesticity was to Esther Smith and her family. Lerner's text is just as scrupulous; an astonishing proportion of his ebullient dialogue springs directly out of the novella's pages, from Alicia's lesson in the proper way to eat ortolans to Gaston's stammered proposal of marriage. Lerner's principal hurdle was the perfect self-containment of Colette's story, which unfolds entirely within Mme. Alvarez' cramped flat and her sister Alicia's intimidating *hôtel particulier.* He resolved it through the most expedient ruse at his disposal—by turning it into *My Fair Gigi.*

Even without any forcing from Lerner, the two plots share certain obvious affinities; both take place at the beginning of the century and focus on the molding of an uninhibited innocent into the humanizing mate of a misogynist who didn't realize how much he needed one. Each Cinderella has a sharp-tongued dragon to school her in deportment, and in Honoré, Lerner creates a Gallic parallel to *My Fair Lady*'s Colonel Pickering, the serene elder chum of the baffled hero. The principal difference between Henry Higgins and Gaston Lachaille is that the Shavian celibate distrusts women because he's never really known any; as a Colette amoralist, Gaston has known far too many of the wrong sort. Yet they vent their bewilderment at the afflictions of love in the same exasperated way—Higgins and Lachaille storm the streets where they live, arguing with themselves in urgent recitatives that try to squelch feelings with logic, and fail.

Gaston's soliloquy is a near-exact equivalent of "I've Grown Accustomed to Her Face," placed earlier in the plot, but then about half *Gigi*'s songs echo *My Fair Lady*'s score in melody or meaning. The rhymed-couplet gossip at Maxim's is the "Ascot Gavotte" with Parisian bitchery substituting for English phlegm; "The Night They Invented Champagne" exchanges "The Rain in Spain's" flamenco for the cancan, but in both, three giddy comrades fly about the sitting room in a sudden burst of joie de vivre. Gigi's tremulous "Say a Prayer for Me Tonight" on the eve of her first night out with Gaston was actually written for Eliza Doolittle to sing before her debut at the Embassy Ball, and then cut during *My Fair Lady*'s pre-Broadway tryout. Its effortless fit into *Gigi*'s plot shows how adroitly Lerner managed to refurbish his own formula.

There's a striking evolution in Lerner's writing for the movies from *An American in Paris* to *Gigi.* His first Freed–Minnelli script channeled his voice into the terse, streamlined conventions of a Metro musical; *Gigi* assumes that his MGM colleagues can adapt their skills to suit the contours of a Lerner libretto. For compelling reasons, Lerner's confident touch had a hypnotic effect on them all. With the Broadway musical at its post-war summit of popular influence and its Hollywood equivalent fast turning into *Jailhouse Rock* or nothing, *Gigi* takes the more palatable route for people like Minnelli and Freed. Five years earlier, *The Band Wagon* had been an unabashed movie spectacular with a theatrical setting; by contrast, *Gigi* feels like a superlative adaptation of a stage smash, with real streetscapes substituted for painted scrims.

The fact that a freshly minted movie could achieve this effect added to *Gigi*'s air of novelty and distinction; yet it also explains why the movie lacks the flowing rhythms of Minnelli's other great musicals. For all the movie's reverence for Colette, its respect for the words of Alan Jay Lerner borders on the worshipful. *Gigi*'s script wavers between the movie impulse to show events and the theatrical necessity of describing those things which happened offstage. In order to give its librettist all due latitude of expression, the movie often compromises by doing both. Throughout *Gigi,* people are forever bounding into some confidant's boudoir for a long chat about some social gaffe we've already seen for ourselves. After dousing his mistress with Veuve Cliquot to avenge her faithlessness, Gaston repairs to Uncle Honoré's to denounce her perfidy; once Gigi rejects Gaston's bid for her to become Liane's successor, Grandmama must dash to sister Alicia's to blurt out every detail of their family disgrace. Even the undeniable polish of this chatter dulls with repetition, and should it clash with the director's instinct to paint Gigi's world rather than talk about it, it's Minnelli who must defer.

Lerner's longwindedness aside, *Gigi*'s fidelity to Colette's own preoccupations guarantees a certain pokiness, since much of what gives this story its special pungence isn't very cinematic. As in many of her works, Colette focuses on that mannerly but brutal barter system which exchanges female sexual compliance for masculine largesse; as *Gigi* is one of her more optimistic stories, sentiment finally subdues commerce. The daily shifts in Gigi's worth in the cocotte trade turn every character into a garrulous speculator, while Minnelli dutifully records the terms of each transaction. Her abrupt retreat from the marketplace is a crucial moment in the story, prompting some of Colette's (and Lerner's) most caustic writing. "To take care of me beautifully means that I should go away from here with you and that I should sleep in your bed," Gigi sadly declares. "And when it's over and done with, Gaston Lachaille goes off with another lady and I have only to go into another gentleman's bed." These are startling words from the heroine of a 1958 movie musical, but by now we've been sitting too long in Grandmama's red parlor to pay full heed to Gigi's distress. The moment is long overdue to run outside into Minnelli's sun-dappled Paris and take another draft of fresh air among the parasoled picnickers.

Despite these longueurs, *Gigi* is a provocative example of the kind of musical only Minnelli knew how to make—a delicate interplay between his seductive candied surfaces and the emotional unease simmering underneath. *Gigi* takes place in a world of matter-of-fact cynicism corseted by a rigid code of etiquette; with Hollywood finally wriggling out of its suffocating self-censorship, Minnelli was free to explore a theme which had long intrigued him, with a candor he'd never been permitted before.

Minnelli's personal convictions are defined by his instinctive empathy rather than concrete ideologies, but as such there's a crypto-feminist strain running through many of his movies. Gigi is the latest in a long line of restive Minnelli women schooled to stifle their feelings as payment for a life of ease. A number of his melodramas center on the urge for self-determination within the confines of marriage, and pose only the bleakest alternatives. For Katharine Hepburn's cowed wife in *Undercurrent,* submission nearly costs her her life; Emma Bovary and *Tea and Sympathy*'s Laura both defy the rules and become outcasts. In deference to the genre, his musicals are more sanguine, featuring heroines who still have time to shape their own fate. Marriage may be the solution but on their own terms. In a Minnelli musical, a happy fadeout means finding the man who wants a partner, not a shadow.

This time, Minnelli upends the usual moral code but the dilemma remains the same. If his other heroines chafe at the prospect of ordinary domestic life, what's in store for Gigi is well-cushioned impropriety. At the film's beginning she is a spontaneous innocent whose free-spirited ways must be tamed to suit her grown-up responsibilities. As with Manuela, her elders forever urge her to stop mooning about and be sensible; without quite saying so, they mean that she must learn the objective value of things, and become a desirable object herself in order to earn her rightful share of life's treats. Gigi is too backward to divine this on her own—she obediently savors Alicia's best vintages and learns the difference between yellow diamonds and topazes, but it's an irrelevant exercise, like the Latin declensions she memorizes at school. She can't quite grasp the logic of Alicia's lessons in appraising the freshness of cigars; after all, she doesn't smoke them.

What's required of Gigi is a double form of deception. By feigning doll-like poise and devotion, she can trick a man into new heights of generosity, while persuading him that each new trinket is a happy little surprise. If the plan goes awry, it's not because Gigi's scruples outweigh her common sense. Her problem is that in addition to her more marketable attributes she's been cursed with sentiment, which has no place in this transaction. Compliant though she tries to be, Gigi is repulsed by Gaston's pledge of love in addition to all the trimmings of a kept life. She's perverse enough to feel that only indifference can justify using a person as a possession; to do this to someone you claim to care for is the one unforgivable obscenity. Despite her training, Gigi can't help being one of those "ordinary people" her aunt describes so contemptuously, and in her milieu this makes her extraordinary indeed.

Of course, in her way Colette was just as practical as Gigi's Aunt Alicia. Gigi's fine feelings are rewarded in a very tangible way, for why squander them on someone too beaten down by life's struggles to appreciate the gesture? *Gigi* is Colette's idea of the best kind of

romantic fable—by marrying her sugar magnate, instead of earning a weekly box of bonbons, Gigi gets to keep the refinery. And like *Gigi*'s author, Minnelli isn't exactly impervious to the pleasures of the senses, either. His bemusement at all this nonchalant naughtiness is what gives the movie its sparkle. For if Gigi's soul must be jeopardized, the least he can do is show how alluring sin really can be.

For all Gigi's disarming coltishness, the film's most arresting characters are its wizened cynics—an old lady whose horizontal career earned her the right to sleep alone with her brilliants at last, and the scamp emeritus whose motto remains, "Stay close to the young and a little rubs off." Aunt Alicia's classes don't do much for Gigi, but they tickle Minnelli no end. She's the essence of calculated femininity, pacing her gold and white rooms in her negligees of ashes-of-rose—too ethereal to be true, until her voice plummets to an imperious baritone to declare that emeralds are a cocotte's only friend. As for Honoré, his zest is as unflagging as Gigi's adolescent energy; he's amused by everything because at his age he knows how ephemeral it all is. Like Alicia, his one faith is in self-preservation, and the best way to ensure it is to keep moving lest emotion make you vulnerable. A fleeting instant of sentiment is all very well, so long as there's no prolonged sequel. In a less sardonic enterprise, his unexpected reunion at Trouville with Mme. Alvarez would cue a tender geriatric subplot and a renewal of their long-discarded vows. But in *Gigi,* "I Remember It Well" means adieu—afterwards Grandmama can only bask in Gigi's reflected glory while Honoré reprises his slightly suspect anthem about the charms of little girls.

These characters are like the permanent street sets on the Metro backlot. There's nothing behind their resplendent façades—what you see is all there is. In *Gigi,* Minnelli reverses the usual Hollywood equation; the buildings are real (most of the time, anyway), but the people are trompe l'oeil apparitions. Of all Minnelli's movies, this is the one which proves most forcefully that style is not mere embellishment—it's an attitude that saturates and defines every frame. For artifice is *Gigi*'s true subject, upstaging Gigi's reformation of the scapegrace Gaston. In the original story we hear about the exploits of the posh set second-hand, through Gigi's exclamation over the latest issue of *Gil Blas.* It's Minnelli's job to show us everything she's missing, and his relish is contagious. He has a perverse respect for all the glamorous silliness he records, because no director knows better than he how much hard work it takes to sustain those debonair poses.

As usual, Minnelli's visual design for the picture was sparked by those artists of the epoch he most admired —Boudin for the seascapes, Seurat's post-Impressionism for Paris at its Sunday leisure, and the caricaturist SEM, whose caustic drawings of Belle Epoque *bon ton* were adapted for *Gigi*'s opening credits. But *Gigi*'s most pervasive models were Ernst Lubitsch's satiny Hollywood-Continental concoctions of the 1930s. Screen operettas such as *The Smiling Lieutenant* and *The Merry Widow* had been escapist in a literal sense, transporting their audiences to the Alt Wien and a Paree that only existed in the imaginations of moviemakers. Consistency gave Lubitsch's deliberate antirealism its special authenticity. His world was populated by the smug idle class and its insolent underlings, would-be lovers and frustrated lechers; their argot is a form of lilting badinage whose relation to everyday speech is like a Monet landscape compared to a snapshot.

In *Gigi,* Minnelli dusted off the Lubitsch lexicon and blended it into his own film vocabulary, and the opening sequence in the Bois de Boulogne sets the tone for everything to come. While carriages and Minnelli's camera canter merrily down a wooded allée, the bystanders form a human frieze of elegant languor, their parasols and walking sticks perched at the requisite rakish angle. Minnelli gives each figure in this *nature morte* its own idiosyncrasies, cutting from hawk-face matrons to impenetrable Amazons and an ancient ex-ingenue with a dyed Titian coiffure. But they are all supernumeraries in a glittering divertissement, just as the bygone milieu they represent prizes perfection of form over the anarchy of feeling.

Gigi is filled with these exquisite marionettes, who are capable of movement or speech but never both at the same time. The lovelies adorning Maxim's drape their plumed and bejeweled forms along the bar in attitudes of forced merriment, but freeze to attention when some new source of scandal strolls past. Gaston's faithless Liane (Eva Gabor) primps and twitters and flirts in a blur of madcap animation, but not a sound issues from her lips—she's an artist in the illusion of gaiety and nothing more. Honoré and Gaston are granted more substance because they pass through this sphere but are not quite of it; Honoré observes it too dispassionately, and Gaston is too weary of everything to join in the charade.

The one true outsider is Gigi, who hasn't been civilized yet at all. At the Bois de Boulogne, she shatters Minnelli's placid settings by larking around and fumbling her schoolbooks. In the Trouville sequence, Minnelli volleys between shots of Gigi scampering over a tennis court and a torpid beauty for whom anything so active as lifting a racket is a vulgar betrayal of her lady-like code. Throughout, she's a fawn among the wax-works, all tremulous instincts and darting movements. Even when she exchanges her schoolgirl plaids for corseted gowns, the essential Gigi is subdued but not defeated. Her debut at Maxim's is a humiliating failure, for no self-respecting kept woman would gush so over Gaston's proffered emerald bracelet with that "miracle of elusive blue." Thanks to Alicia she's gotten the words right, but Gigi's spirit is too gauchely human for her assigned station. Caron as a misfit in the demi-monde meshes perfectly within Minnelli's plan for the movie. In a role a decade her junior, Caron's irresistible schoolgirl act is another vivacious archetype, no deeper than the blasé mime by the cameo players hand-picked by Minnelli to fill out the background.

The lusciously overripe Beaton interiors—from Honoré's café-au-lait Art-Nouveau digs to the reddest room in which a Minnelli heroine ever dwelt—are among the gaudiest baubles in this musical jewel box. But it's Minnelli's original use of the city around him which gives this confection a special artificial sheen. A few other musicals (most notably Stanley Donen's *Funny Face*) had gone to Paris for authentic local color, but essentially they're a tourist's view of the city. Instead, Minnelli chooses those precise architectural elements that will best serve as props in his post-Impressionist high comedy. In his Paris, statues of mythological rape loom over Gigi as she contemp-tuously ponders the hyperactive sex drive of the Parisians; the fussy Beaux Arts fixtures of the Pont Alexandre mirror Gaston's muddled feelings over the new, alluring Gigi. Other American-movies-in-Paris give us the obligatory picturesque cityscape with Eiffel Tower, but in *Gigi* Minnelli shoots it from below, its base casting an oppressive shadow on Gaston as he exclaims in song, "It's a Bore!"

Minnelli uses this tangible world as a boundless stage for sensual abstraction. The climactic reprise to Gaston's soliloquy has no explicit content at all; Gaston is simply a mute figure in the shadows, stalking the night streets as Previn's orchestra rhapsodically plays the title song. Its lush moodiness comes from Minnelli's gift for painting with light—cobblestones washed blue by the moon, Gaston as dapper black silhouette against a sapphire sky and liquid-diamond fountain. In his hands even daylight becomes an element of mystery. The stateliness of his group portraits in the Bois de Boulogne is the more striking because he's framed them with real chestnut trees rustling in the sunshine. Whereas a movie like *Brigadoon* overreached to make the synthetic seem real, *Gigi* gives Minnelli the chance to do something more intriguing. For, like many of the painters he admires, here Minnelli shapes actual landscapes into his own inimitable brand of art.

Subsequent filmmakers have tried to recapture this milieu in a similar way, and each attempt only proved just how masterful Minnelli was. Volker Schlondorff's *Swann in Love* stumbles along the same path, down to the hero's midnight musings on the fatal lure of the opposite sex, but the fin-de-siècle malady of ennui is too vibrant an emotion for him. Where Minnelli is an ambivalent interpreter of this decadent world, Schlondorff wanders through his Proustian Paris with a lugubrious moralist's eye—this really is moviemaking as taxidermy. However, *Gigi* had its own quotient of stylistic lapses, thanks to the forced retreat back to the studio for some of the exteriors. No matter how smoothly Adrienne Fazan blended everything on her moviola, against a brackish pool with neo-neoclassical temple the backlot choruses of "The Parisians" and the title song look like a weird lost reel from *Raintree County*. Hemmed in by the trellised maze of a Metro outdoor-café set, Minnelli just sits back and listens as Chevalier croons two choruses of "I'm Glad That I'm Not Young Anymore" from behind the remnants of his lunch. Whether he was conscious of it or not, *Gigi*'s blend of Broadway and French lit., reins in Minnelli's most freewheeling instincts. This is the only one of his best movie musicals which at times resembles an illustrated soundtrack. Even so, *Gigi* has a particular brittle beauty unmatched by any other movie musical. It's likely to remain the screen's most endearing reverie upon an age once the sole property of French painters and nostalgic reminiscence.

BELLS ARE RINGING

1960

I f the future of the Metro musical looked increasingly cloudy by the mid-fifties, at least Arthur Freed could derive some vicarious pride from what was happening on Broadway at the time. For the two biggest hits of 1956 were both penned by regulars of the Freed Unit: Lerner's *My Fair Lady*, of course, and *Bells Are Ringing*, an original musical comedy by Betty Comden and Adolph Green. Otherwise, these shows had little in common. True to the divergent tastes of their creators, they represented opposite approaches to the craft of the popular stage musical. While Lerner and Loewe sought to elevate Broadway's cultural tone with the kind of classy Anglophilia only American knowhow could pull off, Comden and Green wrote an unrepentant Shubert Alley smash which restored some of the scatterbrained fun musical comedy had increasingly discarded in the pursuit of art.

Bells Are Ringing was in fact precisely what their onscreen counterparts in *The Band Wagon* were trying to fashion for Fred Astaire's Tony Hunter—that famous "light and intimate show . . . with just enough plot to let him do lots of gay and varied numbers." Only, this time the star of this custom-made vehicle was a she—namely Judy Holliday, the most lovable comedienne of her generation. Before Comden and Green's *On the Town* and Holliday's ascent to fame as Billie Dawn in *Born Yesterday*, the three had spent years together as part of a satirical nightclub act called "The Revuers." After winning an Oscar for bringing Billie to the movies, Holliday made a series of sprightly comedies in Hollywood, while Comden and Green wrote *Wonderful Town*, *Peter Pan*, and their various screenplays for MGM. A happy rematch of their talents, *Bells Are Ringing* also marked Holliday's return to the stage as a boundless entertainer who could torch and cha-cha with the same gusto she brought to her clowning.

Its heroine is a switchboard operator for an answering service, who keeps her personal life on hold while plugging into the dreams and disappointments of her clients. She mates randy Siamese cats and also their owners; prescribes mustard plasters for Mme. Grimaldi, the famous coloratura, and plays agent to a mumbling Method actor and a dentist who makes music on his air hose. But Ella's neediest case is Plaza 0 Double-4 Double-3, a playwright with an imminent deadline and terminal writer's block. Desperate to save Jeffrey Moss from himself, she infiltrates his life as the mysterious good fairy Melisande Scott, only to retreat when he falls for this fabricated personality. This whimsy was embellished by a first-rate brace of theatrical talents—Jerome Robbins as director and co-choreographer with Bob Fosse, and savvy tunesmith Jule Styne to provide the requisite lilting ballads and comic patter songs. When it opened on Broadway in November 1956, Comden and Green's just-enough-plot was deemed less-than-sufficient by the *Times'* Brooks Atkinson, who shuddered at the thought of this show minus the excuse of Judy and all her infinite vocal

Judy Holliday and Dean Martin in MGM's Times Square, Bells Are Ringing *(1960)*

impersonations at the telephone console. But this was idle speculation, as Holliday stayed with *Bells Are Ringing* for most of a two-year Broadway run.

Within two weeks of its premiere, the MGM story department had wired the New York office of Freed's desire to acquire the property. As Warners and Paramount reportedly also bid on *Bells Are Ringing*, the rights weren't secured until August 1957, at a cost of $400,000. The ever-diligent legal department noted a vague similarity between this story and two obscure antecedents—a Guy Bolton play called *Guardian Angel* and a French boulevard bauble called *Passy 08-45*. However, the studio dismissed these qualms and went forward regardlessly.

Freed usually succumbed to the temptation of recasting Broadway hits with more photogenic movie names; he had replaced Ethel Merman with Garland and then Betty Hutton for *Annie Get Your Gun*, and substituted Howard Keel for Alfred Drake in *Kismet*. But Holliday's participation was assured from the outset—the part was unimaginable without her and, more to the point, she already had a demonstrable screen following. By the summer of 1958, Minnelli had agreed to direct the picture, and Comden and Green were instructed to turn in the first draft of their refurbished libretto later that fall.

As the show was essentially a situation comedy with songs, nobody expected any unusual obstacles in bringing *Bells Are Ringing* to the screen. But, in fact, a constant atmosphere of tension hung over the production, which was postponed twice before Minnelli began principal photography on October 7 1959. The blame for the delay was attributed mainly to Comden and Green, who suddenly seemed as allergic to the typewriter as their script's hero, Jeffrey Moss. Freed had granted their request to work on *Bells Are Ringing* in New York while they were simultaneously preparing *A Party with Betty Comden and Adolph Green*, a retrospective revue of their work slated to open on Broadway toward the end of 1958. When their first script arrived in October, the producer was appalled to note that it ran 159 pages; with the addition of songs, this version would have been the *Parsifal* of movie musicals. He summarily rejected the draft, ordering a streamlined model by the end of December. Comden and Green had also agreed to pen the lyrics to three new Styne songs by the time Minnelli and Freed arrived in New York for a quick working visit at the beginning of February 1959.

As *A Party* was still playing eight performances a week, it's not surprising that they had nothing to show the California contingent. However, the studio was incensed, and story department head, Kenneth MacKenna, complained of their lax behavior in a curt note to Comden and Green's agent, Irving Lazar. In February, they interrupted *A Party*'s hit engagement to report to the studio for another session with the script. While this version was more manageable, further delays ensued when Holliday took *Bells Are Ringing* on a brief West Coast tour. Minnelli began rehearsals in August 1959, interrupted by location work in New York, which included Susanswerphone's home on East 68th Street—a tumbledown brownstone standing defiant amid the rubble of its demolished neighbors.

Much of the supporting cast was retained from the New York production, including Jean Stapleton as Holliday's spinsterish cousin/employer; foul-minded police detective Dort Clark; and Bernie West's Dr. Kitchell, the musical dentist responsible for deathless rhymes like, "I love your sunny teeth/Your sunny, funny teeth!" For box-office insurance, Sydney Chaplin, an authoritative Jeffrey Moss on the stage, was passed over in favor of Dean Martin, fresh from Minnelli's *Some Came Running* and a star with just the right sly lassitude for the part. Meanwhile, with a bit of fudging, Styne, Comden, and Green came up with their requisite three new songs. "Better Than a Dream," an upbeat Holliday–Martin duet, was actually added to the Broadway production late in the run. The other two were new solos for Martin—"Do It Yourself," substituting for the similar "On My Own" in the stage version, and a ballad called "My Guiding Star."

Minnelli later recalled the three-month shoot of *Bells Are Ringing* as a fairly smooth experience, which was a relative judgment at most. He had just finished two consecutive projects filmed largely in the American hinterlands—Ohio and Indiana for *Some Came Running*, and *Home from the Hill*'s locations in Texas and Mississippi. This was his first picture in over three years made almost entirely on the lot, and after Minnelli's recent rigors, *Bells Are Ringing* must have felt like a working vacation. Nevertheless, the movie was anything but trouble-free. As with Astaire, Minnelli had once again to contend with a moody and obsessively self-critical star in Holliday, who refused to believe his constant praise for her work was anything more than lip service to keep the picture moving.

Meanwhile, Freed still grappled with the picture's stubborn overlength. Having retained a higher than usual quotient of the original's songs, the screen *Bells Are Ringing* threatened to be too much of a good thing. Halfway through shooting, he received a worried memo from Sol C. Siegel, a producer who was the latest to take the hot seat as MGM's production chief. "It looks like we will end up with a three-hour picture based on the footage count to date," he wrote. "I don't see any other way of cutting down except by eliminating a couple of sequences and preferably not those that contain comedy." In early January 1960, with the movie in the can except for the title-song prologue, MGM editing supervisor Margaret Booth reported to Siegel that, without credits and the prologue, *Bells Are Ringing* already ran 131 minutes. Over the next few months, footage was shuffled, excised, and reinserted into the movie with giddy abandon. At one stage, Freed wanted to cut Ella's first-reel blind date, one of the few scenes written from scratch for the screen version, plus the swank cocktail-party sequence, "Drop That Name," the most Minnelliesque moment in the movie. In the end both were retained, unlike Holliday's mock-tragic farce aria, "Is It a Crime?" which was a particular Freed favorite. *Bells Are Ringing*'s first sneak preview in San Francisco went well, except for some grumbling over the interpolated "My Guiding Star," in which Martin sang of his awakened love for Holliday while wandering the dark streets of the city. It sounds like a Brooklyn Heights version of Minnelli's *Gigi* soliloquy, but it slowed up the last part of the picture, and disappeared from the final print.

Compared to the struggles over *Gigi, Bells Are Ringing*'s fine-tuning was a painless process, involving no new footage or major refurbishments. Still, Freed felt dispirited. *Gigi* was destined from the first to be a special undertaking, while this film would turn out to be a sleek revamping of a fluffy stage hit. (Characteristically, Minnelli was too busy to ponder these things, for by this time he was deep in preparations for *Four Horsemen of the Apocalypse,* his most expensive production to date.) Amazingly, little of this battle fatigue showed up on screen. *Bells Are Ringing*'s June opening at Radio City Music Hall was met with an even more buoyant press than the play had received, and huge crowds besides. It broke the Music Hall record for that time of year, grossing over a million 1960 dollars in its seven-week run. However, *Bells Are Ringing* was a quintessentially New York musical at a time when the rest of America seemed interested in neither quality, and its reception elsewhere was far spottier. Moreover, like many movie musicals of the time, save *Gigi,* it had little popular appeal abroad, and with the industry facing soaring budgets and a stagnant domestic box office, the foreign market was increasingly crucial. *Bells Are Ringing*'s estimated final cost came to $3,246,000, then a substantial sum for a musical of comparatively modest scope. As of 1962, its total receipts were $3,502,000, including $681,000 from overseas, leaving an estimated deficit of $1,800,000. It was Minnelli's most unprofitable picture since *The Pirate,* which proved how much escapist tastes had changed. *Bells Are Ringing*'s air of grown-up innocence perfectly suited the traditional MGM public. The problem was, this audience didn't get to the movies much anymore, and the kids who did were more likely to join Connie Francis in Ft. Lauderdale, longing to be *Where the Boys Are.*

Actually, *Bells Are Ringing* is a better example of those hybrid entertainments which flourished briefly at the time and returned in the latter half of the sixties—high-profile Broadway properties that weren't so much adapted for the screen as transcribed onto celluloid. Minnelli had made his share of these by now, and if the form was too confining for uninhibited fantasy, he

knew how to embellish it with tactful craftsmanship. Since Judy Holliday was the show's raison d'être, Minnelli saw no reason to fool around with a successful formula. The camera work by Milton Krasner (Minnelli's new favorite cinematographer, from *Some Came Running* onward) is the most self-effacing of any in the Minnelli–Freed musicals—it's Holliday who energizes the frame, while the camera trails along as an admiring audience for her antics. The script plays like one of Minnelli's romantic comedies, but the numbers by and large preserve the unities of the stage. When Holliday and Martin meet and secretly proclaim that each is "Better Than a Dream," Minnelli doesn't trick up the scene with voice-over monologues of their private thoughts—the stars belt out their alternating choruses within earshot of each other, just as they did in Jeffrey Moss's bachelor pad on stage at the Shubert Theater.

Bells Are Ringing's critical admirers appreciatively noted MGM's fidelity to the original, but it's easy to understand how some of its second-hand conventions might have discomfited those patrons who hadn't managed to catch even the bus-and-truck tour. Movie stars usually didn't strut across the set with their faces tilted stage-front to sell their big numbers, unless they were actually playing vaudevillians. But Holliday's solos at the beginning and end of *Bells Are Ringing* are showstoppers rather than movie climaxes. "It's a Perfect Relationship" takes the musical comedy ingenue's first-act plaint of romantic longing and pitches it for laughs to suit Holliday's self-deprecating temperament. "I'm Going Back" does a cunning variation on that hallowed Broadway staple, the "11 o'clock song"—a solo turn shoved into the plot ten minutes before final curtain, designed to prove how the star earned her billing in the first place.

These specialties are usually meant to induce gooseflesh rather than laughs but, as expected, Comden and Green don't take the bylaws of their trade very reverently. Their lyric lampoons an anthem to home and mammy out of Jolson's Winter Garden days—but instead of Swanee, our star is going back to the Bonjour Tristesse Brassiere Company, where she can hide behind the switchboard and just be "me myself and I." Holliday dashes through everything from a Caucasian cakewalk to a mock-soigné mannequin slouch as she recalls the fun of "a little modeling on the side." Literal-minded moviegoers might have puzzled over just what a shy-type girl like our heroine, Ella Peterson, was *doing* up there, socking across those gags like Mickey-and-Judy auditioning for a spot at the Palace. But it was catnip to Holliday's fans, at a fifth the price of a Broadway seat.

In *Bells Are Ringing,* Holliday is more an irresistible force of nature (or show biz) than a fine-grained comic actress—for that, you'd have to turn back to *The Marrying Kind* or *It Should Happen to You,* two of the black-and-white non-musicals she did with George Cukor.

Minnelli indulges her bent for splay-gaited shtick perhaps a shade too willingly, but then, with first-rate comediennes an elusive breed at any time, it's hard to begrudge his enthusiasm once he had one in front of his CinemaScope lens. Movies like *The Long, Long Trailer* and *The Reluctant Debutante* proclaim Minnelli's contagious admiration for women whose wit is kinetic as well as verbal, and he's masterful at focusing in on those specifics of personality and caste which make them so funny.

Holliday's role is a variation on her usual screen self—the lower-middle-class naif with a New York accent and a heart as big as Central Park. What Minnelli emphasizes as never before is his star's matchless flair for mimicry. Since Ella longs to be liked but has no faith in herself, she only connects with other people as a disembodied phone voice camouflaged to suit the needs of Susanswerphone's subscribers. In concrete terms, this character trait turns the movie into a Holliday gallery of giddy multiple personalities. Every flash on her switchboard sparks a new identity—from the doyenne of La Petite Bergère Restaurant to Santa Claus to Mrs. Van Rensselaer's faux-Mayfair social secretary to good old Mom, the tremble-voiced ancient who's trying to coax Jeffrey Moss off his divan and back to the typewriter. Away from Susanswerphone, Holliday becomes several other people entirely. On her blind date, she's a mute klutz whose overweeningly chic outfit turns to linen flambé after she backs into a waiter. Infiltrating a hipster hangout in search of Blake Barton, she affects sweatshirt and jeans and a Baby Brando growl. Since Ella is patently uncomfortable within her

own skin (not to mention the tightly bodiced bouffant numbers Walter Plunkett designed for her to wear), Holliday makes *Bells Are Ringing* proof farcical that schizophrenia can be fun.

Much of Holliday's appeal during her sadly abbreviated career lay in the fact that her comic genius resided in someone otherwise so ordinary-seeming. From the soft warble of her speaking voice to her candid brown-eyed gaze and her ungirdled hips, she really could have been the girl next door, if you happened to live on the pre-gentrified Upper West Side. *Bells Are Ringing* follows her cue by accentuating the intimate—it's the least pompous of movie musicals in that age of "Glorious Technicolor, Breathtaking CinemaScope and Stereophonic Sound" tweaked by Cole Porter's lyric. Nearly half the film takes place in the dusty clutter of Susanswerphone's basement office, but the effect is cozy rather than claustrophobic. Susanswerphone is a human-scale enclave in an impersonal town, and Minnelli basks in the relaxed interplay between Ella and her surrogate family of co-workers and neighbors. While the relief operator shuffles around shoeless and bitches about the heat, Ella tries out a new dialect and pages through the phone book with her big toe. These aren't the kind of people you usually find in a musical comedy, and Minnelli takes his time to get to know them before venturing out among more usual types.

After their previous libretti for *On the Town* and *Wonderful Town*, *Bells Are Ringing* confirmed that Comden and Green were the musical theater's most eloquent New York chauvinists since Lorenz Hart. They take Manhattan from a romantic worm's eye view. Subliminally, these shows are about the travails familiar to New Yorkers since the days of Peter Stuyvesant—how hard it is to get around town, and how impossible to find a decent place to live, unless you're a successful playwright like Jeffrey Moss. They take place in such glamorous locales as subway cars and taxicabs and grubby basement studios; the main characters subsist on next to no money, kvetch constantly, and can't get over their luck in living in such an exciting, exasperating place. Comden and Green's town is so wonderful because it's the biggest little village in the world. Despite their tough city armor, almost everyone you meet wants to be pals once you get to know them—which you usually do in some production number set on Christopher Street or an avenue on what *Bells Are Ringing* calls "New York's Smart East Side."

With this show, for the first time one of Comden and Green's bargain-basement New Yorkers gets to rub shoulders with her dubious betters on Sutton Place, as the heroine is dragged to a swanky bash in Jeffrey's honor. This Cinderella's problem is not loose high heels but the wrong dress—a cast-off ball gown from Act I of *La Traviata,* courtesy of Susanswerphone subscriber Mme. Grimaldi. There's also the language barrier, for Ella is, as usual, tongue-tied in a crowd, while this elite throng speaks only in rhymed couplets of proper nouns —a Beverly Hills Hotel laundry list of *le tout* show business and lesser allied arts such as literature and high finance. A time-capsule record of late-fifties celebrity-hood, *Bells Are Ringing's* tabloid Almanach de Gotha manages to mention many of the authors' nearest and dearest; amid the odes to Barney Baruch and King Farouk, Alastair Cooke, Lizzie and Eddie, Lucille Ball and Lauren Bacall, Vivien Leigh, Roz Russell and Freddie, there's also room for Arthur Freed, Irving Lazar, and Vincente Minnelli (rhymes with the-former-Grace-Kelly). Ella's contribution to the chatter is to list the famous canines of screen history. When the topic shifts to couture and the enduring value of Chanel and Valentina's "things with good lines," Ella brags about her "things from Klein's." When she wistfully realizes the jig is up and "The Party's Over," the playwright-prince goes to inordinate lengths (i.e., Brooklyn) to try to track her down. When he finds her around the corner from Sutton Place at Susanswerphone's grubby hearth, the happy ending of this Cinderella story is a slight letdown, thanks to Comden and Green's fondness for the New York of hot plates and Murphy beds. It's just so much nicer at Susanswerphone than at Moss's tastefully modern high-rise flat—the best conclusion of all would find the hero typing away in a corner while Ella resumes her calling as fairy godmother to those lost souls buzzing her switchboard.

Considering the movie's adherence to its source, the Comden and Green spirit would have dominated, no matter who had directed it. Yet it's still unmistakably a Minnelli movie—something like *The Clock* with production numbers acted out by pastel-colored cousins to his favorite screen archetypes. Minnelli was drawn to self-doubting heroines whose imaginary alter egos are more confident and glamorous than they could ever be, and his preoccupation with this only increased in the years to come. His final two movies were both portraits of such women, and each concluded with the thought that self-acceptance is the first step toward realizing one's fantasies. Ella's field trip among the upper crust was already a highlight of the play, but Minnelli shapes "Drop That Name" into one of his characteristic lamb-to-the-slaughter set-pieces, in which a gauche outsider is swallowed up and spat out by well-heeled pagans. The scene is cluttered and airless and as blindingly lit as an operating room, the soundtrack clattering with mirthless snickers. In her démodé Minnelli-red dress, Ella is surrounded by Metro's slinkiest starlets in tight metallic-hued sheaths, gliding serenely past his camera with inhuman aplomb. Minnelli always did love a party, but as usual his heroine makes a quick dash for the exit at the first opportunity.

In his lightweight fashion, Jeffrey Moss is a variation on a host of Minnelli heroes of the fifties, from those in *An American in Paris* through *Lust for Life,* with *Two Weeks in Another Town* still to come. As a Broadway hit-manufacturer, Moss's aesthetic grasp may fall short of *Some Came Running's* novelist Dave Hirsh's (much less that of Vincent Van Gogh) but his conflict is the same —he's a thwarted artist whose inability to love is linked to his failure to create. Minnelli stages the playwright's darkest moment in typical manner; Moss croons the Comden–Green pep talk "Do It Yourself" to lure himself back to the grind, but his resolve falters when a long, unsparing glance at the mirror reveals his true self—hungover and burnt-out. The main difference is that, this being musical comedy, instead of losing an ear Dean Martin eventually gets Judy Holliday.

Apart from a few inserted shots, Minnelli doesn't have the luxury of authentic backgrounds to evoke Comden and Green's Manhattan. So instead, he peoples these sound-stage streets with dozens of anonymities as vivid and eccentric as his romantic leads. It's not hard to figure out that his version of Times Square is a facsimile. (One clue is that among its limelit attractions is a certain "Jim Henry's Paradise," the dive in which Rochester and Lena Horne went to perdition in *Cabin in the Sky.*) But the throngs racing past this set testify to his gift for treating extras like quirky character players, who give texture to his frame, rather than just take up space. The energy of the city street sets the tempo for Martin's exultant solo, "I Met a Girl," but Minnelli dispenses with the set entirely. Seen from his high-angle perch, Martin is the central dot in a pointillist sea of people running, laughing, and shoving. These have none of the antic poise of the usual Hollywood bit actors—in their citified way, they resemble the hordes of real midwesterners who surged through the carnival climax to *Some Came Running.*

For all his outré tastes, in one crucial sense Minnelli's alertness to certain realities made *Bells Are Ringing* a more persuasive portrait of the city than the stage version could ever have been. Similar to many Broadway musicals of the 1950s, *Bells Are Ringing*'s ensemble consisted of two dozen homogenized singers and dancers—all young, all pert, nearly all white. Even if it was reconstituted at Culver City, Minnelli's New York is a carefully stirred melting pot of every race and all ages from kids to crones. On stage and screen, the plot stalls fitfully for a subplot involving Ella's boss, Sue, and her faithless Viennese-accented beau, a bookie who poses as a classical record executive. His number, "It's a Simple Little System," is Minnelli's chance to make the comic most of the cross-section of New York types he's assembled. To the meter of a Damon Runyonized Handel oratorio, Eddie Foy Jr. explains to his cronies how to place bets like record orders; meanwhile, Minnelli fills the screen with black matrons and tough guys; a

Arthur Freed, Minnelli, and Judy Holliday in 1959 during a break on Bells Are Ringing *(1960)*

Chinese gamine and a butch *bohémienne* in black leather; dowagers and bag-ladies, bums and businessmen. Minnelli makes sure that for the uninitiated in movie theaters everywhere, these characters distill the idea of New York as forcefully as the high-lifers in *Gigi*'s Maxim's did for Paris.

Not all of *Bells Are Ringing* is so imaginatively fleshed out. Holliday's rendition of Styne's touching ballad "The Party's Over" somehow falls slightly flat—the camerawork and use of the Sutton Place set are utilitarian at best, while the star herself seems a bit remote and muted, having already wrung poignance out of the song 800-plus times on stage. Still, *Bells* is the most ingratiating of Minnelli's lesser musicals. It's ironic that this cheery item was the forerunner of a brace of his final farewells to the medium. *Bells Are Ringing* was the last movie Judy Holliday ever made; after two returns to the theater interrupted by grave sieges of illness, she died in 1965. And nobody at the time imagined that this would be the last Minnelli–Freed musical, least of all the two gentlemen themselves.

Minnelli's last six years at the studio were littered with stillborn musical properties; had they been made, the last phase of his career might have been very different. In 1961, Freed tried to acquire Lerner and Loewe's *Camelot* for Minnelli to direct, but the studio balked at the cost. Minnelli's last contract with MGM, signed the following year, stipulated that the studio would make every effort to obtain the rights to *My Fair Lady,* which would automatically be assigned to him. This time the company made serious bids for this surefire property, but they were once more outbid by Warner Bros. Most frustrating of all was the doomed struggle to make *Say It with Music,* the spectacular Freed meant to be his last hurrah. In 1963, Freed announced he would produce a cavalcade of Irving Berlin songs both new and old— a kind of *Alexander's Ragtime Band* for the sixties. Over the next three years, he and Minnelli struggled in vain to realize this idea. A first-draft script was written by Arthur Laurents (librettist of *West Side Story* and *Gypsy*), with roles penciled in for Robert Goulet, Ann-Margret,

and Sophia Loren. Subsequent scripts were penned by Leonard Gershe (*Funny Face*) and Comden and Green, who stuck with the project the longest. None of them convinced the studio's ever-shifting management, who deemed Freed and his ilk throwbacks to a receding past they'd just as soon forget.

Out of nostalgia for the Freed musical, it's tempting to dismiss their doubts as crassness and arrogance, but these newcomers may have had a point. Men like Joseph Vogel, Robert O'Brien, and Robert Weitman may not have been the measure of the moguls who once made MGM great; still, it's hard to imagine who the audience would have been in those a-go-go times for Berlin's Greatest Hits on a ten million dollar budget. When Minnelli left the studio at the end of 1966 he continued work on a new treatment with MGM writer George Wells. Later on, Freed persevered with Blake Edwards, as new press releases announced first Fred Astaire and then Julie Andrews for this phantom project. But it was never to be—once CBS executive James Aubrey occupied the studio and disposed of most of its assets, *Say It with Music* was history, just like the backlot razed for condominiums. By then it was abundantly clear that the party was over for good; gallantly, Minnelli was one of the last to leave, nursing the dregs of his California champagne.

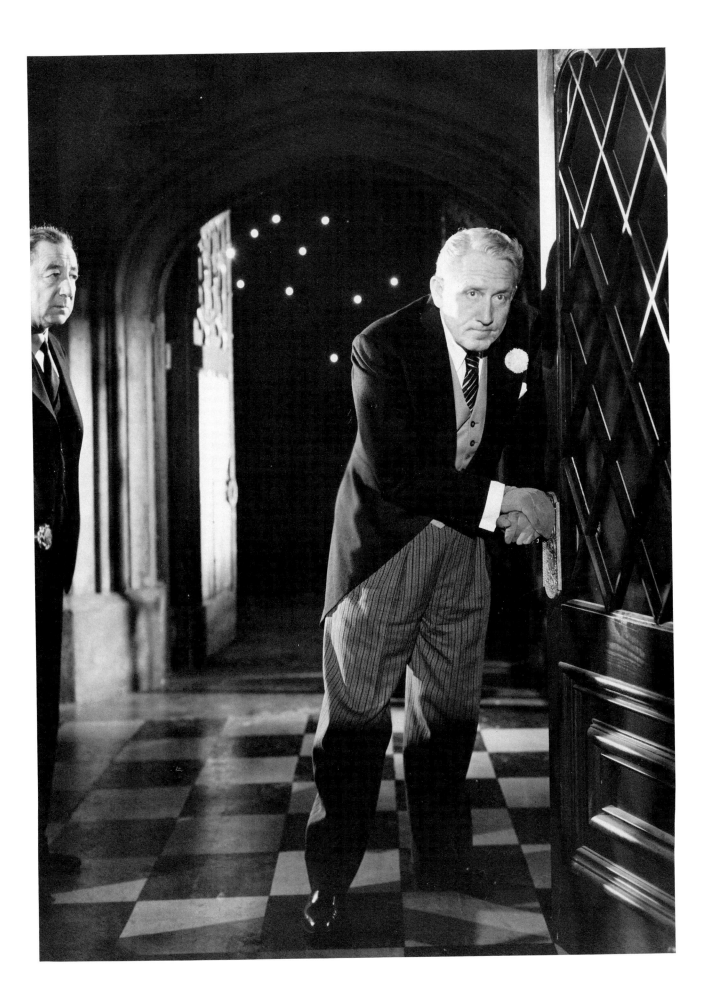

4 Comedies

During Minnelli's first decade at the studio, MGM was noted for other things besides its splendiferous musicals—women's pictures ranging from tony Greer Garson inspirationals to lower-caste romances for Lana Turner; macho vehicles for Clark Gable's surly charm and Robert Taylor's Roman-coin profile; the plush, morbid Victoriana of *Gaslight* and *The Picture of Dorian Gray;* misty-eyed salutes to the Union Jack à la *The White Cliffs of Dover* and *The Green Years;* the love of kids for quadrupeds like Lassie and *National Velvet*'s The Pi; Margaret O'Brien's sniffles and Mickey Rooney's wholesome smalltown randiness. MGM specialized in provincial sentiment and bigtime luxury, both linked to its fervent cult of star personality.

Yet, if the studio had an avid eye for gloss and Class, by the 1940s it had a tin ear for humor. The MGM ethos was too smug to leave room for the anarchy of farce or the skepticism of satire. In the previous decade, the studio had been buoyed by a somewhat homogenized Marx Brothers, the tart teamwork of William Powell and Myrna Loy, and that least typical of Metro stars, Jean Harlow. Both the Marxes and Nick and Nora Charles waned fast, while the late lamented platinum blonde was reincarnated in the bowdlerized form of Ann Sothern's B-picture Maisie.

For a studio that prided itself on the unequaled glory of its constellation of stars, MGM took an unseemly pratfall where its comic contract players were concerned. As Paramount promoted the fortunes of Bob Hope and Goldwyn showcased Danny Kaye, MGM made do with Red Skelton, galumphing his way through recycled Buster Keaton routines of a generation before. Lucille Ball spent much of the forties at Metro but was considered too eccentric for major stardom, so she earned her salary as a red-headed Eve Arden clone, cracking wise along the sidelines. For each of her feminist tussles with Spencer Tracy, Katharine Hepburn was forced to do double penance as a kind of Bryn Mawr Greer Garson, donning *Dragon Seed*'s putty eyelids and raw silk pyjamas, and Clara

Schumann's ladylike widow's weeds for the soporific *Song of Love.* MGM's dream romantic-comedy team was Van Johnson and June Allyson—the box office said so.

Under the circumstances, MGM saw no point in cultivating the handful of master comedy directors who were coddled elsewhere—Preston Sturges was too independent and Ernst Lubitsch a confectioner for gourmet tastes, whose wares cost more and earned less than those of such bread-and-butter purveyors as Norman McLeod or Roy Del Ruth. A witty writer-producer like Joseph L. Mankiewicz left MGM when L. B. Mayer scoffed at his directorial ambitions; by the end of the forties, he was winning Oscars for Fox with *A Letter to Three Wives.* Even a merry director like George Cukor found little to laugh about at Culver City in the 1940s. Between *The Philadelphia Story* (1940) and *Adam's Rib* (1949), he spent his time orchestrating the anguish of Joan Crawford (*A Woman's Face*), Ingrid Bergman (*Gaslight*), Deborah Kerr (*Edward, My Son*) and Hepburn herself (*Keeper of the Flame*). Just as well, for these were scarcely grimmer than his drawing-room farces *Two-Faced Woman* and *Her Cardboard Lover,* which spurred Greta Garbo and Norma Shearer into premature retirement.

As a rising contract director during this decade, Minnelli was expected to adapt to any genre within reason. He'd shown his willingness and aptitude with the range of his first three dramatic films, spanning wartime romance (*The Clock*), contemporary Gothic (*Undercurrent*), and the French provincial mores of *Madame Bovary.* After the Freed musicals, his transition to straight comedy should have been particularly easy, but considerable time went by before he got the chance to prove it. Once he did, Minnelli's comedies became as indispensable to the Metro production lineup in the 1950s as his musicals and melodramas. Many of them were immensely profitable for the studio, and earned considerable critical acclaim in the bargain.

Minnelli enjoyed steering these diversions, partly as a breather from his more imposing projects; from a production point of view, they were simpler to assemble and shoot than his sound-stage dream ballets and dramatic travelogues, which encouraged a more relaxed atmosphere on the set. At the same time, there was nothing frivolous or condescending in his attitude toward these movies. His comedies are in fact a fascinating hybrid of the values he brought to both his musicals and melodramas. Such Metrocolor entertainments as *Designing Woman* and *The Reluctant Debutante* have the stylized verve of Freed Unit production numbers, only here the tempos are set by badinage and genteel slapstick rather than by Gene Kelly's leaps or some Cole Porter song. Like *Meet Me in St. Louis, Father of the Bride* and its sequel take a bittersweet view of the middle-class American hearth. With the sight gags of

The Long, Long Trailer, and *The Courtship of Eddie's Father's* moppet antics, Minnelli echoes the favorite themes of his grimmer films from the period: the boobytrapped lure of material comfort; the unexplored fissures which threaten the most complacent of families. Naturally, the comedies aim for the solace of giggles rather than catharsis, but like his best musicals, they're often darker than they look. For all their satiny wrappings, these movies frequently reinforce one of comedy's basic axioms—that the cue for laughter is someone else's pain.

. . . .

1950   **FATHER OF THE BRIDE and**

1951   **FATHER'S LITTLE DIVIDEND**

Minnelli's first comedy assignment was supposed to be a modest little item with a mouthful of a title—in September 1949, the studio publicity department announced that he would soon start *The Skipper Surprised His Wife,* featuring Robert Walker. Fortunately, something more promising came along, thanks to Pandro Berman, whose *Madame Bovary* had rescued Minnelli from a year's inactivity. Berman was long established as one of Hollywood's most eclectic and discerning producers, and would remain so well into the 1960s. During most of the 1930s he was head of production at RKO, supervising the Astaire–Rogers musicals and Katharine Hepburn's mercurial career. In 1940 Berman transferred to MGM; he remained there for the bulk of his active career, producing *National Velvet, Ivanhoe, The Blackboard Jungle* and *Cat On a Hot Tin Roof* among dozens of other pictures. Berman was known for combining shrewd practical instincts with a sympathetic rapport for the artists he respected. Next to Freed, he was the producer Minnelli worked with most frequently at Metro, mounting many of his subsequent comedies.

Berman's current project was *Father of the Bride,* the latest work of light fiction by Edward Streeter, a best-selling humorist since *Dere Mable,* a collection of the fictional letters home from a typical doughboy published right after World War I. More recent Streeter books had been upscale in tone, and this new effort was a gentle jape at the nuptial rites of upper-middle-class suburbia. It was obviously a perfect property for Metro, the studio which held the patent on the dream of the typical American family as a ruffled corporation lawyer, his imperturbable spouse, their gangly brood and a faithful domestic; as soon as the book appeared in 1948, the film rights were snared for $100,000.

Berman's first task was to assign Frances Goodrich

and Albert Hackett, late of *The Pirate* and *Easter Parade,* to write the screen adaptation. Minnelli was his first choice to direct the film; Berman was proud of the way *Madame Bovary* had turned out, and relied on him to imbue *Father of the Bride's* domestic vignettes with the same resonance and charm he had extracted from *Meet Me in St. Louis.* Minnelli needed no persuading, as the prospect of making a small-scale comedy in a contemporary setting seemed a lark after the rigors of adapting Gustave Flaubert to the screen. Meanwhile, stage actor-director Elliott Nugent had been drafted to helm the luckless *Skipper,* which drifted into obscurity as soon as it was released.

Minnelli and Berman knew at once that Spencer Tracy was the ideal interpreter of their lovably disgruntled title character. In fact, this was in retrospect a more creative stroke of casting than it appeared. Tracy had just begun to assume unmistakably middle-aged roles, and of late only played for laughs when he had Katharine Hepburn around to spar with; in fact, his last Hepburnless comedy had been *Libeled Lady,* made in 1936. Yet *Father of the Bride* almost had to muddle through without him, thanks to an exasperating gaffe by Dore Schary, the new production chief under L. B. Mayer. Schary had offhandedly promised Jack Benny a crack at *Father of the Bride* and, to save the boss's honor, Minnelli was forced to go through the motions of screen-testing the comedian for the part. Out of respect for Benny he did his best, but Minnelli knew that casting him would turn this comedy of sentiment into a showcase for the usual Benny skinflint jokes, keyed for a change to his movie daughter's trousseau instead of to Rochester's salary. The test caused even more trouble than Minnelli had anticipated; upon hearing that others were being considered for it, Tracy abruptly refused the role. As Hepburn and Minnelli had become friends while making *Undercurrent,* he beseeched her to intercede. Over dinner at Hepburn's house, Minnelli managed to persuade Tracy that only he could give *Father of the Bride* the distinction it needed. With that act of diplomacy successfully completed, plans for the movie went forward without a hitch.

As Tracy's daughter, Berman and Minnelli chose seventeen-year-old Elizabeth Taylor, who after five years at the studio had recently launched a precocious career in grown-up parts. They ventured off the lot to find a plausible candidate for the mother of the bride in Joan Bennett. Having spent the thirties as a winsome blonde ingenue and the forties as a sullen temptress with raven tresses, Bennett had now reached the chic matron stage. Berman and Minnelli could scarcely have done better, for in addition to a striking resemblance to Taylor, she and Tracy had a tart, affectionate screen chemistry which veteran moviegoers might have recalled from their first youthful teaming in the wisecracking melodrama *Me and My Gal,* made eighteen years before.

Delighted with his cast and Goodrich and Hackett's script, Minnelli started shooting *Father of the Bride* on January 16 1950. He finished the film exactly a month and a day later—even given the modest physical scale of the movie, this was astonishingly quick for a major Metro release. Minnelli got texture as well as efficiency from cameraman John Alton, a recent B-picture laureate who was used to working fast. The studio felt they had a surefire hit as soon as the first days' rushes were unreeled. Halfway through production on *Father of the Bride,* the story department registered the title, *Now I'm a Grandfather,* for a prospective sequel. On its release in May, the finished film fulfilled all MGM's expectations, for it won unusual acclaim for such an unprepossessing comedy, and proved a boon to the studio's coffers. With domestic returns of $4,150,000 against a budget of about a quarter that sum, the movie was the sixth highest-grossing movie of the year; meanwhile, Oscar nominations were bestowed on Tracy, the script and the picture itself. As for Minnelli, after the shaky times that followed *The Pirate, Father of the Bride* was welcome proof of his value to the studio, and marked the start of the most prolific decade in his career.

Spencer Tracy and Joan Bennett in Father of the Bride *(1950)*

Essentially, Minnelli's first comedy is a streamlined, New Look refurbishment of *Meet Me in St. Louis,* with the spotlight shifted from the lovelorn ingenue to her exasperated dad. In both movies, a series of small family epiphanies give an elastic plot its shape, while the realistic domestic setting sets the tone for the whole. The Smiths and the Bankses alike are defined by the comfortable, well-run American homes in which they live. This is the stage for anything important that happens; every member of the household has a carefully circumscribed role, and no deviant ad-libbing would occur to any of them.

While *Meet Me in St. Louis* looked back wistfully to an age of middle-class stability untroubled by depressions or blitzkriegs, *Father of the Bride* is a Truman-era time capsule, selling the ideal of a return to secure values and suburban comfort. Distinctively flavored though it is by its stars' personalities, the Banks family is the prototype for a dozen fifties sitcoms—so much so that when MGM finally adapted *Father of the Bride* into a TV series in the early sixties, it seemed tediously déjà vu after so many prior small-screen variations on the original movie. Stanley Banks, a.k.a. "Pops," is the compliant breadwinner, soothingly domesticated by the real head of the house, Ellie Banks. Her job is to make things nice, combining immaculate grooming with feminine practicality. Their sons Tommy (teenaged, always hungry) and Ben (collegiate, always borrowing the car) hit their marks on cue, but their big sister the family pet is twenty-year-old Kay, nicknamed Kitten. Her main attribute is energetic American charm, and her sole ambition, matrimony to some likely young man so she can fulfill her destiny as a replica of her own mother. All of them are preternaturally conventional, on a slightly loftier social scale than most folks in the audience.

Inevitably, there's an undertone of smugness to this airbrushed family portrait posed in a white Colonial on a tree-lined street in the second-best part of town. (In this case, Minnelli used a block on N. Alpine Drive in Beverly Hills to stand in for Everydale, U.S.A.) The movie dilutes the Scarsdale-pukka tone of Streeter's book, but there's enough left to reinforce the sense of what an exclusive little enclave the "typical" suburban community could be. It's there in Kay's defiant account of the bloodlines of her betrothed, Buckley Dunstan— "as for his parents . . . they're just as good as you and Mom. They're fine people, and they live in Westbridge. I guess you'll agree that Westbridge is just as good a place as Fairview Manor!" It's certainly discernible in Mrs. Banks' Locust Valley-lockjaw drawl, and the off-handed way she tinkles her little dinner bell when it's time for giggly maid Delilah to serve the coffee.

In later movie dramas, Minnelli would pillory families like this—Frank Sinatra's conformist relations in *Some Came Running;* the repressed, emasculating matriarch that Eleanor Parker plays in *Home from the Hill.*

As someone who himself had lofty ambitions and no pedigree, Minnelli has a keen eye for the subtle gradations of class snobbery, most vividly expressed thus far in his *Madame Bovary.* But this is meant to be a sympathetic comedy, so *Father of the Bride* tweaks these values but spares his characters, who are just flotsam in a materialist tide.

"I always used to think that marriage was a simple affair," the hero mutters at the beginning of the picture, which goes on to prove in relentless detail just how wrong he was. What middle-class weddings are really about is the ostentatious accumulation and display of objects, of which the bride is the most expensive of all. Wedding guests are "reception units" whose function is to consume expensive edibles and bubbly; wedding presents are displayed in their own domestic shrine, serenaded by the MGM Orchestra's droll riff on the March from "Lohengrin." Meanwhile, the bride-to-be is the compliant mannequin for "country suits, blouses, shoes and bags to match, town suits, blouses, shoes and bags to match . . . one hostess dress, four negligees, evening wrap, hats, furs, snuggies, a raincoat, a dozen slips"—a trousseau her father contemplates with mounting horror.

Stanley plaintively asks, "What are people going to say when I'm in the gutter because I tried to put on a wedding like a Roman emperor?" but everyone's too busy to listen. From the moment his daughter's engagement is announced, the Bankses' social status suffers another blow with every passing milestone. Buckley's folks (Moroni Olsen and Billie Burke at her burbliest) turn out to be a lot tonier than the parents of the bride—they've got a *white* servant to open the portals of their Colonial villa. Mrs. Banks' dignity further crumbles in the face of a snotty caterer (Leo G. Carroll) and his Mayfair accent, pronouncing her proposed wedding-reception menu of little cakes and tea sandwiches "what we usually serve for children's parties."

From the beginning, Mr. Banks is the most vulnerable of them all. As played by Bennett and Taylor, the ladies of the household at least sport the natural protective armor of their class, but even in Brooks Brothers suits, Spencer Tracy is nature's rumpled Everyman. Stanley is a particularly likable example of a favorite Minnelli hero—the displaced person, thrust haplessly into a situation he doesn't relish and can't control. For the real story of this movie is not the marriage of his daughter but the slow humiliation of her father, who loses the most cherished person in his life and gets to pay for the privilege.

Stanley narrates the *Father of the Bride,* but he's actually the last to know what's really going on. When his wide-eyed daughter casually announces her plan to wed, Banks hasn't the remotest idea which of her army of suitors she's favored with her hand. (Minnelli does a caustic montage here of this nerds' gallery, swooping in for closeups of a chinless egghead, a scowling radiparched guests. Kay's wedding reception is the usual Minnellian sea of claustrophobic giddiness, and amid the crush and the hubbub, he fails to catch even a glimpse of his daughter before she departs forever. In between, he is insulted by the catering staff, berated by his wife, and half-trampled at the wedding rehearsal. Stanley can't even find relief in slumber, where he is shattered by terrifying visions of himself ruining the High Protestant rites on the happy day.

In dramatic roles, Tracy tended to the pontifical as he got older, particularly later when playing the secular saints of movies like *Bad Day at Black Rock* and *Judgment at Nuremberg*. Even in the Hepburn comedies, his moral clarity and horse sense are the forces which subdue his flighty co-star. So it's especially refreshing to watch this actor play victim for a change, his stoic deadpan the emblem of his unraveling dignity. Most farceurs are light on their feet, but it's Tracy's sheer physical gravity that makes him so funny in this picture; he's a would-be immovable object knocked off his base by malign, irresistible forces. Tracy is a master of the deceptively offhand detail that humanizes a scene—toying with a rice-filled shoe as he surveys the wreckage left by this festive occasion; chewing on his tongue while stuffing himself into a twenty-year-old cutaway. From his impassive gaze to the gruff murmured tones with which he recalls this affair, Tracy's minimalist art is a rebuke to the high-octane energy most actors apply to high comedy.

cal, a rubber-jointed be-bopper and the rest.) The lucky fellow, played by bland Don Taylor, turns out to be "that muscle-bound ham with the shoulders"—plus tennis racquet and too many teeth. When he attempts to assert his paternal prerogatives, the result is universal embarrassment. Over martinis and lunch at the Dunstans', Stanley regales them with hours of cute anecdotes of Kay's childhood before drifting off into an alcoholic snooze. His fireside chat with Buckley about the boy's financial prospects turns into a dozy monologue on the Bankses' exchequer. Usually, however, he doesn't even get the chance to bore his intimates—events are always snatching his cues away. The at-home cocktail hour announcing the engagement finds Stanley closeted in the kitchen making drinks for his

All of which meshes with Minnelli's own intentions, because as with *Meet Me in St. Louis, Father of the Bride*'s buoyant spirit is constantly colliding with its latent pa-

Elizabeth Taylor and Spencer Tracy in Father of the Bride *(1950)*

ABOVE:
Spencer Tracy and Marietta Canty (right) in Father of the Bride *(1950)*

thos. While allowing ample space for the movie's comic set pieces, at every opportunity Minnelli gives a disquieting undertone to the script with two elements banished from most movie comedies—darkness and silence. Shooting *Father of the Bride* in black and white wasn't an unusual choice; in 1950, only musicals and epics tended to be graced by Technicolor. More curious is the shadowy texture of the camera work, which turns this movie into a closet suburban film noir.

More than half of the movie takes place at night, when the family is prey to its worst phantoms—mounting wedding bills, doubts about their future son-in-law's character, a sudden explosion between the engaged couple. Since the mid-thirties, comedies nearly always featured a fizzy score, to cue the audience when they were supposed to be having a good time. But there's no such editorializing here; the Bankses go through their prenuptial trials to the unaccompanied sound of their own agitated voices. This must have been the easiest job contract composer Adolph Deutsch ever had at Metro. The first half of the movie contains no music at all, while the rest comes from an on-screen source and is the bare minimum keyed to the requirements of the story—a church-organ processional, the tinklings of the rented combo at the wedding reception. Deutsch's one sustained musical theme is there for creeps rather than guffaws—the discordant phantom-of-the-opera obbligato which frames Stanley's midnight hallucination of the ceremony to come. This sequence is the most Gothic of all the cold-sweat nightmares in Minnelli's movies, as disturbing in its way as any of the last-reel catharses of his later melodramas. Streeter's novel also features a prenuptial bad dream for Stanley, but it's pretty mild stuff: his formal clothes don't fit, so the wedding party titters and whispers as he marches down the aisle. But the Minnelli version is undiluted Guignol punctuated by the silent screams of the throng—a surreal collage of superimposed images and jagged montage.

Presiding over it all is an extreme closeup of Tracy's haunted eyes, the whites opaque and blinding in a black void. The church floor swims and buckles under the hero's fumbling feet until he's reduced to crawling down the aisle, his morning suit further tattered every time one of his limbs sinks below the surface. The guests are too revolted to laugh, and what a gruesome bunch they are. Shot from below to underscore their grotesqueness, these crones and geezers crane their wizened faces out of the shadows for a better view. (Except that these gargoyles keep their eyeballs in their sockets, they bear an astonishing resemblance to the figures in Max von Sydow's worst delusions in Ingmar Bergman's, *Hour of the Wolf,* made in the late sixties.) Nor are his dear ones any more sympathetic—Ellie hides her face in shame and Kay contorts her face in a horrified shriek, while her bridegroom looks on, sickened. No wonder Stanley wakes up panting; this se-

OPPOSITE:
The Bankses and Dunstans plan for Father's Little Dividend *(1951). Spencer Tracy, Elizabeth Taylor, Don Taylor, Moroni Olsen, Billie Burke, Joan Bennett*

quence gives quite a jolt to the audience as well. The sight of this hero completely debased is no laughing matter. As with Margaret O'Brien's passing traumas in *Meet Me in St. Louis,* Tracy's anxieties are too primal to be dismissed with a vicarious chuckle.

But in the end, a comforting balance is restored. The wedding is *Saturday Evening Post*-perfect, and his daughter even telephones before starting her honeymoon to proffer her heartfelt love and thanks. The movie ends as it began, with Banks exhausted, sunk in his armchair amid the wreckage left by the bridal party.

"Nothing's really changed, has it? " he muses, and in a final gesture of reconciliation, he takes his wife into his arms for a last waltz as their phonograph plays "Goodnight, Sweetheart." Minnelli's camerawork is characteristically fluid throughout, but he saves the big virtuoso shot for the last instant. As Stanley and Ellie dance contentedly inside their white-clapboard haven, Minnelli retreats from them in an endless reverse dolly shot, pulling the camera back through the length of the house and out the French windows to the darkened, wind-stirred garden. It's a genuinely tender moment, distilling the film's mingled emotions of parental devotion and parting. As assigned, Minnelli turned *Father of the Bride* into an ingratiating entertainment with enough realistic detail to give the public a pleasurable shock of recognition. His intimations of trouble are as conspicuous an element in the suburban decor as Ellie's silver-plate coffee service and Stanley's rack of briar pipes; it's just that the audience is too lulled by the movie's charm to notice. Subsequent movies showed that where Minnelli was concerned, the happy nuclear family is a province as mythical as Yolanda Aquaviva's native Patria. Once he left the Bankses behind him for good, Minnelli never again looked on the American household with such serene equanimity.

In the meantime, the dispatch with which the Metro assembly line put together *Father of the Bride*'s sequel shows how efficiently the movie factories still could function in the early 1950s. For a mere $10,000, the studio obtained the rights to a second film using Streeter's characters. As most of *Father of the Bride*'s cast and crew were under contract to MGM, Berman had no trouble reuniting virtually the entire troupe; the only major substitution was Albert Sendrey for Deutsch, to compose the score. The pretext for the sequel was obvious—having survived his daughter's betrothal, Stanley Banks would now suffer through the birth of her first child.

Once Goodrich and Hackett finished the new script

and the stars' intervening commitments had been cleared away, *Father's Little Dividend* was ready to shoot in October 1950. There was, however, one hitch to the timetable—that fall, Minnelli was in the middle of filming *An American in Paris*. Drafting another director to guide *Father* to grandfatherhood would have been more expedient, but Berman counted on him to re-create the luster of the original. Minnelli was intrigued by the challenge of shuttling between two pictures at once; for one thing, acquiescence might buy insurance for the future, showing his bosses what an industrious good sport he could be. With his consent, the studio production department worked out a fiendishly tight schedule for this pair of projects. While the *American in Paris* company took a hiatus between shooting the book and the ballet, Minnelli spent three weeks preparing *Father's Little Dividend* for the cameras. Filming began on October 9 and wrapped up a mere twenty-three days later. Winded but unbowed, he immediately scurried back to Stage 27 to dream once more in Technicolor, dragging John Alton along with him.

By the time Minnelli completed the ballet in January, MGM had already conducted three public previews of *Father's Little Dividend*. The response reaffirmed the appeal of this package, and Minnelli's indefatigable craftsmanship. "Audience chortled throughout. Ending played very well," MGM executive

Lawrence Weingarten cabled Schary after one of these sneak screenings, "Looks like this one will pay the rent." *Father's Little Dividend* opened at Radio City Music Hall in April 1951, less than eleven months after *Father of the Bride*'s premiere there and just about the time it would have taken for the young Dunstans to produce their own offspring. The press liked the sequel nearly as well as the original, and the Directors' Guild awarded Minnelli its quarterly award as best director in that spring's movie season. Fulfilling Weingarten's prophecy, the film returned $3,100,000 against production costs of $941,437.

Father's Little Dividend follows the blueprint of its successful prototype to a fault. Both movies begin in precisely the same way, with Stanley in his armchair fiddling with his shoelace as he confides to the camera all that he's been through over the past few months. Just as he had balked at the prospect of losing a daughter, now he quails to learn he's gaining a grandchild; for him, it's an unwelcome reminder of encroaching age. Where *Father of the Bride* flipped through a snapshot album of Kay's beaux, *Father's Little Dividend* offers a forbidding collage of grandfathers Stanley has known. As before, while Stanley fumes, Ellie bustles—preparing for the baby makes her feel useful again. There's the usual orgy of conspicuous consumption, this time centered on the mother-to-be's baby shower,

Spencer Tracy and Elizabeth Taylor, Father's Little Dividend *(1951)*

and the Dunstans' ferociously polite battle to upstage the Bankses for possession of their mutual grandchild. Kay confides her fears, and her otherwise worry-prone father quells them. He reprises his role as helpless bystander to a furious spat between the youthful couple which threatens all their plans. Later on, Stanley confronts his worst fears of humiliation, which this time take the form of a living nightmare rather than his private dark imaginings—the loss of the baby during an outing with Grandpa in the park. Again, a solemn social ritual makes everything right again; now it's the child's christening, where Stanley learns his name has been bestowed on the littlest future commuter.

Between the expertise of Minnelli and company and the goodwill of a built-in audience, *Father's Little Dividend* couldn't miss. However, it's too busy dogging the footsteps of its successful forebear to achieve a distinctive gait of its own. None of these reprised episodes have quite the same snap as before. Kay and Buckley's midnight quarrel is a more disruptive crisis here than in *Father of the Bride,* but memories of the original undercut its dramatic urgency; you know the scene's going to end in fervent hugs and sobbed mutual apologies while bewildered Father shuffles off into the background, just as it did the first time.

The strain occasionally tells on Tracy, who resorts to an unseemly ration of doleful-eyed mugging to convey Father's perennial high dudgeon. When things get serious, he's further hampered by the moister passages in the script, as in his pious avowal that "when the time comes, you mothers seem to have a courage and a strength you never knew you had." Moreover, while Minnelli's professionalism is evident throughout, his imagination has flagged somewhat the second time around. Considering the atmosphere of haste and distraction in which it was made, it's not surprising that *Father's Little Dividend* lacks the original's nuances of style. Although both had approximately the same budget, the sequel feels more cheaply produced than *Father of the Bride.* The slightly undernourished art direction suits the subject—the young Dunstans' toy-sized starter ranch house with carport and low-slung Contemporary living room suite is a Levittown dream of progressive domesticity. For the sake of speed and expediency, however, the camera work has an overlit flatness found in none of Minnelli's other black-and-white films of the period; it sports the standard utilitarian polish of the second-best Metro product and no more. The addition of a mechanically cheery score behind the action is another conventional touch diluting the movie's freshness. A more central problem is the slack-jawed charmlessness of young husband Don Taylor, who's given more screen time here than in *Father of the Bride.* Stanley's contempt for his son-in-law has only increased on further acquaintance, and the longer Taylor tarries before the camera, the more justified this seems. By the end, one wonders how Minnelli would have extracted laughs from this movie's logical sequel —namely, *Father's Darling Divorcee.*

Still, familiarity bred affection among the fans of the original, who found this a diverting update of the saga. There was one palpable fringe benefit to reuniting this movie family, for, Tracy's occasional comic tics notwithstanding, the rapport between the three stars seems even more assured than before. If Joan Bennett and Elizabeth Taylor were overshadowed by Tracy's quiet bravura in *Father of the Bride,* the sequel gave them both ample chance to shine. In outline, Ellie Banks may be a generic suburban Garden Clubber but Bennett brings real individuality to the part, effortlessly segueing from acidulous sangfroid to dervish-like industry in the flick of a mascaraed eyelash. There's tenderness behind Bennett's brittle chic, as well; early in the film, her hushed reverie on the carefree pleasure of having grandchildren is one of the picture's quiet highlights. Meanwhile, Taylor's performance here is a subtle evolution from the mercurial post-deb she'd played just a year before. In *Father of the Bride,* her loveliness was set off by the character's adolescent volatility italicizing every second word she uttered, but here she makes Kay more fragile and contemplative.

Taylor is fully Tracy's equal in their scenes together, which have a tangible ease and affection few screen fathers and daughters could generate. She's a gentle foil for him as he reminisces on the early months of parenthood, when he feared all his wife's affections would be squandered on their child until he succumbed to her spell himself. Tracy returns the favor while Taylor shows off her confident comic technique in an optimistic report on her obstetrician's progressive ideas—he blanching and stuttering while the expectant mother extolls the fortitude of Primitive Women, who keep their babies "slung on their backs for the first two years of their lives." "You'd carry them around on your back while you were doing your housework and then when it got hungry, you'd swing it around and feed it and then swing it back again," she trills. "It gives the baby a wonderful sense of security."

Minnelli directs these scenes with a minimum of visual fuss, concentrating his energies and our attention on the actors; this latter sequence is filmed in one long medium shot, its rhythms shaped entirely by expectant Kitten and her imploding Pops. Camera action is saved for Stanley's agitation as the desperate hero scours the neighborhood for the missing baby carriage, retrieved by a local cop while he refereed a kids' soccer game. In place of the wistful elegance of *Father of the Bride*'s conclusion, here Minnelli fades to credits with a more facile (and economical) tug to the heart—baby Stanley Banks Dunstan in his christening clothes, beaming appealingly in a star closeup.

For a while there was talk of adding a third chapter to the Bankses' chronicles; considering how lucrative the first two were, MGM would doubtless have rejoiced in bankrolling Stanley Jr. all the way through medical school. However, before any concrete plans took shape, Joan Bennett became embroiled in one of the biggest Hollywood tabloid scandals of the early 1950s. Husband Walter Wanger cornered her agent and alleged lover, Jennings Lang, in a restaurant parking lot and shot him in a rather indelicate place. It was a far cry from the usual round of weddings and babies in the fictitious suburb of Fairview Manor. One of the lesser ramifications of the case was that it spelled the end of *Father III* once and for all. Even under such appalling circumstances, Minnelli was doubtless relieved by this result. Proud though he was of a job ably done, by then he and *Father* had paid dividends enough.

· ·

1954   THE LONG, LONG TRAILER

Two years later, Berman came back to Minnelli with a variation on the *Father of the Bride* model —another Goodrich–Hackett script adapted from a flyweight book, which ribbed the material and emotional stresses of middle-class American wedlock. The differences in this package showed how the relationship between Hollywood and its audience had started to shift by then. *Bride* and *Dividend* featured bona fide movie stars in a property which itself triggered a host of small-screen imitations; *The Long, Long Trailer* tried to wean TV addicts from their sets with the lure of that medium's most beloved attraction—*I Love Lucy*'s Lucille Ball and Desi Arnaz.

For some time the movie industry had loftily chosen to ignore the encroaching competition of television, and MGM was particularly obstinate. But by 1953, even the most ostrich-like insiders conceded that cuts in overhead and defensive slogans like "Movies Are Better Than Ever!" were strategies that alone would only postpone the debacle. This was the year the movies got bigger than ever, trumpeting stereo sound, magnified screens, and 3-D as a challenge to the tinny, flickering gray-and-white images beamed night after night into growing millions of American homes.

Berman's initial contribution to the cause was *Knights of the Round Table*, MGM's first movie in CinemaScope. *The Long, Long Trailer* marked an alternate ruse, of the if-you-can't-lick-'em-coopt-'em variety. Just as the studio had dithered while 20th Century-Fox and Paramount surged ahead with the wide-screen campaign, Metro balked again at Berman's idea. Its executives believed in total segregation from this impudent rival; at the time, MGM contract stars were forbidden to appear on television, even to promote their own movies, for fear of demystifying their aura. The only way the public would get to see Lana Turner or Robert Taylor, they decreed, was by plunking down their change at the neighborhood Loews. By the same token, MGM reasoned that Lucy-and-Desi fanatics would be loath to go out and pay for their antics after seeing them at home for nothing week after week.

In the end, the studio bent to Berman's confidence and proven acumen. Minnelli was finishing up *The Band Wagon* when Berman approached him, and was eager from the start. He enjoyed following his more complex pictures with lighter assignments that took less time to shoot, a regime he followed whenever possible over the next decade. Berman also had little trouble persuading Ball and Arnaz. The movies still held the edge over television in prestige terms, and for them the offer savored of sweet vindication. Early network TV was filled with movie has-beens or never-quite-weres (some things never change), and the Arnazes were no exception. Lucille Ball was forty when *I Love Lucy* premiered in 1951, and after nearly two decades on screen her career had peaked as a Metro second-stringer and Bob Hope's tart-tongued foil in a pair of movies at Paramount. Following a 1940 movie debut, her husband had fared rather less well than that. Apart from a rare dramatic role in war pictures like *Bataan*, Arnaz' Babalu drums turned up sporadically in those

B-picture vaudevilles that couldn't afford Xavier Cugat's fees. To return as full-fledged stars in a movie guided by MGM's most distinguished director was a rare coup, especially on such lucrative terms—a reported $250,000 for their joint services.

Shooting was scheduled to begin on June 18 1953, during the television season's summer hiatus. For Minnelli, making this comedy was in many respects a pleasant reprise of his experience with *Father of the Bride.* Although *The Long, Long Trailer* involved a fair amount of outside location work, Minnelli sped through production in under four weeks, aided by the fact that TV's top comedy team was used to working fast. Ball and Arnaz found a receptive guide and audience in Minnelli, who encouraged them to embroider these tailor-made roles with their special brand of farce. Years later, both warmly recalled his bracing enthusiasm and shrewd instinct for comedy. All welcome news to Berman, who was off in England supervising *Knights of the Round Table* while Minnelli shot *The Long, Long Trailer* at Culver City.

Minnelli's only hassle was a technical dispute with the studio, which Berman tried vainly to resolve in his favor from his temporary outpost at the Borehamwood studios. MGM was determined to distinguish its A-budget entry from Desilu's weekly half-hour sitcom. After briefly toying with the idea of a 3-D Lucy and Desi, the studio decided that at least *The Long, Long Trailer* should be filmed in color—giving audiences their first glimpse of the "dizzy redhead's" true tints since her *Ziegfeld Follies* days. At the time, the studio was dropping the highly saturated Technicolor process in favor of the less complex and expensive Ansco Color system. (Soon, this too would be supplanted by Eastman Color, redubbed Metrocolor on every MGM release that employed it.) Minnelli cabled Berman of his dislike for Ansco's duller spectrum, pointing out among other things that "women's faces in Ansco seem dirty." "Want Minnelli's enthusiasm for picture remain high," Berman wired back to the brass, agreeing with his director and urging the studio to indulge him. MGM declined, and Ansco it remained; a more urgent fight of this nature emerged two years later during the preparation of *Lust for Life.* Nevertheless, this time it was just a minor annoyance. "All filmmaking should be as easy," Minnelli later averred.

To which MGM might have added, all their films should be as profitable. Despite the studio's qualms, *I-Love-Lucy*-mania only whetted moviegoers' curiosity about Lucy and Desi's feature-length romp. After a February 1954 premiere, as usual at Radio City Music Hall, the film amassed domestic rentals of $4,291,000 —more than the hugely popular *Father of the Bride,* and considerably better than the figure achieved by the higher-budgeted *Brigadoon,* released later that year. The critics were also indulgent; ironically, *The Long, Long Trailer* proved that the small screen didn't have

the exclusive patent on up-to-date laughs for the masses.

The Long, Long Trailer demonstrated further that it was possible to remake *Father of the Bride* without recourse to Spencer Tracy or a hefty residual check to Edward Streeter. Its source was a collection of chatty anecdotes culled from a middle-aged couple's year-long trek across the continent—the literary equivalent of a rec room slide show, all picturesque views interspersed with cute candid snaps of the hosts' wacky misadventures, while their guests nod into the martinis. This pair of plucky "trailerites" strive to be Mr. and Mrs. Thoreau on wheels, but the author and wife are the kind of feckless gypsies who accessorize their caravan with hanging copper planters called "ferneries," just like at home. A lot of their merry mishaps turn up in the script, but the chuckly author and his Little Woman disappear altogether. In their stead, Goodrich and Hackett traced in a slightly blurred carbon of TV's Lucy and Ricky Ricardo, here dubbed Tacy [sic] and Nicky Collini. The Arnazes are somewhat less cartoonish (and mirthful) than their sitcom selves, but the chemistry remains the same—one sings, the other takes pratfalls. Her addled "feminine" schemes clash with his bullish male common sense, and sooner or later Desi will explode in Spanish while Lucy has a lot of 'splainin' to do, after those mad-housewife notions of hers lead to domestic disaster.

The trick was to keep this trailer moving forward amusingly, while throwing up enough roadblocks to give the movie a sense of comedic conflict. The Hacketts made do by resorting to a plot structure familiar to the fans of Minnelli's previous two comedies. So, once again, *The Long, Long Trailer* becomes a slapstick tribute to male passivity, in which the breadwinner is beguiled and trapped by the caprices of his energetic better half. Like both *Fathers, The Long, Long Trailer* starts at the end of this saga, as the dismayed hero vents a flashback résumé of the miseries he's endured over the last few weeks. While the Arnazes were actually not that much younger than the book's author and his wife, the script casts them as newlyweds in the manner of the young Dunstans. Pelted with rice and smothered in tissue paper, Arnaz spends the beginning of this movie as a Latin amalgam of father of the bride and luckless bridegroom, an uneasy stooge surrounded by a soprano chorus of nuptial revelry. This shift gives spine to the movie's fragile plot—she's a devotee of life on the open road while he remains an earthbound agnostic, their marriage threatened by their home-on-wheels' every lurch during this slapstick honeymoon.

The Hacketts and Minnelli made sure this was all as solidly crafted as the stellar trailer itself; certainly audiences who expected nothing better than a breezy, bumpy ride with Lucy and Desi got their money's worth. However, this movie is essentially one long, long gimmick that lacks the enduring appeal of *Father of the Bride*. There's no room for the nuances of character that warmed Minnelli's other comedies—understandably, since Arnaz in particular wouldn't have known what to do with them. Playing to strength instead, Minnelli crams the movie with extravagant visual gags. Minnelli's actors often played tug-of-war with the decors for his undivided attention, and this time he had the biggest prop of his career to play with, so the competition was especially fierce. The forty-foot trailer is a farcically malevolent force, literally dwarfing its mortal owners. Once freed of its moorings and barreling down the open road, the trailer becomes a literal running joke. Viewed from the outside, it's an incongruously massive blot on the western landscape; at the same time, Minnelli turns its dollhouse interior into the setting for a post-Marx Brothers riff on claustrophobia, with Arnaz the principal victim. Before the trip begins,

Lucille Ball and Desi Arnaz,
The Long, Long Trailer
(1954)

OPPOSITE:
Desi Arnaz (left), Lucille Ball
in The Long, Long Trailer
(1954)

A moving violation. Lucille Ball tries to cook in the trailer, The Long, Long Trailer *(1954)*

he suffocates in heaps of the bride's nuptial booty, stuffed into every overtaxed cranny they can find. In a scene reminiscent of Tracy's engagement party stint at the bar in *Father of the Bride,* he spends his wedding night shoved into a corner mixing drinks for a flood of thirsty mobile-home aficionados.

As its walls close in on Arnaz, the trailer's rock-and-roll gait turns his helpmate into a human pinball, with the set and Minnelli's camera alike describing full-tilt diagonals worthy of the most expressionistic film. A night in a forest glade ends with a mudbath for Lucy, as gravity hurls her out of the trailer into the sodden muck outside. Her dauntless domesticity prompts the movie's one sustained contribution to the anthology of Ball's classic slapstick routines. While a cheerily vocalizing Arnaz navigates the road, she roosts behind to prepare the evening's gourmet dinner. Before long, the pitching trailer gives a new twist to her technique for tossing Caesar salad, trapping her in an avalanche of flying kitchen utensils and a blizzard of flour. Powerless against the anarchy of this machine for modern living, Ball plummets in stages from doomed aplomb to splay-footed rage. With this episode, Ball triumphantly reaffirmed her stature as the television era's natural successor to Chaplin and Keaton. Minnelli proved her worthy accomplice, even penning Arnaz' operetta-meets-Es-

coffier recitative—the counterpoint to her culinary catastrophe. Till now, movement had spelled poetry in Minnelli movies, this time it recalls the blissful low comedy of pre-talkie farce.

Throughout, Minnelli playfully spices the stew with references to his own movie legacy. Although *The Long, Long Trailer* was built strictly for two, a roster of Minnelli graduates fills its peripheral roles—former father of the groom Moroni Olsen as the avuncular trailer-park manager who reunites the spatting Collinis; *The Clock*'s Keenan Wynn, appearing briefly to play a stoic traffic cop; and *Meet Me in St. Louis'* bumptious housekeeper, Marjorie Main, recast as the cheerfully intrusive neighbor who turns their wedding night into a trailerite cocktail party. While halting traffic in a back-lot town square, the trailer pauses in front of a movie marquee advertising *The Band Wagon;* as Arnaz nervously negotiates a dangerous mountain grade, Ball distracts him by retelling a gloomy movie plot which sounds suspiciously like *Undercurrent.* Minnelli even recycles the sets of an earlier triumph—the trailer's no-contest tussle with a rickety Victorian house takes place on the *Meet Me in St. Louis* street.

But Minnelli's hand is more telling still in the film's broader design—its affectionate but caustic take on the pursuit of material happiness in the America of the 1950s. While *Father of the Bride* satirized the seemingly timeless rituals of suburban life, here he punctures the lure of technology and mobility which possesses a newer, rootless middle class. *The Long, Long Trailer*'s newlyweds are creatures of the automotive age—they first meet at the christening of a new freeway, and seal their joint fate at a mobile home fair touting the gleaming products of American industry. The trailer pit stops where they alight are instant communities featuring all the conveniences of suburban living and none of the civic responsibilities. For an aesthete like Minnelli, the streamlined tackiness of this world is as damning as its improvised impermanence. His pastel views of these highway utopias offer a subversively kitsch version of California Modern; against turquoise skies, the most luxurious trailer haven even has a flagstone swimming pool for its transient homesteaders. Surrounded by her upholstered built-in sofa and gleaming appliances, the slapstick heroine is as fiercely houseproud as Emma Bovary or Ellie Banks. And this is the cue for the movie's central joke, for, however longingly the Collinis muse on the freedom of the open road, they are weighed down by two tons of indispensable creature comforts. The result is that, in the movie's longest set piece, the accumulated bulk of the newlyweds' goods and chattels nearly propels them over the side of a sheer mountain cliff. This episode is a bit too ominous for bellylaughs—for one queasy moment, the overstuffed trailer threatens to annihilate more than just a fledgling marriage.

This chrome and Minnelli-yellow rig is the conspicuous emblem for a theme he understands all too well; namely, the risk of allowing an eye for seductive objects to curdle from affinity into compulsion. On this occasion, detachment lends wit to his moral lesson. One of the reasons Minnelli can treat this as unmitigated farce in contrast to, say, *Madame Bovary*'s domestic tragedy is that he can identify with Emma's romantic aspirations, while he wouldn't be caught dead mooning over something so plebian as a mobile home. This is one of the lowest-calorie concoctions of his career, but Minnelli's flickering irony gives it an occasional kick. With *The Long, Long Trailer,* he made an escapist comedy in which the trip is far worse than the humdrum fate its victims tried to flee.

. . . .

1957　DESIGNING WOMAN

One of the nicer by-products of the rise of television was that it turned every living room Entertainment Unit into a private revival house. Old movies were the cheapest and more expedient broadcast fodder to fill those hours outside of prime time, and soon became the latter-day big screen's most bittersweet competition. So long as millions of Philcos beamed daily doses of Powell and Loy or Gable and Colbert in their 1930s prime, it was tough to persuade fans that movies were better than ever. The genre which prompted especially mournful comparisons was the lost art of sophisticated comedy; the best Hollywood could do was hammer new CinemaScope tailfins on those sleek models first manufactured from Roosevelt's Bank Holiday to Pearl Harbor. During the 1950s, every classic of screwball and sentiment was customized into one of these celluloid Edsels, from *The Awful Truth* (re-titled *Let's Do It Again), My Man Godfrey,* and *It Happened One Night (You Can't Run Away from It)* to *The Lady Eve (The Birds and the Bees), The Women (The Opposite Sex),* and *The Philadelphia Story (High Society).*

In spirit, if not its precise letter, *Designing Woman* was one of the more likable entries in this rash trend. Any resemblance between *Woman of the Year* and this movie's freshly minted script was purely disingenuous; *Designing Woman* looked the last word in Metrocolor glamour, but its soul hankered for the black-and-white days of wisecracks and shoulder pads. Appropriately enough, considering its subject, *Designing Woman* started as a five-page sketch by Metro's reigning woman designer, Helen Rose, who wanted to tailor movie scripts as well as gowns. In 1953, she submitted two story ideas to the studio, neither of them exactly The Newest Look in movie scenarios. The first reads

Gregory Peck and Lauren Bacall at home in Designing Woman *(1957)*

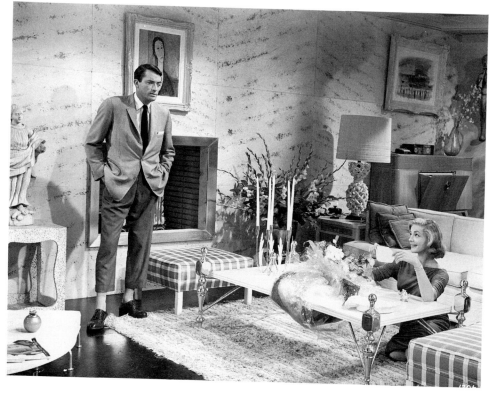

like a hybrid knockoff of the antique musical *Irene* and a Metro effort of the 1940's called *Her Highness and the Bellboy*, and tells of a shy French chambermaid in a New York hotel who does fashion sketches on the side.

This potential Leslie Caron showcase left Rose's bosses cold, but they saw a glimmer of promise in yarn number two. In this, a sleek designer and a rumpled sportswriter meet and wed in haste. They soon realize that her tony set and his cauliflower-eared cronies don't mix, while the reappearance of the groom's erstwhile sweetie, a curvaceous musical-comedy star, nearly lands the pair in the divorce courts. The studio liked the idea of making a movie, any movie, that could be fashioned around a snappy title like Rose's *Designing Woman*. Production head Dore Schary felt that this mutton dressed as Persian lamb might be a likely profitmaker with the right packaging. In fact, he decided to produce it himself, assigning contract writer George Wells to flesh it out into a full-length script.

At Schary's orders, Wells tailored *Designing Woman* to suit the studio's meteoric new star, Grace Kelly. However, it was Kelly's very popularity that forced a fateful delay in the producer's plans. His romantic comedy had to wait its turn behind several lucrative loan-outs to Paramount, plus *High Society* and *The Swan* back at Culver City. By early 1956, with Kelly as bait, Schary had assembled a formidable lineup of talent. Under the direction of Broadway hitmaker Joshua Logan, Kelly's *Rear Window* co-star, James Stewart, eagerly agreed to a rematch, while the studio penciled in Cyd Charisse to play the dancing vamp. From a modest retread of *Woman of the Year*, Schary's package was fast developing into Metro's box office Picture of the Year.

Then Kelly upstaged the studio's plans with a novel plot twist of her own. With regal aplomb, the star announced that as soon as she'd finished with *High Society*, she was taking the romantic lead in a real-life Cinderella story set in Monte Carlo. In retrospect, MGM was remarkably slow to grasp the implications of her announcement. Schary agreed to postpone the start of *Designing Woman* to June, and magnanimously granted her time off for a nice honeymoon like those Liz or Lana enjoyed upon their nuptials to minor Hollywood royalty. Two months after the wedding, Her Serene Highness sent a gracious note to her former boss declining his offer to return to work—as insular principalities went, she preferred Monaco to Hollywood.

Upon Kelly's defection, *Designing Woman* lost its male star and director, as well. Undaunted, Schary scurried to assemble a new troupe of comparable luster. He approached Minnelli, fresh from completing *Tea and Sympathy*, and in fact a more sensible choice than the earthbound Logan. While mulling over available prospects for the disoriented groom, Minnelli and Schary opted to cast violently against type with that preternaturally solid citizen, Gregory Peck. Though hardly renowned for his skill at madcap farce, on the

heels of *Moby Dick* and *The Man in the Grey Flannel Suit*, Peck found the prospect a bracing change of pace and accepted the offer. Peck's deal guaranteed him approval of *Designing Woman*'s leading lady, and he agreed to Minnelli's choice of Lauren Bacall. (By then she was used to picking up Grace Kelly's leavings, having recently replaced her as the feminine lead in Minnelli's *The Cobweb*.) Cyd Charisse was an improbable second fiddle to Bacall in the star hierarchy, so Dolores Gray was substituted and her role refitted accordingly.

Since Gray's pact with MGM had recently lapsed, none of *Designing Woman*'s stars were under contract. Reflecting the trio's respective box-office standing, Peck received $250,000 for his services, while Bacall and Gray were paid $75,000 each. Prominent among supporting roles was the heroine's choreographer pal, a neurotically arty type whose lightfooted ways aggrieved the sportswriter's standards of malehood. For once, Minnelli discarded the standard list of character comedians in favor of the genuine article—dance director Jack Cole, who'd never acted before. Cole also signed to stage Gray's numbers, as he had for *Kismet*. Minnelli drafted cameraman John Alton straight from *Tea and Sympathy*, and encouraged the faithful Preston Ames to conjure up *Designing Woman*'s requisite backlot-Manhattan glamour. Naturally, Helen Rose was selected to design the costumes; after all, the whole thing had been her idea in the first place.

As Schary's particular pet (and one of his last efforts before the Loews Inc. board deposed him in favor of Joseph Vogel), *Designing Woman* got the high-class treatment, afforded twice the shooting schedule and nearly double the budget lavished on previous Minnelli comedies. Shooting began on September 10 1956 and concluded ten weeks later, including a few days' locations at Newport Beach harbor, the Beverly Hills Hotel, and Marineland. After a satisfactory sneak preview in January, *Designing Woman* opened at Radio City Music Hall in May 1957. The movie found a reasonably responsive public, returning $3,750,000

Lauren Bacall at work,
Designing Woman *(1957)*

OPPOSITE:
Dolores Gray, "There'll Be Some Changes Made,"
Designing Woman *(1957)*

against costs of $1,930,313; after distribution, prints, and advertising, and without accounting for subsequent revenues from sales to television, MGM calculated a slight loss of $136,000. Critics viewed it with measured gratitude, observing that *Designing Woman* was about as close as contemporary Hollywood was likely to get to the screwball hits of the past. In this cautious movie age, the fact that *Designing Woman* was first conceived at Metro rather than at Random House or the Theater Guild proved a rare mark of distinction. At the Academy Awards for 1957, George Wells' somewhat shopworn script earned the statuette for Best Original Screenplay; among the also-rans in that category was Fellini's *I Vitelloni.*

In some ways, it was in the more disposable Metro items like *Designing Woman* that Minnelli's value to the

studio shone brightest. The movie sought to perpetuate that glossy ideal of studio-manufactured entertainment which was receding into memory even before the departure of L. B. Mayer. Like so much of that week-in, week-out product which made MGM synonymous with Hollywood in the thirties and forties, *Designing Woman* is a confident A-picture with second-rate aspirations, intent on flinging stardust and production values at the patrons as a substitute for authentic verve and originality. Screenwriter Wells' strategy, logically enough, was to exhume a host of nostalgic commonplaces out of their Depression-age time capsule—tart-tongued working girls, Runyonesque gangsters, scrappy editors stalking copy-strewn newsrooms. His pivotal plot gimmick was a quaint throwback to the days when even the most adult of romantic farces had

171

to be made safe for kiddies of all ages. Heroine Marilla (where did Metro's screenwriters get these names?) waxes furious, not over the prospect of an actual dalliance between her husband and the voluptuous second-lead soubrette—that's next to inconceivable. What vexes her is the thought of what passed between them during his bachelor past, a scruple which might have seemed a trifle obsessive even in some black-and-white diversion, copyright 1935. Nevertheless, the story is cagily constructed to the last reconstituted bit-part archetype. All that's missing is that zesty vernacular wit which made the best thirties comedies treasured emblems of their times.

This was precisely where Minnelli came in handy, for *Designing Woman*'s tired bloodlines didn't faze him a bit. His velvety tempo and droll sense of chic sustain an illusion of high spirits from title credits to final fade-out. *Designing Woman* is never truly funny but it's surprisingly pleasurable to watch, because Minnelli is bent on saturating the screen with effortless glamour if it kills him. Like its thirties' forebears, *Designing Woman* is a vicarious design for living, with the Great White Sets of the deco years supplanted by a gaudy blend of Danish Modern and Decorator French Provincial.

Minnelli's people are to the sophisticated comedy manner born, as befits the Preston Ames' settings they drift through. Mike and Marilla first meet poolside at the Beverly Hills Hotel and set up housekeeping amid the white sectional sofas and bleached antiques of her Park Avenue spread. (You just know she is a woman of taste and refinement, from the modest little Modigliani hanging over her marble fireplace.) Poured into black-jersey sheaths of her own design, the heroine frequently purrs of her love for her metier. While a mannequin stands like a Bonwit Teller Winged Victory awaiting her finishing touch, Marilla's work consists of pacing her Beaux Arts atelier to ponder which kind of white chiffon she should choose to accent her collection. Rival Lori Shannon doesn't have it so bad either —she spends her days undulating through production numbers at a TV studio, and her nights in a fuchsia and chocolate bandbox accessorized with a standard poodle to match. And as the virile opposite to Marilla's soignée heroine, Gregory Peck isn't exactly a bourbon-stained primitive either. In this rarefied Metro universe, clothes make the male as well as the female of the species, and Peck is the best-dressed movie journalist since Rosalind Russell in *His Girl Friday.* Mobsters may threaten his life to squelch a hot story, but they're not nearly so perilous as his spurned fiancée, given to dumping the *specialità della casa* into the lap of his snappy suit while they're lunching at the best restaurant in town.

To sustain the requisite brittleness, attitude is everything, and Minnelli schooled his actors well in the craft of arch behavior. As neither of *Designing Woman*'s stars was the most adroit of physical farceurs, Minnelli carefully rations the quota of slapstick—her screeching collapse at a blood-spattering boxing match, his klutzy parody of choreographer Randy's Broadway-Balinese body language. Wryness is their suit, Bacall narrowing her eyes to a feline slow burn in her best *How to Marry a Millionaire* manner opposite Peck's arched brow and deadpan chortle. Even the tempestuous Gray goes wild in a ladylike manner—turning down the volume of her vibrato to a dangerous whisper, she upends Peck's plate of pasta with a blank ingenue stare and one refined flick of the wrist. The thugs who menace Mike (including a young Chuck Connors) are gangsters according to Lubitsch—soft-spoken and deferent to the ladies; when truly provoked they vent their ire by twisting Peck's patrician nose. Lest this seem too fanciful, Minnelli makes one concession to low comedy in the person of the hero's self-appointed bodyguard, Maxie (Mickey Shaughnessy), a paranoid pugilist whose brains have been scrambled by too many KOs. Maxie sleeps with his eyes open and is pretty comatose when he's awake; a running (or shadow-boxing) moron joke, his motto is "Every time there's trouble, my head . . . I don' like it." Much of this now seems in dubious taste, but Maxie does prompt one of George Wells' genuine laugh lines—when Marilla expresses distaste for the fighter's Neanderthal profile, her husband retorts, "He *has* a nose. It's . . . inside."

With John Alton's complicity, Minnelli gives Shaughnessy's closeups the same care he'd lavish on one of his leading ladies, but to different ends—Maxie is lit from below like Frankenstein's creepy creation. *Designing Woman* is Minnelli's most visually playful comedy, scattered throughout with sprightly camera tricks. Seen through the hero's first-reel hangover, Beverly Hills is a psychedelic landscape of chartreuse palms against Pepto-Bismol skies. Startling jump-cut closeups announce Marilla's discovery that the girl in Mike's ripped-up photo is the sinuous star of the show she's designing. Minnelli's favorite prop, the mirror, is the focus of one of his most elaborate camera setups this side of *Meet Me in St. Louis*. After her ravioli coup de théâtre, Lori pauses to adjust her makeup while Marilla's reflection (in a Minnelli-red ensemble) intrudes to upstage her; the camera tracks backward as the heroine bursts into the restaurant, Lori pausing in the background to appraise the happy bride.

Thanks to its theatrical milieu, *Designing Woman* is the one Minnelli comedy with room for a musical production number, and Gray's specialty is staged with his accustomed verve and subversive wit. As in *It's Always Fair Weather*, Gray plays the beaming, chromium-lunged queen of TV variety. Her big moment here is an excuse for Minnelli to execute two choruses with his recurrent theme of sound-stage grace-under-pressure —instead of *The Bad and the Beautiful*, it's The Loud and the Glamorous. The occasion is a morning run-through of "There'll Be Some Changes Made," during which the star must belt out the song and make love

Minnelli shows Chuck Connors how to twist Gregory Peck's nose, Designing Woman *(1957)*

the script's stock comic situations with certain personal motifs linking *Designing Woman* with both his dramatic films and musicals in unexpected ways.

Designing Woman climaxes with a free-for-all slugfest timed for laughs; this one starts as a sly wink at "The Girl Hunt" ballet from *The Band Wagon,* and ends by foreshadowing the bloody funfair finale from *Some Came Running.* The brawl pitting Mike and Maxie against the fedora-hatted bad guys takes place in that favorite Minnelli hangout, a stage-door alley on the night of a musical comedy premiere. While *The Band Wagon* turned hoofers into stage gangsters, in *Designing Woman* a hoods' rumble is transformed into an impromptu dance routine—once Mike's fists prove unequal to the task, it's Cole's epicene Randy who comes at the goons in sections, his lethal high kicks pulverizing every jaw in sight. Throughout the fracas, Marilla flails about in harm's way until she's suddenly catapulted into a dark corner under a heap of cardboard refuse. Here her plight is just another gag, leaving the heroine with a woozy head, a photogenic smudge on her cheek, and a solicitous husband at her side. But three pictures later, Minnelli recreated this image almost exactly in the last reel of *Some Came Running,* and this time it was no laughing matter. Once Shirley MacLaine's hapless Ginny lies crumpled in the alleyway, it's too late for a tender reconciliation with her alienated spouse; Minnelli next fades gloomily in on her funeral.

Upstaged though it is by the stars' big clinch, Randy's last-reel triumph over the he-men is clearly a vicarious thrill for Minnelli. If there's one character in the world of this movie who matches his own sensibility, this impetuous aesthete is it. Despite limited screen time and Jack Cole's dour, amateurish line readings, Randy is a key figure in the movie's scheme and the only person who ruffles its conventional surface. With him as catalyst, *Designing Woman* dabbles in those questions of gender and identity that Minnelli probed so earnestly in *Tea and Sympathy.*

The real clash in *Designing Woman* is not the standard battle of the sexes but the breach between Mike's blunt male-bounded world and Marilla's trendy, mercurial set, with its sibilant enthusiasms for clothes and the arts. If she quails at the masculine exclusiveness and taste for blood sport among his cronies, he is sickened on learning that her pals include an "excitable type . . . known on his labels as Mr. Chris." Halfway through the film, the two milieus collide when Mike's floating poker game lands at Park Avenue on the same evening as Marilla's at-home reading of the show she's about to design. Minnelli evenhandedly ensures that both sides get their satirical licks; while the card players mutter monosyllabically over their cards, the Broadway bunch twitters in silhouette behind the hostess's translucent screens, exploding with gaiety over such bons mots as "Aunt Agatha, she's done it again!"

to the camera, running between two sets in a two-second dash from Great Lady in pastels to Siren in sea-foam lamé, while studio minions fiddle with her accessories and the perfidious Mike shows up just outside camera range. The content of the number is beside the point—what counts is the carefully timed mayhem that makes it all happen. Within the counterpoint of Minnelli's own tracking eye, the TV camera and microphone boom underscore the song with rolling movements of their own, and you can scarcely tell the chorus boys from the technical crew sprinting around the star to do their jobs on just the right syncopated beat. Under the harried circumstances, Gray's unruffled stance is both the height of show-biz professionalism and a delicious joke. It's another slick demonstration of the Minnelli maxim that whether you're creating art or selling kitsch, hard work is the best fun of all.

Amid all its references to the screwball comedy era—including a contretemps between Peck and Gray's poodle which is a blatant steal from *The Awful Truth*—this movie carries Minnelli's signature throughout. In the wake of his three previous marital comedies, *Designing Woman* squeezes one last laugh out of his bull-at-the-bridal-shower routine, with Peck floundering in the background while a fur-draped cluster of Marilla's pals coos over her pile of booty. Minnelli also inflects

But Minnelli makes it clear where his true sympathies lie. A wisecrack from Mike maligning Randy's manhood prompts the one solemn passage in the movie, as the dancer deflates his smugness by pulling out snapshots of the wife and kids. This little scene is clearly meant for the edification of the audience as well as of *Designing Woman*'s leading man. Minnelli always embraced the socially out-of-sync characters in his movies, because insulated by success though he was, his own eccentric flair made Minnelli a somewhat suspect figure as well. In the pop culture of the mid-fifties, the accusation of unmanliness was a charge as grievous as an affinity for Commies. Minnelli had a personal stake in proving that real men too could wear Cape-

zios; like Randy, with his visions of sea-horse dream ballets, MGM's chief fantasist-in-residence had his own photo album of wives and progeny ready to display on demand. If no moviemaker would dare sanction homosexuality out loud in the 1950s, Minnelli was certainly willing to skewer that sanctimonious virile code which equated imaginative flights like his own as the next thing to idle perversion. In his movies, creativity knows no particular sex and the resourceful artist always gets the last laugh—especially in bonbons like this one. It's Randy's fancy footwork which wraps up the plot, and Minnelli's pizzazz that turns *Designing Woman* into a brightly polished costume bauble.

· ·

1958 THE RELUCTANT DEBUTANTE

Years after MGM ceased attempting new sequels to *Father of the Bride,* the prospect of some new rite-of-passage comedy along the same frolicsome order still brought an acquisitive gleam to its corporate eye. In the mid-fifties, the studio scoured every place from the Bronx to London's Belgravia for this kind of property. First came a working-class variation, with *The Catered Affair,* adapted from Paddy Chayefsky's teleplay. Next, the studio grasped at the opposite end of the social scale with *The Reluctant Debutante* by William Douglas Home, the West End's specialist in High Tory drawing-room comedy, from the post-war age of austerity well into the Thatcher years.

His affectionate dig at the London Season and its toll on one Father of the Deb sounded temptingly like Stanley Banks-in-Mayfair, and MGM's scouts sprinted in pursuit. A Mr. Watling of Metro's London office scurried to appraise the play during its May 1955 tryout in Brighton. An immediate dispatch to Culver City acclaimed it as ''one of the two best English comedies to appear since the war,'' which aroused an astonishing flurry of studio excitement for so gossamer a property. After reading the synopsis, story department chief Kenneth MacKenna passed it on enthusiastically to Dore Schary, declaring, ''I'm sure this is going to be a hit in London and a hit in New York and equally sure it is going to be a hit on our screens.'' MacKenna next cabled no less an authority than Pandro Berman, then in London to supervise his latest Sir Walter Scott extravaganza, *Quentin Durward,* and advised him to take a look at Douglas Home's play himself. Five days later, Berman exhorted his colleagues at home to purchase the rights, dubbing *The Reluctant Debutante* ''excellent material for a successful comedy with class.'' Despite a counterbid from Paramount, MGM acquired this com-

edy for the classy sum of $150,000; the deal was concluded on June 18 1955, scarcely three weeks after the play's West End premiere.

Despite this initial frenzy, nearly three years passed before *The Reluctant Debutante* reached the cameras. For one thing, the studio's agreement called for MGM to co-finance an American production of the play, which the screen version would inevitably follow. In the meantime, Berman and Schary belatedly wondered if Douglas Home's upper-crust whimsy might prove a bit rich for the movie masses, and tried to dream up ways of Americanizing it. Berman's natural instinct was to make this project like *Father of the Bride* only different, with the reliable Frances Goodrich and Albert Hackett transposing it to a New York setting. The Hacketts declined, with the studio's story department concurring that the piece's Britishness was its most distinctive trait. MacKenna associate Marjorie Thorson proposed making it the story of an American father and daughter engulfed in the social whirl of London, noting, ''You might even get some extra humor out of his being an American fish out of water.'' With this in mind, the producer hired Julius Epstein, a Hollywood specialist in adapting literate stage comedies, to write a palatable Anglo-American hybrid. Charles Walters was briefly considered to direct it and, in August 1956, MGM prematurely announced that perky Debbie Reynolds would appear in the teenaged title role.

Two months later the play opened at last in New York, without benefit of any Hollywood gilding. Wilfred Hyde-White and Anna Massey, father and daughter in the London cast, repeated their original roles under Cyril Ritchard's direction. The one star defection was Celia Johnson, who decided to stay home when MGM wouldn't promise her the part of the debutante's eager mother in the screen version as well; Adrienne Allen replaced her. MGM's brass didn't care for the result—MacKenna dismissed Ritchard's approach as "music hall farce"—and neither did Broadway theatergoers. In contrast to its English success, *The Reluctant Debutante* eked out a run of 134 performances, at a total loss of Metro's investment. Berman persevered with his film plans nonetheless, even sending Epstein to London to soak up atmosphere, including a visit to "Josephine Bradley's school for debutantes."

In the fall of 1957, while Minnelli was busy wrapping up *Gigi*, Berman offered Epstein's script to his favorite director of comedies. Although convinced that this transatlantic treatment neutered the play's charm, Minnelli consented to tackle it, on the news of Berman's resolutely English casting coup for the bewildered parents. For the producer was dickering with the newlywed team of Rex Harrison, fresh from his legendary triumph in *My Fair Lady*, and the inimitable comedienne Kay Kendall, who had somehow kept a straight face through Berman's swashbuckling *Quentin Durward* before deliciously letting loose in George Cukor's *Les Girls*. Fortunately for Minnelli, Harrison loathed the present script even more than he did. When Epstein

balked at removing his improvements, Douglas Home himself was hurriedly drafted to refurbish his own text for the screen, a task that continued well into actual production. At Berman's insistence, certain compromises were retained: for the sake of the domestic teenage public, *The Reluctant Debutante*'s younger generation of players had to remain as American as milk shakes. Hence Sandra Dee was now cast as Harrison's daughter, an implausibility explained in the new script by a prior transatlantic misalliance on the part of Harrison's Lord Broadbent (with whom, one wonders—Lana Turner?). For consistency's sake, Dee's fellow Universal Pictures contractee, John Saxon, was chosen as her bongo-playing beau endowed with closet noble bloodlines. For their joint services, Harrison and Kendall received a neat $200,000, while their juniors were snared for $11,000 and $14,900 respectively—barely enough to keep them in hamburgers during *The Reluctant Debutante*'s foreign shoot. Angela Lansbury rounded out the Hollywood contingent in the

Kay Kendall, Angela Lansbury, and Rex Harrison in The Reluctant Debutante *(1958)*

*Minnelli rehearses Kay
Kendall and Rex Harrison for*
The Reluctant Debutante
(1958)

role of Kendall's cat-in-tweeds best chum, with Minnelli choosing the rest of his cast while in London to scout locations at the beginning of 1958.

The choice of Harrison imposed a new set of logistical pressures on this project. After years of dithering, the film had to be rushed to completion by spring, 1958, to free the star for the London run of *My Fair Lady;* however, as a Swiss resident for tax purposes, Harrison couldn't set foot in England until that time, and wasn't too eager to return to America either. This restriction turned *The Reluctant Debutante* into the oddest of all Minnelli's runaway productions. Just five months after he'd left the Paris of Colette's *Gigi*, Minnelli was back to shoot this tribute to Home and Empire with an Anglo-American cast and Franco-American crew. Reunited with faithful cameraman Joseph Ruttenberg, Minnelli settled on art director A. J. d'Eaubonne when Alexandre Trauner proved unavailable. Pierre Balmain gowned Kay Kendall in the height of English chic and Minnelli's favorite leading-lady hues. The director had hoped to spend three weeks of the production schedule in London, but under the circumstances he resorted to the usual Culver City ruse of matching his actors against second-unit back-projection shots, relying on his transplanted stars for the requisite local color.

It took Minnelli just seven rushed weeks to shoot *The Reluctant Debutante*, from mid-February to early April. Minnelli tried not to be distracted by two pieces of disquieting news from home—MGM's efforts to tinker with *Gigi* after its sobering first preview, and his estranged wife Georgette's final decision to file papers

for divorce. Absorbed in the task at hand, he was enraptured by Kendall's boundless charm, energy, and inventiveness, as the press and first-run public would be, once *The Reluctant Debutante* reached the theaters later that summer. Like everyone else on the set, Minnelli grasped nothing of the private tragedy taking place while this giddy farce went before the cameras. Recently, Kendall had rebounded from a sudden, debilitating malady. Just before shooting started, the company was examined for insurance purposes by a doctor from the American Hospital in Paris, who declared that Kendall's case had been "a simple, acute gastroenteritis from which she is now entirely recovered." (In fact, the invalid of the troupe seemed to be Minnelli, recuperating from an upper respiratory infection and a small kidney stone.) Only Harrison knew that his wife's illness was the first symptom of the leukemia which eighteen months later would end her life at the age of thirty-three.

With shooting finished, Minnelli flew to New York for *Gigi*'s world premiere and then back to California to look over Adrienne Fazan's final cut of *The Reluctant Debutante* while preparing for the imminent start of *Some Came Running*. For unreported reasons, a stock score was assembled for the film, with André Previn's *Designing Woman* theme music recycled for *The Reluctant Debutante*'s title sequence. After a smash sneak preview in the suitably posh town of Pasadena, the movie opened at Radio City Music Hall in August 1958. At first, the studio felt its ardor for this property would be amply rewarded. Its opening day racked up the second highest take for a Metro release in the Music Hall's history to date, followed by a first week gross of $192,000; the critics deemed it a much merrier entertainment than the stage original. However, *The Reluctant Debutante*'s eventual audience proved nearly as select as the privileged crowd it satirized. Studio accountants assumed that this was one MGM film which would prove more popular in English-speaking territories abroad than at home, but despite a buoyant London premiere, the British public at large was generally indifferent to the antics of its social betters. Against a production cost of $2,264,909, *The Reluctant Debutante* earned rentals of only $1,943,013 within nine months of its release; a final audit two years later reflecting additional foreign returns placed its deficit at $833,000. Those moviegoers who shared Minnelli's champagne tastes slaked them with *Gigi* instead. Fortunately for Berman's MGM-based Avon Productions, more visceral entertainments like *Cat On a Hot Tin Roof* and *Jailhouse Rock* made up the difference.

Despite its financial failure Minnelli was proud of *The Reluctant Debutante,* and with good reason—as an exercise in style, it's one of the neatest conjuring tricks he ever concocted. Despite the clipped accents of its principals this movie is close kin to many of his lighter Metro entertainments filmed stateside. The ingenue of the title is the latest in Minnelli's worldly innocents, in a line stretching from Esther Smith through Kay Banks to Gigi; she too anxiously scans the dance floor for the absent boy of her heart, and shares youthful confidences with her dad over a midnight glass of milk. More to the point in this case, Minnelli proved you didn't have to stay in Culver City to conjure up that distinctive Metro luster which was his matchless specialty. Working without a staff art director for the first time, he turned the Paris sound stages into a Hollywoodized London of his own confident making. While a local dance band glides through such Metro tunes as "The Boy Next Door," Minnelli fills the wide screen with his accustomed plush textures and glittering light. Significantly, this expatriate project sported a richer studio patina than most of the late 1950s product being turned out on the MGM lot itself.

Still, it's easy to understand why the masses declined the pleasure of *The Reluctant Debutante*'s company. The popular appeal of his previous comedies derived as much from their wish-fulfillment quota as their ration of laughs—Tracy, Ball, and Bacall were figures of fun in an escapist world moviegoers could at least imagine inhabiting themselves. The high-Anglo-Saxon attitudinizing of this farce was caviar for the few, and fish eggs to everyone else. In the egalitarian 1950s, American viewers were more interested in keeping up with Ward and June Cleaver than aping the gentry, while for British audiences now used to a bit of working-class grit in their own movies, this was a reflection of England only Hollywood would have dreamt up.

For *The Reluctant Debutante* is a literal drawing-room comedy with a silken vengeance. Virtually the only person in it who doesn't merit a line in Debrett's is the maid who arranges Kay Kendall's flowers every morning. Lord Jimmy Broadbent is an international banker as witty as he is rich; Lady Sheila, a frantically blurred vision in beige maribou, has champagne where her brains ought to be. Raised in the Colonies though she was, even Jimmy's daughter Jane is preternaturally cosmopolitan. (Like her Brooklyn-born love interest John Saxon, Sandra Dee, late of Bayonne, New Jersey, was carefully coached to bring her diction and demeanor up to snuff. And in fact she got by with surprising poise.) Whatever their given Christian names, everybody calls everybody else "darling" with promiscuous abandon. Their favorite adjective is "divine," applied to anything that isn't positively beastly. The only imaginable trouble in this lofty paradise involves dark mutterings about well-bred girls vilely seduced during stately home weekends. And in this complacent universe, even a suspicious, dark-browed interloper like Saxon turns out to be People Like Us. For in a plot twist worthy of a pre-1914 Victor Herbert operetta, he's revealed to be the new Duke of Positano through the maternal line, with a Florentine palazzo to match. While initially stirred by his bongo drums and talk of primitive mating rituals, the romance between Jane and David turns out to be the primal call of the bluebloods. Upon learning of her intended's lineage, the seventeen-year-old ingenue rises easily to the occasion. "Oh, darling," she sighs with patronizing rapture. "What a lot of housekeeping!" Tumbrels, anyone?

By 1958, all of this was a relic of an age lamented by very few. Yet *The Reluctant Debutante*'s prosceniumarch blitheness clearly amuses Minnelli no end, precisely because it's so wackily stylized. There may well have been an element of nostalgia for Minnelli in this—it's a throwback to the kind of carriage-trade bauble that adorned the Broadway of a quarter-century earlier, when he himself was a transplanted midwesterner in quest of new designs for urbane living. From Kendall's first entrance, *distraite* but soignée in a Minnelli red suit and slouch hat, Minnelli pitches wholeheartedly into *The Reluctant Debutante*'s giddy spirit—so much so that, in some respects, it's the purest comedy he ever made. This time around, no queasy undertones ever cloud the text's airy conceits. Minnelli is too busy keeping the farcical wheels spinning to brake for insights about marital discord, material excesses or the dark musings of the besieged male psyche. *The Reluctant Debutante* marks the only time Minnelli ventured among the upper classes and kept a civil tongue in his head; these characters serenely enjoy their privileges and so, vicariously, does he.

Still, Minnelli is vigilant lest all this slip into well-bred inertia masquerading as high style. By urging on his fleet-footed cameraman and a breathless cast, he turned a verbose script into one of the speediest movies of his career. Minnelli had never before filmed a stage comedy, and so deploys all his cinematic energies to demolish *The Reluctant Debutante*'s theatrical constraints. While the play took place entirely within the Broadbents' London digs, for visual variety Minnelli drags the clan and his audience through a succession of coming-out balls. Utterly at ease now with the dimensions of the CinemaScope frame, he fills it with discreet revelers in their best formal finery, then scrambles the patterns with his camera darting through the throngs. As Sheila and Jimmy anxiously scan the crowd for their errant offspring, Minnelli's breathless tracking shots accelerate the pace, then halt on a dime for the movie's running sight gag—the pair frozen in frustrated mid-gallop as the band strikes up ''God Save the Queen.'' Halfway through the film, Minnelli cooks up a delirious montage to sum up the effects of this social whirl on the stoic Broadbents. As the majordomo intones an assortment of the silliest monickers in the British empire, lovelorn Jane pouts, Sheila shows her spunk on receiving line and dance floor, and the exhausted Jimmy seeks liquid sustenance while trying to stay conscious and vertical at the same time. Douglas Home's fey British languor may have sufficed for the West End; on screen, *The Reluctant Debutante* benefits from its massive transfusion of Hollywood adrenalin.

Minnelli does withdraw to the drawing room for good once it's time to resolve what little plot there is. Fortunately, Kendall and Harrison have enough octane in reserve to keep this engine running in the most confining of circumstances. Minnelli is expert at synchro-

nizing his comedies to suit the natural tempos of his stars, from Spencer Tracy's phlegm to Lucille Ball's frenzies. Here Kendall is the centrifugal force that keeps *The Reluctant Debutante* spinning. During her lifetime she was often and aptly compared to a latter-day Carole Lombard, for, like that queen of thirties screwball comedy, Kendall was that delicious contradiction, a sublimely glamorous figure with the soul of an irrepressible clown. Her clipped, fluty voice was made for genteel repartee, but her elastic frame leaps into knockabout low comedy at the drop of a diamond earclip. Kendall simply can't keep still for an instant—even her clothes vibrate as she sprints and twitters from one imagined crisis to the next. Where Lucille Ball brings an athlete's fearlessness to physical comedy, Kendall turns slapstick into ballet, because, however absurd the situation, a lady must never lose her cool. At the sight of her stepdaughter in the arms of Mr. Wrong, she takes a rubber-legged dive downstairs to a perfect landing, her brain scrambled but coiffure intact. Harrison is the serene foil to her perpetual agitation, and in turn she brightens the saturnine tone which usually marked his screen performances. Even when Douglas Home serves him curdled lines about poached eggs with baleful stares, Harrison makes them seem like souffles. Minnelli complements his two stars with a handful of capable farceurs in the background. In addition to Lansbury, he found a gifted comic juvenile named Peter Meyers to play the object of Kendall's myopic matchmaking—a chinless twit whose hobbies are closet lechery and London's traffic patterns. But in this world where everyone knows his place nobody up-stages its main attraction, Minnelli least of all. If *The Reluctant Debutante* was outmoded the moment it was made, it feels no more dated now than Minnelli's timelier fifties entertainments. Moreover, Kendall's

premature death gives the movie a retrospective luster —her peerless teamwork with Harrison is the stuff of high-comedy legend. Thanks to their chemistry and Minnelli's own deft handiwork, *The Reluctant Debutante* is a relic with sparkle.

· ·

1963

THE COURTSHIP OF EDDIE'S FATHER

The *Reluctant Debutante* was the last of Minnelli's comedies for Pandro Berman. Apart from one final Freed musical, he spent the next four years working in a more solemn vein, making a quartet of melodramas under the supervision of four different producers. Minnelli's latest contract as an MGM staff director lapsed in early 1962, just as he was completing *Two Weeks in Another Town*. By then, he was one of the few directors of any stature in Hollywood still working under this type of arrangement; the practice of keeping high-priced talent under yearly contract was a throwback to the studio's palmy days when the backlot meant standing sets rather than idle real estate. In fact, the new order benefited filmmakers with clout and initiative, which such enterprising types as Hitchcock, Huston, and Wyler had realized for years; as producer-directors, they could develop their own properties and negotiate a cut of the box-office take. But for someone like Minnelli it was a difficult adjustment to make.

At nearly sixty, he'd spent two decades nurtured by a system that, even in eclipse, seemed preferable to the uncertain alternatives. The compartmentalized nature of a place like MGM had always suited Minnelli. He'd never harbored any hyphenate ambitions; so long as he was left alone on the set, Minnelli was quite content to leave the rigors of pitching stories or haggling over budgets to the specialists. This nonchalant attitude had always served him well, for through all the shifting fortunes of the studio somehow the top staff producers invariably dangled their most tempting projects for his consideration. But the MGM of the early sixties was becoming an increasingly alien place. Its last head of production with any hands-on experience as a film-maker, Sol C. Siegel, was eased out in 1961. As a producer who truly admired directors of Minnelli's caliber, Siegel's cardinal sin was his zest for making movies— despite the corporate infighting, during his three-year tenure the studio still managed to turn out a reasonably consistent level of classy product. But the new MGM had different priorities. Under the management of people like Robert Weitman, the Culver City lot was largely given over to grinding out television series, and

for a few years, more MGM releases were produced at the British Borehamwood studio than at home. An annual super-spectacular or two (like 1962's calamitous remake of *Mutiny on the Bounty*, with *How the West Was Won* in the planning stages) was supplemented by a few B-budget efforts to promote the studio's remaining handful of young contract players, essentially the alumni of 1960s *Where the Boys Are*. The last vestiges of MGM's high profile were found in a scant handful of comedies with high-priced free-lance stars, and the occasional prestige item from a Broadway hit or best-seller. (That year's examples were *Sweet Bird of Youth*, planned under Siegel, and the British-based *Lolita*.) Even the old Metro production patina began to show signs of tarnish, thanks to the gradual attrition of its craftsmen through retirement or just plain tired blood.

Nevertheless, Minnelli couldn't yet conceive of a professional future away from Culver City, and the studio was likewise loath to let him go. This was surprising on both sides considering that during the past year the relationship between MGM and its star director had erupted into open conflict for the first time in his long tenure. *Four Horsemen of the Apocalypse*, which premiered as Minnelli's contract expired, was the most trouble-plagued production of his career and immediately came up empty at the box office. Meanwhile, Minnelli and his bosses wrangled bitterly over the final cut of *Two Weeks in Another Town*. Yet in April 1962, they came to terms on a new deal which seemed to reflect Hollywood's recent shifts in power were in Minnelli's favor. Under an exclusive contract to make six films over four-and-a-half years, Minnelli would henceforth be his own corporation, known as Venice Productions (a corrupted combination of his first name with that of his new third wife, Denise). MGM would pay him $3,500 a week with small yearly increments, plus a $75,000 annual fee to Venice Productions, which all told amounted to a slightly higher sum than he'd received under his last contract. Moreover, he was guaranteed twenty-five percent of any net profits earned by those movies MGM financed and distributed; subject to the studio's approval he had the right to select his properties and cast them, to make an unsupervised cut of each completed film through the second preview, and to be consulted at all times thereafter.

Few veteran directors could have asked for more, but the concrete results gratified no one. Only three films out of the prospective six were ever made, each of them safe, conventional projects coasting on star marquee value and Minnelli's automatic craftsmanship. In tangible terms, the dynamics between Minnelli and the studio hadn't changed, except that both were pretty much jogging in place by the early sixties. In effect, he still waited for the studio to come up with the ideas, despite the fact that MGM increasingly shied away from his kind of project. The tired material they did approve for production neutered Minnelli's contractual creative control before he could properly exercise it. Now that he had a personal stake in any eventual profits, Minnelli didn't press unduly to make chancy high-profile projects under the Venice banner. (Freed's *Say It with Music* and the MGM *My Fair Lady* package would presumably have placated Minnelli's ambitions in that direction, had they been made.) Yet his much-vaunted profit clause reaped no rewards despite these precautions. None of the three Venice productions ended in the black, although his Elizabeth Taylor–Richard Burton vehicle, *The Sandpiper,* proved very popular indeed; however, by MGM's calculations, its surplus millions were swallowed up by studio overhead and distribution fees. In 1962, the Venice Productions agreement seemed to confirm Minnelli's unassailable place in the Hollywood hierarchy; in retrospect, it marks the beginning of his slow fade as an active filmmaker.

The Courtship of Eddie's Father was Minnelli's initial film under this pact, and relative to its modest ambitions this intimate comedy proved the most satisfying of the lot. New order or not, this was a property developed through studio channels in the usual manner, with a basic script in place by the time Minnelli came on to helm it. Mark Toby's autobiographical novel dealt with the bumpy readjustment of a recently widowed radio executive and his precocious son; according to publisher Bernard Geis, it was assembled by Toby and friend Dorothy Wilson, who owned the copyright, and then polished by a professional writer. In the book, as on screen, the widower's life is complicated by three contrasting women who, Geis reported to MGM, were different facets of Wilson herself. Metro had favored this kind of cute-but-tart family portrait since the days of L. B. Mayer; at a price of $100,000, the studio acquired the rights three months before the book was published in July 1961.

Nevertheless, its prospects didn't excite Sol Siegel, who was still running the place at the time. He noted that ''despite a very interesting first act, this story is disappointing,'' and predicted it would make a ''little picture'' at best. Even so, five increasingly idle staff producers vied for the chance to make it. Siegel awarded this honor to the indefatigable Joe Pasternak, whose skill at packaging cheerful corn had borne him triumphantly from Kathryn Grayson in the forties to Connie Francis in the sixties. As usual, finding the right screenwriter took a lot more effort. When playwright/humorist Jean Kerr turned it down the studio unsuccessfully wooed Harriet Frank and Irving Ravetch, a writing team accustomed to imposing projects like Minnelli's *Home from the Hill.* Finally, the studio settled on John Gay, who was also an odd choice after such recent jobs as the submarine picture, *Run Silent, Run Deep,* and his co-screenplay credit on *The Four Horsemen of the Apocalypse.*

Gay wrote two drafts of the script during the fall and winter of 1961; astonishingly, even at this late date, an innocuous film such as this faced censorship problems from the Production Code. Specifically, the Code's administrators objected to little Eddie's coy observations about female anatomy, which were modified sufficiently to win the necessary seal of approval. In the spring of 1962, the studio tested various possibilities for the cast, including Jim Hutton from its shrunken contract list to play the lead. Instead, Pasternak set his sights higher, opting for Glenn Ford, whose multi-picture deal with MGM was still in effect. Eager to activate his Venice Productions pact, Minnelli accepted Pasternak's offer to direct, starting work on his return from a career retrospective at London's National Film Theatre in May. With his arrival, the project began to look like a reunion of the late, unlamented *Apocalypse,* but these omens were ignored as the troupe forged ahead.

Minnelli spent several weeks supervising Gay's polish of the script, and with Ford as their dubious box-office magnet, he and Pasternak filled out the cast with a roster of lesser names. Shirley Jones was a predictable choice as the wholesome young widow across the hall, and Paramount loaned Stella Stevens to play Dollye, a sweet but dense tomato in the tradition of *Some Came Running*'s Ginny. Minnelli needed a male Margaret O'Brien for the virtuoso kid lead, and found it in Ronny Howard, late of the film version of *The Music Man* and one of TV's favorite tykes as Opie on *The Andy Griffith Show.* With a production team headed by mainstays Milton Krasner and Adrienne Fazan, Minnelli started shooting *The Courtship of Eddie's Father* on August 1 1962, and completed it the first week of October. After the huge sums lavished on his last two pictures, Minnelli was pressured to keep costs down. Supplemented by stock footage, the story's New York locations were all re-created on the lot, and a wedding sequence was scaled down from a church ceremony to a reception in an apartment used elsewhere in the picture. In the end, the studio spent just under $1,800,000 on the film, Minnelli's smallest budget since the mid-fifties. In fact, the costliest item was his $195,000 directorial fee, with Ford trailing behind at $125,000.

Glenn Ford, Ronny Howard, Shirley Jones, and a dead goldfish in The Courtship of Eddie's Father *(1963)*

The departed Siegel's prophecy that *The Courtship of Eddie's Father* would be just another "little picture" was borne out on its release in June 1963. The movie premiered modestly at the Victoria Theater on Broadway; the critics also managed to contain themselves, divided between those who found its sentimental tone mildly touching and others, uncut treacle. The public's response was equally mild, and the film returned $3,048,000 to the studio, including its first TV rentals, leaving an estimated deficit of $857,000. Even so, the property had a lucrative afterlife for MGM; its homey conceits were ideal for the small screen, and *The Courtship of Eddie's Father* was recycled into a moderately popular weekly sitcom some years later.

Minnelli took on frothier assignments like this as on-the-job therapy in the wake of his more taxing projects. *Two Weeks in Another Town* had stretched into months of behind-the-scenes bloodletting, and the urge to lighten up a little must have been hard to resist. Certainly *The Courtship of Eddie's Father* was modest to a flaw; with its somewhat cut-rate cast and cautiously studio-bound shooting schedule, it was vital neither to Metro's fortunes nor to its director's reputation. Also, it's obvious that Minnelli lowered his own sights to conform to these reduced circumstances. As an exercise in style, this is one of his more negligible movies; his signature brushwork disappears almost entirely under the slapdash slickness which marked most of Joe Pasternak's Metro fodder.

Confined by an A-minus budget, the Panavision panoramas clash with *Courtship's* intimate theme while exposing how undernourished the production really is.

Expediently overlit by the usually imaginative Krasner, *Courtship's* high-rise apartment sets are middle-class ugly without a trace of irony—a jumble of powder-blues and jack o'lantern oranges which normally would have made Minnelli as bilious as the audience. Pasternak's ear for music was notoriously square, and this movie sounds even tackier than it looks. Incorporating a pallid Victor Young theme-song waltz, the score by studio second-rater George Stoll is insistently bland. Like so many studio-spawned entertainments of the early sixties, *Courtship's* business-as-usual polish lagged behind the tastes of the times—too artificial to be true, too antiseptic for fantasy.

Courtship does have one vital element Minnelli's recent comedies lacked—an emotional core worthy of his more serious pictures. Somewhat reminiscent of Frank Capra's 1959 film, *Hole in the Head,* Minnelli's portrait of a widowed father and son focuses on the melancholy implications of this premise. We're introduced to the Corbett household a few days after the death of Eddie's mother, and follow the gradual period of adjustment her survivors endure over the next year in their lives. Under the circumstances, Minnelli ensures that his child protagonist is a much more troubled figure than the usual sitcom moppet. As *Meet Me in St. Louis* previously revealed, he viewed childhood as a minefield of dark imaginings, and Eddie has that morbid sensitivity which marked Margaret O'Brien's Tootie two decades earlier. Playful but acutely intuitive, both brood endlessly over big adult taboos like death or sex, and suffer their sorrows with an intensity their elders have long since learned to suppress.

181

Ronny Howard, Dina Merrill,
Glenn Ford in The Courtship
of Eddie's Father (1963)

Eddie's explosion of grief, early on in the film, is one of the most emotionally startling moments of any Minnelli picture. During a condolence visit from the Corbetts' neighbor, Elizabeth, the adults' casual living-room chat is pierced by a long shriek from Eddie's room. The next shot reveals the child transfixed with horror, staring at the corpse of a goldfish floating on the surface of his aquarium. His convulsions make Tom career out of control as well, shaking and slapping the child to quell his screams. Coming as it does at the end of a deceptively placid first reel, this episode is a deliberate shocker. It's the direct descendant of Tootie's Christmas Eve catharsis among her snowman family, with the same painful meaning—powerless to avert the family upheavals around them, these children vent their troubles on their playthings with a fury that mortifies their elders.

Blessed with juvenile actors as gifted as O'Brien and Howard, Minnelli doesn't stint in exposing the miseries of childhood. In his big scene, Ronny Howard seems literally possessed, winded and trembling from the force of his sobs; just as Garland fought to get her lines out through the static of O'Brien's non-stop keenings, *Courtship*'s grown-up pros have to struggle to restrain

their transported co-star. Once the crisis has passed, Eddie reverts to ordinary everyday worrying. Alert to his father's unhappiness, he tries to distract him by holding solemn "discussions" of the kind Tom used to have with his late wife. Gay's script injects a certain kiddie preciousness into these exchanges, but Minnelli ensures that his smallest actor isn't in on the joke. Howard's freckled, hush-voiced dignity is no laughing matter—his performance is the truest note in the film.

As the film's nominal star, Glenn Ford settles in gracefully as the buttoned-down straight man to *Courtship*'s irrepressible main attraction. Ford was always too phlegmatic a type to become the stuff of legend; of all the mishaps that had plagued Minnelli's *Four Horsemen*, casting him as a tantalizing playboy had proved the movie's coup de grâce. Fortunately, the role in *Courtship* allowed Minnelli to exploit his star's limitations, rather than trying in vain to camouflage them. Mourning becomes an actor like Ford; there was always a pinch of sourness under his decent-Joe movie manner, and this time he has something to be bitter about. He's an inhibited actor playing a man who struggles to master his own feelings, swallowing them down with a strangled gulp. Yet loneliness wells up just the same, under cover of night after Eddie is in bed. Tom's moment of truth is quieter than his son's but just as unexpected, triggered during an idle evening at home in front of the Late Late Show. A rapturous love scene between Gable and Grace Kelly in *Mogambo* reminds him of what he's missed since the death of his wife. Minnelli comes in for the kill by relentlessly cutting between the romantic kitsch on the small screen and several closeups of Ford's rapt face, pinched with deprivation.

Passages like this are almost too poignant for comfort; *Courtship* is meant to be a hybrid of pathos and laughs, but the real urgency of its serious moments makes the movie's antic mood seem calculated. Hollywood comedies of the early sixties were a contradictory lot, homogenized pastel-colored milk shakes stirred with a ring-a-ding-ding swizzle stick. It's no wonder that while Minnelli toiled to follow the rules of the genre, their spirit eluded him. Throughout his work, he had empathized with women while casting a cold eye on the conformist platitudes of hearth and wedlock. His fifties comedies, like *Designing Woman* and *The Reluctant Debutante,* reveled in the quirky wit of their female stars, but *Courtship* assumes a different perspective entirely. This script is a diagram for farce as masculine morality play—men are men and girls are types, and a little child shall lead them.

As Minnelli dutifully lifts the film out of its doldrums, Eddie evolves from bereaved kid to Cupid, and the movie becomes a frolicsome appraisal of the dangers and allure of the Opposite Sex from his knee-high perspective. Like so many of the Doris/Debbie/Shirley comedies of the era, *Courtship* is dedicated to the proposition that lust is cute so long as nobody really does anything about it. John Gay's script adds to this the winsome conceit that even at his tender years, little Master Corbett is All Boy. In their man-to-man talks, a little coaching from Dad makes Eddie himself a pint-sized connoisseur of femininity. After pondering a pinup of Jayne Mansfield, the kid begs to know what "the inches on a lady" means. "Suppose . . . the bust was twenty, what would happen?" muses Eddie, to which his father wittily responds, "Nothing, poor girl." Thirty-six is much better, but for the bust and hips alone; patiently, Dad reminds his son that "if it was 36-36-36, she'd be straight up and down." Despite this mirthful exchange, *Courtship* wants its Good Housekeeping Seal of Approval in the worst way. Eddie's comic books have taught him to watch out for those dames with skinny eyes and big busts, an insight this script heartily endorses. With tongue not so firmly in cheek, the movie follows Eddie's cue in picking the perfect Miss Right for the modern Bachelor Father.

Whatever hapless Dad might prefer, for the sake of a heartwarming fadeout, *Courtship* makes him take vanilla and like it.

You don't even need a tape measure to tote up the attributes of *Courtship*'s three contrasting lovelies—their moral worth is keyed to the color of their coiffures. Representing ash-blonde niceness, neighbor Elizabeth (Shirley Jones) is also endowed with Eddie's favorite kind of big round eyes, and the moist smile of a born nurturer. Perfect marriage material that she is, Elizabeth doesn't work for a living. Instead, she devotes her time to volunteer nursing in a uniform barely distinguishable from her everyday wardrobe. It's in this garb that she makes her first entrance in the movie, bearing a plate of home-made fudge for the freckled little man in her life. Although capable of coy jokes about her "pectoral girdle," after a bit of New Year's bubbly, Elizabeth is most herself as den mother at a kiddie birthday party. This, according to the script, qualifies her to be the ideal life companion for Eddie's father as well.

Yet for most of the picture he prefers the company of lacquered brunette Rita (a bewigged Dina Merrill), although she has eyes so skinny she can barely see out of them. As written, she's a misogynist's emancipated nightmare. As chic as she is practical, Rita is devoted to her trivial vocation of "fashion consultant," and subversively feminist design for living. As she serenely declares on her first night out with Tom, Rita is looking for "the man who'll love me on equal terms. That old saying—behind every man there's a woman? That's not for me. I want to stand right alongside." Nonsense that naturally gets a rise out of her date, who growls, "I'm afraid you're going to have to be satisfied with the vote right now. I don't think that'll ever become a national movement." Nevertheless, he finds her persistent charm and ardor strangely seductive—some men just don't know what's good for them.

While Eddie referees this tug-of-war, redheaded Stella Stevens ambles into view as curvaceous comic relief; she's from the post-Marilyn school of innocent bimbohood, with a cartoon name to match the rest of her attributes. ("Dollye Daly! I like that," chortles Jerry Van Dyke as Tom's pal, the skirt-chasing disc jockey. "It's sort of like Dilly Dally.") Dollye's timidity made her flunk the Miss Montana semifinals, prompting a trip to the big city to pursue a crash course in self-confidence. Beneath her carroty bubble-cut and hyperglandular form she's a kind of idiot savant—you never know what's going to come out of the mouth of this Babe, with her hidden mastery of bowling, trap-drums and civics class facts and figures. In the words of "The Girl Hunt" ballet's Rod Riley, "There was something about this kid that made you want to protect her"; while too flashy for wedlock to a clean-cut type like Tom, Dollye finds a soulmate in Eddie because they share the same seven-year-old point of view.

Minnelli halfheartedly goes along with the gag, his camera even ogling Dollye's rump when she advises her randy admirer that the key to championship bowling lies in the hips. But this chauvinist scenario and his own sensibility make strange bedfellows indeed. He can't help granting a human dimension to these paper dolls, a tendency that finally plays havoc with the smug symmetry of the script. As in *Some Came Running,* Minnelli allows the movie's resident doxy to utterly upstage the demure post-ingenue the hero takes to his heart. You can always tell when a character particularly beguiles him; the camera starts describing its own arcs of delight, sure that the person in the middle of the frame can take the competition. Here Minnelli stars Dollye in the movie's most painstakingly staged sequence—a Times Square spree in the manner of *Bells Are Ringing* and *The Band Wagon.* In one long, infinitely mobile take he follows her through the throngs of a sound-stage penny arcade as she commissions her likeness on a handpainted tie; bestows the prize on Eddie, and chatters of her rustic past and uncertain present to his amused father over orangeade at a hamburger stand. The part held no mysteries for an actress like Stevens, who spent her early career as a second-string hybrid of MacLaine and Monroe. Still, Minnelli's empathy and her own soft-voiced deadpan defuse the smirkiness of the writing—she becomes a disarming eccentric camouflaged as a *Playboy* pipe dream.

Like Dollye, Dina Merrill's sleek Other Woman is a throwback to earlier Minnelli movies, resembling Nina Foch in *An American in Paris* minus the smothering neuroses. In Mark Toby's novel, this character was drawn as an unmistakable shrike, but Minnelli understood the appeal of worldly, confident women like this —after all, he'd married several of them himself. As

Merrill plays her, Rita is unfailingly gracious and sensible, trying her level best to act like a lady while her tiny adversary pulls rank and plays dirty. Eddie's campaign to wean Dad from her clutches is supposed to be piquantly cunning, with lots of adorable closeups of the kid scrunching up his face with disdain at Rita's hopeful approach. But the joke soon curdles—to grown-up eyes, she's a better catch than his beloved Elizabeth, who seems to view marriage as an unpleasant duty nice women endure for the solace of having kids to smother.

Of *Courtship's* three leading ladies, Shirley Jones is the only one as mechanical as the part she's playing, efficiently doling out surrogate-mommy solicitude like tablespoons of cough syrup. In *Home from the Hill,* the domestic paragon played by Eleanor Parker was actually a forbidding creature, full of martyred hurt feelings and thorny virtue. In fact, the heroine of this comedy built to charm is not so very different. She and Eddie's father spend most of the picture snarling at each other; in one of the script's odder notions, this proves that they're meant for each other. According to *Courtship's* preordained happy ending, Eddie gets everything he wants. Dollye has a new protector, Rita is banished to her penthouse purgatory, and he's snared Dad a new wife whose idea of fun is tucking him into bed. It finishes with a lingering shot of Eddie, triumphant at last, but the director's own rapture seems muted at best. The clash between Minnelli's dutiful professionalism and his warring instincts finally makes for inert movie chemistry. Still, burbling below the surface are tantalizing hints of the neurotic melodrama Minnelli might well have made from the same plot—about a towheaded Bad Seed, who leads his gullible elders into a marriage made in hell.

• •

1964 **GOODBYE, CHARLIE**

Nineteen-sixty-three was a frustrating year for Minnelli; for the first time in two decades, he hadn't managed to get a single movie before the cameras. While conferring with Freed on their never-to-be Irving Berlin extravaganza, Minnelli bungled his last chance to direct the screen version of *My Fair Lady.* MGM had tried in good faith to snare this hottest of properties for the Freed–Minnelli team, but quailed when the bidding peaked at the unprecedented sum of five million dollars and counting—far higher than the entire budget on *Gigi.* Nevertheless, Minnelli's hopes revived when, at Lerner and Loewe's urging, a victorious Warner Bros. approached him to come to the Burbank lot and direct the musical anyway. The catch

was money—after spending such a profligate sum on the rights, Jack Warner was in no mood to indulge the artists he'd selected to get the movie made. He offered Minnelli a straight-salary fee, which the director's minions and intimates (Denise Minnelli in particular) deemed a grievous insult to his professional dignity after the hard-won profit cut he'd negotiated at Metro. Mindful of the Hollywood maxim that you're only as good as your last deal, Minnelli upped the ante, at which point Warner calmly called his bluff and drafted the less obstinate George Cukor.

Minnelli found many reasons to regret his ill-advised act of brinkmanship. Throughout their simultaneous tenures at MGM, he and Cukor waged a kind of polite

Tony Curtis revives Debbie Reynolds in Goodbye, Charlie *(1964)*

rivalry, and for the rest of his life a frustrated Minnelli maintained that his *My Fair Lady* would have been a quite different affair from the literal-minded Broadway/ Edwardian tableau that was made without him. While Cukor was thus engaged, for the moment Metro couldn't find anything for Minnelli to do. Out of restless desperation, he grabbed at 20th Century-Fox's offer to direct a Broadway acquisition whose pedigree scarcely matched *My Fair Lady*'s. This was *Goodbye, Charlie*, George Axelrod's gimmicky farce about reincarnation in a Malibu beach house.

Even in crass commercial terms its prospects were questionable; after a lukewarm Broadway premiere in December 1959, the play managed to eke out a three-months run, thanks solely to the marquee lure of Lauren Bacall in her debut as a stage comedienne. As the screen's most glamorous baritone, Bacall brought a certain androgynous logic to the star part—a Hollywood Don Juan who is bumped off by an outraged husband before the play opens, and rematerializes during Act I in the incongruous form of the kind of cutie he's spent his life seducing. Nevertheless, Fox had snared the property in the hope of shaping it to suit Marilyn Monroe, who'd triumphed in the screen ver-

sion of Axelrod's prior smash, *The Seven Year Itch*. However, by the time the studio came around to making *Goodbye, Charlie*, Monroe had been dead for more than a year. Fox next turned to Debbie Reynolds, whose box-office stock had enjoyed a sudden (albeit short-lived) surge after *The Unsinkable Molly Brown* proved the sleeper hit of 1963. The role of Charlie's incredulous but randy one-time crony went to Tony Curtis, who had once before teamed with Reynolds on *The Rat Race*, also an indifferent movie adapted from a flop play.

It's doubtful that even at the outset Minnelli had high hopes for this sour, contrived farce. He certainly expressed doubts about the casting. It was ironic that Minnelli's first movie away from the home lot found him up against the irrepressible Debbie, whom he'd managed to avoid directing through all their years together at Metro. But Fox stood firm, and Minnelli was too eager for work to quibble. MGM, of course, encouraged him to accept, delighted to pass along the financial burden of Venice Productions so long as they had no need of Minnelli's services.

Minnelli took five months, from January through June 1964, to prepare and shoot *Goodbye, Charlie.* He tried to counterfeit the old Metro atmosphere on alien turf by surrounding himself with as many of his long-time colleagues as he could assemble—Krasner as chief cameraman, André Previn to compose the score, costumer Helen Rose, set decorator Keogh Gleason, and art director Jack Martin Smith, who had designed most of Minnelli's films at Metro in the forties. Apart from a few location shots of the beach at Malibu, the film was confined entirely to the Fox lot. (In fact, thanks to the claustrophobically stagebound nature of the story, nearly half of it takes place on one set, representing Charlie's glitzy bachelor lair.) *Goodbye, Charlie* hardly inspired Minnelli to new heights of creativity; his main task was to try to put the brakes on Debbie Reynolds' projectile energy. If no major mishaps took place during the filming of this mechanical farce, Minnelli didn't wreak any miracles either. The film opened its New York showcase run in November 1964, playing three blocks away from the theater where *My Fair Lady* had started its triumphant roadshow engagement a few weeks earlier. The press disdained it as just another stillborn movieland farce; the paying customers were slightly more indulgent, but *Goodbye, Charlie* caused no sensation at the box office either. It may not have been the most ignominious of Minnelli's trio of Venice Productions—*The Sandpiper* probably won that prize—but this strident talkathon proved the dullest of the lot.

Minnelli had generally managed to breathe some wit or acerbity into even the most mechanical of his comedies. In *Goodbye, Charlie,* his stars bounce around the sets like pinballs, but unlike Axelrod's eponymous hero, the script's Charlie is a stiff beyond artificial resuscitation. On stage as on screen, this was the most cynical of morality plays, whose unearthly premise was buried under a barrage of desperate Broadway one-liners. According to Axelrod, Charlie's transsexual fate is the fit punishment for a lifetime of sexual excess; as the unfortunate hero mutters, "It's as though I'd been a gourmet all my life, and suddenly I'm a lamb chop." *The Seven Year Itch* and *Will Success Spoil Rock Hunter* had previously shown that the erotomania of the all-American satyr was Axelrod's favorite comic fetish. There was always a thin line between his own heavy-breathing take on the opposite sex and that of the drooling saps he satirized on stage, but in *Goodbye, Charlie,* the distinction is almost invisible to the naked eye. For, as his newly curvaceous self, Charlie is even deadlier than the male, exchanging new catty wiles for his old wolf whistles. Posing as his own widow, the hero tries to blackmail his respectably wed former bed-mates, a notion just as uproarious in practice as it sounds. His gradual transformation into a woman through and through is less than charming, thanks to Axelrod's cartoon idea of true femininity—all tears, flounces, and trips to the beauty parlor.

The screenplay, by veteran Hollywood boulevardier Harry Kurnitz, preserves the play's dourly antic spirit, adding new wisecracks to compete with Axelrod's limp old ones. ("I don't have to go see Brigitte Bardot movies any more," muses Charlie. "I can just stay home and pull down the shades.") Kurnitz' principal contribution was to open up the play by introducing two characters enamored of the new Charlie: naive Rich Kid with a momma fixation (played by Pat Boone), and the heretofore unseen trigger-happy producer (Walter Matthau), who dispatched the hero to his just

Charlie (Debbie Reynolds) blackmails his exes. Joanna Barnes (left) and Ellen McRae (Burstyn) in Goodbye, Charlie *(1964)*

end in the first place. Their arrival adds extra knots to a story that was muddled from the beginning, but any distraction from this comedy's inert core is welcome.

By amplifying Axelrod's salvos against the loucheness of the Beverly Hills circuit, Kurnitz edged the movie closer to familiar Minnelli territory; in the manner of *The Bad and the Beautiful,* it's peppered with allusions to decades of Hollywood lore, played this time for nervous laughs. Charlie's pre-credits shot in the pants during a party at sea farcically recalls the Thomas Ince scandal of the 1920s; his deadpan, tuber-shaped agent, "Crafty" (Martin Gabel), is an obvious clone of super-dealmaker "Swifty" Lazar, while any resemblance between the late Sir Alexander Korda and the movie's Sir Leopold Sartori, the Hungarian mogul who starts all the trouble, is purely intentional. Minnelli is clearly more at ease skewering the lifestyles of the rich and sleazy than exploiting the yock quotient of *Goodbye, Charlie*'s gender jokes. Joanna Barnes and Ellen McRae (later known as Ellen Burstyn) make a poisonously gracious pair of Hollywood wives, with hilariously outré wardrobes to match. As a below-the-title character player, Matthau neatly trumps the leads —his Sir Leopold is all dangerous Magyar bonhomie, inflected with a smattering of Oxbridge vowels for a spurious touch of class.

Whenever these people are on screen, *Goodbye, Charlie* shows fleeting glints of Minnelli's customary brio. Two sequences freshly minted for the celluloid *Goodbye, Charlie* send up the vulgarity it otherwise succumbs to. Ominously lit by Krasner, the opening orgy a-go-go is sulphurous stuff, a kind of Stateside hangover from the Via Veneto group grope he staged for *Two Weeks in Another Town.* While magnates idly paw their compliant tomatoes, the camera weaves past a frugging starlet toward the stateroom where Charlie disrobes a redhead; as in some demented forties thriller, the style is first-person subjective, shot through the bleary eyes of *Goodbye, Charlie*'s prospective killer. Later on, Minnelli indulges his taste for chichi kitsch as Charlie makes his maiden visit to a Rodeo Drive temple of beauty. It's a West Coast variation on the Park Avenue retreat George Cukor penetrated in *The Women;* the place has the size and swank of an all-girl Baths of Caracalla, flanked by blue frescoes depicting the glory that was backlot Rome. Languid lovelies dangle their toes in tinkly fountains while frantic gossips dart from one cubicle to the next like besmocked hummingbirds. Delighted to find himself on an expansive set for a

change, Minnelli is as animated as they are, sailing his camera past this gilded sorority with a droll flourish.

But even here, the movie's genuine crassness upstages Minnelli's feints at parody. In the script's cheapest gag, the still male-at-heart heroine gets into the spirit of these new surroundings by goosing the nearest available fanny. With her tomboy playfulness stuck at fortissimo, Reynolds' pat is more like a slug—the bit-player object of her affection looks as though she doesn't know what hit her, in more ways than one. It's a sentiment anyone watching *Goodbye, Charlie* can easily relate to. With *The Reluctant Debutante,* Minnelli had mustered considerable verve despite a tinny text trapping his actors on the same living-room set for reels at a time. Five years later, against similar odds, he seems beyond caring.

Whenever Curtis and Reynolds are alone together trading glandular jokes before a back-projected California seascape, *Goodbye, Charlie* feels stage-managed rather than directed. Minnelli keeps everything generically bright and loud and frantic. Having added a few characteristic final touches to the set (for such a crude sort, the late Charlie had awfully good taste in paintings and chinoiserie), he retreats stoically behind the camera while his stars do what comes naturally in clinkers like this. Intent on selling personality-plus, Reynolds and Curtis give an object lesson in what a Nichols and May routine once called "proximity but no relating"; on that sound stage, it's every man for himself. Playing an expatriate novelist, Curtis belts out his ersatz-literate repartee like Cary Grant with thyroid problems and a tin ear. But even he is subdued beside his indefatigable co-star, whose antiseptic-pixie energy increases the hero/heroine's identity crisis at every turn. Flailing and bellowing in oversized p.j.'s, this self-described wolf-turned-lamb chop comes off instead like a dainty if high-strung Lesbian; transformed by pastel war paint and curvy Helen Rose creations, the new Charlie seems less glamorized than embalmed.

But then, the same thing could be said for this whole enterprise. *Goodbye, Charlie*'s onscreen venality is outflanked only by its cynicism, and as a result, Minnelli's last comedy turned out to be his least, as well. Determined to keep working and to adapt to changing tastes he didn't understand, in this mix of tired innuendo and cut-rate glitz Minnelli ended up with a movie that the real-life Charlies, Craftys, and Sartoris might well have embraced as their own.

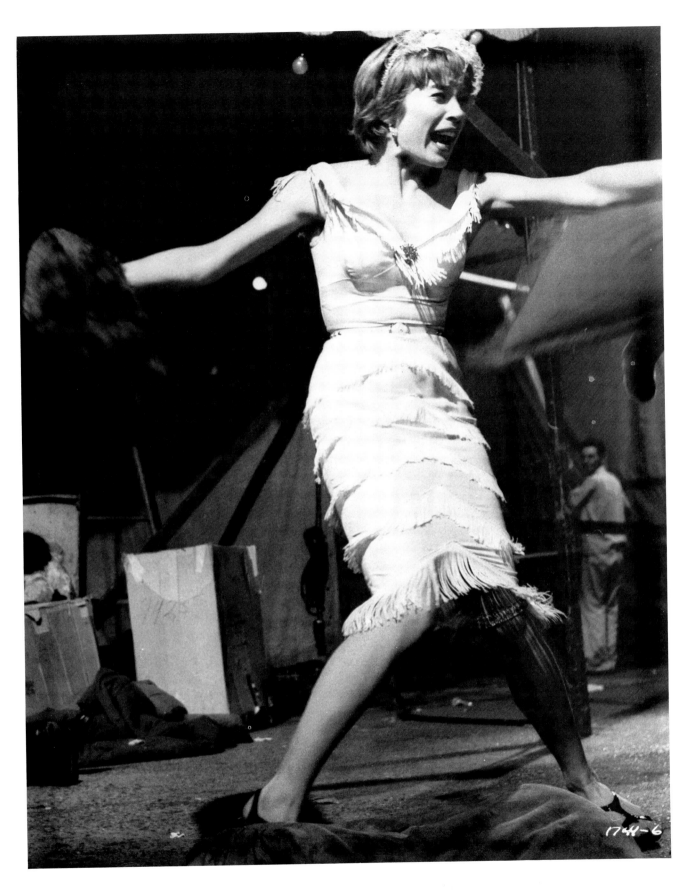

*Dance of death. Shirley
MacLaine in* Some Came
Running *(1958)*

Melodramas

THE CLOCK

While Metro was bound eventually to give Minnelli a serious picture to direct, the opportunity arose sooner than the studio had planned, or he ever expected. Ironically, it was neither Mayer nor Freed who first had the wit to probe this unexplored vein of his talent, but the studio's top musical personality, Judy Garland. With *Meet Me in St. Louis* awaiting release, the adolescent Mickey-and-Judy phase of Garland's career was definitely behind her. Eager for new challenges, she decided it was time to test her gifts as a dramatic actress, and beseeched Freed to find a suitable vehicle. Freed had never before produced a non-musical, but he felt that under the right circumstances the novelty might intrigue her enormous following. Out of the hundreds of properties languishing in the MGM story department slush pile, *The Clock* was a prospect that promised to be both touching and topical.

It was an unpublished short story by Paul and Pauline Gallico about the whirlwind courtship between a white-collar girl and a soldier on two-day leave in New York. Lana Turner generally cornered the studio's patent on love in wartime, but as Freed realized there was no reason why it couldn't serve Garland as well if not better. Minus the usual song cues, heroine Alice Maybery was the tender-hearted girl-next-door of all the musicals they'd done together. Spurred by Garland's enthusiasm, the studio paid $50,000 to Gallico for the rights, after which Freed tapped two contract writers to rough out a script—Joseph Schrank, late of *Cabin in the Sky*, and Robert Nathan, the prolific author of such highflown romances as *Portrait of Jennie*.

From the studio's roster of leading men, Robert Walker was an obvious choice to play Garland's love-struck GI as, whether on loanout for *Since You Went Away* or at home in *See Here, Private Hargrove*, and *Bataan*, Walker's specialty was gangly kids in khaki. Preproduction on *The Clock* started in May 1944. Having just photographed Garland so resplendently in Technicolor for *Meet Me in St. Louis*, George Folsey was immediately drafted to do the same in black and white. At this stage, however, Freed had no intention of add-ing Minnelli to *The Clock*'s creative crew. For one thing, he'd just assigned him to take over *Ziegfeld Follies* from George Sidney; the producer thought one inexperienced artist on this non-singing, non-dancing project was enough. Instead, preproduction began under Jack Conway, an odd candidate indeed for a tender Judy Garland picture. One of MGM's old reliables, Conway did better with rowdy comedies like *Libeled Lady* and virile Gable vehicles on the order of *Boom Town* and *Honky Tonk*.

Perhaps mercifully, Conway's tenure on *The Clock* proved short. In Schrank and Nathan's script, Joe and Alice's brief idyll unfolded against a varied assortment of Manhattan locales, from Times Square and City Hall to the Metropolitan Museum and Central Park. While Garland and company would come no closer to Fifth Avenue than the plywood and canvas version on MGM's Lot 2, Conway was dispatched east with a small crew to film a few reels of fresh background footage, to supplement the usual repertoire of stock shots from the studio library. This turned out to be his first and last contribution to the film. The director became seriously ill on his return to the Coast, and was forced to abandon all work for several months. As a replacement, the studio suggested Fred Zinnemann. Still several years shy of the credits that would make him one of Hollywood's most esteemed filmmakers, he had just marked his graduation from Metro's B-picture unit with the anti-Nazi melodrama *The Seventh Cross*. In retrospect, for Zinnemann to direct Spencer Tracy as a fugitive from fascism wasn't an assignment—it was Kismet. From *High Noon* through *A Man for All Seasons* and *Julia,* he became the screen's specialist in parables on the idealist's fearless struggle in an amoral world. Already, it was a stretch to imagine Zinnemann as the Freed Unit type, but young Metro directors were expected to bend to anything the studio threw at them; when *The Clock* was ready to resume on August 1, Zinnemann had the job.

There was trouble as soon as he walked onto the set. Zinnemann's reserved manner unnerved Garland, who had the distinct impression this boy-meets-girl mood piece was either beyond or beneath him. After taking a close look at the accumulated rushes, Freed decided his star had a point, and closed down production three weeks into shooting. There was some talk of canceling *The Clock* entirely, a prospect everyone concerned wanted to avoid. It was then that Minnelli became a serious contender. Convinced that only he could give her the confidence *The Clock* needed, with Freed's consent Garland approached Minnelli to salvage the film. This was an interesting turnabout—on *Meet Me in St. Louis*, it was he who had cajoled Garland into doing the film. However, Minnelli had strong personal reasons for resisting. Since Garland had broken off the romance they'd begun during *Meet Me in St. Louis* to resume a previous affair with Joseph L. Mankiewicz, the couple had been politely estranged for several months. Their brief reunion for Garland's *Ziegfeld Follies* specialty was strictly professional, and Minnelli wasn't sure he was up to a lengthy reprise.

Nevertheless, the prospect flattered and intrigued him, and its timing was propitious; he'd just finished shooting *Ziegfeld Follies*, with nothing definite on the horizon. After poring through Zinnemann's footage, Minnelli agreed to take over on the proviso that he could start from scratch. He made some changes in the cast, with Ruth Brady taking the place of Audrey Totter as Garland's worldly roommate, and James Gleason brought in to fill the largest supporting part—a sentimental milkman who befriends the lovelorn couple—which Hume Cronyn had been playing for Zinnemann.

Minnelli knew that if this love story were to have the urgency Zinnemann's scenes lacked, he needed to conjure up the mingled loneliness and excitement of the city itself. Clearly, the usual slapdash backlot facsimiles wouldn't suffice. On *The Clock*, he didn't have the luxury of months spent researching the precise look he wanted, as he had enjoyed on *Meet Me in St. Louis*. But Minnelli had other resources this time—the memories stored up from the decade he'd spent in New York. Many of the sets designed for Zinnemann—such as Cedric Gibbons and William Ferrari's extraordinary reconstruction of Pennsylvania Station, which opens and closes the film—were retained, but others were redesigned to match Minnelli's painstaking eye. (A particular favorite was a theater-district spaghetti restaurant trimmed with incongruous Victoriana; he took Garland to dine at the actual spot during their subsequent honeymoon.)

The Clock was the first Minnelli movie to show off his extraordinarily precise way of filling in the human backdrop to his stories with specific and pungent detail. Throughout the rest of his career, he became notorious for spending hours on the set coaching the bit players he'd chosen to populate his frame, giving each a history, a body language of his own. Movie extras were supposed to be homogenized and unobtrusive, but

Minnelli assembled a multiracial, polyglot throng, scurrying through his MGM Manhattan with the self-absorbed purpose of born New Yorkers. It's no insult to the studio's wizard set decorators to note that Minnelli's madding crowds are the most impressive props in the picture.

He also labored hard to stir some urban grit into *The Clock*'s script. According to its central conceit, even a hardhearted town like New York smiles benignly on young lovers; thus, amid all the forces that temporarily separate Joe and Alice, total strangers touched by their ardor constantly drop their protective masks to give the kids a hand. This was an appealing notion, but Minnelli had lived in New York too long to take it quite so literally. He edited the script himself, giving his big-city types a gruffer edge and using velvety closeups and George Bassman's score to substitute for the riper romantic exchanges between Garland and Walker. Nathan objected strenuously to these wholesale prunings, but Freed trusted Minnelli's instincts and refused to interfere. (As it was, in certain passages *The Clock* retained enough goo to choke even Frank Capra.)

The idyllic mood of the story extended to the set as well; Minnelli later remembered this as one of the rare moments when his work and private life were completely in harmony. Success can be a potent aphrodisiac, and their remarkable chemistry as colleagues brought Minnelli and Garland closer together than ever. By the time the film ended around Thanksgiving 1944, they were living together again, just as they'd done during the final weeks of *Meet Me in St. Louis*. In her present frame of mind, Garland was a model of professionalism while shooting *The Clock*. In fact, she assumed the role of behind-the-scenes confidante to co-star Robert Walker, on the rebound from an unhappy collision of his own personal and professional fates—while teamed with him on *Since You Went Away*, his wife Jennifer Jones had left him for its producer, David O. Selznick. During *The Clock*, Walker's off-hours drinking binges marked the start of a self-destructive spiral that would lead to his premature death in 1952. Thanks in part to Garland, Walker nevertheless kept to the task at hand, letter-perfect if a bit bleary-eyed. Engrossed in Garland and the movie, Minnelli failed to heed his distress at the time, which became harder to ignore once the film was in the can and Walker started crashing the Minnelli–Garland home, for comfort.

Thanks to Minnelli, *The Clock* defied its bumpy genesis to everyone's satisfaction. On completion, the final cost came to $1,324,207, even then a reasonable sum considering the seven months and three directors it took to get the movie made. MGM, on viewing the rough assembly of the film, showed its gratitude by rewarding Minnelli with a $25,000 bonus. As with all pictures featuring military characters in those days, it was perused by the War Department on the grounds of "security and propriety," but both the military and

MGM's Stage 27, transformed into Pennsylvania Station, The Clock *(1945)*

Metro brass agreed that for *The Clock*, no retakes would be necessary. The movie premiered in May 1945 to a glowing reception from the New York press. By this late date in the war, Hollywood had turned out dozens of valentines to fresh-faced GIs and their faithful Jills; however, its genuinely lyrical treatment clearly distinguished the film as something special. Released six months after *Meet Me in St. Louis*, *The Clock* solidified Minnelli's acclaim as one of the most accomplished directors of his generation. He dominated the reviews, even among those tabloid critics who usually acted as though the stars directed themselves. More analytical chroniclers, like Manny Farber and James Agee, felt that his observant eye was all that redeemed *The Clock* from the usual Metro-Pollyanna platitudes.

Audiences liked *The Clock* almost as well as the reviewers did. By the end of the year, the film had earned $2,783,000 in domestic rentals—less than the customary returns on a Garland musical perhaps, but ample vindication of Freed's modest gamble. While this gentle film would remain Garland's sole dramatic showcase during her tenure there, it opened up a new world of possibilities for Minnelli. *The Clock* proved what his first screen musicals had been hinting at all along—he

didn't need song cues or dream ballets to transform MGM's star fodder into an expression of his own acute and sensuous way of seeing.

In 1945, nobody had to ask for whom *The Clock* tolled. The whirlwind courtship between two nice, ordinary American kids really celebrated the romance between the moviegoing public and that idealized portrait of itself which made the war worth waging and winning. Yet Minnelli's special vision made something unexpectedly rueful out of the banal archetype of GI-meets-girl. As in *Meet Me in St. Louis*, Minnelli subordinates the plot to a more absorbing story—the relationship between a place captured at a specific moment in time and the people whose lives it defines. Esther's flirtation with the boy next door was the cheerful pretext to explore the nurturing, intimate world of a midwestern suburb at the turn of the century; this love story is really about the urgent mood of a city in wartime, etched with the same extraordinary precision of

191

*Robert Walker and Judy
Garland at City Hall,* The
Clock *(1945)*

detail. By turns exuberant and claustrophobic, his milling panoramas aren't merely a picturesque frame for a simple love story. New York's indifferent hubbub shapes everything that happens to *The Clock*'s anonymous working girl and average GI on leave: edging them closer together for a touch of human warmth, abruptly dividing them in the chaos of the subway at rush hour.

Like King Vidor's masterful *The Crowd,* made at MGM a generation before, this movie offers an indelible panorama of a long-vanished New York—from the Astor Hotel lobby filled with soldiers and their dates on a sweltering night out to a forlorn downtown cafeteria where *The Clock*'s newlyweds face up to their perished dreams over lukewarm soup. Yet its most persuasive essence-of-Manhattan images were shot entirely on the Metro lot. Perched atop his camera boom on MGM's biggest sound stage, Minnelli opens by soaring over the rushing hordes of his mock Pennsylvania Station; somewhere down there is *The Clock*'s young hero, one small human story out of thousands we'll never know about. After singling out Robert Walker for our attention (cadging a light from a commuter played by none other than Arthur Freed), he quickly shows us what the awestruck kid is up against—as the camera looms down on Walker, a tilt-angled collage of the skyscraper city stuns him, driving him back inside the train station. Garland is another mote in the crowd, until they meet in standard movie fashion; he accidentally trips her, and she loses a heel.

Alice's presence makes the city seem a less forbid-

ding place, and in her company Joe samples Manhattan's Sunday afternoon diversions: an open-air ride on a Fifth Avenue bus, the Children's Zoo at Central Park, a visit to the Metropolitan. These early scenes unreel under a technical handicap—the usual Hollywood split between back-projection exteriors and sound-stage-bound actors in the foreground. Minnelli copes by modulating the interplay of his two stars to match the swelter of the city taking its Sunday ease; as a midday sun beats down on the street scene projected behind them, they idly follow the afternoon's natural course.

While the couple gets acquainted, the screenwriters establish who they are in platitudes that could apply to any likely juvenile and ingenue. She's a little secretary in a big office, whose small-town simplicity shines through the poise she's acquired from three years in the big city, while he's the quintessentially endearing hick, with dialogue to match. Joe's most pungent memory of home is the smell of cut grass in the evening after his Dad has mown the lawn, but Minnelli tweaks the sentimental reflexes of the script with some caustic editorializing of his own. The hero's prattle reverberates in the shadow of a stone sphinx, while Alice rubs her tired feet; "Did you have a dog?" she asks quaveringly, but there was no Lassie back home in Indiana to make this mawkish pastorale complete. With so little help from writers Schrank and Nathan, Minnelli relies on the behavioral quirks of his stars to flesh out these archetypes—Garland's nervous, darting gaze complementing Walker's abashed stammer. He orchestrates the tentative silences between them to underscore how vulnerable their connection really is. One casually blurted word could prompt them to separate forever. Minnelli's inventive ruse to reveal Garland's latent dramatic talents was to make her not just songless but speechless. To convey the heroine's shy, contemplative quality, much of the time he built her characterization on her hesitant gestures and the innate tenderness of those expressive eyes.

The pathos emerges from inconsequential details: Alice edgily pacing her cramped apartment while wondering whether she has succumbed to the real thing or that sordid cliché, a serviceman's pickup; her sudden dabbing at a spot on Joe's jacket in mid-spat during their first date. (Minnelli finds room here for another Freed Unit in-joke; the wistful piano player at the Italian restaurant is Roger Edens, Freed's assistant producer and Garland's musical coach.) Having established their attraction in deft realistic strokes, Minnelli shifts mood radically for the couple's first clinch. The occasion is a tranquil midnight stroll through Riverside Park, a prospect that, to a contemporary city dweller, already lifts the movie to the realm of never-never land. At last, Joe and Alice have the town to themselves, and to relish the moment, she invites him to listen to the urban sounds reverberating against the deceptive calm of the park. Suddenly the soundtrack fills with amplified sirens, tugboat whistles, and subway wheels. Garland twirls expectantly, her gestures as dreamily ritualized as in a song cue for a production number, and sure enough the symphony of street noises blends into an MGM heavenly chorale while her eyes widen in wonder. What follows is the most unabashedly passionate moment Minnelli ever filmed. In the movie-music vernacular of the forties, the love theme generally lulls the audience into the right mood of erotic anticipation, but here the stars themselves seem hypnotized by its strains. In gradually magnified closeups, Garland and Walker drift toward the camera and each other, merging into an embrace to a soundtrack crescendo that is the closest a wholesome 1940's love story dares come to orgasm. With Minnelli transfixed behind the viewfinder, Garland's eyebrow twitches ecstatically in mid-kiss as we watch her rite of passage from demure puppy love to sensual adulthood.

In a more conventionally sentimental movie of the era, this scene would serve as the story's climax—the shot to cinch the myth that the thrill of a romance subdues all obstacles. But Minnelli and the city have a few sobering surprises in store. It begins with a bittersweet detour, as the young couple spends the night in the company of a philosopher-milkman, the kind of bighearted curmudgeon who lives on every backlot brownstone street. After he's ko'd by a pugnacious drunk (a droll cameo by Keenan Wynn), they finish Al's deliveries and share his breakfast, dished up by his belligerently loving wife. Although charmingly acted

by gentle-tough guy character player James Gleason and his real-life spouse Lucile, the episode tilts precariously toward cuteness; it's a blue-collar variation of Judge and Mrs. Hardy's love on toast.

Lulled by this warm vision of marital harmony, Joe and Alice decide to share the rest of the day together. Instead, they unwittingly plunge into a wide-eyed nightmare with Minnelli's camera retreating helplessly as they lose each other in the threatening crush of a Grand Central subway platform. Neither has bothered to learn the other's last name; she's trapped on the local while he staggers onto the downtown express. Minnelli's extras scuffle heedlessly around the woebegone lovers, trapped in replicas of the Lexington Avenue line as grim as the real thing. The sense of panic is tangible, amplified by the dark chords of George Bassman's score and nervously intercut shots of Walker and Garland scanning the throng. This sequence is superlatively filmed, culminating in a shot of almost impossible technical difficulty—barreling down the platform, the subway shrieks to a halt on a closeup of Walker's anxious, searching face. Immediately thereafter, Minnelli employs a sly trick to stress the hero's dilemma. The camera pans over what looks like a bird's eye view of the city then pulls back to reveal that it's only a shopwindow cyclorama, as a loudspeaker blares the city's vital statistics, million by million.

Engulfed in another swarm of oblivious New Yorkers, Joe and Alice find each other on the depot steps where they first met and, like their rendezvous in the park, this accident convinces the couple that their love is a unique phenomenon, blessed by the fates. The rest of the movie is an exercise in humiliation, as Minnelli emphasizes how insignificant they are to everyone but themselves. The license bureau at City Hall bursts with couples of every age, race, physical type, and temperament, all but Joe and Alice smugly clutching their blood-test forms. Forced to cool their heels at the city medical office, Alice queasily asks if they could sit elsewhere. The camera pans to reveal the source of her sudden distress—next to her is another worn-out bride in the same off-the-rack dress she's been wearing since the night before. As they scurry back and forth from clinics to city clerks, the movie's title takes on an ominous meaning—time is the enemy, ticking off the minutes before the bureaucrats close up for the night and Joe's leave is over.

In woozy diagonals, Minnelli whips up an expressionistic montage of clock-faces superimposed on civil-servant hatchet-faces; the camera reverts to normal as, at the last possible second, they receive the wedding rite they've been longing for all day. It's a pretty hollow triumph—no ring, no flowers, the bride framed by a thicket of potted palms more appropriate to a funeral home. In an agonized closeup, Alice strains to hear the mumbled ceremony over the din of an elevated train rumbling outside the open window of the municipal building. Their troth officially pledged, she trembles with embarrassment as, in the confusion and relief of the moment, Joe forgets to kiss her. Afterwards, the newlyweds celebrate their nuptial dinner at a greasy spoon, and the bride's frail pluck deflates for good. Following a performance of considerable restraint thus far, Garland unleashes all her latent hysteria, blurting ''It was all so *ugly*'' in a torrent of convulsive sobs. The heroine is beyond comfort and for good reason. The real sorrow is that after all they've been through, Joe and Alice are still strangers with nothing to say to each other.

Attuned though Minnelli is to *The Clock*'s passages of anxiety and despair, to end a Judy Garland picture in a state of such hopelessness would have been an act of heresy. Redemption comes, appropriately enough, in church; having numbly watched a more fortunate pair of newlyweds launched in a blur of pelted rice and congratulations, Joe and Alice sidle into a deserted pew and renew their own vows. This impromptu gesture cements their bond and gives solace to the bride, but as Minnelli films it, the scene is more plaintive than transcendent; sitting in the darkness of the deserted church, they seem smaller and more alone than ever.

The real sop to the fans comes next, in a discreet post-coital interlude the morning after. They spend the last minutes of Joe's furlough in a pantomime of domestic contentment, exchanging coy glances over the breakfast table of their hotel suite. (That they managed to find such luxury accommodations in the midst of wartime Manhattan is *The Clock*'s purest fantasy touch.) In her grown-up negligee, Garland reasserts the movie-star poise she'd subsumed in introverted little Alice, just in time to deliver the reassuring speech that foretells her groom's safe return. ''You're coming back,'' Garland insists, although those who remembered Walker's fate in *Since You Went Away* might not be so sure. ''Whoever up there makes the arrangements for people has done pretty well for us,'' she adds, yet there's an ambiguous disparity between the maxims in the script and what Minnelli's eye chooses to reveal. The young couple may believe in the uniqueness of their destiny, but his camera finds one last occasion to expose how universal that feeling is. Before pausing for Joe and Alice's final farewell, Minnelli tracks past a dozen such partings of soldiers from their various wives and parents and kids—all of whom sustain the hope that they, too, are coming back.

The Clock concludes as it began in Pennsylvania Station, but the symmetry doesn't end there. In a boom shot of staggering panache even for him, Minnelli ascends all the way across the set from the departure gate to the rafters of the depot. Rather than fading out on the comforting image of the heroine's resolute face, *The Clock* takes a God-like view, retreating until she has utterly disappeared in the crowd. Whoever up there makes the arrangements for people has completed His work on Alice, left to her everyday grind after two days of tumult and rapture. Despite the soothing strains of the choir on the soundtrack, the effect is strangely disquieting. With his accent on the uncertainties of life and love in war, and the alienating crush of the metropolis at any time, Minnelli fashioned a happy-ending romance that feels like tragedy.

· ·

1946 **UNDERCURRENT**

Coming as it did on the heels of *Yolanda and the Thief*, *Undercurrent* showed his employers what a versatile good sport Minnelli could be. Too shrewd to insist on surrealist self-expression all the time, if pressed he could turn out a standard-issue box-office thriller with the same dispatch as Mervyn LeRoy. This yarn about Gothic angst among the horsey set was about as far removed from his previous work as he could get. Apart from that abject assignment, *I Dood It*, Minnelli's movies to date had sought quite consciously to advance the art of the popular screen. However, *Undercurrent* boasted no such aspirations—it was made simply to keep its high-priced stars busy and their fans happy, preferably without causing massive embarrassment to either.

Undercurrent's biggest fringe benefit for Minnelli was that it marked his first real collaboration with Pandro Berman, after their passing encounter in the early 1940s. By 1945, the producer was concentrating on dramatic star vehicles, and a story by one Thelma Strabel entitled ''You Were There'' looked like just the ticket. Serialized appropriately enough in the *Woman's Home Companion,* it told of a sheltered New England spinster swept into marriage by a rich and handsome stranger; unbeknownst to her, his brains have been scrambled by a lifelong resentment against his black-sheep brother, and soon the bride becomes the unwilling star of his paranoid fantasies. With its rearing stallions and quaking Negro retainers, ''You Were There'' was something like *Gaslight* in jodhpurs. Considering how lucrative that Cukor film had been for MGM this was no small recommendation, and in March 1945 the studio rewarded Strabel's originality with a check for $25,000.

"You Were There" struck Berman as an expedient solution to MGM's ongoing Katharine Hepburn dilemma—in between her teamings with Tracy, finding material to suit the patrician star was notoriously tough. By now Berman was an expert of sorts, having produced most of her RKO vehicles in the thirties as well as MGM's recent *Dragon Seed,* in which Hepburn played the indomitable spirit of the New China. After that, even casting her as this passive, introverted wallflower seemed plausible—at least in "You Were There" Ann Hamilton was also a Caucasian from New England. Once she accepted the part, Berman began the usual Metro relay race on the script. Over the next few months, the story passed through the hands of a series of woman's-picture specialists, including Helen Deutsch and Marguerite Roberts. However, the final version was written by Edward Chodorov, a playwright who'd shown his aptitude with heroines-in-distress in the Broadway spinetingler *Kind Lady.*

To play Hepburn's ill-humored spouse, Berman thought it would be smart showmanship to cast Robert Taylor, a popular favorite who'd been in uniform and off the screen for two years. His reasons for choosing Minnelli were a little more oblique, and the director himself was surprised when Berman sent him the script. However, he'd certainly shown a sensitive touch with actresses in his handling of Garland, and at the moment, Minnelli was available to start whenever Berman was ready. In 1945, his working pace had slowed down considerably from the three-picture regimen he'd sprinted through the previous year. After completing *Yolanda and the Thief,* Minnelli spent the summer on an extended honeymoon with Garland, followed by the few weeks it took to shoot her episodes for *Till the Clouds Roll By.* By November, he had nothing to do but await the imminent birth of their daughter. His next scheduled picture, *The Pirate,* was on hold pending Garland's recovery and an acceptable script. Unusually for the times, Hepburn's Metro contract granted her veto power over her prospective co-stars and directors, but evidently she was pleased with the

Katharine Hepburn faces herself and her enigmatic husband, Robert Taylor, Undercurrent *(1946)*

*Katharine Hepburn and
Robert Mitchum in*
Undercurrent *(1946)*

package Berman had assembled; during her Christmas holiday in New York, the producer triumphantly cabled Hepburn the news that all commitments had been ironed out with both Taylor and Minnelli.

The film went into production on February 5 1946 under Strabel's original title, which the studio dropped for *Undercurrent*'s more Freudian ring halfway through shooting. *Undercurrent* was a fairly elaborate undertaking: its peripatetic plot shuttled the heroine from back-lot Connecticut to Northern California, Washington, D.C., and to a Maryland estate which from certain angles bore an unmistakable resemblance to Hepburn's family manse in *The Philadelphia Story*. It took Minnelli nearly three months to complete the picture, at a cost of $1,643,772. As even Metro's technicians tended to be typecast according to genre, *Undercurrent* presented Minnelli with a largely unfamiliar crew—most prominently Karl Freund, the camera's master of shadowy expressionism, and Randall Duell, whose job it was to imbue the movie's rustic settings with that outlandish touch of gloss MGM fans had come to expect.

Although hardly transported by the script, Minnelli saw intriguing possibilities in one scene—an ominous homecoming reception for the bride, à la *Rebecca*, in which her fragile self-confidence crumbles on meeting husband Alan's worldly set. He drafted playwright George Oppenheimer to add the right brittle, intimidating buzz to the cocktail chit-chat; meanwhile he struggled to turn Hepburn into the sort of introvert who would quake at the sight of her dowdy self in the bedroom mirror.

Offscreen, as usual, she was the one who cowed everyone else, and Minnelli's most onerous task on

Undercurrent was refereeing the clash of temperaments among his expensive stars. Nearly as touchy as his celluloid alter ego, Robert Taylor bitched that Minnelli had thrown the picture to Hepburn. She in turn exuded disdain for Robert Mitchum, peculiarly cast as the maligned brother who turns out to be a gentle aesthete with a passion for Brahms. Hepburn's hauteur didn't get much of a rise out of Mitchum—most of time he was too exhausted to care. On the cusp of major stardom after years of bit parts and B-westerns, Mitchum was RKO's most valuable new commodity. The studio plotted to take full advantage of his sudden vogue: Mitchum staggered through eighteen-hour workdays to complete one RKO picture plus two loanouts at once during early 1946, of which *Undercurrent* was his morning job.

Throughout all this, Minnelli's personal life brought him a pleasant respite from the tensions on the set. As far as he was concerned, the most memorable event connected with this picture had nothing to do with *Undercurrent*—on March 12 1946, he celebrated the arrival of his first daughter, named Liza May after an Ira Gershwin lyric and Minnelli's late mother. Happily distracted by fatherhood, Minnelli didn't flinch when *Undercurrent* opened in November to the critical reception it deserved. Flacked by MGM as a new high in screen suspense, *Undercurrent* looked like the same old tomfoolery to the press. Yet, thanks to a happy confluence of the times and public taste, the studio had no cause for worry. Movie attendance reached a postwar peak when *Undercurrent* was released, and audiences responded to its blend of offbeat casting, on-the-money production values, and paint-by-numbers plot. By the end of the year, the movie's estimated domestic rentals totaled $3,250,000—ironically, in box office terms this disposable enterprise was one of the most successful dramas of Minnelli's career.

What was it about the times that triggered all those I-married-a-psychotic melodramas which suddenly gripped Hollywood from Victory in Japan through Stalemate in Korea? Intended for a predominantly female audience, these movies may have served as a safety valve for postwar fears of renewed domestic tyranny, after years of relative autonomy while the men were away at the front. *Undercurrent* came fairly early in the cycle, but soon every second woman star this side of Betty Grable found herself recoiling in closeup while her batty and/or homicidal spouse plotted to do her in. Such roles were ideal for soft-voiced glamour types like Loretta Young *(The Stranger)* or Claudette Colbert *(Sleep, My Love, The Secret Fury),* but it was disorienting to watch actresses well-schooled in being deadlier than the male suddenly cower behind the locked doors of their boudoirs—from Ida Lupino *(Beware, My Lovely)* and Joan Bennett *(Secret Behind the Door)* to Barbara Stanwyck *(Cry Wolf, Sorry, Wrong Number)* and Joan Crawford *(Sudden Fear).*

These post-Atomic Gothics were guided by rules as rigid as the Production Code strictures against cussing and double beds, and finally just as soothing. To the undoubted relief of any tenement-bound GI brides in the audience, these beleaguered women were always smart-set darlings by birth or hasty marriage; implicitly, their domestic terror was the excise tax exacted for dwelling in Beekman Place town houses or rustic stately homes. Nevertheless, in the end the wages of luxe were a nervous breakdown but rarely death. For every mustachioed menace who seduced one of these well-heeled innocents into wedlock, some tender and sensitive suitor waited on the sidelines, ready at the fadeout to heal the heroine's traumas and restore her faith in the opposite sex.

Undercurrent resorted to every trick of the trade, embellished with an A-budget ration of woman's-picture plush. Introduced as a Connecticut cricket-on-the-hearth toiling meekly as lab assistant to her scientist father, its film-noir Cinderella endures a shaky transition to Washington hostess and stud-farm chatelaine, draped in tailored gowns by Irene as befit her new station. The heroine's highflown bent for Culture is a peculiarly MGM quirk; contractually, the timbre of a grand piano thrilled L. B. Mayer's great ladies the way a tommygun's staccato did the underworld gents at Warners. After all, this was the studio where even a scarred blackmailer like Joan Crawford in *A Woman's Face* betrayed a shred of humanity by confessing a fondness for classical music—specifically, "most symphonies, some concertos," in her own unforgettable phrase.

Presumably warming up for her forthcoming role as

Clara Schumann in *Song of Love,* the Hepburn of *Undercurrent* is a devotee of one symphony in particular —the Brahms' Third, used as a kind of aural Rorschach test for the movie's dramatis personae. Ann Hamilton's gentle father (familiarly known as "Dink") taught her to play along to his melody at the keyboard, but husband Alan explodes when she dares to try the piece in the drawing room of his ancestral home. He claims that his long-ailing mother died at the piano while performing that very symphony; "I know how much it means to an invalid to be able to play," Ann coos, sympathetically. But the real source of his distress is darker yet— Alan has no aptitude for music, hates it in fact, because brother Michael is the family aesthete, whose affinity for Brahms is matched by his fondness for the same Robert Louis Stevenson verse Ann dotes on. Thus, long before they even meet, Ann and her phantom brother-in-law are clearly each other's destiny. Sure enough, once Alan has been dispatched by a renegade stallion while preparing to bash in his wife's skull, Michael takes Dink's place at the keyboard. At the fadeout, an astonished Ann propels her wheelchair toward the source of those stirring strains, eager once more to resume her place as adoring accompanist to a protective male virtuoso.

Backdated a century, this was precisely the sort of wistful twaddle that set Emma Bovary to brood discontentedly over her own prosaic lot. Three years hence, Minnelli's screen version of Flaubert would debunk this school of lending-library kitsch with caustic relish. But in the meantime, all he could do with *Undercurrent* was play it straight and hope for the best.

Undercurrent represents the dreary underside of that homogenized house style that was the studio system's pride. The Chodorov screenplay is slavishly faithful to its novelette source, reveling in the high-toned locutions that denote refined MGM entertainment. With a title like *Undercurrent,* this movie predictably drowns in pathetic fallacy; the heroine's query about the swimming conditions at a beach near her brother-in-law's ranch prompts stern warnings about riptide. "You can't always see that undercurrent," intones the solemn Michael, disguised for the nonce as a caretaker. "But it's there." In the typical Metro-in-a-minor-key manner, the plot unfolds at a plodding pace, skewed by a characteristically wan string score by the studio's Max Steiner manqué, Herbert Stothart. Freund's photography is likewise utilitarian, its uninflected tones of glossy gloom intent on keeping the creases marring Hepburn's neck and the back-projection views of the California shoreline equally invisible to the audience.

Undercurrent's sole novelty was the promiscuous casting-against-type of its starring trio. In fact, it was an amusing idea to use Robert Taylor's arched sable eyebrows and clipped moustache as the mask of neurotic evil for a change; as the starchiest male idol in Metro's pantheon, his plaster-cast looks were always a dubious substitute for authentic charm. After the first deceptive reels, Taylor barks and glowers, his pale eyes wincing in the expressionist glare of Freund's slashes of white-light-for-derangement. The actor's skin-deep performance actually enhances the dangerous aura surrounding *Undercurrent*'s antihero—his self-conscious virility a sour overcompensation for the hollowness lurking inside.

The fact that the least naturally gifted of *Undercurrent*'s three stars comes off best is a key to what's wrong with the movie. The role of the black-sheep brother who's really a lamb might conceivably have suited someone like Van Heflin, more accustomed to walking his way through one of Metro's tweedy second leads. But saddling the early Robert Mitchum with *Undercurrent*'s radio soap opera maxims was a willful act of sabotage. Sanctimonious lines like "I had no business to feel the way I did about you—my brother's wife," don't trip easily off this plain spoken actor's tongue. Out of self-defense (and sheer exhaustion), Mitchum retreats even further behind that hooded gaze throughout *Undercurrent;* he may look bored, but at least Mitchum's stoic professionalism prevents him from showing the contempt this role richly deserves.

The notion of Mitchum and Hepburn as natural soulmates is one of *Undercurrent*'s most deliriously straightfaced conceits. In all her MGM work after *Woman of the Year,* the romantic chemistry of Hepburn's Tracyless pictures was strictly hypothetical—she seems to shrink inside her skin whenever an unworthy co-star enters her orbit for a closeup clinch. *Undercurrent*'s opening is generic Kate, the bluestocking bachelorette too engrossed in her father's chemical compounds to fuss over the unkempt cut of her coiffure. But once the script veers into paranoia, it's clear that the real misalliance is between Hepburn and *Undercurrent*'s passive heroine. The bride may quake at the prospect of mingling with the big-city swells or presiding over her husband's home, but self-doubt is not the foremost attribute in this star's natural repertoire—some insolent Hepburn gesture invariably intrudes to give the game away. She was a great one for imperiously draping herself along a convenient mantlepiece, and as a hightoned three-fireplace picture, *Undercurrent* provides her with tempting opportunities to assume the pose.

Wide-eyed terror was an alien emotion to Hepburn on screen, thus *Undercurrent*'s would-be suspenseful climax taxes its star to the limit in more ways than one. As a sneering Taylor holds a boulder over her prostrate form, Hepburn obediently pitches in, her tapered hands delicately aquiver as she gasps and shows the whites of her eyes. Paradoxically, she is never so impervious as when striving to mime feminine frailty.

Here and there Minnelli does manage to etch his signature touches into the lacquered surface of this movie. As usual, his most telling prop is the looking glass, a constant reproach to the heroine's flagging self-esteem. Early in the film, Ann trembles at the frowsy sight of herself on the eve of her social debut as Mrs. Garroway, while the bridegroom gazes on smugly behind her. Throughout the cocktail party sequence, reflected images of this elite gaggle of merrymakers mock her from the walls and coffee-table surfaces. It is a characteristic Minnelli set-piece, reappearing with slight variations in a half-dozen later movies. Each over-dressed extra has a distinct, supercharged personality, which fuses with the whirlwind throng gathered around the woebegone heroine; overlapping waves of chatter in some hilarious private code bewilder her and the audience alike. To emphasize Ann's gaucheness, Minnelli reduces the black-and-white spectrum to its starkest minimum; while the other women sport ebony gowns, she blushes in a brown number translating as muddy charcoal.

In Minnelli's more complex movies, clothes and decor help to reveal the quirks of the soul. Although *Undercurrent* purports to be about the deceptive lure of first impressions, its accessories are the only things that matter—what you see is finally what you get. Short of murder, the villain's truly deplorable sin was to thrust his wife into society without the proper wardrobe. Under Alan's tutelage, a trip to the couturier transforms her into a wife worthy of him, but even this exposes his perfidy—in a mild foretaste of *Vertigo,* her chic adornments make Ann the pale replica of a cold-blooded socialite who once spurned him. Alerted to this bombshell, Ann again repairs to the mirror, anxiously comparing herself to the femme fatale in question. Yet here as elsewhere in *Undercurrent* a strange casting gaffe scotches the point, for Hepburn and Jayne Meadows have nothing whatever in common save upper-crust accents to go with their upswept hairdos.

As *Undercurrent* has it, if the right dress defines the woman, a man's castle is what separates the psychos from the misunderstood romantics. Hepburn spends reels of this picture exploring the unfamiliar digs of the Garroway brothers, and what she finds bodes ill for the future of her marriage. Alan's office is massive industrial-moderne, without a single memento of his rise to corporate prominence. "It's not a very personal place," she notes with disappointment—in contrast to Michael's ranch hideaway, which looks "as though it were waiting for someone." While she runs her hand over Michael's guitar, a rack of briar pipes, and the inevitable piano, Minnelli pulls back to take in the whole scene—best summed up as Bel-Air Rustic, with low-slung sofas below flagstone walls. Without a visible trace of irony, this is a hermit's Walden for a latter-day Thoreau, bolstered by a hefty expense account and a clever interior decorator. It is, in fact, the perfect habitat for the bourgeois bohemians who are this movie's mystical lovers, united at last by their passion for the finer things.

Undercurrent's hopeful fadeout is no less synthetic

than everything that precedes it, and an anomaly in Minnelli's career. Enduring love may be the stuff of dream ballets, but it's a dead-end illusion in his later melodramas; if the protagonists survive to the end, the best hope they've got is to reconcile themselves to a solitary future. *Undercurrent* is too faithful to its moist genre to admit of such Hollywood heresies as that. Like everything else in this movie, Minnelli's tonic pessimism is borne away in an undertow of kitsch.

. . . .

1949   MADAME BOVARY

A part from *Meet Me in St. Louis, Madame Bovary* was the film that most profoundly shaped the course of Minnelli's development as a filmmaker, yet it came at a time when he had begun to doubt that his career at MGM had any future at all. After *Undercurrent,* Minnelli returned to his accustomed niche in the Freed Unit to make what he hoped would be the ultimate Minnelli–Garland musical. And in the literal sense of the word, this was exactly what *The Pirate* turned out to be. So when Pandro Berman offered Minnelli the chance for them to make a second picture together, he eagerly set to work after a year of anxious idleness. The project was *Madame Bovary,* and for him the next few months threatened to become a life-collides-with-art intrigue from one of his later inside-Hollywood movies. For while directing the story of a woman whose private phantoms made daily life unendurable for herself, her spouse, and their infant daughter, he lived out a similar scenario in modern dress at home. Minnelli later acknowledged that Garland's retreats into fantasy helped shape his view of Flaubert's capricious, self-destructive Emma.

Like so much of Minnelli's best work, *Madame Bovary* simultaneously exalted the style of moviemaking that made MGM the most prestigious studio in Hollywood, while slyly debunking the moral assumptions that made it also the most conservative. In outline, the film was an Illustrated Literary Classic, a genre Metro exalted particularly in the years before the war with its opulent, statesmanlike homages to Dickens, Tolstoy, Shakespeare and Dumas *fils*. These pictures aimed to please the Emma Bovarys of the 1930s—provincial romantics with pretensions to refinement, whose vicarious movie thrills made their own lives seem doubly wanting in excitement.

As the center of her own glossy showcase, Emma isn't an edifying figure—in fact, she's vivid reproof to the most treasured elements of the MGM myth. Her doomed infatuation with the idea of love is a distortion of Metro's brand of sentimentality; her vanity a domes-

Charles and Emma's rustic wedding. Van Heflin and Jennifer Jones in Madame Bovary *(1949)*

ticated form of the narcissism advertised by Mayer's star attractions, preening in creamily lit closeups. In *Camille* and *Anna Karenina,* Garbo suffered magnificently for a passion larger than herself, but Flaubert's antiheroine is only diminished by hers. If she earns sympathy, it's precisely because Emma's lapses are all too demonstrably human—this faithless wife and negligent mother defies all the feminine ideals MGM movies were in the business of promoting.

Although none of the major studios had tackled this or any other Flaubert work before, *Madame Bovary* had enjoyed several past screen incarnations. In 1932, a shoestring outfit filmed the tale in modern dress under the profane title of *Unholy Love,* featuring silent-movie castaways Lila Lee and H. B. Warner. More prominent was a French version made in 1934 by Jean Renoir, and rarely cited among his better works; the release print was mercilessly pared down from Renoir's intended three hours, and the whole marred by what many felt was the perverse miscasting of matronly stage star Valentine Tessier in the title role. Three years later, Pola Negri played Emma in one of the handful of German talkies she made after sound finished her career in Hollywood; like the Renoir, this unreeled briefly on the U.S. arthouse circuit before the war. Thus, *Madame Bovary* was practically virgin terrain by Hollywood A-picture standards. Following the recent popularity of *Kitty, Forever Amber,* and other hoopskirted wantons of modest literary pedigree, Berman figured Flaubert's combination of class and candor had distinct screen possibilities. It was certainly perfect material for Minnelli. He understood how sensual deprivation and the lure of daydreams made for an obsessive combination—a number of his movies had already touched upon this theme, and his own career was a testament to it.

Berman had just finished an all-star remake of *The Three Musketeers* with writer Robert Ardrey; deciding that anyone who'd tackled one 19th-century French Immortal could handle another, he assigned Ardrey also to prepare the script for *Madame Bovary.* This was a fortuitous choice, for he produced a commendably nuanced reduction of the novel—probably his most distinguished credit in a considerable screenwriting career. Years later, Ardrey abandoned film work to achieve wider fame in the field of popular anthropology. Through books like *African Genesis,* he theorized that aggression was a basic component of the human spirit, the product of our primordial origins. It's possible to see a glimmer of this perspective in the grasping, impulsive Emma Ardrey delineated in this script.

In the late forties, a property like *Madame Bovary* was still vulnerable to censorship. Berman and company feared that even Emma's suicide might be deemed insufficient punishment for her multiple adulteries and more venial sins. Ardrey had to perform an act of sly prestidigitation—to plant Emma's promiscuity in the mind of the beholder while keeping it discreetly out of camera range. To this, the movie's creators added an even more devious ruse. The script was bracketed with a reenactment of Flaubert's own trial for obscenity, in the hope—successful, as it turned out—that the Motion Picture Production Code would be shamed out of emulating the example of the novelist's narrow-minded contemporaries. The prospect of a wholesale ban even affected the way the picture was cast. With Minnelli's assent, Berman initially planned to use Lana Turner in the title role, an implausible idea but at the time consistent with the studio's strategy for its resident glamour girl. Through a series of increasingly ambitious roles in *The Postman Always Rings Twice, Green Dolphin Street* and *Cass Timberlane,* MGM wanted to prove that even if Turner wasn't the next Garbo, she might at least become the new Joan Crawford.

However, industry censors warned that *Madame Bovary* was trouble enough without the handicap of Turner's incendiary screen image; better to bank the fires with some actress whose oomph was tempered by an air of evident refinement. Metro's own Greer Garson and Deborah Kerr were obviously overqualified, but Berman and Minnelli found a happy medium in Jennifer Jones, who, thanks to her mentor David O. Selznick, had had the most contrary career of the 1940s. She'd been beatified by the Academy for playing St. Bernadette of Lourdes, then bared her teeth as the Salomé of the sagebrush in *Duel in the Sun;* at the moment, Jones was again playing the spirit of eternal innocence in *Portrait of Jennie.*

Minnelli agreed that she certainly had the right febrile quality for the part, and negotiations began to obtain her services. Selznick had no trouble envisioning her as Emma either; three years earlier he'd pondered making *Madame Bovary* himself. By the late forties, Selznick was busier brokering the services of the actors he had under contract than producing his own pictures. On this occasion he agreed to release Jones so long as Metro used a couple of his own idle leading men to fill out *Madame Bovary*'s cast. As a result, Emma's noble seducer Rodolphe was assigned to Louis Jourdan, and the young heartthrob of the Swedish screen, Alf Kjellin, made his Hollywood debut as the ambitious clerk Léon under the dubious Anglo-Saxon handle of Christopher Kent. To impersonate Flaubert, Minnelli and Berman settled on saturnine James Mason of the impeccably cultured voice; only Van Heflin, the film's obtusely adoring Charles Bovary, was chosen from the MGM roster of talent.

Minnelli shot *Madame Bovary* from mid-December 1948 through February 1949. MGM was in the middle of one of its periodic economy drives, and particularly after *The Pirate* Minnelli took pains to make *Madame Bovary* stylish without being extravagant. To re-create 19th-century village life at Culver City within a reasonable budget called for considerable imagination. Under

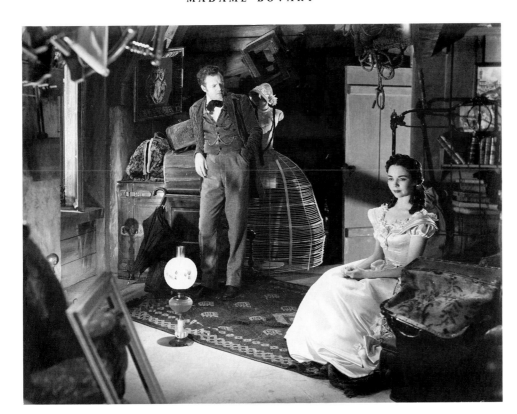

Van Heflin and Jennifer Jones in Madame Bovary *(1949)*

his supervision, Jack Martin Smith's set designs proved a model of canny backlot recycling; the MGM English hamlet with its rustic stone bridge used in every other Greer Garson picture was artfully camouflaged as the quintessentially French town square of Yonville.

Although Flaubert devoted a scant few pages in the novel to the ball at the château, Minnelli's instincts told him that in cinematic terms this would be the dramatic highlight of the picture—the occasion for Emma's illusions and Charles' forebodings to converge in a turbulent sea of music and movement. It was one of the last sequences shot for *Bovary,* and easily the most complicated to stage. Minnelli planned it in the manner of a Freed production number. With dramatic films the practice was to add music to the edited footage, but Minnelli shaped his ball scene to the pre-recorded strains of the "neurotic waltz" he had commissioned from Miklos Rozsa. He insisted on a series of 360-degree pans to convey Emma's perilous exhilaration, which created unending headaches in reconciling Smith's surrounding sets with the mobility Robert Planck's camera needed. But the result was worth their pains—it's one of the more audacious epiphanies in any Minnelli movie.

Undoubtedly, there were times Minnelli wished Rozsa's waltz were the only neurotic thing he had to worry about. As prey to emotional tumult as the character she was struggling to play, Jennifer Jones required constant reassurance; yet the most disruptive forces during *Madame Bovary* weren't directly involved in its making at all. Next to *Gone with the Wind,* Selznick considered Jones his proudest creation, particularly now that after

an intense courtship of several years, she had finally consented to become Mrs. David O. Selznick. Selznick saw himself as producer-by-proxy on every picture she made away from his direct supervision; from the moment Jones was signed, Berman and Minnelli braced themselves for an onslaught of his fabled memos dissecting every aspect of the task ahead, and they weren't disappointed. In daily chapters, Selznick dispensed his appraisal of everything from Flaubert's psychology to the size of Jourdan's part and what he saw as the Metro makeup department's willful attempt to sabotage the "unique loveliness" of his star. Diplomatically, the *Bovary* team bowed to his superior wisdom on the photogenic properties of Jones' eyebrows, and dismissed much of the rest.

Shaking off the problems caused by Minnelli's own marital situation wasn't so easy. Engrossed in work after so many idle months, Minnelli could no longer lavish undivided attention on his wife's troubles, and in her vulnerable state Garland resented it. Her self-pity soured his enthusiasm, and foreshadowed worse to come. *Madame Bovary* went through the usual process of sneak previews and retakes during the spring of 1949, but Minnelli had more urgent responsibilities to cope with—by then his wife was careening toward the most severe crisis of her life. After finishing *In the Good Old Summertime,* Garland staggered through several weeks' work on *Annie Get Your Gun* before suffering a complete collapse in early May. She spent much of the summer at the Peter Bent Brigham Hospital in Boston, treated for, among other things, barbiturate and amphetamine withdrawal; during her convalescence Min-

*Emma at the ball. Jennifer
Jones as* Madame Bovary
(1949)

nelli came east several times to visit her. On Garland's release the Minnellis tried to resume their married life and, gradually, their commitments at the studio, but the ensuing months brought only a temporary reprieve. In June 1950, when Garland failed to report to the set of *Royal Wedding*, MGM abruptly cancelled her contract; shortly thereafter she attempted suicide, with Minnelli as horrified bystander. Before the year was over, they had separated for good.

With his private life a public shambles, the solace of work was crucial to Minnelli, and *Madame Bovary*'s reception signaled a fulfilling new phase in his career. On its premiere in August 1949, critics agreed this was an unusually distinguished film, combining a rare sensitivity to its source with a vivid sense of drama and atmosphere. Perhaps too fatalistic to please the broadest movie public, it still performed respectably enough at the box office, with U.S. returns estimated at $2,000,000 by the end of the year. It was Minnelli's first film since *The Clock* to entirely fulfill both his own hopes and the studio's expectations, giving ample proof of the breadth of his talent. With *Madame Bovary*, his apprenticeship ended for good—Metro now realized that his stylistic flair could enliven the most demanding subjects as well as his fantasies for Freed. Emma's tragedy became the prototype for many of his subsequent dramas—the misfit maddened by the rules and rituals that seem to make life possible for everybody else. Having helplessly witnessed just such a struggle in his private life, Minnelli would spend much of his further career trying to make sense of it.

Minnelli's dramatic movies tend to hold a dark mirror to the themes that animate his musicals, refracting them through a prism which substitutes pessimism for Technicolor. Just as *The Bad and the Beautiful* and *The Band Wagon* would complement each other a few years later, *The Pirate* and *Madame Bovary* make a symmetrically matched pair, chronologically and otherwise. They tell essentially the same story, only with widely divergent consequences. Like *The Pirate*'s Manuela, Emma Bovary is a creature stifled by her environment and her assigned role within it. For each, the main allure of her impending marriage is a material one—a trousseau from Maison Worth for Manuela, a respectable home Emma can call her own. Both heroines are prey to erotic longings fed by a perilous taste in literature, the difference being that, as befits a hopeful genre like the musical, Manuela is liberated by her imagination, while the gravity of daily life brings Emma's adventurous fancies plunging to earth.

The conflict between the urge for self-expression and the pressure to conform is a central one for Minnelli; with his pronounced understanding for the opposite sex, he expresses it with a special intensity when his protagonist is female. "Madame Bovary, c'est moi!" famously declared Gustave Flaubert, a sentiment Minnelli manifestly shares. Yet throughout, he inflects this empathy with an undertone of dispassionate irony. It's there in the detached authorial voice of James Mason, narrating Emma's wayward history; even more so in the way Minnelli defines her visually as an alien figure constantly ill-matched with her surroundings.

The interplay between these two perspectives is what makes this film so intriguing. Like all movie versions of classic fiction, Minnelli's *Bovary* subjects its source to a certain amount of compression. For dramatic emphasis, Rodolphe enters the plot at an earlier stage, initiating Emma to the intoxication of a waltz at the gala ball which seals her restlessness with her lot. Certain characters—Bovary's mother and his first wife—were eliminated entirely, while the faces of expressive character actors like Gene Lockhart and George Zucco served as shorthand for the collection of small-time poseurs and hypocrites Flaubert had sketched with more amplitude.

Virtually every episode in which the heroine does not figure directly has been omitted, but the momentum of Emma's fate remains as inexorable as before. Minnelli's intuition and craft preserve Flaubert's spirit by translating it into a filmic language the mass public of his own time can well understand. "There are thousands of Emma Bovarys. . . . There are hundreds and thousands of women who wish they were Emma Bovary and who have been saved from her fate not by virtue but simply by lack of determination," proclaims Mason/Flaubert in the prologue's courtroom scene. Yet in the person of Jennifer Jones, one thing distinguishes Emma from the common run of women in the world of this movie, and that's star quality. Her beauty, poise, and energy mark her as a creature apart, but also prompt the heroine's fatal delusions. With an actress's born egotism, she imagines herself as the center of a hundred glamorous fantasies; the hitch is that stars don't shape the scenarios assigned to them—their role is to act them out as vividly as possible. Posing in her incongruously sumptuous wardrobe, Minnelli's Emma muses on "Love in a Scotch cottage, love in a Swiss chalet," but she's a leading lady pathetically trapped in the wrong vehicle.

By ignoring this aspect of Emma, cinephobes of a literal turn of mind could easily misread some of Minnelli's tongue-in-cheek contrasts as unintentional Hollywoodisms. Her big entrance in the opening reel is one such moment—graciously preparing breakfast for the young doctor summoned to attend her farmer father, she beams over her omelette pan in an immaculately ruffled white gown. Already, we've been tipped off that this elegant domestic angel is not the "real" Emma, but a cameo turn to titillate her own vanity and dazzle the susceptible Charles. For, unseen by Dr. Bovary during his midnight vigil, in the previous scene Minnelli revealed the girl in her usual guise, bustling in the shadows of the rude farmhouse kitchen, swathed in a smock with a kerchief knotted under her chin.

. . . .

1952

THE STORY OF THREE LOVES —"MADEMOISELLE"

Minnelli stayed aloof from the executive-suite skirmishes that periodically rocked MGM, but they shaped his professional destiny all the same. The Garland affair aside, Minnelli's post-*Pirate* sabbatical took place during a precipitous decline in the studio's output in 1947-48, L. B. Mayer's last year in complete control of studio activities. The New York office brought Dore Schary onto the lot to reactivate its sagging production schedule; *Madame Bovary* was one of the first films he approved. MGM was top-heavy with under utilized talent at the time, and clearly couldn't afford to let staff directors dawdle in their well-appointed offices for long. Certain longtime Mayer loyalists like Clarence Brown distrusted the new order, but with Schary pledging to maintain quality as well as efficiency, Minnelli was happy to oblige.

He was quickly swept up in the studio's accelerating pace, and by the early fifties Minnelli found himself busier than at any time since the end of the war. In 1950-51, he completed his two Spencer Tracy comedies and *An American in Paris*, prepared the *Huckleberry Finn* that never was, and added his signature flourishes to *Lovely to Look At*. Simultaneously, L. B. Mayer was maneuvered into resigning his post, a milestone Minnelli was almost too winded to notice. As the year ended, his agenda for 1952 was filled with two important projects—a behind-the-scenes melodrama about

moviemaking then called *Tribute to a Bad Man*, to be followed by Freed's *The Band Wagon*. The first was to be shot in the spring; meanwhile the studio scrambled to find something suitable to cover Minnelli's then $3,000-a-week salary. The result was a curious item in his directorial career—a miniature fantasy without music called "Mademoiselle," which formed the centerpiece of *The Story of Three Loves*.

Hollywood had tackled few omnibus films in its past —the best-remembered was the 1932 *If I Had a Million*, and then *Tales of Manhattan* a decade later. By the early fifties, however, European imports of this ilk surfaced all over the arthouse circuit, piquing the studios' competitive spirit. They were mostly screen anthologies of some classic short-story writer or other, and after the Somerset Maugham *Trio* and Max Ophuls' De Maupassant homage, *Le Plaisir*, 20th Century-Fox followed suit with an all-American sampler entitled *O. Henry's Full House*. Metro's entry was conceived by producer Sidney Franklin, a studio fixture since the Thalberg days, who chose to soft-pedal the Modern Library angle in favor of the more characteristic attractions of Ars Gratia Artis. His package would sport a brace of star personalities in oversaturated Technicolor suffering through three unrelated tales of thwarted romance.

Originally, Minnelli was to be responsible for two-thirds of *Three Loves*; in November 1951 the publicity

Ricky Nelson and Ethel Barrymore in "Mademoiselle." The Story of Three Loves *(1952)*

OPPOSITE:

Farley Granger and Leslie Caron in "Mademoiselle," The Story of Three Loves *(1952)*

department announced that in addition to "Mademoiselle," he would direct "Why Should I Cry?" about a bad-tempered stage legend humanized by her saintly blind accompanist. Fortunately for him, someone at the studio decided that I. A. R. Wylie's story was worth expanding into a full-length feature. It subsequently reached the screen as the Joan Crawford vehicle, *Torch Song*, directed by Minnelli's perpetual stand-in, Charles Walters. With the loss of "Why Should I Cry?" *The Story of Three Loves* became an unrelieved Cook's Tour of backlot Europe. The Roman setting for "Mademoiselle" was bookended by the London of "The Jealous Lover" and the Paris of "Equilibrium," just down the quai from the spot where Gene Kelly wooed Leslie Caron. Appropriately, the troupe Franklin assembled was as cosmopolitan as possible without benefit of subtitles—starting with the director of the other two stories, Max Reinhardt's son, Gottfried. "The Jealous Lover" featured James Mason and Moira Shearer, the only time Metro managed to snare the elusive ballet star. For "Equilibrium," the studio planned to pair its recently imported Italian waif Pier Angeli with Mexican leading man Ricardo Montalban, but by the time shooting began he had been replaced by Kirk Douglas.

"Mademoiselle" was of course intended for Caron from the beginning, suitably Gallicised from a short story called "Lucy and the Stranger" by Jan Lustig and George Froeschel, two émigré writers at MGM. In its final version, the heroine is the wistful governess for an American family on holiday in Rome, given to reciting Péguy and Verlaine at her eleven-year-old charge. The exasperated kid wishes he could turn instant grown-up and flee her sieges of mushy French verse; yet when an elderly sorceress grants his request for one brief evening, the transformed Tommy awakens to Mademoiselle's beauty of face and soul.

Complementing Caron was a truly eclectic cast. As the two Tommys, animated little Ricky Nelson of the TV-sitcom family grew rather incongruously into the languid Farley Granger; Zsa Zsa Gabor adorned the bit part of a worldly barfly who vamps the hero before his rendezvous with Mademoiselle; while none other than Ethel Barrymore lent her air of imperious tongue-in-cheek to fairy godmother Mrs. Pennicott. For Minnelli, directing the grandest theatrical dame of them all was the most delightful fringe benefit of "Mademoiselle"; he was enchanted by her unflappable spirit and professionalism. For Miss Barrymore's first and most important scene, he enshrined her in an Italian-Gothic set worthy of an expatriate Miss Havisham—a tumble-down villa basking in the sound-stage alfresco of a velvety Roman twilight. The Metro art department performed its customary marvels for Minnelli, capped by a luscious series of matte shots by special-effects master Warren Newcombe re-creating the Forum and the Baths of Caracalla. Less specific were the back-projection views used to illustrate Granger and Caron's carriage

ride through the city; six months later these subbed for Central Park as Fred Astaire and Cyd Charisse rode a hansom midway through *The Band Wagon*. The soundtrack for "Mademoiselle" indulged in some creative recycling of its own, with the *Madame Bovary* waltz Minnelli had so relished turning up prominently in Rozsa's new score for this picture.

"Mademoiselle" was the first of these *Three Loves* to reach the cameras, and Minnelli worked through his episode with dispatch, completing it on a three-week schedule in February 1952. Nevertheless, Franklin soon discovered the financial drawback of projects like this; with the standard ration of stars and settings multiplied by three, *The Story of Three Loves* also cost more than the average feature. By the time Reinhardt filmed his two segments MGM had spent a total of $2,498,112, enough to cover one of Freed's song-and-dance spectaculars. Dubious about the popular appeal of what was essentially an inflated arthouse movie, the studio kept *The Story of Three Loves* on the shelf for nearly a year, finally opening it at Radio City Music Hall in March 1953 on the heels of *The Bad and the Beautiful*. Despite its relatively novel form and opulent packaging, *The Story of Three Loves* was received indifferently by the press and public alike, earning only $1,350,000 in its domestic run. A dozen years later, MGM fared somewhat better with *The Yellow Rolls Royce*, following the same recipe of international stars in novelettish love stories, but shot this time against authentic continental backdrops.

Minnelli managed to imbue "Mademoiselle" with a

few characteristic touches to distinguish it from the Reinhardt episodes; here and there are glimmerings of lyricism and whimsy beyond the powers of his dour colleague. Nevertheless, *The Story of Three Loves* has a faintly embalmed quality and no wonder—it's haunted by the phantom of Irving Thalberg, still hovering over the backlot fifteen years after his demise. In the truest MGM spirit, this movie's delusions of superiority rest on the fact that any resemblance to real people, locations, and emotions is strictly unintentional. Mere mortals may be afflicted by chaotic carnal impulses, but the half-dozen lovelorn souls in this trio of featurettes are beyond anything so messy as sex. They drift across the screen and around each other like wistful wraiths, miming that exquisite heartbreak only a luscious close-up can assuage.

These are stateless persons, whose polyglot cadences are smoothed into the exquisite tones any Stateside movie fan would instantly recognize as Class. The continental capitals in which they emote are sound-stage essence-of-Europe, settings more pungently photogenic than the actual places could ever be. And just as you'd expect, *The Story of Three Loves* serves up a high-carbohydrate buffet of continental culture in easily digestible tidbits. The opening, "Jealous Lover," is an hors d'oeuvre of ballet and Good Music, chiefly the Rachmaninoff "Rhapsody on a Theme by Paganini." "Equilibrium" is itself a Culver City Rhapsody on a Theme by Sartre, as a suicidal refugee plucked from the Seine by a guilt-ridden circus aerialist becomes the catalyst for the moral regeneration of her savior. To refresh the palate before the Existentialist course, "Mademoiselle" serves up ambrosial Gallic verse in a sumptuously fake Roman place setting.

Masked by a rich sauce of production values, two-thirds of these three loves are still yesterday's leftovers. With frail Moira Shearer once again strapped into slippers that will pirouette her to an early grave, "The Jealous Lover" baldly replicates *The Red Shoes,* with James Mason standing in for Anton Walbrook as her martinet impresario. "Equilibrium" recalls a somewhat obscure source—Julien Duvivier's wartime anthology, *Flesh and Fantasy,* that concluded with a Big Top yarn in which love defeated morbid karma, embodied on that occasion by Charles Boyer and Barbara Stanwyck.

Though less obviously derivative, "Mademoiselle" is also lukewarm mush. Like *The Clock,* this movie brings together two lonely innocents in a city of strangers, but the emotional urgency that propelled Minnelli's first dramatic effort eludes him here. Fables like this soar or disintegrate on their charm quotient, and "Mademoiselle" founders on the perverse notion that the heroine's anemic pedantries are irresistibly fetching. Skeptical viewers might wonder why an eleven-year-old boy is cooped up in a Roman hotel room reading gloomy Gallic poetry, yet "Mademoiselle" implies that little Tommy's resentment is the height of kiddie callousness. Granted the wish to become an "old man of 25" for a night, he accidentally encounters the fey governess, still weeping over Verlaine. At this point, girl and movie alike could use a touch of his philistine bluntness. Instead, this tuxedoed transient succumbs to her thrall, and soon two moist-eyed somnambulists are proclaiming their love in slow verse and even slower motion.

It's a Technicolor object lesson on just how dangerous a little learning can be. Despite Minnelli's loving camera work with Caron, Mademoiselle is every bit the hypersensitive drip little Ricky Nelson thinks she is. If Caron and Granger seem made for each other nonetheless, it's because both sport the same hypnotized expression, cowed by the stilted sentiments they've been instructed to utter. Their love scene is lifeless until the dialogue defers to Miklos Rozsa's violins, and the actors become anonymous specks in the director's decorative scheme. Minnelli caps a succession of soft frescoes of Rome by night with a lovely bit of surrealistic trumpery—a giddying overhead shot of Granger running down a gaslit alley before the spell can be broken, dwarfed by an equestrian statue out of *An American in Paris.* For these fleeting seconds, "Mademoiselle" is transported to the Eternal City (of Minnelli's imagination), a dream without a ballet.

The appearance of Ethel Barrymore halfway through the story is a bracing tonic. As long as she's on screen, "Mademoiselle's" high-flown sentiments give way to astringent comedy, with its director's eager complicity. For her fairy godmother is a very Minnellian sort of witch—an acidulous elegant who presides over a landscape of crumbling baroque archways and sunken Roman pediments, quaffing Darrogue from a Venetian glass that disintegrates at her touch. Like *Gigi*'s Aunt Alicia, Mrs. Pennicott is at once the star and *metteur-en-scène* of her miniature domain. Age has its compensations—the serenity of egotism for one thing, and an Olympian irony wasted on the young. The little boy who interrupts her solitude is that most welcome of companions, a credulous audience. Regally indicating Miss Schneider, her obedient watchdog, the grande dame reveals how she subdued the overweening German governess who blighted her own youth. Tommy's plight is a welcome occasion to indulge her sensuous love of self. Mrs. Pennicott announces serenely that to achieve the spell which would liberate him from Mademoiselle, the boy must invoke her name on the stroke of eight: "I love to hear it pronounced, it intoxicates me," she croons. Vain, brusque, and seductive by turns, this otherworldly old party gives Minnelli's veteran star the chance to show off some special sorcery of her own; the merry malice of that Barrymore voice slices through this movie's conceits like a stiletto.

At the time, "Mademoiselle" was a mere trifle to fill Minnelli's idle weeks between more important things. It touched a personal chord in him nonetheless, because the figure of Mrs. Pennicott personified an essential Minnelli theme—the power of the imagination to subdue the strictures of daily life, rather than submit to them. As he himself grew older the lure of this axiom grew stronger still, and "Mademoiselle" would serve as a rough draft for his last testament as a filmmaker. With *A Matter of Time,* Minnelli again wove a fable about an aged eccentric who initiates a frustrated innocent to the lure of dreams. After a quarter-century, the supernatural comic relief of "Mademoiselle" be-

comes a cue for pathos in *A Matter of Time;* by then, the director's own professional glories had receded into memory, like the amorous exploits of the ravaged countess. If neither film sustained the transcendent quality Minnelli sought, each did achieve a fleeting grandeur with the same heartfelt image—a reclusive old lady enveloped in the sapphire light of a Roman dusk, contemplating the mysterious promise of the darkness to come.

. . . .

1952 THE BAD AND THE BEAUTIFUL

Less than six weeks after polishing off his brief stint on "Mademoiselle," Minnelli started shooting what became his most honored dramatic film to date. The first and best of his four portraits of the movie business, *The Bad and the Beautiful* above all celebrates the tempestuous joys of collaboration—that fusion of divergent crafts and temperaments into a disciplined team bent on making vivid popular art. Certainly *The Bad and the Beautiful* exemplified its own theme. Apart from his musicals, this was Minnelli's best sustained exercise in idiosyncratic style—a delirious interplay of light and shadow in perpetual motion, something rarely seen in American movies since the advent of

Orson Welles. Yet the blueprint for Minnelli's fancies had been carefully sketched out months before he started dreaming up that infinity of dolly shots. While he supplied the texture, it was a newly hired staff producer named John Houseman who decided to turn a prosaic tale culled from a woman's magazine into this valentine to Hollywood's love for its own scapegrace ways.

Following his stint in the late thirties as Orson Welles' impresario at the Mercury Theater, the restless Houseman had led a checkered career on both coasts. After collaborating on the *Citizen Kane* script and a brief spell at the Selznick studio, Houseman spent most of

Starting small. Kirk Douglas in The Bad and the Beautiful *(1952)*

the war supervising the Voice of America's broadcasts to Europe. For the rest of the decade, he shuttled between directorial jobs on Broadway and fitful attempts at producing movies out west. During that time he was responsible for a handful of memorable pictures—*The Blue Dahlia, Letter from an Unknown Woman,* and *They Live by Night* among them—but his relationship with the industry establishment was mutually wary at best. People in the trade viewed Houseman as a leftish, highbrow outsider who disdained mass tastes and the production-line esprit de corps; alighting at three studios in five years, he in turn found the task of psyching out his employers' caprices a wearisome business.

Nevertheless, while at RKO he found Dore Schary a more responsive production chief than most; so when his own contract there lapsed and after another New York detour to direct *King Lear,* Houseman accepted Schary's offer to make pictures under his supervision at MGM. He tested the waters with *Holiday for Sinners,* a small-scale melodrama set in New Orleans during Mardi Gras. Modesty was a virtue that alas went unappreciated at a studio like Metro, and Houseman pledged to think bigger the next time around.

Eventually, he came across something called ''Me-

morial to a Bad Man'' in the February 1951 issue of the *Ladies' Home Journal.* This told of a just-deceased and unlamented Broadway producer whose legacy is a deathbed letter to three protégés reminding them that for all his sins, they owe their careers to his exasperating genius. In his short story, George Bradshaw had obviously been inspired by that Shubert Alley terror Jed Harris, whose premature demise was a case of collective wishful thinking. A few years earlier, the movies had already eulogized the still-extant Harris with a Robert Montgomery picture called *That Saxon Charm.* Even Bradshaw's central gimmick was a new twist on a commonplace movie hook that, as Houseman later observed, dated at least to the jigsaw-flashback style of Herman Mankiewicz' script for *Citizen Kane.* (Not to mention brother Joseph's kaleidoscopic account of another Broadway egomaniac in *All About Eve.*) But one element caught Houseman's eye. In ''Memorial to a Bad Man,'' the producer's victims had fled to the West Coast to elude his clutches; by shifting the entire action to Hollywood, Houseman could refashion this yarn into a lively chronicle of the film industry's recent past.

Once Houseman successfully pitched his idea to Schary, MGM acquired the rights to this and an earlier,

OPPOSITE:
*Kirk Douglas, Paul Stewart,
Vanessa Brown, and Barry
Sullivan crash a Hollywood
party in* The Bad and the
Beautiful *(1952)*

similar Bradshaw story called "Of Good and Evil" for $11,500. To fashion a script along the lines he wanted, Houseman tapped Charles Schnee, late of *They Live by Night* and subsequently lured to MGM by Schary as a producer-writer of B-pictures. Schnee set to work with energy and dispatch, resurrecting Bradshaw's antihero as an exiled has-been, grasping for a comeback. In the original story, the people surrounding the Jed Harris clone are clichés with little color or individuality—an unflappable First Lady of stage and screen, a stage manager turned bicoastal producer-director. Encouraged by Houseman to heighten backlot gossip with his own imagination, Schnee redrew them from scratch. The saga of dynamic, obsessive Jonathan Shields now paralleled the rise of David O. Selznick, down to such details as the bankrupt death of his mogul father. (In consequence, Selznick's lawyers briefly considered suing MGM to halt production on grounds of libel.) Shields' star discovery Georgia Lorrison was, like Diana Barrymore, the slattern offspring of a legendary but dissolute Shakespearean actor. The sad difference was that Georgia's real-life model never achieved anything like the screen eminence of her fictional counterpart.

Houseman was delighted with the result, its title altered slightly to *Tribute to a Bad Man.* He submitted the script for Minnelli's consideration, although the two men scarcely knew each other at the time. It was a calculated move to give Houseman's project the éclat he wanted; after *An American in Paris* and *Father of the Bride,* Minnelli was the studio's hottest directorial property. Fortunately, he warmed to the script as well as to Houseman's stimulating personality, and the rest of the package quickly fell into place.

Minnelli and Houseman found themselves in total agreement when they came to cast the picture. While the studio tried to pressure them to settle on an in-house star for Shields, both insisted on free-lancer Kirk Douglas. The leading female role belatedly gave Minnelli the chance to find out what he could do with Lana Turner. When she'd been dropped from *Madame Bovary,* Minnelli did some preliminary work on Turner's 1950 vehicle, *A Life of Her Own,* but in the end this sob story about the affairs of a New York mannequin was directed by George Cukor. Metro character actor Barry Sullivan was initially picked for the Southern novelist-turned-screenwriter whose story climaxes the picture, but when Dick Powell angled for the role, Houseman and Minnelli reassigned Sullivan as the young director who serves as the first pawn in the hero's game plan for success. As a change from all the tweedy gents he customarily played at MGM, Walter Pidgeon cam-

paigned to play Harry Pebbel, Shields' put-upon studio manager. No stretch of imagination was required to cast Gaucho, a tireless Latin lover onscreen and off. He was tailor-made for Gilbert Roland, known as Amigo to his cronies, and whose amatory exploits over a quarter-century in Hollywood made Gaucho's pale in comparison. Gloria Grahame completed the stellar cast as the writer's wife who becomes Gaucho's last conquest; she and Houseman came to be acquainted during her tempestuous marriage to his friend and directorial colleague, Nicholas Ray.

By its very nature, plus an odd quirk of timing, the project took on a special resonance for Minnelli. After all, this was a group portrait of driven, creative types whose private affairs are entirely enmeshed with their professional concerns; eventually they must learn that the only lasting fulfillment is to be found in work. Minnelli had his own reasons for subscribing to such sentiments; the final decree of his divorce from Judy Garland was granted on April 8 1952, the day before he started shooting *Tribute to a Bad Man.*

Underscoring this irony was the air of commitment and energy that immediately seized the set. Everybody involved sensed that *Tribute to a Bad Man* was going to be something special; its eight weeks of filming gathered an exciting momentum as Minnelli, Houseman, and Schnee vied to outdo each other in embellishing the picture with new tidbits from their collective store of movie memories. Wittily staged by Minnelli, the making of Shields' first triumph, "The Doom of the Cat Men," was Houseman's tribute to his friend, Val Lewton, the genius of the B-thriller at RKO in the 1940s. It was Minnelli who thought up the movie-within-the-movie that makes Georgia a star—a Czarist extravaganza of the sort that Garbo once adorned at Metro. (He was obviously bemused as well by "The Proud Land," the flop variation on *Gone with the Wind* that marks Shields' directorial debut; six months later, posters advertising this fiasco appear all over the sets of *The Band Wagon.*)

As they viewed their workaday surroundings with fresh eyes, Minnelli and company tried to capture the surreal properties of a studio in repose—the vast, dark expanses of an empty sound stage at night, the mountains of props piled up like discarded toys in a gargantuan attic. Working for the first time with cameraman Robert Surtees, he reveled in the life-meets-art gamesmanship this project demanded. Visitors to the set were titillated by the spectacle of Minnelli crouched up near the rafters, zooming at another camera boom, itself swooping to shoot some Lana-as-Georgia tableau as florid as any scene in a real Minnelli movie.

To balance the somewhat verbose quality of Schnee's script, Minnelli propelled his camera through every scene with hyperactive aplomb. In the manner of *Madame Bovary,* Minnelli used the techniques he'd honed in his musicals to punch up the picture's emotional highlights. Georgia's lonely prowl around the set of her stellar debut was choreographed to David Raksin's bluesy sax-and-strings theme music, composed in advance for the purpose. In the script, the leading lady's professional triumph coincides with her personal disintegration, as Shields bluntly rejects her advances after their picture's successful premiere. When Schnee conceived the scene, Georgia was merely to drive off tearfully in a quick fadeout to despair, but Minnelli chose instead to heighten it into a wordless tour-de-force. With the car mounted on a rain-pelted turntable, Minnelli whipped up a queasy crescendo of concentric movement—Lana flailing inside the careening chassis while Minnelli threw lightning bolts and madly hurtled his camera from the windshield to the driver's seat. It was an audacious variation on the wheels-within-wheels strategy with which he twirled sets and people in the *American in Paris* ballet—here adapted to very different ends.

While sowing his technical oats, Minnelli also forged an easy rapport with his cast, and despite the constellation of egos assembled there were none of the traumas that marred some of his previous films. His male star's mercurial, angst-flecked energy at once earned Douglas the place in Minnelli's melodramas that Gene Kelly held in his musicals—a kind of extroverted projection of the director's own mix of ambition and melancholy. His approach to acting matched Minnelli's flamboyance as a filmmaker, and they understood each other from the start. If Minnelli occasionally needed to persuade Douglas to bank his fires a bit, with his leading lady the challenge was to penetrate the protective smokescreen of her customary diva poise. No stranger to the professional self-doubts of her character, to everyone's surprise Turner worked very hard indeed. In response, Minnelli took a page from Schnee's text, using tact, patience, and praise to extract a performance in prime Jonathan Shields manner. More than satisfied with the result, the role earned Turner the warmest press of her career thus far. While it's hard to swallow the movie's claim that she could ever be Hollywood's "best actress" as well as its "best box office," here she does give off a flash of real Hollywood tinsel, rather than the dull gloss of a standard Turner star turn.

Tribute to a Bad Man was completed on June 4 1952. The studio was pleased in equal measure by the quality of Minnelli's rushes and the tightness of Houseman's budget, which totaled a mere $1,558,263. The only thing MGM didn't like about *Tribute to a Bad Man* was the title—according to the marketing department, it smacked of sagebrush and threw away Lana Turner's name value. Publicity chief Howard Dietz came up with the substitute, a florid paraphrase of F. Scott Fitzgerald, which Houseman for one cordially loathed.

Nevertheless, as MGM's first big movie of the year, it was *The Bad and the Beautiful* that adorned the marquee of Radio City Music Hall in January 1953. Under

any title it proved a solid popular hit, returning $484,000 in net profit from total rentals of $3,373,000. Despite a general chorus of praise for the acting and Minnelli's keen eye, the consensus in the press was more subdued. Like many of his subsequent melodramas, *The Bad and the Beautiful* played against a growing critical taste for that false naturalism allegedly bringing new maturity to the American screen—a combination of high dudgeon and low-cal visuals. Some reviewers dismissed it as too unabashedly made-in-Hollywood to take an objective bead on the film capital's secret sins. Sobersides like Bosley Crowther in the *New York Times* and Hollis Alpert in *Saturday Review* seemed to miss the standard ration of movie moralizing. They couldn't decide whether Shields was meant to be seen as an out-and-out louse or not. If so, his offscreen triumph at the final fadeout was mighty disturbing. Surely anyone as unprincipled as he must lose sleep mulling over his catalogue of crimes—why didn't *The Bad and the Beautiful* show any of that?

Somehow, the movie establishment had no trouble reconciling these matters. Screened in Los Angeles in time for the 1952 Oscars, *The Bad and the Beautiful* earned six nominations, winning in each category save Best Actor. As usual when he directed a serious picture, the Academy neglected to cite Minnelli, but *The Bad and the Beautiful*'s reception abroad brought further compensations. As *Die Stadt der Illusionen,* it triumphantly opened the 1953 Berlin Film Festival; in Paris, *Les Ensorceles* prompted new panegyrics from the Minnelli cultists at *Cahiers du Cinéma,* longing to make their own movies about the passion and tumult of life on a film set. And when Minnelli and Houseman united for the last time to make *Two Weeks in Another Town* a decade later, the nostalgic legacy of *The Bad and the Beautiful* haunted every frame.

If the early 1950s marked the golden age of anything in Hollywood, it was in the realm of elegiac self-reflection. The blacklist, television, the rise of talent agencies as movie packagers and the forced divestiture of theater chains haunted the industry's present and clouded its future. With the glory days receding quicker than you could say CinemaScope, there was no more tempting moment to indulge in a nostalgic wallow. A host of retrospective movies emerged; each staking out its own particular terrain—the withering irony with which *Sunset Boulevard* contrasted the leopard-skin twenties and the gray-flannel fifties, *Singin' in the Rain*'s vivacious retake of the talkie revolution. Soon to come was the grandiloquent pathos of the updated *A Star Is Born,* set in a make-believe modern Hollywood where the worst thing a studio mogul could contemplate was still the slow dive of a contract luminary from the box-office firmament into the surf off Malibu.

The pictures in this cycle were so vivid that, paradoxically, they proved it was still possible to make enduring movies in the troubled here and now. *The Bad and*

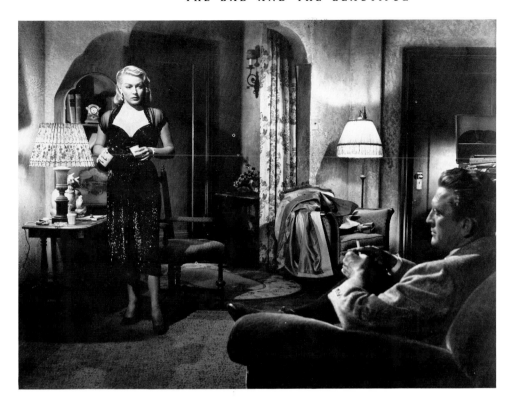

Lush meets louse. Lana Turner and Kirk Douglas in The Bad and the Beautiful *(1952)*

the Beautiful complemented the others by recording the eighteen-year rise and fall of an independent producer from the Depression to the day before yesterday—roughly the same arc spanned by David O. Selznick, whose biggest triumphs also lay behind him. Along the way, it took the usual license with movie chronology. Big-time Latin lovers in the "Gaucho" mold went out when synchronized sound came in, and imaginative B-horror flicks like *The Doom of the Cat Men* were a staple of the war years, not the mid-thirties; Jonathan Shields produces his Civil War epic a decade after Selznick's made all others superfluous. Like most 1950s movies set any time later than the Wall Street Crash, *The Bad and the Beautiful* fudges period niceties of clothes and coiffure, relying on the occasional jalopy or nostalgic tune to conjure up the passing parade. Apart from one shot of the Beverly Hills Hotel, Minnelli doesn't bother to orient the fans with the usual stock views of Hollywood landmarks—like the films-within-a-film, his melodrama unfolds within the soundproofed walls of a movie set.

In fact this film reeks of artifice in every frame, which is what gives *The Bad and the Beautiful* its perverse authenticity. It parallels the sort of picture its cast of characters would make themselves, since the only reality they recognize is the kind you learn from the screen. The plot turns on the romantic conceit that, in a company town manufacturing illusion, art and life are inextricable. Minnelli makes sure that we can't tell the difference either, since the producer-hero and his volatile crew are as prone to actorish poses as the cast of a Jonathan Shields spectacular.

The work ethic is the one moral code in this hermetic environment with any meaning. Collaboration substitutes for comradeship, and whatever betrayals and hurt feelings explode between takes, in the end all that counts is up there on the screen. To fulfill his celluloid visions, the movie's antihero stage-manages the fates of everyone around him; he hands over his best friend's pet project to a more seasoned director; coaxes a big-time performance out of a fledgling actress by cynically exploiting her infatuation for him, and engineers an ill-starred affair for a Southern flirt so her screenwriter husband can work in peace. By the movie's epilogue, virtually none of them has any private life left. But that's trivial compared to the fact that each has climbed to the peak of his profession, due in no small part to a shove from Shields. His ultimate defense is, in the words of his steadfast yes-man Harry, "On every list of the ten best films ever made, there are always two or three of Jonathan's." The reminder is more persuasive than any contrite apologies from Shields, whose long-distance pitch for the blockbuster to cap their joint careers draws his three victims to the phone like iron filings to a magnet.

Like the heroes of so many of his later melodramas, Shields is defined by his lonely compulsions. Incapable of real intimacy, he has cronies but no true companions, and confuses sex with aggression and contempt. Jonathan's tussles with his leading lady end not in a kiss, but with her lying limp in his grasp, a bundle to be tossed into her solitary bed or a convenient swimming pool. "Maybe I like to be cheap once in a while," he spits at the horrified Georgia, explaining why he'd rather spend the night of their premiere with a slatternly starlet who makes no claim on his feelings. The

Kirk Douglas rejects Lana Turner in The Bad and the Beautiful *(1952)*

only fulfillment he seeks or finds is on a sound stage. In a rare reflective moment, he uses the vocabulary of seduction to describe his calling, from the first flush of desire to post-coital depression. "When I make a picture it's like romancing a girl," he muses. "You see her, you want her, you go after her—the big moment! Then the letdown, every time, every picture, the after-picture blues." The difference is that no woman could ever spark the charge he gets from producing. When Shields can't make pictures he ceases to exist, disappearing from view until at the finale he's just a disembodied force at the other end of a transatlantic call, trying to resurrect his career.

Minnelli had little trouble comprehending the creative single-mindedness of a man like Shields. Yet it's ironic that he chose to celebrate a mogul whose intrusive, hands-on methods would drive any self-respecting director to distraction. Unlike the producers who supervised Minnelli's own films, Shields dominates the set as well as the executive suite, coaching his actors and checking the camera angles. His directors are privileged to yell "Action" and "Cut," but it's Shields who calls the shots. This portrait drew on the fund of Selznickiana known to everyone in Hollywood—his Svengali relationship with Jennifer Jones, and the directorial relay race which marked the making of *Gone with the Wind* and *Duel in the Sun* under his impatient supervision.

But once Shields decides he may as well stage his masterpieces himself, the hubris is more than Minnelli can bear. When Shields objects that a scene-in-progress lacks punch, the director in his employ tries to give him a crash course in film technique. "A picture all

climaxes is like a necklace without a string—it falls apart," he declares. "To direct a picture, a man needs humility. Do you have humility, Mr. Shields?" He doesn't, of course, and the result bombs: "no tension, no timing, no pace," in his own chagrined words. Every craft has an indispensable function in this curiously egalitarian world, and what destroys Shields is not his Machiavellian way with people, but the self-delusion that his gifts transcend his lack of training.

In this spirit, Minnelli reserves a wry chortle for directors with an overweening sense of their own importance. The Von Stroheim clone Von Ellstein is an imperious Teutonic poseur, his humility speech notwithstanding. Just as pompous is that dour Brit Henry Whitfield, who directs Georgia's first triumph. As played by dapper Leo G. Carroll, the Hitchcockian reference would be easy to miss were it not for the steely middle-aged matron (Kathleen Freeman) who parrots his words and dogs his every step—a rather nasty caricature of the Master's wife, Alma Reville.

These peripheral strokes give texture to *The Bad and the Beautiful*'s narrative triptych. The first panel is devoted to Shields' directorial protégé, Fred Amiel, who is self-effacing to a flaw—accomplished and devoted to his work but congenitally incapable of blowing his own horn. Minnelli introduces this paragon indulging in his own favorite pastime—laying out a breathless dolly shot from atop his camera boom. But the resemblance ends there, for Minnelli resisted endowing Amiel with his own characteristic eccentricities. This matter-of-fact professional wears conservative suits to the set and is the only member of the troupe with a conventionally happy home life. As played by stolid Barry Sullivan, he's quite the dullest of *The Bad and the Beautiful*'s principals. Considering the turmoil in Minnelli's private affairs at the time, the tranquillity of a solid citizen like Amiel must have looked attractive indeed.

The novelist-turned-screenwriter James Lee Bartlow, whose saga takes up the final third of the movie is also a sketch in mezzotints—detached, sardonic, the inevitable pipe clenched in his thoughtful jaw. He and Amiel are Shields' introverted foils; their temperaments are channeled into their work. *The Bad and the Beautiful*'s women, however, are a more mercurial lot, whose incessant role-playing turns every moment into a movie vehicle of their own devising. In an insinuating performance by Gloria Grahame, the screenwriter's wife Rosemary is a natural supporting player who longs to play the lead in her real-life adventures. This demi-Bovary is mistress of the vivacious simper, never more demure than when she vamps her husband into accepting a trip to Hollywood. "James Lee," she drawls, "you have a very naughty mind—I'm happy to say!" and his superior novelist's brain notwithstanding, James Lee is powerless against her silken wiles. Shields sees through the performance at once, but can't help admiring the misplaced energy that goes into it. His task is to distract her with a new leading man so James Lee can brood at his typewriter in peace.

For all his professorial qualms, James Lee earns a comfortable niche in Hollywood, but Rosemary's flair for theatrics fails to mask her amateur standing. Her offscreen death in a plane crash while carousing with Gaucho is as neat a case of *deus ex machina* as anything James Lee could invent in a script. Her infidelity aside, Rosemary's capital offense was her charming frivolousness; the Hollywood of *The Bad and the Beautiful* is too serious a place to make room for dilettantes. "She interfered with your work, she wasted your time, she wasted you. You're better off without her," Jonathan bellows at his grieving screenwriter and, coldblooded as it sounds, from a professional standpoint his logic is unassailable.

The movie's central vignette showcases Shields' greatest creation, Georgia Lorrison, who acquires the right priorities the hard way. Like Jonathan, she is the spawn of a Hollywood dynasty, destined from birth to make her mark in the movies. Just as Shields dematerializes once his livelihood slips away, Minnelli surrounds Georgia in darkness until she finds her calling. When first seen in flashback as a loveless teenager, she's just a disembodied pair of legs dangling drunkenly from the rafters of her abandoned family manse. The crucial difference between the two is that Jonathan's ego impels him to surpass the achievements of Shields Senior, while the insecure Georgia careens down the dissolute path forged by her famous father.

Her pedigree ensures that Georgia is "born to live by make-believe," as Shields notes sardonically—it's her

curse and her salvation. Until he takes her in hand, Georgia drifts as a failed bit player whose most colorful performances unreel in the privacy of her photogenically sordid bungalow. There she plays the sad loose dame out of a dozen films noir, swilling hooch and bartering her favors, but there are other roles in her repertoire. Clothes make the girl—snuggled in Shields' oversized bathrobe after he sobers her up with a dunk in the pool, she becomes the baby-voiced gamine with a crush on Daddy. "Love is for the very young," he quips in a vain attempt to keep her at arm's length, but the irony is lost on Georgia. What the producer calls her "star quality—Lorrison quality" is the combination of a face that the camera loves and a vacuously malleable psyche. Woo her between takes and she'll glow like a woman in love for her closeups; treat her like a star and odds are she'll become one.

Appropriately, Georgia's crash course in the tricks of the trade has less to do with acting technique than diva attitude: how to wear a major gown with authority, using a cigarette as a prop for seduction. Herself the ultimate movie-factory creation, Lana Turner had spent her career mastering lessons like these; her synthetic sincerity turns Georgia's rise into a Pirandellian imitation of life.

For an insider like Minnelli these ironies are irresistible, and he flexes every strategy he's got to confound his heroine even further. On a deserted sound stage or in Shields' inner sanctum, wherever Lana/Georgia goes a key light magically picks out the planes of her face from the surrounding murk. His camera leaps upward past Georgia on the set acting her big monologue to the hushed admiration of the studio technicians, and in a parallel movement plummets to earth as she sweeps into view at the premiere, playing the overnight sensation. Georgia wants to perform a real-life love scene at Jonathan's retreat, but the set has been dressed for a different movie; it's a haunted house stalked by its very own Cat Woman. ("I saw the picture—thought you were swell," croons Shields' undulating groupie who, unlike Georgia, has no trouble differentiating life from celluloid fancies.) Retreating in horror, Georgia totters decorously toward her car and oblivion. Even at wit's end, she instinctively remembers to walk like a star the way Shields taught her. And when she finally explodes in a fit of uninhibited despair, Minnelli accompanies her catharsis with his showiest celluloid fakery—flashing lights and buckets of fake rain glorify this shrieking blur of rhinestones and ermine.

Georgia emerges from this trauma a star through and through—preternaturally poised, absurdly glamorous. In her dressing room between takes for what looks like an Arthur Freed version of *Der Rosenkavalier*, Georgia reposes in powdered wig and black-spangled breeches as casually as if they were curlers and lounging pajamas. At the movie's conclusion, she halts dramatically in mid-flight from Shields Productions, an arm's length away from an extension phone in the darkened vestibule. Something irresistible draws her, and it's not just the voice of the Master. For there's that key light again, fixed on the receiver waiting for Georgia to assume her rightful place in its glow. Fred and James Lee crowd her in on either side, but there's no contest—blonde screen deities have their prerogatives, and with tongue in cheek, Minnelli respects them.

This self-referential playfulness is what gives *The Bad and the Beautiful* its particular zest. Scene after scene is a kind of show-and-tell about the craft of moviemaking, as Shields mouths his axioms and Minnelli illustrates their power. While dreaming up *The Doom of the Cat Men,* Jonathan muses, "The dark has a life of its own. In the dark, all sorts of things come alive," which is Minnelli's cue to kill all the lights save the desk lamp which pinpoints the producer's hand in a *danse macabre.* Later on, the producer slashes away at James Lee's script and comes up with a mute scenario of his own: "We move the camera in close on her . . . she's too emotional to be able to speak, and what she's feeling, we'll leave for the audience to imagine." Sure enough, at *The Bad and the Beautiful*'s final fadeout

Minnelli's camera moves in close on Georgia, and what she's feeling—curiosity, longing, excitement—the audience imagines from Lana Turner's darting glance and the spectral light poised on her cheekbones.

No one relishes this gamesmanship more than Minnelli; with every adrenalin-propelled dolly shot, he lets us know that there's no fun like the hard labor of making movie magic. Like *The Faraway Mountain, The Proud Land,* and the rest of Shields' imaginary legacy, *The Bad and the Beautiful* aspires neither to high art nor newsreel naturalism. By its own example, this black-and-white fantasia celebrates the energy and showmanship that made the studio system flourish. Minnelli and his troupe hoped to perpetuate that spirit in the act of commemorating it, which adds a retrospective note of pathos to the movie's upbeat fadeout. For by 1952, the Shieldses and Lorrisons were fading fast, and the Hollywood they knew was less and less the self-contained community that had nurtured them. Still protected within MGM's walls, Minnelli sustains his illusions with all the conviction he can muster, gallantly whistling in the dark.

. . . .

1955   # THE COBWEB

Spurred by the success of *The Bad and the Beautiful,* over the next two years Houseman staked out a special terrain for himself at MGM. His productions of Joseph Mankiewicz' *Julius Caesar* and Robert Wise's *Executive Suite* won wide praise as the last word in Hollywood taste and craft. In fact, both films shrewdly updated that revered specialty of the studio's distant Thalberg era—the star-laden ensemble piece, combining mass appeal and classy aspirations. After these variations on *Romeo and Juliet* and *Dinner at Eight,* Houseman's next project also proved a quintessentially 1950s rehab of another Depression-age classic. In 1931, More Stars Than There Were in Heaven learned about love and loss in *Grand Hotel;* in 1955, *The Cobweb* sequestered a new generation of luminaries within the plush confines of a private mental institution.

Its source was a critically admired first novel by William Gibson, writing under the pseudonym of William Mass. Later the author of such hit plays as *Two for the Seesaw* and *The Miracle Worker,* Gibson had steeped himself in *The Cobweb*'s hospital milieu during his wife's long tenure on the staff of the Menninger Clinic. At Houseman's urging, MGM acquired the book for $55,000 shortly after its publication in 1954. Meanwhile, he entrusted the adaptation to John Paxton, whose scripts for *Crossfire* and *The Wild One* had shown

a lively flair for topical melodrama. Houseman was eager to work with Minnelli again, and had no trouble persuading him to rejoin forces on this project. Since their last teaming, he'd directed two musicals for Freed, punctuated by his Lucille Ball farce. After spending most of 1954 in dispiriting pursuit of *Brigadoon* and the elusive *Green Mansions,* Minnelli was ready to clear the dry-ice fog out of his head and focus on something grittier. Like *The Bad and the Beautiful, The Cobweb* sought to reveal the inside workings of a closed society, and the conflicts of people whose professional lives compensate for their emotional isolation. Its psychiatric setting may have had a perverse fascination for him after the years of nursing Garland through her troubles, and certainly its bizarre plot played right to his own idiosyncrasies. In Gibson's book, the simmering hostilities between the clinic's patients and warring factions among its staff erupt over a seemingly trivial matter of taste—the choice of a new set of drapes for the patients' lounge. Notoriously subject to his own frustrated twitches should a prop on the set offend his eye, Minnelli of all directors truly believed that decor was the mirror of the soul.

He brought to this film the same vigor and enthusiasm that had sparked *The Bad and the Beautiful,* but there were troubled auguries from the beginning. Prevailing censorship taboos clamped a straitjacket on the novel's characters. Paxton was forced to eliminate the homosexuality of one inmate, and turn the central romance between an art therapist and her miserably wed

boss into a chaste but guilt-ridden affair ending in his humbled return to the hearth. In the hope of undoing some of the damage, Minnelli persuaded MGM to bring Gibson out to rework the dialogue and supervise the set for accuracy. Despite his valuable contributions, Minnelli never got quite the script he wanted.

Casting the picture was another headache, eventually prompting the first rift between Minnelli and his producer. In spring 1954, MGM optimistically announced a glittering assembly of its contract stars for *The Cobweb*'s marquee—Robert Taylor and Lana Turner to play the chief doctor and his neglected spouse, and Grace Kelly as the woman who comes between them. Houseman additionally hoped to snare James Dean, fresh from his debut in *East of Eden,* for the key role of Stevie, an affection-starved teenager under the hero's care. However, by late fall when the script was ready to shoot, Taylor and Turner had found other things to do. Minnelli and Houseman settled on Richard Widmark in an imaginative switch from his usual film noir low-lifes at 20th Century-Fox, pairing him with their favorite household troublemaker, Gloria Grahame. Dean balked at the paltry fee Metro and his home studio Warner Bros. had worked out for his services, so as a rather pallid substitute, MGM proposed

OPPOSITE:

Pier Angeli in the test for the never-filmed Green Mansions *(1954)*

The pet patient and the doctor's wife. John Kerr and Gloria Grahame in The Cobweb *(1955)*

John Kerr, signed to a contract after his Broadway success in *Tea and Sympathy*.

With a month to go before *The Cobweb*'s starting date, Grace Kelly also defected. Having just raced through four pictures in succession, the star informed her employers that she was too exhausted to tackle another one; Minnelli and Houseman hurriedly agreed on Lauren Bacall as a replacement. Meanwhile, each came up with intriguing ideas for the film's supporting roles. Minnelli summoned Oscar Levant to lend his neurotic baggage to the formerly gay, now mother-fixated Mr. Capp, and Houseman persuaded Lillian Gish to make her first film appearance in six years as the asylum's blunt, reactionary administrator, Miss Inch. Their clash came when Minnelli insisted on Charles Boyer to play Widmark's antagonist, an authoritarian psychiatrist in decline thanks to his excesses with women and drink. (Ironically, Boyer had achieved Hollywood stardom with a role virtually identical to Widmark's in the 1935 *Private Worlds*, the American screen's first serious treatment of psychiatry.) Houseman strenuously objected, on the grounds that the star's roué charm and Gallic accent would add a redundant red herring to an already overburdened script. He grudgingly conceded when Minnelli refused to consider anyone else, but Houseman wasn't so indulgent in the skirmishes to come.

Nevertheless, a deceptive calm prevailed as Minnelli launched *The Cobweb*'s seven-week shoot in early December 1954. Although the cast hadn't quite the box-office luster MGM originally hoped for, Minnelli's troupe was both gifted and responsive to his direction. On his first non-musical to use both color and CinemaScope, Minnelli was fortunate to have the reliable George Folsey behind the camera to ease the transition. *The Cobweb*'s subject matter didn't call for Minnelli's most dynamic visual strategies, apart from one climactic sequence—Stevie's anguished escape from the asylum. For this scene, Minnelli needed music even more ''neurotic'' than Rozsa's *Madame Bovary* waltz, and he got it in the dissonant brasses of the theme provided by Leonard Rosenman, the one *East of Eden* alumnus Houseman was able to snare for *The Cobweb*. With its edgy, propulsive series of tracking shots through marsh and field, this moment is a dry run for the boar hunt in *Home from the Hill*, another breathless fresco of an adolescent boy running in search of himself.

Striking though this footage was, as Minnelli's rushes arrived from the lab Houseman became apprehensive. With its sprawling tangle of incidents and relationships, *The Cobweb* threatened to far exceed the standard length for a Metro dramatic feature, and Minnelli's penchant for long takes and atmospheric detail was making matters worse. Just as *The Bad and the Beautiful*'s story of camaraderie on the set extended behind the scenes, this time the director-producer team butted heads in a turf war worthy of the movie's warring shrinks. Minnelli emerged with a rough clocked at two and a half hours, and announced that as far as he was concerned, *The Cobweb*, was ready for release. Houseman insisted on sweating thirty minutes out of it, and when Minnelli refused to cooperate, he and editor Harold F. Kress did the job without him. On viewing the result, its now-overwrought director exploded at Houseman, accusing him of willful sabotage.

The old guard. Charles Boyer and Lillian Gish in The Cobweb *(1955)*

OPPOSITE LEFT:
Gloria Grahame puts up her drapes, The Cobweb *(1955)*

OPPOSITE RIGHT:
Richard Widmark rips them down, The Cobweb *(1955)*

As expected, Schary sided with *The Cobweb*'s producer and it was his 124-minute cut which MGM sneak-previewed in April 1955. This screening went better than any of them had expected. Despite mutterings from the peanut gallery ("Buy Venetian blinds and have done with it," proclaimed one preview card preserved in the studio files), its first audience greeted *The Cobweb* with considerable enthusiasm, singling out Lillian Gish's feisty performance as the highlight of the movie. Nonetheless, the studio wasn't convinced of its popular appeal, and scheduled the New York premiere for Loews' State rather than the more prestigious and lucrative Radio City Music Hall. The press gave it a promising launch, generally agreeing that its distinguished cast and Minnelli's compassionate modulation of the theme compensated for the knotted skeins in *The Cobweb*'s plot. One demurral came from *Variety*, which chided MGM for making a movie too tasteful for its own good; the trade journal predicted that any patron willing to spend two hours shut up in a loony bin expected more bolts and jolts for his money. As things turned out, *Variety* psyched out the movie-going public more accurately than a Rorschach test. In its general release *The Cobweb* earned back approximately $1,500,000 in domestic rentals, considerably less than MGM spent to produce it. For most of those involved, the outcome didn't justify the behind-the-scenes turmoil; later on, the best William Gibson could say for it was that nothing in the finished film made him ashamed of his involvement. Fortunately, circumstances didn't allow the spat between Minnelli and Houseman to fester into an out-and-out feud. Within

weeks of hurling invective at each other over the moviola, the chastened pair was immersed in plans for the most challenging project of their joint careers—the life story of Vincent Van Gogh.

As much as any of his other melodramas, *The Cobweb* illustrates the forcefulness of Minnelli's directorial personality. Out of Gibson's novel and the starry ensemble Houseman had assembled, he wove a dense fabric of the themes that preoccupied him in film after film—the artist as outsider; work as balm for personal disappointment; the individual's struggle to reconcile his existential loneliness with the need to become part of a community. Within this fresco of an extended family in crisis, Minnelli constantly emphasizes how isolated each of its members really is. Whether inmates, would-be healers, or their mates, *The Cobweb*'s half-dozen principal characters all nurse their private quota of pain, and then strike out reflexively at the nearest moving target. As star patient Stevie quips early in the film, "you can't tell the patients from the doctors"; what makes *The Cobweb* more unsettling still is that you can't distinguish the director from either of them, so completely does Minnelli identify with this tangle of collective hysteria.

There's good reason why the clinic in this movie resembles no such institution on earth, Gibson's on-the-set counsel notwithstanding. This is a custom-tailored snake pit where Minnelli himself might feel at home. The patients' group sessions play out like his customary party scenes gone sour—a nervous mix of chatty cosmopolitans and flinching wallflowers. The film's most conspicuous cases for treatment—diagnosed or otherwise—sport those obsessions that made *The Cobweb*'s creator the filmmaker he was. Seconds after the title credits have faded from view, we are plunged into a brief encounter between Karen McIver and her husband's young charge which could only take place in Minnelliland. Before you can say Oedipal transference, they discourse on the symbolism of flowers ("Isn't it enough that they have color and form?" she sullenly deadpans as only Gloria Grahame could) and on the tormented genius of Les Fauves. The gladioli on the back seat of Karen's station wagon inspire the kid to brood over André Derain's deathbed cry, "some red, show me some red . . . and some green!" Which is more or less what Minnelli had been screaming at the Metro art department for years.

In the hands of any other director, the ensuing tempest over the library curtains would have receded to its proper place as a plot device—the catalyst which ignites the latent tensions among *The Cobweb*'s volatile inhabitants, and all the more ironic for its triviality. Paxton methodically spells out the real troubles in a round of confessional duologues inflected with the latest 1950s brand of psychobabble—from art therapist Meg Rinehart to dipsomaniac Mr. Capp, chances are that it was smothering mommy or unfeeling dad who made them what they are. Yet Minnelli can't resist embroidering this theme with samples from his draper's catalogue. His sundry window treatments don't just distract from a loquacious script; the way these people see "color and form" individualizes them for Minnelli as succinctly as a fingerprint. The drab cotton panels bought by Vicky Inch reflect her barren inner life, while Karen's "Chippendale rose on antique satin" is the mark of her frustrated femininity; Stevie's washes of bright color over anxious ink cartoons combine his teenaged exuberance with the bleak perspective that got him committed in the first place. Wherever she goes, Karen brings her talisman fabric swatch along—tossing it on the marital bed she and McIver rarely share, proffering it to her husband's psychiatrist-rival over a furtive cocktail. When both men ignore this expression of her taste, she feels herself utterly rejected, just as Stevie's climactic destruction of his drawings is a sublimated form of suicide. If this is pathological, its director knew all the symptoms first-hand. Played absolutely straight throughout, the motif becomes Minnelli's own form of on-the-lot occupational therapy.

For Minnelli cultists, this type of audacity is what distinguished him from his more earnest, literal-minded peers. To those who don't share his credo, two insistent hours of interior-decoration-as-truth-serum is bound to seem a trifle unbalanced. Even when the curtains are nowhere to be seen, *The Cobweb*'s plush Metro accessorizing gives these scenes something of a split personality—all those tasteful pastel decors and well-groomed star performers take some of the visceral kick out of the plot. The tentative illicit romance between Widmark and Bacall unreels in a siege of long one-take talkathons, with Minnelli waiting idly for his actors to shut up so he can move the camera again. His restlessness shows through in the oddest moments; a flamboyant boom shot of Bacall's house at night is inserted for no discernible reason save that, amid so much verbal intrigue, he hasn't had the chance to stretch his legs for reels at a time. Stevie's disappearance is a welcome distraction, if only because it gets Minnelli out-of-doors in search of some dramatic tableau to fill his panoramic screen. He finds it in a rain-swollen river swarming with would-be rescuers, while red-lights-for-danger flicker in the gloom.

The Cobweb has other fitful compensations. In contrast to the often flatfooted writing, the movie's structure has a certain sardonic, fugue-like elegance to it; from one sequence to the next, its highstrung characters change partners in an endless roundelay of connivance, betrayal, and high dudgeon. There are zestful performances from Lillian Gish, whose non-stop peevishness is a tonic change from her customary beatific self, and from Charles Boyer, deliberately pathetic as a hollow man who's coasted on charm for far too long. Most striking of all is Gloria Grahame's portrait of a mad housewife, twitching with rage beneath her Better Homes and Gardens façade.

Thanks in part to Grahame's natural eccentricity, *The Cobweb*'s scenes of domestic purgatory are far more harrowing than the climactic *Walpurgisnacht* at the clinic. *The Cobweb* offers the first bitter taste of Minnelli's ever-deepening cynicism on the state of family life in the affluent 1950s: *Tea and Sympathy, Some Came Running* and *Home from the Hill* are littered with respectable couples who observe the proprieties but loathe each other, usually with a complement of shell-shocked kids in the background. The McIver household in *The Cobweb* is the perfect setting for a misbegotten marriage. By day it has the sterile upscale hominess of a W. J. Sloane's window display, and by night it shifts to mock-Colonial Gothic—doctor and wife sulk in the shadows of their respective bedrooms, while their solemn little boy plays chess against himself. No wonder daughter Rosie wants to be a patient when she grows up. Compared to this fragmented family unit, the hospital is a utopia of togetherness and harmony.

Minnelli's bleak take on the story is so persuasive that the Production-Code-imposed reconciliation at the end seems doubly arbitrary. A scrawled legend in yellow announces "The trouble was over" across Karen's chintz drapes, now an improvised bed for the prodigal inmate; but after all the excitement, *The Cobweb* feels like six characters in search of a catharsis which never quite comes. Its mixture of psychosexual angst and textile whimsies is the kind of distinctive failure only Minnelli could make; still, in this straitjacket of a script, Minnelli wasn't able to explore a pure red and green delirium of his own.

· ·

LUST FOR LIFE

For the rest of his life, Minnelli regarded *Lust for Life* as his toughest challenge and one of his prouder achievements—perhaps the most visually evocative movie he ever made, in service of a subject he passionately identified with. Minnelli's deepest affinities as a filmmaker converged in this treatment of Vincent Van Gogh's life—from the link between emotional isolation and the creative impulse expressed in the medium Minnelli so revered, to the urge to use color as a psychological tool, plus his special sensitivity to the social landscape and cultural legacy of France.

In many crucial aspects, *Lust for Life* nevertheless marked a departure from everything he had tackled to date. While producers like Freed often developed properties with Minnelli in mind, this was the only film he himself initiated during more than two decades at MGM. His first film based on fact and shot primarily in actual locations, *Lust for Life* gave Minnelli the chance to fuse his imagination with a realistic sense of place and mood. On the Continent, Minnelli began to work in a freer, more improvised style, reshaping his ideas to respond to these fresh surroundings. This exhilarating but rigorous experience left a profound mark on the film, for in the wake of *The Bad and the Beautiful, An American in Paris,* and *The Band Wagon,* this is the grimmest of Minnelli's self-portraits in code. For *Lust for Life* is really about his own compulsive zest for work, to the almost painful exclusion of everything else.

The property had had a long and jinxed history at the studio before Minnelli decided to tackle it. First published in 1934, Irving Stone's fictionalized portrait of the artist was purchased by MGM for $120,000 in late 1946, after a new edition of the book proved a runaway best-seller. Several staff producers, including Sam Zimbalist, Voldemar Vetleguin, and Arthur Freed jousted for this prize, each assigning a rival screenwriter to bear his colors. However, the unrelievedly somber nature of Van Gogh's saga defeated them all, and by the end of 1947, various treatments written by Richard Llewellyn, Dalton Trumbo and Irving Stone himself lay unmourned in the morgue of the MGM story department. Several times Freed girded himself for a new assault; in 1950 he proposed resuscitating *Lust for Life* with Richard Brooks as its writer-director, but nothing tangible came of this. Two years later, Kenneth MacKenna reported that the project had stalled, but in 1953 the unexpected popularity of *Moulin Rouge,* John Huston's film biography of Toulouse-Lautrec, made *Lust for Life* an attractive proposition again.

An independent producer named Willis Goldbeck then approached the studio with an intriguing package —a Jean Renoir *Lust for Life* starring Van Heflin, which Goldbeck would finance, film in Europe, and allow MGM to distribute in the States for a fee of $300,000. Metro initially favored this deal as an expedient way to salvage something from this project, but his own bud-

Kirk Douglas and miners' wives in the Borinage, Lust for Life *(1956)*

getary problems forced Goldbeck to abandon the project in March 1954. In the meantime, *Lust for Life*'s impatient author put in his bid to purchase back the rights from MGM and get the movie made himself. According to this scenario, Italian moguls Carlo Ponti and Dino De Laurentiis were ready to bankroll *Lust for Life* with Yul Brynner, Marlon Brando, or Kirk Douglas in the lead. Stone's director of choice was Jean Negulesco—a Sunday painter in the post-Impressionist manner, whose directorial palette leaned more toward *Three Coins in the Fountain*. However, these negotiations eventually petered out as well. By the fall of 1954, MGM was essentially back where it had started, with vague murmurings from Arthur Freed that *Lust for Life* remained on his dream agenda.

After eight years the clock was winding down fast on this property; Stone's contract stipulated that if the screen version were not completed by early January 1956, all rights would revert to him. Meanwhile, in early 1955, an item in the trades announced that a new production company set up by Kirk Douglas had a rival film on Van Gogh in the works, to be directed by the persistent Negulesco. If either prospect came to pass, the considerable sums spent to develop *Lust for Life* would have to be written off as a dead loss. Under the circumstances, Dore Schary was eager to listen when Minnelli dashed from his labors on *The Cobweb* and confided his eagerness to make the film himself. In his memoirs, the director claimed it was his idea to team up with Houseman against the boss's suggestion of another, unnamed staff producer; according to Houseman, the pair approached Schary together. In any case,

they pledged to leave *The Cobweb*'s frictions behind in order to concentrate on this exciting new collaboration.

Casting the picture proved the least of their problems—in physique and temperament Douglas couldn't be bettered as Van Gogh, and co-opting him for *Lust for Life* also scotched the star's competing designs on the role. Houseman and Minnelli also agreed that Anthony Quinn's blunt sensuality would make a provocative Paul Gauguin. The most urgent matter was to find what had eluded everyone thus far—the dramatic spine of Van Gogh's life story. Houseman later asserted that he had Norman Corwin in mind from the start to tackle this problem, but studio records show that the first writer approached was Robert Ardrey, who'd done such a skillful job with *Madame Bovary*. However, Kenneth MacKenna reported that Ardrey declined with regret, noting that "after a lot of study he could not find any satisfactory dramatic structure. He feels that most of the story goes on inside the man and does not lend itself to objective exposition." MGM next approached Daniel Taradash *(From Here to Eternity)*, without success, before at last signing Corwin at the end of January 1955. Although Corwin's was a sporadic and not unusually distinguished screen career thus far—his most conspicuous credit being the 1951 Jane Wyman weepy, *The Blue Veil*—he sported unusual qualifications for the job. As one of radio's most prolific writers, Corwin had won considerable notice for his vivid recreations of historical figures and events.

In fact, his solution emulated the shape and sound of a dramatic broadcast, narrating Van Gogh's peripatetic struggles by means of the lifelong correspondence

Pamela Brown and Kirk Douglas, Lust for Life *(1956)*

OPPOSITE:
Minnelli and John Houseman at MGM

between the artist and his forebearing brother, Theo. This approach seemed perfect to Minnelli, who had been studying the letters for inspiration. Nevertheless, MGM warned Houseman that an exasperating legal obstacle loomed ahead to further complicate the task for Corwin. The Van Gogh correspondence was the property of the artist's namesake, Theo's surviving son, who abhorred the prospect of these Hollywood vulgarians appropriating the family legacy. Although the present Vincent Van Gogh couldn't stop the film from being made, he was bound to sue if a single phrase from the letters appeared in the *Lust for Life* script.

Undeterred, Corwin forged ahead, with Minnelli supervising his progress whenever he could leave his whirling dervishes on the *Kismet* set. With his encouragement Corwin hacked away at the book's more dubious conceits, including the phantom sweetheart Stone had given Van Gogh as a sop to the conventional sentiments of his readers; the result adhered more closely to the historical record than Stone's novel had done. While Corwin tried to conjure up an authentic voice for Van Gogh, Minnelli and Houseman struggled to reconcile the artist's vision with the technological palette at their disposal. Two years earlier MGM had abandoned both the standard rectangular screen and Technicolor, the media best suited to reproduce the shape and texture of Van Gogh's work. Now that CinemaScope was the format of choice in movie theaters everywhere, the studio refused to shoot *Lust for Life* any other way. Whether he liked it or not, Minnelli had to figure out how to cram Van Gogh's canvases into a frame better suited for the processional in a Giotto fresco.

When it came to the color film stock to be used, *Lust for Life*'s producer/director team refused to submit so easily. Lately the process of choice at MGM, Eastmancolor's pastel spectrum couldn't master the sunflower yellows and cobalt blues so characteristic of Van Gogh. After dropping its contract with Technicolor, MGM had briefly used another alternative, the Ansco process.

Minnelli had resisted it at the time, but now found its hues richer and more adaptable than its pallid successor's. The studio grudgingly conceded his point after looking over test footage shot in both, and finally agreed to use Ansco for the negative, with the release prints to be done in Eastman. However, having lost the Hollywood competitive wars, the Ansco company had halted production of their coveted stock, and thus MGM emptied its warehouses of every remaining scrap of film.

Meanwhile, the studio's legal department scoured the globe for Van Gogh's far-flung work, pleading with collectors from Edward G. Robinson in Beverly Hills to Moscow's Museum of Modern Art to allow the use of his paintings on screen. Those chosen to adorn Van Gogh's studios in Arles and elsewhere were painstakingly faked; others appeared in closeup inserts punctuating the scenes of Van Gogh at work, their final selection and placement to be decided by Minnelli after *Lust for Life* was shot and assembled. A photographic crew spent months shuttling from private galleries to museums on three continents, shooting the canvases with still portrait cameras; the transparencies were then themselves filmed at Culver City with specially fitted movie cameras devised by MGM's John Arnold. Two artists were hired to execute the ersatz Van Goghs —one to provide the finished paintings, the other to double the onscreen brushwork for Kirk Douglas. Meanwhile, to avoid glaring factual gaffes, Houseman hired Impressionism scholar John Rewald, of The Museum of Modern Art, to serve as the film's historical consultant throughout preproduction.

Minnelli was determined to stress the interplay between Van Gogh's work and his natural surroundings in every frame of the movie. In the wake of *Moulin Rouge*'s striking, on-the-spot reproduction of the fin-de-siècle Left Bank, he and Houseman had no trouble persuading MGM to shoot *Lust for Life* on location. But their task was infinitely more complicated than anything John Huston had faced. As an aside in Corwin's script ruefully noted, Toulouse-Lautrec "would never leave Paris," while their haunted hero never stood still. Before they were through, the *Lust for Life* troupe would follow his traces from the coal mines of the Belgian Borinage and his homeland in the Dutch countryside through Amsterdam and Paris to the landscapes of Provence and the Ile-de-France where Van Gogh spent his productive, tormented final years. Thanks to *Kismet*, Minnelli wasn't free until midsummer but the fields and vineyards ripening under the Southern sun waited for no man, not even these intrepid trespassers from Culver City's *Ecole des Beaux Arts*. Thus, Houseman worked out a shooting schedule of near-military precision, and prayed that both the elements and his director would stick to the scenario. From necessity, the script was shot in reverse order, with the company gradually trekking north as the weather grew colder. Throughout the spring of 1955, production scouts from MGM's European offices fanned out in search of the right locations. With a few months to go before principal shooting could begin, Joseph Ruttenberg flew to Arles to photograph the orchards in bloom —the first sight Van Gogh had described on arriving in the South. Still trapped in his backlot Baghdad, Minnelli was thrilled with the footage Ruttenberg brought back with him, and knew that they would make beautiful pictures together, once *Kismet* was behind them.

With so much of the film to be shot on the Continent, MGM expediently decided to assemble the bulk of the *Lust for Life* cast from its English base at Borehamwood. Thus Houseman left for London at the beginning of July to survey the terrain, subject to Minnelli's final accord. With his shrewd eye for talent, the producer picked a distinctive group of character players largely unfamiliar to American moviegoers. As the sodden prostitute with whom Van Gogh made a foredoomed stab at domesticity, Pamela Brown was the antithesis of the Hollywood loose lady—stocky and introverted, with the icy baritone that had stirred theatergoers in Christopher Fry's *The Lady's Not for Burning*. The last role to be filled was Theo, which, though less colorful than Gauguin, was the longest part in the script next to Vincent Van Gogh himself. All sorts of actors from both sides of the Atlantic were considered, from Arthur Kennedy and David Wayne to John Gregson and Dirk Bogarde. With ten days to go before shooting was to begin, Minnelli and Houseman decided the West End's James Donald had the right quality of furrow-browed sensitivity.

Lust for Life's director finally arrived bleary-eyed in London on July 22, less than seventy-two hours after calling his last shot on Arthur Freed's *Arabian Nights*. Exhausted though he was, Minnelli had little time for rest. *Lust for Life* was to start shooting in France by August 2, and all the European casting and locations had to be finalized. As if this weren't enough, Minnelli found himself without a cinematographer. After his back-to-back assignments of that first trip to Arles as well as *Kismet*, Ruttenberg decided belatedly that *Lust for Life*'s long shoot abroad would be too taxing. Minnelli was exceedingly fortunate to obtain the ace British cinematographer Freddie Young in his place—from the moment they met, he was buoyed by Young's painstaking sensitivity to his ideas, and by the cameraman's own inventiveness.

Three days after Minnelli landed, he was off to Belgium to check out the locations Houseman had scouted, then on to Paris and the South of France for more of the same. At last, he returned to Auvers-sur-Oise outside of Paris for the first day's shoot, filming what was virtually the last scene in the finished film— Van Gogh's suicide while painting *Wheat field with Crows*. The company spent a week in the district to shoot the Quatorze Juillet fête underscoring Van

Gogh's desperate alienation, and some establishing shots of the garden of Dr. Gachet, the physician and art patron who harbored Van Gogh during his final crisis. In these sequences, as in many others during *Lust for Life*'s trek southward, Minnelli insisted whenever possible on using the precise locales Van Gogh had known and described in his letters to Theo.

After a couple of days at the Francoeur Studios in Paris for some interior shots, the *Lust for Life* troupe hit the highways for three weeks' work in Provence, commencing in Arles. Destroyed by Allied bombardments during the war, Van Gogh's yellow house had to be reconstructed from scratch, but with slight refurbishments virtually everything else Minnelli shot was as it had been in the artist's time, sixty-five years before— including the asylum at St. Rémy where he recuperated after his breakdown in Arles. The immediacy of it all spurred Douglas to burrow into his role with a positive frenzy, which Minnelli rapturously encouraged. As before, they established a remarkable creative shorthand on the set—so much so that on his belated arrival on location, a bristling Anthony Quinn felt the odd man out. Meanwhile, Minnelli's vivid first-hand impressions of Van Gogh's world prompted daily changes in the script, focusing mostly on his quarrelsome cohabitation with Gauguin and subsequent commitment at St. Rémy. With Corwin in California, this task fell to Houseman and his associate Jud Kinberg. Their efforts exasperated MGM's Joe Kaplan, assigned to supervise *Lust for Life* abroad and report back regularly to Culver City on its progress. On August 17 he sourly informed the studio, "at this writing I still do not have a finished script. I can tell you, at this point, the script is already much too long. Maybe they are going to cut it down. But when? After we have shot it?"

Thus started a transoceanic squabble that lasted long after the *Lust for Life* troupe retreated home to Culver City. Every few days, Houseman shipped the rushes to a special Ansco lab in Houston for processing and then to be perused at the studio by Schary. Everyone agreed

Rex Harrison and Kay Kendall in The Reluctant Debutante *(1958)*

RIGHT:
Kay Kendall and Rex Harrison in a tête-à-tête, The Reluctant Debutante *(1958)*

*Sandra Dee, Kay Kendall,
and Rex Harrison face the
London season in* The
Reluctant Debutante *(1958)*

227

Dollye and her drums. Stella Stevens in The Courtship of Eddie's Father *(1963)*

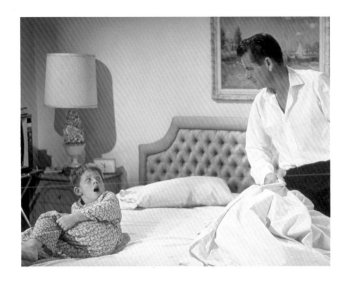

Bedtime story. Ronny Howard and Glenn Ford in The Courtship of Eddie's Father *(1963)*

Glenn Ford greets the guests at Eddie's birthday party. The Courtship of Eddie's Father *(1963)*

*Charlie invades a Beverly
Hills beauty parlor. Debbie
Reynolds (right) in*
Goodbye, Charlie *(1964)*

RIGHT:
Vincent paints Dr. Gachet in Minnelli's sound-stage garden. Kirk Douglas and Everett Sloane in Lust for Life *(1956)*

ABOVE:
Van Gogh's final bout of despair. Kirk Douglas in Lust for Life *(1956)*

Wade relaxes with his hounds and a beer. Robert Mitchum and George Hamilton in Home from the Hill *(1960)*

Tension on the set. Kirk
Douglas broods while
Rosanna Schiaffino explodes,
Two Weeks in Another
Town *(1962)*

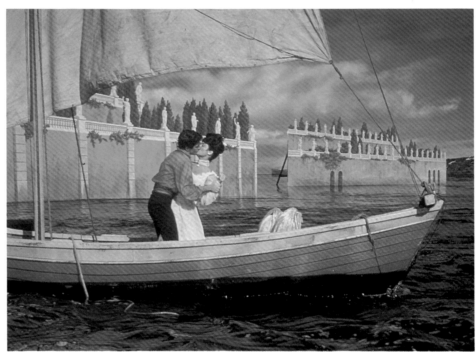

*George Hamilton tussles with
Rosanna Schiaffino in the
movie-within-the-movie of*
Two Weeks in Another
Town *(1962)*

Minnelli's censored Roman orgy. Kirk Douglas and Cyd Charisse (center) in Two Weeks in Another Town *(1962)*

RIGHT:
Kirk Douglas admires Cyd Charisse's taste in diamonds. Two Weeks in Another Town *(1962)*

Elizabeth Taylor and Richard Burton steal an illicit moment of peace, The Sandpiper *(1965)*

BELOW:
Liza Minnelli's rich fantasy life in A Matter of Time *(1976)*

240

H682-106

the footage was spectacular, but that there was going to be far too much if Houseman didn't tighten the reins on Minnelli. On August 22, Schary anxiously cabled Houseman, "Just a few minutes ago I received the final script on *Lust for Life* which measures 148 pages. I urge you again, John, to do something about the length of this film, as I am truly alarmed at the prospect of shoot-ing quantities of film which will wind up as wasted money. . . . Otherwise, we'll wind up with the same experience we had on *Cobweb,* where the film was cut and the cutting must have made subtle changes which unfortunately affected some of the reception to the film." Houseman immediately replied, "Painfully aware truth your two cables. Please believe continuous intense thought being given and action being taken to reduce script while maintaining . . . balance and dra-matic values we all want."

These pressures and an ever-mounting budget exac-erbated the already tense atmosphere between *Lust for Life*'s director and producer. Despite the unavoidable vagaries of location work, Minnelli refused to let any-thing distract him from his Anscocolor brushwork—not even Houseman's need to keep MGM's cumber-some caravan moving at an efficient pace. The two men

OPPOSITE:
1955, Minnelli directing Anthony Quinn and Kirk Douglas in Lust for Life *(1956)*

Van Gogh and Gauguin in Arles. Kirk Douglas and Anthony Quinn in Lust for Life *(1956)*

had previously shown an odd tendency to imitate the emotional timbre of whichever film they were working on, and *Lust for Life* proved no exception. This time, Houseman fell into the role of fuming pragmatist à la Theo, steeled against Minnelli's outbursts of stamp-ing and stuttering—the petulant aesthete who was damned if he'd come in from the fields until his canvas was finished. Prudently, they resolved to keep all squabbles within the family as much as possible. This required more tact than usual, for the *Lust for Life* team was simultaneously starring in a movie of its own—a promotional short Schary had commissioned Jud Kin-berg to shoot during their sojourn abroad, intended to celebrate their seamless teamwork in the service of Van Gogh's legacy.

When not miming sweetness and light for the sake of Kinberg's "Van Gogh: Darkness into Light," House-man hounded Minnelli to speed things up and MGM to do its part to ease his burden. A crucial aspect on

241

The Red Café. Kirk Douglas in Lust for Life *(1956)*

any Minnelli picture was the rapport with his belea-guered art director, which broke down totally on *Lust for Life*. The local expert hired by Houseman balked at executing Minnelli's elaborate visual schemes, to his increasing fury. "I realize that enormous demands are made by Minnelli on an art director," Houseman duly wrote the studio, "but as regards the sets to be designed and built in Culver City, I think you must face the fact that Minnelli categorically refuses to work with Hans Peters and that if Peters remains on the picture we shall have catastrophic trouble. Minnelli's attitude is quite violent and unfortunately not to be changed." MGM promised to put the steadfast Preston Ames at his dis-posal once the *Lust for Life* unit returned home. Min-nelli's admiration for Freddie Young was as vehement as his resentment of Peters, but in this instance the studio was powerless against the Hollywood cinema-tographers' guild's insistence on replacing him with a paid-up local member.

While these battles were being waged by transatlan-tic cable, *Lust for Life* concluded the French leg of its campaign on September 6, with three weeks in the Low Countries still to follow. At Schary's long-distance urging, Minnelli and Houseman huddled en route to pare away at these early episodes in the Van Gogh saga, although some of the most striking material in the picture still remained to be shot. They spent four hurried days filming Douglas and Pamela Brown around the canals of Amsterdam, and in a Dutch studio recreating the *Potato Eaters* tableaux with local extras who bore an astonishing resemblance to the peasants of Van Gogh's time. The troupe then moved to the village of Nuenen, where Van Gogh's father had served

as pastor. Interiors were shot in the original parish house, but the rainy September weather kept inter-rupting Minnelli's efforts to capture the surrounding landscapes. After ten days of fighting the elements, the company packed up for Belgium, with one important Dutch sequence—Vincent's thwarted marriage pro-posal to his cousin Kee—rescheduled for Culver City.

By now harmony was restored between Minnelli and his producer, but this last location nevertheless turned out to be the toughest chapter of the trip. The Borinage of the 1950s remained no less grimy and cheerless than it was when Van Gogh left it—an asset for the picture but cold comfort to *Lust for Life*'s worn-out crew after nearly two months on the road. As a stoic Douglas fought off fatigue and a throat infection, Minnelli spent several obstinate days at the bottom of a mine shaft trying to film Van Gogh's descent among the workers. But finally he gave up after Young insisted the scene was impossible to light; spliced together with the footage they'd taken above ground, this too would be recreated back in Hollywood.

With two days in a Brussels sound stage to round out the Borinage scenes, *Lust for Life*'s European shoot ended at last on September 29. Back in Hollywood, Minnelli picked up where he'd left off exactly a week later. Members of his British-inflected cast were trans-ported to Hollywood to complete their roles, supple-mented by local actors Everett Sloane (Dr. Gachet), Henry Daniell and Madge Kennedy (Van Gogh's par-ents). *Lust for Life* posed a continuity nightmare, cutting from Van Gogh's moonlit wanderings through Arles to his lonely sound-stage digs filmed five thousand miles away and several weeks later. Thanks to the dedication of his star, getting Douglas to sustain his fervor was the least of Minnelli's problems. Behind the camera, he had a mostly new technical crew to contend with, required to fill in the movie's jigsaw gaps in hues identical to those daubed by the craftsmen Minnelli left behind in Europe. To shoot those moody Old World interiors, the studio paradoxically tapped Russell Harlan, whose forte was the wide open spaces of westerns like Howard Hawks' *The Big Sky*. It's a tribute to his virtuosity (plus Minnelli's own keen eye) that, with rare lapses, Harlan's footage blended so imperceptibly into the reels Freddie Young had filmed abroad.

Minnelli meanwhile proved as exacting at home as he'd been on location, taking two additional months to complete *Lust for Life.* Once the sets were struck and the actors dismissed, he concentrated on the film's great inanimate subject—the blowups of the paintings themselves. From the first, Minnelli planned to mingle art and historical incident in a manner that no movie had attempted to date. Such biographies tended toward a doggedly literal-minded approach, with unvarying dissolves from establishing shots of the artist at his easel into the triumphant fadeout on the finished work. Instead, Minnelli sought a terse shorthand to capture the way a painter transforms reality to suit his private vision. Throughout *Lust for Life,* he juxtaposed his recreated 19th-century vistas with flashes of Van Gogh's own resplendent, individual perspectives on what we've just seen, without pausing to explain or editorialize. For months, he and Houseman discussed this intricate, painstaking process, and there was only one editor on MGM's staff whom Minnelli trusted to execute it to his satisfaction—his old ally Adrienne Fazan. At his urging, Houseman campaigned to get her while they were still shooting in Europe, reminding the studio that the movie's "montages and rhythmic patterns and combinations of painting and drama are much like musical numbers." With Fazan at the moviola and *Tea and Sympathy* on hold until he was ready, for once Minnelli had the time to assert his directorial prerogatives and actively participate in the editing.

By mid-January 1956, they had assembled *Lust for Life*'s rough cut—just past the studio's original deadline with Stone, who'd graciously extended it on receiving an additional $35,000 fee. Pleased with the result but worried about its popular reception, Schary nurtured the movie through three sneak previews before releasing it to theaters. At its first screening, *Lust for Life* played well but somewhat sluggishly, which resulted in the excision of a final scene devoted to Van Gogh's funeral. (Norman Corwin was particularly relieved to see this go, telling Schary that "visually, the profusion of flowers makes it look, to me, like a gangster's funeral.") After the second sneak, Schary ordered further small trims, plus retakes on the scene in Theo's Paris apartment in which he defends his scapegrace brother to the starchy owner of the gallery where he

works. With Minnelli by this time midway through *Tea and Sympathy,* George Cukor was summoned to shoot this material, which took less than a week to complete. After its enthusiastic reception at the last preview, Schary pronounced himself satisfied, but Minnelli waged a last campaign to restore a few cut sequences, particularly Gauguin's first scene in Arles, at the Red Café. "I hope that you will look on this not as the petulance of a director wanting to restore some shots which he fancies show him off but as a man who loves this picture and believes in it," he urged in a memo to Schary. "The scene is entertaining. The audience loves Gauguin. He lights up the whole picture when he appears. . . . Most important, the proprietor's 'crazy redhead' talk establishes Van Gogh as the subject of gossip by the townspeople." With *Lust for Life* already running 122 minutes, Minnelli's reasoning didn't sway Schary—the scene stayed on the cutting room floor.

"I wish you luck on commercial success," one patron had scrawled at the third sneak preview. "You already have an artistic one." MGM spent the next several months trying to ensure that the one didn't preclude the other. To trumpet its aesthetic stature, *Lust for Life* was launched in a deliberately un-Metro manner. The world premiere took place at the Edinburgh Arts Festival in August 1956; a September benefit screening for the Metropolitan Museum of Art served as its New York vernissage, preceding a commercial run at the Plaza Theater, which usually favored subtitled imports over Metro's domestic vintage. With this approach aimed at the cultured few, MGM also figured a way to cultivate the philistines. The publicity department came up with a campaign fraudulently hinting that the artist's lust for life was more ecstacy than agony—a lurid "Impressionist" poster of Van Gogh ravishing a tousled model on the floor of his atelier, with a plaster cast of the Venus de Milo posed in the background for inspiration. This was precisely the cliché of bohemian passion its creators had tried so scrupulously to avoid. Minnelli and Houseman were naturally appalled, but had no say in the matter. However, Kirk Douglas took his own form of revenge by confiding to the press that the key to Van Gogh's lonely soul was his latent homosexuality. A furious publicity department ordered the star henceforth to keep his goddamn motivation to himself—*Lust for Life* was going to be a tough enough sell without his help.

Yet no matter how Metro sold it, *Lust for Life* remained an arthouse sensation on a CinemaScope budget. Its critical reception was everything Minnelli and company could have wished, but where the mass audience was concerned, even the rave reviews made the movie sound like a class outing, with the *Christian Science Monitor* citing "Mr. Minnelli's sense of color and pictorial composition" and the *New Yorker* drily praising it as "one of the few films about artists to demonstrate that the camera can follow the lead of those it attempts to portray." The year-end awards enshrined the film as MGM's big prestige item for 1956: Douglas was awarded the New York Film Critics' prize and Quinn subsequently won the Best Supporting Actor Oscar, with additional nominations meted out to Norman Corwin, the art direction team, and *Lust for Life*'s star. But Metro's ledgers showed that Impressionism didn't play so well at drive-ins as it had at the Academy of Motion Picture Arts and Sciences; in its domestic run, the movie earned approximately $1,600,000 in rentals, offset by a comparatively warmer popular reception abroad. *Lust for Life*'s sunburst fadeout also marked the last blaze of glory at MGM for several of its key participants; while the accolades mounted, Schary was ousted by a new Loews Inc. management team, upon which event Houseman also left the studio, to return four years later under less auspicious circumstances. But after a trio of disappointing movies, *Lust for Life* was just the invigorating jolt Minnelli needed to propel him into the most confident phase of his career.

Among art lovers inured to Great Lives as told by Hollywood middlebrows, the very idea of a *Lust for Life* is bound to provoke skepticism. The title alone is bad enough; add to this the prospect of Kirk Douglas gritting his gleaming choppers in CinemaScope while Miklos Rozsa whips the MGM Orchestra to a frenzy, and it portends a lust for showmanship far stronger than any fealty to art. Certainly, the notorious facts of Van Gogh's life were the stuff of celluloid hokum, no matter how austerely painted—his frustrated affairs, his creative self-doubts, and climactic self-mutilation are straight out of some mad-artist Grand Guignol.

In fact, the movie adheres to the basic outline of Van Gogh's final years with unusual fidelity, despite the elisions necessary to any feature film. Yet scrupulous as it is, *Lust for Life* doesn't try for an objective, comprehensive rendering of its subject, any more than *The Bad and the Beautiful* records the craft of moviemaking with newsreel accuracy. Minnelli's enthusiasm for the material prompted a stylistic rigor and consistency remarkable even by his own standards. In turn, his angle of vision shaped Van Gogh's life into a portrait as idiosyncratically his as the painter's own canvases of the farm laborers of Provence. Coming at the midpoint of his career, *Lust for Life* is his most penetrating treatment of the artist, whose bittersweet fate it is to see the world through a different prism than the contented run of ordinary mortals.

While a certain romantic masochism inevitably clings to this archetype, Minnelli stoutly resists sentimentalizing him. His hero is no misunderstood victim of a callous world; prone to inchoate outbursts and heedless monomania, Van Gogh is the one whose social instincts are fatally impaired. (With his voice pitched to an aggressive wheedle, Douglas induces a reflexive cringe every time he speaks.) Vincent's ego-

tism is fueled by an exquisite sensitivity to his own pain, rather than the burden of genius. From his widowed cousin Kee to Paul Gauguin, he repels affection by the blind intensity with which he demands it. Vincent's aesthetic improvidence and weepy emotionalism mark him as a deviant from the prevailing code of masculine behavior. Antithetical impulses confound him at every turn; Van Gogh's longing for the comforts of family life and his empathy for humble miners and peasants and their "nobility of toil" clash with the single-minded pursuit of his solitary (and elitist) profession. He admiringly writes to Theo that the potato-eaters he draws partake honestly of the fruit of their labors; yet so long as Vincent lives, he depends on his brother's largesse to subsidize a painter's life. Work gives Vincent a reason to keep on living, but also propels him to self-destruction, as the gap between what he perceives and his ability to render it faithfully becomes too unbearable to contemplate.

For Minnelli, the need to create is too primal to dissect or comprehend—it's the process of refining that vision that fascinates him. Accordingly, the movie begins almost two-thirds into Van Gogh's life, with the first exploration of his powers at the age of twenty-five while serving as lay preacher in the Borinage. Vincent's headlong immersion in the grime and suffering around him affronts the church, and his tentative charcoal sketches are an outlet for the Christian compassion he's otherwise barred from expressing. From these opening scenes onward, the artist's subjective relationship to his environment becomes *Lust for Life*'s real subject, as Minnelli shows us the world strictly as Van Gogh apprehends it. Until the painter discovers the transfiguring qualities of light and color in his work, Minnelli limits his own spectrum accordingly. Even in sunshine, an impenetrable blue-gray haze hovers over the collieries and slagheaps of the Borinage; with its impasto of dirt over crumbled plaster and the same brackish light angled over his straw pallet, Van Gogh's hovel itself looks like an artful canvas inspired by real-life destitution. In all weathers, the same lush green tone saturates the Dutch farm village where Van Gogh twice retreats to quell his despair; the Hague, scene of his liaison with the prostitute-laundress Christine, is a nighttime place of murky canals and smoke-blackened dives—daylight brings only the dankness of a storm on the beach where he insists on posing his fed-up mistress. From his peasant subjects to the dour ministers and burghers of the Van Gogh family and even the bedraggled Christine, everyone in Vincent's world dresses in black or "the good, dark color of our Dutch earth." Minnelli films these interior scenes in the manner of Flemish genre paintings, with shadows clinging to the whitewashed walls.

Van Gogh's arrival in Paris coincides with an exhibition of Impressionist paintings. Suddenly, Minnelli fills the screen with their exuberant pastels, and after

Wheat field with crows. Kirk Douglas in Lust for Life *(1956)*

forty minutes of subdued Northern tones this is as much a jolt to our senses as it is to Van Gogh's. "If they're right, then everything I've done is wrong," he exclaims to Theo, and sets forth to absorb even more. Apart from the view out of Theo's window, Minnelli doesn't lavish us with Parisian panoramas. His Vincent is dazzled by the fervor of this new, bold artistic circle rather than the place itself, so the city we see is a microcosm of studios and galleries, alternating with radiant closeups of the oils themselves. Minnelli gives us and Van Gogh alike a crash course in the crosscurrents of Impressionism, from Pissarro advising the novice to translate "light into the language of paint" to Seurat putting the finishing touches to . . . *La Grande Jatte* while bragging that "everything I do is worked out in advance, with mathematical accuracy through precise scientific methods." Gauguin is most formidable of all, bellowing, "You are all so busy imitating each other's tricks, you've forgotten what painting is about," as he strides darkly around Père Tanguy's shop.

Unintentionally, these scenes have the musty whiff of the official Salon about them, with Minnelli's bewhiskered bit-part actors striking attitudes of high artistic dudgeon, as they mouth such unwieldy Corwinisms as "Cezanne! King of the Unsaleables!" Fortunately, Minnelli caps it all with a more idiomatic touch. On a grassy bank in the Bois, Gauguin tells his new friend of his single-minded approach to painting, warning him that "friends, comfort, family, if they interfere with your peace to work, you cut them off!" A troubled Vincent listens dubiously, while in the background Minnelli places a tableau that sums up all the

small pleasures Van Gogh has so painfully missed until now—a happy family unit idly enjoying a Sunday picnic together. As Van Gogh leaves for the South "to see nature under a clearer sky," Minnelli concludes this Paris interlude with a shot of Theo face-to-face with Vincent's self-portrait, musing, "I wonder if there'll ever come a happy time for him." Minnelli lingers on the gaunt intensity of that painting, underscoring just how unlikely that prospect is.

Minnelli postpones our view of Provence's clearer sky until Van Gogh discovers it on the spring morning that follows his arrival. This is *Lust for Life*'s one moment of pure lyricism, as tracking shots of dappled branches in blossom shift triumphantly to the artist's glowing blue and white landscapes. As the setting for Vincent's greatest productivity and worst bouts of despair, the Arles sequence summons up Minnelli's most characteristic motifs as well. His montages of Van Gogh at his easel and trudging through the countryside celebrate the physical exertion creative work demands. In *The Bad and the Beautiful*, Douglas as Jonathan Shields bounded muscularly through the sound-stage shadows to pursue his personal muse; his Van Gogh stars in an alfresco variation on the same theme. Where Shields' medium was darkness, Van Gogh is intoxicated by the blazing summer light that fills *Lust for Life*'s Cinema-Scope frame.

All Minnelli's aesthete-protagonists are consumed by their work, but the compulsion drives Van Gogh to breaking point—that place where his genius and illness intersect. *Lust for Life* captures his shifts of mood in the flicker of a dissolve—disrupting the long-shot pastorales of Vincent in the fields with ominous, tight closeups of his sweat-drenched face squinting up at the sun. ''These colors give me an extraordinary exaltation,'' Vincent writes to his brother: ''lemon yellow, sulphur yellow, greenish yellow'': tones that happen to spring naturally from Minnelli's palette as well. But when solitude and fatigue overtake the painter, this sensitivity to color becomes obsessive, cueing Minnelli to saturate the screen with tints of a queasy intensity— deep sapphire for the waters of the bay where Van Gogh paints *Starry Night;* red for the *Night Café* of his absinthe stupors. Minnelli treats the latter painting as his hero's key creation and no wonder—what Vincent describes as its swirls of ''blood red and dark yellow'' are an agonized distortion of the cerise and buttercup hues that haunt Minnelli's more lighthearted fancies elsewhere. Leaping at Gauguin's eye from a pile of Vincent's canvases, or reflected in the looking glass behind the straight-razor quivering in the artist's hand, the *Night Café* is horror intensified by color—a bad dream unrelieved by dance.

Like the central figures in *The Band Wagon, The Bad and the Beautiful,* and even *The Cobweb,* Minnelli's Van Gogh needs the fraternity of others who share his mission. Despite his hope of turning his lonely Yellow House into a haven for other artists, he is destined to remain a community of one, divided against himself. Throughout *Lust for Life,* Vincent self-destructively pursues the very people incapable of returning his devotion, picking at their deepest taboos until they're forced to reject him. With Gauguin's arrival at Arles this pattern reaches its most disastrous phase, for the new object of his suit is his complete temperamental opposite; bluntly practical and allergic to emotional entanglements, Gauguin exudes a masculine self-assurance Van Gogh utterly lacks.

Minnelli shapes their relationship into a desperate same-sex parody of a marriage gone sour. Assuming the part of the clinging, neglected *hausfrau,* Vincent unerringly provokes Gauguin. Their first evening together ends in a squabble over the meaning of art, pitched at the heat of a lovers' quarrel. This passionate dialectic between Gauguin's cult of intellectual control and Van Gogh's flailing emotionalism fizzles to an uneasy truce, but Minnelli's symbolic autumn mistral battering their claustrophobic studio hints at worse to come. In the vineyards, at home, and in the alleyways of the town, Vincent suffocates his housemate with manic philosophical babble, and the deeper into himself Gauguin tries to retreat, the more aggressively the other grabs at him for any human reaction, hostility included. Minnelli plunges the screen into blackness at Gauguin's departure, as Vincent stalks his quarry through the night streets. In silent closeup, his face is a blurred mask of longing and paralyzed rage, rejection festering into self-disgust. Minnelli paints Vincent's subsequent disintegration in the same lurid yellows

and reds the artist had poured into his *Night Café.* The sun-hypnotized artist is mocked by the pale facsimile of a gas globe assaulting his sight three times over: in the deserted street, on his canvas, and finally in the studio lamp that mercilessly exposes his agony to himself. The camera pans from the object of Van Gogh's obsession to Minnelli's special fetish, the mirror, and halts there without a flinch to record Vincent's misery magnified in its gaze. His eyes slammed shut, he presses his skull against his reflection in the vain hope of obliterating it. Unable to bear the sight of himself any longer, he drops from view but the camera stays on the mirror, still reflecting the lamp and the red canvas that symbolize his pain. With a curdled scream, he paces to the mirror once more, blood flowing from his ear in grisly homage to the hues of the *Night Café.*

Minnelli records this torment and the numbed inertia that follows without presuming to parse the cause —the artist's recurring maladies are as intrinsic to him as his talent, and just as inexplicable. *Lust for Life* depicts the final period of Van Gogh's life as the deceptive quiet before the storm, his bursts of creativity inevitably knotting into derangement. Prescribed tranquillity and moderation by the doctors of the asylum at St. Rémy, in resuming work Van Gogh at once embraces life and prefigures his final collapse. As the script spells out too explicitly in an exchange between Vincent and the nun who nurses him, *The Mower* is ''any man struggling in the heat to finish his work. It's the figure of death.'' New canvases fill the screen—serene landscapes at first, succeeded by the whirling brushstrokes of cypresses and shooting stars that foretell another crisis. On a final visit to Theo in Paris, a mirror once again records his collapse, but this time he's just a mote in its distant reflection. At Auvers, Dr. Gachet counsels Vincent that ''work is the only medicine there is,'' but as usual the artist downs an overdose. While Minnelli flings the Auvers paintings at the screen, a letter from Vincent warns his brother that he's working ''in haste from day to day as a miner does when he knows he's facing disaster.''

A canvas of the local town hall decked out for Bastille Day dissolves into a picture of the real thing, which sets the stage for Minnelli to retouch one of his own earlier paintings in a new and bitter light. This small-town celebration conjures up a carefree episode from the *American in Paris* ballet, *pompiers,* skylarking school-kids, carousel and all. But spoiling the joyous symmetry is the hunched figure of Van Gogh, stumbling wretchedly against the carefree tide. While an oompah band delights the crowd filling the sunlit background, Vincent quivers miserably and alone in a shadowy bistro. It's the last succinct view of his fathomless alienation, and in his despair he flees to that fateful wheat field to work. As the crows rise out of nowhere to attack Vincent amid the sun-yellow grain, Minnelli endows the scene with a hallucinatory menace—we see this landscape through the artist's paranoid eye. His frenzied focus on Van Gogh's last burst of concentration is the most plaintive image in the film. Daubing his brush back and forth between the abstract swirls of color on the palette and the anxious strokes on his canvas, Vincent realizes at last that while painting expresses his pain, it won't ever alleviate it. The report of his gun breaks the noonday silence of the half-harvested field. Following the historical record as well as standard Hollywood practice, Van Gogh lingers long enough for a deathbed farewell with his brother, helpless as always to save Vincent from himself. Minnelli closes with an abstract image to transcend the gloom of this denouement—pulling back from *The Mower,* the camera takes in a crazy-quilt collage of Van Gogh's masterpieces until they fill the entire expanse of the panoramic screen. After this sober recording of the suffering that went into it, Van Gogh's legacy is nevertheless a cause for celebration. With his own vibrant pictures, Minnelli paid his subject the highest tribute he could bestow. In *Lust for Life,* Van Gogh becomes that poignant figure "in the bright daylight with the sun flooding everything in a light of pure gold"—the human center of a deeply felt work of art.

1956 TEA AND SYMPATHY

Robert Anderson's play about the tender liaison between a schoolmaster's neglected wife and a persecuted pupil summed up all the odd contradictions in the American theater and its public alike during the postwar years. While passionately proclaiming the right to defy convention for the sake of self-fulfillment, *Tea and Sympathy* itself conformed to every rule of shrewd Broadway stagecraft. Praised for his candor, Anderson's real trump was a flair for shocked, pregnant silences which hinted at those urges nice people knew about but preferred not to discuss out loud. Overnight, his final *coup de théâtre* became the most notorious star curtain line since Blanche Dubois surrendered to the kindness of strangers. Years from then, when playgoers talked about this—and they certainly did—they were very kind indeed. For once Laura started unbuttoning her blouse, the audience could safely embrace the play's hero as well. He was normal all right, just a slightly different kind of normal from the boys who hounded him. In the midst of the McCarthy era, *Tea and Sympathy* deftly channeled liberal anxieties away from the political sphere to matters of personal identity. With homosexuality substituting for Communism, Anderson created the perfect allegory for nice people with clean consciences—a portrait of the innocent falsely accused of committing the unmentionable.

The first hit of the 1953-54 theater season, *Tea and Sympathy*'s cachet was further enhanced by the smart packaging of its premiere production. Under Elia Kazan's direction the play marked Deborah Kerr's New York stage debut after seven years in Hollywood, and she gave the era's definitive portrait of sensitive young matronhood. As a snob hit with an exploitable subject, *Tea and Sympathy* left half of Hollywood with their tongues hanging out, particularly movie executives of Dore Schary's sentimental-progressive bent. Within days of its opening he urged the New York office to sew up the rights, but his request set off warning bells in Loews Inc.'s executive suite.

The hitch was that in the early fifties, what looked mildly daring on Broadway seemed unimaginably outré to the movie industry, still bound by its antiquated Production Code. The first cracks in the system appeared in 1953, when independent producer-direc-

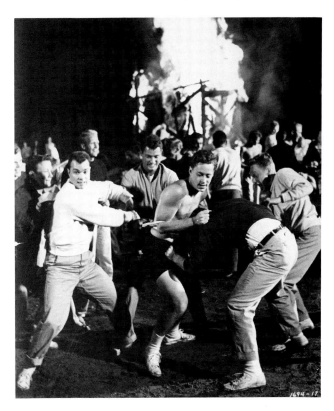

Pariah at the bonfire. John Kerr (center) in Tea and Sympathy *(1956)*

Tom learns to walk like a man. John Kerr and Darryl Hickman in Tea and Sympathy *(1956)*

OPPOSITE:
Lady and the tramp. Deborah Kerr and Norma Crane (left) in Tea and Sympathy *(1956)*

tor Otto Preminger refused to excise that filthy word "virgin" from his Broadway-adapted *The Moon Is Blue,* and released the film with a Condemned rating from the Catholic Legion of Decency, and without an MPAA seal of approval. However, the majors were still too wary of the consequences to follow Preminger's lead. Where *Tea and Sympathy* was concerned, New York informed Culver City that not even Loews' own theater chain would dare book the picture without the sanction of the Production Code.

So began three years of negotiations to reconcile Laura and Tom's illicit romance and the gospel according to the MPAA. Upon MGM's obsequious request, in October 1953, Production Code officials Geoffrey Shurlock and Jack Vizzard left for New York to give the play their expert appraisal, with half their expenses paid by the studio. On their return, Schary got the bad news—in its present form, *Tea and Sympathy* was indeed verboten as screen material. During a conference on the Culver City lot, Vizzard informed Loews' executive Robert Vogel, story department head Kenneth MacKenna, and Schary that "the ending of this story was unacceptable on the grounds that it was a justification of adultery"; worse was the play's homoerotic innuendo, "in view of the fact that the Code forbids even the *inference* of sex perversion." In his notes from that meeting, Vizzard scrupulously recorded MGM's plea of good faith and pure intentions. "Mr. Schary protested that he did not want to bring up the question of homosexuality. He wished rather to center the boy's problem on the fact that he was an 'off-horse' . . . that he was a non-conformist." Schary had a desperate brain-wave, the first of many drafted over the next few years, to sanitize Anderson's smoldering finale. Why couldn't Laura's husband burst in on the couple at the crucial moment, mused Schary, thwarting the act in letter if not in spirit? With the bland acknowledgment that this was "quite a departure from that which the play contains," a skeptical Vizzard advised Schary that his problems had just begun.

MGM might have surrendered, had it not been for a sudden flurry of rival bids from Paramount, John Huston's production company, and—in an ironic example of déjà vu—Samuel Goldwyn. (When he'd set out to film Lillian Hellman's *The Children's Hour* in the thirties, industryites expressed shock that he would make a movie about lesbians. "So," retorted Goldwyn, "we'll turn them into Americans." Which, in fact, is precisely what he did.) Despite Metro's head start, the competition raised the ante to the then-astonishing sum of $400,000, of which $300,000 would be withheld until Anderson turned in a filmable script costing MGM an additional fee of $25,000. The playwright obliged with an eleven-page treatment designed to open up his text for the screen and defuse the censors at the same time. On July 19 1954, MGM announced that *Tea and Sympathy* was theirs; three days later the studio received a note from the ever-vigilant Legion of Decency, warning of dire consequences unless the play were purged of all offense.

These threats notwithstanding, MGM intended to evoke the stage version as faithfully as possible. *Tea and Sympathy* was inconceivable without Deborah Kerr, a major box-office attraction as well as its ideal interpreter. In a break from the usual movie practice, producer Pandro Berman also decided to use her lesser-known New York co-stars—Leif Erickson as her coarse husband, and John Kerr, who'd just played his first woebegone screen teenager in Metro's *The Cobweb*. The new element was Minnelli, summoned by Berman early in his preparations for the film. Apart from the sure rapport they'd established on three prior movies together, no director was more naturally equipped to understand the hero's predicament than he—an unabashed aesthete whose values also collided with the masculine mind-set of his surroundings.

Although Berman assembled his package by January 1955, a long wait loomed before production could start. Following *Tea and Sympathy*'s national tour, Deborah Kerr was scheduled to do the screen version of *The King and I,* while Minnelli's back-to-back commitments on *Kismet* and *Lust for Life* would tie him up through the rest of the year. In the meantime, there was plenty of work in store on the script. The first thing to go was the hint that the schoolmaster's persecution of Tom was prompted by his own closet homosexual instincts. MGM was delighted with Anderson's first complete draft. Thanks to his scrupulous euphemisms and a few carefully placed acts of contrition, Kenneth

MacKenna happily memoed Schary that "only the most narrow interpretation of the Code . . . could possibly deny us approval." But MacKenna's optimism proved sadly unfounded. In a letter dated March 25 1955, Geoffrey Shurlock turned MGM down flat, declaring "the problem of the boy is still fear that he may be a homo-sexual [sic]. And the wife's giving herself to him in adultery still appears to us to violate the Code."

So it was back to the typewriter for Anderson, armed with new instructions from the studio—to satisfy Shurlock, the wages of Laura's sin required her death after all. The playwright spent months struggling with this unwelcome twist in the scenario. In August he wrote Berman and MacKenna, "I am only unhappy about Laura's dying . . . I think she might have become a nurse and very possibly been killed in Korea . . . if she must die. . . . Why haven't all the sordid adulteresses died in the pictures? I think maybe on this point we have given way too far." In this letter Anderson reminded his colleagues, "as you know I have long entertained another idea, which keeps the apology but also keeps her alive." No less weary of truckling to the MPAA's demands, Berman encouraged him to try out this latest compromise.

Anderson thus turned his story into an extended flashback, recalled by the adult Tom during his tenth class reunion. At the end, he encounters his former scourge, now a lonely, hollow-eyed wreck; whereupon the schoolmaster bitterly hands him a note from the long-vanished Laura. In Deborah Kerr's most tremulous tones, she debunks the nostalgic account of their affair which Tom has set down in his successful first novel. The harsh truth is that their careless rapture shattered both her husband's life and Laura's own self-respect; even for Tom this moment of weakness was wrong, terribly wrong, a descent to base instinct when patience and time would have cured all his problems. After all the pressures of the past year, Anderson's solution utterly contradicted everything that preceded it; the only consolation was that if he hadn't played along, the studio would have been forced to come up with something even worse. Berman summoned him west to pitch his new ending personally to the MPAA, and, as MGM had hoped, this gesture did the trick. In September, Geoffrey Shurlock affirmed that with these changes *Tea and Sympathy* indeed met the demands of the Code, subject to a final perusal of the completed film.

Minnelli was thousands of miles away during this last stage of maneuvers, pursuing the spirit of Vincent Van Gogh in the South of France. With the first cut of *Lust for Life* assembled in mid-January 1956, the exhausted director took a six-week break from studio duties—his first paid vacation in six years. On return, he and Anderson spent a month together for one last polish on the script, trying to make something palatable out of that accursed coda. After two years of behind-the-scenes hassles, the filming of *Tea and Sympathy* that spring came as something of an anticlimax—at just over six weeks it took less time to shoot than any of Minnelli's other dramatic features. Having performed the play together several hundred times, *Tea and Sympathy*'s stars didn't need much coaching from Minnelli to get to the heart of the matter. Compared to his logistical nightmares on *Lust for Life*, conjuring up a New England campus in Hollywood was almost a holiday in itself. Apart from a few days' location work at the beach and a nearby country club, Minnelli didn't even have to leave the studio.

Nevertheless, with Anderson's help he opened up the action considerably, finding new ways to dramatize the contrast between Laura's comforting hearth and the harassment Tom endures whenever he ventures outside. A spectacular example was the pagan frenzy of the school's homecoming bonfire, shot over several nights on the backlot in the manner of the Halloween sequence from *Meet Me in St. Louis*. Minnelli lavished particular care on the scene of Tom's humiliating failure with the town trollop—alluded to on stage but not shown. He turned it instead into the film's cathartic moment, goading a reluctant John Kerr to writhe into a froth of masochistic agony. But, as on Broadway, everything led up to Laura's redemptive embrace. With a great part of the plot necessarily confined to the student residence hall, Minnelli felt that this of all scenes called for a more evocative setting. His inspiration was a mist-filtered sound-stage glade worthy of *Green Mansions*—a poetic touch its wistful hero might well appreciate, but a bit overripe as far as Anderson was concerned.

Six weeks after Minnelli wrapped up *Tea and Sympathy* it was ready for the usual sneak preview ritual, which went smoothly despite the imposed note of repentance at the end. The first audience seemed oblivious to the movie's purported shock value ("A lot of cute boys," gushed one patron. "John Kerr is very much like James Dean."), but once again the censors stepped in to shield the public from corruption. The

MPAA demanded a six-line cut in the love scene, that the studio wheedled down to four. The Legion of Decency complained instead about the movie's sins of omission. Unless the epilogue were amended to stress the boy's guilt as well, *Tea and Sympathy* would receive a Condemned rating; even with a Production Code seal, this would scare off the big theater circuits. Anderson had no choice but to submit. This new cloud provoked an intercontinental flurry of calls and cables as the speech bounced from the reluctant playwright in New York to the studio for Schary's approval, then on to London for Deborah Kerr to loop during her holiday abroad before landing back in Hollywood as a new splice on the soundtrack.

However, Anderson's draft wasn't stern enough to suit the Catholic board, which then proposed penning a version of its own. MGM's New York office was willing to do anything to take the heat off, but Berman had reached the end of his patience. "The last reel of this picture will be ridiculous and in my opinion should be laughed at by audiences," he furiously cabled Arthur Loew in New York. "It is a sad state of affairs when they can not only tell us what to say but how to say it and write propaganda in their language to disseminate for them . . . I wish we could accept their C rating and keep our pride." Already immersed in work on *Designing Woman*, Minnelli let his producer do the screaming for both of them. Two days later Anderson added his voice to the chorus. "If we give in on this, for me, I never want to see the picture again," he lamented, "and will consider it a very sad and sour conclusion to an otherwise wonderful experience." To their relief Loews Inc. called the Legion's bluff and won a B rating ("Morally Objectionable in Part for All"), a lesser taint they could all live with. Anderson told Loew he was "heartened by your courage," but after all their compromises, this victory had a distinctly hollow ring.

Ten days after *Lust for Life*'s gala premiere further uptown, *Tea and Sympathy* opened at last at Radio City Music Hall. Naturally, the critics made sarcastic merry over the Production Code's restrictions, with *Time* magazine noting, "the censor seems in most instances to have used the fig leaf for its own eye patch." *Tea and Sympathy* nevertheless remained the kind of movie the metropolitan press instinctively favored—a deep genuflection toward that superior medium, the theater. Thus it won wide praise as the latest of Hollywood's baby steps toward maturity, with Minnelli lauded in the *Herald Tribune* as elsewhere for his "quiet and compassionate" treatment of Anderson's theme. Actually, in the wake of its advance word, all that quiet compassion may well have come as a letdown to many moviegoers; while doing respectable trade, *Tea and Sympathy* created no special sensation at the nation's box offices. Against a total cost of $1,818,688, it earned rentals of $2,184,558 plus an additional million abroad. Whetted by the visceral thrills of Minnelli's more flamboyant pictures, the European press had a hard time understanding what the fuss had been about. Compared to *Lust for Life,* it seemed rather a tempest in a teapot after all.

Of all Minnelli's 1950s dramas, *Tea and Sympathy* is most purely a time-capsule relic of its era. Like the original play, it shrewdly mines that decade's primal anxieties—the fear of having one's life ruined by unjust accusations, of not fitting in with the lonely crowd. As *Tea and Sympathy* would have it, Tom's predicament is distressing precisely because at heart he's a "regular fellow" who doesn't deserve the scorn he attracts. Tom isn't really effeminate at all (much less h-m-s-x-al)— just shy, sensitive, and intellectual, which admittedly in those times were qualities almost as suspect. (In fact, as played by John Kerr, the hero's worst offense against convention seems to be congenital lethargy.)

From the depths of his cultivated soul, Minnelli clearly relishes exposing the he-men who make Tom's life so miserable as the idiots they are. He directs the boy's schoolmates as a kind of masculine-hysteric geek chorus—always roughhousing in bare-chested packs, noisy and messy and puerile. As exemplars of male middle-age, their admiring elders are no less contemptible. Tom's father, played in a perpetual cold sweat by Edward Andrews, is craven and emotionally constipated, and Laura's husband Bill all extrovert bloat and bluster. (Minnelli's disdain for Bill's type shows through perhaps too overtly in Erickson's performance; he's so boorish it's impossible to divine how a sensitive soul like Deborah Kerr's Laura could have married him in the first place.) The overt heterosexuality of the students and alumni of Chilton Prep is indistinguishable from closet misogyny, or worse. Normal means sexually segregating themselves from the women at the local beach, and the peak of good clean fun is the victory Bonfire and Pajama Fight, in which the seniors strip the nightclothes off the compliant new boys. According to the convoluted logic of this varsity drag, it's a privilege reserved for real guys; the hero's garments remain intact until his roommate Al takes pity on him and jumps in to save Tom's honor by ripping his pajamas to shreds.

Appalled, Minnelli devotes the first half of *Tea and Sympathy* to this nonsense, and so long as he concentrates on the forces arrayed against Tom, the movie is insidiously entertaining. One by one, he enumerates the arbitrary strictures of butch behavior—crewcuts and team sports as opposed to tousled hair plus a solitary taste for classical music, and constant vigilance lest your true nature reveal itself. In the political climate of the day, the movie's most daring scene hints at broader issues than the mere false charge of unmanliness: Laura confronts Tom's one wavering chum, asking how he would like it if she decided to spread innuendos about him. "How easy it is to smear a person," Laura muses, reminding him that one whispered allu-

sion to "suspicious characteristics" and you're blackballed (or red-baited) from the charmed circle of conformists. At the same time, Minnelli sees the bleak humor in all this, particularly when Al sets out to show the bewildered Tom how a real man walks; considering his own lolling gait, the director might well have deliberated taking some lessons of his own.

This sequence takes place in the school's music conservatory, under an imperious bust of Beethoven. Throughout his expository Act I, Minnelli gracefully frees the text from the stage play's constraints, although sharp-eyed movie devotees might well recognize the boundaries of the MGM backlot. (The exclusive prep school's main hall is the same red-brick Victorian pile that housed *The Cobweb*'s inmates; the rest of the campus is strictly Arthur Freed U., former home of *Best Foot Forward* and *Good News.*) Nevertheless, this group portrait of teenaged tyranny is blunted by Anderson's tentative grasp of the vernacular, sanitized further by the demands of the Production Code. Discarding those riper epithets permitted on Broadway, the worst thing Tom's persecutors can come up with is the oft-repeated "Sister Boy," an odd locution if there ever was one.

Unfortunately, as the conflict builds, *Tea and Sympathy*'s proscenium-archness asserts itself ever more insistently. By now Minnelli is hard-pressed for excuses to venture outside Laura's sitting-room and, worse yet, he can't get the sitting-room gentility out of his lead actress. MGM's unusual fealty to the original stage cast curiously backfires here; having played the part for so long, Deborah Kerr strains to bring fresh cadences to her lines, with the perverse result that Laura's impassioned moral rectitude sounds more stilted than ever. Her plummy vowels and long metronomic pauses turn a phrase like "Manliness is also tenderness . . . and gentleness . . . and . . . consideration," into a solo dirge for unaccompanied cello. Part of the problem is Minnelli's notion of what becomes a lady most; somehow his movies tend to equate refinement with a kind of plaster-cast poise. Kerr's rhetorical inflections are further exposed by the slightly adenoidal underplaying of our hero. If her great lady mannerisms go over the top, her co-star is an actor who fails utterly to command the screen, as John Kerr's lackluster subsequent career attested.

With the censors hovering anxiously at their backs, Laura and Tom's long-awaited clinch generates no sparks at all; Mrs. Reynolds keeps that cardigan buttoned while the dazed boy reclines in Minnelli's misty column of forest-cathedral light. The director does what he can to take the curse off that despised coda, filling the screen with rustling autumn leaves and the mournful chords of a Mozart violin concerto, but it's really beyond hope. However righteously it condemns the hypocrisy of bigots, in the end *Tea and Sympathy*'s courage is as frail as its own digestible little convictions.

• •

1958   **SOME CAME RUNNING**

In 1951, James Jones made one of the most startling literary debuts of the post-war era with *From Here to Eternity,* his novel about barracks life in Hawaii on the eve of World War II. Jones' best-seller won the National Book Award and subsequently became a celebrated movie, prompting great speculation as to what this much-hyped first-novelist would do for an encore. The answer was six years in coming—a weighty opus whose veiled subject was Jones' own second-book slump. Its hero, Dave Hirsh, is a dissolute writer just discharged from the Army, who makes a misbegotten odyssey back home to Parkman, Illinois (Indiana in the film), a cheerless hamlet rather like the one that spawned Jones. Over the next three years and twelve hundred-odd pages, Hirsh tussles with the suffocating midwestern boosterism of his elder brother Frank, a bad case of *nostalgie de la boue* compelling him to hook up with tawdry Ginny of the local brassiere factory, and the chilly call of the mind embodied by town intellectual Gwen French, whose sexual urge is as blocked as Dave's muse.

Nearly a year before *Some Came Running* emerged off Scribner's presses, the publisher dispatched a terse synopsis to Hollywood. Hoping, as did Scribner's, that lightning would strike twice for Jones, MGM snatched up the movie rights in January 1957 with a bid of $250,000. By its November publication date, the book's advance fanfare as a thinking man's *Peyton Place* was drowned out by a chorus of catcalls from the nation's book reviewers. With near unanimity, they derided it as a self-indulgent wallow in gross excesses of every sort, gaseous philosophizing included. Nevertheless, MGM remained convinced that there was a vivid big-screen melodrama buried somewhere under Jones' verbiage. Sol C. Siegel, a high-profile producer recently elevated to Schary's former post, resolved to supervise the film himself. Two screenwriters were assigned the unenviable task of turning *Some Came Running* into a feature-length script—John Patrick, late of such contrastingly frothy Siegel entertainments as *High Society* and *Les Girls,* and Arthur Sheekman.

Metro originally announced that Glenn Ford would star in the film. While Ford was a perfectly plausible actor for the part, at some point Siegel had an even better box-office idea. Five years before, *From Here to Eternity* had sparked Frank Sinatra's meteoric screen comeback, establishing him for the first time as a forceful dramatic performer. In successive serious pictures like *The Man with the Golden Arm* and *The Joker Is Wild,* Sinatra distinguished himself as a self-destructive misfit, on the James Jones model. Having recently signed to do three films for MGM, the star agreed to launch the deal with *Some Came Running* (as a reflection of his

increasing clout, Sinatra's fee was a then-resounding $400,000 against ten percent of the gross).

This was the package Siegel proffered Minnelli in the spring of 1958, as he returned from the French shoot of *The Reluctant Debutante.* Added to the attraction of directing a star of Sinatra's caliber, Jones' hero was Minnelli's favorite male archetype—the artist divided against himself. MGM wanted to get *Some Came Running* in motion as quickly as possible, so Minnelli drew up an unusually tight production schedule—six months from preliminary script to a Hollywood premiere in time for Oscar consideration at the end of 1958. June and July were spent securing the rest of the players and preparing for a midsummer start on location.

Minnelli sought a troupe both congenial to Sinatra and compatible with the small-time low-lifes and provincial burghers of Jones' book. Chief among the former is the hero's boon companion, an itinerant gambler named 'Bama Dillert. Sinatra crony Dean Martin had just made his dramatic debut in *The Young Lions,* and Minnelli thought his languid irony would also suit *Some Came Running.* He went farther afield in quest of the film's wayward female lead. In the book, Ginny is the receptacle for all of Jones' misogynist contempt—a dimwitted slut as physically unappetizing as she is morally deficient. There were no obvious Ginnys among Hollywood's well-groomed female stars, but then in 1958, Shirley MacLaine was not yet quite of the latter company. Under contract to producer Hal Wallis, she'd run the gamut from Jerry Lewis' love interest in *Artists and Models* to the screen's least likely Hindu princess in *Around the World in 80 Days* on loan-out to Mike Todd, without finding a niche for her unconventional looks and offhandedly gauche acting style.

However, Minnelli thought her youthful eccentricity could lend poignance to Jones' female albatross, abetted by a generous suggestion from Sinatra—a shift in the story's violent conclusion making Ginny rather than *Some Came Running*'s hero the victim of an assassin's bullet. MGM was delighted with Minnelli's casting inspiration, in part because at that stage in her career MacLaine commanded less than a tenth of what Sinatra had cost. Most of this paltry sum went to Wallis in any case, and to pique the producer MacLaine put off her arrival on the *Some Came Running* set until the last moment. Without benefit of the usual battery of makeup tests, Minnelli was forced to improvise Ginny's bedraggled Kewpie-doll look on the spot. Nevertheless, MacLaine seized this opportunity with enormous zest. *Some Came Running* launched her as Hollywood's lovable hoyden, a 1950s child-woman somewhat lower on the evolutionary scale than the blithe continental gamine patented by Audrey Hepburn.

Meanwhile, *Some Came Running* offered new challenges to Minnelli as well. After spending so much of his time on location in Europe, this was his chance to rediscover America from atop his camera boom. Until recently, the movie's small-town atmosphere would have been counterfeited on the backlot as a matter of course. But the expansive horizons of the Cinema-Scope era broadened audience expectations as well—by the late fifties, authentic backgrounds were fast becoming the rule, with sound-stage fakery an increasingly conspicuous anachronism. Hence, after scanning the Mid-West for a suitably evocative setting, in August MGM dispatched the *Some Came Running* company to Madison, Indiana, for three weeks of exteriors.

This was a curious semi-homecoming for Minnelli, who'd made his own precocious escape from an Ohio town similar to this without a backward glance. Blessed now with a return ticket to Hollywood, he trained an avid eye on Madison's scruffy downtown of brick storefronts and bar-and-grills, and the manicured residential quarters of the town's country-club set. During the war, its inhabitants had starred in an O.W.I. documentary as the model American community, but

Ginny entertains. Frank Sinatra, Shirley MacLaine, Dean Martin, Carmen Phillips in Some Came Running *(1958)*

that was nothing compared to the excitement of greeting an MGM unit in full pomp. As a mere director, Minnelli was left alone to ferret out his impressions, but for *Some Came Running*'s more conspicuous personalities this Indiana sojourn turned into an extremely confining few weeks in another town. Sinatra and his entourage encamped in a house adjacent to the motel overrun by the rest of the movie crew. With MacLaine tagging along as female mascot, between working hours they holed up for the sort of marathon male bonding Dave and 'Bama indulge in throughout *Some Came Running*'s script. Meanwhile, Sinatra was besieged from all sides by curious (and often amorous) locals, triggering outbursts from the star that startled both the town fathers and the members of the press who converged on Madison to cover the shoot.

Minnelli ignored these peripheral tensions in his customary manner, but his matter-of-fact immersion in the task at hand finally collided with Sinatra's rising pique. For *Some Came Running*'s climax, Minnelli had planned something to rival the *Bovary* ball and Lana's smash-up for centrifugal excitement—a brass-scored, neon-lit carnival concluding not with a sound-stage samba as in *Yolanda and the Thief,* but in an alfresco hail of bullets. Madison's main street was rigged with working props assembled from circuses and amusement parks throughout the region. Conspicuous among these was a huge Ferris wheel, around which Minnelli had carefully choreographed the accelerating tensions of the scene. Despite hours of shuffling hundreds of extras and his stellar trio about like chessmen, to Minnelli's dismay the glittering tableau he had in mind refused to fall into place. Suddenly the director had his brainstorm—dismantle everything and move

the Ferris wheel six feet. Minnelli thought he'd found the perfect practical solution to a visual problem, but after cooling his heels half the night, it was just a psychotic whim to Sinatra. He stormed off the set in a fury, and it took all Minnelli's powers of diplomacy to get him to return for the offending shots, and in fact complete the picture at all.

Tempers cooled once they returned to California for the last seven weeks of production. Eager to restore harmony with his star, Minnelli accommodated Sinatra's night-owl habits by adopting a noon-to-eight p.m. work regimen for the rest of the shoot. Thanks to this comparative innovation, he managed to wrap up the picture on October 21, six days ahead of schedule. Despite the longueurs of its source, *Some Came Running* prompted none of the editing-room struggles that had buffeted *The Cobweb, Lust for Life,* and *Gigi.* The Patrick–Sheekman script deftly telescoped the action from three years to several weeks, meanwhile paring away the novel's digressive flashbacks and peripheral characters; under the circumstances, at 134 minutes *Some Came Running* was a model of streamlined storytelling.

By December 4, Adrienne Fazan had completed the final cut in time for a highly successful sneak preview. After its Oscar-qualifying Los Angeles engagement, the movie opened at Radio City Music Hall in January 1959 to the most divided reception earned by a Minnelli drama since *Undercurrent.* The strangest rebuke came from the *Saturday Review,* baffled that a literary light like *Some Came Running*'s hero could be prey to such gutter habits as drinking, gambling, and consorting with tramps. While praised in some quarters, Min-

Death stalks the carnival.
Steven Peck in Some Came
Running *(1958)*

A B O V E :
Lady and the tramp II.
Shirley MacLaine and
Martha Hyer in Some Came
Running *(1958)*

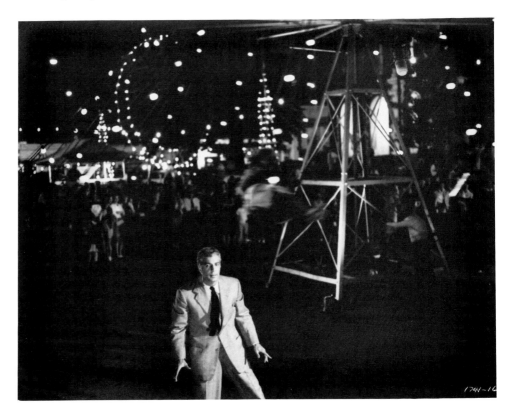

nelli's own stylistic contradictions came in for more general licks. The movie's deliberate blend of psychological portraiture and unabashed melodrama confused those reviewers who expected serious directors to express themselves in somber half-tones. *Some Came Running*'s audacious finale invited the most blistering attacks of all, with Bosley Crowther lamenting that Minnelli had to "hoke up" an absorbing story with "grotesque action and phantasmagoric stuff with colored lights." Yet compared to the novel's scathing press the critical consensus here was practically triumphant, with better news still to come. With four nominations for *Some Came Running* added to *Gigi*'s nine, Minnelli dominated the 1958 Academy Awards competition in breathtaking fashion, and the film enjoyed solid commercial success at domestic box-office returns of $4,500,000 against a $3,161,021 budget. Among its lesser distinctions, *Some Came Running* spurred a siege of so-called Rat Pack movies featuring various permutations of the Sinatra–Martin–MacLaine clique, which exploited the popular legend of their offscreen camaraderie with increasing self-consciousness. For Minnelli, the movie demonstrated a flair for contemporary Americana as distinctive as his take on fin-de-siècle France. Within a few months, he would once again set out for the hinterlands, pursuing the even darker vision of *Home from the Hill.*

Like the novel which inspired it, *Some Came Running* is the prodigal's revenge on the caste-ridden backwater that spawned him. The difference is that Minnelli substituted his own jaundiced imagery for Jones' tortured verbiage—while only marginally subtler, the movie is infinitely more digestible. From *Lust for Life* onward, Minnelli's farflung travels infused his work with a renewed vigor, and *Some Came Running* demonstrated that no locale was too prosaic to stimulate his eye. Out of a few panoramas spanning the downtown hub of an ordinary midwestern county seat, Minnelli builds an atmosphere of stifling melancholy and foreboding which pervades even those interiors shot later in Culver City. The hungover contempt with which the prodigal black sheep regards his erstwhile home town goes double for *Some Came Running*'s director, who had also escaped before inertia got the better of his wanderlust.

Some Came Running is a particularly lively example of that 1950s movie staple, the Hollywood melodrama as pop anthropology. Its acute sense of place mirrors the looming contrasts of the social terrain Minnelli surveys. In their colonnaded houses high above the town, the prosperous elect like Dave's brother Frank lead lives of well-heeled anxiety, terrified lest some unconscious misstep tumble them from their perch. Meanwhile, the drifters, drunks, and other proles spend their idle hours tanking up at a grubby downtown bar and clandestine poker mill. If the gentlemen of Parkman, Illinois, are distinguished from the inferior classes by their tight white collars and hearty air of industry, their

women belong entirely to two distinct species: ladies, recognizable by their immaculate grooming and impenetrable frigidity, and trollops, whose status is advertised by their tight garments, lax grammar, and what-the-hell morals. Theoretically, the twain never meet, and when Ginny pays a surprise call on Gwen French in her classroom, the CinemaScope screen is barely wide enough to encompass them both. In practice, there's a special limbo reserved for those respectably raised young females depraved enough to acknowledge their own erotic stirrings, much less indulge them; once caught, they suffer immediate banishment and permanent disgrace. This is the fate which greets Frank Hirsh's restless secretary after an ill-advised foray with her boss to the local Lover's Lane, and which his teen-aged daughter Dawn barely averts thanks to her Uncle Dave's intervention. Well-traveled hipster though he is, as a self-styled "expert on tramps" there are certain codes even Dave respects—namely, that none of his own flesh and blood should turn into one. By his own sodden example, Dave demonstrates that a self-declared bum can still sport the instincts of a gentleman.

This psychosexual schizophrenia was something of a given in the 1950s, which Minnelli tacitly perpetuated in movies like this one, *Tea and Sympathy,* and *Home from the Hill.* Now as then, the contrast between the relative naturalism of *Some Came Running*'s setting and its broadly sketched characters disconcerts many viewers. A certain amount of exaggeration naturally comes with the territory; more to the point, these Babbitts and the lower orders represent the call of opposites tugging at *Some Came Running*'s morbidly passive hero. A semi-alcoholic lapsed intellectual—his credentials established by a closeup of the Portable Editions of Steinbeck, Faulkner, and Wolfe lying atop his GI duffel bag—Dave Hirsh spends the entire picture shuttling uneasily between two parallel worlds, at home in neither. Affluent jeweler Frank Hirsh (Arthur Kennedy) and wife Agnes (Leora Dana) are an appalling pair, given to gooey endearments before company and venomous hisses on the rare moments that they're trapped alone together. Obsessed with appearances and fanatically self-absorbed, the Hirshes are incapable of sincere thought or deed; the one thing that affords Frank a residue of sympathy is his hangdog randiness, which brittle Agnes could never stoop to satisfy.

Dave's raffish cronies are a much livelier bunch—evident right away from their snappy haberdashery. Sporting a white Stetson permanently atilt on his head and Dean Martin's best whiskey-drenched drawl, 'Bama is a cynical philosopher/cardsharp for whom most men are fools and all women pigs. His contempt extends to his own future, dissolving in the bottom of a bottle; apart from poker, 'Bama's one gift is a talent for friendship with a rare kindred spirit like Dave. As for Ginny, in outline she's merely that hoariest of theatrical conceits, the dim doxy of boundless heart.

"What am I, a tramp or something?" bleats the tousled pickup after a night sprawled out in the Greyhound bus that brought Dave from Chicago to Parkman. It's strictly a rhetorical question, and the laugh is predictably on her. True to her breed, Ginny carries the tackiest accessories this side of Stella Dallas —moulting boas, sateen souvenir pillows, and best of all a purse in the shape of a floppy-eared hound. There's a mutt-like quality in her abject adoration for Dave as well; too dumb to dissemble, Ginny is the only person in the world of this movie who aims to please, and means what she says. Gradually, Minnelli molds her from the butt of sniggery jokes to a sad symbol of female masochism. He willingly distorts the dramatic line of the picture's second half to showcase Ginny's pathos and, not incidentally, the emotional virtuosity of his star. *Some Came Running* offers MacLaine a succession of Oscar-begging arias in both major and minor keys. Ginny's impromptu drunken chorus of "After You've Gone" in a Terre Haute nitery also prompts Minnelli's most playful use of wide screen and depth of focus, highlighting MacLaine's ear-bending torch against the smooth harmonies of the boy trio hired to keep the patrons happy. Ginny soon runs the gamut from exhibitionism to self-sacrifice to utter abasement. "Dave, be in love with me," she begs, with MacLaine squeezing her eyes shut while crushing her co-star in an excess of desperate affection. Grateful that this outburst has momentarily stanched his sarcasm, Ginny shows her devotion by tidying up the masculine squalor of his furnished room. "Butcha gotta remember, I'm human," she chirps while pitching into her new-found chores. Ginny may remain defiantly bigger than life, but this is a plea Minnelli takes very much to heart.

Where *Some Came Running* stumbles badly is in the depiction of Ginny's opposite number—the schoolteacher whose sexual reserve stirs Dave like a perverse aphrodisiac. With her fine mind, distinguished lineage, and cultivated taste in literature, Gwen French is supposed to represent all the civilized values which lie dormant in Dave until he can give up his dissipated ways and regain a measure of self-confidence. Yet reflecting an era when intellectuals were viewed as oddities at best, *Some Came Running* pitches some peculiar notions about the way academic types talk and behave. Characteristically, Minnelli marks the Frenches as creatures apart by their distinctive taste in interior design. With pardonable pride, Gwen ushers Dave into their favorite room in the family manse—a hybrid kitchen/hearth/library whose mixture of first editions and copper pots is a madcap tribute to the principle of *mens sana* in *House Beautiful.*

At home in this domain, Gwen's father is the soul of high-domed bonhomie, given to such locutions as "Let me fix you a martini that's pure magic." Yet he's positively plain-spoken compared to his corseted offspring. Apparently, sexual deprivation combined with a high

IQ have done strange things to Gwen's syntax, compelling her to say things like, "Your hands on me aren't the least persuasive," as she intercepts a forward pass from the frustrated hero. Throughout, Martha Hyer plays Gwen like a pod-person refugee from *Invasion of the Body Snatchers*—as though an inhibited libido were some exotic form of shellshock.

Minnelli can't seem to decide whether Gwen's stubborn chastity is admirable or aberrant—unlike Jones, who concluded his novel with Gwen's visit to a gynecologist to be clinically deflowered once and for all. Nevertheless, her deadpan propriety raises a subversive chuckle at the most inappropriate moments, particularly when she compliments Dave on "his very exciting talent" while he's bent on a more primal form of stimulation. This inadvertent double-entendre puts an extra spin on the heady seduction scene which follows, with Gwen sobbing in silhouette while Dave picks the hairpins out of her schoolmistress's bun. Repulsed by Dave's wild ways and her own heretofore untapped sensuality, Gwen eventually breaks off their relationship, an act which serves as an ironic mirror image of Dave's mistreatment of Ginny. However, Gwen's thoroughgoing weirdness takes all the poignance out of the situation; even in the giddy realm of romantic melodrama, love is rarely so blind as the hero's unrequited yen for this chilly schoolmarm.

Fortunately once she's dispensed with the movie regains its momentum. Dave's impulsive wedding to Ginny recalls the dispirited nuptial scene in *The Clock*, with the bride again languishing for a kiss that never comes. Their union takes place against the backdrop of the Parkman centennial carnival, which, like the amusement park climax of Hitchcock's *Strangers on a Train*, serves as an incongruously giddy setting for sudden death. Minnelli sets up the premise for his paroxysmal finale at the beginning of the film; for all his passivity, Dave unwittingly attracts violence, whether at the hands of Ginny's discarded boyfriend or the knife-wielding loser in one of 'Bama's poker games. Yet the movie's sudden shift in style comes as an audacious jolt. For his climax, Minnelli hurtles the movie from melodrama to the realm of nightmarish abstraction—it's like "The Girl Hunt" ballet shot with real bullets.

A blast of brass on the sound track announces the would-be killer, knocking back his booze in a choreographed rictus of depravity while Minnelli fills the screen with a blaze of red light. It's the kind of stylized moment which could only be confected on a sound stage, or so one assumes—until the camera pans a few feet to reveal the main street of this Indiana town in full festive pomp. Minnelli's most stunning brand of applied artifice follows, as he turns this real place into a CinemaScope hallucination. While frantically cutting between the hunter and his unsuspecting quarry, Minnelli crams his frame with disquieting contrapuntal movements—spinning lights and milling crowds and carnival roustabouts setting up their booths, all aswirl in his breathless lateral tracking shots. Juxtaposed with the stalking gunman, Minnelli's carnival pastimes acquire an encroaching sense of peril—flashes of light from a shooting gallery, a merry-go-round casting ghostly shadows against a lavender wall, the adenoidal tout pitching her slice-and-dice French fry contraption. Insidiously, favorite cherry reds and yellows become the colors of rage and danger. After this propulsive build-up the denouement is chillingly sudden, with Ginny flung lifelessly to the ground like a discarded puppet. The whole sequence is masterfully designed to exploit the horizontal proportions of the wide screen, culminating in its last sorrowful images—Dave gently arranging Ginny's body in an attitude of repose, her head at rest on the cushion he bought her during their spree in Terre Haute.

Minnelli dissolves from neon-pierced darkness to daylight for *Some Came Running*'s brief epilogue, but the despair lingers nonetheless. The mourners at Ginny's funeral stand alone in silence, contemplating her pointless death and the loneliness that confronts them all. The movie ends on a tentative note of transcendence, as Minnelli tracks past the funeral to fade out on a stone angel monument gazing down on the green valley below. Of all his tortured characters, Ginny is the lucky one, for death has granted her a measure of peace which will forever elude her survivors. *Some Came Running* may be pulp fiction, but Minnelli's eye gives it a sense of amplitude its sprawling source never achieved.

1960

HOME FROM THE HILL

Hollywood's taste for probing the hidden anxieties in small-town family life dates back at least to the 1942 *Kings Row*; however, by the late fifties this trend had escalated into an obsession, magnificent or otherwise. Amplified from mass marketed novels onto the magnetic tracks of the panoramic screen, movies like *Written on the Wind, Peyton Place,* and *No Down Payment* were the studios' titillating antidote to that complacent prime-time vision of American domesticity the networks beamed into living rooms week after week. While television celebrated wise moms and befuddled dads antiseptically cohabiting on Anystreet, U.S.A., the domestic miseries of these Hollywood movies had a specific address, and somehow sex lay at the root of them all. In these scenarios, New England villages and Texas hamlets were the usual geographic magnets for sin, with some competition from California's new suburban Levittowns. As the town fathers succumbed either to booze or satyriasis, their wives' frustrations congealed into pure contempt; meanwhile, to substitute for those nurturing bonds long since dissolved at home, the members of a bewildered younger generation tumbled into plenty of trouble of their own.

It was a far cry from the tepid platitudes of Mickey-and-Judy, which may help explain why MGM took so long to catch up with the era's favorite brand of melodrama. While *Some Came Running*'s setting and subplot used certain of these elements, *Home from the Hill* was the first Metro film to assemble all the staples of the genre. Its source was a first novel by William Humphrey, set in the east Texas of his birth; published in 1957, the book earned a warm welcome from the literary establishment, who dubbed Humphrey a promising acolyte in the Faulkner school of virile, evocative regionalism. More to the point where Hollywood was concerned, *Home from the Hill*'s chronicle of a divided family's poisoned legacy read like lively screen material. MGM's story department eagerly recommended the book to the studio's executives, who purchased it in January 1958 for $45,000 plus a small cut of the profits, a month after Knopf's publication date.

Once the rights were secured, Sol Siegel added the film to his own production schedule, to follow *Some Came Running.* The studio originally thought of Clark Gable as the ideal match for *Home from the Hill*'s hypermasculine patriarch, Wade Hunnicutt, whose Texan *droits de seigneur* extend from wild game to loose females. Although no longer under contract to MGM and by then in his late fifties, Gable remained one of the industry's most formidable stars. Meanwhile, the book's literary lineage clearly influenced Siegel's choice of screenwriters for this project; having just shaped a pair of Faulkner stories into the popular hit *The Long, Hot Summer* at 20th Century-Fox, the married team of Irving Ravetch and Harriet Frank Jr. were summoned to MGM to work on *Home from the Hill.*

Their adaptation updated the period from the 1930s to the present, and gave a conciliatory inflection to the story's coda as balm for Humphrey's tone of inexorable tragedy. Wade and his disdainfully genteel wife, Hannah, play out their marital miseries in a tug-of-war over son Theron, himself an unlucky mixture of their irreconcilable natures. In the book, Wade had also spawned innumerable bastard offspring, and the Ravetches' main innovation was to combine these into the newly minted character of Rafe, the film's most resilient figure and a vital dramatic contrast to the pallid Hunnicutt heir. Siegel wanted Minnelli for *Home from the Hill* from the first, but it was the Ravetches' contribution that convinced him to accept; as far as he was concerned, their script considerably enhanced a problematical novel. This film and *The Long, Hot Summer* established the Ravetches as Hollywood's most reliable chroniclers of life South-by-Southwest, ranging from *Hud* and *The Reivers* through *Conrack* and *Norma Rae*.

With *Some Came Running* in the can, by early 1959 production on *Home from the Hill* geared up in earnest. By this time, Gable was supplanted by Robert Mitchum, with teary-voiced Eleanor Parker typecast as his self-martyring consort. (Hannah Hunnicutt's perpetual air of ladylike dudgeon may have been fueled by Parker's own sense of injustice; she received a mere $75,000 for *Home from the Hill* against Mitchum's $200,000 and a slice of the gross.) As there were few established names young enough to play Wade's sons, Minnelli opted for relatively untried talent. Rafe marked George Peppard's first important film role, after a pair of minor screen appearances and the young romantic lead in the stage comedy *The Pleasure of His Company*. New Metro contract juvenile George Hamilton had even less acting experience, but Minnelli thought his precociously urbane manner would translate well into Theron's callow confusion. *Home from the Hill* was supposed to mark the screen debut of Yvette Mimieux, a teenaged hopeful being groomed by the studio, but her role was cut from the final print. As the local girl abandoned by Theron and cherished by his half-brother, Minnelli selected the grave-faced Luana Patten, a former child actress for Disney, and assigned

the part of her grieving father to Everett Sloane.

Since Minnelli's location work had proved one of *Some Came Running*'s conspicuous assets, Siegel planned similar embellishments for *Home from the Hill*. Between the geographical demands of the story and the outsized length of the Ravetches' script, next to *Lust for Life* this was Minnelli's longest and most complicated shoot for a non-musical to date. The Hunnicutts' domain was recreated in and around Oxford, Mississippi, coincidentally the home town of William Faulkner. Minnelli had barely deposited his *Gigi* Oscar in Beverly Hills before dashing to the Deep South to start *Home from the Hill* on April 9. On studio orders, Siegel reluctantly stayed behind to concentrate on his general administrative duties, handing over direct supervision of *Home from the Hill* to Edmund Grainger. Most of the film's exteriors were shot during these hectic first three weeks, with Siegel enthusiastically praising the footage Minnelli sent back to the studio. "The rushes I saw today in the cemetery looked really wonderful," he cabled his director in Oxford, "one of the finest emotional scenes I've seen in a long time." The month of May was spent back on the lot filming the interiors, plus one scene left over from the Mississippi location— the pre-dawn hunt which opens the film, unpersuasively counterfeited inside a Metro sound stage.

In June, the *Home from the Hill* company hit the road again for two weeks in Texas to make one of Minnelli's characteristically propulsive set-pieces—the boar hunt which marks Theron's rite of passage toward a manhood in his father's image. The sulphurous swamp and its surrounding woods actually combined two locations near Paris and Clarksville—author Humphrey's birth-

George Peppard, Constance Ford, and Robert Mitchum in Home from the Hill *(1960)*

OPPOSITE:
Robert Mitchum, George Hamilton, and Eleanor Parker in Home from the Hill *(1960)*

place. With its headlong tracking shots through dense thickets, the scene called on all of cameraman Milton Krasner's virtuosity. The boars themselves were an unlovely addition to the usual Minnelli menagerie of swans, poodles, and peacocks—but then, with its copperheads and mosquitoes and semi-tropical humidity, this was hardly the Paris of Minnelli's *Gigi* either. Two tuskers were shipped from a Hollywood animal trainer at a salary of $750 a week, rather more than *Home from the Hill*'s human ingenue was getting; unused to the rigors of long distance travel, one of them (named Bijou) died en route. Minnelli took ten days to shoot a sequence that would occupy less than five minutes of screen time. The production manager supervising the shoot tattled of Minnelli's slowness to the studio, which then threatened to summon the company back to Hollywood, until Mitchum intervened on his behalf.

It took six more weeks at MGM to complete *Home from the Hill.* Throughout, Minnelli marveled at Mitchum's self-deprecating professionalism, and the extraordinary empathy and nuances he brought to the part. (Their collaborative rapport was also apparent to Siegel, who halfway through production admiringly memoed Grainger, "I don't remember when I've seen

Mitchum handled so well." Siegel was less sanguine about Eleanor Parker, whose Southern accent seemed excessively cornpone to him.) Minnelli relished performers like Mitchum and Kirk Douglas who brought their own imaginative resources to the task at hand with a minimum of fuss. If there was going to be any dithering on the set he would be the one to do it, rearranging the props and plotting his dolly shots. Peppard was the first Actors' Studio alumnus he'd ever directed, and his Method drove Minnelli to near-madness. The young actor doggedly worked his way through the emotions of the moment while the cameras turned, a process that struck Minnelli as a self-indulgent waste of time. His impatience in turn riled Peppard, convincing him that Minnelli was one of those crass Hollywood hacks they'd warned him about in New York. At one point, he seriously threatened to walk off the picture. Yet the daily rushes showed what a sensitive performance Peppard was giving despite their differences, and by the time shooting ended on August 7 they had a guarded truce. Peppard subsequently earned extraordinary personal notices for his work in *Home from the Hill* that predicted a first-rank star career which never quite materialized.

259

Minnelli finished the film with a few weeks to spare before he was due to report to Arthur Freed for *Bells Are Ringing.* As prepared for release by *The Cobweb*'s editor Harold Kress, *Home from the Hill* weighed in at a massive 150 minutes, but this time the studio didn't blink—everyone felt the story's inexorable momentum justified its unusual length. A November sneak preview played exceedingly well, but Metro chose to hold off the film's release until March 1960. This decision to open an important film during the traditionally slow Lenten season infuriated Siegel, who registered his "firm conviction that MGM is not getting the best of it when it comes to merchandising our pictures," adding that even the successful *Some Came Running* might have earned more with a pushier marketing campaign.

The movie's Radio City Music Hall premiere took place during New York's worst late-winter blizzard in ten years. Despite kudos for Mitchum and Peppard and an occasional nod to Minnelli's "keen eye for the bits and pieces of Americana," in Arthur Knight's words, *Home from the Hill* won a frosty welcome from the press. The *Christian Science Monitor*'s description of its "mishmash of murder, adultery, misalliance and illegitimacy" set the prevailing tone. By 1960 critical palates were sated with these house-divided melodramas, reinforcing the prejudice that any movie choosing to focus on such a multitude of sins had to be pretty disreputable itself. The film's main support came from the Hollywood trade journals, which accurately predicted a prosperous career for *Home from the Hill* in the nation's theaters, and its subsequent foreign release followed the same pattern. With Minnelli in attendance at the start of a long European vacation, *Home from the Hill* was the official U.S. entry in the Cannes Film Festival in May—unveiled at the crest of the *nouvelle vague,* this quintessential Hollywood offering earned dismissive reviews and no prizes.

Back home, the movie also came up empty in the 1960 Oscar nominations, although Mitchum and Peppard were both cited that year by the National Board of Review. Nevertheless, on both sides of the Atlantic, *Home from the Hill* made up in profits what it lacked in prestige, Siegel's apprehensions notwithstanding. Brought in for a relatively economic $2,406,570, the film returned $5,610,627, of which a surprisingly high two million came from its engagements abroad. With the subsequent addition of a lucrative TV sale, this proved the last Minnelli movie to end up on the black-ink side of Metro's ledgers during his tenure there. At the time, its success reinforced the studio's belief that Minnelli could make something memorable out of whatever he tackled. This confidence would lead next to *The Four Horsemen of the Apocalypse,* and the worst debacle of his career.

With *Home from the Hill* Minnelli traveled far beyond the usual boundaries of his imagination. Compared to this Texas country of Winchesters and hound dogs and blood vendettas, the Arles of Van Gogh or even *Kismet*'s Baghdad took shape right in his own backyard. Having concentrated so often on citified artists and well-bred ingenues with hyperactive fantasy lives, for an aesthete like Minnelli the blunt-spoken, danger-courting man's man at the center of *Home from the Hill* was the real exotic. As such, *Home from the Hill* shows off both the breadth and the limits of his professional craft. Thanks to a few shots of good ol' boys lolling in a real down-home town square and a soundtrack-full of twanged vowels from his complement of crease-faced character actors, this movie manages just enough local color to pass muster with those folks sitting in the balconies of the Loews' circuit up north. But try as he may, Minnelli is no Howard Hawks; *Home from the Hill*'s emotional intensity comes from the way he transplanted this material to that wilderness of the heart he understood so well. For all his high-speed stalking and shooting in the Texas dawn, the bloodiest conflicts take place as usual in the great indoors where families destroy each other. And though Minnelli doesn't flinch from the Texas Gothicisms of illicit sex and homicidal rage which fuel the plot, *Home from the Hill*'s pervasive mood is an elegiac regret for the failures of love and the limitations of kindness.

This lengthy narrative is bracketed by two acts of violence against Mitchum's willful patriarch. It begins with a gunshot blast to his shoulder from a young redneck he has cuckolded, and culminates with his bloody

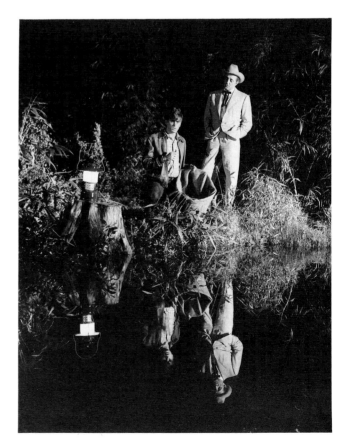

George Peppard and Eleanor Parker. The final scene from Home from the Hill *(1960)*

OPPOSITE:
George Hamilton and Robert Mitchum in Home from the Hill *(1960)*

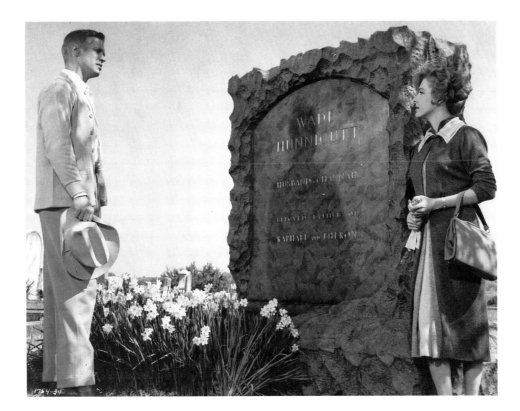

murder, ironically for the one act of sexual poaching he didn't commit. With his banked, virile authority, Mitchum can't help but dominate the movie as effortlessly as he commands the lesser mortals in his private domain—by force of personality as well as sheer physical size, he looms above everyone else in the world of this movie. Yet the character of Wade is the most compelling figure in the background of the conflict that really concerns Minnelli. Like *The Cobweb* and *Tea and Sympathy* this is a rite-of-passage movie, which focuses on the struggles of two young men to measure themselves against a baffling, arbitrary code of adult male behavior.

A kind of backwoods *Dance of Death, Home from the Hill* dissects the legacy of a destructive marriage, with Wade and wife Hannah embodying the perilous opposites of sexual role-playing—his male aggression colliding against her feminine repression. With a few verbal parries and thrusts, the Ravetch/Frank script deftly sketches in the history of these scarred veterans of an eternal domestic war. Confronted by the evidence of Wade's compulsive infidelity at the beginning of their life together, Hannah retaliates by denying him all human contact from that time onward. The one issue of this arid union is their son Theron, conceived before Hannah's disillusionment and seventeen as the movie begins. Wade conceded Theron's upbringing to Hannah, to cinch his wife's grudging consent to remain in the household as his nominal consort, and the teenager we see is the model son of an overprotective mother's fondest dreams—soft-spoken and deferent, desperately eager to please.

Yet now that he's on the brink of physical maturity, Theron's gentleness is an affront to his father's masculine pride. The credulous kid becomes the butt of a practical joke engineered by Wade's inferiors—dragged to the marshes to hunt for the mythical snipe, he is left literally holding the bag and whistling in the dark. Exasperated, Wade's guarded truce with Hannah now erupts into open warfare over their son's destiny. Contemptuously surveying a butterfly collection and other souvenirs of Theron's protracted childhood, he lays down the law to his offspring. "Let me show you how a man lives," he mutters, which is Minnelli's cue to pan in wonderment over the most macho interior his camera ever captured. Rifles and hunting trophies of every species line the walls; next to a blazing open hearth is a man-sized easy chair the color of fresh-killed meat—a perversion of Minnelli-red. Beer in hand, Wade swaggers to his throne and takes his ease, lounging with his legs apart while his pack of hound dogs shuffles obediently to heel. It's a picture of pure male arrogance, which Minnelli clearly finds both magnetic and repellent.

Theron submits unquestioningly to his father's campaign to initiate him into "the company of men"; abetted by Rafe, his father's young and trusted hired hand, he proves a quick study in both marksmanship and the cool nerve it takes to make a first-rate hunter. "What every man hunts out there is himself," Wade tersely advises his son; according to this virile ethos, Theron's true test comes when he is entrusted with the killing of a wild boar, heretofore his father's exclusive prerogative in the territory. This is also Minnelli's chance to flex his directorial sinews, and the mortal chase which follows is one of the most exhilarating passages of tour-de-force moviemaking in his entire canon. Racing to keep up with the hunter and his hounds, Minnelli's camera sprints wildly under a deceptively cheerful sun toward the danger lurking in the darkest recesses of a primeval wood. In this metaphor-fraught landscape, the worst horrors remain unseen; the camera's lurching apprehension reflects our own, as from an impassable thicket, birds scatter in fright and the shrieks of animals in deadly combat rend the soundtrack. Beauty and terror are inseparable here. Theron's journey takes him past a quicksand swamp emanating yellow fumes of a hue rich enough to enrapture Van Gogh. (In filming this picturesque Texas locale, Minnelli typically opted to improve on nature, ordering his crew to fill the air with ever more vividly tinted fumes, until the screen achieved the magical haze of Kelly and Caron's dry-ice embrace in his *American in Paris* ballet.) This is Sulphur Bottom, of which Rafe warned the lad, "you walk in there and you'll never walk out"; it's a tempting symbol, but Minnelli wisely resists its facile lure. This curtain of smoke hovers on the periphery of the frame at various intervals, but nobody actually ventures inside—for *Home from the Hill*'s characters, the real threat of oblivion comes from within.

In a chilling closeup, the boar charges the camera until Theron fells it with one shot, but Wade's exultant pride in his son turns out to be tragically premature. His lessons in this male cult of the outdoors are as incomplete an education as Hannah's lifelong course in Southern gentility; by depriving each other of intimacy throughout their marriage, both Hunnicutts have unwittingly stunted Theron's grasp of the pleasures and responsibilities that make up a normal adulthood. After this escapade, *Home from the Hill* shifts to more serious business—Theron's timid courtship of Libby, a spirited local beauty. This blue-jeaned Romeo and Juliet bask in the tenderest love scenes Minnelli had staged since *The Clock,* against settings that underscore Theron's increasing self-confidence. Their first meeting alone takes place in the Hunnicutt attic, surrounded by the discarded playthings of his childhood; their consummation follows in a corner of that forest he conquered. But their idyll is brief; naively, Theron can't understand the blunt hostility of Libby's father to their romance, but his own mother clears up the mystery. Determined to shatter her son's sudden idolatry of Wade, Hannah blurts out the family secrets from which Theron had always been shielded. For not only has Wade's lechery made him the enemy of every self-respecting husband and father in the county, but Wade's boon companion Rafe is none other than the bastard issue of one of his numberless casual liaisons.

Hannah's revelation is even more potent than she intends—it alienates Theron from both his parents while poisoning his chances for a serene future with Libby. "They kill each other a little at a time . . . tore me in half that way every day of my life," he seethes while disentangling himself from the girl whose passionate devotion is precisely what Theron needs; "that's what they call love and being a family." In the act of repudiating Wade, Theron unwittingly follows in his muddy boot-tracks. After his outburst, Libby has too much pride to tell him that she is expecting a child —a second generation of Hunnicutt bastards.

While Theron gradually disintegrates, Minnelli's attention turns to the parallel saga of Rafe's lonely journey toward a maturity his over-privileged half-brother will never achieve. As in *Some Came Running, Home from the Hill*'s group portrait of a loveless household is enclosed within a larger landscape of near-feudal social distinctions, of which Rafe is the principal victim. Tersely, Minnelli introduces this theme by capturing the community in the throes of a curious local ritual—spring-cleaning at the town cemetery, where class barriers are memorialized for eternity. As Bronislau Kaper's score strikes up a perversely merry jig, the camera pans past Hannah and the town worthies sweeping the underbrush from the imposing monuments erected to their forebears. Minnelli then cuts across the road to a plot of graves so overgrown with weeds that the scattered markers are barely visible; this is "Reprobates' Field," and the only person who bothers to tend it is Rafe, in memory of his disgraced mother. When Theron visits Rafe's solitary shack to share what he has learned, his half-brother delivers an anguished monologue describing a lifetime of "hangin' around" on the sidelines while the legitimate Hunnicutt heir reaped the benefits of his station.

Yet as *Home from the Hill* unreels, it's clear that so far as Minnelli is concerned Rafe is the lucky one—spared the wrangling that haunted Theron's youth, he has no lessons in parental pathology to unlearn. With his innate strength of character and an unfulfilled need for companionship, Rafe is the one male figure in this movie who realizes that men also have a capacity for tenderness. By marrying Libby and embracing her child as his own, he can create a family to satisfy his own nurturing instincts.

In brutal contrast, both Hunnicutts are destroyed by the law of the hunt which defined them as men. Wade is gunned down in his den, surrounded by the mounted game that brought him such pride; after avenging his father's death, Theron disappears forever into the green wilderness where his adolescence ended. Throughout *Home from the Hill*'s two and a half hours, Minnelli's quietly foreboding tone makes the explosions at the finale seem as inevitable as fate. What elevates *Home from the Hill* from crude formula to something like the grandeur of tragedy is his compassion for these victims of their own creed. Wade's hubris lay in his blinkered belief that his profligate ways concerned him and no one else; Hannah smothered her child with the affection she had stubbornly denied her-self. The unexpected element in the story is the warm fraternal bond Minnelli draws between the two half-brothers. In light of Theron's basic decency, his wasted youth is that much more painful to witness. Although somewhat marred by Parker's theatrical tics as Hannah —her throaty drawl and quivering eyebrows working overtime to sell her Southern-matron brand of distress —the interplay between Minnelli's acting ensemble is as sensitively judged as in any film he ever made.

With pitiless logic, Minnelli's epitaph for this shat-tered family fades out on the Hunnicutt gravesite. *Home from the Hill*'s final image is one of those compositions for which CinemaScope was invented. At left is the huge red slab commemorating Wade's death, the names of both sons etched into the stone as his grieving survivors; on the right Hannah and Rafe walk off to-gether, hoping to make sense of the rest of their lives. Hollywood chronicles of American domestic life don't get grimmer than this—by the time he was emotionally equipped to make *Home from the Hill,* Minnelli had come a long way from *St. Louis.*

- -

THE FOUR HORSEMEN OF THE APOCALYPSE

1962

As its era's prime candidate in the *Heaven's Gate* sweepstakes, *The Four Horsemen of the Apocalypse* was a bad idea that became deadlier at every step. Four years' work and seven and a half million squandered dollars later, no one volunteered to take the main rap for this calamity, but there was plenty of blame to go around. If Minnelli and the film's eventual star had only trusted to instinct and shown the guts to turn it down, *Four Horsemen* might have remained just an-other executive-office brainstorm-of-the-month. But even at the twilight of the studio era, it was hard to shake the creed that if the forces at Metro were so insistent, surely they knew what they were doing. Once Minnelli got involved, a terrible momentum kept *Four Horsemen* staggering forward until the movie was slaughtered by the press, its remains paraded before scattered mourners at theaters around the nation.

It was mainly the fault of *Ben Hur,* and MGM's de-luded adherence to the lightning-strikes-twice philos-ophy of moviemaking. In 1958, the studio was marshaling all its forces for a remake of this 1926 Judeo-Christian-Roman spectacle. Just as the origi-

Glenn Ford goes gaucho,
The Four Horsemen of the
Apocalypse *(1962)*

nal nearly broke the bank in the studio's infancy, the new version was going to be the most monumental, spendthrift extravaganza in its corporate history, dwarfing even *Quo Vadis.* If *Ben Hur* could be refurbished for the wide-screen era, why not exhume another well-remembered relic from the age of silent epics? In fact, the original *Four Horsemen* predated MGM itself. Rex Ingram's 1921 screen version of Vicente Blasco Ibañez' best-seller was the notable achievement of Metro Pictures, one of the three lesser units that merged in 1924 to form MGM; it earned a permanent niche in movie annals as the vehicle that sparked the Valentino craze.

Exploiting this legendary title from the twenties had the ring of a likely notion. (It certainly could have been worse—say, an all-star *Greed* in Metrocolor and stereophonic sound.) But one wonders if anybody concerned took a good hard look at the original movie. The truth was that in contrast to *Ben Hur*, this property had little to recommend it to latter-day audiences. While *Ben Hur*'s pagan sweep and haloed reverence exerted an ageless kitschy appeal, *Four Horsemen* was the time-capsule artifact of a specific era. In 1921, this parable of an Argentinian playboy finding redemption in the trenches of No Man's Land was both exotic and topical; it vividly conjured up the traumas of a recently buried past. But for the grandchildren of *Four Horsemen*'s original fans, World War I was neither romantic nor tragic —just quaintly remote.

Moreover, the only thing truly outsized about this movie was the erotic allure of its male star. The first *Ben Hur* had also enshrined a Latin heartthrob in Ramon Novarro, but in the 1920s and 1950s alike, just about any sinewy type with a soulful gaze would have

sufficed—what propelled the picture to triumph were all those floating galleys and speeding chariots. Star charisma, however, had been the first *Four Horsemen*'s specific raison d'être. Scenarist June Mathis tailored it expressly to elevate Valentino above the anonymous ranks of third-billed gigolos; forty years on, the only thing anybody remembered about the movie was Rudy's smoldering tango. Needless to say, sheiks of the pampas were an extinct and unlamented species in the Eisenhower era. The closest modern equivalent was Elvis, far too low-rent a type for a prestige opus on the order of this apocalypse.

So MGM found itself gearing up to recreate one of the great personality showcases in Hollywood history, without having the slightest notion of who was going to star in it. Somehow, this lapse in logic deterred neither Joseph Vogel, presiding over the New York office, nor Sol Siegel back in Hollywood. Nor did they balk upon learning that MGM had allowed the rights to this property to lapse decades before. Sometime after Blasco Ibañez' death in 1929, his estate resold *Four Horsemen* to a local outfit called Moctezuma Film, which now cheerfully bartered it back to MGM for the sum of $200,000 in blocked pesetas.

In June 1958, the studio announced its acquisition to the press. Although MGM's plans for *Four Horsemen* remained tantalizingly vague, one thing was certain— after the recent box-office flops of such World War I movies as Selznick's *A Farewell to Arms* remake and *Paths of Glory*, this story would need to be updated to a punchier period. With this in mind, Kenneth MacKenna approached none other than Graham Greene with an offer to write a "rather free treatment" of the novel for the screen, an honor which Greene declined. MGM veteran Robert Ardrey subsequently accepted the job and spent the first half of 1959 hammering together a lengthy first draft; as the studio decreed, he redrew the dashing Julio as An Argentinian in (Occupied) Paris, uncertainly poised between Fascism and the Resistance during WW II. Meanwhile, Siegel gave the plum of supervising *Four Horsemen* to Julian Blaustein, a recent arrival on the lot who, like his boss, had put in years of yeoman work at 20th Century-Fox.

This foretold trouble even at this early stage. Although his record at Fox ran the gamut from *The Day the Earth Stood Still* to *Desiree,* Blaustein had yet to produce a film on the scale MGM envisioned for *Four Horsemen.* He'd never coped with the vagaries of an extensive European shoot, or the whims of a director as eminent as Minnelli. If Blaustein seemed overmatched, Ardrey wasn't challenged nearly enough. Thanks to the studio's guidelines, his treatment was the last word in 1942 Underground Chic—a tonier version of the I-Spit-at-the-Gestapo scripts Joan Crawford was doing before she decamped from Metro for Warners and greater glory.

With Minnelli at liberty after completing *Bells Are Ringing* for Arthur Freed in early 1960, this was the draft Siegel dangled hopefully before him. It's easy to understand why the studio expected Minnelli to turn this dross into the gold-plated lead that Oscars were made of. After all, Paris had always inspired the poet in him, and in his two latest melodramas, Minnelli managed to generate sparks from the most prolix of plots. Following their two years of intense collaboration, Siegel's admiration for his gifts had no limit.

Why Minnelli succumbed is harder to fathom. He knew that Blasco Ibañez' characters made no sense wrenched out of their original context, despite Siegel's insistence on swastikas or nothing. It was flattering to be told how indispensable his taste and talent were; perhaps Minnelli had begun to believe his own inhouse publicity by this time. Trusting to Siegel's acumen and a pledge to overhaul the script, Minnelli agreed to tackle *Four Horsemen* after *Home from the Hill*'s Cannes premiere and a few weeks' vacation in Italy.

Having secured Minnelli, MGM now applied pressure to assemble the cast, despite much floundering for a plausible Julio. Early on, Blaustein had considered Dirk Bogarde, then making his Hollywood debut as Franz Liszt in *Song without End;* he also confided to Siegel that he'd heard "marvelous things about Monty Clift in Spiegel's picture [*Suddenly, Last Summer*] and in the one he is now shooting with Kazan [*Wild River*]. What I hear is that he's behaving as a professional and looks wonderful." Both actors were a far cry from the rakish expatriate ranchero of Ardrey's script. Eventually Blaustein proposed a different approach—gambling on some intriguing new personality, as the original movie had.

MGM then pondered giving this plum to George Hamilton, who sported minimum qualifications of youth and dark looks and was extremely cheap besides, thanks to his beginner's contract with the studio. During his sojourn in Rome Minnelli met Alain Delon, who'd made a smoldering first impression on the art-house circuit in René Clement's *Purple Noon,* and he thought this eminently photogenic *jeune premier* might well have the right chemistry for the part. But Delon's international appeal and his command of English were untried commodities at the time, and nobody paid much heed to Minnelli's suggestion. For several months, the most serious candidate for Julio was Horst Buchholz, the young German matinee idol engaged that summer to seduce and abandon Leslie Caron in the Hollywoodization of Marcel Pagnol's *Fanny* trilogy.

But 1960 wasn't 1921, and the prospect of risking a relative novice like Buchholz made MGM very nervous indeed. At last, Joseph Vogel proposed the path of least resistance—Glenn Ford, who had recently renewed his multi-picture deal with the studio at a quite reasonable fee as established names went. MGM had a lot riding on Ford's presumed hold on the public; he had just completed its expensive remake of *Cimarron.* With this super-western in the can, Ford was available and willing, and if Blaustein didn't acquiesce the studio would have to find something else for the actor to do at $150,000 per. Vogel didn't seem to care that Ford was a ludicrous choice—indelibly American and, at forty-two, a generation too old to play the sinuous hero.

Four Horsemen's producer was naturally appalled; from his preproduction base in Paris Blaustein begged Siegel to intercede. "My hope has been that Mr. Vogel can be made to see that *Four Horsemen* is a major chance for something unusual and that Glenn standardizes it, makes it just another big Hollywood production with a great title. . . . With him, we're playing it safe, and to play it safe these days is to take the biggest of possible risks. . . ." Still on vacation in Rome, Minnelli chose to stay out of this tug-of-war, and his passivity at this crucial moment may have fatefully tipped the balance. Blaustein told Siegel, "while Vince says he will accept either Glenn or Buchholz . . . he repeated that he would be glad to take Glenn if you decide on him as a matter of *company policy.* In other words, if New York feels a name is needed, Vincente will go along with the decision. But on an artistic basis his feelings are more for Buchholz whom he would be glad to work with without a test." Soon the word arrived from New York—no Ford, no picture. Minnelli's the-studio-is-usually-right credo rarely extended to anything as critical as casting; this time his reluctance to rile the bosses overruled his judgment.

Vogel's insistence meant that the script had to be overhauled as much for practical as dramatic reasons. Siegel noted that Julio had been written as "a young man of perhaps 22 or 3 or 4. Now that we know Glenn

Ford is playing the role we must think of Julio as Aly Khan—an Argentinian who is also cosmopolitan." Robert Ardrey pitched in for two hectic weeks of rewrites, but more drastic work and a fresh eye were needed. At Minnelli's request MGM tried to lure Terence Rattigan, then the West End's toniest dramatist, to do a new adaptation but he declined, as did Irwin Shaw.

In early August, Minnelli left Rome for Paris to assemble his crew and scout locations. With no time to spare, MGM settled on a professional screenwriter who wouldn't be so fastidious. Fresh from his labors on the Clark Gable–Burt Lancaster submarine picture *Run Silent, Run Deep,* John Gay was ordered to fly straight to Paris and read the old script en route. On his arrival, Minnelli urged him to virtually disregard Ardrey's work, but Blaustein ordered caution, insisting that at least the old version gave them something tangible with which to plan the shooting schedule and budget. This sparked the first in a series of increasingly ferocious rows between *Four Horsemen*'s director and producer. In early September, Blaustein complained to Siegel in Culver City that "Vincente was in a state of panic about the script. Now it's my turn . . . John Gay has done yeoman work in tackling material totally unfamiliar to him. But never did I realize how little Vincente liked about the script. . . . No longer do we have a romance in the 'classical' style. Instead we have a more modern approach to a love story. This is probably a good change considering that Glenn Ford is hardly a romantic figure. . . . Vincente feels that you and he have been in total agreement about the script and will accept these suggestions more readily from you." He concluded with the prophetic postscript that "another of the problems—mine—is to maintain the morale of a very sensitive director whose talent is most valuable to the picture. I just have to be careful that in doing a service to Vincente I am not doing a disservice to the picture." Characteristically, Siegel backed Minnelli, informing Blaustein "I am afraid you have no choice but to go down the path Minnelli and Gay have chosen. I am aware that it means we will be shooting before the script is completed."

With or without a script, MGM had still to find a polyglot cast to suit Blasco Ibañez' complicated family tree of intermarried Frenchmen, Germans, and Argentinians, while somehow complementing Glenn Ford. The Gallic branch was headed by Julio's cynical hedonist father Marcelo Desnoyers, a role Minnelli reserved for his favorite Parisian, Charles Boyer. What followed was a retake of Minnelli's casting battles during *The Cobweb.* The New York office squawked that Boyer wasn't worth his $100,000 price tag, adding that "the sales department does not repeat not regard him as plus value particularly in co-star billing position." The studio proposed Jean Gabin, despite the fact that he hadn't worked in English for twenty years; having

compromised with Ford, Minnelli insisted on Boyer no matter what. The sales department notwithstanding, MGM was lucky to get him. By the time the movie was released, Boyer had scored an Oscar nomination for his role in the popular *Fanny,* and next to Ford he was virtually the only name in *Four Horsemen* that meant anything to moviegoers.

Hungarian-born Paul Lukas, who'd won an Oscar a generation before as a staunch antifascist in *Watch on the Rhine,* was signed as his goose-stepping brother-in-law, Karl von Hartrott, at a quarter Boyer's fee. MGM was eager to snare Steve McQueen to play Lukas' equally Nazified son Heinrich, but *Four Horsemen*'s shooting schedule conflicted with the young actor's western series for television, so the studio bowed to ethnic logic and chose Karl Boehm, son of the great conductor. The most colorful role in the script was that of the lusty Argentine patriarch, Madariaga; since there was no actor living truly old enough to play Glenn Ford's grandfather, Siegel offered it to Lee J. Cobb, who'd spent half his career hiding behind grizzled toupees and rubber-cement wrinkles.

With Ford as ostensible box-office insurance, MGM decided to cast his illicit love, Marguerite, on the basis of merit and chemistry alone. Even so Ingrid Thulin was an obscure choice, although by then she'd achieved some fame outside her native Sweden, thanks to Ingmar Bergman's *Wild Strawberries* and *Brink of Life.* The fact that the heroine was French and Thulin Nordic didn't seem to worry anyone, all accents east of New York being interchangeable so far as the studio was concerned. Thulin's test for Marguerite, shot in London that August, convinced MGM to sign her to a five-year, five-picture commitment to follow this American breakthrough. The obvious plan was to launch Thulin as a new Ingrid Bergman for the 1960s, and in the hope that movie history would repeat itself (or that time had stood still) MGM even paired her with Paul Henreid, once more a Resistance hero and cuckolded spouse à la *Casablanca*'s immortal Victor Laszlo. If Henreid was somewhat geriatric for the type by now, this only emphasized the relative allure of Glenn Ford as his rival for Marguerite's affections. As things turned out, Thulin's Hollywood debut was greeted less like Ingrid Mach II than Anna Sten in CinemaScope, and MGM never exercised its option on her services.

With this dispiriting lineup in place Minnelli turned to other, equally daunting matters—the massive physical requirements of the picture. As counterpoint to the Julio–Marguerite romance and the hero's crisis of conscience, *Four Horsemen* aimed for the definitive movie

OPPOSITE:
Ingrid Thulin and Paul Henreid in The Four Horsemen of the Apocalypse *(1962)*

treatment to date of the 1940s siege of Paris—troops, tanks and all. Even so, studio executives blanched at the preliminary budget estimate of $4,750,000—a figure which would soon prove to be ludicrously optimistic. While they pondered whether it was more economical to complete the movie at Culver City or Borehamwood, shooting started at the Place de l'Opéra on October 2 1960. The infinity of Paris locations planned for *Four Horsemen* made Minnelli's *Gigi* shoot seem like child's play in retrospect, and this time the French government treated MGM's invading army with a contempt worthy of the script's jackbooted occupation force. At first, Blaustein was refused permits to stage any street scenes involving large crowds, much less extras in Nazi uniform. For many, the sight of German officers parading down the Champs Elysées only fifteen years after the war—particularly for the sake of a frivolous Hollywood spectacular—was an affront to recent memory.

De Gaulle's Fifth Republic had even more pressing reasons to ban a sequence Minnelli mapped out of a spontaneous Resistance uprising near the Sorbonne— the fear that in the midst of the darkest period of the Algerian conflict, life might imitate art. "There was an actual student riot against de Gaulle last Sunday," Blaustein wrote Siegel on October 7, to explain *Four Horsemen*'s halting start. "Three days ago, France and Germany signed a military pact which will allow Germany to have military bases in France. This has not been made public yet, but the police are girding for extensive riots throughout Paris once the word is published. . . . We have also been told that de Gaulle has been irritated by what we've been doing here in the streets. . . ." Weeks of frantic maneuvering brought compromises on both sides—Minnelli tabled his riot for the time being, and the German march through the Place de l'Etoile was mostly staged out of harm's way, on a boulevard in Versailles.

For expediency's sake, MGM tried to convince Minnelli to leave these panoramic shots to his second-unit director, but he insisted on supervising the work himself. (One inducement was the chance to work with the great Georges Perinal, cameraman for the second unit while Milton Krasner was occupied with the first.) Having been roped into the picture against his better judgment and then conceded too much on the casting, Minnelli brooked no interference on the set. If MGM wanted a romantic epic in his resplendent manner, they were going to have to pay for it with their accustomed largesse of time and money. His cavalier perfectionism irritated Blaustein no end, but Siegel took pains to stroke his touchy director at regular intervals. "The rushes I have seen with the Nazis sitting in the sidewalk café were perfectly wonderful," he wrote Minnelli from California three weeks into shooting. "There is no substitute for reality. . . . I know you helped create many of the fine things in the script with

John Gay. . . . I appreciate more than I can ever say your contribution to the script."

Despite Siegel's encouragement, Minnelli's mood mostly remained as dour as the sodden autumn weather. (Unintentionally, the chill gray skies over Paris became one of *Four Horsemen*'s few realistic touches.) He dragged his cast from the Eiffel Tower through the Tuileries to Notre Dame, the Ile St. Louis and the Gare de l'Est, with a second foray to Versailles to shoot a Ford–Thulin love scene, and several days at a stone farmhouse in the nearby countryside for the film's explosive finale. Minnelli took eight weeks to wrap up his *Four Horsemen* locations; with two-thirds of the picture still to go, by December the prospective budget had shot up to $6,500,000. To exert some control over these terrifying sums, Siegel decided to summon the troupe back to Culver City rather than shooting the remainder at the British lot. After a five-day hiatus *Four Horsemen* resumed in Hollywood on December 6, by which point Minnelli and Blaustein's mutual distrust had congealed into outright contempt.

Although impressed with the footage Minnelli brought back from France, his drawn out tempos began to worry Siegel. "His entrances and exits are much too slow," the studio head memoed Blaustein. "I want to alert Minnelli about the necessary pace required in a picture of this kind. I will try to alert him to the necessity of coming into scenes when they are underway, rather than his customary method of shooting each scene as though it was a first act." Still, if Blaustein thought he'd found an ally in his skirmishes with his recalcitrant director, the next few weeks disabused him of that hope. As the picture settled in for what looked like a long winter on the back lot, Siegel championed Minnelli while bearing down ever harder on *Four Horsemen*'s hapless producer. "It appears that we are headed for about a five-hour picture. This is not a gross exaggeration," he snapped in a memo which landed on Blaustein's desk New Year's Eve. "I would be remiss, as head of the studio, if I did not do something about it, and by something I mean dramatic. . . . I think Vincente is doing a wonderful job directing this picture, and it seems a pity so much of his enormous effort and talent will go to waste if we are forced to drop one hour of the film."

Siegel's praise prompted howls of outrage from Blaustein. "I, for one, am fed up with Minnelli's insistence on having *everything* his own way," he exploded in reply. "We've lived through his overshooting in Paris, including the criminal expenditure on the Versailles episode. We've had the experience with the Gestapo prison and we've had the department store scene. Now we're about to have a retake of a scene that we already know is too long." Minnelli chose to ignore these front-office fireworks; the atmosphere on the set was dire enough as it was. While Blaustein's hostility doubtless made things worse, in retrospect the producer had good reason to feel frustrated. For all his absorption in detail, Minnelli's most successful movies always managed an efficient cruising speed before the cameras. In deference to *Four Horsemen*'s scope, Minnelli was kept on a looser rein than usual and with less pressure from the studio his customary decisiveness seemed to elude him. Not since *The Pirate* had he lingered so long over a project, and this time the delays couldn't be blamed on the vagaries of some tempest-tossed star.

Repeatedly, he insisted on reshooting completed sections of the script, which lay stillborn no matter how many times he tackled them. The crucial love scenes in particular played out as if they'd been stage-managed by an anesthesiologist—Thulin wandered blankly through the art department's lavish sets like the displaced person she was, while Ford hid behind the same impassive deadpan whether wooing her or parrying with the enemy.

The impenetrable chill on the set was an ironic contrast to the recent developments in Minnelli's personal life. During his vacation in Italy the previous summer, he had made the acquaintance of Denise Giganti, a glamorous Yugoslavian-born divorcée approximately half his age. She became his constant companion once *Four Horsemen* summoned him to Paris, and by the time the production was dismantled for the trip back home, they were engaged to be married. Minnelli and his third wife exchanged vows in an impromptu ceremony in Palm Springs on New Year's Eve, 1960. While the second Mrs. Minnelli had never quite adjusted to the social rigors of Beverly Hills, its caste system held no terrors for the vivacious Denise, who immediately staked out her claim as one of the town's social leaders.

This pleasurable tumult didn't alter the grim situation Minnelli faced during working hours. The feuds behind the scenes were more dramatic than anything being captured by his cameras. Toward the end of February, Minnelli shot a pivotal sequence in which Julio tussles bitterly with his fascist cousin Heinrich in the sleek setting of a Paris night club. Siegel praised the rushes effusively, but for Blaustein this was the final straw. "The mood between Julio and Heinrich is *completely* wrong," he fumed in a memo to the studio head. "More and more I see the mounting effects of the lack of communication between Minnelli and me. . . . If Minnelli chooses to ignore both you and me, the very least we have the right to expect is that he study the script." Blaustein's accusations against his eminent director exasperated Siegel, and he dispatched a swift retort. "I completely disagree with your analysis of the film Minnelli shot. . . . May I add that I also see the mounting effects of the lack of communication between you and Minnelli. As far as I am concerned, Minnelli has an excellent perspective of the characters and the method of telling the story. . . . I resent having to carry this additional burden which was thrust on

me. I think you should examine yourself very carefully with regard to your attitude toward creative people. . . . For whatever reason, the bridge between you and Minnelli was destroyed."

By now, the movie's original shooting timetable had faded into memory. After its early October start, the studio had planned to complete principal photography by February 15, considering this a spendthrift indulgence as it was. Yet Minnelli didn't disband his unit until the end of March. MGM hoped *Four Horsemen* would be ready for release by the end of 1961, but the lethargy that plagued this project from its outset clung to the very end. Between May and July, Minnelli reshot several reels of footage, including much of the German march into Paris with which he'd started the previous October, Ford playing gaucho on a backlot Patagonia, and that jinxed Left Bank student riot. He also devised the one sequence in the picture which really whetted his imagination—the ghost riders of Conquest, War, Pestilence, and Death, spurring their steeds through sulphurous expanses of sound-stage stratosphere. Minnelli had hired Tony Duquette to design the intricate armor for this symbolic quartet, plus a matching set of Four Horsemen andirons to adorn the hearth of the Madariaga hacienda; now he spent two weeks shaping this galloping ballet, the horses mounted on parallel treadmills while Minnelli poured on the smoke and colored lights.

At the beginning of August Minnelli declared himself done at last, exactly a year after he'd first begun work on the picture. But the apocalypse wasn't over yet. Two months later, MGM finally scheduled a sneak preview in Santa Barbara, and the response was as funereal as they had feared. One discerning patron noted on his preview card, "the film would have been wonderful shown in 1946-48, but it is too late in the century"; more bluntly, another remarked, "you have a turkey unless you liven it up." Audience reaction to the cast was particularly devastating. Apart from Lee J. Cobb, the only figures to elicit any excitement were Conquest, War, Pestilence, and Death themselves.

Nobody had the strength to go through another siege of retakes, and besides, by then Minnelli had fled to Rome to start *Two Weeks in Another Town*. Since the look of the film was apparently beyond help, MGM began to fiddle with the soundtrack instead. André Previn was hurriedly commissioned to compose a new background score to replace Alex North's. Meanwhile, the studio shook its collective head over the comatose line readings from *Four Horsemen*'s imported leading lady. The daily rushes had revealed Thulin's English as perfectly intelligible; however, strung together into a two and a half hour film, her dialogue sounded monotonously uninflected. The only option was to bring in another actress to dub for her—a common enough practice in Europe, but practically unheard of in Hollywood (movie musicals excepted) since the beginning of talkies. This thankless task went to Angela Lansbury, who late in October spent a week modulating her own tones to blend with those bits from Thulin's tracks deemed salvageable. (To an attentive ear the results were curious indeed; in some passages, Marguerite #1 starts a sentence, and Marguerite #2 completes it.)

Two more months of desultory juggling and trims brought *Four Horsemen*'s final cost to $7,590,775, double Minnelli's biggest budget to date. The studio arranged to hold the world premiere at the scene of the crime, in Paris—a newsworthy gambit, and far enough away so that the publicity department could squelch the word if the locals got restless. To everyone's amazement, the international film journalists assembled for the January 17 1962 opening generally greeted *Four Horsemen* with awe and admiration. The popular film weekly *Cinémonde* exclaimed that "Minnelli's virtuosity is simply dazzling," to which *Die Welt* added, "No director ever before caught the psychological situation of World War II so strongly in his grip"; most astonishing, Italy's authoritative newspaper , the *Corriere della Sera,* insisted that "the picture is of the utmost reality," and even Paris' resident American arts reporter Thomas Quinn Curtiss called it "a commendable achievement" in the international edition of the *Herald Tribune.*

Perhaps MGM should have used its French-subtitled prints for the domestic run as well. In deference to its imposing subject, the studio launched *Four Horsemen* at home with a benefit screening in Washington, attended by the diplomatic community and a sheaf of congressmen. Unused to these attentions from Hollywood, the seat of government went all out to welcome the interlopers from the movie capital: Senator Keating from New York and California Democratic Senator Clair Engle crossed party lines to co-host a luncheon for Minnelli and Ford, while the French ambassador's wife presided over a bi-lingual tea in the director's honor.

After all the official hoopla, *Four Horsemen* seemed more anticlimax than apocalypse by the time it limped into New York's Loews' State in March. Strangely, while their continental equivalents found its *echt*-Hollywood grandeur rather thrilling, to American critics freshly exposed to the European New Wave, *Four Horsemen* was the embalmed relic of a fallen movie empire. "It hardly seems possible that at the same time Resnais was making *Marienbad,* MGM was working on a remake of *The Four Horsemen of the Apocalypse,*" sniffed Philip T. Hartung in the pages of *Commonweal;* the *Saturday Review*'s Hollis Alpert summed up the consensus with the plaint, "All one can say is, 'Why, why, why?' " Ordinary moviegoers in turn behaved as if all that Pestilence and Death might be catching, and *Four Horsemen* failed dismally at the box office. In the wake of lesser calamities such as Ford's *Cimarron* and Jeffrey Hunter as Jesus in *King of Kings,* it contributed mightily to Siegel's imminent downfall as Metro production chief; Blaustein in turn never made a picture at the

*Minnelli and Glenn Ford
filming in the Paris Metro,*
The Four Horsemen of the
Apocalypse *(1962)*

studio again. Fortunately for Minnelli, MGM had a sufficient quota of executives under the rope to dismiss his contribution to the crime. Every director was entitled to one fiasco in his career, and he emerged from this one shaken but relatively unscathed; the real bloodshed came soon enough during his *Two Weeks in Another Town.*

The Four Horsemen's vital missing element should have been obvious before Minnelli exposed a foot of film. For there was simply no compelling reason for this movie to exist—its theme had been explored many times previously with far greater impact, and this lugubrious misalliance of actors hardly warranted such an elaborate reprise. From a technical standpoint, *Four Horsemen* is one of the slickest productions Minnelli ever directed, scrupulously embellished with his signature grace notes: giddy party scenes and moonlit strolls by the Seine, even a few lectures on Art Appreciation thanks to Julio and Marcelo's taste for post-Impressionism. Yet no amount of artificial respiration could revive something as stubbornly inanimate as this.

Worse still, for long stretches even Minnelli's own best instincts appear to have deserted him. *Four Horsemen* never quite recovers from the phoniness of its opening scenes, set in Culver City, Argentina. While *Yolanda*-ish music cranks away on the soundtrack,

Minnelli stages a tacky pan-Latin fiesta; at its center, a white-maned Cobb and his middle-aged grandson Ford make chumps of themselves dancing a pampas jig in floppy gaucho costumes. (The director's one kindness here is to keep their feet out of camera range, focusing instead on Ford's congealed gaze as he navigates a flaccid tango.) In desperation, Minnelli overdresses the spectacle in a way similar to the soggier moments in *Kismet,* with a bevy of his feathered friends —shooting this hacienda revelry through a perchful of cockatoos and parrots.

But once the music stops, the director discards ornithology for high theatrics. When Cobb, respectfully called The Old One, learns that half of his brood are Nazi sympathizers, lusty grandpa becomes King Lear, and the weather darkens accordingly. ''A curse on my seed,'' he bellows while a monsoon batters the French windows of his family seat. The clouds part to reveal the riders of the apocalypse, prompting a cry of ''Death! Death!'' from the prescient Old One, who then expires in the downpour. These figures do indeed resemble Duquette's apocalypse andirons writ gargantuan, since they're far too quaintly sculpted to inspire the expected mix of awe and foreboding. No wonder Ford seems more befuddled than usual in his star closeup.

This may have been the last word in 1921 dramaturgy, but forty years on even CinemaScope and a high-fidelity soundtrack can't salvage galloping hokum like this. *Four Horsemen*'s tragedy centers on the disintegration of a proud dynasty—a pretext compelling enough for the Minnelli melodramas that preceded it. But this ensemble of German, French, Hungarian and Hollywoodian players interact like a failed summit conference rather than a family in crisis. One expects to find Minnelli on firmer ground once the action shifts to a France on the verge of World War II, and his opening shots of the Place de l'Etoile at night encircled by a galaxy of headlights do have some of the old American-in-Paris brio. Whenever they venture outdoors, Minnelli and his two cinematographers capture the mist-diffused light of the city as eloquently as any émigré troupe on location before them. (By contrast, the interiors shot at the MGM studio are as garishly illuminated as a Chevrolet showroom.)

But there's a crucial error in judgment that sabotages Minnelli's requisite Occupation atmosphere. Perversely, *Four Horsemen*'s most contemporary touches are found in the wardrobe and hair styles of its cast— apart from the occasional snood on the head of some fleeting extra, everyone sports the last resplendent word in 1961 finery. This up-to-date fashion parade tends to distract from *Four Horsemen*'s theme of doomed love in bad times; then again, the banality of the plot and its trapped players beg for all the diversionary tactics Minnelli can muster. The Gay/Ardrey script mingles uneasily the clichés of two generations;

the coy candor of the early sixties permits Julio and Marguerite to cohabit, but in deference to the censors they never touch except when vertical and fully clothed. Meanwhile, *Four Horsemen*'s Nazi lore is a throwback to a thousand wartime thrillers. Julio bravely joins the Resistance because *au fond,* ''a man has to take sides''; for dramatic contrast *Four Horsemen* dusts off that fascinating fascist, the monocled Kommandant, who slavers over the lusciously Aryan Marguerite.

Apart from the stalwart Boyer, a professional who could rise above any turgid occasion, Minnelli's cast ranges from dull to worse, and it's apparent that his usual instinct for handling actors was deadened by the grind of *Four Horsemen*'s year-long shoot. The silliest performances come from the opposite ends of the Madariaga clan—Lee J. Cobb's Old One is uncured ham, and as his grandchild, Chi-Chi, Yvette Mimieux is the essence of Valley Girl masquerading as a Sorbonne student activist. Thulin is lost from her very first scene, as Angela Lansbury's unmistakable tones issue gaily from her mouth. Even in the fitful moments when the soundtrack restores her own voice, Thulin's spirit is absent without leave. She's supposed to register desire and remorse in alternate doses, but the only expression she can muster is sheer benumbed terror at her professional predicament.

Neither Thulin nor the equally robotic Ford are helped by their assigned dialogue, written in the Esperanto of movie mush. (''The world . . . and the war . . . move on. . . . Passions . . . are sometimes spent,'' she haltingly informs her beloved Julio on their last night together.) To compensate for this romantic vacuum, Minnelli resorts to sumptuous displays of sound and light. When Julio and Marguerite meet for an afternoon rendezvous at Versailles, the chill autumnal radiance of the photography and the violin obbligato of André Previn's gorgeous love theme almost camouflage the fact that nothing is going on between these two actors.

On several occasions, Minnelli alludes to the bigger conflagration which dwarfs this affair with the use of striking double-exposure montages—a blend of authentic wartime images with his own artfully faked shots, and drenched in disquieting monochromes. (One of these, depicting the siege of Warsaw, bows to Eisenstein's Odessa Steps sequence, as jagged closeups of a horrorstruck woman in spectacles collide with panoramas of exploding bombs.) Yet even this misfires, for the vitality of these episodes only emphasizes how ossified the rest of the film really is. By nature as apolitical as his Julio, Minnelli couldn't summon up the passion and ferment *Four Horsemen*'s subject matter required. By the time the movie was done, he'd learned that the fifth horseman was named Failure.

. . . .

1 9 6 2

TWO WEEKS IN ANOTHER TOWN

After the *Four Horsemen* debacle, everything about *Two Weeks in Another Town* promised a return to form for Minnelli. Reunited with the team who helped mount his most admired dramatic successes, it offered Minnelli the chance to spend two months in one of his own favorite towns, in pursuit of a theme he well understood. All of which made the painful struggles to get the film done and its eventual failure even more dispiriting. An insidious lack of conviction clouded the project from the start, reinforced later on by a chronic case of battle fatigue that even the picturesque Roman locations couldn't dispel. As if this weren't enough, the movie got trapped in the crossfire of MGM's escalating front-office wars. Mangled by the studio, skewered by the press, and spurned by moviegoers, *Two Weeks in Another Town* was a more revealing worm's-eye view of creative self-doubt and the erosions of time than its key players ever intended.

It took considerable maneuvering to turn Irwin Shaw's novel into *The Bad and the Beautiful's Little Dividend*; in its original form, the story's only link to Minnelli's 1952 melodrama is its equally withering take on the neuroses that afflict the inmates of the movie industry. Shaw's hero Jack Andrus is a man in vigorous middle age whose acting career was cut short in his youth by a wartime injury and his own waning ambition; now (rather implausibly) a military adviser to NATO, he is summoned to Rome by his former Svengali, a great director on the skids, to supervise the dubbing on the cheesy epic this filmmaker vainly hopes will salvage his career. A fortnight in this gilded snake pit inoculates Andrus forever against the corrupt allure of his former calling; in the end the chastened hero returns to Paris, his cool-headed French wife and the relative tranquillity of his diplomatic post. Like James Jones' *Some Came Running*, this was not one of its author's punchier efforts, but Shaw's best-selling track record virtually guaranteed a movie sale even before its scheduled publication date in 1960. Agent Irving Lazar auctioned *Two Weeks in Another Town* to the highest bidder while the book was still in galleys, and MGM snapped it up for the relatively paltry sum of $55,000. This purchase coincided with another minor milestone: in December 1959, MGM announced that John Houseman had agreed to resume producing pictures for the studio after a three-year absence. Considering Houseman's proven aptitude with Hollywood stories, Sol Siegel decreed that *Two Weeks in Another Town* was the project to launch this new contract.

However, a six-month strike by the Writers' Guild temporarily tabled these plans. By the time it was set-tled, Houseman opted to proceed first with a more modest undertaking—a domestic drama called *All Fall Down* from a script by William Inge, featuring Warren Beatty and Eva Marie Saint under John Frankenheimer's direction. Nonetheless, in the summer of 1960 the studio drew up a wish list of stars to adorn *Two Weeks in Another Town*. Although arguably a decade too old for the part, Clark Gable was Siegel's first choice to play the toughened survivor at the center of Shaw's story. In the novel, the waning director is a charismatic Irishman named Delaney, and it occurred to Siegel that reuniting Gable with Spencer Tracy for the first time in two decades would be an intriguing stroke of showmanship. With these two, *Two Weeks in Another Town* would have recalled an MGM legacy even more distant and nostalgic than *The Bad and the Beautiful*; certainly, this stellar combination promised a tone far different from the extroverted angst that saturated every frame of the movie Minnelli eventually made. However, Siegel's idea died with Gable, felled by a sudden heart attack in November 1960.

Meanwhile, Houseman bowed to logic by giving Charles Schnee the novel to adapt. However, life since *The Bad and the Beautiful* had not been kind to him, and his halting progress on *Two Weeks in Another Town* foretold trouble for everyone concerned. It took Schnee nearly a year to compose a treatment, and two full drafts before Houseman had a halfway satisfactory shooting script. Part of the problem undeniably lay with Shaw's novel and its relatively inert hero, suffering from what was at worst a tame mid-life crisis. Whatever the outcome of his tumultuous Roman holiday, in the book Andrus had little to lose or gain by the experience; a secure job and a well-tempered marriage await him once he's gotten the klieg lights and his former amanuensis out of his system. Even so, Schnee had managed to do much more with far less when handed George Bradshaw's skimpy *Memorial to a Bad Man* back in 1951.

Through Houseman, Siegel suggested they raise the stakes by making Andrus a more desperate character, and the screenwriter took him at his word. As Schnee reshaped the plot, a hellish marriage and Hollywood's gaudy corruptions had propelled Andrus into a complete physical and mental breakdown; he's spent the last several years walled up in a private institution rather than usefully ensconced at NATO, and this

OPPOSITE:
Kirk Douglas and Oscar,
Two Weeks in Another
Town *(1962)*

fourth-rung job on a third-rate movie represents his last chance for sanity and self-esteem. In the book, the lubricity of these Californians in exile and the Mediterranean laissez-faire of the locals made a sexually combustible combination. Andrus indulges in a restorative fling with a generous-hearted Roman girl also desired by the picture's narcissistic young star, while the director compulsively beds down his complaisant leading lady, to the fury of his shrewish spouse. In this spirit, the relative candor of Schnee's first draft prompted howls of dismay from the MPAA, still bent on preserving the old Hollywood of twin beds and tat-for-tit moral retribution.

"The code recognizes that men and women engage in premarital and extramarital relationships and agrees that stories dealing with these aspects of human behavior may be told if presented in a way which recognizes that these liaisons are immoral," Geoffrey Shurlock reminded Joseph Vogel in a stern letter to the studio dated January 25 1961. "The script in discussion here presents a panorama of affairs interlocked and overlapping in a way that would seem to indicate that the moral law was suspended, if not actually abolished, during the writing of this script. It is difficult to conceive that fornication could be any more casually portrayed than is done here. The portrayal of free and easy sexual intercourse is so graphically depicted herein that any pretense of presenting it in a moral light would appear to be almost ludicrous."

Of course, the ludicrous thing was Shurlock's own choleric tone, the last gasp of an institution desperately out of touch with the temperament of the age. The MPAA's idea of what constituted the graphic depiction of free and easy sexual intercourse paled next to the barebottomed hijinks of the average Bardot export playing in cities all over America—often distributed by subsidiaries of the same studios still ruled by the Production Code's commandments. But this broadside from Shurlock drew flinches from MGM president Joseph Vogel, who was himself part of the old order. As far as he was concerned, there were enough headaches running the studio without having a dirty movie on his hands. With Vogel and the censors hovering anxiously over his shoulder, Schnee went back to work. In June, a temporarily placated Vogel informed Houseman that the Code people were "highly enthusiastic over the ingenious way in which serious Code problems have been licked in the new script." (Apparently, fornication

*Kirk Douglas and Edward G.
Robinson in* Two Weeks in
Another Town *(1962)*

OPPOSITE:
*Kirk Douglas and Cyd
Charisse in* Two Weeks in
Another Town *(1962)*

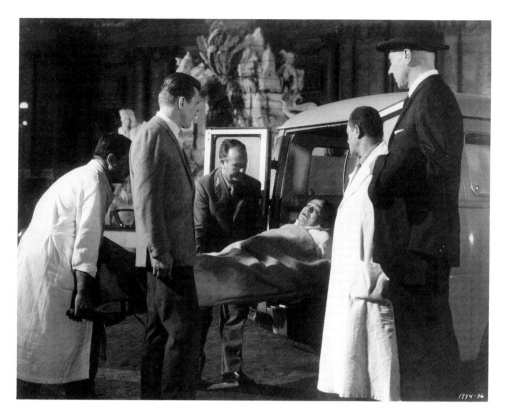

was okay as long as it took place offscreen and thus did not corrupt the innocent.) Vogel kept an ominously vigilant eye on the proceedings from then on.

Armed with Schnee's new draft, Houseman easily persuaded Kirk Douglas to head the cast of *Two Weeks in Another Town,* which served as further inducement for Minnelli to agree to direct; underscoring the *Bad and the Beautiful* connection, David Raksin was hired to compose the music. The fee for Douglas came to half a million dollars against ten percent of the gross, while Minnelli and Schnee each commanded over two hundred thousand apiece. With these figures added to a projected 81-day shooting schedule, MGM estimated that *Two Weeks in Another Town* would cost over four million dollars—a startling contrast to the relatively modest sums it had taken to make *Some Came Running* and *Home from the Hill* just two or three years earlier. This was a general trend of the times; the real problem was that box office receipts hadn't expanded accordingly. Reeling from the projected cost, MGM threatened to cancel the picture unless Houseman pared this sum by at least twenty percent. He played along, but in the end the budget inched past the studio's original estimates anyway, thanks partly to Minnelli's increasing slowness behind the camera, which stretched production to nearly four months.

As a slight consolation, once Douglas was signed the rest of the cast proved a relative bargain. With a name change from Delaney to Kruger for plausibility's sake, the role of the director went to Edward G. Robinson, whose $100,000 salary was far lower than Spencer Tracy's would have been. The feminine lead, vastly

expanded from the book, was Andrus' predatory former wife Carlotta; Minnelli selected Cyd Charisse, whose dangerous females had usually been confined to the realm of dream ballets. Considering her a histrionic lightweight and a dubious box office asset since the eclipse of the movie musical, Houseman was skeptical of this coup and Douglas opposed it outright, but Minnelli's enthusiasm prevailed. *Two Weeks in Another Town* would be Charisse's first MGM picture since her contract had expired five years before. Her salary was a tenth her co-star's, and her billing commensurately modest; at Douglas' insistence Charisse would be listed after the title on all prints and advertising. After considering Jo Van Fleet to play the director's formidable wife, the studio settled on Claire Trevor, who thus got in a few belated licks of her own, fifteen years after Robinson knocked her around in *Key Largo.* MGM's resident boy ingenue George Hamilton headed the picture's younger generation of decadents as Davie Drew, petulant scourge of the screen. Houseman and Minnelli chose a real Italian starlet, Rosanna Schiaffino, to play his film-within-the-film leading lady, while the bigger role of Douglas' wistful Roman playmate went to Daliah Lavi, an Israeli actress based in Italy.

So far, so good. In late August 1961, Minnelli flew to Rome for six weeks of preproduction work, followed shortly by Houseman. Amid all the preparations, they failed somehow to address *Two Weeks in Another Town*'s most vulnerable point—the stridency of the shooting script. In retrospect, giving such an assignment to Schnee was an insensitive move, as from a psychological standpoint he was desperately overqualified for the job. While the brutal symbiosis between the philandering has-been director and his paranoid spouse was a feature in the Shaw novel, as amplified by Schnee this subplot bore a queasy resemblance to the screenwriter's own domestic hell. At a climactic point in the script, Clara Kruger halfheartedly attempts suicide—a gesture calculated to induce pangs of remorse from her otherwise contemptuous husband. Shockingly, Mary Schnee went this character one better, actually killing herself just as the movie was going before the cameras in October 1961. Obviously, Schnee was in no state to grapple with the nuances of the script; if anything, this tragedy only validated its scathing view of wedlock Hollywood style.

Working a continent away, Schnee's colleagues were naturally stunned by the news, but meanwhile each had his own burdens to contend with. As Houseman later acknowledged in his autobiography, the zest which fueled his first stint as a Metro producer had flagged perceptibly, and he was hard-pressed to exert the requisite authority over this sprawling project. This lethargy and Minnelli's own state made for an ill-timed match, for at nearly sixty, the year misspent on *Four Horsemen of the Apocalypse* had exerted a more severe toll on the director than he cared to admit. Whenever under unusual strain or stumped by a resistant script, Minnelli instinctively took refuge in his flair for sensuous surfaces, and tended to let the rest fend for itself. Hence in early October he shot reel after moonlit reel

around the Piazza Navona, the Spanish Steps, Trastevere, and the Via Veneto, which never looked lovelier while the cast strolled somewhat aimlessly in the foreground. Minnelli wanted this version of Rome-by-night to out-Fellini *La Dolce Vita,* while MGM would have settled for *The Bad and the Beautiful* on Roman Holiday, and feared that he was giving them *The Four Horsemen* Go Latin instead. With his own job on the line, Sol Siegel was in no mood to indulge him this time around. Siegel's cables to Minnelli complained that the footage he'd seen thus far lacked energy, and urged him to speed up his work pace. "It is a fresh story of today and requires that kind of treatment," he argued. "You caught a wonderful spirit in *Some Came Running* and *Home from the Hill. . . . Two Weeks* needs the same care and attention." With obvious exasperation, he continued, "We have been criticized by our Board of Directors regarding our expensive productions. I am asking for your utmost cooperation, Vincente, to go over your schedule in Rome in order to cut it down to the number of days originally allotted to you."

Nevertheless, Minnelli stretched the 19-day location schedule to nearly a month, riling the studio by shooting scenes of the Excelsior Hotel and his Roman starlet's Minnelli-red apartment on the spot when they might have been done more expediently in Culver City later. The momentum continued to flag once the company resumed work at MGM on November 9; it took eleven more weeks to get *Two Weeks* in the can. Sets constructed for *Lady L,* a George Cukor costume picture tabled at the last minute, were recycled for *Two Weeks'* film-within-the-film. Meanwhile, Minnelli dusted off his trusty *Bad and the Beautiful* turntable and replaced Lana Turner's sedan with a spiffy new convertible for Charisse and Douglas to careen about in. One of the last scenes to be shot was his Fellini-inflected variation on an old Minnelli trademark—a wild party with the depressed hero as nauseated odd-man-out. As he conceived this bacchanale, a collection of jet-set decadents lolled about in a narcotic stupor while an erotic tableau unfolded for their jaded delectation, just outside camera range. Minnelli took particular pride in this sequence, aiming to combine his customary elegance with a jolt worthy of this "fresh story of today." Vogel, however, was outraged that any MGM movie would contain such smut, however implicit, and vowed to expunge it personally, if necessary.

The dispirited audience response at two sneak previews in the spring of 1962 only strengthened his resolve; in the meantime, Minnelli's staunchest ally Sol Siegel had been deposed as production head in favor of Robert Weitman, who was a more compliant organization man. At Vogel's orders, *Two Weeks* was handed to the studio's supervising editor Margaret Booth for drastic surgery—her specialty on the lot since the days of *Greed.* Minnelli's genteel orgy was slashed until it resembled a mass hangover the morning after a night that never was. Also gone was a melancholy monologue for Charisse which, like Nina Foch's excised final scene from *An American in Paris,* was meant to explain what made this destructive jet-setter tick. Without it, the character was just a gratuitous shrew; in fact, Booth's wholesale cuts had the perverse effect of making the movie's cast of neurotics more sordid than ever. Stripped of all motivation, they seemed merely nasty for the hell of it.

As *Two Weeks'* director, and the person held responsible for its worst excesses, Minnelli was naturally not consulted about any of this. What really revealed Vogel's contempt for the project was the fact that nobody told Houseman what was happening either—the deed was done while the producer was in Europe supervising *The Cool of the Day,* his next (and last) film for the studio. Furious at this slight to his professional dignity, Houseman shot off an imperious memo to the legal department on his return. "These changes were at no time discussed with me and in spite of our formal request the negative was cut without me or my associate producer having had a chance to review the changes," he fumed. "In thirty years of my accumulated reputation in the American theatre, film and television fields, I have taken full artistic responsibility for all the works which bore my name. *Two Weeks in Another Town* in its present form does not represent my work and I cannot permit my name to appear as its producer."

In response, the studio grudgingly allowed Houseman to re-edit the footage himself, always within the guidelines decreed by Vogel. As with *The Cobweb,* his complicity greatly upset Minnelli, and Kirk Douglas loyally backed the director up with an impassioned protest of his own. But Houseman had little choice in the matter—*Two Weeks* was going to be mutilated with or without his consent, and the best he could do was make the cuts as inconspicuous as possible. Anxious to shore up his shaky position at the studio, Houseman agreed to put his name back on the picture, dismissing Minnelli's rancor as an impractical fit of pique. "Obviously, there is nothing to be done about this," he wrote to Weitman, "and I am deeply grateful to you for letting me restore some of the lacerations performed by our leader." So the movie conceived in tribute to their first joint triumph faded out in an atmosphere of recriminations and disillusionment. It was the bitterest experience in Minnelli's twenty years at the studio.

Without undue fanfare, *Two Weeks in Another Town* premiered in August 1962. Its dismal reception exceeded all expectations—in spite of the movie's obvious flaws, the venomous tone of the reviews still came as a shock. Like the officers of the Production Code, the New York press apparently considered it a capital offense to make a movie about such unpleasant people. Always a champion of moral uplift and regeneration, the *Times'* Bosley Crowther sniffed, "when a

group of top American filmmakers goes all the way to Rome to make a picture about the sort of Hollywood rejects who sometimes get involved in this sort of trash and then make it as trashy as the worst stuff, it is time for loud and pained complaint." After noting that "*Two Weeks in Another Town* leaves no stomach unturned in its dutiful recital of banalities about movie making," the *Herald Tribune's* Joseph Morgenstern found Minnelli's decision to punctuate the film with an excerpt from *The Bad and the Beautiful* particularly galling. "This inside joke is enough to remind us that these people have done better, and know better. Shame on them."

Moviegoers seconded the critics' disdain. Worldwide, the picture earned rentals of $1,913,399—less than half what it cost to make, and far below *The Bad and the Beautiful's* returns in pre-inflation 1952 dollars. MGM estimated its total losses at $3,662,892, a figure nearly as ignominious as *The Four Horsemen's* dismal returns earlier the same year. *Two Weeks in Another Town* did attract a few champions among the young disciples of André Bazin's *politique des auteurs,* who considered the movie a deliberately outrageous testament to Minnelli's gift for melodrama. Writing in *Film Culture,* Peter Bogdanovich blithely proclaimed it superior to *La Dolce Vita* in every respect. Even Minnelli was nonplussed by such effusive praise—after all, he was no fan of *Two Weeks'* final cut himself.

Protected by his new Venice Productions contract, Minnelli emerged with his career more or less intact but his prestige tarnished. In his remaining years there, he never again commanded the unique status he had so long enjoyed at MGM. No longer an irreplaceable member of a team which in any case had ceased to exist, Minnelli was just another veteran director among many, his reputation on the line with every film he managed to make. At that, he proved one of *Two Weeks in Another Town's* more fortunate survivors, for the fallout from this fiasco was considerable. Sol Siegel having been ousted several months earlier, in 1963 it was Vogel's turn to get his walking papers from the board of directors; shortly thereafter, Houseman gratefully left MGM for good. By then, fate had added an epilogue to this whole affair too tragically neat for the hokiest movie scenario. In December 1962, a heart attack killed Charles Schnee at the age of 46—fourteen months after his wife's death, and shortly after *Two Weeks in Another Town* concluded its ill-attended run on the Loews' circuit.

Early into *Two Weeks,* the shrink treating Jack Andrus gives us a quick résumé of the hero's case history. Among other afflictions, he's been buffeted by "manic depressive psychosis, compulsive violence, delusional episodes, alcoholism acute and chronic." It's all reminiscent of that doll of Tootie Smith's with her four fatal diseases when, as her pal the iceman pointed out, "it only takes one." That's what ails *Two Weeks in Another*

*Kirk Douglas, Minnelli, and
John Houseman in Rome to
shoot* Two Weeks in
Another Town *(1962)*

Town as well; it's got satyriasis, nymphomania, latent homosexuality, suicidal episodes and paranoid hysteria both acute and chronic, when just one mental malady per customer would have sufficed. Meanwhile, *Two Weeks'* creative crew suffered from a case of *The Bad and the Beautiful.* To so deliberately invite comparison with this movie was fatal enough for the Minnelli–Houseman team—but *Two Weeks in Another Town* compounds the error by evoking some of *The Cobweb*'s stray neuroses, and perhaps a dollop or two from *Lust for Life* for good measure. Everyone is too engrossed in looking anxiously over their shoulders to get a firm bead on the script in their hands.

"You and I made some good ones—yes, and a couple of great ones," Kruger ruefully reminds his fallen star, while caressing Andrus' tarnished Academy Award. And the director pounds the point home with a nostalgic screening of their greatest joint triumph, which is Minnelli's cue to exhume an excerpt from *The Bad and the Beautiful* for his own retrospective pleasure, and ours. With these incestuous inside references, it's tempting to view Maurice Kruger as Minnelli's own unvarnished portrait. He may well have feared earning Kruger's epithet as the self-imitating "prototype of the obsolete Hollywood talent"; after the *Four Horsemen* debacle, Minnelli doubtless suffered through his own 2 a.m. blues, wondering "how can a man go wrong and not know why." His empathy is palpable in those moments when Kruger faces his own decline, which are among *Two Weeks'* least stridently directed. This explains perhaps why Minnelli stresses Kruger's pa-

thology so insistently elsewhere, lest his own identification with the character become too close for comfort.

In fact, *Two Weeks* is another Minnelli–Houseman movie in which the wrong folks end up locked inside the asylum. As fleshed out with Edward G. Robinson's customary pugnaciousness, Kruger is a master manipulator with an irrepressible streak of cruelty, usually vented on those too vulnerable to retaliate. His principal victim is the hotheaded young star of their faltering epic, and the last in Minnelli's long line of hypersensitive young men. Although played with appropriate callowness if not much charisma by George Hamilton, Davey Drew is really John Kerr resurrected; denounced for effeminacy like *Tea and Sympathy*'s hero, he turns self-tortured runaway in an episode which virtually replicates the climax from *The Cobweb*.

Two Weeks in Another Town is fairly bursting with depraved females, from Kruger's nasty spinster assistant to his "lawful wedded nightmare" and the lubricious Carlotta. Apparently, Minnelli was powerless against the venom of Schnee's script. Such wholesale misogyny has no precedent in Minnelli's movies, and his discomfiture shows in the one-note caricatures he extracted from *Two Weeks'* obedient actresses. Claire Trevor rants and brays to the point of apoplexy, and with her skin-tight black plumage and hair lacquered to extinction, Charisse purrs and undulates like a transvestite in heat. Daliah Lavi's sensuous local lass is meant to serve as antidote to all this feminine bitchery, but she's merely a chauvinist's dream girl, no more nuanced than the movie's assortment of vixens. Selflessly giving herself to the neediest man of the moment, this Magdalene in white is drawn to *Two Weeks'* hero because he's damaged goods—twice she ardently caresses the scar on his cheek, souvenir of the Carlotta-induced auto wreck that got him committed in the first place. Yet Veronica-what's-the-difference, as she calls herself, appears to have no thoughts or needs of her own, an impression reinforced by Lavi's stunned rendering of her lines.

More amusing, if equally one-dimensional, is Rossana Schiaffino's volcanic diva, with her ceaseless torrents of Italian invective. In fact, *Two Weeks* itself catches fire whenever Minnelli drops the off-the-set agonies to concentrate on the everyday craziness of putting a movie together. Having suffered through enough such crises in his time, his gibes at the language-gap vagaries of runaway production have the comic ring of truth. As always, going on location whetted Minnelli's appetite, which fitfully grants *Two Weeks* some luster of its own. His Via Veneto exhibitionists rival Fellini for flamboyant absurdity and the fountains in the Piazza Navona inspire woozy flights of improvi-

sation in the best Minnelli manner, with closeups of Bernini's pagan statuary angled to ape the mental state of his disintegrating hero.

Unfortunately, all this is just window-dressing for the lurid heart of the matter. While Douglas glowers balefully on instruction, *Two Weeks* unfolds its schematic tale of decline and regeneration. As if to prove that even paranoiacs have enemies, the script piles betrayal on top of perfidy; before long, its cynicism seems no less glib than that unlamented MGM sentimentality of yore.

Inevitably, *Two Weeks'* shellshocked hero must next career down that same highway-to-oblivion Georgia Lorrison took so memorably. For all Minnelli's This-Is-Cinerama swerves and jolts, it's not as cathartic a trip the second time around—just longer and noisier, with wanton Carlotta shrieking in the passenger seat. While Minnelli's craftsmanship is as assured here as in any film he ever made, this portrait of the new Hollywood is less a blistering exposé than a stubborn lesson in the law of diminishing returns.

• •

1965 # THE SANDPIPER

This silliest of all Minnelli's melodramas was conceived for the most mercenary of motives—to exploit the Taylor–Burton scandal à go-go at the peak of its tabloid fascination. By blending their patented screen images with stray bits from Somerset Maugham's *Miss Thompson*, independent producer Martin Ransohoff concocted the "original" story for *The Sandpiper* all by himself—the ill-starred misalliance between a voluptuous free spirit and a married clergyman whose tight white collar belies an untapped capacity for passion. To flesh this into script form, Ransohoff cannily hired two formerly blacklisted screenwriters in succession; however distasteful the task, after years of financial drought Dalton Trumbo and Michael Wilson weren't in a position to be choosy. The producer also had little trouble luring the Burtons to play what was essentially a feature-length preview-of-coming-attractions touting the fan magazine version of their private affairs. At $1,500,000 plus a cut of the gross for their joint services, the price was right. They did stipulate, however, that Ransohoff hire a director of comparable luster to guide them through this soapy scenario with as much dignity as possible.

Ransohoff eagerly agreed to their terms, and in June 1963 he announced that William Wyler would direct *The Sandpiper* as a Columbia release. (If nothing else, the producer deserved credit for fast reflexes; this deal

made the papers before the Burtons' notorious *Cleopatra* had its public premiere.) At some point, Wyler understandably entertained second thoughts and dropped out of the project; in the meantime, Ransohoff had signed a multi-picture deal with MGM. By then the Burtons had already earned the studio a small fortune with an airport-lounge rehab of *Grand Hotel* called *The V.I.P.s.*, and Metro was delighted to package a new personality showcase to their measure.

This, of course, was where Minnelli came in. He was certainly eminent enough to satisfy the Burtons, and as eminently available. Following his loanout to Fox to do *Goodbye, Charlie*, Minnelli had no tangible projects on the horizon to justify the weekly stipend MGM was committed to pay his Venice Productions whether he worked or not. Minnelli harbored no illusions about the merits of *The Sandpiper*'s script, but he had compelling reasons of his own for taking the job. After two studio-bound comedies in a row, at least this deluxe endeavor would take him off the lot again with the time and budget to indulge his professional wanderlust. Besides, he hadn't been associated with a real moneymaker in several years, and *The Sandpiper* was

OPPOSITE:
Elizabeth Taylor at Big Sur,
The Sandpiper *(1965)*

as close to a sure thing as one could find in 1964; it promised to shore up his commercial standing in the industry, and turn that elusive profit-sharing clause in his contract from the hypothetical to the probable. More irresistible yet, *The Sandpiper*'s stars seemed eager indeed to get him, inviting Minnelli for a visit in New York during the run of Burton's *Hamlet* to discuss the prospect. From *Brigadoon* to *Four Horsemen of the Apocalypse*, this sort of flattery had gotten him in trouble before, and despite his qualms Minnelli proved susceptible once again.

With the Burtons in hand a supporting cast was almost irrelevant, but Minnelli and Ransohoff mustered a respectable lineup all the same. Eva Marie Saint accepted the thankless part of the pastor's steadfast beige-on-beige wife for equal star billing and one-tenth Richard Burton's half-million salary. The heroine had a neglected suitor as well, in the person of a surly artist who specializes in wood sculptures of her nude form. Apparently it was Taylor herself who had the odd idea of offering this role to Sammy Davis Jr. Apart from his questionable erotic appeal, the script was really too flimsy to support the added weight of an interracial liaison. Minnelli and Ransohoff vehemently objected and instead cast the dour but more plausible Charles

Bronson. As Taylor's equally unfettered love child, Minnelli cast James Mason's small son Morgan in his first and last movie role, while *Meet Me in St. Louis'* Boy Next Door Tom Drake turned up in a small part as a colleague of Burton.

To protect the Burtons' salaries from the long arm of British and American Internal Revenue, *The Sandpiper*'s base of operation was a French sound stage. Faking the west coast of Bohemia at the Boulogne-Billancourt Studios held no terrors for Minnelli, who had made *The Reluctant Debutante* there six years earlier; besides, there were worse places than Paris to spend a couple of working months. To ensure the requisite made-in-Hollywood gloss, he brought along with him a top-grade crew of long-time colleagues from the home lot. *The Sandpiper* was Minnelli's eighth straight collaboration with cameraman Milton Krasner. George W. Davis and Urie McCleary, who'd designed most of Minnelli's movies after *Gigi*, dreamed up the driftwood-and-macramé interiors for Taylor's beachfront retreat; his favorite costumer Irene Sharaff (also responsible for Taylor's *Cleopatra* look) assumed the task of transforming the star into Big Sur's most glamorous beatnik. The trip to Paris was preceded by a month of location work; MGM considered substituting a beach

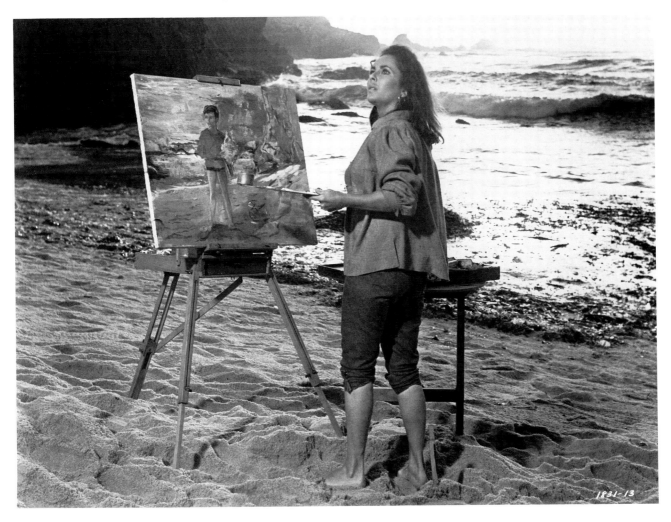

*Richard Burton, Elizabeth
Taylor, James Edwards in*
The Sandpiper *(1965)*

*Richard Burton, Elizabeth
Taylor, James Edwards in*
The Sandpiper *(1965)*

in Corsica for California, but in the end Minnelli spent September 1964 filming the rocky coastline between Carmel and Big Sur after all. This footage was meant to convey the heroine's Thoreau-like communion with the natural world around her; the least you could say for Krasner's gold-lit seascapes was that they made for a fetching travelogue.

The Sandpiper troupe flew to Europe in early October, and during the two months they spent in Paris, the making of this movie assumed its proper place as a sideshow to the Burton media circus. The most famous couple in the world was besieged by paparazzi and hordes of the civilian curious wherever they went, with a hapless Minnelli trampled in their wake. For what it was worth, he asserted his customary authority during working hours, for even if MGM and the press had cast him as the most conspicuous supernumerary in the Burtons' entourage, at least the two stars were too professional to rub it in.

Minnelli finished principal photography at the beginning of December. After a sneak preview in January, he reshot part of a Taylor–Burton love scene at a motel in Encino, using doubles for his long-departed stars. *The Sandpiper's* final budget came to $5,200,000, even then a substantial sum for a non-road show attraction; as a comparison, Ransohoff's Steve McQueen vehicle *The Cincinnati Kid*, released by MGM around the same time, cost two million dollars less to produce. With exhibitor interest at fever pitch, the studio scheduled the film as its big summer release with a steamy campaign to match. ("She gave men a taste of life," the ads panted, ". . . that made them hunger for

more!") *The Sandpiper* opened at Radio City Music Hall, the first Minnelli film to do so since *Bells Are Ringing,* and predictably racked up huge attendance figures. If any picture was critic-proof this was it, which was fortunate for Metro because the reviews were unanimously derisive. "How wanly Art imitates Life," muttered *Time* magazine's anonymous reporter, while the *Herald Tribune's* Judith Crist dubbed *The Sandpiper* "the most perfectly awful movie of the past several seasons." The press was too busy giggling over the script's fatuities and the overripe curves Taylor displayed in her semi-nude scene to single out Minnelli's contribution to the movie's deadpan merriment. One compassionate note was sounded by the *Village Voice's* auteurist critic, Andrew Sarris. Lamenting Minnelli's diminished status in the new Hollywood hierarchy, he observed that "Metro's most flamboyant stylist in the forties and fifties has been reduced to accepting assignments at the whim of an alleged actress he virtually started on the road to stardom. . . . The little men with the big cigars will credit the Burtons for the good business and blame Minnelli for the bad reviews," although he was "the only person connected with the production who has ever shown any genuine feeling and flair for the medium."

There was a certain sad truth to Sarris' musings. For an artist of Minnelli's pride, *The Sandpiper's* box-office success was a humiliation in itself—its dreadful reputation actually helped sell the picture, as moviegoers flocked to see if it was really as laughable as everyone had said. To add injury to insult, Minnelli never saw any of the profits he'd so eagerly anticipated. Next to

Doctor Zhivago, The Sandpiper was MGM's biggest grossing film of 1965, returning $6,200,000 in domestic rentals and an additional four million in foreign and television revenue. According to the studio's complicated accounting formulas, this left the picture $1,500,000 short of recoupment. Its stars earned their slice off the top all the same, and immediately went on to redeem their artistic standing with Mike Nichols' film version of *Who's Afraid of Virginia Woolf?* All Minnelli got out of *The Sandpiper* was another body blow to his already tottering prestige.

The saddest thing about *The Sandpiper* is the way traces of Minnelli's handiwork still show through—it's a deadpan self-parody of his other movies about lonely artists and the siren call of nonconformity. To give him credit for something, Minnelli's reach never exceeds the grasp of his painter protagonists. In *Lust for Life,* he surrounded Van Gogh with a film worthy of its subject; *The Sandpiper* is as bad as the motel-art oils of seagulls and little boys turned out by its strong-willed heroine.

From Laura's opulently scruffy surfside home to the dress-extra free spirits who let it all hang out at Big Sur's Nepenthe, *The Sandpiper*'s view of subterranean life is exactly what you'd expect from a sixty-year-old director who'd tarried at Metro too long. The best he could do was prevent his actors from telegraphing their contempt for the ridiculous things they had to say in scene after sodden scene. Just when you think nothing could top Taylor's metaphor-fraught claim that, "the only way you can tame a bird is to let him fly free," her co-star trumps her by begging the deity to "grant me some small remembrance of honor," once the temptation of the Taylor flesh proves too irresistible. Frankly, all the much-touted heat between these two remains strictly in the mind of the *Photoplay*-sated beholder. Their on-screen affair is strictly business—two high-priced celebrities sleepwalking through their preordained paces.

After *The Night of the Iguana,* audiences were attuned to the sight of Burton as a man of the cloth brought low by desire, but at its most delirious *The Sandpiper* came up with some new frissons for the inveterate Liz-watcher. Stuffed into an endless wardrobe of lavender-on-lavender sportswear, she smooches with Burton while a wounded fowl nests in her raven tresses, and fends off a randy ex-lover by brandishing a dainty hatchet while her breast heaves furiously inside a violet-blue bra. Taylor even delivers a proto-feminist monologue earnestly decrying the barrenness of the married woman's lot, while the Big Sur surf pounds the sand of her own private cove. Inadvertently, Minnelli turns this unabashed star vehicle into an iconoclastic black comedy, but the joke wears thin long before the minister and his illicit beloved go their separate soulful ways. By then the moment was overdue for MGM and its house director to part company as well, while Minnelli retained some small remembrance of honor of his own.

Minnelli with Hirschfeld caricature, 1983

6 Finales

With three pictures still to go under his Venice Productions deal with MGM, Minnelli remained idle under contract for nearly two years after completing *The Sandpiper.* For a time he occupied himself with the studio's projected musical remake of *Goodbye, Mr. Chips,* originally planned to star Rex Harrison talk-singing an André Previn score. But the material didn't really interest him, and Minnelli opted instead to concentrate on Freed's pipe-dream Irving Berlin cavalcade *Say It with Music.* (When the refurbished *Chips* finally reached the screen in 1969, it was Peter O'Toole who mumbled his way through a new batch of songs by Leslie Bricusse, under the direction of Herbert Ross; the film was a critical and commercial disaster.) Throughout 1965 into the following year, MGM offhandedly strung Minnelli and Freed along, tabling each successive draft of the script without quite mustering the guts to kill the project altogether. The successful 1966 reissue of *Gigi* only emphasized how remote the glory days of the MGM musical really were; by Hollywood's accelerated hourglass the eight years since its premiere were a creative lifetime and several studio regimes ago. *Gigi*'s producer-director team was history, as far as MGM's current caretakers were concerned, and only tact kept them from saying so.

Since MGM had no particular desire to put Minnelli to work on anything else, his contract lapsed by mutual consent in November 1966. The studio grudgingly agreed to allow him to continue working with writer George Wells on yet another draft of the Berlin project without payment, noting that he and MGM were ''under no mutual obligation'' whatever. Out of loyalty to Freed, Minnelli persevered for a few months before finally giving up. (Resuscitated one last time by Blake Edwards, *Say It with Music* was finally laid to rest in 1969 when new MGM chief James Aubrey effectively dismantled the studio.) On this anticlimactic note, Minnelli left the lot for good after twenty-six years; his one bittersweet consolation was that at this stage, there really wasn't much to leave.

Minnelli got a welcome boost to his morale when the 1967 Cannes Film Festival invited him to preside over its jury. While in Europe, he received an unexpected offer from Broadway's prolific and mercurial producer David Merrick—the chance to direct his first stage musical since the 1939 *Very Warm for May.* Minnelli had been wooed by several similar proposals during his MGM years; the most intriguing, *The Golden Apple,* was a musical adaptation of Homer's *Odyssey,* and winner of the 1954 New York Drama Critics' Circle award. Until now, he'd been far too engrossed in making movies to be seriously tempted, but with nothing forthcoming in Hollywood, the idea of recharging his energies in the medium of his first great successes seemed attractive indeed.

The show in question may not have been as ambitious as Jeffrey Cordova's adaptation of *Faust,* but the dark portents were there all the same. Tentatively entitled *Façade,* it was meant to be a sober yet sumptuous retelling of the Mata Hari legend, crafted by a youngish trio with a scant list of Broadway credits behind them —librettist Jerome Coopersmith, responsible for the Sherlock Holmes musical *Baker Street;* composer Edward Thomas, and lyricist Martin Charnin, then a decade shy of his popular smash *Annie.* Despite its operetta-ish World War I setting, the script's antiwar sentiments ostensibly lent the show some Viet Nam-era resonance; however, *Façade*'s main appeal for Minnelli was its promise of period spectacle and the provocatively elusive nature of its heroine. Production plans began to take shape in the summer of 1967, and to ease his director's transition back into the theater, Merrick assembled a group of seasoned stage professionals with whom Minnelli had happily collaborated in Hollywood. Chief among these were choreographer Jack Cole, whose dances would run the gamut from Mata Hari's celebrated cooch to an Act II Interrogation Ballet, and the great Irene Sharaff to drape the stellar spy in appropriately glittering undress. Merrick raised a budget of $500,000, then the high-standard figure for a splashy Broadway musical; most of the money came from RCA Victor, which planned to record the show.

Right away there were signs of trouble. As their singing-dancing seductress, Merrick and Minnelli unaccountably cast an obscure movie starlet who could do neither. Austrian-born Marisa Mell had recently appeared as Marcello Mastroianni's playmate in *Casanova '70,* which hardly qualified her to command the central role in a Broadway musical; Mell's principal attributes

• •

ON A CLEAR DAY
YOU CAN SEE FOREVER

Alan Jay Lerner's *On a Clear Day You Can See Forever* was the most eagerly anticipated show of the 1965-66 theatrical season, despite a bumpy gestation —its original composer Richard Rodgers dropped out in favor of the lyricist's *Royal Wedding* collaborator, Burton Lane; while out of town, *On a Clear Day*'s leading man Louis Jourdan had also defected, ceding to understudy John Cullum. Nevertheless, it represented Lerner's first stage work since *Camelot* as well as the star breakthrough for Barbara Harris, the late Judy Holliday's natural successor as Broadway's most endearing musical comedienne. The plot confected by Lerner was a romantically tall tale of reincarnation, shuttling between the English Restoration and present-day New York. While under hypnosis to stop smoking, an insecure kook named Daisy Gamble gives way to the irresistible spirit of her former self, the seductive adventuress Melinda Wells, who bewitches the doctor of parapsychology who has unleashed her.

It didn't take ESP to see the link between *On a Clear Day*'s cynical professor awakened to love by his déclassé guinea pig and *My Fair Lady;* however, Lerner sans George Bernard Shaw failed to mesmerize Broadway's opinion-makers. Despite panegyrics for Harris and kind words for Lane's melodies, *On a Clear Day* was dismissed as a distinct letdown thanks largely to its cumbersome libretto. In a season which also included *Man of La Mancha, Mame* and *Sweet Charity,* this expensively mounted show lasted eight months on Broadway. Lerner's reputation still awed Hollywood, however, and Paramount secured the movie rights for a reported $750,000, before the end of *On a Clear Day*'s run.

In fact, Paramount had an inordinate amount riding on Lerner's art, having already committed to the big-screen version of his western musical *Paint Your Wagon.* With its author serving as co-producer with studio executive Howard W. Koch, *On a Clear Day* took shape as a comparatively modest undertaking by the profligate standards of the time, allotted less than half *Paint Your Wagon*'s $20,000,000 budget. As the show offered little in the way of presold appeal, Paramount cast about for an indelible personality to fill the star part. This called for an idiosyncratic singing actress suited equally to play a period voluptuary in the flashbacks and the wistful underdog of her latter-day reincarnation. Box office logic if little else prompted Koch to offer the role to Audrey Hepburn; once she declined he aggressively pursued Barbra Streisand instead. Although ideal for the part, from a commercial standpoint Streisand was then something of a calculated risk. Despite her meteoric rise in the theater and as a

recording artist, Streisand's appeal with movie audiences had yet to be confirmed. After completing the London run of *Funny Girl,* she was committed to recreating this Broadway triumph on screen, with the celluloid version of *Hello, Dolly!* to follow; neither had started production when Koch persuaded her to do *On a Clear Day You Can See Forever.*

With its star otherwise engaged, Paramount tabled all plans for *On a Clear Day* until well into 1968. Meanwhile, Lerner campaigned hard to get his favorite screen director hired as well. Although Minnelli hadn't set foot in a sound stage for five years or made a musical in ten, Lerner still felt that no one could match his sensitivity for the form. As Streisand had been signed first, her consent was an essential part of the package. Fortunately, Minnelli always warmed to bigger-than-life personalities of her stripe, and his genuine enthusiasm at the prospect of working with Streisand won her over immediately. Once that was settled, he persuaded Lerner to make some major refurbishments of the original libretto, particularly the period sequences. At Minnelli's request, they were updated a century to the Napoleonic era, which he found more photogenic, while Lerner also raised the dramatic ante for Melinda's erotic dalliances with a climactic trial for treason and murder. To Minnelli's delight, Lerner persuaded Cecil Beaton to create the Empire designs for the flashbacks; it was all soothingly reminiscent of their happy collaboration on *Gigi* ten years before.

With preproduction scheduled for the fall of 1968, Paramount had considerable trouble casting the shrink distracted by Streisand's schizoid Eliza. Clearly subordinate to the heroine, the role was written as one extended slow burn with song cues, which probably explains why first choice Richard Harris turned it down. Undaunted, Koch aimed even higher by offering it to Frank Sinatra and even Gregory Peck, who, whatever his vocal deficiencies, at least suited Hollywood's notion of what an egghead was supposed to look like. When both declined, perennial Francophile Lerner suggested Yves Montand. Although his *chansonnier* charm always lost something in translation, Montand had at least proven a gallant foil to the likes of Monroe and MacLaine in his previous American films. *On a Clear Day*'s hero had been Gallicized briefly before by Jourdan during the stage tryout, and Lerner hoped Montand's continental cool would spark the right

OPPOSITE:
Yves Montand and Barbra Streisand, On a Clear Day You Can See Forever *(1970)*

chemistry of opposites with the madcap exhibitionism of a star like Streisand. Besides, his name might help sell the film to an overseas market usually allergic to American movie musicals.

Where the domestic movie public was concerned, a great deal had happened in the three years between *On a Clear Day*'s Broadway run and its impending screen incarnation. The sixties' youthquake had reached even Alan Jay Lerner's ears, and he halfheartedly transcribed some of this dissonance to his distinctly unhip screenplay. Allusions to student unrest now buzzed around his musical-comedy campus, but the most visible concession to the times was a newly interpolated character—Daisy's stepbrother, an itinerant semi-hippie adorned with sideburns and an acoustic guitar. It was Minnelli who matched this dubious cliché to an obscure and suitably unconventional actor named Jack Nicholson, then a second-billed biker, acid-tripper and general-purpose maniac in Roger Corman drive-in movies. When *On a Clear Day* finally reached the theaters, *Easy Rider* had made a subversive counterculture icon out of Nicholson, and his presence on the sidelines of a Barbra Streisand musical seemed weird indeed. But at the time, getting this part was a step out of the exploitation-flick ghetto toward the big time, and it

wouldn't take long for the movie establishment to conform to Nicholson's mold instead.

On a Clear Day finally went before the cameras on January 6 1969, for what was scheduled to be an 82-day shoot. Although the film paired Minnelli with a new art director in John de Cuir, his cameraman was another link to his halcyon days at MGM; he had last worked with Harry Stradling on *The Pirate*, two decades earlier. A Los Angeles park provided the rose-garden location for Streisand's solos, "Hurry! It's Lovely Up Here" and the title song, which opened and closed the film; the interiors for the flashback and contemporary stories alike were constructed mostly on the Paramount lot. From the moment filming started, the company braced for fireworks between Minnelli and his volatile star, who had earned a reputation in the trade for bluntly challenging the authority of the eminent directors she had worked with. Instead, harmony reigned; where a martinet like William Wyler brooked little discussion of artistic matters with mere performers once the cameras turned, Minnelli always nurtured a collaborative spirit with his stars, and encouraged the Streisand penchant for contributing her own ideas to the part. While her confidence and enthusiasm stimulated Minnelli, his laissez-faire attitude stranded those performers less secure than she was. Struggling with a rather dour role in an idiom not his own, Montand needed all the help he could get, while cool fish-out-of-water Nicholson found himself directed by someone whose ideas of beats and hipsters were shaped by *The Sandpiper.*

Enraptured by Streisand, Minnelli took special pains to make her shine in the flashback sequences, in which neither Montand nor Nicholson appeared. In Lerner's revised script, Barbra/Melinda meets the scapegrace love of her life during a banquet in George IV's Royal Pavilion at Brighton. Initially, Koch planned to construct a facsimile at the studio, until de Cuir estimated that re-creating its Arabian Nights splendors on the lot would be costlier than sending the company across the Atlantic to shoot the real thing. In late April, *On a Clear Day*'s principal crew accordingly flew to England. Minnelli was ravished by what he found there; he enjoyed nothing more than turning a real-life wonderland into the stuff movie dreams are made of. A decade earlier, he'd reanimated Maxim's into a bejeweled fin-de-siècle demimonde. With Cecil Beaton once more at his side, Minnelli filled the Royal Pavilion with a Regency fantasia of dress-extra Beau Brummels and Emma Hamiltons, dominated by a turbanned Streisand in crystal and silver décolletage.

To make this *Gigi* revisitation complete, Minnelli's reveries on the set were once again clouded by a sudden change of scenario in his personal life. For the first time since their marriage, wife Denise chose not to accompany him while shooting a film abroad. On arriving in England, he learned that she had embarked on a new relationship; after their eventual divorce, the third Mrs. Minnelli married mercantile king Prentis Cobb Hale, conquering San Francisco society with the same aplomb she had deployed in Beverly Hills. As a young bachelor in the 1930s, Minnelli had deflected the matchmaking efforts of his friends by whimsically citing his fear of "the Minnelli curse"; in the wake of three failed marriages, he wondered whether there hadn't been something to it after all. Sadly, 1969 was a year of sobering goodbyes for Minnelli. On June 22, not long after he returned home from England to complete *On a Clear Day,* Judy Garland died suddenly in London, of an apparently accidental barbiturate overdose.

Despite his private heartaches, Minnelli had a job to do. Work was his refuge, and considering his increasing idleness in the late sixties, it was fortunate that *On a Clear Day* came along when it did. The Brighton shoot was bracketed by two sieges of intensive location work in New York, oddly enough a new experience for him; except for a few pick-up shots in *Bells Are Ringing,* Manhattan was one place on the map Minnelli had always counterfeited on some MGM sound stage. The hero's big solo, "Come Back to Me," inspired Minnelli to mount the most vertiginous tracking shot of his hy-

permobile career. Taking a leaf from the airborne first-act finale in New York bay of Wyler's *Funny Girl,* he replaced his crane boom with a helicopter swooping around a wind-blown Montand, rhapsodizing from the roof of the Pan Am building. Minnelli punctuated this number with shots of Streisand scampering through a sheaf of picturesque midtown locations, from the East Side across Fifth Avenue to the fountain at Lincoln Center, the water synchronized to spurt on musical cue like the Place de la Concorde cascades in *Gigi.*

Paramount hoped to shoot a brief student demonstration sequence on the campus of Columbia University, but having barely survived the real thing less than a year earlier, the college trustees were hardly prepared to indulge the fancies of a Hollywood film crew. When Fordham University also turned down the honor, the studio gave up and hurriedly arranged to fake the scene back west. Nevertheless, Minnelli captured an excess of riches during this New York sojourn; in fact the stylish footage taken in Central Park zoo and the sculpture garden of The Museum of Modern Art never made it to the final cut. Production closed on the Paramount lot in early June. Although the film had run several weeks over, compared to many super-musicals of the day the making of *On a Clear Day* was a model of speed and efficiency. For Minnelli it was his most satisfying project in years, but after viewing the rough assembly Paramount wasn't quite so sanguine. Initially, the studio had scheduled a fall 1970 road-show premiere for its Streisand vehicle, calculated at nearly a year after *Hello, Dolly!*'s Christmas 1969 release. But over the intervening months, it became clear that the musical cycle was fast wearing out its popular welcome; despite Streisand's following and the tentatively up-to-date trappings of the script, *On a Clear Day* seemed an unlikely prospect to buck the trend. Accordingly, its opening was pushed up to the summer, and the running time trimmed by fifteen minutes to accommodate a continuous-run policy.

Three musical sequences disappeared from the film at this stage. "Wait Till We're Sixty-Five," a rooftop duet for Daisy and her uptight fiancé (played by Larry Blyden), had been a small-scale production number tricked up with prisms and multi-colored gels fusing mild psychedelia with a palette reminiscent of Minnelli's 1930s stage revues. The others featured two of the four new songs Lerner and Lane had written for the film. Minnelli conceived "ESP" as one of *On a Clear Day*'s most flamboyant moments, a montage of Streisand's past and future incarnations permitting her to warble several languages while parading about in fashions both antique and 21st-century mod. Jack Nicholson had been lumbered with "Who Is There Among Us Who Knows?" a ballad as meandering as its title. Although this curiosity subsequently appeared on a compilation album of cut songs from movie musicals, filmgoers were spared his adenoidal crooning to a

Jack Nicholson serenades Barbra Streisand. A cut sequence from On a Clear Day You Can See Forever *(1970)*

hummed counterpoint from Streisand. Paramount's prunings were so hurriedly executed that when *On a Clear Day* opened, half the publicity photos displayed outside New York's Loews' State were from scenes no longer in the movie.

While better on balance than a skeptical studio had expected, the reviews for *On a Clear Day* ran the gamut from contempt to qualified rapture. Most lamented Montand's displaced-person star turn and the tired blood of the present-day sequences in general; depending on whom one read, Streisand's bravura constituted the pinnacle of her film career to date or else a testament to her unbridled egomania. However, virtually everyone felt that *On a Clear Day*'s most stubborn time-tripper was not Lerner's heroine, but Minnelli himself. Certainly, his kind of sensuous escapism had never been so generally out of fashion as it was on the cusp of the seventies. For would-be modernists defending the medium from the clutches of corrupt old Hollywood, Minnelli's quest for style represented a bankrupt phoniness the screen was well rid of. Thus *Time* decreed, "he puts his star through all that is passé," while *Newsweek*'s Joseph Morgenstern dismissed Minnelli and Harry Stradling as "custodians of a defunct tradition," adding that "they, far more than poor Daisy Gamble, are haplessly trapped in the present."

Others saw him instead as the noble keeper of a guttering flame; if there were no longer any room for the unabashed artifice Minnelli reveled in, then that was the movies' loss. In the *Village Voice*, Molly Haskell wrote admiringly that "through distancing and stylization, and with the right mixture of pageantry and parody, Minnelli has suggested a contemporary world which is set in quotation marks, and a historical one in double quotations." The *New York Times'* Vincent Canby proclaimed *On a Clear Day* "the first Barbra Streisand movie to suggest—even briefly—that she is capable of playing something other than Fanny Brice in the seven stages of woman. . . . Minnelli's love of decor transforms the movie into very real fantasy." When Canby described the Brighton episode as "lush lyricism from Minnelli's *Yolanda and the Thief* period," the comparison was meant as a wistful compliment.

In a year dominated by movies like *M*A*S*H* and *Five Easy Pieces,* nostalgia didn't mean much to that majority of moviegoers far younger than *Yolanda* itself. Defensively, Minnelli later wrote, "it was not my greatest musical success, but neither was it Paramount's greatest musical failure," which was indeed an accurate appraisal. Shortly after his movie opened the studio launched *Darling Lili,* Blake Edwards' own ill-starred variation on the *Mata Hari* mystique; at double the cost of *On a Clear Day* it proved a complete financial bust, effectively ending the first phase of Julie Andrews' Hollywood career. By contrast, thanks to Streisand's tenacious personal following, if little else, Minnelli's film earned domestic returns of $5,350,000. While a modestly respectable sum, it was hardly enough to improve Minnelli's stock as a bankable commodity.

With this movie, Minnelli was burdened by handicaps that would have daunted a director half his age. Reflecting the era's wariness toward the old conventions of the movie musical, *On a Clear Day* uneasily grafts its songs onto a plot resembling nothing so much as a sitcom version of *The Three Faces of Eve.* As Dr. Chabot hypnotizes Daisy to awaken her former selves through reel after reel, the viewer's eyelids begin drooping as well. According to the movie's central whimsy, Marc and Daisy are karmic lovers whose current incarnations clash—he yearns for the Melinda that was while she pines for the shrink that is, but they'll happily mate at last in some future lifetime. Unfortunately, thrown together on the Paramount lot in 1969 A.D., Streisand and Montand seem scarcely to be professional acquaintances, let alone destiny's pawns. (Minnelli's camera strategies are no help either—relying on alternating closeups in their shared scenes, he rarely shows them together in the same shot.)

Streisand was always the epitome of the self-contained star, whose onscreen rapport with her leading men tended to the theoretical. Even so, Montand presented special obstacles of his own. Removed from his natural habitat on the French concert stage, Montand's debonair appeal damply unglues under the fierce gaze of the Panavision camera. Chabot is a coolheaded intellectual with a skeptical mind and a romantic soul, but Montand is too concerned with making his lines intelligible to worry about any of that. In his obvious discomfiture, Montand seems foolishly square and prematurely middle-aged; under the circumstances, Daisy's infatuation for the doctor is more perverse than her psychic skill for finding lost objects and making flowers grow.

Undaunted, Minnelli concentrates on Streisand. As the latest in his constellation of extrovert singing comediennes, she displays all the feminine aplomb he admired most in his movie-musical divas. Streisand freaks and Barbra-phobes alike were forced to concede that under Minnelli's indulgent eye, *On a Clear Day* was a multiple-personality showcase for her fabled virtuosity and then some. As Daisy, she serves up a cartwheeling sample of Brooklyn-inflected shtick, while her Melinda is a swan-necked odalisque out of some lost painting by Ingres.

In the contemporary episodes, Minnelli's directorial gallantry plays havoc with the already dubious logic of Lerner's script. Daisy is supposed to be an unprepossessing shlemiel of a girl—disgruntled by her contrast with the late Melinda, Chabot calls Daisy a "caterpillar . . . this little nothing of a creature." Yet in whatever guise, the last thing this star lacks is temperament; moreover, in her kicky coordinates by Arnold Scaasi, Barbra looks every inch the thoroughly mod fashion plate. Bellbottomed jeans and long ironed-out hair may serve the collegiate extras milling about in the background, but our heroine sports enough outsized millinery to accessorize an updated remake of *Gigi.*

As it hopscotches between two centuries, *On a Clear Day*'s own split personality dwarfs any identity crisis endured by Daisy. It's glaringly apparent that while the plot keeps tugging Minnelli back to the miniskirted present, he'd rather lose himself forever in Melinda's boudoir wars of 1812. In its final form, *On a Clear Day*'s Brighton sequences were substantially pared away; although prominently billed in the credits, *Lust for Life*'s Pamela Brown flits by as a monarch's consort and disappears. Nevertheless, the scenes which remain have an opulent grace that conjures up MGM's heyday if not quite the age of Napoleon. For the lush Lerner–Lane ballad "Love with all the Trimmings," Minnelli intercuts glowing closeups of Melinda and her newest conquest across the banquet table, capping the song's reprise with a sensual tracking shot encircling the couple as they hungrily embrace. Later, he pitches Streisand's soliloquy "He Isn't You" in a more rueful key, as Melinda ponders the vagaries of love in her neo-Classical salon with ormolu accents. In between, Minnelli sends up the then-recent hit *Oliver!* with a cartoon-Dickensian account of Melinda's orphanage upbringing—all sound-stage coal-soot and cobblestones.

Even this parody is sumptuously lit and designed, while the contemporary episodes unreel in a solid fluorescent glare against sets as flagrantly fake as the Regency ones, but not nearly so alluring. Minnelli's own standards of escapist glamour don't jive with the movie's halfhearted feint at the counterculture; in the trendy here and now, the director has a hard time divining what passes for chic any more, let alone whether he likes any of it. The lengthy sessions in Dr. Chabot's study, allow ample opportunity to ponder how ugly the room is—a migraine blend of marble steps and woodsy bookshelves with space age-contempo furniture. For reasons that only a meager budget could justify, Streisand's culminating torch of "What Did I Have that I Don't Have" is awkwardly crammed within this tacky space, when it might better have prompted a Minnelli prowl through lonely streets in the manner of *Gigi*'s title number. With its expansive helicopter shots of the city and frantic jump-cutting, Montand's big moment aims to show how up-to-date Minnelli could be. Although it's indeed nice to be outdoors for a change, all this gimmickry trumps his performers, and wears Minnelli out before he's gotten through the song's second chorus.

At final fadeout, Streisand sings her farewells from the void, superimposed against an expanse of pink and gray clouds. In *The Four Horsemen of the Apocalypse,* a like device foretold destruction and death, but here it's supposed to convey an infinity of hope. While Daisy had her future lives to look forward to, Minnelli was still glancing backward. With its tale of a woman whose subconscious identity outshines her waking self, *On a Clear Day* is a direct descendant of some of Minnelli's brightest entertainments, from *The Pirate* through *Bells Are Ringing.* But the times weren't ripe for this latest incarnation. As *On a Clear Day*'s star climactically laments, she's "out of date and outclassed, by my past," and despite Streisand's distilled exuberance and Minnelli's own fitful bursts of dazzlement, the movie gravely hinted at the same predicament for its director.

• •

1976   A MATTER OF TIME

Despite the tepid reception accorded *On a Clear Day*, Minnelli refused to concede that his active filmmaking career had come to a close, and over the next few years he worked hard to develop two new projects at Paramount. Each was the biography of a flamboyant woman celebrity from the 1920s who met an untimely end—the Bessie Smith story, intended for Tina Turner, and the life of Zelda Fitzgerald, to be adapted from Nancy Milford's acclaimed book with Liza Minnelli as its star. Neither film got past the preliminaries, thanks to growing doubts that Minnelli still had the stamina to direct and also, in the latter case, an impasse over the rights to the Fitzgerald property. Any qualms Hollywood's power brokers had about entrusting a major film to a veteran of his vintage and temperament were reinforced by a sharp decline in Minnelli's health during the early 1970s. As a lifelong chain-smoker whose idea of physical exercise was riding a camera boom, he suffered a series of minor strokes which further knotted his chronic stutter and increasingly clouded his memory; around the same time, a near-fatal chest ailment necessitated an operation to remove part of one lung. In light of this growing frailty, as he approached seventy Minnelli's lifelong habit of fibbing about his age backfired in an unexpected way; for a man reputed to be only in his early sixties, he seemed prematurely *hors de combat*.

With little to occupy him, Minnelli did what comes naturally to semi-retired celluloid legends—in 1974 he published his memoirs, *I Remember It Well*, penned in collaboration with professional ghost writer Hector Arce. By then, his happiest distraction was basking in the reflected glory of his daughter Liza's achievements as a screen actress and concert personality. The pair had always enjoyed an exceptionally close relationship; both before and after the breakup with Garland, Minnelli was a doting parent who took an active role in the rearing of his firstborn. Throughout her childhood, Liza was a welcome fixture on the sidelines of practically every Minnelli set, and in their free time together, he avidly encouraged his daughter's talent and her flair for fantasy. In early adulthood, she relied frequently on her father's loving professional counsel, and later claimed that her performance as Sally Bowles in *Cabaret* was much influenced by his insights into the period and on movie-musical craft in general. Father and daughter had long nurtured a mutual hope to collaborate on a movie someday, and following the collapse of *Zelda*, Minnelli was spurred to seek other prospects. Even so, their eagerness did have its limitations—at one time or another various would-be backers approached the Minnellis with the idea of mounting the Judy Garland story, a notion that appalled them both.

For years Minnelli had been interested in Maurice Druon's 1954 novel, *La Volupté d'etre*, translated into English as *The Film of Memory*. Inspired by a fabled international decadent of the 1910s, the Marchesa Luisa Casati, it chronicled the last days of a former *grande horizontale* who once subdued a generation of

Charles Boyer and Ingrid Bergman, A Matter of Time *(1976)*

financiers, warriors and literati, plus the inevitable crowned head or two. Residing in a third-rate Roman hotel, La Sanziani relives these triumphs as if they were tomorrow, encouraged by an awestruck chambermaid who then embarks on her own adventures inspired by the Countess's example. As *La Contessa,* Paul Osborn's 1965 stage adaptation starring Vivien Leigh had expired during a pre-West End tour of the British provinces. Nevertheless, the story's bittersweet whimsies haunted Minnelli, who had presided over more than his share of Technicolored masked balls during a glorious if rapidly receding prime; besides, with a certain shift in emphasis the role of the waif-like maid Carmela struck him as a worthy acting challenge for Liza.

Unfortunately, Hollywood fairy godfathers like Arthur Freed had long since gone the way of La Sanziani's protectors, and Minnelli struggled hard to adapt to the new, pragmatic order of things. In the bewildering world of independent movie packaging, it was up to him to chase down the rights to the property, commission a script, and dig up the necessary financing. First, he entrusted the screen treatment to John Gay, twice his writing colleague during the latter years at MGM. Gay's principal innovation was to shift Carmela from appreciative bystander to the center of the Countess's time-travel reveries.

Reinforcing the aura of auld lang syne which clung

to this package, Minnelli joined forces with *Home from the Hill*'s producer Edmund Grainger and his partner Jack H. Skirball, another grizzled veteran of the industry's bygone age. Dutifully, they pitched the picture all over town, but even with Liza Minnelli's presumed box-office lure this low-concept fantasy was rejected by each of the majors in turn. As a last resort, the team dispatched its now dog-eared script to Hollywood's equivalent of ground zero: American-International Pictures, purveyor of bikers, bikinis and buckets-of-blood to the nation's drive-ins. AIP president Samuel Z. Arkoff decided a prestige novelty on this order might enhance his schlockmaster image in the trade, and he showed his largesse by allocating five million dollars to produce it—a relative pittance by A-picture standards, but a record budget for AIP. Grateful that his professional drought had at long last ended, Minnelli blithely signed a contract which failed to guarantee him any control over the film's final form—a lapse he would have reason to regret.

With due fanfare, in the fall of 1975 Arkoff announced that under the working title of *Carmela,* the Minnelli project would commence before the end of the year, to be shot entirely on location in Rome and Venice. Minnelli flew to Europe to scout locations and assemble a cast and crew—notably an actress who could conjure up the Countess's otherworldly mystique. Luise Rainer and Valentina Cortese headed Minnelli's intriguing list of candidates, but AIP insisted on a more impressive name for the marquee and, as things turned out, Arkoff's choice of Ingrid Bergman would prove the one positive contribution he was to make.

As a sentimental coup, Minnelli persuaded Charles Boyer out of retirement for one scene opposite his former co-star, as the Countess's long-estranged husband. He assigned other supporting roles to a polyglot blend of Europeans—a cast which conjured up four decades of movie history. For the tiny part of one of La Sanziani's admirers, Minnelli chose Amedeo Nazzari, the Italian screen's premier heartthrob during the Mussolini era, and for her industrialist lover, Spanish character actor Fernando Rey; Bergman's daughter Isabella Rossellini made her debut appearance as a nurse at the Countess's deathbed, while Tina Aumont—offspring of Jean-Pierre and the late Maria Montez—assumed the considerably bigger role of the chambermaid's citified cousin. As his cameraman, Minnelli was lucky to obtain the services of the gifted Geoffrey Unsworth, who had previously photographed Bergman in *Murder on the Orient Express* and Liza Minnelli in both *Cabaret* and *Lucky Lady.*

Although *Carmela* was never conceived as a musical, Liza specialists John Kander and Fred Ebb were summoned to contribute a pair of songs, one of which would provide the film's eventual title. (Somewhere along the way, the heroine's name also changed from Carmela to Nina.) Meanwhile, with the start of production looming Minnelli and Arkoff continued to tangle over the script. In the novel, Druon paralleled the event of the Countess's death with her protégé's discovery by a De Sica-like movie auteur, pointing vaguely at a hopeful future for the girl. Gay's scenario had faithfully followed this line, but Arkoff decreed that the climax needed something more socko. Reluctantly, Minnelli agreed to throw a few scenes together showing Nina as a consecrated screen legend, while privately muttering his intention to snip them out of the final cut.

After a six-year hiatus, an undeterred Minnelli plunged happily into work. Directing his daughter and a tireless professional like Bergman was as joyful as he'd expected, and Minnelli got his usual kick from discovering locations that trumped his own mental mirages; the standout here was the Venetian Palazzo Ca' Rezzonico, where he staged Nina's most opulent imaginary incarnation. But *A Matter of Time*'s long Roman winter became a rather grueling experience for all concerned. The fourteen-week shooting schedule expanded to nearly five months and, to AIP's dismay, the budget ballooned accordingly. Italian work stoppages and laboratory glitches caused frequent halts to the production, but inevitably the delays were blamed largely on Minnelli's waning powers of authority.

At the peak of his career, he'd relied on an army of MGM technicians who knew what he was after almost before he asked for it; now he was saddled with an unfamiliar crew, inadequate resources, and a language barrier that only compounded the effect of Minnelli's recent neurological disorders on his always capricious powers of speech. While his daughter usually managed by experience and osmosis to intuit what he wanted, the effort was a great deal harder for the rest of the troupe. Minnelli had always enjoyed acting out bits of business for his cast's benefit, but now these charades became a dire necessity, with not infrequent black-comedy consequences. On one occasion, he ordered a supporting player to copy his gestures exactly; the actor duly aped him, right down to a nervous twitch at the lips—Minnelli's on-the-set trademark since his MGM days.

The most grievous clash between the hardheaded Arkoff and his up-in-the-clouds director came about once post-production work began. Back in America that spring, Minnelli's first rough assembly of the material he'd shot struck Arkoff as endless and incoherent; while the director had a clear vision of the film's ultimate shape, he was incapable of explaining it to the producer's satisfaction. Arkoff declared that Minnelli's input was no longer required—he would supervise the rest of the job himself. Bowing to the ensuing cries of protest from both Minnellis, he conceded his director one last chance to pull together his version—an agreement AIP honored more in letter than in spirit. For when Minnelli asked for alternate takes and additional footage to be sent from the Roman labs, the studio refused. He could use only the material from the first assembly and not a frame more. It was an impossible task and upon viewing the result, Arkoff made good his earlier threat. He hacked away at the story, throwing out much of the flashback material and eliminating one character entirely—the Countess's confidante, played by Italian stage star Anna Proclemer. To compensate, he tossed in some travelogue snaps of Rome that Minnelli hadn't even shot; most damaging of all, Arkoff disfigured the movie's structure by enclosing the story within those shots of Nina-as-diva, which turned the whole mess into a kind of fourth-rate *A Star Is Born.*

In Hollywood, Arkoff's actions turned *A Matter of Time* into a fleeting cause célèbre. Martin Scorsese organized a petition signed by nearly every major director in the business protesting this shabby treatment of an artist of Minnelli's stature, and he arranged to have the broadside published in the trades. Although touched by this gesture of support, Minnelli realized that he had no practical recourse in the matter—the film was out of his hands for good. After all the hope and effort he'd lavished on *A Matter of Time,* its outcome was deeply demoralizing. Minnelli knew this might well be his last opportunity to direct, and he harbored no illusions as to the picture's eventual reception. For the remainder of his life, Minnelli couldn't bear to watch the version AIP released—that would have been the most painful disillusionment of all.

AIP booked *A Matter of Time* to open at Radio City Music Hall on October 7 1976, which further emphasized what a throwback the movie was; by then, only the mustiest of old-fashioned "family" entertainments played the Music Hall. The stage show during its engagement was an all-Gershwin potpourri of the sort Minnelli himself might have confected there forty years earlier. The New York notices went beyond disappointment to outright fury, as if *A Matter of Time*'s creators had deliberately perpetrated some crime against art. Surprisingly, the most compassionate review came from the *New Yorker*'s Pauline Kael, previously not the most ardent Minnelli fan. "From what is being shown to the public, it is almost impossible to judge what the tone of [Minnelli's] film was, or whether it would have worked at any level," she wrote. "But even if his own version was less than a triumph, that was the film I wanted to see—not this chopped-up shambles," Kael continued, and went on to devote half her column to Bergman's undimmed majesty as the old countess. *A Matter of Time* had only a perfunctory release after its premiere engagement, resulting in a near-complete financial loss.

It's curious the way properties showcasing geriatric European cousins to Auntie Mame attracted a whole generation of Hollywood elder statesmen during the 1970s; chronologically, *A Matter of Time* came in between George Cukor's *Travels with My Aunt* and Billy Wilder's *Fedora,* both of which also enshrined an eccentric former beauty musing on the delicious excesses which marked her youth. All three sported the most characteristic traits of their creators, from Cukor's quick-witted badinage to the acid iconoclasm of Wilder's best post-*Sunset Boulevard* manner, and the rueful romanticism Minnelli brought to *A Matter of Time.* Each in its own way was a self-portrait in code, whose intimations of mortality are made bearable by transposing them to the fictional persona of some time-ravaged glamour girl. Unfortunately for these bittersweet retrospectives of gilded days, by the 1970s nostalgia wasn't what it used to be either. Despite the odd kind word from a few auteurist critics, the Cukor and Wilder films fared scarcely better with the public than Minnelli's did.

It's probable that even had *A Matter of Time* been faultlessly realized, the film would have sorely tested an audience unused to this brand of anachronistic fantasy. As things turned out, its obtrusive technical shoddiness brought Minnelli's delicate aspirations crashing to earth—never before had a picture with his name on

it so lacked professional polish. In his previous Roman busman's-holiday, *Two Weeks in Another Town,* an on-the-skids director instructs his crew to attend to "that Kruger sound"—the aural richness that always set his pictures apart. Minnelli's production crew on *A Matter of Time* was apparently tone-deaf; the sound track is marred by the lukewarm sludge of Nino Oliviero's score and atrocious post-dubbing that gives the same flat, anonymous American cadences to all of these on-screen Romans save the three stars and Isabella Rossellini. Even the Kander–Ebb songs are an unwarranted intrusion, stylistically out of sync and shoved arbitrarily into the crevasses of the plot.

Thanks in large part to Arkoff's intervention, *A Matter of Time* looks little better than it sounds. From the opening's disjointed collage onward, the film appears to have been edited with a cleaver. Minnelli's reluctance to shoot this foolish prelude was more than justified; dolled up like a dress-extra cocotte out of *Gigi,* Liza twitters about in a frantic series of meaningless poses. The postcard vistas Arkoff so stubbornly inserted have one discernible purpose—to justify the long location shoot to the production's accountants. These montages don't just interrupt an already truncated script; their insistently mod zooms and tilted pans clash glaringly with the stately rhythms of Minnelli's footage. (When the editor splices together a shaky hand-held shot of the pigeons of Rome with one of Minnelli's graceful tracks into a closeup of his daughter, it's as though we are in two different cities.) In the novel's cleverest structural conceit, the Countess traveled through her memories in reverse order as in a film run backwards, lulled by the recollections of childhood as death overtakes her. But the ham-fisted cutting blunts all of this, turning La Sanziani's ravings into a random muddle.

Visually, the movie falters even in those areas over which Minnelli exerted some control. The Countess's faded chamber is a refuge for him as well as La Sanziani; whenever Minnelli ventures outside into the real-life streets of shops and trattorias the images turn flat and tentative, as if his fancies disintegrated under the harsh scrutiny of natural light. Both indoors and out, the movie unreels in a continual time-warp. About halfway through the film a remark from the screenwriter-in-residence indicates the year as 1949, while up to now the clothes and general demeanor of the cast placed *A Matter of Time* at the day before yesterday, 1975. Costuming the recent past in present-day dress was an expedient of old Hollywood, and one Minnelli had resorted to in both *The Four Horsemen of the Apocalypse* and parts of *The Bad and the Beautiful.* But it's particularly distracting here, as this tale needed all the specifics of time and place he could muster to enhance its wispy charm.

A Matter of Time's failures go even deeper than that —its very theme strikes an unsavory note when it

Liza Minnelli time-travels to Venice, A Matter of Time *(1976)*

means to inspire. The Countess's lessons in love, luxe and self-fulfillment may dazzle the credulous Nina, but all she's really being taught is how to be a gold-digging narcissist. (Even Gigi knew there was more to life than the jewels and other bibelots greedily amassed by her Aunt Alicia.) Whether in 1975, 1949 or La Sanziani's heyday, "to be desired and conquer," in the Countess's imperious phrase, wasn't the noblest of feminine ambitions. From the Countess's perspective (and by extension Minnelli's), any other existence is too drab to contemplate. She greets Nina's hope for a modest marriage with disdain, muttering, "a chemist's shop, a chemist's house, a chemist's *children*," which speaks less of her high standards than the script's unexamined snobbery. The Countess's aphorisms about life ("Take everything you can from life, it never gives anything back") and death ("No one dies unless we wish them to. . . . Time doesn't exist") are cultured pearls at best, but Minnelli caresses them as if they were priceless, bestowing these gifts on Nina to contemplate in wonder.

The Countess's more tangible castoffs are just as unbecoming. When Liza was small, as a special Christmas treat her father would dress her up in miniature costumes adapted from his movies, and *A Matter of Time* is a kind of perverse grown-up variation on that childhood masquerade. While the script proclaims that "the world worships an original," too often Minnelli nearsightedly imposes his own rarefied notions of glamour, negating those very properties that had made his daughter a star. When Liza as Nina appropriates the Countess's memories as well as her clothes, her mentor's femme-fatale posture demands an unseemly stretch for an actress whose natural keynote is quicksilver energy. One of the film's most ill-conceived im-

ages shows Nina's imaginary transformation into La Sanziani sporting full courtesan regalia—a slinky black-and-white gown swathed in fur and brilliants, topped with an aigretted turban. Absurdly grand on Bergman, the ensemble looks like a Halloween get-up wrapped around Liza Minnelli, turning this fantasy into unwitting comedy.

Liza is more in her element as the big-hearted gamine of Nina's workaday self, but even here the combination of Minnelli's paternal pride and his customary indulgence of star ladies with big personalities occasionally does her in. The script offers two big emotional arias of the sort that won Minnelli her first Oscar nomination for *The Sterile Cuckoo*. Nina's feminist tirade at the screenwriter who discovers her and the screen test which leads her to stardom each describes the same virtuoso parabola, from waiflike vulnerability to gritty self-assertion. In both cases, her spontaneous cascade of tears is too calculated for comfort—a cue for applause rather than the tug at our collective heart both Minnellis intended.

Yet despite so many blunders and miscalculations, for those who care about Minnelli's movie legacy *A Matter of Time* is a touching last farewell to the obsessions of three decades. It is in fact Minnelli's own film of memory, surveying his most treasured motifs as if its director knew there would never be another time to express them. As testament to his lifelong gallantry, its dual heroines are Minnelli's tenderest female archetypes—the vulnerable innocent who attains self-fulfillment in dreams, and the elderly elegant consoled by the relics from her prime. Nina inspires a return to his favorite colors; dressed in buttercup-yellow for most of the film, she eventually reclines in the last Minnelli-red boudoir he'd ever confect. His heroine's first glimpse of the tumult of moviemaking conjures up the ghosts of *The Bad and the Beautiful,* as Minnelli once again adjusts his key lights and races down those sound-stage corridors with giddy abandon. "The mirror must be beautiful, too," intones the Countess as she inducts Nina into the cult of the looking-glass that has hypnotized Minnelli's characters since *Cabin in the Sky.* As ever, this enigmatic object can bring sorrow as well as enchantment to its beholder. *A Matter of Time*'s most arresting sequence finds La Sanziani catching a glimpse of her reflection in a brief, tragic instant of clarity—weeping with shock at the ravaged face which stares back at her.

And every so often Minnelli achieves moments which not only evoke his past, but nearly equal it. Disguised for the nonce by a cap of platinum-waved hair and a black-and-white *maquillage* like a continental kabuki, Bergman is every inch the creature of glorious melancholy Minnelli intended, and somehow her innate sturdiness adds an extra, reckless quality to the

character's willful derangement. La Sanziani's senses are sharpest at that hour when the afternoon sun wanes and starlings flock through the Roman skies, and so is Minnelli's delicate, wordless poetry. The sight of this old lady sitting rapt in the shadows of evening is more eloquent than any of her *carpe-diem* pronouncements. The Countess's final encounter with her long-discarded husband recalls the "I Remember It Well" vignette from *Gigi,* but played here in a more astringent key. No reconciliation is possible between this deluded creature and a rueful realist like Boyer, whose spectral elegance looks as if it might crumble at a touch.

Although the scene is squandered toward the movie's beginning rather than at the climax where it should be, all of Minnelli's former delicacy and sureness of touch glimmer briefly here. Later on, he once more rises to the occasion for his daughter's benefit. Savoring the dregs of the Countess's Venetian masque, Nina casts off her Marie Antoinette finery while liveried flunkeys sweep up several tons of multicolored stream-

The Minnellis in 1975 on the set of A Matter of Time *(1976)*

ers. With that, Liza launches into an insinuating slow version of "Do It Again," courtesy of Minnelli's favorite composers, the brothers Gershwin. Between the witty excess of the setting and the effortless sophistication of the song, it's a fanciful fragment worthy of Minnelli's Arthur Freed days. Unfortunately, most of the scant souls who saw *A Matter of Time* on its original release were too distracted by the surrounding wreckage to notice.

"My work . . . in the final analysis, is the story of my life," Minnelli wrote in the last pages of his autobiography. "Let them inscribe on my tombstone what they could about any craftsman who loves his job: 'Here lies Vincente Minnelli. He died of hard work.'" Instead, Minnelli spent the last decade of his life adjusting as equally as possible to the role of artist emeritus. In the cozy second-floor study of his house in Beverly Hills, he would paint and read, and graciously receive that new and unfamiliar species, the dogged film scholar. Retrospectives of his work proliferated on two continents and when his health permitted, Minnelli happily attended to bask in the accolades. Although official honors from his own country eluded him—neither the American Film Institute, Kennedy Center, nor the Film Society of Lincoln Center saw fit to bestow a career-achievement award on Minnelli during his lifetime—the director of *Madame Bovary, Lust for Life,* and *Gigi* was made a Commander of Arts and Letters by the government of France and was later inducted into the *Légion d'honneur*; Italy chimed in with the City of Rome award.

Perhaps the most gratifying homage of all came from that emerging generation of filmmakers who had grown up with his movies. Regarded as hopelessly outmoded in the sixties and early seventies, Minnelli's brand of headlong artifice was suddenly embraced by such high-profile directors as Martin Scorsese and Francis Coppola. Scorsese's *New York, New York* lovingly re-created the enclosed world of Minnelli's musicals and melodramas, while even an oddity like Coppola's *One from the Heart* evoked the stylized crowds-and-neon tumult of his set pieces from *Some Came Running* and *Bells Are Ringing*. In time, music video directors such as Julian Temple would tip their hats to his production numbers on the small screen as well as in the movies, with such films as *Absolute Beginners*.

Minnelli's final years brought certain personal consolations as well. After an extensive courtship, in 1980 he embarked on his fourth and most tranquil marriage to Lee Anderson, an elegant Scotswoman long resident in Los Angeles. Her tender care sustained Minnelli through all the illnesses to come, and doubtless extended his life. Occasionally visited by his younger daughter, Christina, who had settled in Mexico, Minnelli remained as close as ever to his firstborn, who kept her father up-to-date on new trends in pop culture by introducing him to such chums as Michael Jackson. On his eightieth birthday, in 1983, Minnelli was fêted with a gala retrospective at the Palm Springs Desert Museum and, with Liza at his side, he in turn regaled his friends and the other swells in attendance with a debonair rendition of the Gershwins' "Embraceable You." Although largely confined to his house thereafter, over the next three years he would occasionally turn up on the Beverly Hills circuit. One of Minnelli's last public appearances, in the spring of 1986, was at a Directors' Guild dinner for Akira Kurosawa.

On July 25 1986, Vincente Minnelli died in his sleep at home of complications from pneumonia and emphysema. The funeral five days later was one of those grand ceremonials Hollywood reserves for its departed greats. Three generations of show business notables crowded into a Forest Lawn chapel which uncannily resembled one of his own sets for *Brigadoon*. The eulogies were given by Gregory Peck and Kirk Douglas; in his remarks, Douglas noted that despite all their years of collaboration and friendship, there remained a private core to Minnelli's nature which he could never quite penetrate. Which was just as well, for perhaps that secret place was where this director's art came from, and Minnelli would have been the last person capable of explaining its mystery. His movies endure as both his own composite self-portrait and a glass that reflects the time and place that nurtured him. And as Minnelli proclaimed in his last celluloid farewell, the mirror must be beautiful, too.

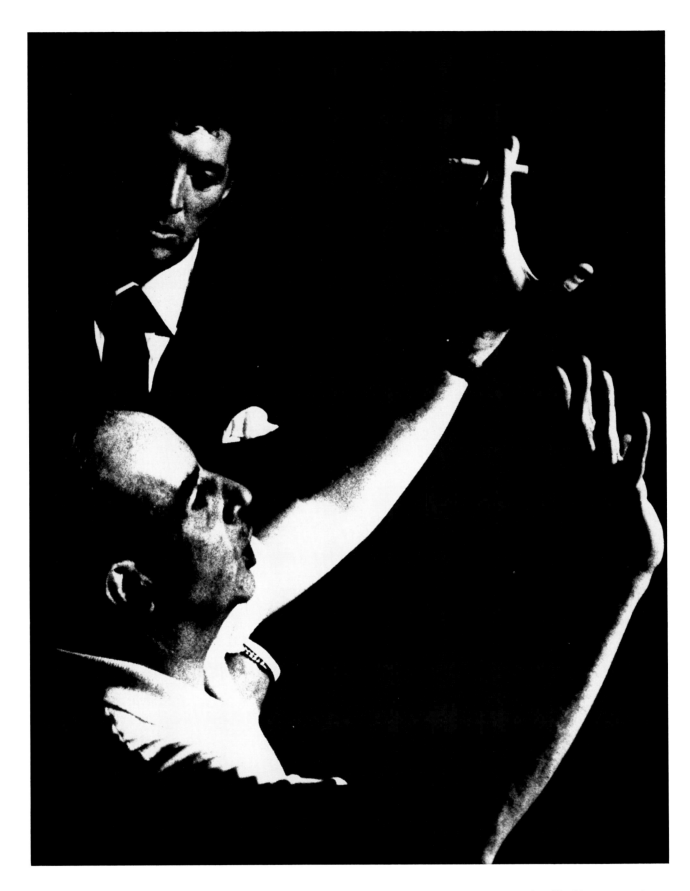

Minnelli with Dean Martin
on the set of Some Came
Running *(1958)*

7 Filmography

1943   **C A B I N   I N   T H E   S K Y**

Cabin in the Sky

Producer: Arthur Freed, associate Albert Lewis. Screenplay: Joseph Schrank, from the musical play by Lynn Root (book). John Latouche (lyrics), Vernon Duke (music): "Taking a Chance on Love," "Honey in the Honeycomb," "Cabin in the Sky." Additional songs by Harold Arlen and E. Y. Harburg: "Happiness Is Just a Thing Called Joe," "Life's Full of Consequence," "L'il Black Sheep." "Going Up" by Duke Ellington. Photography: Sidney Wagner. Art direction: Cedric Gibbons, assisted by Leonid Vasian. Set decoration: Edwin B. Willis, assisted by Hugh Hunt. Musical direction: George Stoll. Musical adaptation: Roger Edens. Orchestrations: George Bassman. Choral arrangements: Hall Johnson. Recording direction: Douglas Shearer. Editor: Harold F. Kress. Costumes: Irene, assisted by Shoup. Men's wardrobe: Gile Steele. Cast: Ethel Waters (Petunia Jackson), Eddie "Rochester" Anderson (Little Joe Jackson), Lena Horne (Georgia Brown), Louis Armstrong (The Trumpeter), Rex Ingram (Lucius/Lucifer, Jr.), Kenneth Spencer (Rev. Green/The General), John W. "Bubbles" Sublett (Domino Johnson), Oscar Polk (The Deacon/Fleetfoot), Mantan Moreland (First Idea Man), Willie Best (Second Idea Man), Fletcher "Moke" Rivers (Third Idea Man), Bill "Poke" Bailey (Bill), Ford L. "Buck" Washington (Messenger boy), Butterfly McQueen (Lily), Ruby Dandridge, (Mrs. Kelso), Nicodemus (Dude), Ernest Whitman (Jim Henry), The Hall Johnson Choir. 96 minutes.

1943   **I   D O O D   I T**
Producer: Jack Cummings. Screenplay: Sig Herzig and Fred Saidy, adapted from 1928 film *Spite Marriage*. Photography: Ray June. Art direction: Cedric Gibbons, associate Jack Mar-

tin Smith. Set decoration: Edwin B. Willis, associate Helen Conway. Art direction for musical presentation: Merrill Pye. Musical direction: George Stoll. Songs by Don Raye, Gene de Paul, Lew Brown, Ralph Freed, Sammy Fain, Count Basie, Cole Porter, Vernon Duke, John Latouche, Ted Fetter, Leo Robin, Richard Myers: "Star Eyes," "So Long Sarah Jane," "One O'Clock Jump," "Swingin' the Jinx Away," "Taking a Chance on Love," "Jericho." Arrangement of "Jericho": Kay Thompson. Editor: Robert J. Kern. Choreography: Bob Connolly. Recording direction: Douglas Shearer. Costume supervision: Irene, associate Irene Sharaff. Men's costumes: Gile Steele. Cast: Red Skelton (Joseph Rivington Reynolds), Eleanor Powell (Constance Shaw), Richard Ainsley (Larry West), Patricia Dane (Suretta Brenton), Sam Levene (Ed Jackson), Thurston Hall (Kenneth Lawlor), Lena Horne (Herself), Hazel Scott (Herself), John Hodiak (Roy Hartwood), Butterfly McQueen (Annette), Marjorie Gateson (Mrs. Spelvin), Andrew Tombes (Mr. Spelvin), Jimmy Dorsey and his Orchestra, Helen O'Connell, and Bob Eberley. 101 minutes.

I Dood It

1944   **M E E T   M E   I N   S T.   L O U I S**
Producer: Arthur Freed. Screenplay: Irving Brecher and Fred F. Finkelhoffe, based on stories published in *The New Yorker* by Sally Benson. Cinematography: George Folsey. Technicolor direction: Natalie Kalmus, Henri Jaffa. Art direction: Cedric Gibbons, associates Lemuel Ayers and Jack Martin Smith. Set decoration: Edwin B. Willis, Paul Huldschinsky. Songs by Hugh Martin and Ralph Blane: "The Boy Next Door," "The Trolley Song," "Have Yourself a Merry

Meet Me in St. Louis

Little Christmas," "You and I," and traditional standards. Editor: Albert Akst. Costumes: Irene Sharaff. Makeup: Jack Dawn. Choreography: Charles Walters. Musical adaptation: Roger Edens. Musical direction: George Stoll; Lennie Hayton. Orchestrations: Conrad Salinger. Recording direction: Douglas Shearer. Cast: Judy Garland (Esther Smith), Margaret O'Brien (Tootie Smith), Mary Astor (Anna Smith), Lucille Bremer (Rose Smith), Tom Drake (John Truitt), Marjorie Main (Katie), Leon Ames (Alonzo Smith), Harry Davenport (Grandpa), June Lockhart (Lucille Ballard), Henry H. Daniels, Jr. (Lon Smith Jr.), Joan Carroll (Agnes Smith), Hugh Marlowe (Colonel Darly), Robert Sally (Warren Sheffield), Chill Wills (Mr. Neeley). 113 minutes.

1945 THE CLOCK

Producer: Arthur Freed. Screenplay: Robert Nathan and Joseph Schrank, from a story by Paul and Pauline Gallico. Photography: George Folsey. Art direction: Cedric Gibbons, William Ferrari. Set decoration: Edwin B. Willis, associate Mac Alper. Musical score: George Bassman. Editor: George White. Special effects: A. Arnold Gillespie and Warren Newcombe. Costume supervision: Irene, associate Marion Herwood Keyes. Recording direction: Douglas Shearer. Cast: Judy Garland (Alice Maybery), Robert Walker (Corporal Joe Allen), James Gleason (Al Henry), Keenan Wynn (Drunk), Marshall Thompson (Bill), Lucile Gleason (Mrs. Al Henry), Ruth Brady (Helen). 90 minutes.

The Clock

1945 YOLANDA AND THE THIEF

Producer: Arthur Freed. Screenplay: Irving Brecher, based on a story by Jacques Thery and Ludwig Bemelmans. Photography: Charles Rosher. Art direction: Cedric Gibbons and Jack Martin Smith. Set decoration: Edwin B. Willis, associate Richard Pefferle. Musical direction: Lennie Hayton. Orchestrations: Conrad Salinger. Songs by Arthur Freed and Harry Warren: "This Is a Day for Love," "Angel," "Will You Marry Me?," "Yolanda," "Coffee Time." Editor: George White. Special effects: A. Arnold Gillespie and Warren Newcombe. Costumes: Irene Sharaff. Miss Bremer's gowns: Irene. Choreography: Eugene Loring. Technicolor direction: Natalie Kalmus, associate Henri Jaffa. Recording direction: Douglas Shearer. Makeup: Jack Dawn. Cast: Fred Astaire (Johnny Parkson Riggs), Lucille Bremer (Yolanda Aquaviva), Frank Morgan (Victor Budlow Trout), Mildred Natwick (Aunt Amarilla), Mary Nash (Duenna), Leon Ames (Mr. Candle), Ludwig Stossel (School teacher), Jane Green (Mother Superior), Remo Bufano (Puppeteer), Francis Pierlot (Padre), Leon Belasco (Taxi driver), Ghislaine Perreau (Gigi), Charles La Torre (Police Lieutenant), Michael Visaroff (Major Domo). 108 minutes.

Yolanda and the Thief

1944 ZIEGFELD FOLLIES
Released 1946

Producer: Arthur Freed. Photography: George Folsey, Charles Rosher, Ray June. Art direction: Cedric Gibbons, Merrill Pye, Jack Martin Smith, Lemuel Ayers. Set decoration: Edwin B. Willis, associate Mac Alper. Musical direction: Lennie Hayton. Musical adaptation: Roger Edens. Orchestrations: Conrad Salinger and Wally Heglin. Vocal arrangements: Kay Thompson. Songs by Arthur Freed and Harry Warren; George and Ira Gershwin; Ralph Blane and Hugh Martin; Kay Thompson and Roger Edens; Philip Braham and Douglas Furber. Choreography: Robert Alton. Editor: Albert Akst. Puppet sequence photographer: William Ferrari. Puppets: Leo and Florence Bunin. Costume supervision: Irene. Costume design: Irene Sharaff, Helen Rose. Technicolor direction: Natalie Kalmus, associate Henri Jaffa. Recording direction: Douglas Shearer. Makeup: Jack Dawn. Hair stylist: Sydney Guilaroff. SEQUENCES Introduction: William Powell (Florenz Ziegfeld). Animated Sequence: Bunin's Puppets, di-

Ziegfeld Follies

rected by Norman Taurog. "Pink Number" ("Bring On the Beautiful Girls"): Lucille Ball, Fred Astaire, Cyd Charisse, Virginia O'Brien. "A Water Ballet": Esther Williams. "Number Please": Keenan Wynn, directed by Robert Lewis. "Traviata": James Melton and Marion Bell, dance direction by Eugene Loring, costumes by Sharaff. "Pay the Two Dollars": Victor Moore and Edward Arnold. "This Heart of Mine": Fred Astaire and Lucille Bremer. "Fanny Brice Wins a Sweepstake Ticket": Fanny Brice, Hume Cronyn, and William Frawley, written by David Friedman, directed by Roy Del Ruth. "Love": Lena Horne, directed by Lemuel Ayers. "When Television Comes": Red Skelton, directed by George Sidney. "Limehouse Blues": Fred Astaire, Lucille Bremer, costumes by Sharaff. "A Great Lady Has an Interview": Judy Garland, dance direction by Charles Walters. "The Babbitt and the Bromide": Fred Astaire and Gene Kelly. "Beauty": Kathryn Grayson. 110 minutes.

1946   UNDERCURRENT

Producer: Pandro S. Berman. Screenplay: Edward Chodorov, based on a story by Thelma Strabel. Photography: Karl Freund. Art direction: Cedric Gibbons, Randall Duell. Set decoration: Edwin B. Willis, associate Jack D. Moore. Editor: Ferris Webster. Musical score: Herbert Stothart. Costume su-

Undercurrent

pervision: Irene. Recording direction: Douglas Shearer. Makeup: Jack Dawn. Hair stylist: Sydney Guilaroff. Cast: Katharine Hepburn (Ann Hamilton), Robert Taylor (Alan Garroway), Robert Mitchum (Michael Garroway), Edmund Gwenn (Prof. "Dink" Hamilton), Marjorie Main (Lucy), Jayne Meadows (Sylvia Lea Burton), Clinton Sundberg (Mr.

Warmsley), Dan Tobin (Prof. Joseph Bangs), Kathryn Card (Mrs. Foster), Leigh Whipper (George), Charles Trowbridge (Justice Putnam), James Westerfield (Henry Gilson), Billy McLain (Uncle Ben). 116 minutes.

1946   TILL THE CLOUDS ROLL BY

Judy Garland numbers "Who," "Look for the Silver Lining," "Sunny" directed by Vincente Minnelli. Producer: Arthur Freed. Directors: Richard Whorf, George Sidney. Story: Guy Bolton. Adaptation: George Wells. Screenplay: Myles Connolly, Jean Holloway. Songs by Jerome Kern (music) and Oscar Hammerstein II (lyrics): "Who," "Sunny"; and Buddy DeSylva, "Look for the Silver Lining." Musical direction: Lennie Hayton. Orchestrations: Conrad Salinger. Vocal arrangements: Kay Thompson. Musical numbers staged by Robert Alton. Directors of photography: Harry Stradling, George Folsey. Technicolor direction: Natalie Kalmus, associate Henri Jaffa. Editor: Albert Akst. Recording direction: Douglas Shearer. Art directors: Cedric Gibbons, Daniel E. Cathcart. Set decoration: Edwin B. Willis, Richard Pefferle.

Till the Clouds Roll By

Special effects: Warren Newcombe. Montages: Peter Ballbusch. Costume supervision: Irene. Costume design: Helen Rose. Men's costumes: Valles. Hair stylist: Sydney Guilaroff. Makeup: Jack Dawn. Cast: Judy Garland (Marilyn Miller), Robert Walker (Jerome Kern), Lucille Bremer (Sally), Joan Wells (Sally as a girl), Van Heflin (James I. Hessler), Paul Langton (Oscar Hammerstein II), Dorothy Patrick (Mrs. Jerome Kern), Mary Nash (Mrs. Muller), Harry Hayden (Charles Frohman), Paul Maxey (Victor Herbert), Rex Evans (Cecil Keller), William "Bill" Phillips (Hennessy), Van Johnson (Band leader), June Allyson, Angela Lansbury, Ray McDonald (Guest stars), Maurice Kelly, Cyd Charisse, Gower Champion (Dance specialty), Ray Teal (Orchestra conductor), Wilde Twins (Specialty), Byron Foulger (Frohman's secretary), William Halligan, Tony Martin, Dinah Shore, Kathryn Grayson, Virginia O'Brien, Lena Horne, Caleb Peterson, Bruce Cowling ("Showboat" number), Kathryn Grayson, Johnny Johnston, Lucille Bremer, Frank Sinatra, Virginia O'Brien, Lena Horne, Tony Martin ("Finale"). 137 minutes.

1948   THE PIRATE

Producer: Arthur Freed. Screenplay: Albert Hackett and Frances Goodrich, based on the play by S. N. Behrman, as produced by The Playwrights' Company and The Theater Guild. Photography: Harry Stradling. Art direction: Cedric Gibbons, Jack Martin Smith. Set decoration: Edwin B. Willis, associate Arthur Krams. Musical direction: Lennie Hayton. Orchestrations: Conrad Salinger. Choreography: Robert Alton and Gene Kelly. Songs by Cole Porter: "Niña," "Love of My Life," "Mack the Black," "You Can Do No Wrong," "Be a Clown." Editor: Blanche Sewell. Costume supervisor: Irene. Costume design: Tom Keogh, executed by Karinska. Technicolor direction: Natalie Kalmus, associate Henri Jaffa. Recording direction: Douglas Shearer. Makeup: Jack Dawn. Hair stylist: Sydney Guilaroff. Paintings: Doris Lee. Cast: Judy Garland (Manuela), Gene Kelly (Serafin), Walter Slezak (Don Pedro Vargas), Gladys Cooper (Aunt Inez), Reginald Owen (the Advocate), George Zucco (the Viceroy), Lester Allen (Uncle Capucho), Lola Deem (Isabella), Ellen Ross (Mercedes), Mary Jo Ellis (Lizarda), Jean Dean (Casilda), Marion Murray (Eloise), Ben Lessy (Gumbo), Jerry Bergen (Bolo), Val Setz (Juggler), Cully Richards (Trillo), Gaudsmith Brothers (Specialty), Nicholas Brothers (Specialty dance). 102 minutes.

The Pirate

1949   MADAME BOVARY

Producer: Pandro S. Berman. Screenplay: Robert Ardrey, based on the novel by Gustave Flaubert. Photography: Robert Planck. Art direction: Cedric Gibbons, Jack Martin Smith. Set decoration: Edwin B. Willis, associate Richard A. Pefferle. Music: Miklos Rozsa. Editor: Ferris Webster. Special effects: Warren Newcombe. Costumes: Walter Plunkett, Valles. Choreography: Jack Donohue. Recording direction: Douglas Shearer. Makeup: Jack Dawn. Hair stylists: Larry Germain, Sydney Guilaroff. Cast: Jennifer Jones (Emma Bovary), James Mason (Gustave Flaubert), Van Heflin (Charles Bovary), Louis Jourdan (Rodolphe Boulanger), Christopher Kent (Léon Dupuis), Gene Lockhart (J. Homais), Frank Allenby (Lhereux), Gladys Cooper (Mme. Dupuis), John Abbott (Mayor Tuvache), Henry Morgan (Hyppolite), George Zucco (Dubocage), Ellen Corby (Félicité), Eduard Franz (Roualt), Henri Letondal (Guillaumin), Esther Somers (Mme. Lefrançois), Frederic Tozere (Pinard), Paul Cavanagh (Marquis D'Andervilliers), Larry Sims (Justin), Dawn Kinney (Berthe), Vernon Steele (Priest). 115 minutes.

Madame Bovary

1950   FATHER OF THE BRIDE

Producer: Pandro S. Berman. Screenplay: Albert Hackett and Frances Goodrich, based on the novel by Edward Streeter. Photography: John Alton. Art direction: Cedric Gibbons, Leonid Vasian. Set decoration: Edwin B. Willis, Keogh Gleason. Music: Adolph Deutsch. Editor: Ferris Webster. Costumes: Helen Rose (women); Walter Plunkett (men). Recording direction: Douglas Shearer. Makeup: Jack Dawn. Hair stylist: Sydney Guilaroff. Cast: Spencer Tracy (Stanley T. Banks), Joan Bennett (Ellie Banks), Elizabeth Taylor (Kay Banks), Don Taylor (Buckley Dunstan), Billie Burke (Doris Dunstan), Leo G. Carroll (Mr. Massoula), Moroni Olsen (Herbert Dunstan), Melville Cooper (Mr. Tringle), Taylor Holmes (Warner), Paul Harvey (Rev. Galsworthy), Frank Orth (Joe), Rusty Tamblyn (Tommy Banks), Tom Irish (Ben Banks), Marietta Canty (Delilah). 93 minutes.

Father of the Bride

1951   FATHER'S LITTLE DIVIDEND

Producer: Pandro S. Berman. Screenplay: Albert Hackett and Frances Goodrich, based on characters created by Edward Streeter. Photography: John Alton. Art direction: Cedric Gibbons, Leonid Vasian. Set decoration: Edwin B. Willis, associate Keogh Gleason. Music: Albert Sendrey, conducted by George Stoll. Editor: Ferris Webster. Costumes: Helen Rose.

Recording direction: Douglas Shearer. Makeup: William Tuttle. Hair stylist: Sydney Guilaroff. Cast: Spencer Tracy (Stanley T. Banks), Joan Bennett (Ellie Banks), Elizabeth Taylor (Kay Dunstan), Don Taylor (Buckley Dunstan), Billie Burke (Doris Dunstan), Moroni Olsen (Herbert Dunstan), Richard Rober (Police Sergeant), Marietta Canty (Delilah), Rusty Tamblyn (Tommy Banks), Tom Irish (Ben Banks), Hayden Rorke (Dr. Andrew Nordell), Paul Harvey (Rev. Galsworthy), Richard Rober (Police Sergeant), Frank Faylen (Policeman), Beverly Thompson (Nurse), Donald Clarke (the Dividend). 82 minutes.

Father's Little Dividend

1951 AN AMERICAN IN PARIS

Producer: Arthur Freed. Screenplay: Alan Jay Lerner, based on his story. Photography: Alfred Gilks. Ballet photography: John Alton. Art direction: Cedric Gibbons, Preston Ames. Set decoration: Edwin B. Willis, associate Keogh Gleason. Music: George Gershwin. Musical direction: Johnny Green, Saul Chaplin. Orchestrations: Conrad Salinger. Choreography: Gene Kelly, assistant Carol Haney. Lyrics by Ira Gershwin: ''I Got Rhythm,'' ''Embraceable You,'' ''S'Wonderful,'' ''Nice Work If You Can Get It,'' ''By Strauss,'' ''Tra-La-La,'' ''Our Love Is Here to Stay,'' ''Concerto in F,'' ''Liza,'' ''I Don't Think I'll Fall in Love Today,'' ''Bidin' My Time,'' ''How Long Has This Been Going On?,'' ''I'll Build a Stairway to Paradise'' (lyrics by E. Goetz and B. G. DeSylva). Editor: Adrienne Fazan. Montage sequences: Peter Ballbusch. Spe-

An American in Paris

cial effects: Warren Newcombe, Irving Ries. Costume design: Orry-Kelly. Beaux Arts Ball costumes: Walter Plunkett. Ballet costumes: Irene Sharaff. Technicolor direction: Henri Jaffa, James Gooch. Recording direction: Douglas Shearer. Makeup: William Tuttle. Hair stylist: Sydney Guilaroff. Gene Kelly's paintings by Gene Grant. Cast: Gene Kelly (Jerry Mulligan), Leslie Caron (Lise Bourvier), Oscar Levant (Adam Cook), George Guetary (Henri Baurel), Nina Foch (Milo Roberts), Eugene Borden (Georges Mattieu), Martha Bamattre (Mathilde Mattieu), Mary Young (Old woman dancer), Ann Codee (Thérèse), George Davis (François), Hayden Rorke (Tommy Baldwin), Paul Maxey (John McDowd), Dick Wessel (Ben Macrow). 113 minutes.

1952 THE STORY OF THREE LOVES
''Mademoiselle'' Sequence
Released 1953

Producer: Sidney Franklin. Screenplay: Jan Lustig, George Froeschel, based on a story by Arnold Phillips. Photography: Charles Rosher, Harold Rosson. Art directors: Cedric Gibbons, Preston Ames. Music: Miklos Rozsa. Editor: Ralph E. Winters. Costumes: Helen Rose. Recording direction: Douglas Shearer. Makeup: William Tuttle. Hair stylist: Sydney Guilaroff. Cast: Ethel Barrymore (Mrs. Pennicott), Leslie Caron (Mademoiselle), Farley Granger (Tommy), Ricky Nelson (Tommy at age twelve), Zsa Zsa Gabor (Girl at bar). (Total running time: 112 minutes.)

The Story of Three Loves

1952 THE BAD AND THE BEAUTIFUL

Producer: John Houseman. Assistant director: Jerry Thorpe. Screenplay: Charles Schnee, based on short stories by George Bradshaw. Photography: Robert Surtees. Art direction: Cedric Gibbons, Edward Carfagno. Set decoration: Edwin B. Willis, Keogh Gleason. Music: David Raksin. Editor: Conrad A. Nervig. Special effects: A. Arnold Gillespie, Warren Newcombe. Costumes: Helen Rose. Recording direction: Douglas Shearer. Makeup: William Tuttle. Hair stylist: Sydney Guilaroff. Cast: Lana Turner (Georgia Lorrison), Kirk Douglas (Jonathan Shields), Walter Pidgeon (Harry Pebbel), Dick Powell (James Lee Bartlow), Barry Sullivan (Fred Amiel), Gloria Grahame (Rosemary Bartlow), Gilbert Roland (Victor ''Gaucho'' Ribera), Leo G. Carroll (Henry Whitfield), Vanessa

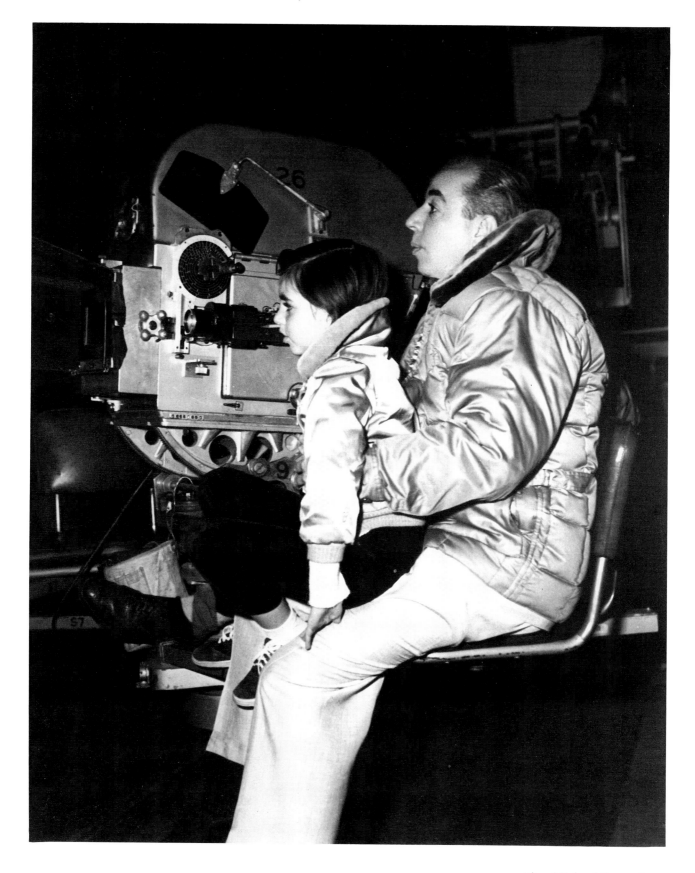

*Liza visits her father on the
set in the early 1950s*

The Bad and the Beautiful

Henri Jaffa, Robert Brower. Print process: Ansco Color. Recording direction: Douglas Shearer. Makeup: William Tuttle. Hair stylist: Sydney Guilaroff. Cast: Fred Astaire (Tony Hunter), Cyd Charisse (Gabrielle Gerard) with vocals dubbed by India Adams; Oscar Levant (Lester Marton), Jack Buchanan (Jeffrey Cordova), Nanette Fabray (Lily Marton), James Mitchell (Paul Byrd), Robert Gist (Hal Benton), Thurston Hall (Colonel Tripp), Ava Gardner (Herself), LeRoy Daniels (Shoeshine man), Madge Blake (Gushy woman), Sue Casey (Tall woman in penny arcade), Matt Mattox (Specialty dancer), Dee Trunell and Jimmie Thompson (Troupe members), Steve Forrest (Man), Dee and Eden Hartford, Julie Newmar (Girls in "Private Eye" number). 112 minutes.

Brown (Kay Amiel), Paul Stewart (Syd Murphy), Sammy White (Gus), Elaine Stewart (Lila), Ivan Triesault (Von Ellstein), Peggy King (Singer), Louis Calhern (voice of Mr. Lorrison), Jonathan Cott (Assistant director), Lucille Knox (Blonde with "Gaucho"), Kathleen Freeman (Miss Marsh), Marietta Canty (Ida), Steve Forrest (Young actor with Georgia), Perry Sheehan (Secretary), Robert Burton (Director McGill), Bob Carson (Casting director), Barbara Billingsley (Lucien), Dorothy Patrick (Arlene), Francis X. Bushman (Speaker). 118 minutes.

1953   **THE BAND WAGON**

Producer: Arthur Freed, associate Roger Edens. Assistant director: Jerry Thorpe. Screenplay: Betty Comden, Adolph Green, adapted from Broadway revue (1931) with songs by Arthur Schwartz (music) and Howard Dietz (lyrics). Photography: Harry Jackson, George Folsey. Art direction: Cedric Gibbons, Preston Ames. Set decoration: Edwin B. Willis, Keogh Gleason. Musical numbers designer: Oliver Smith. Musical direction: Adolph Deutsch. Orchestrations: Conrad Salinger, Skip Martin, Alexander Courage. Songs by Dietz/Schwartz: "A Shine on Your Shoes," "You and the Night and the Music," "By Myself," "Dancing in the Dark," "Triplets," "New Sun in the Sky," "I Guess I'll Have to Change My Plans," "Louisiana Hayride," "I Love Louisa," "That's Entertainment," "The Girl Hunt Ballet." Editor: Albert Akst. Special effects: Warren Newcombe. Costumes: Mary Ann Nyberg. Choreography: Michael Kidd. Technicolor direction:

The Band Wagon

1954   **THE LONG, LONG TRAILER**

The Long, Long Trailer

Producer: Pandro S. Berman. Assistant director: Jerry Thorpe. Screenplay: Albert Hackett and Frances Goodrich, based on the novel by Clinton Twiss. Photography: Robert Surtees. Art direction: Cedric Gibbons, Edward Carfagno. Set decoration: Edwin B. Willis, Keogh Gleason. Music: Adolph Deutsch. Editor: Ferris Webster. Special effects: A. Arnold Gillespie, Warren Newcombe. Costumes: Helen Rose. Color consultant: Alvord Eiseman. Print process: Ansco Color. Recording direction: Douglas Shearer. Makeup: William Tuttle. Hair stylist: Sydney Guilaroff. Cast: Lucille Ball (Tacy Collini), Desi Arnaz (Nicholas Carlos Collini), Marjorie Main (Mrs. Hittaway), Keenan Wynn (Policeman), Gladys Hurlbut (Mrs. Bolton), Moroni Olsen (Mr. Tewitt), Bert Freed (Foreman), Madge Blake (Aunt Anastacia), Oliver Blake (Mr. Judlow), Perry Sheehan (Bridesmaid). 96 minutes.

1954   **BRIGADOON**

Producer: Arthur Freed. Associate producer: Roger Edens. Assistant director: Frank Baur. Screenplay: Alan Jay Lerner, based on the musical play, book, and lyrics by Lerner, music by Frederick Loewe: "The Heather on the Hill," "Waitin' for My Dearie," "Almost Like Being in Love," "I'll Go Home with Bonnie Jean," "Down on MacConnachy Square," "Brigadoon." Photography: Joseph Ruttenberg. Art direction: Cedric Gibbons, Preston Ames. Set decoration: Edwin B. Willis, Keogh Gleason. Musical direction: Johnny Green. Orchestrations: Conrad Salinger. Choral arrangements: Robert Tucker. Choreography: Gene Kelly. Editor: Albert Akst.

Brigadoon

Special effects: Warren Newcombe. Costumes: Irene Sharaff. Color consultant: Alvord Eiseman. Print process: Ansco Color. CinemaScope. Recording direction: Dr. Wesley C. Miller. Makeup: William Tuttle. Hair stylist: Sydney Guilaroff. Cast: Gene Kelly (Tommy Albright), Van Johnson (Jeff Douglas), Cyd Charisse (Fiona Campbell), Elaine Stewart (Jane Ashton), Barry Jones (Mr. Lundie), Hugh Laing (Harry Beaton), Albert Sharpe (Andrew Campbell), Virginia Bosler (Jean Campbell), Jimmy Thompson (Charlie Chisholm Dalrymple), Tudor Owen (Archie Beaton), Owen McGiveney (Angus), Dee Turnell (Ann), Dody Heath (Meg Brockie), Eddie Quillan (Sandy), George Chakiris (Dancer). 108 minutes.

1955   THE COBWEB

Producer: John Houseman, associate Jud Kinberg. Assistant director: William Shanks. Screenplay: John Paxton; additional dialogue: William Gibson, based on the novel by Gibson. Photography: George Folsey. Art direction: Cedric Gibbons, Preston Ames. Set decoration: Edwin B. Willis, Keogh Gleason. Music: Leonard Rosenman. Editor: Harold

The Cobweb

F. Kress. Costumes: uncredited. Color consultant: Alvord Eiseman. Print process: Eastmancolor. Graphic design execution: David Stone Martin. Recording direction: Dr. Wesley C. Miller. Makeup: William Tuttle. Hair stylist: Sydney Guilaroff. Cast: Richard Widmark (Dr. Stewart McIver), Lauren Bacall (Meg Faversen Rinehart), Charles Boyer (Dr. Douglas

N. Devanal), Gloria Grahame (Karen McIver), Lillian Gish (Victoria Inch), John Kerr (Steven W. Holte), Susan Strasberg (Sue Brett), Oscar Levant (Mr. Capp), Tommy Rettig (Mark), Paul Stewart (Dr. Otto Wolff), Jarma Lewis (Lois Y. Demuth), Adele Jergens (Miss Cobb), Edgar Stehli (Mr. Holcomb), Sandra Descher (Rosemary), Bert Freed (Abe Irwin), Mabel Albertson (Regina Mitchell-Smythe), Fay Wray (Edna Devanal), Oliver Blake (Curly), Olive Carey (Mrs. O'Brien), Eve McVeagh (Shirley), Virginia Christine (Sally), Jan Arvan (Mr. Appleton), Ruth Clifford (Mrs. Jenkins), Myra Marsh (Miss Gavney), James Westerfield (James Petlee), Marjorie Bennett (Sadie), Stuart Holmes (Mr. Wictz). 124 minutes.

1955   KISMET

Producer: Arthur Freed. Assistant director: William Shanks. Screenplay: Charles Lederer, Luther Davis, adapted from the musical play; book: Lederer and Davis, based on the novel by Edward Knobloch. Music and lyrics by Robert Wright and George Forrest, adapted from themes by Aleksandr Borodin: "Stranger in Paradise," "Rahadlakum," "And This Is My Beloved," "Sands of Time," "Not Since Ninevah," "Baubles, Bangles, and Beads," "Fate," "Bored," "Gesticulate," "Night of My Nights," "The Olive Tree." Photography: Joseph Ruttenberg. Art direction: Cedric Gibbons, Preston Ames. Set

Kismet

decoration: Edwin B. Willis, Keogh Gleason. Music supervision: André Previn, Jeff Alexander. Orchestrations: Conrad Salinger, Alexander Courage, Arthur Morton, conducted by Previn. Musical staging and choreography: Jack Cole. Editor: Adrienne Fazan. Special effects: Warren Newcombe. Costumes: Tony Duquette. Color consultant: Charles K. Hagedon. Print process: Eastmancolor. CinemaScope. Recording direction: Dr. Wesley C. Miller. Vocal supervision: Robert Tucker. Makeup: William Tuttle. Hair stylist: Sydney Guilaroff. Cast: Howard Keel (Hajj, the Poet), Ann Blyth (Marsinah), Dolores Gray (Lalume), Vic Damone (Caliph), Monty Woolley (Omar), Sebastian Cabot (Wazir), Jay C. Flippen (Jawan), Mike Mazurki (Chief policeman), Jack Elam (Hassan-Ben), Ted de Corsia (Police subaltern), Reiko Sato, Patricia Dunn, Wonci Lui (Princesses of Ababu), Julie Robinson (Zubbediya). 113 minutes.

1956   LUST FOR LIFE

Producer: John Houseman, associate Jud Kinberg. Assistant director: Al Jennings. Screenplay: Norman Corwin, based on

Lust for Life

the novel by Irving Stone. Photography: F. A. Young, Russell Harlan. Art direction: Cedric Gibbons, Hans Peters, Preston Ames. Set decoration: Edwin B. Willis, Keogh Gleason. Music: Miklos Rozsa. Editor: Adrienne Fazan. Costumes: Walter Plunkett. Color consultant: Charles K. Hagedon. Print process: Metrocolor. CinemaScope. Recording direction: Dr. Wesley C. Miller. Makeup: William Tuttle. Hair stylist: Sydney Guilaroff. Cast: Kirk Douglas (Vincent Van Gogh), Anthony Quinn (Paul Gauguin), James Donald (Theo Van Gogh), Pamela Brown (Christine), Everett Sloane (Dr. Gachet), Niall MacGinnis (Roulin), Noel Purcell (Anton Mauve), Henry Daniell (Theodorus Van Gogh), Madge Kennedy (Anna Cornelia Van Gogh), Jill Bennett (Willemien), Lionel Jeffries (Dr. Peyron), Laurence Naismith (Dr. Bosman), Eric Pohlmann (Colbert), Jeanette Sterke (Kay), Toni Gerry (Johanna), Wilton Graff (Rev. Stricker), Isobel Elsom (Mrs. Stricker), David Horne (Rev. Peeters), Noel Howlett (Commissioner Van Den Berghe), Ronald Adam (Commissioner de Smet), John Ruddock (Ducrucq), Julie Robinson (Rachel), David Leonard (Camille Pissarro), William Phipps (Emile Bernard), David Bond (Seurat), Frank Perls (Pére Tanguy), Jay Adler (Waiter), Laurence Badie (Adeline Ravoux). 122 minutes.

1956   TEA AND SYMPATHY

Producer: Pandro S. Berman. Assistant director: Joel Freeman. Screenplay: Robert Anderson, based on his play pro-

Tea and Sympathy

duced on stage by The Playwrights' Company. Photography: John Alton. Art direction: William A. Horning, Edward Carfagno. Set decoration: Edwin B. Willis, Keogh Gleason. Music: Adolph Deutsch. Editor: Ferris Webster. Wardrobe for Miss Kerr: Helen Rose. Color consultant: Charles K. Hagedon. Print process: Metrocolor. CinemaScope. Recording director: Dr. Wesley C. Miller. Makeup: William Tuttle. Hair stylist: Sydney Guilaroff. Cast: Deborah Kerr (Laura Reynolds), John Kerr (Tom Robinson Lee), Leif Erickson (Bill Reynolds), Edward Andrews (Herb Lee), Darryl Hickman (Al), Norma Crane (Ellie Martin), Dean Jones (Ollie), Jacqueline de Wit (Lilly Sears), Tom Laughlin (Ralph), Ralph Votrian (Steve), Steven Terrell (Phil), Kip King (Ted), Jimmy Hayes (Henry), Richard Tyler (Roger), Don Burnett (Vic). 122 minutes.

1957   DESIGNING WOMAN

Producer: Dore Schary, associate George Wells. Assistant director: William Shanks. Screenplay: George Wells, from a suggestion of Helen Rose. Photography: John Alton. Art direction: William A. Horning, Preston Ames. Set decoration: Edwin B. Willis, Henry Grace. Music: André Previn. Musical staging: Jack Cole. Song by Overstreet, Higgins, and Edwards: "There'll Be Some Changes Made." Editor: Adrienne

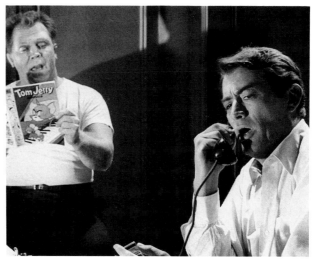

Designing Woman

Fazan. Special effects: Warren Newcombe. Gowns by Helen Rose. Color consultant: Charles K. Hagedon. Print process: Metrocolor. CinemaScope. Recording direction: Dr. Wesley C. Miller. Makeup: William Tuttle. Hair stylist: Sydney Guilaroff. Cast: Gregory Peck (Mike Hagen), Lauren Bacall (Marilla Hagen), Dolores Gray (Lori Shannon), Jack Cole (Randy Owen), Tom Helmore (Zachary Wilde), Mickey Shaughnessy (Maxie Stulz), Sam Levene (Ned Hammersmith), Chuck Connors (Johnny O.), Edward Platt (Martin J. Daylor), Alvy Moore (Luke Coslow), Jesse White (Charles Arneg), Carol Veazie (Gwen). 118 minutes.

1958   GIGI

Producer: Arthur Freed. Assistant directors: William McGarry, William Shanks. Screenplay: Alan Jay Lerner, from the novel by Colette. Photography: Joseph Ruttenberg. Art

Gigi

direction: William A. Horning, Preston Ames. Costumes, scenery, and production design: Cecil Beaton. Set decoration: Henry Grace, Keogh Gleason. Music: Frederick Loewe. Musical direction: André Previn. Orchestrations: Conrad Salinger. Lyrics by Alan Jay Lerner: ''Thank Heaven for Little Girls,'' ''It's a Bore,'' ''The Parisians,'' ''She's Not Thinking of Me,'' ''The Night They Invented Champagne,'' ''I Remember It Well,'' ''Say a Prayer for Me Tonight,'' ''I'm Glad I'm Not Young Anymore,'' ''Gossip,'' ''Gigi.'' Vocal supervisor: Robert Tucker. Editor: Adrienne Fazan. Color consultant: Charles K. Hagedon. Print process: Metrocolor. CinemaScope. Recording direction: Dr. Wesley C. Miller. Makeup: William Tuttle, Charles Parker. Hair stylists: Guillaume, Sydney Guilaroff. Cast: Leslie Caron (Gigi), vocals dubbed by Betty Wand; Maurice Chevalier (Honoré Lachaille), Louis Jourdan (Gaston Lachaille), Hermione Gingold (Mme. Alvarez), Eva Gabor (Liane d'Exelmans), Jacques Bergerac (Sandomir), Isabel Jeans (Aunt Alicia), John Abbott (Manuel). 116 minutes.

1958 **THE RELUCTANT DEBUTANTE**

Producer: Pandro S. Berman. Assistant director: William McGarry. Screenplay: William Douglas Home, based on his play. Photography: Joseph Ruttenberg. Art direction: A. J. d'Eaubonne. Set decoration: Robert Christides. Dance music and arrangements: Eddie Warner and his Orchestra. Editor: Adrienne Fazan. Wardrobe for Sandra Dee: Helen Rose. Wardrobe for Kay Kendall, Angela Lansbury, and Diane

The Reluctant Debutante

Clare: Pierre Balmain. Print process: Metrocolor. CinemaScope. Sound mixer: Guy Rophe. Makeup: Jean-Paul Ulysse. Cast: Rex Harrison (Jimmy Broadbent), Kay Kendall (Sheila Broadbent), John Saxon (David Parkson), Sandra Dee (Jane Broadbent), Angela Lansbury (Mabel Claremont), Peter Myers (David Fenner), Diane Clare (Clarissa Claremont). 94 minutes.

1958 **SOME CAME RUNNING**

Producer: Sol C. Siegel. Assistant director: William McGarry. Screenplay: John Patrick, Arthur Sheekman, based on the novel by James Jones. Photography: William H. Daniels. Art direction: William A. Horning, Urie McCleary. Set decoration: Henry Grace, Robert Priestley. Music: Elmer Bernstein. Song by Sammy Cahn (lyrics) and James Van Heusen (music): ''To Love and Be Loved.'' Editor: Adrienne Fazan. Costumes: Walter Plunkett. Color consultant: Charles K. Hagedon. Print process: Metrocolor. CinemaScope. Recording direction: Franklin Milton. Makeup: William Tuttle. Cast: Frank Sinatra (Dave Hirsh), Dean Martin ('Bama Dillert), Shirley MacLaine (Ginny Moorehead), Martha Hyer (Gwen French), Arthur Kennedy (Frank Hirsh), Nancy Gates (Edith Barclay), Leora Dana (Agnes Hirsh), Betty Lou Keim (Dawn Hirsh), Larry Gates (Prof. Robert Haven French), Steven Peck (Raymond Lanchak), Connie Gilchrist (Jane Barclay), Ned Wever (Smitty), Carmen Phillips (Rosalie), John Brennan (Wally Dennis). 134 minutes.

Some Came Running

1960 **HOME FROM THE HILL**

A Sol C. Siegel Production. Producer: Edmund Grainger. Assistant director: William McGarry. Screenplay: Harriet Frank, Jr., Irving Ravetch, based on the novel by William Humphrey. Photography: Milton Krasner. Special effects: Robert R. Hoag. Art direction: George W. Davis, Preston Ames. Set decoration: Henry Grace, Robert Priestley. Music: Bronislau Kaper. Conductor: Charles Wolcott. Editor: Harold F. Kress. Costumes: Walter Plunkett. Color consultant: Charles K. Hagedon. Print process: Metrocolor. CinemaScope. Recording direction: Franklin Milton. Makeup: William Tuttle. Hair stylist: Sydney Guilaroff. Cast: Robert Mitchum (Wade Hunnicutt), Eleanor Parker (Hannah Hunnicutt), George Peppard (Rafe Copley), George Hamilton (Theron Hunnicutt), Luana Patten (Libby Halstead), Everett Sloane (Albert Halstead), Anne Seymour (Sarah Halstead), Constance Ford (Opal Bixby), Ken Renard (Chauncey), Ray Teal (Dr. Reuben Carson). 150 minutes.

Home from the Hill

1960 BELLS ARE RINGING

Producer: Arthur Freed. Assistant director. William McGarry. Screenplay: Betty Comden, Adolph Green, adapted from their musical play (music by Jule Styne). Photography: Milton Krasner. Art direction: George W. Davis, Preston Ames. Set decoration: Henry Grace, Keogh Gleason. Musical adaptation and conducting: André Previn. Orchestrations: Alexander Courage, Pete King. Songs by Comden/Green/Styne: "Just in Time," "The Party's Over," "I'm Goin' Back (Where I Can Be Me)," "It's a Perfect Relationship," "Drop that Name," "Do It Yourself," "Hello, Hello There," "It's a Simple Little System," "Mu-Cha-Cha," "Better than a Dream." Editor: Adrienne Fazan. Costumes: Walter Plunkett. Choreog-

Bells Are Ringing

raphy: Charles O'Curran. Print process: Metrocolor. CinemaScope. Recording direction: Franklin Milton. Makeup: William Tuttle. Hair stylist: Sydney Guilaroff. Cast: Judy Holliday (Ella Peterson), Dean Martin (Jeffrey Moss), Fred Clark (Larry Hastings), Eddie Foy, Jr. (J. Otto Prinz),

Jean Stapleton (Sue), Ruth Storey (Gwynne), Dort Clark (Inspector Barnes), Frank Gorshin (Blake Barton), Ralph Roberts (Francis), Valerie Allen (Olga), Bernie West (Dr. Joe Kitchell), Steven Peck (First gangster), Gerry Mulligan (Ella's blind date). 126 minutes.

1962 THE FOUR HORSEMEN OF THE APOCALYPSE

Producers: Julian Blaustein. Assistant directors: Erich von Stroheim Jr., Eric Hurel, Jacques Bertraud. Screenplay: Robert Ardrey, John Gay, from the novel by Vicente Blasco Ibáñez. Photography: Milton Krasner. Second unit: Georges Perinal. Art direction: George W. Davis. Urie McCleary, Elliot Scott. Set decoration: Henry Grace, Keogh Gleason. Four Horsemen figures designed by Tony Duquette. Music: André Previn. Editors: Adrienne Fazan, Ben Lewis. Montages: Frank Santillo. Special effects: A. Arnold Gillespie, Lee LeBlanc, Robert R. Hoag. Choreography: Alex Romero. Costumes: René Hubert, Walter Plunkett, and (for Thulin) Orry-Kelly. Print process: Metrocolor. CinemaScope. Makeup: Charles Parker, William Tuttle. Hair stylist: Sydney Guilaroff. Cast: Glenn Ford (Julio Desnoyers), Ingrid Thulin (Marguerite Laurier), Charles Boyer (Marcelo Desnoyers), Lee J. Cobb (Julio Madariaga), Paul Henreid (Etienne Laurier), Karl

The Four Horsemen of the Apocalypse

Boehm (Heinrich von Hartrott), Paul Lukas (Karl von Hartrott), Yvette Mimieux (Chi-Chi Desnoyers), Harriet McGibbon (Luisa Desnoyers), Kathryn Givney (Elena von Hartrott), Richard Franchot (Franz), Brian Avery (Gustav), Albert Rémy (François), George Dolenz (General von Kleist), Marcel Hillaire (Armand Dibie), Stephan Bakassy (Colonel Kleinsdorf), Nestor Paiva (Miguel). 153 minutes.

1962 TWO WEEKS IN ANOTHER TOWN

Producer: John Houseman, associate Ethel Winant. Assistant director: Erich von Stroheim, Jr. Screenplay: Charles Schnee, based on the novel by Irwin Shaw. Photography: Milton Krasner. Art direction: George W. Davis, Urie McCleary. Set decoration: Henry Grace, Keogh Gleason. Editors: Adrienne Fazan, Robert J. Kern, Jr. Special effects: Robert R. Hoag. Music: David Raksin. Wardrobe for Cyd Charisse: Pierre Balmain. Color consultant: Charles K. Hagedon. Print process: Metrocolor. CinemaScope. Recording direction: Franklin Milton. Makeup: William Tuttle. Hair stylist: Sydney Guilaroff. Cast: Kirk Douglas (Jack Andrus), Edward G. Robinson (Maurice Kruger), Cyd Charisse (Carlotta), George Hamilton (David Drew), Daliah Lavi (Veronica), Claire Trevor (Clara), James Gregory (Brad Byrd), Rosanna Schiaffino (Barzelli), Joanna Roos (Janet Bark), George Macready (Lew Jordan), Mino Doro (Tucino), Stefan Schnabel (Zeno), Vito Scotti (Assistant director), Tom Palmer (Dr. Cold Eyes), Erich von Stroheim, Jr. (Ravinski), Leslie Uggams (Chanteuse), 107 minutes.

Two Weeks in Another Town

1963   THE COURTSHIP OF EDDIE'S FATHER

Producer: Joseph Pasternak. Assistant director: William McGarry. Screenplay: John Gay, from the novel by Mark Toby. Photography: Milton Krasner. Art direction: George W. Davis, Urie McCleary. Set decoration: Henry Grace, Keogh Gleason. Music: George Stoll. Song by Victor Young and Stella Unger: "The Rose and the Butterfly." Editor: Adrienne Fazan. Costumes: Helen Rose. Print process: Metrocolor. Panavision. Recording direction: Franklin Milton. Makeup: William Tuttle. Hair stylist: Sydney Guilaroff. Cast: Glenn Ford (Tom Corbett), Ronny Howard (Eddie Corbett),

The Courtship of Eddie's Father

Shirley Jones (Elizabeth Marten), Dina Merrill (Rita Behrens), Stella Stevens (Dollye Daly), Roberta Sherwood (Mrs. Livingston), Jerry Van Dyke (Norman Jones), John La Salle Jazz Combo. 117 minutes.

1964   GOODBYE, CHARLIE

20th Century-Fox. Producer: David Weisbart. Assistant director: David Hall. Screenplay: Harry Kurnitz, based on the play by George Axelrod, produced on the stage by Leland Hayward. Photography: Milton Krasner. Art direction: Jack Martin Smith, Richard Day. Set decoration: Walter M. Scott, Keogh Gleason. Music: André Previn. Orchestrations: Al Woodbury. Songs by Dory Langdon (lyrics) and André Previn (music): "Goodbye, Charlie," "Seven at Once." "Seven at Once" sung by Jerry Wallace. Editor: John W. Holmes. Special effects: L. B. Abbott, Emil Kosa, Jr. Costumes: Helen Rose. Print process: Deluxe. Recording direction: W. D. Flick, Elmer Raguse. Makeup: Ben Nye. Hair stylist: Margaret Donovan; executed by Christine Widmeyer. Miss Reynolds' hairstyles: Sydney Guilaroff. Cast: Tony Curtis (George Tracy), Debbie Reynolds (Charlie), Pat Boone (Bruce Minton), Walter Matthau (Sir Leopold Sartori), Joanna Barnes (Janie), Ellen McRae (Franny), Laura Devon (Rusty), Martin Gabel (Morton Craft), Roger C. Carmel (Inspector), Henry Madden (Charlie Sorel), Myrna Hansen (Starlet), Michael Romanoff (Patron), Antony Eustrel (Butler), Michael Jackson (Himself), Donna Michelle (Guest on yacht). 117 minutes.

Goodbye, Charlie

1965   THE SANDPIPER

Producers: Martin Ransohoff, John Calley. Assistant director: William McGarry. Screenplay: Dalton Trumbo, Michael Wilson, based on the story by Martin Ransohoff, adapted by Irene and Louis Kamp. Photography: Milton Krasner. Wildlife photography: Richard Borden. Art direction: George W. Davis, Urie McCleary. Set decoration: Henry Grace, Keogh Gleason. Music: Johnny Mandel. Song by Johnny Mandel and Paul Francis Webster (music and lyrics): "The Shadow of Your Smile." Editor: David Bretherton. Costumes: Irene Sharaff. Print process: Metrocolor. Panavision. Recording direction: Franklin Milton. Makeup: William Tuttle. Hair stylist: Sydney Guilaroff. Cast: Elizabeth Taylor (Laura Reynolds), Richard Burton (Dr. Edward Hewitt), Eva Marie Saint (Claire Hewitt), Charles Bronson (Cos Erikson), Morgan Mason (Danny Reynolds), Robert Webber (Ward Hendricks), Tom Drake (Walter Robinson), James Edwards (Larry Brant), Torin Thatcher (Judge Thompson), Douglas Henderson (Phil Sutcliff), Peter O'Toole (Voice). 116 minutes.

The Sandpiper

1970   ON A CLEAR DAY YOU CAN SEE FOREVER

Paramount Pictures. Producers: Howard W. Koch, Alan Jay Lerner. Assistant director: William McGarry. Screenplay and lyrics: Alan Jay Lerner, based on his musical play. Photography: Harry Stradling. Production design: John de Cuir. Set decoration: George Hopkins, Raphael Bretton. Music: Burton Lane. Choral arrangements: Joseph J. Lilley. Music arrangements and conducting: Nelson Riddle. Lyrics by Alan Jay Lerner: "On a Clear Day (You Can See Forever)," "Come Back to Me," "Hurry, It's Lovely Up Here," "What Did I Have That I Don't Have?," "Love with All the Trimmings," "He Isn't You," "Melinda," "Go to Sleep." Editor: David Bretherton. Costumes: Cecil Beaton, Arnold Scaasi. Choreography: Howard Jeffrey. Print process: Technicolor.

On a Clear Day You Can See Forever

Sound: Benjamin Winkler, Elden Ruberg. Makeup: Harry Ray. Hair stylist: Frederick Glaser. Cast: Barbra Streisand (Daisy Gamble), Yves Montand (Dr. Marc Chabot), Bob Newhart (Dr. Mason Hume), Larry Blyden (Warren Pratt), Simon Oakland (Dr. Conrad Fuller), Jack Nicholson (Tad Pringle), John Richardson (Robert Tentrees), Pamela Brown (Mrs. Fitzherbert), Irene Handl (Winnie Wainwhistle), Roy Kinnear (Prince Regent), Peter Crowcroft (Divorce attorney), Byron Webster (Prosecuting attorney), Mabel Albertson (Mrs. Hatch), Laurie Main (Lord Percy), Kermit Murdock (Hoyt III), Elaine Giftos (Muriel), John Le Mesurier (Pelham), Angela Pringle (Diana Smallwood), Leon Ames (Clews), Paul Camen (Millard), George Neise (Wytelipt), Tony Colti (Preston). 129 minutes.

1976   A MATTER OF TIME

American International Pictures. Executive producers: Samuel Z. Arkoff, Giulio Sbarigia. Producers: Jack H. Skirball, J. Edmund Grainger. Production executive: Steve Previn. Screenplay: John Gay, based on the novel *Film of Memory* by Maurice Druon. Photography: Geoffrey Unsworth. Produc-

A Matter of Time

tion design: Veniero Colasanti, John Moore. Music: Nino Oliviero; arrangements: Carlo Esposito. Conductor: Bruno Canfora. Songs by Fred Ebb and John Kander (music and lyrics): "A Matter of Time," "The Me I Haven't Met Yet" and George Gershwin (music), B. G. DeSilva (lyrics): "Do It Again." Editor: Peter Taylor. Post production: Salvatore Billitteri. Sound: Franca Silvi. Makeup: (Bergman, Minnelli) Christina Smith. Hair stylist: (Minnelli) Liz Gaylor. Cast: Liza Minnelli (Nina), Ingrid Bergman (the Countess), Charles Boyer (Count Sanziani), Spiros Andros (Mario Morello), Tina Aumont (Valentina), Anna Proclemer (Jeanne Blasto), Gabriele Ferzetti (Antonio Vicaria), Arnolda Foa (Pavelli), Orso Maria Guerrini (Gabriele D'Orazio), Fernando Rey (Charles Van Maar), Amadeo Nazzari (Countess's admirer), Isabella Rossellini (Nurse). 97 minutes.

8 *Bibliography*

MINNELLI'S ART WORK
Book illustrations:

Casanova's Memoirs. Edited by Joseph Monét. Drawings by Vincente Minnelli. New York: The Van Rees Press, 1930.

Reproductions of Minnelli's Theater Designs:

"Décors pour Broadway." *Positif* (Paris), vol. nos. 200–202 (Dec 1977–Jan 1978), pp. 102–105.

Houghton, Norris. "The Designer Sets the Stage: I. Norman Bel Geddes. II. Vincente Minnelli." *Theater Arts Monthly* (New York), vol. 20, no. 10 (Oct 1936), pp. 776–788.

"Vincente Minnelli. The Whole Show but the Actors." *Theater Arts Monthly* (New York), vol. 20, no. 1 (Jan 1936), pp. 37–46.

WRITINGS BY MINNELLI
Autobiography

Minnelli, Vincente, with Hector Arce. *I Remember It Well.* Garden City, New York: Doubleday, 1974.

MONOGRAPHS

Brion, Patrick, Dominique Rabourdin, and Thierry de Navacelle. *Vincente Minnelli.* Paris: Hatier/5 Continents, 1985.

Campari, Roberto. *Vincente Minnelli.* Series: Il Castoro Cinema, no. 43/44. Rome: La Nuova Italia, 1977.

Casper, Joseph Andrew. *Vincente Minnelli and the Film Musical.* New York: Barnes, 1977.

De la Roche, Catherine. *Vincente Minnelli.* The New Zealand Film Institute/Film Culture (U.S.A.), 1959.

MGM

Crowther, Bosley. *The Lion's Share: The Story of an Entertainment Empire.* New York: Dutton, 1957.

Eames, John Douglas. *The MGM Story: The Complete History of Fifty-four Roaring Years.* New York: Crown, 1979; rev. ed., 1982.

MGM MUSICALS

Fordin, Hugh. *The World of Entertainment: Hollywood's Greatest Musicals. The Freed Unit at MGM.* Garden City, New York: Doubleday, 1975. Reprinted as: *The Movies' Greatest Musicals: Produced in Hollywood USA by the Freed Unit.* New York: Ungar, 1984.

Knox, Donald. *The Magic Factory: How MGM Made "An American in Paris."* New York: Praeger, 1973.

OPPOSITE:
Minnelli wearing Légion d'honneur *award given to him by the French Government*

MUSICALS (STAGE)

Bordman, Gerald. *American Musical Theatre: A Chronicle.* New York: Oxford University Press, 1978.

Francisco, Charles. *The Radio City Music Hall.* New York: Dutton, 1979.

Green, Stanley. *Ring Bells! Sing Songs! Broadway Musicals of the 1930's.* New Rochelle, New York: Arlington House, 1971.

MUSICALS (FILM)

Delamater, Jerome. *Dance in the Hollywood Musical.* Ann Arbor, Mich.: UMI Research Press, 1981.

Green, Stanley. *Encyclopaedia of the Musical Film.* New York: Oxford University Press, 1981.

Hirschhorn, Clive. *The Hollywood Musical.* New York: Crown, 1981.

Sennett, Ted. *Hollywood Musicals.* New York: Abrams, 1981.

Springer, John. *All Talking! All Singing! All Dancing! A Pictorial History of the Movie Musical.* New York: Citadel Press, 1966.

Taylor, John Russell, and Arthur Jackson. *The Hollywood Musical.* New York: McGraw-Hill; and London: Secker & Warburg, 1971.

INTERVIEWS WITH MINNELLI

Aprà, Adriano. "Conversazione con Vincente Minnelli." *Filmcritica* (Rome), vol. 12, no. 114 (Oct 1961), pp. 542–545.

Bachmann, Gideon. "The Nostalgia Express: Gideon Bachmann Interviews Two Minnellis and a Bergman." *Film Comment* (New York), vol. 12, no. 6 (Nov–Dec 1976), pp. 19–20.

Bitsch, Charles, and Jean Domarchi. "Entretien avec Vincente Minnelli." *Cahiers du Cinéma* (Paris), vol. 13, no. 74 (Aug–Sept 1957), pp. 4–18.

Diehl, Digby. "Directors Go to Their Movies: Vincente Minnelli and *Gigi*." *Action* (Hollywood: Directors Guild of America), vol. 7, no. 5 (Sept–Oct 1972), pp. 2–10.

Domarchi, Jean, and Jean Douchet. "Rencontre avec Vincente Minnelli." *Cahiers du Cinéma* (Paris), vol. 22, no. 128 (Feb 1962), pp. 3–13.

Film Notebooks (Univ. of Calif. at Santa Cruz) (Winter 1978). "A Conversation with Vincente Minnelli," pp. 2–10.

Higham, Charles, and Joel Greenberg. *The Celluloid Muse: Hollywood Directors Speak.* London: Angus & Robertson, 1969.

Lehman, Peter, Marilyn Campbell, and Grant Munro. "Two Weeks in Another Town: An Interview with Vincente Minnelli." *Wide Angle* (Athens, Ohio), vol. 3, no. 1 (1979), pp. 64–71.

Schickel, Richard. *The Men Who Made the Movies. Interviews with Frank Capra, George Cukor, Howard Hawks, Alfred*

Hitchcock, Vincente Minnelli, King Vidor, Raoul Walsh, and William A. Wellman. New York: Atheneum, 1975.

Serebrinsky, Ernesto, and Oscar Garaycochea. "Vincente Minnelli Interviewed in Argentina." *Movie* (London), no. 10 (June 1963), pp. 23–28.

Shivas, Mark. "Method: Vincente Minnelli." *Movie* (London), no. 1 (June 1962), pp. 20–24.

ARTICLES ABOUT MINNELLI & HIS FILMS

Alexandre, Jean-Lou. "*Ars gratia artis* ou Minnelli existe-t-il?" *Cinéma 9* (Paris), nos. 7 and 8 (1970).

"American Report: Vincente Minnelli." *Cahiers du Cinéma* (Paris), vol. 25, nos. 150–151 (Dec 1963–Jan 1964), p. 59.

Anderson, Lindsay. "Minnelli, Kelly, and *An American in Paris.*" *Sequence* (London), no. 14 (New Year 1952), pp. 36–38.

Aprà, Adriano. "Solitudine di Vincente Minnelli." *Filmcritica* (Rome), no. 134 (June 1963), pp. 343–350.

Beaton, Cecil. "Beaton's Guide to Hollywood." *Films and Filming* (London), vol. 5, no. 4 (Jan 1959), pp. 9, 31.

Carey, Gary. "Vincente Minnelli and the 1940s Musical." *Cinema: A Critical Dictionary. The Major Filmmakers.* Vol. 2. Edited by Richard Roud. New York: Viking; London: Secker & Warburg, 1980.

Chaumeton, Etienne. "L'Oeuvre de Vincente Minnelli." *Positif* (Paris), vol. 2, no. 12 (Nov–Dec 1954), pp. 37–45.

Cinema (Beverly Hills, Calif.), vol. 2, no. 6 (July–Aug 1965).

Fieschi, Jacques. "Mémoire musicale." *Cinématographe* (Paris), no. 34 (Jan 1978), pp. 14–18.

Gavin, Arthur E. "Location-shooting in Paris for *Gigi.*" *American Cinematographer* (Hollywood), vol. 39, no. 7 (July 1958), pp. 424–425, 440, 442.

Genné, Beth Eliot. "Vincente Minnelli's Style in Microcosm: The Establishing Sequence of *Meet Me in St. Louis.*" *Art Journal* (New York: College Art Association of America), vol. 43, no. 3 (Fall 1983), pp. 247–254.

Gilks, Alfred. "Some Highlights in the Filming of . . . *An American in Paris.*" *American Cinematographer* (Hollywood), vol. 33, no. 1 (Jan 1952), pp. 18–19, 36–39.

Goldman, William. *The Season: A Candid Look at Broadway.* New York: Harcourt, Brace & World, 1969; reprinted New York: Proscenium/Limelight, 1984.

Goodwin, Joe, and Karen Swenson. "One More Look at *On a Clear Day You Can See Forever.*" *Barbra Quarterly* (Los Angeles), no. 9 (Fall 1982), pp. 20–33.

Johnson, Albert. "The Films of Vincente Minnelli." Part I: *Film Quarterly* (Berkeley, Calif.), vol. 12, no. 2 (Winter 1958), pp. 21–35; Part II: *Film Quarterly,* vol. 12, no. 3 (Spring 1959), pp. 32–42.

Johnson, Albert. "A Visit to *Kismet.*" *Sight and Sound* (London), vol. 25, no. 3 (Winter 1955–56), pp. 152–156.

Krasner, Milton. "My Color Photography of *The Sandpiper.*" *American Cinematographer* (Hollywood), vol. 46, no. 7 (July 1965), pp. 428–431.

Laura, Ernesto Guido. "Vincente Minnelli." *Filmlexicon degli autori e delle opere.* vol. 4. Rome: Edizioni di Bianco e Nero, 1961.

Lightman, Herb A. "*The Four Horsemen.*" *American Cinematographer* (Hollywood), vol. 43, no. 4 (Apr 1962), pp. 222–223, 250, 252–253.

Mayersberg, Paul. "The Testament of Vincente Minnelli." *Movie* (London), no. 3 (Oct 1962), pp. 10–13.

Moritz, Charles, ed. *Current Biography Yearbook 1975.* New York: H. W. Wilson, 1975, 1976.

Morris, George. "One Kind of Dream. George Morris on *A Matter of Time.*" *Film Comment* (New York), vol. 12, no. 6 (Nov–Dec 1976), p. 21.

Morris, George. "Vincente Minnelli." *International Film Guide. 1978.* Edited by Peter Cowie. London: Tantivy Press; South Brunswick and New York: A. S. Barnes, 1977.

Perelman, S. J. "A Couple of Quick Ones. Two Portraits: 1. Arthur Kober. 2. Vincente Minnelli." *The Stage* (New York), vol. 14 (Apr 1937), p. 66. Reprinted in Perelman collections *Crazy Like a Fox* (New York: Random House, 1945), and *The Best of S. J. Perelman* (New York: Random House/Modern Library, 1947).

Siegel, Joel E. " 'Love Is the Exception to Every Rule, Is It Not?': The Films of Vincente Minnelli and Alan Jay Lerner." *Bright Lights* (Los Angeles), vol. 3, no. 1 (1980), pp. 7–11, 19, 34.

"The Rise and Fall of the Musical." *Films and Filming* (London), vol. 8, no. 4 (Jan 1962), p. 9.

Yates, Penny, ed. *The Films of Vincente Minnelli.* New York: The Thousand Eyes/Zoetrope, Number 4 (1978).

MINNELLI'S ASSOCIATES & COLLABORATORS

Astaire, Fred. *Steps in Time.* New York: Harper & Row, 1959.

Astor, Mary. *A Life on Film.* New York: Delacorte Press, 1967.

Beaton, Cecil. *The Restless Years. Diaries 1955–63.* London: Weidenfeld & Nicolson, 1976.

Basinger, Jeanine. *Gene Kelly.* New York: Pyramid, 1976.

Carey, Gary. *Judy Holliday. An Intimate Life Story.* New York: Seaview Books, 1982.

Cutts, John. "On the Bright Side. An Interview with Charles Walters." *Films and Filming* (London), vol. 16, no. 11 (Aug 1970), pp. 12–18.

Douglas, Kirk. *The Ragman's Son.* New York: Simon & Schuster, 1988.

Duke, Vernon. *Passport to Paris.* Boston: Little, Brown, 1955.

Finch, Christopher. *Rainbow. The Stormy Life of Judy Garland.* New York: Grosset & Dunlap, 1975.

Fordin, Hugh. *Getting to Know Him. A Biography of Oscar Hammerstein II.* New York: Random House, 1977.

Haney, Lynn. *Naked at the Feast: A Biography of Josephine Baker.* New York: Dodd, Mead, 1981.

Harvey, Stephen. *Fred Astaire.* New York: Pyramid, 1975.

Harvey, Stephen. "Stanley Donen Interviewed by Stephen Harvey." *Film Comment* (New York), vol. 9, no. 4 (July–Aug 1973), pp. 4–9.

Haskins, James, with Kathleen Benson. *Lena. A Personal and Professional Biography of Lena Horne.* New York: Stein & Day, 1984.

Hauduroy, Jean-François. "Writing for Musicals. Interview with Betty Comden and Adolph Green." *Cahiers du Cinéma in English* (New York), no. 2 (1966), pp. 43–50.

Henreid, Paul, with Julius Fast. *Ladies Man. An Autobiography.* New York: St. Martin's Press, 1984.

Hirschhorn, Clive. *Gene Kelly. A Biography.* Chicago: Regnery, 1974; 1984.

Horne, Lena, and Richard Schickel. *Lena.* Garden City, New York: Doubleday, 1965.

Houseman, John. *Final Dress.* New York: Simon & Schuster, 1983.

Houseman, John. *Front and Center.* New York: Simon & Schuster, 1979.

Houston, Penelope. "Interview with John Houseman." *Sight and Sound* (London), vol. 31, no. 4 (Autumn 1962), pp. 160–165.

Johnson, Albert. "Conversation with Roger Edens." *Sight and Sound* (London), vol. 27, no. 4 (Spring 1958), pp. 179–182.

Lerner, Alan Jay. *The Street Where I Live: The Story of My Fair Lady, Gigi, and Camelot.* New York: Norton, 1978.

Levant, Oscar. *The Memoirs of an Amnesiac.* New York: Putnam, 1965.

Lillie, Beatrice; aided and abetted by John Philip; written with James Brough. *Every Other Inch a Lady.* London and New York: W. H. Allen, 1973.

MacLaine, Shirley. *"Don't Fall Off the Mountain."* New York: Norton, 1970.

Martin, Tony, and Cyd Charisse. As Told to Dick Kleiner. *The Two of Us.* New York: Mason/Charter, 1976.

Nogueira, Rui. "Dalton Got His Film." *Cinéma 71* (Paris), no. 158 (July–Aug 1971), pp. 89–108.

Rabourdin, Dominique. "Entretien avec Leslie Caron." *Positif* (Paris), no. 180 (Apr 1976), pp. 39–47.

Rose, Helen. *Just Make Them Beautiful.* Santa Monica, Calif.: Dennis-Landman, 1976.

Rózsa, Miklós. *Double Life. The Autobiography of Miklós Rózsa.* New York: Hippocrene Books, 1982.

Sauvage, Pierre. "Entretien avec Charles Walters." *Positif* (Paris), nos. 144–145 (Nov–Dec 1972), pp. 16–33.

Sharaff, Irene. *Broadway and Hollywood Costumes Designed by Irene Sharaff.* New York: Van Nostrand Reinhold, 1976.

Spencer, Charles. *Cecil Beaton Stage and Film Designs.* New York: St. Martin's Press, 1975.

Strasberg, Susan. *Bittersweet.* New York: Putnam, 1980.

Thomas, Tony. *The Films of Kirk Douglas.* Secaucus, N.J.: Citadel Press, 1972.

Thomas, Tony. *Harry Warren and the Hollywood Musical.* Secaucus, N.J.: Citadel Press, 1975.

Turner, Lana. *Lana. The Lady, the Legend, the Truth.* New York: Dutton, 1982.

Vickers, Hugo. *Cecil Beaton. The Authorised Biography.* London: Weidenfeld & Nicolson, 1985.

Viviani, Christian. "Souvenirs d'un directeur de la photographie." *Positif* (Paris), no. 142 (Sept 1972), pp. 68–81.

Winer, Stephen. "Dignity—Always Dignity! Betty Comden and Adolph Green's Musicals." *The Velvet Light Trap* (Cottage Grove, Wisc.), no. 11 (Winter 1984), pp. 29–32.

Zec, Donald, and Anthony Fowles. *Barbra: A Biography of Barbra Streisand.* New York: St. Martin's Press, 1982.

ART REFERENCE

LeMarie, Jean. *Who Was Van Gogh?* Transl. by James Emmons. Geneva: Editions d'Art, Albert Skira, 1968. (Dist. by World Publishers, Cleveland, Ohio.)

Rewald, John. *Post-Impressionism: From Van Gogh to Gauguin.* 2nd edition. New York: The Museum of Modern Art, 1962.